Sports and Exercise in Midlife

American Academy
of Orthopaedic Surgeons
Seminar

Sports and Exercise in Midlife

Edited by
Stephen L. Gordon, PhD
Chief, Musculoskeletal Diseases Branch
National Institute of Arthritis and Musculoskeletal and Skin Diseases
National Institutes of Health
Bethesda, Maryland

Xavier Gonzalez-Mestre, MD
Director of Research Programs
Institut d'Estudis de la Salut
Department of Health and Social Security
Catalunya, Spain

William E. Garrett, Jr, MD, PhD
Associate Professor of Orthopaedic Surgery and Cell Biology
Duke University
Durham, North Carolina

with 80 illustrations

Seminar
Catalunya, Spain
July 1992

Supported by the
National Institute of Arthritis and Musculoskeletal and Skin Diseases

and the
Institut d'Estudis de la Salut, Generalitat de Catalunya

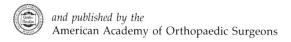

and published by the
American Academy of Orthopaedic Surgeons

American Academy of Orthopaedic Surgeons
6300 North River Road
Rosemont, IL 60018

Staff

Executive Director:
Thomas C. Nelson

Director, Division of Education:
Mark W. Wieting

Director, Department of
Publications:
Marilyn L. Fox, PhD

Senior Editors:
Bruce Davis
Lynne Shindoll

Associate Senior Editors:
Joan Abern
Jane Baque

Production Manager:
Loraine Edwalds

Assistant Production Manager:
Kathy M. Brouillette

Editorial Assistants:
Susan Baim
Sharon Duffy
Katy O'Brien
Sophie Tosta

Publications Secretaries:
Geraldine Dubberke
Em Lee Lambos

Library of Congress Cataloging-in-Publication Data

Sports and Exercise in Midlife/edited by Stephen L. Gordon, PhD, Xavier Gonzalez-Mestre, MD, and William E. Garrett, Jr, MD, PhD, supported by the American Academy of Orthopaedic Surgeons, the National Institute of Arthritis and Musculoskeletal and Skin Diseases, the National Institutes of Health, and Institut d'Estudis de la Salut, Generalitat de Catalunya.

ISBN 0-89203-078-X
LC 94-70109

Seminar Participants and Contributors

Nils-Holger Areskog, MD, PhD*†
Professor, Head
Department of Clinical Physiology
Faculty of Health Sciences
Linköping, Sweden

Jose L. Bada, Jr, MD†
Senior Resident
Instituto ASEPEYO
Barcelona, Spain

Montserrat Bellver, MD†
Centre d' Alt Rendiment
Barcelona, Spain

Josep Borrell, MD*†
Director Médico Instituto ASEPEYO
Barcelona, Spain

Erin L. Boynton, MD, FRCSC†
Lecturer
Department of Surgery
University of Toronto
Toronto, Canada

Joseph A. Buckwalter, MD*†
University of Iowa
Orthopaedics Department
Iowa City, Iowa

Maria Isabel Covas, MD, PhD†
Servicio de Laboratorio
Hospital del Mar
Laboratori de Referéncia de Catalunya
Barcelona, Spain

Ramon Cugat, MD*†
Professor Asociado Universidad
    Autonoma de Barcelona
Muta Montanesa de Barcelona
Mutalidad de Futbolistas Espanoles,
    Delegacion Catalana
Hospital Universitario del Mar
Barcelona, Spain

R. Curco, PhD†
Centre D'Alt Rendiment
Sant Cugat del Vallés
Barcelona, Spain

Xavier Cusco, MD†
Orthopaedics
Clinice del Pilar
Barcelona, Spain

Bruce H. Dobkin, MD*†
Professor, Department of Neurology
University of California, Los Angeles
School of Medicine
Los Angeles, California

Roberto Elosua, MD†
Department D'Epidemiologia i Salut
    Pública
Barcelona, Spain

Eugenio Diaz Ferreiro, MD*
Servicio de Traumetologia y Cirugia
    Ortopédica
Ciudad Sanitaria Vall d'Hebron
Barcelona, Spain

Gerald M. Finerman, MD*†
Professor
Department of Orthopaedic Surgery
UCLA School of Medicine
Los Angeles, California

Montse Garcia, MD†
Researcher
Clinica Del Pilar
Barcelona, Spain

William E. Garrett, Jr, MD, PhD*†
Associate Professor of Orthopaedic
    Surgery and Cell Biology
Duke University
Durham, North Carolina

James G. Garrick, MD*†
Director, Center for Sports Medicine
Saint Francis Memorial Hospital
San Francisco, California

Roger M. Glaser, PhD*†
Director, Institute for Rehabilitation
    Research and Medicine
Professor of Physiology and Biophysics
Wright State University School of
    Medicine
Dayton, Ohio

Xavier Gonzalez-Mestre, MD*
Director of Research Programs
Institut d'Estudis de la Salut
Department of Health and Social Security
Catalunya, Spain

Stephen L. Gordon, PhD*†
Chief, Musculoskeletal Diseases Branch
National Institute of Arthritis and
   Musculoskeletal and Skin Diseases
National Institutes of Health
Bethesda, Maryland

James E. Graves, PhD†
Associate Professor and Chair
Department of Health and Physical
   Education
Syracuse University
Syracuse, New York

Charles Y. Guezennec, MD, PhD*†
Chief Division Physiologie-Métabolique
CERMA
Centre d'Essais en Vol
Brétigny Sur Orge, France

William J. Jason, MD†
UCLA School of Medicine
Department of Orthopaedic Surgery
Los Angeles, California

Peter Jokl, MD*†
Professor of Orthopaedics and
   Rehabilitation
Chief, Section of Sports Medicine
Yale School of Medicine
New Haven, Connecticut

Xavier Juan, MD†
Mutualidad de Futbolistas Españoles
Barcelona, Spain

William J. Kraemer, PhD*†
Associate Professor of Applied Physiology
Director of Research
Center for Sports Medicine
Pennsylvania State University
University Park, Pennsylvania

Robert E. Leach, MD*†
Editor
American Journal of Sports Medicine
Waltham, Massachusetts

Wayne B. Leadbetter, MD*†
Visiting Scientist, Naval Medical Research
   Institute
Wound Repair Enhancement Division
Bethesda, Maryland

David T. Lowenthal, MD, PhD*†
Professor of Medicine, Pharmacology, and
   Exercise Science
University of Florida
Director, Geriatric Research, Education
   and Clinical Center
VA Medical Center
Gainesville, Florida

Jaume Marrugat, MD, PhD*†
Department d'Epidemiologia i Salut
   Pública
Institut Municipal D'Investigacio Medica
Barcelona, Spain

Juan Carlos Monllau, MD†
Resident, Orthopaedics
Hospital
Girond, Spain

Robert C. Mulholland, MB, FRCS*†
Special Professor, Orthopaedic and
   Accident Surgery
University of Nottingham
Nottingham, United Kingdom

Antonio Navarro, MD, PhD*†
Professor of Orthopaedics
Hospital of Traumatology, Vall d'Hebron
Barcelona, Spain

Timothy D. Noakes, MB ChB, MD*†
Liberty Life Chair of Exercise and Sports
   Science
Director, MRC/UCT Bioenergetics of
   Exercise Research Unit
Department of Physiology
University of Cape Town Medical School
Observatory, South Africa

Andre J. Premen, PhD†
Health Scientist Administrator
Division of Extramural Affairs
National Heart, Lung, and Blood Institute
National Institutes of Health
Bethesda, Maryland

Pedro Pujol, MD*†
Head of Nutrition Department
Centre d'Alt Rendiment
Barcelona, Spain

James C. Puffer, MD*†
Professor and Chief
Division of Family Medicine
UCLA School of Medicine
Los Angeles, California

Ralph K. Requa, MSPH†
Research Director
Center for Sports Medicine
San Francisco, California

S. Ribas, MD†
Biologist-Nutritionist
Technical Department
Casa Santiveri S.A.
Barcelona, Spain

Alan D. Rogol, MD, PhD*†
Professor of Pediatrics and Pharmacology
University of Virginia Health Sciences
  Center
Charlottesville, Virginia

Loring B. Rowell, PhD†
Professor, Departments of Physiology and
  Biophysics and Medicine (Cardiology)
University of Washington School of
  Medicine
Seattle, Washington

Angel Ruiz-Cotorro, MD†
Mutualidad Futbolistas Catalana
Barcelona, Spain

E. Sanchez, PhD†
Centro de Alto Rendimiento Deportino
Saint Cugat
Barcelona, Spain

Isabel Sanudo, MD*
Hospital Clinic Rehabilitation Service
Faculty of Medicine
Barcelona, Spain

Anthony Schepsis, MD†
Associate Professor of Orthopaedic
  Surgery
Boston University Medical Center
Boston, Massachusetts

Ramon Segura, MD, PhD†
Professor, Medical School
University of Barcelona
Barcelona, Spain

Josep Ricardo Serra Grima, MD*†
Cardiology Department
Hospital de San Pau
Barcelona, Spain

Nicolás Terrados, MD, PhD*†
Sports Medicine Center
Fundación Deportiva Municipal
Avilés, Spain

Charles M. Tipton, PhD*†
Department of Exercise and Sport
  Sciences
University of Arizona
Tucson, Arizona

Arthur C. Vailas, PhD*
Professor and Chair
Department of Kinesiology
University of Wisconsin-Madison
Madison, Wisconsin

Carlos Vallbona, MD*†
Distinguished Service Professor and
  Chairman, Department of Community
  Medicine
Professor of Rehabilitation and Family
  Medicine
Baylor College of Medicine
Houston, Texas

J. Nardi-Vilardaga, MD, PhD†
Servcio de Traumatologia y Cirugia
  Ortopedica
Hospital de Traumatologia y
  Rehabilitacion
Ciudad Sanitaria y Universitaria, Vall
  d'Hebron
Barcelona, Spain

Jaime Vilaro, MD†
Mutualidad de Futbolistas Españoles
Barcelona, Spain

Ilkka Vuori, MD, PhD*†
UKK Institute for Health Promotion
  Research
Tampere, Finland

Donna L. Wheeler, PhD†
Director of Research
Oregon Health Sciences University
Division of Orthopaedics and
  Rehabilitation
Portland, Oregon

Savio L-Y. Woo, PhD†
Ferguson Professor of Orthopaedics and
  Vice Chairman for Research
Professor of Mechanical Engineering
Department of Orthopaedic Surgery
University of Pittsburgh
School of Medicine
Pittsburgh, Pennsylvania

*Seminar Participants
†Contributors to Volume

Table of Contents

Preface

On July 20-24, 1992 the National Institute of Arthritis and Musculo-skeletal and Skin Diseases (NIAMS), National Institutes of Health, and the Research Program, Institut d'Estudis de la Salut, Generalitat de Catalunya, Spain, sponsored a Workshop on Sports and Exercise in Midlife. The concept for this endeavor emerged while Xavier Gonzalez-Mestre, MD, Director of Research Programs at the Institut d'Estudis de la Salut (IES), Department of Health in Catalunya, was on a training assignment with me at the NIAMS. Both of us had reached midlife while maintaining a strong scientific and personal interest in sports and exercise activities. It appeared that there was limited information available to guide participants, clinicians, or investigators in sports and exercise as they relate to the midlife population. Using the international setting of the 1992 Olympics in Barcelona, Spain, this workshop became a Cultural Olympic Event with an internationally recognized group of scientists and clinicians participating.

The organizing committee, in addition to Dr. Gonzales-Mestre and myself, included William E. Garrett, Jr, MD, PhD, Duke University; Gerald M. Finerman, MD, University of California at Los Angeles; Antonio Navarro, MD, PhD, Hospital of Traumatology (Vall d'Hebron), Barcelona, Spain; and Pedro Pujol, MD, Centre d'Alt Rendiment, Barcelona, Spain. Dr. Gonzalez-Mestre and I served as co-chairpersons.

I would like to thank Marilyn Fox, PhD, Director of the Department of Publications, who was responsible for organizing and managing this project. Lynne Shindoll and Bruce Davis, senior editors, Joan Abern and Jane Baque, associate senior editors, and Leslie Neistadt copyedited the manuscripts, and Loraine Edwalds, production manager, and Kathy Brouillette, assistant production manager, oversaw the smooth flow of manuscripts through the production process. I would also like to acknowledge the efforts of Sophie Tosta, Sharon Duffy, Susan Baim, and Katy O'Brien, editorial assistants; and Geraldine Dubberke and Em Lee Lambos, publications secretaries.

Abstracts were prepared by each participant and distributed before the meeting to facilitate discussions during the workshop. Four major areas were covered in the presentations: epidemiology, physiologic response to participation, training programs, and treatment of injuries. Within the physiologic response and training portions, a broad range of perspectives were included: aerobic fitness, musculoskeletal fitness, endocrine response, nutrition, and neurologic response. Three special presentations were incorporated to consider functionally impaired individuals. Part of the discussion period was devoted to developing recommendations for future research directions. These future recommendations will appear after the four major content sections of the book.

Based on the original workshop premise, that information should be available to guide midlife individuals (and their physicians) in more successful participation in sports and activities, the concluding portion of each discussion was devoted to answering hypothetical, "practical" questions that may be asked of a doctor by those currently exercising or considering an exercise program. The organizing committee developed six questions that were considered by the workshop participants. The list of questions and the composite answers are provided in the concluding portion of this book.

Both formal discussion periods and conversations during breaks led to some comprehensive, possibly philosophical, thoughts regarding this workshop. The broadest definition of midlife spanned from 35 to 65 years of age. The general consensus was that we should not be concerned with a rigorous effort to define the exact limits of midlife or establish intermediate categories; eg, young midlife. There was a broad belief that fitness may be achieved by a combination of energetic activities of daily living and specific exercise activities. Any constructive action taken by individuals toward attaining fitness is beneficial. Unfit people can and should work toward a healthier lifestyle and better fitness. Maintained throughout life, fitness activities can alleviate many of the decreases in function attributed to aging. Most participants believed that some of these age-related effects may, in fact, be strongly related to a gradual disuse response as much as to aging itself. The occurrence of injury during sports and exercise was recognized as an acceptable risk associated with these activities. Most injuries are mild to moderate in severity and have no long-term aftereffects. Alternative exercises are recommended rather than total withdrawal from activity following injury. Clinical investigators were optimistic about the many physiologic and psychological benefits of special exercise programs and equipment for many functionally impaired individuals.

There was a generally accepted concept that the sports and exercise activities of midlife individuals should be viewed as a fun part of a healthy life-style. These activities should not be perceived as a required chore necessary to achieve fitness. The competitive aspects should be de-emphasized, which may in turn reduce injuries. In making the closing remarks at this workshop, Professor Albert Oriol Bosch, Director, Institut d'Estudis de la Salut in Catalunya, made the following observation regarding excessive competitiveness: "If you were a champion athlete in your youth, there is nothing further to prove. If you were not, midlife is not the time to prove it."

Stephen L. Gordon, PhD

Section One

Epidemiology of Sports Activity and Injury in Midlife

Chapter 1

Prevalence of Sports Activity and Injury in North America

James G. Garrick, MD
Ralph K. Requa, MSPH

Assessing either the extent of participation in fitness activities or the resulting injuries in individuals in their midlife years is a difficult task. For a variety of reasons, these individuals have, for the most part, escaped the scrutiny of epidemiologic research. While promoting the virtues of cardiovascular fitness enhancement, the medical community and exercise physiologists have all but ignored the musculoskeletal consequences of these fitness activities.

One approach to gathering epidemiologic data about adult fitness activities is to combine information from medical facilities with participation data from other sources. Unfortunately, in the United States, there is no single reliable source describing the population's involvement with fitness activities—much less its problems with injuries.

The most frequently quoted source of information regarding adult fitness activities is the Census Bureau's Statistical Abstract of the United States.[1] Under "participatory sports" the following are listed as the ten most popular sports: swimming, exercise walking, bike riding, camping, freshwater fishing, bowling, exercising with equipment, basketball, aerobic exercising, and volleyball, with participation ranging from a high of 70.4 million to a low of 25.1 million. These data suggest that a significant proportion of the population is involved in some form of fitness activities. However, these data are inflated in that the numbers include individuals who have participated in these activities only a single time during the course of a year.

The meaningful data base regarding sports and fitness activities generally covers three categories of activities: those associated with a high risk of injury; those involving team competition; and those with youthful participants. High-risk activities such as skiing provoke interest because the consequences are not only medically obvious but are of economic importance to both the participants and society. Team activities attract interest because they are easier to study than individual sports. For example, a soccer team consists of a group of participants who can be readily identified, contacted, and questioned or examined. Youth activities such as (American) football attract interest not only because of the high risk of injury, but also because participants are under the guidance of adults who bear some responsibility for the consequences.

Unfortunately, the activities for which we have some epidemiologic data represent only a small fraction of the fitness endeavors of the adult in midlife. The two exceptions to the above categories are running and aerobic exercise. However, even in these relatively extensively studied activities, we have only highly focused "snapshots" of data.

Powell and associates[2] examined epidemiologic data concerning running injuries. They noted that while there is an abundance of information regarding the relative frequencies of various injuries, which may even allow the generation of hypotheses regarding injury causes, such reports do not provide incidence rates or identify risk factors or even high-risk runners. Among the few epidemiologic studies allowing a calculation of rates within a clearly defined population at risk, there are data suggesting that age was associated (either positively or negatively) with running injuries.

Similarly, we attempted to examine the literature concerning aerobic exercise injuries.[3] Like Powell, we encountered difficulties in establishing incidence rates. In many instances, the population at risk was poorly defined, and the published reports of aerobic exercise injuries were simply anecdotal accounts of experiences in a medical practice. The few studies that did identify the population at risk failed to reveal any significant association between age and risk of injury.

Beyond data regarding running and aerobic exercise, we must rely on data gathered at medical facilities that provide care for the recreational athlete and fitness participant. Over the past 13 years, our facility has provided care for over 40,000 sports injuries. The ten activities most frequently cited by patients as the cause of these problems are presented in Table 1. Due to a lack of exposure data, there is no way of assessing whether large numbers of injuries reflect a disproportionate number of participants or a hazardous activity. Running is probably a reflection of the former and skiing the latter.

All of the activities shown in Table 1 have a high proportion of injuries, and presumably participants, in midlife. There appears to be a trend toward lessened participation with advancing years, except for individuals active in tennis, walking, and golf. However, one of the dangers of extrapolating participation trends from injury data is that the relatively high proportion of injuries in the older age groups may not represent a high level of participation, but rather increasing hazards to the older individual.

Table 1 Injury rates (percent) by age and sport at the Center for Sports Medicine 1979 to 1992

Sport	Age of Participants (years)						Total %
	0-20	21-30	31-40	41-50	51-60	61+	
Running	9.4	23.3	31.6	25.6	8.3	1.8	20.3
Tennis	7.8	7.0	21.4	37.0	15.6	11.3	9.6
Basketball	27.4	34.2	19.2	13.0	4.8	1.4	5.4
Aerobic exercise	5.6	26.1	32.4	26.1	7.0	2.8	5.3
Walking	5.8	16.7	20.3	21.0	21.7	14.5	5.1
Ballet	44.7	30.3	12.9	9.8	1.5	0.8	3.0
Weight training	7.1	22.0	38.6	22.8	6.3	3.1	4.7
Alpine skiing	12.1	25.8	25.8	25.0	7.3	4.0	4.6
Cycling	8.8	26.3	31.3	22.5	10.0	1.3	3.0
Golf	7.5	9.1	22.7	25.8	15.2	19.7	2.5

When these data are examined with regard to the age of the individual injured, it becomes apparent that injury patterns are more a function of the activity than the age of the participant. For example, ankle sprains among basketball players are common across all age groups. Likewise, knee sprains among skiers and patellofemoral dysfunction among runners, aerobic dancers, cyclists, and walkers appear to have no predilection for particular age groups.

Bowling, volleyball, and swimming—activities listed among the ten most popular participatory sports—are notably absent from the list of activities producing the most sports injuries. This absence is surprising because sport-specific epidemiologic studies would suggest that the injury rates associated with volleyball and swimming are substantially higher than those seen in walking and golf. The exclusion of volleyball and swimming from the list of injury-producing activities may be a reflection of the participants' level of exposure, or lack thereof. Playing volleyball at a family picnic or going to the beach are activities that are unlikely to produce injuries, but would qualify one as a sport participant from the standpoint of Census Bureau surveyors.

Faced with the many problems associated with investigating fitness activities in a global fashion, we decided to examine the activities in which a group of committed fitness advocates participated. We defined a committed fitness participant as one who participated in aerobic exercise for at least three 45-minute sessions per week or in more than one major fitness activity for at least four 45-minute sessions per week. Subjects were recruited from 15 San Francisco area fitness clubs and agreed to participate in weekly telephone contacts in order to document both fitness activities and injuries. Injuries were defined as any musculoskeletal complaint arising from participation in fitness activities. The injuries were further subcategorized as those resulting in limiting fitness activities and/or requiring formal medical treatment.

There were 986 participants who completed the study. They were followed for an aggregate of 10,582 weeks of activity (11 weeks per participant average) and over 60,000 hours of participation. While most participants were in their 20s and 30s (the median age was 32 years), more than 150 were in their 40s, and nearly 60 were over the age of 50.

There were 525 injuries recorded during the course of the study, of which 475 were sports-related for an injury rate of 7.83/1,000 hours of activity (475/60,629). Of these injuries, 69% resulted in "time loss," interfering with fitness activities and/or the activities of daily living. The injury rate for time-loss injuries was 6.61/1,000. Seventy-three (13.9%) of the injuries and complaints resulted in the participant seeking formal medical treatment.

Injury rates for various activities are presented in Table 2. Overall numbers of injuries were highest for team sports, including basketball and racquetball, and running, intermediate for tennis and aerobic exercise, and lowest for stationary cycling, golf, swimming, walking, and individual toning/calisthenics. In aggregate, team sports had the highest injury rates (15.99), followed by classes (11.32), individual sports (9.77), aerobic exercise (6.62), weights (6.33), and cardiovascular exercise equipment (3.17).

Injury rates for males and females were identical for individuals aged 29 and under. Males aged 30 to 39 had an overall higher injury rate than females of the same age (10.3 versus 7.6, < 0.05), perhaps because males are more likely to participate in activities with a higher risk of injury, such as basketball and racquetball. Injury rates for males declined slightly after age 30, but rates for females remained relatively constant with increasing age.

One of the more striking findings was that a substantial proportion of the injuries occurred to previously injured anatomic regions (only 40% of the injuries were acute). Over 15% of individuals with knee, ankle, foot/toes, low back, and shoulder injuries had a positive history of injury to that same anatomic region. Viewed another way, individuals with a history of injury to any of the above-mentioned anatomic regions were twice as likely to reinjure the same area than those who had no such history.

Discussion

Because of a general lack of information about fitness activities for adults in midlife, it is difficult to make generalizations concerning the hazards associated with participation in such activities. While it is generally accepted that any activity that enhances cardiovascular fitness is "healthy," our ability to assess the net cost of such enhancement is deficient. Although the negative consequences of fitness enhancement—injuries—are rarely life threatening (and the benefits are often life prolonging), injuries are nonetheless costly in terms of both utilization of medical resources and lost productivity.

Table 2 Injury totals and rates by sport

Activity	Total Number of Injuries	Rate/ 1,000 Hr	Time Loss Injuries	Rate/ 1,000 Hr	Hours
Aerobic dance	90	6.62	63	4.63	13,600
Class					
Dance—Other	10	10.20	5	5.10	981
Yoga	3	7.20	2	4.80	417
Other (shaping or sculpting, ski conditioning, martial arts, etc)	15	13.93	12	11.15	1,077
Cardiovascular exercise equipment					
Cycles—stationary	6	1.77	5	1.48	3,387
Cross-country ski exercise equipment	1	4.66	1	4.66	215
Rowing machines	4	7.06	3	5.30	567
Stair climbers	16	2.95	9	1.66	5,424
Treadmills	7	6.36	6	5.45	1,101
Weights					
Free weights	36	4.26	31	3.66	8,459
Weight machines (Cybex, Nautilus, Pyramid, Universal, etc)	22	5.46	17	4.22	4,031
Individual					
Cycling	13	6.01	8	3.70	2,165
Roller skating	3	20.94	3	20.94	143
Running	71	14.74	52	10.79	4,818
Skiing (Alpine)	18	8.25	17	7.79	2,182
Walking	8	2.01	7	1.76	3,983
Other (golf, swimming, etc)	54	14.21	43	11.32	3,799
Team					
Basketball	24	18.31	18	13.73	1,311
Racquetball	6	14.00	6	14.00	429
Tennis	9	7.74	6	5.16	1,163
Other (softball, volleyball, etc)	24	23.16	17	16.41	1,036
Nonsports related	50		43		
Unknown	10		4		

Injuries sustained by individuals in midlife are particularly significant because their effects extend beyond an inability to participate in fitness activities. Unlike school-age youth and the elderly, an injury to an individual in midlife may mean a loss of work productivity and thereby influence the ability to earn a living. In addition, such injuries may preclude or discourage participation in other fitness activities.

Powell and associates[2] reported that among serious runners, 37 of each 100 would be injured per year. We estimated that among the fitness participants in our investigation there would be 129 injuries per 100 participants per year, of which 75% would result in time loss (based on 150 hours of participation per year). While these data suggest that fitness activities in general, and running in particular, are more hazardous than previously documented, one must bear in mind the differing definitions of injury.

In our study of fitness participants, an "injury" was any complaint, 25% of which did not result in any change in the participant's activity. Of those injuries that did result in some change in fitness regimen (time loss), the majority required only that the individual make changes in specific fitness tasks, for example, avoiding a particular lift in weight training or avoiding a particular step in aerobic exercise.

In the studies of runners, the definition of an injury was more constrained and involved substantially more disability. In the three studies quoted in most detail in the Powell Report,[2] to qualify as an "injury" the problem had to be severe enough to either preclude running for at least a week or result in taking medication, decreasing mileage, or consulting a health professional.[4-6]

In an effort to place injury rates in a similar context, we can look at time loss injuries among our runners using a definition similar to that used by Koplan and associates.[4] They noted that more than one third cited an injury that at least diminished mileage over a year of running. Our definition of time loss injuries, those that altered or stopped participation, was similar. The rate of time loss injury among our participants who ran was 10.79/1,000 hours or 43.3/100 study-person-years, which is somewhat higher than that noted by Koplan and associates.[4] Our study participants may have differed from runners selected from participants in a road race, because we required our subjects to engage in more than one major fitness activity. Few participated regularly in road races. Whether this had an effect on their rate of injury is not known.

Although few investigators have examined the influence of prior orthopaedic problems on injury rates, this appears to be a problem of some magnitude. Theoretically, it should become a greater problem with advancing age, as the older participant has had more exposure and therefore more opportunities to be injured. However, we found no evidence of increasing injury rates with advancing age. One explanation for this finding may be that those individuals with prior or repeated injuries are more likely to stop participating in fitness activities; this observation is supported in part by the fact that older patients did not give a history of having more injuries than their younger counterparts.

Among the more optimistic findings in the investigation of fitness participants was the fact that most injuries were of gradual onset or the result of overuse. Such injuries are not only less likely to result in long-term medical problems but also more likely to respond to injury prevention efforts. Almost without exception, investigators examining the causes of overuse injuries have found that "training errors" are the major factor. Thus, education programs offer a potential means of injury prevention.

One of the more discouraging findings is that only a relatively small proportion of the population of the United States considered to be in midlife participates in any meaningful, regular fitness program. It is also disturbing that the information we have concerning both participation and injury rates comes from the middle and higher socioeconomic classes. Virtually no information exists regarding fitness activities among the economically deprived—the group that might conceivably benefit most from regular participation in a fitness program.

References

1. U.S. Department of Commerce, Bureau of the Census. *Statistical Abstract of the United States 1990, The National Data Book*, ed 110. Washington, DC.
2. Powell KE, Kohl HW, Caspersen CJ, et al: An epidemiological perspective on the causes of running injuries. *Phys Sportsmed* 1986;14:100-114.
3. Garrick JG, Requa RK: Aerobic dance: A review. *Sports Med* 1988;6:169-179.
4. Koplan JP, Powell KE, Sikes RK, et al: An epidemiologic study of the benefits and risks of running. *JAMA* 1982;248:3118-3121.
5. Pollock ML, Gettman LR, Milesis CA, et al: Effects of frequency and duration of training on attrition and incidence of injury. *Med Sci Sports* 1977;9:31-36.
6. Blair SN: Running injuries: Rates, risk factors and prevention. *Med Sci Sports Exerc* 1985;17:xii.

Chapter 2

Prevalence of Sports Activity and Injury in Europe

Carlos Vallbona, MD

In view of the growing importance of sports and leisure time physical activity as a means to attain optimal physical fitness, maintain health, and prevent cardiovascular and other diseases, it is appropriate to review the epidemiologic evidence gathered by European investigators in support of recommendations to increase the current level of community participation in leisure time physical activity. This goal has been translated into specific outcome objectives, which are incorporated with few changes into several national health plans for the year 2000.[1-3] The high prevalence of sedentariness and the low level of participation in leisure time physical activity in midlife have been well documented in the majority of industrialized nations, and it was fitting that a workshop be devoted to a scientific analysis of issues related to sports, physical activity in general, and injury in midlife. This workshop could not have been more timely if we consider that just a few days after the Symposium, the XXV Olympic Games focused the world's attention on the high level of physical fitness and performance exhibited by elite young athletes from all over the world.

The objectives of this review paper are the following: (1) to review the historic interest in physical activity and exercise by European physicians and investigators; (2) to present survey data on the prevalence of sedentariness and leisure time physical activity in European populations; (3) to analyze the results of studies of physical fitness in selected European populations; (4) to discuss the relationship between physical fitness and physical activity during work and leisure time; (5) to review data on the protective value of physical activity against cardiovascular morbidity and mortality; and (6) to summarize epidemiologic data on some risks and injuries attributable to exercise.

Historic Interest in Physical Activity and Exercise by European Physicians and Investigators

The European medical community has had a historic interest in the physiology of exercise and its value in preventive medicine. The ancient Greeks acknowledged the value of exercise as illustrated in the doctrine that Xenophon probably learned from Socrates, which asserts that physical exercise helps to postpone deterioration in the power of thinking by preventing ill health.[4] Similarly, by 400 BC, Hippocrates wrote the following statement which has been extensively quoted:[5] "All parts of the body, which are designed to serve a function, will remain in good health, grow and reach an advanced age if they are used in moderation. However, if they are not used, they tend to become diseased, cease to grow, and age prematurely."

Various writers of the Middle Ages and early Renaissance wrote on the value of "hygienic exercise," especially Galen, who in his book *On Hygiene* discussed the importance of physical activity in keeping with Hippocrates' admonitions.[6]

Perhaps the first book devoted solely to the value of physical exercise that included specific recommendations for people at all age groups was written by Cristobal Mendez, a physician from Jaen, Spain, who in 1553 published the *Libro del Excercisio Corporal* (Book of Bodily Exercise) based on his own information and experiences, guided, in turn, by the knowledge, observations, and experience of numerous predecessors. Indeed, in the prologue of his book, he makes extensive reference to Aristotle, Averroes, and Celsus, in addition to Galen, Pliny, Plutarch, and Ptolemy.[7] Only three copies of this book are known to exist, one at Yale University and two at the National Library of Madrid. Two quotes from Cristobal Mendez are particularly relevant: "The easiest way of all to preserve and restore health without diverse peculiarities and with greater profit than all other measures put together is to exercise well." "I will speak of the great utility of the exercise of walking, and I do not find a more proven one and necessary one than this because it can be done in a very easy way and without too much trouble or too many inconveniences."

About 16 years after Mendez's book, another treatise on exercise was published by Gerolamo Mercuriale under the title *Artis Gymnasticae Apud Antiquos* (The Art of Gymnastics Among the Ancients). In his treatise he makes reference to 96 different authors, although he does not count Mendez among them. It is likely that the short interval between the publication of the two books did not give Mercuriale an opportunity to learn about the Spaniard's publication.[6,8]

Claude Bernard, the founder of modern physiology, was undoubtedly very conscious of the importance of physical activity and exercise as illustrated in the following statement from one of his letters to Madame Raffalovich:[9] "In all things, the good and the bad are nothing but the extremes; moderate exercise gives strength, forced exercise weakens those with a nervous temperament."

By the end of the nineteenth century there was a great deal of popular interest in performing the rhythmic physical exercises widely known throughout Europe as "Swedish gymnastics." The reestablishment of the modern Olympiad in 1896, which promoted a spirit of competition in sports and physical performance, ignited the world. The subsequent proliferation of the practice of an ever-growing variety of sports in leisure time sparked a great deal of interest on the part of European physiologists as detailed in a review article by P-O Åstrand.[10] The interest was shared immediately by physiologists in America and other parts of the world. The landmark contributions of Irma Åstrand,[11] P-O Åstrand,[12-15] Bergström,[16] and others to the understanding of the physiologic responses to graded exercise and the quantification of physical fitness in military recruits paved the way for an active period of investigation beginning after World War II.

Perhaps the first important epidemiologic observation was made in the members of England's "Fellowship of Cycling Oldtimers," a 50-year-old organization of cyclists 50 years of age and older—75% of whom were still cycling at the time of the study. They exhibited a striking decrease in coronary heart disease in relation to the general population, particularly after 75 years of age.[17]

Two important epidemiologic studies were published in the 1950s. Logan[18] reported on the relationship between socioeconomic status and cardiovascular mortality, and subsequently Morris and associates[19,20] published the first large-scale population study of the value of physical exercise in preventing fatal cardiovascular disease in British civil servants and London bus drivers.

The conclusions of these studies were supported by important case control and cohort studies conducted in large population samples by American and Canadian epidemiologists. The First International Conference on Physical Activity and Cardiovascular Health was held in Toronto in 1966. This conference did much to unify concepts and adopt reasonably standardized methodologies for the quantitative assessment of cardiovascular endurance and physical fitness.[21] Some of these methodologies were applicable to epidemiologic studies that quantitated the growing prevalence of sedentariness in population groups and the deterioration of physical fitness of midlife adults in the industrialized countries. Similarly, the conference provided a stimulus to the implementation of therapeutic exercise programs aimed at improving the physical fitness of persons with ischemic heart disease, respiratory disease, and other disabilities. The more recent Second International Conference on Exercise, Fitness and Health, which was also held in Toronto, in 1988, led to a consensus of current knowledge to be shared by professionals in a variety of disciplines including physiology, epidemiology, sports medicine, preventive medicine, rehabilitation medicine, nutrition, and psychology.[22]

Interestingly, manned space exploration, which began with the first cosmonaut, Yuri Gagarin, and the first astronaut, Alan Shepard, in 1961, posed important research questions on the adaptation to zero-gravity environments and the value of physical exercise as a means to prevent any deleterious physiologic consequences of living in a zero-gravity environment. In this regard, the studies published by the British investigator Cuthbertson in 1929[23] represent the beginning of an equally feverish period of investigations that analyzed in detail the cardiovascular and metabolic consequences of bedrest in healthy persons[24-27] and in healthy persons submitted to simulated zero-gravity environments,[28-30] as well as in paralyzed persons.[31]

Prevalence of Sedentariness and Leisure Time Physical Activity in European Populations

Over the last three decades, several epidemiologic studies have been conducted in European populations to document the extent to which groups of individuals are physically active at work and during leisure time, the relationship between the level of physical activity and physical fitness, and more importantly, how these factors relate to cardiovascular morbidity and mortality. Most of the published studies carried out in midlife populations have pursued more than one of the above objectives, but regardless of scope, they contain abundant information from which it is possible to extract data on the prevalence of physical activity at work and during leisure time (or conversely, the prevalence of sedentariness) in several European countries.

Most of the papers published since 1970 include data that have been gathered through interview surveys of individuals in specific populations, predominantly in the working environment, but some in general populations. It should be recognized that surveys based on self-reported data do not yield as valid information as those based on objective measurements. Table 1 lists the papers that in the opinion of this reviewer, seem to be based on acceptable methodologic survey principles in spite of some selection biases clearly recognized by the authors of these studies.[32-43] In most instances, the bias results from having surveyed only men or industrial workers (who usually were male).

It can be concluded from all these studies that the prevalence of moderate or high levels of physical activity during leisure time in the industrialized populations of Europe is undesirably low with a correspondingly high prevalence of sedentariness, which has increased slightly in some populations in the last decade. It is also clear from the above studies that sedentariness is usually associated with other cardiovascular risk factors, such as smoking, hypertension, obesity, alcohol consumption, and poor nutritional habits.[44] This association may, in part, explain the relationship between physical activity and cardiovascular morbidity and mortality.

Table 1 Prevalence of high leisure time physical activity (Europe)

Author	Country	Year	Population	N Subjects	Sex	Age (years)	Prevalence (%)	Comment*	Ref.
Hickey et al.	Ireland	1969-72	Industry; general	15,171	M	25-74	22	a	32
De Backer et al.	Belgium	1981	Industry	1,513	M	40-55	27	a,b	33
Holme et al.	Norway	1981	General	15,000	M	40-49	24	a,c	34
Bjartveit	Norway	1983	General—rural	>60,000	M-F	35-49	15-32	a	35
Tuxworth et al.	United Kingdom	1979-86	Industry	1,394	M	35-60	28	a,b	36
Mundal et al.	Norway	1982	Industry General	2,109	M	40-60	5-11	a,b,c	37
Tuomilehto et al.	Finland	1970-85	General	3,975	M	25-64	23	a	38
Johansson et al.	Sweden	1981-88	General	7,495	M	47-55	16	a,c	39
Sobolski et al.	Belgium	1968-85	Industry	2,363	M	40-55	33	a,b,d	40
	Slovakia	1985	Industry	1,995	M	40-55	27		
Heinemann & Zerbes	Germany (East)	1989	General	119	M	25-34	15-24	a	41
Viljanen et al.	Finland	1991	General—urban	778	M-F	25-55	10-15	a,b	42
de Cambra et al.	Catalunya	1990	General	1,025	M-F	15-65	21		43

*a. Shows association of sedentariness and other risk factors
b. Studies relationship with physical fitness
c. Studies relationship with cardiovascular disease
d. Includes in definition subjects whose leisure time work was ≥418 kJ/day

Physical Fitness of Selected European Populations

A limited number of studies have been conducted to document the level of physical fitness in European populations. The fact that the literature is sparse in this area is not surprising, because the methodology to quantitate physical fitness, expressed according to different parameters (maximal oxygen consumption, maximal heart rate, cumulative work and power capacity, energy expenditure, heat produced, muscular strength, explosive muscular effort, muscular performance time, endurance, etc) requires the use of rather sophisticated techniques, and in some instances, can pose definite risks to untrained subjects.[45-47] Table 2 presents studies that have been carried out according to well-accepted and valid methodologic principles.[33,36,40,44,48-50] It can be inferred from the above studies that the observed level of physical fitness in the European populations is quite similar to that of the Canadian population and somewhat higher than that of several American populations. The European studies also document the decline in physical fitness that occurs with age, as one would expect from cross-sectional and cohort studies.

Relationship Between Physical Fitness and Physical Activity During Work and Leisure Time

The studies presented in Table 2 also show that there is a relationship between physical activity during leisure time and physical fitness,

Table 2 Population studies of physical fitness (Europe)

Author	Country	Year	Population	N Subjects	Sex	Age (years)	Physical Fitness*	Comment**	Ref.
Erikssen & Rodahl	Norway	1979	Industry	1,835	M	40-59	CW 110 kJ 7 Mets	a,b	48, 49
De Backer et al.	Belgium	1981	Industry	1,505	M	40-55	112 W 7 Mets	c,d	33
Tuxworth et al.	United Kingdom	1979-86	Industry	1,394	M	35-60	25-37 $\dot{V}O_2$max ml/kg/min	b,c,e	36
Sobolski et al.	Belgium	1968-85	Industry	2,363	M	40-55	1.48 W/kg 6-7 Mets	c	40
	Slovakia	1985	Industry	1,995	M	40-55	1.52 W/kg 7 Mets	c	40
Shvartz & Reibold	Seven European countries	up to 1986	General	(141 population samples)	M-F	6-75	40 $\dot{V}O_2$max ml/kg/min	b	50
Lie et al.	Norway	1987	General	2,014	M	40-59	160 MHR 11 Mets	b	44

* Expressed in different units: CW = cumulative work; kJ = kilojoules; Mets = multiples of metabolic activity at rest; MHR = maximum heart rate; $\dot{V}O_2$max ml/kg/min = maximum oxygen consumption milliliter per kilogram per minute; W = watts.

**a. Shows seasonal variations
  b. Shows decline with age
  c. Shows relationship with leisure time activity (low order)
  d. Shows relationship with work activity (low order)
  e. Shows higher values for cyclists

but such a relationship is much less evident or nonexistent between physical activity during work and physical fitness.[36,42] It has been pointed out that the lack of relationship may be due to the narrow spectrum of physical activity at work in all the industrialized nations and to the low percentage of individuals who participate in work activities that impose high energy demands.

Protective Value of Physical Activity Against Cardiovascular Morbidity and Mortality

A few European cohort studies have collected data on the relationship between physical activity and cardiovascular morbidity and mortality. Table 3 lists some of the published studies.[34,39,44,51-53] Most show that individuals who are very active during leisure time indeed have decreased morbidity and mortality, but this may result from the fact that these individuals tend to have fewer risk factors associated with cardiovascular disease, such as smoking, hypertension, obesity, excessive caloric and saturated fat intake, and alcohol consumption.[18,33,37,54-56] The results of univariate analyses of the protective effect of physical activity are somewhat inconclusive. There is no evidence of any significantly favorable relationship between increased physical activity at work and decreased cardiovascular morbidity and mortality, and in fact, one study shows that cardiovascular morbidity is increased in persons whose jobs require high levels of physical activity.[34] There is, however, statistical evidence in favor of a univariate

Table 3 Studies of association between physical activity, physical fitness, and cardiovascular disease

Author	Country	Year	Years of Follow Up	Population	N Subjects	Sex	Age (years)	Comment*	Ref.
van Saase et al.	The Netherlands	1956-88	32	Athletes	1,259 (62,113 person-years)	M-F	30 at entry	a	52
Morris et al.	United Kingdom	1968-78	8-10	Industry	18,000	M	40-64	a	53
Lie et al.	Norway	1972	7	General	1,832	M	40-59	c	44
Holme et al.	Norway	1981	4	General	15,000	M	40-49	a,b	34
Johansson et al.	Sweden	1981-88	12	General	7,495	M	47-55	a	39
Pocock et al.	United Kingdom	1987	6	Industry	7,735	M	40-59	b	51

*a. Shows a decrease related to leisure physical activity
 b. Shows an increase related to worktime physical activity
 c. Shows a decrease related to high physical fitness

relationship between high physical activity at leisure time and decreased cardiovascular morbidity and mortality. Multivariate analyses conducted by some authors demonstrate that a rather small percentage of the variance in the incidence or prevalence of cardiovascular disease may be augmented by physical activity alone, but as shown by the studies of Table 3, such a contribution appears to be greater when physical activity at leisure time is analyzed together only with smoking, hypertension, and obesity.

The exact pathophysiologic mechanisms by which physical exercise may prevent the incidence of cardiovascular disease and some of its manifestations (especially arrhythmias) have not been elucidated, but one potentially protecting effect may be an improved blood flow, which has been documented by Ernst.[57] This would be in addition to the well-documented favorable changes in the lipid profile that occur as a result of physical activity.[58] As yet, there is no conclusive evidence of increased coronary blood flow as a result of physical exercise alone, but several studies have shown that a decrease in coronary plaque size may occur under the influence of several cholesterol-lowering interventions, including one that tested the value of changing lifestyle habits (including physical exercise).[59] One should also consider the possibility of improved small vessel coronary blood flow not shown by traditional large vessel angiography.

Health Risks and Injury Attributable to Exercise

Undoubtedly, whenever several organs or physiologic systems are subjected to extraordinary work demands during physical activity, there is a certain health risk involved, especially in individuals whose functional capacity or physical fitness is not optimal. In general, however, the benefit/risk ratio is so favorable that physicians and professionals in sports medicine do not believe that exercise is deleterious, except for the occurrence of musculoskeletal injuries, which only rarely lead to permanent disability, at least in the general population.[60-62]

Sudden death can and does occur in individuals during exercise.[61,63,64] For the last several years, and as a result of the extraordinary publicity that the media (especially television) have devoted to sports activities, the general population has viewed images of severe injuries and even sudden death as they occurred. The most dramatic of these injuries is sudden death, especially when it occurs in prominent athletes.[65-67] Because millions of persons have witnessed fatal incidents during organized sports, the erroneous conclusion has been reached that sudden death represents an important health hazard of physical exercise. This is simply not the case considering its low incidence. Cousteau,[68] in a publication dealing with the issue of sports after 50 years of age, alludes to the fact that sudden death is a danger of sports activities after age 40, but clearly, its incidence is quite low considering that in 1989, more than 20 million French persons of all ages practiced sports more or less regularly, including a significant number in midlife.[68] Similarly, in a study of a general population of adult joggers, Thompson and associates[69] found only one death per 400,000 hours of activity.

It has become evident from several studies that sudden death associated with vigorous exercise occurs mainly in individuals who have had preexisting risk factors (such as listed in Outline 1) or proven cardiac disturbances. In postmortem pathologic studies, the preexistence of coronary artery disease or valvular heart disease has been documented in virtually all cases. In a study of 60 deaths associated with the sport of squash, Northcote and associates[70] were able to study in depth 53 cases with a certified cause of death. Coronary heart disease was listed in 51 cases, valvular heart disease in four, cardiac arrhythmia in two, and hypertrophic cardiomyopathy in one. Only two deaths from noncardiac causes were observed in this series. Forty-five of those who died had reported chest pain prior to death, and 22 of them were known to have been previously diagnosed as having at least one condition related to the cardiovascular system (hypertension in 14 of the subjects). A high prevalence of other cardiovascular risk factors was found in those who died from coronary artery disease. Northcote and associates[70] also reported that there may be 2.5 million people in the United Kingdom who play squash once or more a month, but through press reports and a retrospective mail survey of sports centers throughout the United Kingdom, they documented that only 89 sudden deaths had occurred over a period of 7 years, thus confirming the extremely low incidence of sudden death in the demanding sport of squash.

The incidence of arrhythmias in athletes has been studied by Huston and associates,[71] and the data are shown in Table 4. Hanne-Paparo and Kellermann[72] also documented the frequency of ar-

Outline 1 Possible risk factors for sudden death in exercise and sport

Drug addiction: cocaine, amphetamines, tobacco, alcohol
Athlete heart
Family history of ischemic heart disease
Hypertension
Hyperlipidemia
Prolongation of QT time (familiar)
Arrhythmias
Marfan's syndrome

Table 4 Incidence of arrhythmias in athletes

	General Population (%)	Athletes* (%)
Arrhythmias		
Sinus bradycardia	24	50-85
Sinus arrhythmia	2.4-20	14-69
Wandering pacemaker	—	7-19
A-V block		
1°	0.7	33-64
2° Mobitz I	0.003	0.1-10
3°	0.0002	0.002
Nodal rhythm	0.06	0.03-7
Premature ventricular beats	0.1	0.2-2.5

*Sport variable according to different authors
Reproduced with permission from Huston TP, Puffer JC, Rodney WM: The athletic heart syndrome. *N Engl J Med* 1985;313:24-32.)

rhythmias in athletes and in controls during continuous electrocardiographic monitoring (Table 5). The European literature on this topic also includes some studies on the relationship between physical exercise and cardiac arrhythmias in athletes, as well as in healthy subjects.[73]

A thorough analysis of the incidence of injuries in sports participants and the prevalence of disability resulting from such injuries is beyond the scope of this paper. The reader is referred to a well-documented article on the methodologies used to assess the etiology of sport injuries.[74] Unfortunately, the European (as well as the non-European) literature on studies specifically carried out to analyze the incidence and prevalence of sports injuries in midlife is almost nonexistent. However, one important aspect of disability of particular interest in midlife is the suspected high prevalence of osteoarthritis in physically active persons.[75,76] An association between sports activities and osteoarthritis was pointed out by Baetzner[77] in 1936. However, American authors such as Lane and Fries[78] point out that the impact loading on weightbearing joints in running does not necessarily cause osteoarthritis. Recently, Professor Ernst[79] of the University of Vienna reviewed the existing evidence available in the Euro-

Table 5 Frequency of arrhythmias in athletes and controls during ECG monitoring

	Controls	Athlete
Heart rate		
Average lowest heart rate	45	3
Average highest heart rate	137	12
Arrhythmias (Prevalence %)		
Sinuspause > 2 secs	6	3
1° A-V block	14	37
2° A-V block (type I)	6	23
2° A-V block (type II)	0	9
Nodal rhythm	0	20
Premature ventricular beats	43	33
>5 PVC/hour	6	0
Ventricular tachycardia	6	0

(Reproduced with permission from Hanne-Paparo N, Kellermann JJ: Long-term Holter ECC monitoring of athletes. *Med Sci Sports Exerc* 1981;13:294-298.)

pean, American, and Canadian literature and concluded that "(1) all moderate exercise is better than no exercise; (2) only very excessive running may be harmful to the hips; (3) normalization of weight is mandatory when applicable."

It has been reported that midlife women who participate in long distance running may have a tendency to develop anemia and secondary amenorrhea.[80] Although this side effect has been well documented, it has been equally well documented that conditioning exercises decrease the incidence of premenstrual tension.[81] Thus, the benefits of a well regulated program of physical exercise may outweigh the risks.

Conclusions

A few studies suggest a relationship between participation in physical activities at leisure time and positive health attitudes.[82] Unfortunately, however, these studies point to a significant lag between positive attitudes towards exercise and the actual practice of such exercise. This has been documented by American investigators.[83] A more recent publication elaborates on this issue, pointing out that a population may be divided into four sectors according to their level of knowledge of, attitudes toward, and behavior in relation to specific health habits.[43] The distribution curve of the population may be normal or skewed toward one or the other extreme. Figure 1 depicts such distribution. Individuals to the left of the curve have no knowledge of, nor any favorable attitude toward good health habits, nor do they practice them. To the right of the curve, the individuals are knowledgeable about good health habits, have favorable attitudes towards them, and practice them. According to this model, a favorable shift of the population from a level of poor knowledge, attitude, and behavior to one of good knowledge, attitude, and behavior occurs

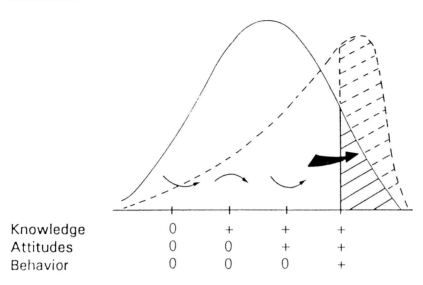

Knowledge	0	+	+	+
Attitudes	0	0	+	+
Behavior	0	0	0	+

Fig. 1 *Relationship between knowledge, attitude, and behavior. Shifting to the right in the case of physical exercise would yield more people participating in these activities. (Adapted with permission from de Cambra S, Serra L, Tresserras R, et al: Activitat física i promoció de la salut: Llibre Blanc (Physical activity and health promotion: White Paper). Generalitat de Catalunya, Departament de Sanitat I Seguretat Social. (Barcelona, Catalonia, Spain) March 1991.)*

very gradually. Initially, there is improvement in the level of knowledge, followed by improvement in attitudes, and a subsequent acquisition of appropriate health behaviors. The health belief model proposed by Becker and associates[84] is also applicable to the analysis of an individual's or a population's beliefs on the value of participation in physical exercise programs.[43]

The compilation of the newly acquired epidemiologic knowledge of the relationship between physical exercise, avoidance of risk factors, and prevention of cardiovascular disease has provided the rationale for a variety of future population-based interventions similar to those currently in progress in various parts of the world.[85] Their purpose is to promote leisure time physical activity and sports so as to improve the physical fitness and cardiovascular endurance of persons of all ages. Interventions have been inaugurated in several European communities, most notably those of The Netherlands, United Kingdom, Scandinavian countries, and Catalunya, Spain, as well as in a group of communities participating in the Healthy Cities Project, organized and coordinated by WHO.[86-88] Although the results are not yet available, it is hoped that they will be quite convincing in demonstrating the health benefits and the minimal risks of carefully planned health exercise programs and motivating midlife individuals to change their increasingly sedentary lifestyles in favor of greater leisure time participation in physical activities and sports. The ultimate goals are to decrease the prevalence of obesity, ischemic heart disease, diabetes, and other illnesses directly or indirectly related to sedentariness; to decrease the age-adjusted mortality rates; to decrease morbidity due to cardiovascular disease and other chronic conditions; and eventually to increase the number of years of healthy life (as well as the general quality of life).

References

1. Public Health Service. Healthy people 2000: National health promotion and disease prevention objectives: Full report, with commentary. Washington, DC, US Department of Health and Human Services, Public Health Service 1991, DHHS Publication No. (PHS)91-50212.

2. Salleras LS, Via-Redons JM: Setting targets for health policy: The Catalonian approach. Departament de Sanitat i Seguretat Social: Generalitat de Catalunya, 1992.

3. World Health Organization: Regional Office for Europe. *Targets for Health for All: Targets in Support of the European Regional Strategy for Health for All.* Copenhagen, WHO, 1985.

4. McIntosh PC: *Sport in Society.* London, England, CA Watts, 1963.

5. Schmid M: Wesen und aufgabe der Gerontologie in medizingeschichtlicher Sicht. Bericht Symposion der Deutschen Gesellschaft für Gerontologie (Nürnberg, 1973). Banaschewski, München, 1974.

6. Guerra F: (Prologue to the English translation): Méndez C, Kilgour FG (eds): *Book of Bodily Exercise.* New Haven, CT, Elizabeth Licht, 1960. Translated by Guerra F.

7. Méndez C: *Libro del Exercicio Corporal* (Book of Bodily Exercise). Sevilla, 1553.

8. Mercuriale G: *Artis Gymnasticae Apud Antiquos Celeberrimae* (The Art of Gymnastics among the Ancients). Venetiis, (City), Apud Juntas (publisher), 1569.

9. Bernard C: *Lettres A Madame R.* Publication of the Claude Bernard Museum: St-Julien en Beaujolais.

10. Åstrand P-O: Human physical fitness with special reference to sex and age. *Physiol Rev* 1956;36:307-335.

11. Åstrand I: Aerobic work capacity in men and women with special reference to age. *Acta Physiol Scand* 1960;49(suppl 1969):1-92.

12. Åstrand P-O, Rodahl K: *Textbook of Work Physiology: Physiological Bases of Exercise,* ed 3. New York, NY, McGraw-Hill, 1986.

13. Åstrand P-O, Christensen EH: Aerobic work capacity, in Dickens F, Neil E (eds): *Oxygen in the Animal Organism.* New York, NY, Pergamon Press, 1964, pp 295-314.

14. Åstrand P-O, Slatin B: Plasma and red cell volume after prolonged severe exercise. *J Appl Physiol* 1964;19:829-832.

15. Åstrand P-O: Aerobic work capacity during maximal performance under various conditions. *Circ Res* 1967;20(suppl 1):I202-I210.

16. Bergström J, Hermansen L, Hultzman E, et al: Diet, muscle glycogen and physical performance. *Acta Physiol Scand* 1967;71:140-150.

17. Blocker WP: Fellowship of Older Timers Cyclists. Personal communication.

18. Logan WPD: Mortality from coronary and myocardial disease in different social classes. *Lancet* 1952;1:758-759.

19. Morris JN, Heady JA, Raffle PAB, et al: Coronary heart-disease and physical activity of work. *Lancet* 1953;2:1053-1057.

20. Morris JN, Kagan A, Pattison DC, et al: Incidence and prediction of ischaemic heart-disease in London busmen. *Lancet* 1966;2:553-559.

21. Shephard RJ: Proceedings of the International Symposium on Physical Activity and Cardiovascular Health held in Toronto, Ontario, Canada, October 11-13, 1966. *Med Assoc J* 1967;96:695-696.

22. Paffenbarger RS Jr, Hyde RT, Wing AL: Physical activity and physical fitness as determinants of health and longevity, in Bouchard C, Shephard RJ, Stephens T, et al (eds): *Exercise, Fitness and Health: A Concensus of Current Knowledge*. Champaign, IL, Human Kinetics Books, 1990, chap 3, pp 33-48.

23. Cuthbertson DP: The influence of prolonged muscular rest on metabolism. *Biochem J* 1929;23:1328-1345.

24. Deitrick JE, Whedon GD, Shorr E: Effects of immobilization upon various metabolic and physiologic functions of normal men. *Am J Med* 1948;4:3-36.

25. Saltin B, Blomqvist G, Mitchell JH, et al: Response to exercise after bed rest and after training. *Circulation* 1968;38(suppl 5):VII1-78.

26. Taylor HL, Erickson L, Henschel A, et al: The effect of bed rest on the blood volume of normal young men. *Am J Physiol* 1945;144:227-232.

27. Whedon GD; Deitrick JE, Shorr E: Modification of the effects of immobilization upon metabolic and physiologic functions of normal men by the use of an oscillating bed. *Am J Med* 1949;6:684-711.

28. Beckman EL, Coburn KR, Chambers RM, et al: Physiologic changes observed in human subjects during zero G simulation by immersion in water up to neck level. *Aerospace Med* 1961;32:1031-1041.

29. Graveline DE, Barnard GW: Physiologic effects of a hypodynamic environment: Short-term studies. *Aerospace Med* 1961;32:726-736.

30. Graybiel A: Symptoms resulting from prolonged immersion in water: The problem of Zero G asthenia. *Aerospace Med* 1961;32:181-196.

31. Vallbona C: Bodily responses to immobilization, in Kottke FJ, Stillwell GK, Lehmann JF (eds): *Krusen's Handbook of Physical Medicine and Rehabilitation*, ed 3. Philadelphia, PA, WB Saunders, 1982, chap 52.

32. Hickey N, Mucahy R, Bourke GJ, et al: Study of coronary risk factors related to physical activity in 15,171 men. *Br Med J* 1975;3:507-509.

33. De Backer G, Kornitzer M, Sobolski J, et al: Physical activity and physical fitness levels of Belgian males aged 40-55 years. *Cardiology* 1981;67:110-128.

34. Holme I, Helgeland A, Hjermann I, et al: Physical activity at work and at leisure in relation to coronary risk factors and social class: A 4-year mortality follow-up: The Oslo study. *Acta Med Scand* 1981;209:277-283.

35. Bjartveit K, Foss OP, Gjervig T: The cardiovascular disease study in Norwegian counties: Results from first screening. *Acta Med Scand* 1983;675(suppl):1-184.

36. Tuxworth W, Nevill AM, White C, et al: Health, fitness, physical activity, and morbidity of middle aged male factory workers I. *Br J Ind Med* 1986;43:733-753.

37. Mundal R, Erikssen J, Rodahl K: Assessment of physical activity by questionnaire and personal interview with particular reference to fitness and coronary mortality. *Eur J Appl Physiol* 1987;56:245-252.

38. Tuomilehto J, Marti B, Salonen JT, et al: Leisure-time physical activity is inversely related to risk factors for coronary heart disease in middle-aged Finnish men. *Eur Heart J* 1987;8:1047-1055.

39. Johansson S, Rosengren A, Tsipogianni A, et al: Physical inactivity as a risk factor for primary and secondary coronary events in Göteborg, Sweden: *Eur Heart J* 1988;9(Suppl L):8-19.

40. Sobolski JC, Kolesar JJ, Kornitzer MD, et al: Physical fitness does not reflect physical activity patterns in middle-aged workers. *Med Sci Sports Exerc* 1988;20:6-13.

41. Heinemann L, Zerbes H: Physical activity, fitness, and diet: Behavior in the population compared with elite athletes in the GDR. *Am J Clin Nutr* 1989;49(suppl 5):1007-1016.

42. Viljanen T, Viitasalo JT, Kujala UM: Strength characteristics of a healthy urban adult population. *Eur J Appl Physiol* 1991;63:43-47.

43. de Cambra S, Serra L, Tresserras R, et al: Activitat fisica i promoció de la salut: Llibre Blanc (Physical activity and health promotion: White Paper). Generalitat de Catalunya, Departament de Sanitat I Seguretat Social. (Barcelona, Catalonia, Spain) March 1991.

44. Lie H, Mundal R, Erikssen J: Coronary risk factors and incidence of coronary death in relation to physical fitness: Seven-year follow-up study of middle-aged and elderly men. *Eur Heart J* 1985;6:147-157.

45. Cardus D: Exercise testing: Methods and uses. *Exerc Sport Sci Rev* 1978;6:59-103.

46. Nygard C-H, Lupajärvi T, Ilmarinen J: Musculoskeletal capacity of middle-aged women and men in physical, mental and mixed occupations: A 3.5 year follow-up. *Eur J Appl Physiol* 1988;57:181-188.

47. Standardized Test of Fitness. Government of Canada (Fitness and Amateur Sport), Ottawa, 1981.

48. Erikssen J, Rodahl K: Seasonal variation in work performance and heart rate response to exercise: A study of 1,835 middle-aged men. *Eur J Appl Physiol* 1979;42:133-140.

49. Erikssen J: Physical fitness and coronary heart disease morbidity and mortality: A prospective study in apparently healthy, middle aged men. *Acta Medica Scand Suppl* 1986;711:189-192.

50. Shvartz E, Reibold RC: Aerobic fitness norms for males and females age 6 to 75 years: A review. *Aviat Space Environ Med* 1990;61:3-11.

51. Pocock SJ, Shaper AG, Cook DG, et al: Social class differences in ischaemic heart disease in British men. *Lancet* 1987;2:197-201.

52. van Saase JL, Noteboom WM, Vandebroucke JP: Longevity of men capable of prolonged vigorous physical exercise: A 32 year follow up of 2259 participants in the Dutch eleven cities ice skating tour. *Br Med J* 1990;301:1409-1411.

53. Morris JN, Everitt MG, Pollard R, et al: Vigorous exercise in leisure time: Protection against coronary heart disease. *Lancet* 1980;2:1207-1210.

54. Dai SF, Marti B, Rickenbach M, et al: Sports correlate with positive living habits: Results from the population survey the Swiss MONICA project. *Schwei Z Sportmed* 1990;38:71-77.

55. Morris JN: Exercise and the incidence of coronary heart disease. *Prim Cardiol* 1992;18:62-69.

56. Pekkanen J, Marti B, Nissinen A, et al: Reduction of premature mortality by high physical activity: A 20-year follow-up of middle-aged Finnish men. *Lancet* 1987;1:1473-1477.

57. Ernst E: Influence of regular physical activity on blood rheology. *Eur Heart J* 1987;8(suppl G):59-62.

58. Seals DR, Hagberg JM, Hurley BF, et al: Effects of endurance training on glucose tolerance and plasma lipid levels in older men and women. *JAMA* 1984;252:645-649.

59. Ornish D, Brown SE, Scherwitz LW, et al: Can lifestyle changes reverse coronary heart disease? The Lifestyle Heart Trial. *Lancet* 1990;336:129-133.

60. Haskell WL, Montoye HJ, Orestein D: Physical activity and exercise to achieve health-related physical fitness components. *Public Health Rep* 1985;100:202-212.

61. Blair SN, Kohn HW, Goodyear NN: Rates and risks for running and exercise injuries: Studies in three populations. *Res Q Exerc Sport* 1987;58:221-228.

62. Siscovick DS, LaPorte RE, Newman JM: The disease-specific benefits and risks of physical activity and exercise. *Pub Health Rep* 1985;100:180-188.

63. Firor WB, Faulkner RA: Sudden death during exercise: How real a hazard? *Can J Cardiol* 1988;4:251-254.

64. Gregoire JM, Caminiti G, Messin R: Sudden death in athletes. *Rev Med Brux* 1990;11:272-277.

65. Opie LH: Sudden death and sport. *Lancet* 1975;1:263-266.
66. Opie LH: Letter: Exercise, sport and sudden death. *Lancet* 1975;1:71-73.
67. Opie LH: Letter: Long-distance running and sudden death. *N Engl J Med* 1975;293:941-942.
68. Cousteau JP: Which sports after 50 years of age? *Annales de Cardiol Angeiol* 1989;38:623-625.
69. Thompson PD, Funk EJ, Carleton RA, et al: Incidence of death during jogging in Rhode Island from 1975 through 1980. *JAMA* 1982;247:2535-2538.
70. Northcote RJ, Flannigan C, Ballantyne D: Sudden death and vigorous exercise: A study of 60 deaths associated with squash. *Br Heart J* 1986;55:198-203.
71. Huston TP, Puffer JC, Rodney WM: The athletic heart syndrome. *N Engl J Med* 1985;313:24-32.
72. Hanne-Paparo N, Kellermann JJ: Long-term Holter ECG monitoring of athletes. *Med Sci Sports Exerc* 1981;13:294-298.
73. Mølgaard H, Srensen KE, Bjerregaard P: Minimal heart rates and longest pauses in healthy adult subjects on two occasions eight years apart. *Eur Heart J* 1989;10:758-764.
74. Walter SD, Sutton JR, McIntosh JM, et al: The aetiology of sport injuries: A review of methodologies. *Sports Med* 1985;2:47-58.
75. Burry HC: Sport, exercise and arthritis. *Br J Rheumatol* 1987;26:386-388.
76. Puranen J, Ala-Ketola L, Peltokallio P, et al: Running and primary osteoarthritis of the hip. *Br Med J* 1975;2:424-425.
77. Baetzner W: *Sport und Arbeitsschäden*. Leipzig, Germany, G Thieme, 1936.
78. Lane NE, Fries JF: Relationship of running to osteoarthritis and bone density. *Compr Ther* 1988;14:7-15.
79. Ernst E: Editorial. Jogging—for a healthy heart and worn-out hips? *J Intern Med* 1990;228:295-297.
80. Bullen BA, Skrinar GS, Beitins IZ, et al: Induction of menstrual disorders by strenuous exercise in untrained women. *N Engl J Med* 1985;312:1349-1353.
81. Prior JC, Vigna Y, Sciarretta D, et al: Conditioning exercise decreases premenstrual symptoms: A prospective controlled six month trial. *Fertil Steril* 1987;47:402-408.
82. Owen N, Lee C: *Why People Do and Do Not Exercise*. South Australia, Department of Recreation and Sport, 1984.
83. Mason JO, Powell KE: Editorial: Physical activity, behavioral epidemiology and public health. *Public Health Rep* 1985;100:113-115.
84. Becker MH, Drachman RH, Kirscht JP: A field experiment to evaluate various outcomes of continuity of physician care. *Am J Pub Health* 1974;64:1062-1070.
85. Vanden-Auweele Y: Physical activity and sports as health promoting behavior in middle age. *Tijdschrift Voor Gerontologie en Geriatrie* 1988;19:289-295.
86. Uitenbroek DG, McQueen DV: Leisure time physical activity behavior in three British cities. *Sozial und Praventivmedizin* 1991;36:307-314.
87. Vuori I: The cardiovascular risks of physical activity. *Acta Med Scand* 1986;711(suppl):205-214.
88. Aaro LE, Eriksen R, Henriksen G, et al: To be in good trim: A campaign for the promotion of physical activity in Sogn and Fjordane 1983-84. *Tidsskrift for Den Norske Laegeforening* 1987;107:2417-2420.

Chapter 3

Biological Effect of Physical Activity on the Serum Lipid Profile: The MARATHOM Study

Jaume Marrugat, MD, PhD
Maria Isabel Covas, MD, PhD
Roberto Elosua, MD

Physical activity has been referred to as "an agent with lipid-lowering, antihypertensive, positive inotropic, negative chronotropic, vasodilating, diuretic, anorexigenic, weight reducing, cathartic, hypoglycemic, tranquilizing, hypnotic, and antidepressive" properties.[1] The range of age this affirmation applies to has not been specified; therefore, it may be assumed that all people meeting the required physical capabilities would benefit from the qualities of physical activity.

On the other hand, many risk factors have been identified for the development of ischemic heart disease (IHD). Hypertension, diabetes, hypercholesterolemia, cigarette smoking, and overweight are independent risk factors for such disease; conversely, high levels of high-density lipoprotein (HDL) cholesterol seem to be associated with a low incidence of IHD.[2] Some of these risk factors may be modified by different procedures. Among them, physical activity plays an important role in the control of the lipid profile. The purpose of the present work is to discuss the effects of exercise on serum lipids and to present the preliminary results of the MARATHOM study, which is aimed at finding a threshold in the amount of physical activity required to keep the serum lipid profile within low cardiovascular risk levels.

Plasma Lipids

Plasma lipids are transported by lipoproteins containing apolipoproteins and lipids including triglycerides (TG), cholesterol, cholesteryl esters, and phospholipids. A number of plasma lipoproteins have been identified so far. Four major lipoproteins are involved in the bloodstream transport of lipids: chylomicrons, very low density lipoproteins (VLDL), low-density lipoproteins (LDL), and HDL. Triglycerides are transported by chylomicrons and VLDL. Some 70% of cholesterol is transported on LDL, and approximately 20% on HDL.[3]

High-density lipoprotein is primarily synthesized in the liver and the intestine. This stage is called nascent HDL, and it acquires cholesterol from tissues. The enzyme lecithin cholesterol acyltransferase (LCAT) catalyzes the esterification of cholesterol to cholesteryl esters that enter into the hydrophobic core of HDL.[4] Nascent HDL particles are converted to spherical particles with the same density as the HDL3 subfraction, and these are later transformed into large HDL2 particles. HDL2 also can be converted back to HDL3 either by removing triglycerides and phospholipids by means of hepatic lipase[5] or by transfering of cholesteryl esters into VLDL and LDL. This process is termed reverse cholesterol transfer.[6]

An impressive amount of evidence has been accumulated that proves the relationship between lipids and atherosclerosis.[7-10] The involvement of atherosclerosis in the pathogenesis of IHD has also been well established.[11,12] Diet and drugs have been effective in lowering levels of total cholesterol[13,14] as a preventive approach. As mentioned, it has been suggested that the protective effect of physical activity against IHD is achieved in part through favorable modification of the risk factor profile (blood pressure, body mass index, lipids).[15,16]

Changes of Serum Lipids With Exercise

Exercise exerts on plasma lipids and lipoprotein both immediate and long-term effects that reduce the risk of IHD.

Immediate Lipidic Response to Exercise

Immediate responses have been studied mostly under experimental conditions of endurance activity. These effects include a decrease in serum levels of TG, VLDL linked to TG, and VLDL linked to cholesterol, with an increase in HDL, the HDL2 subfraction of HDL, and LCAT concentrations.[17-22] Removal of free cholesterol from the lipoprotein surface creates a concentration gradient that favors the net transfer of cholesterol from cell membranes of peripheral tissues to the surface of lipoprotein, and later to the lipidic core by LCAT action.[23] The increase in HDL is inversely correlated with serum TG[24] and fat clearance.[22] Increased activity of both hepatic lipoprotein lipase (LPL) and posthepatic LPL has also been reported.[25-27] These changes have been observed a short time after exercising, and may persist for 1 to 4 days.[28]

HDL3 baseline levels were not different in trained and untrained men[29]; however, increases in this cholesterol subfraction after exercise have been demonstrated in untrained but not in trained people.[30,31] After prolonged strenuous physical exercise, an increase in apoprotein A-I (Apo A-I) has been observed.[32] Other authors do not report changes in serum Apo A-I nor in apoprotein A-II (Apo A-II) (the main protein components of HDL); nonetheless, changes in their distribution between HDL subfractions have been found[29] that support the hypothesis of the conversion from HDL3 to HDL2.

LPL is the rate-limiting enzyme in the hydrolysis of TG-rich lipoproteins that regulates the transfer of lipidic surface material to HDL during and after endurance exercise.[33] The magnitude of the plasma TG response to immediate or long-term exercise is highly and inversely influenced by preexercise values[34]; in other words, substantial decreases in plasma TG occur only in people with raised preexercise values of these lipids.

Lipidic Response to Regular Exercise

Changes in serum lipids related to regular exercise are similar to those associated with a short-term exposure to exercise, plus a decrease in total cholesterol (TC), LDL, and the TC/HDL ratio.[35] Changes in HDL and LDL cholesterol are correlated with changes in total body mass index and percentage of body fat.[36] The major regular exercise effect on plasma cholesterol seems to be an increase in HDL as a result of endurance training, which is probably related to the increase in LPL activity and TG catabolism.[37] Regular exercise has been shown to increase chylomicron clearance, which is in turn inversely related to high levels of circulating HDL.[38]

LPL may assist in supplying free fatty acids to active muscle. The trained state is characterized by an increased flux of fatty acids and smaller pools of adipose tissue. This flux is reflected by smaller, more metabolically active adipose cells in smaller adipose tissue depots. Peak blood concentrations of free fatty acids (FFA) and ketone bodies are lower during and following exercise in trained individuals, probably due to increased capacity of the skeletal musculature to oxidize these energy sources.[33] Trained individuals oxidize more fat and less carbohydrate than untrained subjects when performing submaximal work of the same absolute intensity. Moreover, in nontrained men an increase of FFA has been reported after exercise.[39]

The acute TG decrease seems to be explained by the accelerated catabolism resulting from increased LPL activity.

An enhanced insulin sensitivity and improved glucose tolerance suggest that exercise training is associated with an improvement in glucose metabolism.[34,40] Decreased VLDL-TG synthesis may also occur in response to an increase in tissue insulin sensitivity.[41] Insulin is the major determinant and stimulant of LPL. Thus, it is likely that the enhancement of insulin sensitivity would lead to a more efficient lipolytic system with a consequent decrease in the TG concentration. This lipolytic action increases HDL levels. A positive relation between insulin sensitivity and HDL has also been described.[42] The low body fat content of endurance-trained athletes also contributes to lower TG concentration through the same mechanism.[42]

Endurance training is associated with increases of both the lipid and protein components of HDL2, the less dense of the HDL subfractions, whereas reports on the HDL3 subfraction are still controversial: studies reporting decreased,[43] increased,[44,45] or no changes[46] in HDL3 in association with exercise are available. These inconsistencies may relate in part to the large variability in laboratory methods of determining the HDL2 and HDL3 subfractions.[47] Metabolic studies using autologously labeled ^{125}I-HDL[48] have concluded that higher HDL levels in active men were associated with increased HDL apoprotein survival, although apoprotein synthetic rates were virtually identical to those of sedentary men. Increased LPL activity and lower activity of hepatic triglyceride lipase—an enzyme that participates in delipidation and clearance of HDL particles—have been proposed as the mechanisms that contribute to HDL survival.[24,48]

Ischemic Heart Disease and Exercise

The exercise dose (intensity, duration, and frequency) and total time required to maintain serum blood lipids and lipoproteins levels at low IHD risk remains controversial. There is general agreement that resistive high intensity training is an effective means to influence serum lipid levels,[49-51] independent of changes in maximum oxygen consumption ($\dot{V}O_2max$) during exercise tests, in body weight, or in body composition.[52] Exercise intensity greater than 5 kcal/min and a total energy expenditure of 1,000 to 1,499 kcal/week are some tentative threshold doses of exercise effective for prevention of IHD and promotion of health.[53,54]

Some studies have shown that strength exercise or habitual physical activity of light intensity are not a major determinant of serum lipid levels.[51,55] However, there is experimental and epidemiological evidence supporting the hypothesis that risk of IHD can be further reduced with light or moderate intensity physical activity, including working around the home and yard, walking, or practicing sports (30 to 60 min/day, 150 to 300 kcal/day).[53,56]

Factors that have been described as interacting with or confounding the relationship between physical training and serum lipids include diet, alcohol consumption, cigarette smoking, age, length and intensity of training, $\dot{V}O_2max$, body weight, and percent body fat.[35] Life-style-related variables (diet, physical activity, alcohol and cigarette consumption), age, sex, and body mass index explain 16% to 26% of the variance in cardiovascular risk. Furthermore, lifestyle variables are significantly and independently related to serum lipid levels.[57]

As a consequence of the interest in the primary prevention of IHD, sedentary people are advised to become more active. The origin of this interest lies in the accumulated evidence of the protective effect of physical activity on this condition.[15,58-61] The pattern of the associations found between lack of physical activity and risk of coronary heart disease supports a "dose-response" effect.[62] The association is stronger when comparing a "very active group" to a sedentary group[62]; and the explanation for the low magnitude of the relationship (as measured with a relative risk) in some studies is the relatively low activity level of the active group.[63]

The extent to which the protective effect of physical activity is produced through changes in serum lipoproteins is an attractive field for epidemiological research.

The MARATHOM Study

According to the relationship between physical activity and serum lipoproteins, and to the lower incidence of IHD among active and very active people, it is reasonable to aim epidemiological research at the hypothesis that there is a beneficial dose-response effect of physical activity on serum lipids.

The MARATHOM (Medida de la Actividad física y su Relación Ambiental con Todos los lipidos en el Hombre) study was designed to assess the amount and type of leisure-time physical activity required to keep serum lipid levels within those regarded as low IHD risk.

Subjects and Methods

Only men 20 to 60 years of age have been considered in the study. Subjects were selected by stratified sampling from three levels of physical activity in leisure time: sedentary (average energy spent in physical activity lower than 143 kcal/day), active (average energy spent in physical activity between 143 and 286 kcal/day), and very active (average energy spent in physical activity greater than 286 kcal/day). For analysis purposes, recruitment was also stratified in two age groups: 20 to 40 years and 41 to 60 years. The aim of this stratified recruitment was to obtain a sample with a wide range of both physical activity practices and ages.

Subjects with any known pathology (specifically, neoplasia, cardiovascular pathologies, diabetes, hyperlipidemia, abnormal basal electrocardiogram, abnormal effort electrocardiogram, obesity [body mass index >31 kg/m²], drug abuse, or chronic pharmacologic treatment) were excluded.

Sample Size

An alpha risk of 0.05 and a beta risk of 0.20 in a two-tailed test were accepted. A standard deviation of 43 mg TC per deciliter was used for sample size calculation (as reported in a reference work on total cholesterol among Spanish men).[64] Sample size was calculated to enable us to detect an epidemiologically relevant difference of 16 mg/dl between the mean TC in the subgroups of interest. To detect this between-groups difference in TC as statistically significant, 114 subjects were needed in each of the six subgroups. Thus, the total sample size was 684 subjects. Substitution of nonresponders was applied systematically because no biases were expected from the study characteristics.

So far, 461 men have been recruited: 179 of them are bank employees and 282 are marathon runners. Recruitment in the very active group has been completed, but subjects in the lower activity groups will continue to enter the study until the sample size in these strata is achieved.

Measurement of the Amount of Physical Activity: The Minnesota Leisure Time Physical Activity Questionnaire

The Minnesota Leisure Time Physical Activity Questionnaire (LTPAQ) was developed and tested by Taylor and associates in 1978.[65] It was designed to measure the amount of energy spent in physical activities in leisure time during the last 12 months.

The questionnaire is administered by a trained interviewer. The participant is asked to mark those physical activities that he practiced over the past year, out of a list of suggested activities. A code of intensity has been assigned to each physical activity, meaning how much energy per minute is spent while the activity is being performed. The interviewer records how many times the activity is performed each month and the time (in minutes) spent in each session. With simple calculation, the annual amount of energy spent in leisure time physical activity is estimated in kcal/day. The interview lasts about 20 minutes.

Physical activities are classified, according to the intensity of the amount of energy spent, into the following categories: light (intensity code of energy spent between 2 and 4 kcal/min), medium (intensity code of energy spent between 4.5 and 5.5 kcal/min), and heavy (intensity code of energy spent greater than or equal to 6 kcal/min). The energy spent in light, medium, and heavy physical activities completes the information about the amount and quality of physical activities performed by each participant.

Diet Questionnaire

The MARATHOM study includes a three-day recall self-administered questionnaire that requires the participant to declare all the food consumed over any three days in the last week, including drinks. The analysis of the responses provides a reasonable description of sources of calories for each participant as well as its quantitative contents of certain specific nutrients (full fats, saturated fats, monounsaturated and polyunsaturated fats, cholesterol, proteins, carbohydrates, fiber, caffeine, vitamins, Na, K, Mg, and Zn).[66]

The alimentary data collected in the questionnaire are converted into nutritional data using a specific program (The Professional Diet Balancer-Nutridata software, 1987, version 2.1).

Exercise Test

A maximum exercise test, following Bruce's protocol, was performed by all 461 participants. Continuous 12 conventional leads electrocardiographic monitoring was performed throughout the exercise and four minutes postexercise. Moreover, systolic blood pressure was also monitored during the exercise.

Laboratory Measurements

The following biochemical parameters were measured: glucose, TC, TG, HDL cholesterol, and LDL cholesterol. Glucose was determined via the glucose oxidase method, TC via the cholesterol oxidase-peroxidase method, and TG via the enzymatic ultraviolet method. HDL cholesterol was determined by precipitating VLDL cholesterol and LDL cholesterol with polyethylene glycol at different concentrations and pH, dissolved in a 0.1 M phosphate buffer and measuring the soluble or supernatant cholesterol. LDL cholesterol was determined by precipitating LDL cholesterol with dextran sulfate, measuring the supernatant (or soluble) cholesterol (SCH), and calculating with the formula: LDL = TC - SCH.

Other Measurements

The baseline heart rate, 12 lead electrocardiogram (ECG), and blood pressure in supine position were recorded. Height and weight were measured with the subjects barefoot and wearing light clothing. Body mass index was calculated as weight (in kg) divided by height (in meters) squared. Age in years was also recorded.

Statistical Analysis

For bivariate correlation, Spearman's correlation was used. The Kruskal Wallis and Mann-Whitney U-Test were used for comparison of continuous variables between groups that departed from normal.

Table 1 Distribution of subjects in the MARATHOM study by age and activity level groups

Ages (years)	Sedentary	Active	Very Active	All Levels of Activity
20-40	37	48	163	248
41-60	50	44	119	213
All ages	87	92	282	461

Sedentary: <143 kcal/day
Active: 143-286 kcal/day
Very active: >286 kcal/day

Results

Eighty-seven sedentary, 92 active, and 282 very active men have been recruited so far (248 subjects aged 20 to 40 years and 213 aged 41 to 60 years) (Table 1). Mean age of all participants was 40.4 years with a standard deviation (SD) of 9.2.

Statistically significant differences have been found in the analysis of variance between the very active, active, and sedentary subjects in weight, height, body mass index, baseline heart rate, alcohol consumption, and biochemical laboratory findings (Table 2). Very active subjects were younger (39.3 years, SD 8.9) than those in the sedentary group (43.1 years, SD 8.4). Total cholesterol was lowest among very active subjects, as well as TG, LDL cholesterol, and the ratio of total cholesterol to HDL cholesterol. Conversely, HDL cholesterol was significantly higher in the very active group compared to the active and sedentary groups (p <0.01) (Table 2). A statistically significant higher alcohol consumption among sedentary people was found.

When comparing subjects aged 20 to 40 years (248 individuals) with those aged 41 to 60 years (213 individuals), the older group had higher BMI, total cholesterol, LDL cholesterol, triglycerides, and the ratio of total cholesterol to HDL cholesterol. In contrast, they showed a lower heart rate and HDL cholesterol (Table 3).

When the analysis was stratified by age and physical activity level, the lipid parameters were found to change steeply across sedentary, active, and very active groups of younger subjects (Table 4). Body mass index, alcohol consumption, baseline heart, and the ratio of TC to HDL were higher among less active subjects compared to their more active counterparts (Table 4).

In the older stratum of subjects, the mean values of age and body mass index in the sedentary group were very similar to those of active people. Although not statistically significant, total cholesterol, LDL cholesterol, and TG were higher, and HDL cholesterol and the ratio of TC to HDL cholesterol were lower in the active groups than in the sedentary group. The opposite, expected result was observed in the very active group.

Table 2 Characteristics of MARATHOM study groups of physical activity

Parameters	Sedentary (1) Mean ± SD n = 87	Active (2) Mean ± SD n = 92	Very Active (3) Mean ± SD n = 282	Global Mean ± SD	p
Age (years)	43.105 ± 8.378	41.250 ± 9.729	39.303 ± 8.925	40.423 ± 9.168	1-3*
Weight (kg)	76.933 ± 11.067	76.988 ± 9.653	69.966 ± 8.078	72.734 ± 9.648	1-3,2-3†
Height (cm)	170.581 ± 6.165	172.389 ± 8.084	172.675 ± 6.609	172.220 ± 6.896	1-3*
BMI (kg/m²)	26.412 ± 3.392	25.946 ± 2.842	23.420 ± 2.232	24.513 ± 2.942	1-3,2-3*
HR	75.256 ± 13.589	71.348 ± 12.302	65.557 ± 11.518	68.588 ± 12.701	1-3,2-3*
Alcohol (g/day)	27.275 ± 26.210	17.706 ± 19.910	15.636 ± 20.735	18.145 ± 22.036	1-2,1-3*
Glucose	88.660 ± 17.893	86.136 ± 14.369	89.822 ± 11.379	88.846 ± 13.459	2-3†
Total chol	223.189 ± 36.961	220.881 ± 41.327	200.144 ± 37.693	208.692 ± 39.670	1-3,2-3*
HDL-chol	48.358 ± 13.883	45.085 ± 9.807	53.988 ± 12.617	51.108 ± 12.859	1-3,2-3*
LDL-chol	148.404 ± 33.503	152.695 ± 41.154	129.110 ± 36.146	137.542 ± 38.164	1-3,2-3*
Triglycerides	130.750 ± 62.100	120.051 ± 84.670	82.942 ± 39.187	99.405 ± 59.436	1-3,2-3*
T-chol/HDL	4.968 ± 1.619	5.197 ± 1.811	3.913 ± 1.227	4.373 ± 1.548	1-3,2-3*

SD, standard deviation; BMI, body mass index; HR, heart rate; HDL, high-density lipoprotein; LDL, low-density lipoprotein; chol, cholesterol; T-chol/HDL, the ratio of total cholesterol to HDL cholesterol; n, group size.
*$p<0.01$
†$p<0.05$
Sedentary: <143 kcal/day
Active: 143-286 kcal/day
Very active: >286 kcal/day

Table 3 Characteristics of the study participants stratified by age

Parameters	20-40 Years Mean ± SD n = 248	41-60 Years Mean ± SD n = 213	p
Weight (kg)	71.999 ± 9.472	72.734 ± 9.648	NS
Height (cm)	173.318 ± 6.520	170.702 ± 7.126	<0.0005
BMI (kg/m²)	23.962 ± 2.792	25.275 ± 2.981	<0.0005
HR	69.650 ± 13.101	67.101 ± 11.995	0.043
Alcohol (g/d)	17.907 ± 22.639	18.473 ± 21.232	NS
Glucose	88.761 ± 12.860	88.959 ± 14.266	NS
Total chol	200.571 ± 37.390	219.455 ± 40.187	<0.0005
HDL chol	52.294 ± 13.319	49.537 ± 12.097	0.044
LDL chol	129.944 ± 37.065	147.488 ± 37.423	<0.0005
Triglycerides	89.689 ± 46.709	112.122 ± 71.033	0.001
T-chol/HDL	4.144 ± 1.617	4.677 ± 1.400	<0.0005

SD, standard deviation; BMI, body mass index; HR, heart rate; HDL, high-density lipoprotein; LDL, low-density lipoprotein; chol, cholesterol; T-chol/HDL, the ratio of total cholesterol to HDL cholesterol; n, group size

On the other hand, total energy expenditure and energy expenditure in heavy physical activity correlated better with all serum lipidic parameters than with energy expenditure in moderate or light physical activity (Table 5). The correlation is inverse for total cholesterol, LDL cholesterol, triglycerides and the ratio of TC to HDL cholesterol, and direct for HDL cholesterol.

Discussion

Despite the fact that the recruitment has not been completed in the MARATHOM study, the preliminary results suggest that the maxi-

Table 4 Characteristics of subjects in the MARATHOM study stratified by physical activity level and age group

	Sedentary (1) Mean ± SD	Active (2) Mean ± SD	Very Active (3) Mean ± SD	p
20 to 40 years				
Age (years)	35.650 ± 5.475	33.429 ± 5.526	33.107 ± 5.163	1-2(*);1-3(**)
BMI (kg/m²)	26.443 ± 3.401	24.997 ± 2.408	23.004 ± 2.261	1-2(*);1-3,2-3(**)
HR	77.350 ± 15.165	74.542 ± 12.609	66.408 ± 11.685	1-3,2-3(**)
Alcohol (g/day)	31.000 ± 31.138	19.565 ± 21.294	14.943 ± 20.544	1-3(**)
Glucose	87.650 ± 16.229	87.769 ± 17.406	89.255 ± 11.130	2-3(*)
Total chol	220.700 ± 40.592	207.846 ± 42.009	194.123 ± 33.847	1-3(*)
HDL chol	45.300 ± 12.162	45.154 ± 11.739	55.302 ± 13.250	1-3, 2-3(**)
LDL chol	147.000 ± 39.518	143.615 ± 43.589	122.467 ± 33.295	1-3,2-3(*)
Triglycerides	137.947 ± 46.440	101.000 ± 57.258	78.895 ± 39.120	1-2,1-3(**):2-3(*)
T-chol/HDL	5.300 ± 1.992	5.081 ± 2.326	3.172 ± 1.151	1-3,2-3(**)
41 to 60 years				
Age (years)	49.464 ± 5.088	49.404 ± 5.523	47.652 ± 5.426	1-3(*)
BMI (kg/m²)	26.385 ± 6.422	26.916 ± 2.9452	23.987 ± 2.070	1-3,2-3(**)
HR	73.435 ± 11.925	67.864 ± 11.078	64.405 ± 11.235	1-2(*);1-3(**)
Alcohol (g/day)	24.227 ± 21.256	15.848 ± 18.469	16.877 ± 21.115	1-2,1-3(*)
Glucose	89.273 ± 19.048	84.848 ± 11.560	90.706 ± 11.784	2-3(*)
Total chol	224.697 ± 35.149	231.151 ± 38.341	209.529 ± 41.551	1-3(*);2-3(**)
HDL-chol	50.212 ± 14.696	45.030 ± 8.164	51.941 ± 11.354	2-3(**)
LDL-chol	149.212 ± 31.143	159.848 ± 38.284	139.368 ± 38.175	2-3(**)
Triglycerides	126.606 ± 69.890	135.061 ± 99.525	89.191 ± 38.747	1-3,2-3(**)
T-chol/HDL	4.767 ± 1.338	5.288 ± 1.303	4.225 ± 1.284	1-3(*);2-3(**)

SD, standard deviation; BMI, body mass index; HR, heart rate; HDL, high density lipoprotein; LDL, low density lipoprotein; chol, cholesterol; T-chol/HDL, the ratio of total cholesterol to HDL cholesterol; n, group size; 37, 48, and 163 for sedentary, active, and very active 20 to 40 year olds and 50, 44, and 119 for sedentary, active, and very active 41 to 60 year olds.
*$p<0.05$
**$p<0.01$
Sedentary: <143 kcal/day
Active: 143-286 kcal/day
Very active: >286 kcal/day

Table 5 Spearman's correlation coefficient between energy expenditure in physical activity and serum lipids and glucose

	Glucose	T-chol	HDL-chol	LDL-chol	Triglycerides	T-chol/HDL
Energy expenditure in PA	0.152	−0.317	0.317	−0.335	−0.401	−0.432
Energy expenditure in heavy PA	0.158	−0.337	0.364	−0.376	−0.402	−0.482
Energy expenditure in medium PA	0.050	−0.118	0.046	−0.110	−0.094	−0.093
Energy expenditure in light PA	0.069	−0.027	−0.035	−0.002	−0.107	−0.002

PA, physical activity; Chol, cholesterol; T-chol, total cholesterol; HDL, high density lipoprotein; LDL, low density lipoprotein; T-chol/HDL, total cholesterol / HDL cholesterol ratio.

mum benefit of physical activity is achieved in the very active level of exercise. However, no attempt has been made, on this occasion, to test the main hypothesis of MARATHOM: to find a threshold of amount and quality of exercise required to maintain the serum lipid profile within low cardiovascular risk levels. The hypothesis that such a threshold exists will be tested in a multivariant analysis, adjusting the effect of physical activity for its intensity and quantity, fat intake (as measured with the diet questionnaire), age, body mass index, and alcohol and cigarette consumption.

The Minnesota Leisure Time Physical Activity Questionnaire was successfully validated by the authors (comparing its results with those of the effort test) for its use among Spanish men at the beginning of the study (unpublished data).

As already mentioned, the recruitment in lower physical activity levels has not been completed and, consequently, the very active group is more heavily weighted. This may introduce a difficulty in the interpretation of these preliminary results. Nonetheless, some general observations may be discussed: in the analysis stratified by age and activity group, the body mass index changes between activity groups parallel those of total cholesterol, LDL cholesterol, triglycerides, and HDL cholesterol. This suggests that the potential benefit of physical activity is achieved in part through the changes in lipids provoked by weight loss, a result that is in agreement with other authors.[36,67]

Age is a confounder for the relationship between activity group and serum lipid profile. The younger group of participants seemed to benefit dramatically from physical activity according to the level of exercise. In contrast, among subjects aged 41 to 60, the active group had higher levels of total cholesterol, LDL cholesterol and triglycerides, and lower levels of HDL cholesterol than the sedentary group. This suggests that other factors, such as diet, may be confounding this relationship. The hypothesis that older people may need more exercise to obtain a substantial modification of their serum lipids is also plausible. The anticipated benefits of exercise were observed in the very active group of the older population.

Although it is not yet possible to answer the major question of the MARATHOM study on defining a threshold in the amount of physical activity necessary to keep the lipids within the levels of low risk of IHD, a gross estimate of this boundary may be provided. The only group that showed a statistically significant difference in all serum lipids was the very active. Moreover, the mean total cholesterol in this group is clearly under the recommended limits for prevention of cardiovascular diseases[68] in all strata of analysis. The active group was defined by an expenditure of at least 284 kcal/day in any kind of physical activity (approximately 2,000 kcal/week). Other authors have already proved that an expenditure over 2,000 kcal/day reduces the risk of a heart attack[15]; whereas, more recently, it has been suggested that the limit might be lower (1,000 to 1,500 kcal/day).[54]

On the other hand, the intensity of physical activity (an estimation of its quality) may be the cornerstone of its effectiveness in the control of serum lipids. The best correlation with serum lipids has been obtained in individuals who spent most of the energy in physical activity that required more than 6 kcal/min. This agrees with other authors who noted that the appropriate intensity of physical activity for preventive purposes should be over 5 kcal/min.[55]

Physical activity is the most natural nonpharmacological way to control a multiplicity of cardiovascular risk factors. Therefore, an appropriate and clear answer to the issues presented in this work is required in order to optimize preventive community interventions. The MARATHOM study was designed to contribute to this task, but it will be necessary to wait until the end of 1993 for the final results.

References

1. Roberts WC: An agent with lipid-lowering, antihypertensive, positive inotropic, negative chronotropic, vasodilating, diuretic, anorexigenic, weight-reducing, cathartic, hypoglycemic, tranquilizing, hypnotic and antidepressive qualities. *Am J Cardiol* 1984;53:261-262.

2. Gordon T, Castelli WP, Hjortland MC, et al: High density lipoprotein as a protective factor against coronary heart disease: The Framingham Study. *Am J Med* 1977;62:707-714.

3. Braunwald E (ed): *Principles of Cardiology*. Philadelphia, PA, WB Saunders, 1992.

4. Francone OL, Gurakar A, Fielding C: Distribution and functions of lecithin: Cholesterol acyltransferase and cholesteryl ester transfer protein in plasma lipoproteins: Evidence for a functional unit containing these activities together with apolipoproteins A-I and D that catalyzes the esterification and transfer of cell-derived cholesterol. *J Biol Chem* 1989;264:7066-7072.

5. Flier JS, Underhill LH, Eckel RH: Lipoprotein lipase: A multifunctional enzyme relevant to common metabolic diseases. *N Engl J Med* 1989;320:1060-1068.

6. Slotte JP: HDL receptors and cholesterol efflux from parenchymal cells. *Eur Heart J* 1990;11(1Suppl E):212-217.

7. Keys A: Coronary heart disease in seven countries. *Circulation* 1970;41(Suppl1):I1-I211.

8. Keys A, Aravanis C (eds): *Seven Countries: A Multivariate Analysis of Death and Coronary Heart Disease*. Cambridge, MA, Harvard University Press, 1980.

9. Kannel WB, Castelli WP, Gordon T: Cholesterol in the prediction of atherosclerotic disease: New perspectives based on the Framingham Study. *Ann Intern Med* 1979;90:85-91.

10. Ross R: The pathogenesis of atherosclerosis: An update. *N Engl J Med* 1986;314:488-500.

11. Fuster V, Badimon L, Badimon JJ, et al: The pathogenesis of coronary artery disease and the acute coronary syndromes (1). *N Engl J Med* 1992;326:242-250.

12. Fuster V, Badimon L, Badimon JJ, et al: The pathogenesis of coronary artery disease and the acute coronary syndromes (2). *N Engl J Med* 1992;326:310-318.

13. Carmena R: Dieta y colesterol sérico. *Med Clin (Barc)* 1989;92:56-59.

14. Brown WV: Review of clinical trials: Proving the lipid hypothesis. *Eur Heart J* 1990;11(Suppl H):15-20.

15. Paffenbarger RS Jr, Wing AL, Hyde RT: Physical activity as an index of heart attack risk in college alumni. *Am J Epidemiol* 1978;108:161-175.

16. Johansson S, Rosengren A, Tsipogianni A, et al: Physical inactivity as a risk factor for primary and secondary coronary events in Göteborg, Sweden. *Eur Heart J* 1988;9(Suppl L):8-19.

17. Folsom AR, Caspersen CJ, Taylor HL, et al: Leisure time physical activity and its relationship to coronary risk factors in a population-based sample: The Minnesota heart survey. *Am J Epidemiol* 1985;121:570-579.

18. Danner SA, Wieling W, Havekes L, et al: Effect of physical exercise on blood lipids and adipose tissue composition in young healthy men. *Atherosclerosis* 1984;53:83-90.

19. Brownell KD, Bachorik PS, Ayerle RS: Changes in plasma lipid and lipoprotein levels in men and women after a program of moderate exercise. *Circulation* 1982;65:477-484.

20. Puzo J, Casasnovas JA, Lapetra A, et al: Estudio de los parámetros lipidicos de dos poblaciones juveniles con diferente actividad física. *Rev Clin Esp* 1988;182:124-126.

21. Dufaux B, Order U, Muller R, et al: Delayed effects of prolonged exercise on serum lipoproteins. *Metabolism* 1986;35:105-109.

22. Sady SP, Thompson PD, Cullinane EM, et al: Prolonged exercise augments triglyceride clearance. *JAMA* 1986;256:2552-2555.

23. Williams PT, Albers JJ, Krauss RM, et al: Associations of lecithin: Cholesterol acyltransferase (LCAT) mass concentrations with exercise, weight loss, and plasma lipoprotein subfraction concentrations in men. *Atherosclerosis* 1990;82:53-58.

24. Kiens B, Lithell H: Lipoprotein metabolism influenced by training-induced changes in human skeletal muscle. *J Clin Invest* 1989;83:558-564.

25. Kantor MA, Cullinane EM, Herbert PN, et al: Acute increase in lipoprotein lipase following prolonged exercise. *Metabolism* 1984;33:454-457.

26. Lampman RM, Santinga JT, Savage PJ, et al: Effect of exercise training on glucose tolerance, in vivo insulin sensitivity, lipid and lipoprotein concentrations in middle-aged men with mild hypertriglyceridemia. *Metabolism* 1985;34:205-211.

27. Lithell H, Schele R, Vessby B, et al: Lipoproteins, lipoprotein lipase and glycogen after prolonged physical activity. *J Appl Physiol* 1984;57:698-702.

28. Berger GM, Griffiths MP: Acute effects of moderate exercise on plasma lipoprotein parameters. *Int J Sports Med* 1987;8:336-341.

29. Kuusi T, Kostiainen E, Vartiainen E, et al: Acute effects of marathon running on levels of serum lipoproteins and androgenic hormones in healthy males. *Metabolism* 1984;33:527-531.

30. Goldberg L, Elliot DL: The effect of physical activity on lipid and lipoprotein levels. *Med Clin North Am* 1985;69:41-55.

31. Kantor MA, Cullinane EM, Sady SP, et al: Exercise acutely increases high density lipoprotein-cholesterol and lipoprotein lipase activity in trained and untrained men. *Metabolism* 1987;36:188-192.

32. Lamon-Fava S, McNamara JR, Farber HW, et al: Acute changes in lipid, lipoprotein, apolipoprotein, and low-density lipoprotein particle size after an endurance triathlon. *Metabolism* 1989;38:921-925.

33. Askew EW: Role of fat metabolism in exercise. *Clin Sports Med* 1984;3:605-621.

34. Goldberg AP: Aerobic and resistive exercise modify risk factors for coronary heart disease. *Med Sci Sports Exerc* 1989;21:669-674.

35. Tran ZV, Weltman A, Glass GV, et al: The effect of exercise on blood lipids and lipoproteins: A meta-analysis of studies. *Med Sci Sports Exerc* 1983;15:393-402.

36. Williams PT, Wood PD, Krauss RM, et al: Does weight loss cause the exercise-induced increase in plasma high density lipoproteins? *Atherosclerosis* 1983;47:173-185.

37. Stucchi AF, Terpstra AH, Foxall TL, et al: The effect of exercise on plasma lipids and LDL subclass metabolism in minature swine. *Med Sci Sports Exerc* 1991;23:552-561.

38. Cohen JC, Stray-Gundersen J, Grundy SM: Dissociation between postprandial lipemia and high density lipoprotein cholesterol concentrations in endurance-trained men. *Arterioscler-Thromb* 1991;11:838-843.

39. Hespel P, Lijnen P, Fagard R, et al: Changes in plasma lipids and apoproteins associated with physical training in middle-aged sedentary men. *Am Heart J* 1988;115:786-792.

40. Seals DR, Hagberg JM, Hurley BF, et al: Effects of endurance training on glucose tolerance and plasma lipid levels in older men and women. *JAMA* 1984;252:645-649.

41. DeFronzo RA, Ferrannini E: Insulin resistance: A multifaceted syndrome responsible for NIDDM, obesity, hypertension, dyslipidemia, and atherosclerotic cardiovascular disease. *Diabetes Care* 1991;14:173-194.

42. Donahue RP, Orchard TJ, Becker DJ, et al: Physical activity, insulin sensitivity, and the lipoprotein profile in young adults: The Beaver county study. *Am J Epidemiol* 1988;127:95-103.

43. Williams PT, Krauss RM, Wood PD, et al: Lipoprotein subfractions of runners and sedentary men. *Metabolism* 1986;35:45-52.

44. Hespel P, Lijnen P, Fagard R, et al: Effects of training on the serum lipid profile in normal men. *Drugs* 1988;36(Suppl2):27-32.

45. Northcote RJ, Canning GC, Todd IC, et al: Lipoprotein profiles of elite veteran endurance athletes. *Am J Cardiol* 1988;61:934-936.

46. Raz I, Rosenblit H, Kark JD: Effect of moderate exercise on serum lipids in young men with low high density lipoprotein cholesterol. *Arteriosclerosis* 1988;8:245-251.

47. Cheung MC, Alberg JJ: Characterization of lipoprotein particles isolated by immunoaffinity chromatography: Particles containing A-I and A-II and particles containing A-I but no A-II. *J Biol Chem* 1984;259:12201-12209.

48. Thompson PD, Cullinane EM, Sady PS, et al: High density lipoprotein metabolism in endurance athletes and sedentary men. *Circulation* 1991;84:140-152.

49. Cullinane E, Siconolfi S, Saritelli A, et al: Acute decrease in serum triglycerides with exercise: Is there a threshold for an exercise effect? *Metabolism* 1982;31:844-847.

50. Haskell WL: Exercise-induced changes in plasma lipids and lipoproteins. *Prev Med* 1984;13:23-36.

51. Leclerc S, Allard C, Talbot J, et al: High density lipoprotein cholesterol, habitual physical activity and physical fitness. *Atherosclerosis* 1985;57:43-51.

52. Hurley BF, Hagberg JM, Goldberg AP, et al: Resistive training can reduce coronary risk factors without altering VO$_2$ max or percent body fat. *Med Sci Sports Exerc* 1988;20:150-154.

53. Leon AS: Physiological interactions between diet and exercise in the etiology and prevention of ischaemic heart disease. *Ann Clin Res* 1988;20:114-120.

54. Drygas W, Jegler A, Kunski H: Study on threshold dose of physical activity in coronary heart disease prevention: Part I. Relationship between leisure time physical activity and coronary risk factors. *Int J Sports Med* 1988;9:275-278.

55. Fang CL, Sherman WM, Crouse SF, et al: Exercise modality and selected coronary risk factors: A multivariate approach. *Med Sci Sports Exerc* 1988;20:455-462.

56. Van der Eems K, Ismail AH: Serum lipids: Interactions between age and moderate intensity exercise. *Br J Sports Med* 1985;19:112-114.

57. Marti B, Dai S, Rickenbach M, et al: Total cholesterol, HDL-cholesterol and blood pressure in relation to lifestyle: Results of the first population screening of the Swiss MONICA Project. *Schweiz-Med-Wochenschr* 1990;120:1976-1988.

58. Jennings G, Nelson L, Nestel P, et al: The effects of changes in physical activity on major cardiovascular risk factors, hemodynamics, sympathetic function, and glucose utilization in man: A controlled study of four levels of activity. *Circulation* 1986;73:30-40.

59. Pekkanen J, Marti B, Nissinen A, et al: Reduction of premature mortality by high physical activity: A 20-year follow-up of middle-aged Finnish men. *Lancet* 1987;1:1473-1477.

60. Slattery ML, Jacobs DR Jr: Physical fitness and cardiovascular disease mortality: The US Railroad Study. *Am J Epidemiol* 1988;127:571-580.

61. Kannel WB: Factores de riesgo en la enfermedad coronaria: Experiencia del seguimiento durante tres décadas del estudio Framingham. *Hipertensión y Arterioesclerosis* 1989;1:77-86.

62. Berlin JA, Colditz GA: A meta-analysis of physical activity in the prevention of coronary heart disease. *Am J Epidemiol* 1990;132:612-628.

63. Paffenbarger RS Jr, Hyde RT, Jung DL, et al: Epidemiology of exercise and coronary heart disease. *Clin Sports Med* 1984;3:297-318.

64. Segura A, de Mateo S, Gutierrez J: Epidemiología de los factores de riesgo cardiovascular en un area de Castilla - La Mancha. *Rev Latina Cardiol* 1986;7:377-385.

65. Taylor HL, Jacobs DR Jr, Schucker B, et al: A questionnaire for the assessment of leisure time physical activities. *J Chron Dis* 1978;31:741-755.

66. Hurren CA, Stockley L, Broadhurst AJ: An abbreviated food table using food groups for the calculation of energy, protein, fat, carbohydrate, total sugars, starch, and dietary fibre. *Nutr Res* 1987;7:15-25.

67. Wood PD, Stefanick ML, Dreon DM, et al: Changes in plasma lipids and lipoproteins in overweight men during weight loss through dieting as compared with exercise. *N Engl J Med* 1988;319:1173-1179.

68. Ministerio de Sanidad y Consumo: Consenso para el control de la colesterolemia en España. Madrid, Spain, Publicaciones del Ministerio de Sanidad y Consumo, 1989.

Chapter 4

Environmental Risk Factors of Exercise and Sport Injuries

Ilkka Vuori, MD, PhD

Exercise and sport are some of the most popular leisure time activities among midlife individuals, and their popularity is increasing in many countries.[1,2] Most sports carry an inherent risk of injury. Most exercise and sport injuries are either acute traumatic or overuse injuries to the musculoskeletal system, but a small number affect the internal organs, especially the cardiovascular system, and these injuries are often serious. It is known that injury is often reported as a reason for discontinuation of exercise and sports. In order to increase the adoption of and adherence to exercise, the risk of even minor injuries should be minimized.

In exercise and sport, injury is the result of a sudden or long-term mismatch between the loading imposed on the individual by circumstantial or external (extrinsic) factors and the individual's capacity to cope with that load as determined by personal or internal (intrinsic) factors.[3] Some of the circumstantial risk factors arise from the physical, chemical, and psychosocial environment of exercise and sport.

An environmental risk factor may be direct and a primary cause of injury, for example, cold in cold injuries. However, it may be only contributory, for example, heat causing sweating, dehydration, fatigue, impaired neuromuscular coordination, and, thus, increased propensity to fall. Internal and external risk factors interact; their effects may be additive or subtractive.

Aging may increase the risk of exercise and sport injuries because many physiologic changes associated with increasing age decrease the capacity to withstand or avoid excessive stress.[4-8] Some of the changes associated with increasing age are caused by biologic aging, for example, decreasing elasticity of collagenous tissues and decreased nerve conduction velocity. However, many changes are caused in part by changes in behavior, for example, decreasing aerobic power and muscle strength may be the result of a reduced amount and intensity of physical activity.[8] In this way aging may also lessen the risk of injury, because the speed, power, strength, and duration of exercise and sport performances usually decrease with age.

The aim of this review is to examine how age or age-related biologic, psychosocial, and behavioral changes interact with environmental factors to affect the risk of injury in exercise and sport. This examination must rely mainly on reasoning, because there are virtually no epidemiologic data comparing the incidence of various injuries in different environmental conditions by age, while adjusting for other factors such as physical fitness, health, and experience. Thus, the magnitude and even the direction of the influence of age on the risk of injury depends on multiple factors and varies greatly among individuals.

Environmental Risk Factors

Environmental risk factors of exercise and sport injury can be classified as shown in Outline 1.

The incidence and severity, and thus, the impact of different environmental factors varies greatly in different sports and in different geographic locations. Therefore, any of the risk factors may be important in some circumstances and for some populations. However, if the importance of the risk factors is estimated on the basis of the number of people exposed, opportunities to avoid them or to be protected from them, and the severity of the resulting injuries, heat is the most significant environmental risk factor, the worst enemy of an exerciser, seconded possibly by cold.

Interactions of Age and Environmental Risk Factors

The interactions of age and environmental risk factors may relate to the exposure, and to the chances of modifying the exposure by protective or compensating measures. The exposure can change with age, according to the changes in participation rates in different sports and where and how they are practiced. The effects of the exposure and the possibility of modifying them can change with age according to physiologic or pathophysiologic changes caused by or related to aging.

Heat

The number of midlife individuals exposed to heat may be increasing because of the greater participation in exercise and sport in warm climates during vacations and retirement. The risk of exercise-related heat injuries is especially high in long-distance runs in hot climates, but problems may occur even in rather mild conditions.[9]

The physiology and pathophysiology of heat tolerance in exercise and their determinants have been thoroughly studied.[10-13] In order to maintain thermal equilibrium, the extra heat generated by

Outline 1 Environmental risk factors for exercise and sport

Physical (and Chemical) Media
  Air
    temperature: heat, cold
    humidity: high (and low)
    movement: wind
    pressure: low (O_2 partial pressure)
    brightness (visibility): low (and high)
    impurities: pollution
  Water
    temperature: low (high)
    movement: waves, currents
    pressure: high (O_2, N_2 partial pressure)
    brightness (visibility): low
    impurities
Boundaries of the Medium
  Horizontal
    surface: qualities
  Vertical
    walls, fences, precipices, gorges, etc.
Obstacles in the Medium
  Natural
    stationary (trees)
    moving (people)
  Constructed
    stationary (poles, fences)
    moving (machines)
The Psychosocial Environment
  Rules, regulations, and standards
    supervision and enforcement
  Competitiveness
  Behaviors (risk taking)

muscular activity and absorbed from solar radiation must be dissipated. When the temperature is above 20°C, the main method of heat loss is evaporation. The extra heat load produced by an intensively exercising midlife athlete may be 1,000 kcal/h or even more; and 500 to 600 kcal is lost when one liter of sweat is completely evaporated from skin. The sweating rate in prolonged athletic activity may be over 1 l/h, causing hypotonic fluid loss mainly from the extracellular space.[14] At the same time, blood flow to the skin increases and causes cardiac output to increase. In intense exercise in a hot climate, blood flow to the skin may be 15% to 25% of the cardiac output, which may cause a reduction in muscle blood flow, especially if the total cardiac output decreases from hypovolemia and reduced venous return.[10]

The effects of heat depend not only on temperature, but also on humidity and movement of the air. High humidity, ie, water vapor in the air, decreases the evaporation of sweat and increases the heat load. An air stream caused by wind or movement of the body increases both the evaporation of sweat and the convection of heat.

A physiologically relevant way to express temperature is the so called "effective" temperature, measured as wet bulb globe tempera-

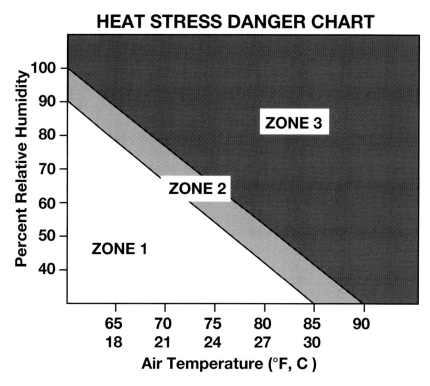

Fig. 1 *Heat stress danger chart. Zone 1: no special risks of exercise-heat injury, normal heat stress precautions. Zone 2: moderate risk for susceptible individuals, less intense and shorter bouts of exercise with more frequent fluid intake. Zone 3: great risk, exercise should be rescheduled to a cooler part of the day. (Modified from Fox EL, Mathews DK: The Physiological Basis of Physical Education and Athletics, ed 3. Philadelphia, PA, WB Saunders, 1981.)*

ture (WBGT). This index does not allow for air movement, however, which can have substantial influence on effective temperature. For example, a relative air speed of 5 m/s can lower the effective temperature by 5°C to 7°C in a moderate climate. When WBGT exceeds 28°C, it is recommended that marathon runs be cancelled. At WBGT of 23°C to 28°C the risk of heat illnesses in vulnerable subjects is high, and at 18°C to 23°C the risk is moderate.[15] The heat stress danger zones by temperature and humidity are shown in Figure 1.

Exercise in heat can cause four conditions. Syncope is transient fainting or light-headedness. It occurs most often when exercise is abruptly stopped while blood is pooled in the muscles of the lower extremities and in dilated skin vessels. Consequently, venous return is diminished and cardiac output remains insufficient for adequate brain circulation. Predisposing factors are dehydration with consequent hypovolemia, and lack of acclimatization.

Cramps are painful muscle tightening and spasms during or after intense, prolonged exercise in heat. They are caused by overexertion of the muscles, dehydration, and electrolyte loss. Predisposing factors are existing sodium depletion and lack of acclimatization.

Exhaustion is a serious exercise heat injury resulting from dehydration or hyponatremia. Body temperature is elevated, but sweating continues either profusely, or, in case of severe dehydration, at a reduced rate. The symptoms are fatigue, muscular weakness, lightheadedness, nausea, vomiting, and headache. The predisposing factors are dehydration, negative sodium balance, and lack of acclimatization.

Heat stroke is extreme hyperthermia, a medical emergency, caused by thermoregulatory failure. There is profound central nervous system dysfunction, which is not spontaneously reversible. Predisposing factors are the same as those listed above.

Some researchers suggest that age by itself may not be a major factor in decreasing heat tolerance or increasing the risk of exertional heat syndromes,[16-18] but contrasting views are presented.[12,19] However, because poor physical condition, insufficient training, obesity, chronic diseases, and use of drugs may decrease heat tolerance in exercise and acclimatization to heat,[20] older individuals are more likely than younger individuals to belong to the groups having decreased heat tolerance. Thus, in practice, heat may be a more significant environmental risk factor in the midlife than in the young exercising population, but each person's risk is unique and risk must be assessed on an individual basis.

Cold

Exposure to cold in exercise and sport is not limited to the most northern and southern regions of the globe; cold also is prevalent at high altitudes, where hiking, mountaineering, and downhill skiing are practiced by large numbers of midlife individuals. The popularity of these sports is increasing. Local or generalized hypothermia may occur even in temperatures much above 0°C if heat loss is great because of humid, windy weather and wet clothing, and heat generation is decreased because of fatigue.[21-23] The effects of cold are increased by the air stream, because of increased evaporation and convection, and by humidity, because of decreased insulation provided by the clothing and increased evaporation. The combined effects of temperature and air stream on heat loss are measured in the wind-chill factor (Table 1). Thus, a temperature of −4°C and a wind speed of 16 km/h (4.4 m/s) equals a wind-chill factor of −12°C. However, the danger zones in Table 1 apply to cooling of exposed skin of sedentary persons, and the risk is greatly reduced by windproof clothing and intensive muscular activity.[24]

The risk of hypothermia is especially great in water because of the high thermal conductivity of water, which results in cooling at a

Table 1 Cooling power of wind on exposed flesh expressed as an equivalent temperature under calm conditions

Wind speed* (m·s⁻¹)	Actual Temperature (°C)												
	10	5	0	−5	−10	−15	−20	−25	−30	−35	−40	−45	−50
	Equivalent Chill Temperature (°C)**												
Calm	10	5	0	−5	−10	−15	−20	−25	−30	−35	−40	−45	−50
2	9	4	−1	−6	−11	−16	−21	−26	−32	−37	−42	−47	−52
4	5	−1	−7	−13	−19	−25	−31	−37	−43	−49	−55	−61	−67
6	3	−4	−10	−17	−23	−30	−37	−43	−50	−56	−63	−69	−76
8	1	−6	−13	−20	−27	−34	−41	−48	−55	−62	−69	−76	−83
10	0	−8	−15	−22	−30	−37	−44	−51	−59	−66	−73	−81	−88
12	−2	−9	−17	−24	−32	−39	−47	−54	−62	−69	−77	−84	−92
14	−2	−10	−18	−25	−33	−41	−48	−56	−64	−72	−79	−87	−95
16	−3	−11	−19	−26	−34	−42	−50	−58	−65	−73	−81	−89	−97
18	−3	−11	−19	−27	−35	−43	−51	−59	−67	−75	−83	−90	−98
20*	−4	−12	−20	−28	−36	−44	−52	−60	−68	−76	−84	−91	−99

Little danger
In events of less than 5 h with dry skin; maximum danger from false sense of security (WCI<1400)

Increasing danger
Danger from freezing of exposed flesh within 1 min (WCI 1400–2000)

Great danger
Flesh may freeze within 30 s (WCI>2000)

*Wind speeds >20 m·s⁻¹ have little additional effect. WCI, wind chill index.
**The actual thermometer reading (°C) and wind speed (m·s⁻¹) are used to calculate an equivalent chill temperature (see Gonzalez RR. Work in the north: physiological aspects. Artic Med Res 1986;44:7–17).
(Reproduced with permission from Gonzalez RR: Work in the North: Physiological aspects. *Arctic Med Res* 1986;44:7-17.)

rate 20 to 30 times higher than that in the air.[21] A number of physiologic effects of cold relevant to exercise and sport are shown in Figure 2.

Cold exposure may cause specific cold injuries, such as frostbite, trench foot, and hypothermia,[22] and increase respiratory and cardiac symptoms in susceptible subjects.[25-27] In addition, cold may increase the risk of musculoskeletal injuries and cardiac complications. A study on sudden cardiac deaths in exercise revealed that these deaths were most numerous in cross-country skiing (Table 2).[28,29]

In order to see if these deaths might be related to cold, my associates and I collected information on all autopsied sudden cardiac deaths in Finland in two years (n = 791) and the meteorologic data at the time and place of the death. The results showed that the temperature and especially the wind-chill factor (W-CF) were significantly lower (−2°C, −9 W-CF) on the days when five to six sudden deaths occurred compared to days when no (+4°C, −0.6 W-CF), one to two (+3.8°C, −0.4 W-CF), or three to four (+2.8°C, −1.0 W-CF) sudden deaths occurred (Vuori et al, unpublished), supporting the findings of other studies suggesting that the incidence of cardiovascular events is increased in cold weather in susceptible subjects.[25]

The critical temperature for many exercises and sports is about −23°C; below that temperature the combined effects of cold and air stream caused by activities such as running, bicycling, and skiing can rapidly produce frostbite of the exposed parts and cause severe

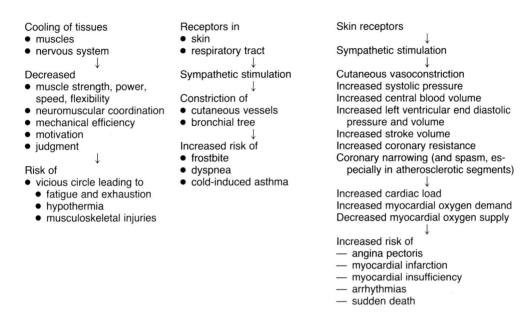

Fig. 2 *Physiologic responses and health risks related to cold exposure.*

Table 2 Incidence of sudden cardiovascular death from exercise for Finnish men, aged 40-69 years, expressed as the number of exercise sessions in millions per death

| Age group, yr | Jogging, Running | | Cross-country Skiing | | Soccer/Basketball/Volleyball | |
	Number of deaths	Exercise sessions in millions per death	Number of deaths	Exercise sessions in millions per death	Number of deaths	Exercise sessions in millions per death
40-69	17	4.1	34	1.1	6	3.3
50-69	12	4.7	61	0.7	1	10.3

irritation of the airways and eyes. A Swiss recommendation of cold limits in sports is −15°C for cross-country skiing of 30 to 50 km and −18°C for shorter distances, and −20°C for downhill skiing.[30]

Aging may increase the risk associated with cold. Aging reduces vasoconstriction and blunts cold perception,[31] and it is associated with decreased fitness and physiologic reserves; decreased flexibility and neuromuscular coordination; and increased musculoskeletal, respiratory, cardiovascular, and metabolic morbidity. These factors may increase the risk of cardiovascular events, musculoskeletal injuries, severe fatigue, and hypothermia.

Altitude

The physiologic effects of altitude begin to appear above 1,500 m. The decreased O_2 pressure leads to hyperventilation, dehydration, and decreased plasma volume, resulting in increased heart rate and cardiac output at submaximal exercise levels. These effects are increased by cold and dry air. The $\dot{V}O_2max$ may decrease slightly between 1,000 and 2,000 m; and above 2,000 m it decreases an average of 3% for each 300 m, although individual variation is large.[24] Thus, especially during the first three weeks at altitude, aerobic performance capacity is decreased in most individuals; the decrement increases with increasing altitude.[11,12,21,32,33]

Acute health effects of altitude begin to appear around 2,000 m, but the individual variation is wide. The symptoms of acute mountain sickness include headache, dizziness, irritability, nausea, vomiting, insomnia, and poor appetite. The symptoms may begin during the first two to four hours and usually within the first 24 hours, and they last for two to three days. High altitude pulmonary edema causing severe breathlessness, coughing, chest discomfort, and often copious sputum excretion begins to appear above 3,000 m, following the same time course as acute mountain sickness. Life-threatening cerebral edema, appearing as severe headache, disorientation, hallucinations, and coma, is a risk above 4,000 m. Months of residence at moderate altitude may lead to chronic mountain sickness, which appears as weakness, plethora, and congestive heart failure.[21,32]

The risk of health consequences related to high altitude may increase with aging because of decreased physiologic reserves and increasing prevalence of chronic cardiorespiratory and metabolic diseases. On the other hand, healthy midlife individuals do not suffer acute mountain sickness more severely or more often than young people.[32,34] It is likely that up to 3,000 to 5,000 m, the limiting factor for physical performance is muscular fatigue and, thus, the heart may not be maximally loaded.[32] Thus, increasing age without concomitant illnesses seems not to increase significantly the risk of injury in exercise and sport at moderate altitude.[34] However, heat and especially cold are often combined with altitude, and the effects of these factors may be additive in determining the risk of injury.

Air Pollution

Air pollution is a growing problem for exercisers and athletes of all ages in many countries. The most common forms of air pollution are reducing and oxidant smog.[35] Reducing smog is produced by burning carbon fuels, such as coal. It contains sulfur oxide, sulfur trioxide, and smoke particles, and causes bronchospasm, paralysis of ciliae in the airways, production of sputum, airway collapse, increased risk of infection, and increased work of breathing. The oxidant smog is produced by motor vehicle exhaust under the influence of sunlight. This smog contains carbon monoxide, hydrocarbons, ozone, and nitrogen oxides. It causes formation of carboxyhemoglobin, impairment of oxygen transport and oxygen dissociation, reduction of $\dot{V}O_2max$, irritation of the eyes and respiratory tract, and even asthmatic attacks, headache, and deterioration of visual acuity, mental functions, and motivation. The exposure to air pollutants is increased during intensive exercise as a result of increased breathing, and the risk of harm to performance and health is similarly increased.[11,33,36]

Aging alone does not increase the harmful effects of air pollution. Because the effects of air pollution depend partly on the intensity of breathing and, thus, on the intensity of exercise, air pollution may actually cause even fewer problems for healthy midlife individuals than for young exercisers. On the other hand, the increased work of breathing caused by aging and the greater prevalence of respiratory and cardiac diseases increases the risk of harmful effects of air pollution in the midlife population.

Physical Surroundings

The surface qualities and natural or constructed obstacles on the grounds greatly influence the risk of injuries.[37] It is obvious that reaction and movement time, speed, neuromuscular coordination, flexibility, agility, visual acuity, and accommodation, as well as endurance, all tend to decrease with aging,[8] and these changes tend to increase the risk of fatigue, falls, slips, and collisions. These risks may be offset by decreased speed, power, and competitive spirit of the performances with aging. The likely result of all these factors is that the risk of musculoskeletal injuries increases with age in maximal performances requiring high speed or power or complex skills, especially in unfavorable surroundings, but in "age-adjusted" performances, this may not be true.

Selection of Sports Activities

Prevention of exercise and sport injuries is possible as demonstrated in soccer[38] and in downhill skiing,[39] but it is a demanding task requiring careful planning, multi-disciplinary approach, and long-term interventions.[40-43] The effective prevention of exercise injuries must be based on detailed and sport-specific knowledge of risk factors, including their statistical power, their prevalence in the target populations and in the practiced sports, their mechanisms of action, and ways of reducing them by avoidance, protection, or compensation. This knowledge, which is limited, helps to reduce the incidence of injuries, but does not eliminate them entirely; the chain of events and the involved factors usually are not well-enough known, cannot be sufficiently influenced,[3,44,45] and are partly unpredictable.[46]

Even limited results may be worth the effort, however, and even on the basis of deficient knowledge, it is possible to plan a useful strategy for sport injury prevention. One way to formulate such a strategy is to divide it into various approaches: (1) behavioral approach, referring to instruction, education, and communication on individual, group, and population levels, (2) technical approach, describing the development and use of protective equipment and safe materials, and (3) organizational approach meaning development, implementation, and enforcement of rules, regulations, norms, and other measures.[47,48] In many, if not in most serious attempts to prevent exercise and sport injuries, all these approaches must be used intensively and for a lengthy period.[40-42]

Sports can be classified into groups according to their suitability for midlife individuals. The most suitable exercises and sports are brisk walking and hiking; sports including walking as the most strenuous part, such as golf; keep-fit activities at home or in guided groups; and home activities such as gardening, dancing, and swimming, as well as cycling and cross-country skiing in safe environments. Tennis, possibly in applied forms, and table tennis are among the most suitable ball games for midlife individuals. Fortunately, in terms of fitness and health benefits, these activities are among the most effective. The medium group includes sports requiring faster, stronger, or more skillful movements or great structural or functional endurance like badminton, squash, volleyball, Alpine skiing, and running. The least suitable sports are those requiring great speed, power, fast turns, and good balance, especially combined with the characteristics of the medium group and those that also include body contact and collisions, especially in a highly competitive spirit. These sports include boxing, soccer, football, rugby, basketball, ice hockey, weight lifting with maximal weights, and many track and field disciplines.

Recommendations for Midlife

The following statements and recommendations concerning the risk of exercise and sport injuries and their prevention in the midlife population seem warranted.

Midlife subjects are not a homogeneous population. The different rates of biologic and behavioral aging and the different degrees of functional and structural impairment and morbidity, as well as the individual differences in their abilities for exercise and sport, are even greater than among younger subjects. These differences emphasize the need for highly individual risk assessment, which includes a medical check-up with special emphasis on the musculoskeletal system and the cardiorespiratory organs and evaluation of functional abilities such as strength, flexibility, coordination, balance, vision, and hearing. A graded exercise-ECG test is recommended.[49] Appropriate measures should be taken to correct or compensate for deficiencies, for example, suitable spectacles, good shoes with orthotics if necessary, and adjustment of medication. Detailed schemes exist for assessment of the individual readiness for exercise and sports.[15,22,49,50]

In general, the biologic phenomena related to aging increase the risk of both acute and overuse injuries and are additive to the environmental risk factors. Therefore, maximal efforts, especially those requiring great speed and power are not recommended.

A majority of midlife individuals interested in exercise and sport are relatively healthy and, in general, the functional and structural impairment resulting from aging is not yet major. Therefore, the risk due to age itself is not greatly increased, and a too protective or too prohibitive approach in general information and in individual counseling should be avoided. A key point to emphasize is to begin exercise very gradually and with basic activities, especially after prolonged inactivity, in order to develop the necessary fitness and skills for more demanding performance.

Midlife individuals should pay special attention to the general and age-specific recommendations to avoid exposure to environmental risk factors, to protect against them, and to decrease their effects. These recommendations include the following: Thorough stretching and warming-up before and gradual cessation and thorough cooling-down after each exercise session are even more important for midlife athletes than for young athletes. Allowing sufficient time for recovery both during an exercise session and between sessions is necessary because the processes for structural and functional recovery and repair slow down with age. Efficient prevention of fatigue should be emphasized for two reasons. First, aging as such and the poorer physical fitness of many midlife exercisers places them at increased risk of hypoglycemia, glycogen depletion, and dehydration leading to fatigue. Second, fatigue associated with the detrimental effects of aging on many organ systems, decreasing their tolerance and reserves, as well as the increased morbidity, increase the risk of injury. Many environmental factors increase the risk of fatigue development, and fatigue under the conditions may lead to more serious consequences than in favorable conditions in younger subjects. Thus, athletic activities in extreme environments should be avoided.

Previous heat tolerance and any history of heat injuries should be assessed. Obese and unfit persons should be informed of their increased risk of poor heat tolerance. Acclimatization by exercising with mild to moderate intensity in heat for four to seven times improves heat tolerance markedly. Intensive activity should be done only in a well-tolerated temperature and humidity area (Zone 1, Fig. 1). Clothing during exercise should be light-colored, shiny, scanty, and loose-fitting, and should allow sweat evaporation. Wet clothes should be changed as often as possible. Fluid should be taken before, during, and after exercise. During intensive exercise, cool fluid should be taken several times during an hour, about 200 ml at a time. It should contain some carbohydrate and a small amount of sodium, especially in prolonged activities.

Enhanced cold sensitivity due to cold-induced asthma, previous cold injuries, or Raynaud's syndrome should be assessed. Cold injury can be prevented by increasing heat production and decreasing heat loss. Therefore, the general advice is to keep moving and to keep properly clothed and dry. It is worth emphasizing that systemic and local hypothermia can develop even in intensive exercise, like marathon running in warm temperature, from heat loss caused by a high sweat-evaporation rate and insufficient protection against air stream and moisture. The risk of serious hypothermia is especially great in prolonged strenuous efforts in open areas in windy, moist, and cool climates such as those in which mountain hiking, cycling, skiing, and canoeing are practiced. Fatigue leading to decreased heat production may be disastrous in these conditions.

Warming up, preferably indoors, prevents cooling at the beginning of exercise. Continuous movement is needed to prevent subsequent cooling, which emphasizes the importance of physical and mental endurance in cold conditions. Rest breaks should be taken in a shelter or when wearing a well-insulated, wind-protective jacket. Proper clothing provides sufficient, but not excessive insulation, permeability to the water vapor of evaporating sweat, and protection of exposed or cold-sensitive areas (head, ears, nose, neck, fingers, sides of the chest, breasts, groin, and feet). Layered clothing is the best solution for the insulation and permeability requirements. It includes tightly fitting underwear of preferably synthetic material, which allows the sweat to be absorbed to the next layer, leaving the skin and underwear relatively dry. The middle layer is loose-fitting, well-insulating, and sweat permeable. Wool and synthetic materials are suitable fabrics. The outer layer is wind-protective and water-repellent, but water vapor-permeable, for example, Goretex.®

A key point for effective cold protection is to keep the clothing as dry as possible by efficient ventilation, by adjusting the insulating layer according to the activity and temperature, and by wearing a protective outer layer. The other way to keep the clothing dry is to avoid overly intensive bursts of activity. In cold, snow, and wet conditions, shoes should be protected by a special cover or by socks or a plastic bag.

Adequate food intake (in shelter) is important both to produce heat and to maintain endurance. Heavy exercise causes intensive sweating, even in cold conditions, and the fluid loss is increased markedly by breathing cold, dry air. Thus, adequate fluid intake is important in cold weather. Smoking and alcohol consumption increase the risk of fatigue and cold injuries.

The increased cardiorespiratory requirements at altitude increase the risk of injury resulting from cardiorespiratory diseases; these risks should be carefully assessed. Ascent to altitude above 2,000 m is not advisable for individuals with poorly controlled angina, congestive heart failure, hypertension, or pulmonary insufficiency that causes dyspnea, even in light activity. Sufficient acclimatization decreases the risk of injury and other harmful effects of altitude. Acclimatization can be enhanced by sufficient fluid intake to compensate for dehydration and by avoiding activities and measures that cause sympathetic stimulation, such as smoking, alcohol, and caffeine intake and strenuous activities.

Summary

The risk of injury in exercise and sport is only slightly or moderately increased in healthy midlife individuals by aging alone. The risk may increase markedly because of the additive effects of environmental factors increasing the demand for various performance qualities and reserve capacity. Aging is associated with increased prevalence of diseases affecting physical performance directly or indirectly, and the combination of the effects of normal aging, diseases, and environmental factors may increase the risk of injury to an unacceptably high level. The risk level can and should be assessed individually, especially when midlife individuals ignorant of their health status consider beginning exercises or sports requiring substantially greater strength, speed, power, endurance, or skills than their previous activities, and especially when these activities will be performed in demanding environmental conditions.

For the majority of even high-risk individuals, there is a variety of exercise and sport that can be practiced safely for health, fun, and well-being. The former state president of Finland, Urho Kaleva Kekkonen, stated that "All reasons given not to exercise are excuses." That may be quite true.

References

1. Powell KE, Stephens T, Marti B, et al: Progress and problems in the promotion of physical activity, in Oja P, Telama R (eds): *Sport for All*. Amsterdam, Elsevier Science Publishers, 1991, pp 55-73.

2. Bouchard C, Shephard RJ, Stephens T (eds): *Physical Activity, Fitness, and Health: Consensus Statement*. Champaign, IL, Human Kinetics Publishers, 1993.

3. van Mechelen W: *Aetiology and Prevention of Running Injuries*. University of Amsterdam, 1992. Thesis.

4. Shephard RJ: *Physical Activity and Aging*. London, Croom Helm, 1978.

5. Fries JF, Crapo LM: *Vitality and Aging: Implications of the Rectangular Curve*. San Francisco, CA, W H Freeman and Company, 1981.

6. Spirduso WW, Eckert HM (eds): *Physical Activity and Aging*. American Academy of Physical Education Papers No. 22. Champaign, IL, Human Kinetics Books for the American Academy of Physical Education, 1989.

7. Stamford BA: Exercise and the elderly. *Exerc Sport Sci Rev* 1988;16:341-379.

8. Siegel AJ: Exercise and aging, in Strauss RH (ed): *Sports Medicine*, ed 2. Philadelphia, PA, WB Saunders, 1991, chap 34, pp 529-543.

9. Hughson RL: Heat stroke in northern climates, in Sutton JR, Brock RM (eds): *Sports Medicine for the Mature Athlete*. Indianapolis, IN, Benchmark Press, 1986, chap 13, pp 145-149.

10. Rowell LB: Cardiovascular adjustments to thermal stress, in Shepherd JT, Abbound FM (eds): *Handbook of Physiology. Section 2. The Cardiovascular System*; Vol 3. Peripheral circulation and organ blood flow. Part 2. Bethesda, MD, American Physiological Society, 1983, pp 967-1023.

11. Haymes EM, Wells CL: *Environment and Human Performance*. Champaign, IL, Human Kinetics Publishers, 1986.

12. Åstrand P-O, Rodahl K: *Textbook of Work Physiology. Physiological Bases of Exercise*, ed 3. New York, NY, McGraw-Hill, 1986.

13. Hales JRS, Richards DAB (eds): *Heat Stress: Physical Exertion and Environment*. Amsterdam, Elsevier Science Publishers, 1987.

14. Noakes TD: Fluid replacement during exercise. *Exerc Sport Sci Rev* 1993;21:297-330.

15. Mellion MB, Shelton GL: Safe exercise in the heat and heat injuries, in Mellion MB, Walsh WM, Shelton GL (eds): *The Team Physician's Handbook*. Philadelphia, PA, Hanley & Belfus, 1990, chap 11, pp 59-69.

16. Kenney MJ, Gisolfi CV: Thermal regulation: Effects of exercise and age, in Sutton JR, Brock RM (eds): *Sports Medicine for the Mature Athlete*. Indianapolis, IN, Benchmark Press, 1986, chap 12, pp 133-143.

17. Pandolf KB: Air quality and human performance, in Pandolf KB, Sawka MN, Gonzalez RR (eds): *Human Performance Physiology and Environmental Medicine at Terrestrial Extremes*. Indianapolis, IN, Benchmark Press, 1988, pp 591-629.

18. Yousef MK: Heat tolerance and exercise capacity in old age, in Hales JRS, Richards DAB (eds): *Heat Stress: Physical Exertion and Environment*. Amsterdam, Elsevier Science Publishers, 1987, pp 367-382.

19. Kenney WL, Hodgson JL: Heat tolerance, thermoregulation and ageing. *Sports Med* 1987;4:446-456.

20. Hughson RL: Hyperthermia, hypothermia and problems of hydration, in Shephard RJ, Åstrand P-O (eds): *Endurance in Sport*. Oxford, Blackwell Scientific Publications, 1992, chap 42, pp 458-470.

21. Sutton JR: Exercise and the environment, in Bouchard C, Shephard RJ, Stephens T, et al (eds): *Exercise, Fitness and Health: A Consensus of Current Knowledge*. Champaign, IL, Human Kinetics Books, 1988, chap 16, pp 165-178.

22. Paton BC: Cold injuries, in Strauss RH (ed): *Sports Medicine*, ed 2. Philadelphia, PA, WB Saunders Company, 1991, chap 24, pp 359-388.

23. Bracker MD: Environmental and thermal injury. *Clin Sports Med* 1992;11:419-436.

24. Pandolf KB, Young AJ: Environmental extremes and endurance performance, in Shephard RJ, Åstrand P-O (eds): *Endurance in Sport.* Oxford, Blackwell Scientific Publications, 1992, chap 27, pp 270-282.

25. Vuori I: The heart and the cold. *Ann Clin Res* 1987;19:156-162.

26. Houdas Y, Deklunder G, Lecroart J-L: Cold exposure and ischemic heart disease. *Int J Sports Med* 1992;13(suppl 1):S179-S181.

27. Regnard J: Cold and the airways. *Int J Sports Med* 1992;13(suppl 1):S182-S184.

28. Vuori I, Suurnäkki T, Suurnäkki L: Liikuntaan liittyvän äkkikuoleman riski ja syyt (Cases and risk of sudden death in exercise and sports. English summary.) *Duodecim* 1983;99:516-526.

29. Vuori I: The cardiovascular risks of physical activity. *Acta Med Scand* 1986;(suppl 711):205-214.

30. Lereim I: Sports at low temperatures. Federation Internationale de Ski, Worbstrasse 210, Postfach, CH-3074 Gumligen, Switzerland.

31. Cooper KE, Ferguson AV: Thermoregulation and hypothermia in the elderly, in Pozos RS, Wittmers RL (eds): *The Nature and Treatment of Hypothermia.* Minneapolis, MN, University of Minnesota Press, 1983, chap 3, pp 35-45.

32. Houston CS: Altitude sickness, in Strauss RH (ed): *Sports Medicine,* ed 2. Philadelphia, PA, WB Saunders, 1991, chap 25, pp 389-408.

33. Pyke FS, Sutton JR: Environmental stress, in Bloomfield J, Fricker PA, Fitch KD (eds): *Textbook of Science and Medicine in Sport.* Champaign, IL, Human Kinetics Books, 1992, pp 114-133.

34. Balcomb AC, Sutton JR: Advanced age and altitude illness, in Sutton JR, Brock RM (eds): *Sports Medicine for the Mature Athlete.* Indianapolis, IN, Benchmark Press, 1986, chap 19, pp 213-224.

35. Shephard RJ: Athletic performance and urban air pollution. *Can Med Assoc J* 1984;131:105-109.

36. Folinsbee LJ: Ambient air pollution and endurance performance, in Shephard RJ, Åstrand P-O (eds): *Endurance in Sport.* Oxford, Blackwell Scientific Publications, 1992, chap 44, pp 479-486.

37. Flynn RB: Sports surfaces, in Mellion MB, Walsh WM, Shelton GL (eds): *The Team Physician's Handbook.* Philadelphia, PA, Hanley & Belfus, 1990, chap 9, pp 47-56.

38. Ekstrand J: *Soccer Injuries and Their Prevention.* University of Linköping, 1982. Dissertation.

39. Eriksson E, Danielsson K: Ski injuries in Sweden—the value of a national survey, in Staff PH (ed): Nordisk idrettsmedisinsk kongress. Beitostølen 27.-30. mars, 1977, pp 135-141.

40. Backx FJB: *Sports Injuries in Youth: Etiology and Prevention.* University of Utrecht, 1991. Thesis.

41. van Kernebeek E: Evaluation report "Sports injuries, how to prevent them." Oosterbeek, 1992.

42. van Mechelen W: Running injuries: A review of the epidemiological literature. *Sports Med* 1992;14:320-335.

43. van Mechelen W, Hlobil H, Kemper HC: Incidence, severity, aetiology and prevention of sports injuries: A review of concepts. *Sports Med* 1992;14:82-99.

44. Lysens RJ, de Weerdt W, Nieuwboer A: Factors associated with injury proneness. *Sports Med* 1991:12:281-289.

45. Hoeberigs JH: Factors related to the incidence of running injuries: A review. *Sports Med* 1992:13:408-422.

46. Meeuwisse WH: Predictability of sports injuries. What is the epidemiological evidence? *Sports Med* 1991:12:8-15.

47. de Vent TGM: Sports injuries prevention by information and education. Consumer Safety Institute. Report no 51. Amsterdam 1988.

48. van Vulpen AT: Council of Europe coordinated research project, "Sports injuries and their prevention." Oosterbeek, NISGZ, 1989.

49. American College of Sports Medicine. *Guidelines for Exercise Testing and Prescription*, ed 4. Philadelphia, PA, Lea & Febiger, 1991.

50. Sutton JR, Brock RM (eds): *Sports Medicine for the Mature Athlete*. Indianapolis, IN, Benchmark Press, 1986.

Section Two

Physiologic Response to
Athletic Participation

Chapter 5

Cardiovascular Adjustments to Exercise and Physical Conditioning in Midlife

Loring B. Rowell, PhD
Charles M. Tipton, PhD

Introduction

Physical conditioning refers to cardiovascular and metabolic adaptations to high loads placed regularly on these two systems. The respiratory system may adapt somewhat,[1] but the most important adaptations are in the cardiovascular system and in the oxidative metabolic capacity of skeletal muscle.[2,3] Physical conditioning requires the activity of a large muscle mass over prolonged periods of time at intensities that require 60% to 70% of the highest possible whole-body oxygen uptake ($\dot{V}O_2$).[4] The adaptations occur in the young and the old, in men and women, and they can be evaluated in terms of functional criteria or performance criteria. These criteria are quite different and their differences have led to substantial confusion. The questions to be answered here are the following: How well do midlife men and women adapt to physical conditioning and how are these adaptations achieved?

Functional Criteria for Adaptation to Physical Conditioning

Functional Criteria Versus Performance Criteria

Maximal Oxygen Uptake ($\dot{V}O_2$max)　　The most important functional criterion in this discussion is the $\dot{V}O_2$max, which is a measure of the functional capacity of the cardiovascular system. It is enhanced by physical conditioning through the effects of exercise in increasing maximal cardiac output and muscle blood flow, maximal stroke volume, and total and regional oxygen extraction or systemic arteriovenous oxygen difference (A-$\dot{V}O_2$ difference).

　　In contrast, performance criteria, which are discussed in more detail later, describe the ability to perform work at specified rates and durations. Performance criteria describe work capacity or endurance rather than cardiovascular function. The primary determinants of work capacity or performance are metabolic, and these determinants reside in the active muscles as long as the delivery of oxygen by the cardiovascular system is adequate. Increases in work performance are associated with metabolic adjustments in skeletal muscle during physical conditioning, and these adjustments greatly exceed any changes in cardiovascular function.

Therefore, the factors that increase $\dot{V}O_2max$ are not necessarily the same factors that increase work performance. Up to a point, of course, the $\dot{V}O_2max$ is a determinant of work performance (ie, $\dot{V}O_2max$ must be high enough to ensure adequate oxygen delivery). Nevertheless, $\dot{V}O_2max$ can be unaffected by a number of stresses that severely impair work performance.[3,5] Conversely, work performance can be increased (within limits) without improvement in $\dot{V}O_2max$. The point is that $\dot{V}O_2max$ is not a reliable index of performance, and performance is not a reliable index of functional capacity.[3,5] The emphasis here is on the functional capacity, or $\dot{V}O_2max$.

The Cardiovascular Determinants of $\dot{V}O_2max$ According to the Fick principle, a restatement of the law of conservation of mass,

$$\dot{V}O_2max = HR_{max} \times SV_{max} \times A\text{-}VO_2 \; diff_{max} \qquad \text{(Equation 1)}$$

where $\dot{V}O_2max$ is the product of maximal values for heart rate (HR), stroke volume (SV), and systemic A-VO$_2$ difference. The maximal A-VO$_2$ difference is determined by the arterial oxygen content and the mixed venous or pulmonary arterial oxygen content. The subsequent discussion will examine these determinants in order to dissect out the factors that are potential limitations to oxygen transport and to show how these factors can be altered by conditioning. If these are true limiting factors, then they must be the sites of adjustment to physical conditioning, as well as the sites responsible for the decline in $\dot{V}O_2max$ with aging.

Metabolic Determinants of $\dot{V}O_2max$ In normal individuals, the capacity of skeletal muscles to consume oxygen exceeds the capacity of the cardiovascular system to deliver oxygen to the muscles when they are extremely active.[3,6] If the metabolic capacity of an active muscle were a determinant of the $\dot{V}O_2max$, then the statement that $\dot{V}O_2max$ is a measure of the functional capacity of the cardiovascular system would be incorrect, and Equation 1 would not be an adequate description of its determinants. The simplest proof rests with two observations. First, raising the arterial oxygen content (widening A-VO$_2$ diff$_{max}$ in Equation 1) raises $\dot{V}O_2max$, and second, at $\dot{V}O_2max$, the addition of more active muscles does not raise $\dot{V}O_2$. In the first case, if metabolism were a limit, $\dot{V}O_2$ would not be expected to rise, but it does; whereas in the second case, $\dot{V}O_2$ would be expected to rise, but it does not.

Age Differences in $\dot{V}O_2$max The decline in $\dot{V}O_2$max with age has been recognized for a long time. Rates of decline range from those that would extrapolate to zero $\dot{V}O_2$max (and death) by late midlife, to more encouraging estimates showing decline to be as low as 0.2 ml kg^{-1} min^{-1} $year^{-1}$ (as opposed to a high of 1.43 ml kg^{-1} min^{-1} $year^{-1}$). Historically, many investigators observed a more or less uniform decline of 0.4 to 0.5 ml kg^{-1} min^{-1} $year^{-1}$.[7] This decline is less in women, approximately 0.2 to 0.35 ml kg^{-1} min^{-1} $year^{-1}$.

Although most age comparisons have been cross-sectional, even the longitudinal studies reveal large differences from the "usual" pattern of decline. Prediction of the decline is complex because of age-related changes in weight and body composition and changing patterns of physical activity. The higher incidence of cardiovascular and respiratory disease with increasing age is another complication. It appears that in active people, the decline is slow from 20 to 60 years of age and speeds up after 60 years; whereas in sedentary individuals, the decline is rapid in the 20s and 30s due to inactivity and increased weight; the rate of decline becomes less thereafter. In short, simply averaging the rate of decline over several decades can be meaningless.[7]

Again, it is the factors that normally limit the uptake of oxygen that would be expected to cause a decline in oxygen uptake with advancing age. Most agree that the age-dependent decline in maximal heart rate is the major cause because it contributes much more to the decline in maximal cardiac output than does the decline in stroke volume.[8] Figure 1 shows average rates of decline in $\dot{V}O_2$max and its determinants in 98 sedentary men and 104 sedentary women and reveals what has become a traditional picture of how $\dot{V}O_2$max declines. Maximal A-VO_2 difference, which is not shown in Figure 1, has been reported in some studies to be narrowed in older individuals.[9] Direct measurements of arterial and pulmonary-arterial oxygen contents in 23 healthy individuals (12 normal men aged 20 to 64 years and 11 normal women aged 28 to 61 years) at $\dot{V}O_2$max did not suggest a lower-than-normal maximal total extraction of oxygen.[8] Some have assigned this putative decline in maximal oxygen extraction to a reduction in muscle mass.[10]

Gerstenblith and associates[11] have questioned whether the age-related decline in stroke volume shown in Figure 1 actually occurs in healthy individuals. An investigation of older subjects screened for coronary arterial disease and hypertension yielded the surprising result that maximal cardiac output and stroke volume did not decrease in midlife or old age. However, both the screening of subjects and the use of gated radionuclide angiocardiography to estimate stroke volume and cardiac output may have contributed to this result. For example, when conventional direct Fick or indicator dilution tech-

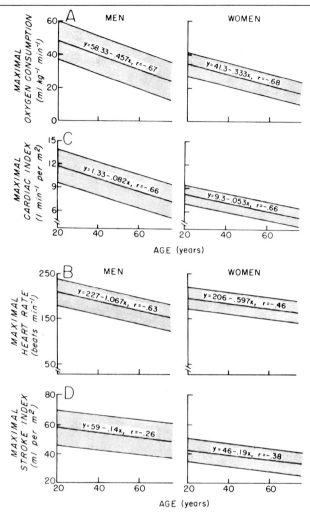

Fig. 1 *Normal range (mean + 2 SD) of maximal oxygen consumption and its determinants in 98 normal sedentary men 20 to 73 years of age, and 104 normal sedentary women 20 to 70 years of age. Measurements of cardiac output were made by direct Fick method in 12 normal men 20 to 64 years of age (mean 45.6 years) and 11 normal women 28 to 61 years of age (mean 50.9 years). (Adapted with permission from Hossack KF, Bruce RA: Maximal cardiac function in sedentary normal men and women: Comparison of age-related changes. J Appl Physiol 1982;53:799-804.)*

niques are used to measure cardiac output, stroke volume is calculated by dividing heart rate and cardiac output. In this case, the error in cardiac output measurement is divided by heart rate. Radionuclide angiocardiography determines stroke volume, which is multiplied by heart rate to derive cardiac output. Errors in stroke volume determination are multiplied by heart rate.

A series of investigations from Lakatta's group has revealed important effects of aging on human left ventricular function during exercise.[11] End-diastolic volume appears to increase more in older subjects, but left ventricular end-systolic volume does not decrease to the same extent as in younger subjects. This means that end-systolic volume is greater and the fraction of diastolic volume ejected on each contraction (ejection fraction) is lower in older than in younger individuals during exercise. Stated differently, the ejection fraction increases less from rest to exercise in older than in younger individuals. (The errors in determining the ratio of end-systolic:end-diastolic volume or ejection fraction are far smaller than errors in measuring absolute volumes by radionuclide angiocardiography.) The lower ejection fraction in the elderly appears not to be caused by greater ventricular afterload inasmuch as Gerstenblith and associates[11] did not observe higher arterial pressure in older subjects. Parenthetically, this latter finding appears to be at odds with their unique finding of higher maximal cardiac output in older individuals; the combination of higher cardiac output and lower muscle mass and muscle vascular conductance would lead to a higher pressure.

The lower ejection fraction in older subjects during strenuous exercise could be explained by a reduction in myocardial contraction force caused by decreased inotropic responsiveness of the left ventricle. Gerstenblith and associates[11] reported a decline in β-receptor binding affinity on white blood cells with increasing age. They hypothesized that a generalized decrease in β-adrenergic modulation of cardiovascular function occurs with aging, making the hemodynamic responses of older individuals resemble those of younger subjects after β-receptor blockade. A reduction in circulating catecholamines during exercise is not a factor; if anything, plasma catecholamine levels are higher in older than in younger individuals during strenuous exercise.

It is not clear at what age this decline in ventricular function becomes significant. Gerstenblith and associates[11] saw significant changes in 21 men aged 45 to 64 years. Higginbotham and associates[12] found no age-related declines in indices of ventricular performance during mild to peak exercise when seven men aged 40 to 50 years were compared with ten men in their third decade and seven men in their second decade. There were no significant correlations between age and stroke volume, end-diastolic and end-systolic volumes (all indexed to body surface area), ejection fraction, peak ejection rate, or pulmonary artery wedge pressure. Although midlife lowered peak heart rate and cardiac output, it had no significant effect on left ventricular pressure, volume, and contractile force.

In addition to its effects on heart rate and cardiac output, aging could also reduce $\dot{V}O_2max$ by narrowing A-VO_2 difference (see above). This narrowing could stem from reductions in arterial oxygen content or higher-than-normal mixed venous oxygen content. An increased diffusion limitation between the alveolus and pulmonary capillaries, mismatches between alveolar ventilation and perfusion, or possibly increased pulmonary arteriovenous shunting could raise the alveolar-arterial oxygen difference and lower arterial P_{O_2} and oxygen content. Mixed venous oxygen content, on the other hand, would be raised (and A-VO_2 difference narrowed) by distributing a smaller-than-normal percentage of cardiac output to active muscle at $\dot{V}O_2$max. Normally, about 85% of maximal cardiac output is distributed to working muscle. This high percentage is made possible by augmented sympathetic vasoconstrictor outflow that reduces blood flow to the major nonexercising regions in proportion to the fraction of $\dot{V}O_2$max required. For example, splanchnic and renal blood flows are reduced by 70% to 80%.[5] The high total systemic extraction of oxygen also requires highly efficient oxygen extraction by active muscle. For maximal extraction efficiency, the conditions for diffusion of oxygen from the muscle capillaries to the mitochondria must be optimal.

In summary, it is generally agreed that the decline in $\dot{V}O_2$max with age is mainly attributable to gradual declines in maximal heart rate and cardiac output and to some decline in stroke volume as well. A progressive reduction in β-adrenergic function may cause a slow deterioration of left ventricular function. There is no general agreement on whether the maximal A-VO_2 difference narrows with age in individuals without pulmonary disease or peripheral vascular disease. In theory, a proportionately greater reduction in muscle mass than in maximal cardiac output could cause a smaller maximal A-VO_2 difference (ie, larger fraction of cardiac output perfusing inactive regions).

Range of Adjustment in $\dot{V}O_2$max In young, midlife, and old individuals, physical conditioning increases $\dot{V}O_2$max. The large range of $\dot{V}O_2$max in normal young people as shown in Figure 2 includes values from the most sedentary individuals, as well as some of the world's elite endurance athletes. In five different longitudinal studies on 35 normally active individuals (ie, neither sedentary nor actively conditioning themselves; $\dot{V}O_2$max approximately 45 ml kg^{-1} min^{-1}), the rise in $\dot{V}O_2$max averaged approximately 15% in response to 2 to 3 months of physical conditioning.[5,13] Figure 3 suggests that aging has little effect on the magnitude of the adjustment in $\dot{V}O_2$max. For example, when 15 men aged 38 to 52 years were conditioned for 8 weeks, $\dot{V}O_2$max rose from 36 to 42 ml kg^{-1} min^{-1}; the average increase was 14%. The range of adjustment, which depended on the initial value, was 5% to 31%.

Among the most important factors for determining the size of increase in $\dot{V}O_2$max is its initial value before conditioning. Figure 3 shows results summarized from three studies on healthy young men and compares their responses with those of subjects aged 34 to 40 years and 41 to 50 years.[14] In all age groups, the percentage improvement was greatest when the initial values for $\dot{V}O_2$max were low, and improvement was least when initial $\dot{V}O_2$max was high. An exception may be in old subjects (60 to 71 years). Their average increase of 24%

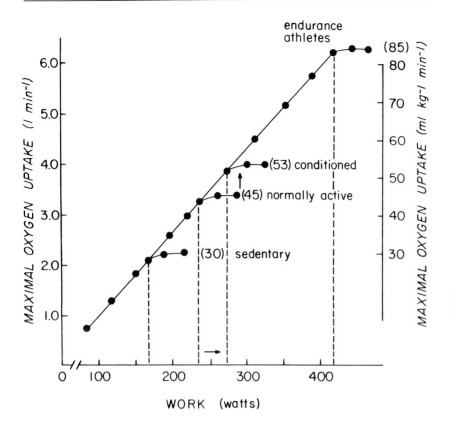

Fig. 2 *Range of values for $\dot{V}O_2$max in normal young people having different levels of regular physical activity from sedentary to elite endurance athletes. The range over which $\dot{V}O_2$max increases in normal individuals with months of physical conditioning is small in comparison. The plateau of $\dot{V}O_2$ with increasing work rate is the basis for an objective determination of $\dot{V}O_2$max. (Reproduced with permission from Rowell LB:* Human Circulation: Regulation During Physical Stress. *New York, NY, Oxford University Press, 1986.)*

in $\dot{V}O_2$max over a 12-month period was not closely related to the low and narrowly distributed initial values.[15]

Extension of the conditioning period for longer periods increases $\dot{V}O_2$max further.[16] For example, when a 6-month period of low-intensity conditioning was extended for an additional 6 months in subjects approximately 63 years old, $\dot{V}O_2$max, which had increased by 12% in the first six months, rose an additional 18% for a total of 30% at the end of one year.[10]

Another way of viewing the effect of physical conditioning on $\dot{V}O_2$max as individuals age is to examine the extent to which the rate of decline in $\dot{V}O_2$max might be attenuated by conditioning. From his own studies and a review of the literature, Hagberg[4] concluded that

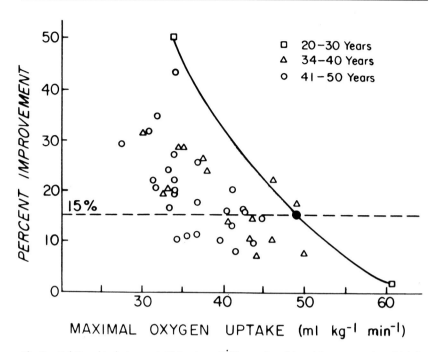

Fig. 3 *Relationship between initial value of $\dot{V}O_2$max (x-axis) and the percent by which it increases during physical conditioning in three age groups depicted by symbols. The curve shows average improvement relative to initial value in young men (20 to 30 years) in several studies.[5,13,19] (Adapted with permission from Saltin B: Physiological effects of physical conditioning. Med Sci Sports 1969;1:50-56.) (Reproduced with permission from Rowell LB: Human Circulation: Regulation During Physical Stress. New York, NY, Oxford University Press, 1986.)*

conditioning could reduce the decline in $\dot{V}O_2$max from 10% per decade in sedentary men and women to 5% per decade.

How Physical Conditioning Increases $\dot{V}O_2$max

Equation 1 indicates that $\dot{V}O_2$max can be increased by raising the maximal values of heart rate and stroke volume, and therefore, cardiac output, and also by raising arterial oxygen content and by reducing mixed venous oxygen content—ie, expanding the systemic A-VO_2 difference.

Factors That Normally Limit $\dot{V}O_2$max

The factors that normally limit $\dot{V}O_2$max must be the ones that are altered so as to permit an increase with conditioning. It is unlikely that any single step could be the limiting factor simply because there are three determinants of $\dot{V}O_2$max in the Fick equation (Equation 1).

At $\dot{V}O_2max$, 90% of the oxygen that moves by forced convection and by diffusion through the pulmonary and cardiovascular systems is consumed by active skeletal, respiratory, and cardiac muscles. As oxygen is transferred from the atmosphere through the lung to skeletal muscle mitochondria, distinct anatomic barriers are encountered in the cardiovascular and respiratory systems. Four potentially important limiting steps proceeding from lungs to active muscles are as follows: (1) Oxygen is transferred by convection from the atmosphere to alveoli by pulmonary ventilation. Normally, pulmonary ventilation does not limit $\dot{V}O_2$; however, when $\dot{V}O_2max$ increases to high values during physical conditioning, the primary changes are in the cardiovascular system, with little adaptation in the pulmonary system.[1] (2) Diffusive transfer of oxygen across the alveolus into the red blood cells can limit $\dot{V}O_2max$ when pulmonary ventilation does not increase enough to reduce alveolar PCO_2 and raise alveolar PO_2.[1] This reduces systemic A-VO_2 difference by decreasing arterial oxygen content. These limitations sometimes appear in normal young individuals after physical conditioning; they have not been reported in midlife or older subjects. (3) Convective transfer of oxygen by blood pumped by the left ventricle to the active muscles is commonly the most important factor limiting $\dot{V}O_2max$ in all age groups. (4) Diffusive transfer of oxygen across the capillary, cellular, and mitochondrial membranes is another important factor that limits $\dot{V}O_2max$ by affecting the systemic A-VO_2 difference. Because most of the cardiac output is directed to active muscle, its oxygen extraction will have the greatest impact on systemic A-VO_2 difference. Active diversion of blood flow away from nonexercising regions by sympathetic vasoconstriction is quantitatively less important because their fraction of cardiac output is so small.[3,5] These two factors together control the maximal systemic A-VO_2 difference, which is, along with maximal cardiac output, a primary determinant of $\dot{V}O_2max$.

The most important determinants of oxygen extraction by the muscles are as follows: (1) capillary density and numbers of capillaries per muscle fiber; (2) the number of capillaries per area of tissue; and (3) the area of tissue perfused by each capillary. Each of these factors is increased by physical conditioning,[17] and is essential in the adaptation to exercise and the rise in $\dot{V}O_2max$. Grimby and associates[18] found muscle capillary density in 78- to 81-year-old men and women to be 347 per mm^2 and 358 per mm^2, respectively. The number of capillaries per muscle fiber was 1.61 and 1.40, respectively. Kayser and associates[17] observed similar values in normal sedentary young subjects. These findings indicate that there is little change in muscle capillary density or diffusion distances with aging. Also, the activity of important mitochondrial enzymes appeared to be unaffected by age, giving credence to the suggestion that a coupling between capillary density and oxidative potential of the muscle may persist throughout our lifetimes.[18]

An additional point that bears importantly on the question of why $\dot{V}O_2max$ declines with aging concerns the relationship between $\dot{V}O_2max$ and total active muscle mass. $\dot{V}O_2max$ is thought to be reached in humans when only about 50% of the total muscle mass is active; the ability of humans to raise cardiac output is not sufficient to supply oxygen to a greater mass of active muscles during maximal exercise. If this concept is true, then a gradual decline in muscle mass with aging would appear not to explain the fall in $\dot{V}O_2max$ unless the muscles themselves become abnormal due, for example, to metabolic disease or very low oxidative enzyme activity.

Limiting Factors That Adjust to Physical Conditioning

Physical conditioning of healthy young sedentary individuals for 2 to 3 months raised $\dot{V}O_2max$ by 16% to 33% as a consequence of equal increases in maximal cardiac output and in maximal A-VO$_2$ difference.[5,13,19] The increase in maximal cardiac output was due entirely to increments in stroke volume; maximal heart rate was unaffected.

Any generalization stating that increases in maximal cardiac output and A-VO$_2$ difference contribute equally to increments in $\dot{V}O_2max$ during conditioning is not uniformly applicable. For example, in midlife men[20,21] and women,[22] the rise in $\dot{V}O_2max$ with conditioning was due almost entirely to increases in maximal stroke volume and cardiac output, whereas A-VO$_2$ difference was unaltered.

Seals and associates[10] came to another conclusion concerning the mechanism of increased $\dot{V}O_2max$ when they conditioned 11 men and women who were 63 years old. The 30% increase in $\dot{V}O_2max$ over one year could be explained from the calculated increase in A-VO$_2$ (maximal cardiac output, which is extremely difficult to measure, was estimated from maximal heart rate and stroke volume measured at submaximal $\dot{V}O_2$). Inasmuch as the increase in cardiac output with conditioning is directed to active muscle, in which oxygen extraction is highest, the failure of Hartley and associates[20] to see a rise in oxygen extraction at $\dot{V}O_2max$ is puzzling. The problem here is that methodological variability becomes magnified at $\dot{V}O_2max$ irrespective of the method for measuring cardiac output (again, direct measurements of arterial and pulmonary arterial oxygen content in unconditioned older subjects revealed normal maximal A-VO$_2$ differences).[8] If precision of measurement were greater, it is expected that contributions from increases in stroke volume and extraction of oxygen would be observed because of the changes in the heart and skeletal muscle evoked by the adaptation.[3,5,23]

How Stroke Volume and A-VO$_2$ Increase

Stroke Volume   Gerstenblith and associates[11] have proposed that a down-regulation of β_1-adrenoreceptors in the heart could reduce cardiac performance with aging. They forecast an increase in stroke vol-

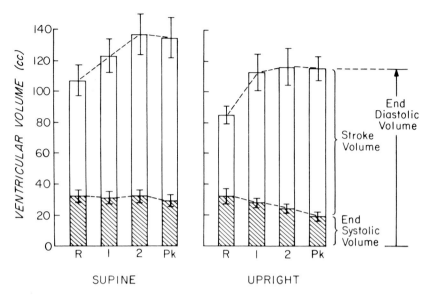

Fig. 4 *Left ventricular volumes (by radionuclide scintigraphy) at rest and at three levels of supine and upright exercise in normal young subjects. Exercise was mild (1), moderate (2), and at "peak" levels (Pk). Attention is directed to the fall in end-systolic volume, the rise in end-diastolic volume, and the increase in ejection fraction from 65% (rest) to 85% (Pk exercise). Higginbotham and associates[12] observed similar responses in middle-aged men. (Adapted with permission from Poliner LR, Dehmer GJ, Lewis SE, et al: Left ventricular performance in normal subjects: A comparison of the responses to exercise in the upright and supine positions. Circulation 1980;62:528-534.) (Reproduced with permission from Rowell LB: Human Circulation: Regulation During Physical Stress. New York, NY, Oxford University Press, 1986.)*

ume with age and duration of exercise not seen by others who used different methods for measuring cardiac output. If up-regulation of β_1-adrenoreceptors attended conditioning in midlife subjects, would it improve ventricular performance and increase cardiac output?

Cardiac contractility   In healthy and normally active young people, changes in myocardial contractile force seemed not to be a primary mechanism for increasing stroke volume. The findings of Poliner and associates[24] (Fig. 4) in young men (mean age, 26 years), and Higginbotham and associates[12] in 20- to 50-year-old men, showed that ventricular contraction force increases with exercise intensity. However, the ejection fraction is so high at $\dot{V}O_2$max (85% or more), and left ventricular end-diastolic volume is so low that it would be difficult to visualize (and also difficult to measure) further significant improvement.[25]

Ventricular afterload   Physical conditioning is usually unaccompanied by significant changes in arterial pressure (which may decrease slightly) or ventricular afterload.[3,5,10,13] When maximal cardiac output is increased, this means that conditioning is accompanied by an adjustment that matches total vascular conductance to maximal cardiac output. It also means that conditioning is accompanied by an increase in muscle vascular conductance.

Ventricular preload   Physical conditioning may or may not increase total blood volume. The question is whether such an adjustment in volume is necessary to raise stroke volume by the Frank-Starling or length-tension mechanism. Ventricular filling pressure increases with vigorous exercise, but it is not known if conditioning further augments the rise in filling pressure.[3] Whatever is finally concluded about the effects of conditioning on blood volume, one crucial observation stands out: simply cutting the pericardium affords improvements in stroke volume and cardiac output similar to those acquired after months of physical conditioning. For example, in a healthy midlife man in whom the pericardium was excised during surgery to abolish a chronic tachycardia and to implant a pacemaker, stroke volume could rise dramatically during exercise. For example, when heart rate was held constant by controlling his pacemaker, cardiac output still rose normally when $\dot{V}O_2$ increased. The rise in cardiac output from 6 to 16 l/min ($\dot{V}O_2$ = 2 l/min) was achieved by an abnormally large rise in stroke volume from 70 to nearly 170 ml.[23]

The above finding appears to signify that before conditioning, filling pressure was already higher than needed to improve stroke volume, and therefore, further increases in stroke volume must be limited mechanically by the pericardium. This would explain, for example, why acute volume expansion by autotransfusion of whole blood did not increase stroke volume during maximal exercise despite a 7-mm Hg increase in central venous pressure.[26]

Could the frequent increases in ventricular filling pressure during physical conditioning have gradually stretched the pericardium so that the heart slowly responds to a filling pressure that has been adequate to increase stroke volume all along? Studies of the mechanical properties of the pericardium in dogs reveal that this tissue grows (ie, pericardial mass increases, the tissue does not simply stretch) when filling pressure is increased in dogs over 3 weeks or longer by arterial venous fistulae.[27]

Arteriovenous Oxygen Difference   There are three possible explanations for the increase in total oxygen extraction that accompanies physical conditioning. First, the arterial oxygen content may increase. Actually, the tendency is for it to decrease slightly.[5,16] Second, greater vasoconstriction in nonexercising organs (eg, kidneys) could further reduce mixed venous oxygen content. However, vasoconstriction of these organs is essentially maximal at $\dot{V}O_2$max both before and after physical conditioning.[3,5] Third, there is increased extraction of oxygen by active muscle, which may be achieved in two ways. The fraction of cardiac output distributed to active muscle may be increased, so that the percentage of oxygen extracted from blood will also increase. This possibility is supported by longitudinal studies, which show that during maximal exercise, total leg blood flow increases in parallel with the rise in $\dot{V}O_2$max and that femoral A-VO$_2$ difference widens as well.[2] Another way to increase oxygen extraction by the muscle, and a critical adaptation to conditioning, is to increase muscle capillary density. Capillary density, leg blood flow, and $\dot{V}O_2$max all increase in approximate proportion after several months of conditioning.[28] One important aspect of the capillary proliferation is that the increase in total capillary blood volume minimizes the fall in capillary mean transit time caused by the increase in muscle blood flow. When mean transit time for red blood cells through the capillaries becomes too short, oxygen extraction is reduced because the time for unloading and diffusion of oxygen is too brief. In addition to a fine balance among muscle blood flow velocity, capillary blood volume, and mean transit time; the aforementioned shrinkage in diffusion distances along with the greater number of capillaries per muscle fiber are also essential to augment oxygen extraction.

We lack direct measurements of microcirculatory adjustments in skeletal muscle of midlife individuals before and after conditioning. Inasmuch as midlife individuals show the same magnitudes of increase in $\dot{V}O_2$max as younger people, and they achieve these increases by similar expansions of A-VO$_2$ difference (as well as by increased cardiac output), these microcirculatory adjustments in muscle must occur in the older individuals also. Their muscles clearly extract more oxygen from each liter of blood they receive after they are physically conditioned. Hagberg and associates[29] reported that maximal A-VO$_2$ differences in young (26 years old) and midlife (56 years old) master athletes were the same, and that their values were higher than those of a sedentary control group of individuals, also 56 years old.

Metabolic Adaptations in Skeletal Muscle

Metabolic Adaptations and $\dot{V}O_2$max

It was pointed out earlier that the metabolic capacity of skeletal muscle is not a factor limiting $\dot{V}O_2$max in healthy, normally active individuals. It is necessary to activate only approximately 50% of human muscle mass to reach maximal cardiac output and $\dot{V}O_2$max. In humans (but possibly not in some other species) the capacity of skeletal muscle to vasodilate and consume oxygen exceeds the pumping capacity of the heart and its ability to transport oxygen to the muscles.[3,5,28]

Biochemical studies of human muscle biopsy samples also indicate that the oxidative capacity of muscle far exceeds the rate at which oxygen could be supplied by the heart.[28] Nevertheless, physical conditioning increases the quantity of mitochondrial enzymes within the muscle and the muscle's oxidative capacity.[28,30] Others have made similar observations in nonhuman species and have concluded that these metabolic adjustments within the muscle contribute to the increase in $\dot{V}O_2$max.[23] Although this could be true in some species, it is clearly not the case in humans.

Metabolic Adaptations and Work Capacity

At the beginning of this paper, a brief differentiation was made between functional criteria for adaptation and performance criteria. The functional criteria have been spelled out. $\dot{V}O_2$max is such a criterion and is not a criterion of performance. Clear distinctions between functional and performance criteria are frequently not made, so there may be confusion. The crucial discrimination is that the metabolic adjustments in skeletal muscle determine the great changes in work capacity (eg, 300%), whereas the cardiovascular adjustments determine the small (eg, 15% to 30%) increases in $\dot{V}O_2$max. These distinctions can be made by looking at the way automobiles are tested. Performance criteria establish how far the vehicle can travel on 40 liters of fuel; the industry may call these economy races or tests. Functional criteria establish the maximal power that the vehicle's engine can develop, but they say nothing about how far it can go or how efficiently it will perform.

The increased content of oxidative enzymes and the enhanced metabolic potential of the conditioned muscles are essential to the dramatic increases in work capacity.[30,31] The enzyme changes ensure that a greater fraction of the pyruvate formed during glucose metabolism can be oxidized in the mitochondria. This explains the marked reduction in lactate release seen in both the young and old[32] after physical conditioning. Also, a greater fraction of the active acetate needed for the oxidative reactions of the tricarboxylic acid cycle can be provided by β-oxidation of free-fatty acids. These adaptations spare muscle glycogen during prolonged exercise and enhance the ability of the conditioned muscles to oxidize greater amounts of free-fatty acids. The data of Essen-Gustavsson and Borges[33] and Grimby and associates[18] suggest that these adaptations persist through midlife to old age.

Acknowledgments

I am grateful for the assistance of Pam Stevens for manuscript and illustration preparation, and Carol Taylor for photographing the illustrations. Two major reviews covering changes in cardiovascular function with aging were published recently.[34,35]

Work from this laboratory was supported by National Heart, Lung, and Blood Institute Grant HL-16910.

References

1. Dempsey JA: J.B. Wolffe memorial lecture: Is the lung built for exercise? *Med Sci Sports Exerc* 1986;18:143-155.
2. Saltin B, Rowell LB: Functional adaptations to physical activity and inactivity. *Fed Proc* 1980;39:1506-1513.
3. Rowell LB: *Human Circulation: Regulation During Physical Stress.* New York, NY, Oxford University Press, 1986.
4. Hagberg JM: Effect of training on the decline of V02 max with aging. *Fed Proc* 1987;46:1830-1833.
5. Rowell LB: Human cardiovascular adjustments to exercise and thermal stress. *Physiol Rev* 1974;54:75-159.
6. Andersen P, Saltin B: Maximal perfusion of skeletal muscle in man. *J Physiol (Lond)* 1985;366:233-249.
7. Buskirk ER, Hodgson JL: Age and aerobic power: The rate of change in men and women. *Fed Proc* 1987;46:1824-1829.
8. Hossack KF, Bruce RA: Maximal cardiac function in sedentary normal men and women: Comparison of age-related changes. *J Appl Physiol* 1982;53:799-804.
9. Julius S, Amery A, Whitlock LS, et al: Influence of age on the hemodynamic response to exercise. *Circulation* 1967;36:222-230.
10. Seals DR, Hagberg JM, Hurley BF, et al: Endurance training in older men and women: I. Cardiovascular responses to exercise. *J Appl Physiol* 1984;57:1024-1029.
11. Gerstenblith G, Renlund DG, Lakatta EG: Cardiovascular response to exercise in younger and older men. *Fed Proc* 1987;46:1834-1839.
12. Higginbotham MB, Morris KG, Williams RS, et al: Regulation of stroke volume during submaximal and maximal upright exercise in normal man. *Circ Res* 1986;58:281-291.
13. Clausen JP: Effect of physical training on cardiovascular adjustments to exercise in man. *Physiol Rev* 1977;57:779-815.
14. Saltin B: Physiological effects of physical conditioning. *Med Sci Sports* 1969;1:50-56.
15. Kohrt WM, Malley MT, Coggan AR, et al: Effects of gender, age, and fitness level on response of V02 max to training in 60-71 yr olds. *J Appl Physiol* 1991;71:2004-2011.
16. Ekblom B: Effect of physical training on oxygen transport system in man. *Acta Physiol Scand (Suppl)* 1968;328:1-45.
17. Kayser B, Hoppeler H, Claassen H, et al: Muscle structure and performance capacity of Himalayan Sherpas. *J Appl Physiol* 1991;70:1938-1942.
18. Grimby G, Danneskiold-Samsoe B, Hvid K, et al: Morphology and enzymatic capacity in arm and leg muscles in 78-81 year old men and women. *Acta Physiol Scand* 1982;115:125-134.
19. Saltin B, Blomqvist G, Mitchell JH, et al: Response to exercise after bed rest and after training. *Circulation* 1968;38(suppl 5):1-78.
20. Hartley LH, Grimby G, Kilbom A, et al: Physical training in sedentary middle-aged and older men: 3. Cardiac output and gas exchange at submaximal and maximal exercise. *Scand J Clin Lab Invest* 1969;24:335-344.
21. Saltin B, Hartley LH, Kilbom A, et al: Physical training in sedentary middle-aged and older men: II. Oxygen uptake, heart rate, and blood lactate concentration at submaximal and maximal exercise. *Scand J Clin Lab Invest* 1969;24:323-334.
22. Kilbom A: Physical training in women. *Scand J Clin Lab Invest* 1971;119:1-34.

23. Rowell LB: *Human Cardiovascular Control*. New York, NY, Oxford University Press, 1993.

24. Poliner LR, Dehmer GJ, Lewis SE, et al: Left ventricular performance in normal subjects: A comparison of the responses to exercise in the upright and supine positions. *Circulation* 1980;62:528-534.

25. Blomqvist CG, Saltin B: Cardiovascular adaptations to physical training. *Annu Rev Physiol* 1983;45:169-189.

26. Robinson BF, Epstein SE, Kahler RL, et al: Circulatory effects of acute expansion of blood volume: Studies during maximal exercise and at rest. *Circ Res* 1966;19:26-32.

27. Freeman GL, LeWinter MM: Pericardial adaptations during chronic cardiac dilation in dogs. *Circ Res* 1984;54:294-300.

28. Saltin B, Gollnick PD: Skeletal muscle adaptability: Significance for metabolism and performance, in Peachey LD, Adrian RH, Geiger SR (eds): *Handbook of Physiology: Skeletal Muscle*. Baltimore, MD, Williams & Wilkins, 1983, sect 10, pp 555-631.

29. Hagberg JM, Allen WK, Seals DR, et al: A hemodynamic comparison of young and older endurance athletes during exercise. *J Appl Physiol* 1985;58:2041-2046.

30. Gollnick PD, Saltin B: Significance of skeletal muscle oxidative enzyme enhancement with endurance training. *Clin Physiol* 1982;2:1-12.

31. Gollnick PD, Riedy M, Quintinskie JJ, et al: Differences in metabolic potential of skeletal muscle fibres and their significance for metabolic control. *J Exp Biol* 1985;115:191-199.

32. Seals DR, Hurley BF, Schultz J, et al: Endurance training in older men and women: II. Blood lactate response to submaximal exercise. *J Appl Physiol* 1984;57:1030-1033.

33. Essen-Gustavsson B, Borges O: Histochemical and metabolic characteristics of human skeletal muscle in relation to age. *Acta Physiol Scand* 1986;126:107-114.

34. Lakatta EG: Cardiovascular regulatory mechanisms in advanced age. *Physiol Rev* 1993;73:413-467.

35. Folkow B, Svanborg A: Physiology of cardiovascular aging. *Physiol Rev* 1993;73:725-764.

Chapter 6

Autonomic and Central Nervous System Effects of Physical Exercise

Nils-Holger Areskog, MD, PhD

Introduction

Physical training enables the body to adapt to the demands of increased physical activity. Characteristic of this adaptation is the training-induced bradycardia seen both at rest and during exercise at submaximal work loads. This lowered heart rate (HR) has traditionally been attributed to altered autonomic nervous activity.

By blocking both the sympathetic and vagal cardiac nerves, the intrinsic heart rate (IHR) can be measured. At the University of Linköping, IHR has been investigated experimentally in rats and in humans to measure the effects of and the mechanisms behind the change in IHR due to physical training.

It is well known that long-term adaptation to high altitude results in a lower maximal HR compared with the HR at sea level. However, this inhibition of maximal HR can be reset instantaneously by breathing air enriched with oxygen.

Increasing age reduces the maximal HR during exercise by about one beat per minute (bpm) for each year after the age of 25. It is not known whether there are any neural mechanisms or whether there is a change in the peripheral circulatory regulation with increasing age.

By stimulating muscle contraction or peripheral afferent nerves, it is possible to provoke long-lasting circulatory effects, such as blood pressure reduction in the post stimulatory phase. It is not known which mechanisms elicit these effects.

Physically well-trained people of all ages have been described as more mentally stable—possibly less depressed and less inclined to drug and alcohol abuse. Are there any physiologic mechanisms to explain these observations? One possibility is that the endogenous opioid systems in the central nervous system are modulating the autonomic nervous system.

In the following chapter, the circulatory changes induced by endurance exercise, high altitude, and age, and attributed to alterations in autonomic nervous regulation are reviewed along with some recent work on the activation of central endogenous opioid systems by exercise.

The Autonomic Nervous System and Training-Induced Bradycardia

Badeer[1] suggested that training caused a change of the autonomic balance in the regulation of HR, leading to bradycardia at rest that by itself caused further adaptation during exercise. However, Nylander[2] found that rats treated with the adrenergic beta-blocker metoprolol to produce a constant bradycardia at rest did not develop an exercise bradycardia or a lowered IHR (lowered HR after vagal and sympathetic blockade). Furthermore, training after sympathectomy did not result in any reduction in IHR, implying that intact adrenergic nerves seem to be essential for the development of a decreased IHR. Training in combination with atropine treatment[3] in rats resulted in a resting bradycardia and a lower IHR. From these rat studies, it appears that the development of training bradycardia depends partly, but not exclusively, on autonomic nervous effects. It is possible that increased venous return and higher levels of metabolites from working muscles during a longer period of endurance training might elicit structural myocardial changes (eg, enlargement of the atria responsible for the decrease in IHR).

In man, there is a dominating vagal influence on resting HR. During work, the sympathetic influence dominates, resulting in a higher HR. At submaximal work loads (HR ≥ 120 bpm at sea level), there is virtually no vagal influence on the HR. However, in a study at Mount Everest, Bengt Saltin, Gabrielle Savard, and I[4] found that after long-term adaptation to an altitude of at least 5,200 m a s l (meters above sea level) there is still vagal activity up to the maximal work load.

After a short period of endurance training, there is increased vagal and decreased sympathetic tone, contributing to the relative bradycardia during training. In order to further investigate the role of the altered autonomic cardiac balance after training, we studied[5] IHR in man after a short-term period of endurance training and found a decrease in IHR at submaximal work load, but not at rest or at maximal work load. In another study[6] comparing competitive elite male bicyclists who had performed intense endurance training for several years and untrained men, we found a clear difference between the trained and untrained men, in HR at rest and at all exercise levels. These findings suggest a nonautonomic component in the training-induced bradycardia, which results in an average HR that is 17 bpm lower at rest, 16 bpm lower at submaximal load, and 11 bpm

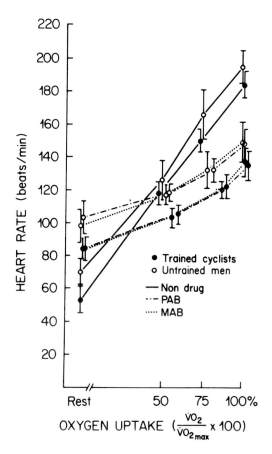

Fig. 1 *Heart rate in trained and untrained men at rest and during exercise requiring approximately 50%, 75%, and 100% of maximal oxygen uptake, without treatment and with autonomic blockade. Means + 1 SD PAB = Propranolol + atropine-blockade. MAB = Metoprolol + atropine-blockade. (Reproduced with permission from Lewis SF, Nylander E, Gad P, et al: Non-autonomic component in bradycardia of endurance trained men at rest and during exercise. Acta Physiol Scand 1980;109:297-305.)*

lower at maximal loads without autonomic-blocking drugs. After combined parasympathetic and beta-adrenergic blockade with atropine and propranolol, HR was lower in the trained group at rest and at all levels of exercise. In the trained group, HR was 19 bpm lower at rest, 10 bpm lower at submaximal load, and 13 bpm lower at maximal load than in the untrained group (Fig. 1). All differences between the trained and untrained groups were significant. After autonomic blockade maximal HR was 46 bpm lower in the trained group, and 49 bpm lower in the untrained group, a statistically insignificant difference.

Most investigators have attributed the bradycardia of endurance training to increased vagal tone and decreased beta-adrenergic influence.[7] However, our data indicate that in humans, there is also a lower IHR in trained than in untrained individuals, in spite of the fact that our elite cyclists were on an average five years younger than the sedentary men (21 and 26 years of age, respectively). This finding is surprising because it has been shown both in man and in rats[8,9] that IHR decreases with age. The time span from resting to maximal HR was not significantly different in the two groups (131 and 125 bpm, respectively). Thus, intense endurance training does not seem to increase the time span, but only causes a downward parallel shift in the curve for HR increase from rest to maximal work.

Hence, our studies revealed a nonautonomic component of the training bradycardia in well-trained men that might be related to cardiac enlargement, eg, atrial dilatation, possibly causing an inhibition of the firing rate of the sinoatrial pacemaker in response to stretch.

The Autonomic Nervous System and Cardiovascular Adaptation to High Altitude

With acute exposure to altitude, sympathetic activity is markedly enhanced both at rest and during work, as reflected by elevated plasma epinephrine and norepinephrine levels. This enhanced sympathetic activity may indicate the need to maintain blood pressure at a relatively normal level in spite of the very pronounced vasodilation in the muscle during exercise. Also, maximal oxygen uptake and peak blood lactate levels during exhaustive exercise are lowered.

During the Swedish Mount Everest expedition in 1987,[4] we studied the mechanisms responsible for lowering the maximal HR, especially the roles of the autonomic nervous system and the available oxygen supply. Maximal HR decreases in proportion to the increase in altitude. With increasing altitude, the effectiveness of the sympathetic nervous system is inhibited, and the plasma norepinephrine levels at maximal work load decrease. Figure 2 shows a comparison between plasma norepinephrine levels in "Operation Everest" (the American simulated Everest expedition in a low-pressure chamber) and our findings at Mount Everest with comparable results.[10-12] However, the mechanisms behind these changes are controversial and not well understood. Is the central activation of the sympathetic nervous system inhibited by hypoxia, is peripheral neurotransmission inhibited, or is feedback from the working muscles lacking? If norepinephrine levels are correlated with maximal HR, there is also close agreement between our findings and those of the simulated Everest operation.

At sea level, the exercise-induced rise in HR up to 110 to 120 bpm is due to withdrawal of parasympathetic influence on the sinus node. Thereafter, sympathetic nervous activity elevates the HR to the maximal levels. Adaptation to long-term stay at high altitude inhibits the effectiveness of the sympathetic nervous system, and plasma

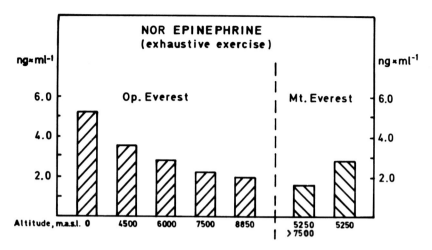

Fig. 2 *Plasma norepinephrine levels during exhaustive work at different altitudes.* **Left**, *"Operation Everest."* **Right**, *"Swedish Mount Everest expedition." (Reproduced with permission from Wahlund E, Weng P, Areskog N-H, et al: På världens tak: Rapport från den svenska Mount Everest-expeditionen. [At the top of the world: A report from the Swedish Mount Everest expedition.] Läkartidningen 1988;85:3161-3169.)*

norepinephrine levels at maximal work load are considerably reduced. On the other hand, the vagal activity after atropine blockade is relatively increased and vagal activity is not withdrawn during intense exercise at high altitude, in contrast to sea level (Fig. 3). The altered balance between the sympathetic and parasympathetic nervous systems may be a dominant cause of the lowered maximal HR at high altitude.

Atropine-induced parasympathetic blockade caused a HR increase of approximately 20 bpm at rest and with exhausting exercise, in contrast to sea level work. However, the maximal work performance did not increase after blockade in spite of the HR increase.

Within a few seconds, supplemental oxygen at maximal load resulted in a HR increase (Fig. 4). It was then possible to considerably increase the maximal work load. The maximal work performance and maximal HR then approached the values seen at sea level.

Adrenergic beta-blockade decreased maximal HR by approximately 20 bpm with a concomitant reduction in maximal work performance. Compared to adrenergic beta-blockade at sea level, the drop in HR was slightly less. After supplemental oxygen, there was an increase in HR and in maximal work performance, although the values were not significantly different from the controls. Tables 1 and 2 summarize our findings regarding HR and blood pressure at rest and at 100 W work level.

The physical work performance of our climbers at 5,200 m a s l was reduced by almost half when compared to work at sea level, and

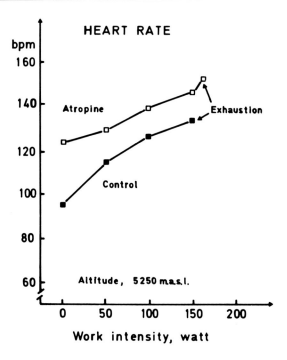

Fig. 3 *Heart rates at rest and during exercise after vagal blockade compared to controls at an altitude of 5,250 m above sea level (m a s l).*

Table 1 Heart rate (HR) and blood pressure (BP) at rest and at 100 W (watts) work level (n = 10)

Conditions	At Rest HR (bpm)	BP (mm Hg)	At 100 Watts HR (bpm)	BP (mm Hg)
Sea level (n=4)	63	135/80	104	148
Altitude (n=6)	88	121/92	129	156
Beta-blockade (n = 3?)	95→81	112/86	110	128
Atropine (n = 3?)	85→112	103/80	150	133

maximal HR was 30 to 60 bpm lower. Climbers who had been at 6,400 m a s l for a long time had a lower maximal HR than those who remained in base camp at 5,200 m a s l. In contrast to sea level, we did not find any significant differences between maximal oxygen uptake for one- and two-legged work, respectively. A surprising finding was a tendency to higher HR after one-legged work compared to two-legged work, which fits well with Bengt Saltin's hypothesis that the amount of working muscular mass influences the inhibition of HR during exercise in chronic hypoxia. In some two-legged tests in

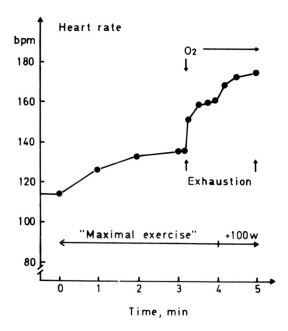

Fig. 4 *Effect on exercise heart rate of oxygen supply at exhaustion at 5,200 m a s l.*

Table 2 Heart rate (HR), systolic blood pressure (BP), work level (WL), blood lactate (HLa), and norepinephrine (NE) values at maximal work (n = 10)

Conditions	HR (bpm)	BP (mm Hg)	WL (watts)	HLa (mM)	NE (ng•ml^{-1})
Sea level (n = 4)	173	205	310	8.4	6.6
Altitude (n = 6)	141	175	183	5.3	2.9
+ O$_2$	163	—	324	6.8	5.6
Beta-blockade	123	144	175	6.1	3.4
+ O$_2$	137	—	324	6.9	4.8
Atropine	165	162	183	5.9	3.8
+ O$_2$	170	—	331	7.8	5.8

well-adapted individuals, a paradoxical HR reaction was seen: a sudden decrease in HR with increasing load and a considerable fall in blood pressure. This reaction might be due to insufficient sympathetic activity or dominant vagal activity.

To conclude, chronic exposure to altitude lowers maximal HR and maximal cardiac output, causing reduced maximal oxygen uptake and decreased aerobic work performance. Lung function is probably closely tied to the altered regulation of the cardiovascular system. There is no reason to increase pulmonary blood flow, because that would result in a further reduction in the arterial oxygen saturation. A decreased maximal HR seems, then, to be beneficial for oxygen transport and also to protect the heart from ischemia due to high HR.

Hyperventilation, which results in a lowered P_{CO_2} in combination with a low arterial P_{O_2}, may trigger the autonomic regulation of HR and stimulate increased parasympathetic and decreased sympathetic activity during exercise. However, signals from the working extremity muscles seem to influence maximal HR. A larger working muscle mass probably produces a lower maximal HR. Thus, the maximal pump capacity of the heart is reached with only a small fraction of the muscle mass exercising after long-term adaptation to chronic hypoxia at an altitude above 5,000 m. The influence of the sympathetic nervous system on the heart is reduced, as indicated by the low plasma catecholamine levels and the relatively smaller effect of adrenergic beta-blockade compared to sea level. The parasympathetic nervous system has a relatively more powerful effect on the heart during work when compared to sea level because atropine blockade increased the maximal HR.

Does the lowered maximal HR protect the heart itself, or is a pump with low cardiac output and high oxygen content the best strategy when the diffusion of oxygen is limiting the maximal oxygen consumption, or do the signals from the working muscles play an essential role in optimizing circulation during severe hypoxia? We cannot answer these questions today. Further studies of the mechanisms behind the regulation of maximal HR inhibition are warranted. The very fast increase of the maximal HR after supplemental oxygen speaks in favor of an autonomic nervous system adaptation. This adaptation may be related to low P_{O_2}, but it might also be related to low P_{CO_2} from chronic hyperventilation at high altitude.

Age-Induced Circulatory Changes

One of the well-known factors contributing to the reduction in physical work performance during early midlife is the decreasing maximal HR with age. From the age of 25, about one bpm per year is lost. As was mentioned earlier, this might be due in part to decreased IHR resulting from age. This decreased maximal HR is one of the main reasons for the lowered maximal oxygen uptake with increasing age, because it usually is not compensated for by increased stroke volume.

This decreased maximal HR occurs in spite of increased sympathetic activity in elderly individuals compared to young ones, at least at rest, reflected by both increased catecholamine levels in plasma and by direct recording of sympathetic nervous activity.[13] However, in the standing position, sympathetic nervous outflow to the leg muscles was increased less in the elderly than in young individuals. The net effect on the target organ decreases with age; this may be due to down-regulation of adrenergic receptors or fewer receptors.

However, apart from the decreased maximal cardiac output with age, there also seems to be a change in regulation of blood flow to the exercising muscles, which results in a relative hypoperfusion in the elderly (Bengt Saltin, MD, personal communication, 1992). This type of hypoperfusion of the legs, resulting in a rise in blood lactate levels during exercise, also is seen in patients with chronic heart failure.[14] It is possible that increased skeletal muscle vessel resistance during exercise serves to maintain both the arterial blood pressure and the perfusion of important nonexercising regions if the cardiac output response is limited in relation to the demands.

Evidence for a Central Neurotransmitter System in Endurance Training

Important circulatory effects result from regular endurance training, including a reduction in blood pressure at rest, especially in patients with hypertension. After endurance work, there is also a temporary reduction in blood pressure, lasting for several hours. This reduction in blood pressure is more marked and has a longer duration in hypertensive joggers.[15]

For a long time it has been known that many joggers of all ages experience positive effects of physical training, including a general sense of well-being. Many athletes experience a euphoric effect of training.[16] Some decades ago, several psychiatrists around the world started to use physical training as treatment for certain depressive and anxiety states.[17] It also is known that endurance work can increase the pain threshold in a manner resembling the effects of transcutaneous nervous stimulation. All these effects can be due to an activation of central opioid systems triggered by discharge from mechanoreceptor afferent nerve fibers originating in the exercising skeletal muscles.

Thoren and associates[18] in Gothenburg have considerably increased our knowledge about these effects, mainly through experiments on spontaneous hypertensive rats. Thoren and associates[18] recently reviewed this research; in the following paragraphs, their data are cited and compared with data on humans derived from other research groups.

Structurally, the opioids resemble the exogenous opiates used by man through millennia for their euphoric and analgesic effects. The opioids are divided into three groups: endorphins, enkephalins, and dynorphins. Among the endorphins, there are alpha, beta, and gamma forms. Beta-1 endorphin has been studied the most in exercise because it is involved in the autonomic nervous control of blood pressure, pain perception, and body temperature. Another independent beta-endorphin system originates from the anterior pituitary gland, which also produces ACTH. It is important that the hypothalamic beta-endorphin production occurs independently of the stress-related release of beta-endorphin and ACTH, which is reflected in the beta-endorphin levels found in peripheral blood. This discrepancy between brain endorphin concentrations and peripheral blood levels may be one reason for conflicting data in the literature regarding opioid effects and exercise.

There are specific opioid receptors both in the cardiovascular system and in the periphery of the sympathetic nervous system.[19] They inhibit peripheral sympathetic transmission, altering the balance between the sympathetic and parasympathetic systems, and resulting in bradycardia and hypotension. Naloxone has been used as an opioid antagonist, but in high doses it may lose its specificity for opioid receptors. In many studies, naloxone did not abolish circulatory and metabolic responses to exercise, but that may be due to the use of inadequate doses.

Hoffmann and associates[20] found that the concentration of beta-endorphins in cerebrospinal fluid of rats was significantly increased in trained animals compared to sedentary controls up to 48 hours after the end of exercise, supporting the concept of long-lasting opioid effects of exercise on the central nervous system. What are the mechanisms behind this response? Interesting experiments by the same group in Gothenburg,[21,22] using sciatic nerve stimulation in rats, have revealed that during stimulation, there was the expected increase in sympathetic outflow, blood pressure, and HR that is produced during exercise by activation of neural afferents from leg muscles. After stimulation there was a long-lasting increase in the pain threshold and reduced brain norepinephrine synthesis; both effects were blocked by naloxone, indicating involvement of the opioid system. There was also a behavioral depression without baroreflex tachycardia and decreased sympathetic neural outflow. Because both the circulatory and behavioral effects could be blocked by naloxone and by centrally acting serotonin antagonists, the studies support the important role of the central nervous system endorphins for the effects after nerve stimulation in contrast to the effects during nerve stimulation (Fig. 5). Similar effects are produced by direct gastrocnemius muscle stimulation (Fig. 6).[23] In man, Droste and associates[24] found a transient elevation in dental pulp pain threshold after short-term exhaustive physical exercise. The elevation in pain threshold was not directly related to plasma endorphin levels and it was not affected by naloxone, which may be the result of inadequate dosing.

Thoren and associates[18] hypothesize that ergoreceptors in the muscles activated during exercise have a paradoxical influence on the autonomic nervous system. Brief exhaustive exercise excites sympathetic neural outflow and causes withdrawal of cardiac vagal tone, leading to increases in HR, blood pressure, and cardiac output, and improved oxygen delivery to the exercising muscle without involvement of the opioid systems. However, after prolonged stimulation of ergoreceptors, the central opioid system is activated, leading to inhibition of the sympathetic nervous system, evident mainly during re-

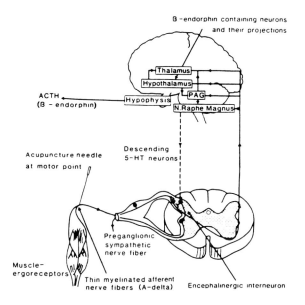

Fig. 5 *A hypothetical scheme of how muscle exercise might influence central and peripheral opioid concentrations, affecting pain threshold and blood pressure. (Reproduced with permission from Thoren P, Floras JS, Hoffmann P, et al: Endorphins and exercise: Physiological mechanisms and clinical implications.* Med Sci Sports Exerc *1990;22:417-428.)*

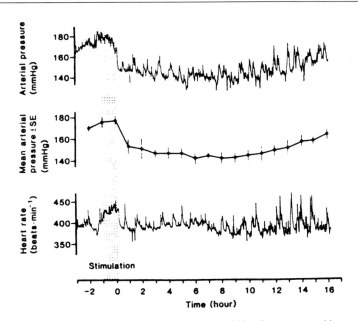

Fig. 6 *Changes in arterial blood pressure, mean arterial blood pressure, and heart rate induced by stimulation of the gastrocnemius muscle of a spontaneously hypertensive rat. (Reproduced with permission from Hoffmann P, Thoren P: Electric muscle stimulation in the hind leg of the spontaneously hypertensive rat induces a long-lasting fall in blood pressure.* Acta Physiol Scand *1988;133:211-219.)*

covery after cessation of work and favoring the restoration of energy stores. The increased pain threshold contributes to the sense of well-being in spite of fatiguing exercise.

Finally, a few words about the long-term effects of exercise on blood pressure. It is well-known that aerobic exercise programs reduce the cardiovascular effects of both physical and mental stress. Such programs have been used as treatment for hypertensive patients, especially those with labile hypertension. There is a decrease in the blood pressure of hypertensives in the immediate post-exercise period.[25] However, after months of endurance training, there is also a chronic lowering of blood pressure. According to Thoren and associates,[18] it is not unlikely that this response after physical exercise is due to activation of the central opioid systems. We can now recommend physical training as a therapeutic treatment for hypertension, based not only on long-held belief, but also on convincing empiric research.

References

1. Badeer HS: Cardiovascular adaptations in the trained athlete, in Lubich T, Venerando A (eds): *Sports Cardiology*. Bologna, Aulo Gaggi Publisher, 1980, pp 3-12.

2. Nylander E: Intrinsic heart rate: Investigations in training-induced bradycardia in rats and humans. *Linköping University Medical Dissertations*, 1981, p 114.

3. Hughson RL, Sutton JR, Fitzgerald JD, et al: Reduction of intrinsic sinoatrial frequency and norepinephrine response of the exercised rat. *Can J Physiol Pharmacol* 1977;55:813-820.

4. Areskog N-H, Saltin B, Savard G: The role of the autonomic nervous system for exercise limitation at high altitude. *Acta Physiol Scand* 1988;134(suppl 575):40.

5. Lewis S, Thompson P, Areskog N-H, et al: Endurance training and heart rate control studied by combined parasympathetic and beta-adrenergic blockade. *Int J Sports Med* 1980;1:42-49.

6. Lewis SF, Nylander E, Gad P, et al: Non-autonomic component in bradycardia of endurance trained men at rest and during exercise. *Acta Physiol Scand* 1980;109:297-305.

7. Scheuer J, Tipton CM: Cardiovascular adaptations to physical training. *Annu Rev Physiol* 1977;39:221-251.

8. Jose AD, Collison D: The normal range and determinants of the intrinsic heart rate in man. *Cardiovasc Res* 1970;4:160-167.

9. Corre KA, Cho H, Barnard RJ: Maximum exercise heart rate reduction with maturation in the rat. *J Appl Physiol* 1976;40:741-744.

10. Reeves JT, Groves BM, Sutton JR, et al: Operation Everest II: Preservation of cardiac function at extreme altitude. *J Appl Physiol* 1987;63:531-539.

11. Houston CS, Sutton JR, Cymerman A, et al: Operation Everest II: Man at extreme altitude. *J Appl Physiol* 1987;63:877-882.

12. Wahlund E, Weng P, Areskog N-H, et al: På världens tak: Rapport från den svenska Mount Everest-expeditionen. [At the top of the world: A report from the Swedish Mount Everest expedition.] *Läkartidningen* 1988;85:3161-3169.

13. Iwase S, Mano T, Watanabe T, et al: Age-related changes of sympathetic outflow to muscles in humans. *J Gerontol* 1991;46:M1-5.

14. Sullivan MJ, Knight JD, Higginbotham MB, et al: Relation between central and peripheral hemodynamics during exercise in patients with chronic heart failure: Muscle blood flow is reduced with maintenance of arterial perfusion pressure. *Circulation* 1989;80:769-781.

15. Wilcox RG, Bennett T, Brown AM, et al: Is exercise good for high blood pressure? *Br Med J* 1982;285:767-769.

16. Appenzeller O: Editorial: What makes us run? *N Engl J Med* 1981;305:578-580.

17. Morgan WP: Affective beneficence of vigorous physical activity. *Med Sci Sports Exerc* 1985;17:94-100.

18. Thoren P, Floras JS, Hoffmann P, et al: Endorphins and exercise: Physiological mechanisms and clinical implications. *Med Sci Sports Exerc* 1990;22:417-428.

19. Illes P, Bettermann R, Ramme D: Sympathoinhibitory opioid receptors in the cardiovascular system, in Buckley JP, Ferrario CM, Lokhandwala MF (eds): *Brain Peptides and Catecholamines in Cardiovascular Regulation*. New York, NY, Raven Press, 1987, pp 169-184.

20. Hoffmann P, Terenius L, Thoren P: Cerebrospinal fluid immunoreactive beta-endorphin concentration is increased by voluntary exercise in the spontaneously hypertensive rat. *Regul Pept* 1990;28:233-239.

21. Yao T, Andersson S, Thoren P: Long-lasting cardiovascular depression induced by acupuncture-like stimulation of the sciatic nerve in unanaesthetized spontaneously hypertensive rats. *Brain Res* 1982;240:77-85.

22. Yao T, Andersson S, Thoren P: Long-lasting cardiovascular depressor response following sciatic stimulation in spontaneously hypertensive rats: Evidence for the involvement of central endorphin and seretonin systems. *Brain Res* 1982;244:295-303.

23. Hoffmann P, Thoren P: Electric muscle stimulation in the hind leg of the spontaneously hypertensive rat induces a long-lasting fall in blood pressure. *Acta Physiol Scand* 1988;133:211-219.

24. Droste C, Greenlee MW, Schreck M, et al: Experimental pain thresholds and plasma beta-endorphin levels during exercise. *Med Sci Sports Exerc* 1991;23:334-342.

25. Bennett T, Wilcox RG, Macdonald IA: Post-exercise reduction of blood pressure in hypertensive men is not due to acute impairment of baroreflex function. *Clin Sci* 1984;67:97-103.

Chapter 7

Fluid Balance Before and During Exercise

Timothy David Noakes, MB ChB, MD

Introduction

The idea that one should drink during exercise, especially long distance running, is of recent origin. This is surprising, given that it had already been established by the early military studies[1] that fluid ingestion aided performance and prolonged survival during exercise in the desert heat.

Thus the advice given to marathon runners of the early 1900s included the following caveats: "Don't take any nourishment before going seventeen or eighteen miles. If you do you will never go the distance. Don't get in the habit of drinking and eating in a Marathon race; some prominent runners do, but it is not beneficial."[2] Famous runners of this era echoed these sentiments. American Joseph Forshaw, who finished fourth in the 1908 and tenth in the 1912 Olympic marathon with a time of 2:49:49, had written: "I know from actual experience that the full (marathon) race can be covered in creditable time without so much as a single drop of water being taken or even sponging of the head."[2]

Fifty years later, some individuals had not changed their advice. Jim Peters, who may have been the greatest marathoner of all time,[3] enunciated the conventional wisdom of his day in the following statement:[4] ". . .(in the marathon race) there is no need to take any solid food at all and every effort should also be made to do without liquid, as the moment food or drink is taken, the body has to start dealing with its digestion, and in so doing some discomfort will almost invariably be felt." Another famous ultra-distance runner who set world records at 30, 40, and 50 miles in 1954 confirmed that this advice was widely accepted: "In those days it was quite fashionable not to drink, until one absolutely had to. After a race runners would recount with pride "I only had a drink after 30 or 40 kilometres." To run a complete marathon without any fluid replacement was regarded as the ultimate aim of most runners, and a test of their fitness" (J Mekler, 1991, personal communication). This athlete who

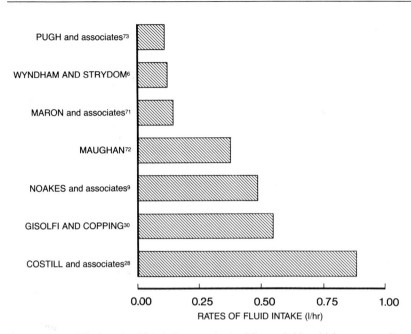

Fig. 1 *Rates of fluid intake (l/hr) during exercise in different field and laboratory studies in competitive athletes. Note that prior to 1985, competitive marathoners seldom drank more than 100 ml/hr during competition. In contrast to the other studies, those of Gisolfi and Copping[30] and Costill and associates[28] were performed in the laboratory. This would explain the higher rates of fluid intake.*

once competed in a 100-mile race in which he first drank only after 75 miles, confirmed that this approach was still popular when he had run his last competitive ultramarathon race in 1969.

That these ideas could ever have held credence, let alone so recently, may seem absurd to the modern exercise physiologist. But the fluid requirements of athletes has attracted scientific interest only since the early 1970s (Fig. 1). Virtually all the textbooks of exercise physiology and sports medicine published before 1970 contain little or no reference to this topic; one of the first to include a section on fluid replacement during exercise was the monograph of Costill.[5] Yet many studies showing the importance of adequate fluid replacement, especially during industrial and military activities in the heat, had already been published. Possibly a landmark scientific study that extended these beliefs to sports was that of the South African physiologists, Cyril Wyndham and Nick Strydom.[6]

In their study, Wyndham and Strydom[6] found that athletes who became dehydrated by more than 3% during a series of 32-km foot races had elevated post-race rectal temperatures. As also found by Adolph,[1] there was a linear relationship between the athletes' levels of dehydration and their post-race rectal temperatures, at least for

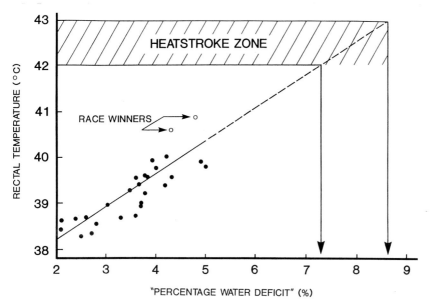

Fig. 2 *A linear relationship between rectal temperature after two 32-km foot races and percentage water deficit was reported by Wyndham and Strydom.[6] Note (1) that the highest rectal temperatures were found in the race winners; (2) that heatstroke could only be expected in runners who were dehydrated by between 7% and 8.5%; (3) that the highest levels of dehydration in these runners were 5%; and (4) that their rectal temperatures ranged between 38.3 and 41.0 C.*

levels of dehydration greater than 3% (Fig. 2). The authors concluded (1) that the level of dehydration was the most important factor determining the rectal temperature during prolonged exercise so that (2) the avoidance of dehydration would be the critical factor in preventing heat injury during prolonged exercise.[6,7] Interestingly, the title of their article, "The danger of an inadequate water intake during marathon running," was misleading because the study identified no such danger. Figure 1 shows that despite significant levels of dehydration, rectal temperatures were well below those measured in persons with heatstroke. Furthermore, of all the athletes, the race winners were the most dehydrated and had the highest rectal temperatures (Fig. 1). Thus, a more appropriate title for their article might have been: "Remarkable resistance to detrimental effects of dehydration in competitive marathon runners."

Although the basis for some of their conclusions has been challenged,[8-10] there is no doubt that it was especially this study[6] that stimulated the modern interest in the role of fluid replacement during exercise. The detrimental effects of dehydration are now well established (Table 1). Less well established are the real medical risks imposed by dehydration developing during exercise[11] and the influence of the aging process on fluid balance during and after exercise.

Table 1 Physiological changes attenuated by fluid ingestion during prolonged exercise

Impaired physical performance
Increased serum Na^+ concentration
Increased serum osmolality
Reduction in plasma volume
Increased rectal temperature
Increased heart rate
Reduced skin blood flow
Increased perception of effort
Increased serum hormone activities

Modern Studies of Fluid Loss and Fluid Ingestion During Exercise

Two experimental models have been used to study the effects of fluid loss and fluid intake on physiologic responses during exercise.

Fluid loss (hypohydration) induced either by the administration of diuretics, or exposure to sauna, or fluid restriction *before* exercise, produces physiologic effects that are more marked than those that result from the form of dehydration that develops voluntarily *during* exercise when the rate of fluid loss exceeds the rate of fluid ingestion.[12,13] In particular, the reduction in plasma volume and in physical performance for a given level of dehydration is greater with hypohydration.[12-15]

For this reason, the result of the hypohydration studies, which are reviewed in detail elsewhere,[16] are perhaps most relevant for activities in which subjects deliberately dehydrate themselves before exercise, usually to make a specific competitive weight. This review focuses principally on studies of exercise-induced dehydration.

The Effect of Exercise-Induced Dehydration on Physical Performance

The balance of evidence indicates that the ingestion of water enhances performances both during very prolonged exercise of low intensity and during exercise of somewhat higher intensity but shorter duration. However, this effect may be somewhat less than that achieved when the fluid contains carbohydrate either alone[17] or with electrolytes.[18,19] Possibly the most consistent finding is that fluid ingestion markedly reduces the perception of effort during both low[1] and high intensity exercise.[20] It is also probable that exercise performance during high intensity exercise is impaired at levels of dehydration that do not influence performance at lower exercise intensities.[1]

Physiologic Effects of Progressive Dehydration During Prolonged Exercise

Plasma volume falls during prolonged exercise; the fall is least when the rate of fluid ingestion equals the rate of fluid loss.[21] The ingestion of sodium-containing solutions may prevent the fall in plasma volume more effectively than the ingestion of pure water.[22]

Similarly, the rise in serum osmolality and serum electrolyte concentrations is least when the rate of fluid ingestion equals the rate of fluid loss. The rise in serum osmolality and serum sodium concentration correlates with the rise in esophageal temperature[23] and may be the stimulus for the reduction in sweating that develops at the higher levels of dehydration.[24] This suggests that an important goal of fluid ingestion during exercise may be to prevent changes in serum osmolality or serum sodium concentrations.[25]

Sweat rate during exercise is not influenced by the level of dehydration during exercise, at least at levels of dehydration less than about 5%.[24] Hyperhydration before exercise increases the sweat rate during subsequent exercise.

The exercise-related rise in rectal temperature is attenuated by fluid ingestion during exercise.[1,15,21,23,26-31] The rise is least when the rate of fluid ingestion approximates the sweat rate.[23,31] However, the magnitude of this effect of fluid ingestion on the rise in rectal temperature is relatively small[9] so that its real physiologic relevance may be questioned.

Hypohydration before exercise also reduces rectal temperature during subsequent exercise.[32] Heart rate is increased[2,27,31,33,34] and stroke volume reduced in proportion to the fluid deficit that develops during exercise.

Fluid ingestion maintains higher rates of forearm blood flow during exercise[15,23] and of forearm and calf blood flow at rest during prolonged heat exposure.[35] The reduction of forearm blood flow is proportional to the level of dehydration.[23] Hence, fluid ingestion during exercise may attenuate the development of hyperthermia by maintaining skin blood flow.[15]

Perception of effort during exercise is increased in proportion to the fluid deficit.[23] Even partial fluid replacement has a significant effect on the perception of effort during exercise of high intensity.[20]

Plasma concentrations or activities of the fluid and electrolyte regulating hormones, specifically atrial natriuretic peptide (ANP), antidiuretic hormone (ADH - also arginine vasopressin - AVP), aldosterone, and renin, increase during prolonged exercise.[36-39] In general, ADH activities rise in response to increasing serum osmolality,[39,40] whereas plasma renin activity may follow changes in either plasma or extracellular fluid volumes.

Fluid ingestion during exercise reduces the hormonal activities and concentrations during exercise; concentrations are further reduced when subjects hyperhydrate prior to exercise.[37]

Renal function during prolonged exercise such as marathon running is unaffected by levels of dehydration less than 4% and is enhanced during recovery in those who retain fluid during exercise.[41] The classic studies also found that renal function was not influenced by levels of dehydration less than 7%.[1] Anuria has been reported in one runner who drank inadequately and lost 11% of her body weight during an 88-km ultramarathon.[42]

Dehydration impairs gastric emptying[43] and could theoretically limit fluid replacement during prolonged exercise. In contrast, intestinal absorption may increase when blood volume falls.[44] But gastric emptying should not limit fluid replacement during exercise because high rates of gastric emptying can always be achieved with the appropriate drinking patterns.[45] It is more probable that fluid absorption by the small bowel could limit fluid replacement, especially when only plain water is ingested at high rates during prolonged exercise.

Influence of the Exercise-Related Fall in Plasma Volume on Physiologic Responses During Exercise

It seems that the prevention of any rise in the serum osmolality or the serum concentration of the plasma volume explains why fluid ingestion attenuates the rise in rectal temperature during exercise.[15] Maintenance of the pre-exercise serum sodium concentration and serum osmolality prevents any reduction in skin blood flow.

The progressive rise in heart rate and fall in stroke volume during exercise, termed cardiovascular drift, is not due solely to the fall in plasma volume, as both are reduced more by fluid ingestion than by intravenous fluid infusion during exercise.[15] Complete prevention of cardiovascular drift during exercise requires that glucose also be infused intravenously.[21] I have proposed that especially the rise in oxygen consumption during prolonged exercise results from a catecholamine-mediated stimulation of metabolism that is prevented by glucose infusion.

Optimum Rates of Fluid Intake During Exercise

The evidence so far presented suggests that the principal aim of fluid ingestion during exercise is to prevent any rise in serum osmolality or serum sodium concentrations. A secondary goal is to prevent any change in plasma volume. Yet few studies have considered the interacting influences of the rates of fluid loss and fluid ingestion, and the composition of the ingested solution on changes in these variables during exercise. Rather, it has been assumed that the optimum rate of fluid ingestion is always that which equals the rate of fluid loss. But is it clear that most subjects do not voluntarily replace all the fluid lost during exercise.[1] It is, therefore, appropriate first to discuss the factors that influence the rates of fluid loss and fluid ingestion during exercise because this discussion may identify those exercising conditions in which the development of voluntary dehydration is more likely. The possible effects of the nature of the ingested fluid on changes in serum osmolality and plasma volume under these conditions will also be briefly considered.

Rates of Fluid Loss During Exercise

The rate of sweat loss, which is the principle determinant of fluid loss from the body during exercise, is determined principally by the metabolic rate.[10,46-51] At least in running, the metabolic rate is determined by the body mass and the running speed; in nonweightbearing activities like cycling, the velocity of movement becomes the principal determinant of the metabolic rate. Barr and Costill[52] have predicted sweat rates for subjects of different masses at different speeds. Their prediction is that sweat rates will seldom be greater than 1.2 l/hr in runners weighing less than 70 kg. Such high sweat rates are probable only in runners of 80 kg or more running faster than 12 km/hour (Fig. 3). The finding that sweat rates measured in runners during long distance races are seldom greater than 1.2 l/hr[9] confirms the general accuracy of these predictions.

The rates of fluid intake during exercise vary considerably but are seldom more than about 500 ml/hr except in subjects cycling in the laboratory when they are forced to ingest fluid at high rates. Hence one conclusion might be that the subjects voluntarily choose to drink about 500 ml/hr during exercise with little likelihood that rates will be greater than 1 l/hr, except under laboratory conditions.

But as these rates of fluid ingestion are less than sweat rates, voluntary dehydration develops at least during those activities lasting less than about 6 hours. In longer events, especially those lasting many days, there is a tendency for body weight to increase during exercise.

It is generally assumed that all fluid ingested during exercise would be absorbed. However, the assumption that the small bowel has an unlimited capacity for both fluid and energy assimilation is currently under review.[53] At present the maximum rates of small bowel fluid and glucose absorption either at rest or during exercise are not known. But there is information to suggest that these rates may be sufficiently low to limit optimum fluid and carbohydrate replacement[54-56] during exercise. Clearly, unless the maximum rates of fluid absorption by the small bowel are known, it is difficult to prescribe how much fluid should be ingested during exercise.[57]

The Role of Sodium Chloride Ingestion

The predictions of Adolph and Dill[58] that the fluid deficit which develops during exercise is corrected only when the sodium chloride deficit has been corrected so the "water cannot be held until the missing osmoles are made good"[59] has been confirmed by the detailed studies of Nose and associates.[60-64] The essential conclusion from these studies is that the sodium content of the extracellular space must regulate the extracellular fluid volume.[61,65] As a result, the extracellular fluid volume must contract whenever a sodium deficiency develops. This explains why serum sodium concentrations re-

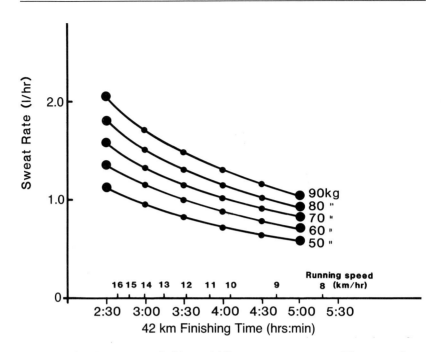

Fig. 3 *Predicted sweat rates of athletes of different masses running at different speeds.*

main constant (or increase slightly) during prolonged exercise when both sodium and water are lost, even if plain water in limited amounts is replaced.[66]

It follows that an important benefit of ingesting sodium chloride during or after exercise might be better maintenance and more rapid restoration of the extracellular volume and possibly also the plasma volume,[22,37,67,68] although this is not always found.[33,69] This effect would be enhanced by the addition of carbohydrate, which further increases the rate of fluid absorption from the solution ingested during exercise.[70]

The Influence of Aging

Most human physiologic functions alter with age. Yet most of the studies of the physiological effects of dehydration and of fluid balance during exercise were performed on younger athletes. Thus, it might be asked whether the findings reviewed in this manuscript are applicable to persons of all ages.

There is no reason to suspect that older persons are better able to resist the detrimental effects of dehydration, already described (Table 1); logic would suggest that the effects of dehydration would be greater in older persons. Clearly this is an important question that invites scientific evaluation. The practical value of this finding would be to establish whether older persons should be particularly careful to prevent the development of dehydration during exercise.

Similarly, it is not known whether the rates of fluid loss during exercise are influenced by aging. It is unlikely that the fundamental dependence of sweat rate on metabolic rate is greatly influenced by aging. Hence the general relationship among running speed, mass, and sweat rate depicted in Figure 3 is probably applicable for most age groups. Aging may influence the relationship only in as much as older persons tend to be heavier and to exercise at lower intensities. Hence it is probable that fluid requirements during exercise become less as persons age, simply because they tend to exercise less intensively.

Just as there are few data on the rates of intestinal fluid absorption in healthy persons, so too are the effects of aging on this process largely unknown. But it is also likely that individual variation in rates of intestinal fluid absorption exceed the magnitude of change induced by aging.

Summary

Current evidence indicates that adequate fluid ingestion during exercise enhances athletic performance; prevents a fall in plasma volume, stroke volume, cardiac output, and skin blood flow; maintains serum sodium concentrations and serum osmolality; lowers rectal temperature and the perception of effort; and prevents a progressive rise in heart rate. Rates of sweating and urine flow are not influenced by fluid ingestion. The evidence suggests that the maintenance of serum osmolality and serum sodium concentrations at pre-exercise levels is the important determinant of these beneficial effects of fluid ingestion on cardiovascular function and thermoregulation. The provision of glucose in the ingested solution may be necessary to optimize performance; glucose ingestion, which enhances fluid and sodium absorption in the small bowel, may also prevent a progressive rise in oxygen consumption during exercise. Sweetened carbohydrate-containing drinks may also increase fluid intake during exercise, thereby minimizing voluntary dehydration.

Therefore, the optimum solution for ingestion during exercise should provide carbohydrate, probably at rates of about 1 g/min, and electrolytes in concentrations which, when drunk at the optimum rate, maintain serum osmolality and plasma volume at pre-exercise levels by replacing exactly the water and electrolytes lost from the extracellular space. At present, the composition of the fluid that will optimize electrolyte and fluid replacement of the extracellular space is not established. Neither are the optimum rates of fluid ingestion during exercise known. At low sweat rates (<1 l/hr) it is probable that all the lost fluid can and should be replaced; rates of fluid ingestion needed to offset higher sweat rates may exceed the maximum intestinal absorptive capacity for water. Furthermore, high rates of fluid intake (>1 l/hr) are achieved with difficulty during exercise, especially when running, and are likely to lead to feelings of abdominal discomfort possibly due to the accumulation of unabsorbed fluid in the small bowel or colon. Practicing to drink regularly during training might reduce the severity and frequency of these symptoms, possibly by increasing intestinal absorptive capacity.

There are no studies to show that aging significantly influences the physiologic effects of dehydration, the relationship between the metabolic rate and the sweat rate, or the capacity of the intestine for fluid absorption.

Hence, until additional evidence becomes available, it would seem that advice regarding fluid replacement during exercise should be similar for athletes, regardless of their ages.

Acknowledgments

This work was supported by the Medical Research Council of South Africa, the Harry Crossley and Nellie Atkinson Research Funds of the University of Cape Town, G.W. Leppin (Pty) Ltd, Wander AG Bern Ltd and the South African Sugar Association. The manuscript is a condensed version of the author's more complete review.[11]

References

1. Adolph EF: *Physiology of man in the desert*. New York, NY, Interscience Publishers, 1947.

2. Sullivan JE: *Marathon running*. New York, NY, American Sports Publishing Company, 1909.

3. Noakes, TD: *Lore of Running*, ed 3. Champaign, IL, Leisure Press, 1991.

4. Peters JH, Johnson J, Edmundson J: Modern middle and long-distance running. London, Nicholas Kaye, 1957.

5. Costill DL: *A scientific approach to distance running*. Los Altos, CA, Track and Field News, 1979.

6. Wyndham CH, Strydom NB: The danger of an inadequate water intake during marathon running. *S Afr Med J* 1969;43:893-896.

7. Wyndham CH: Heat stroke and hyperthermia in marathon runners. *Ann N Y Acad Sci* 1977;301:128-138.

8. Noakes TD: The collapsed endurance athlete—time to rethink our management? *Sports Training Med Rehab* 1991;2:171-191.

9. Noakes TD, Adams BA, Myburgh KH, et al: The danger of an inadequate water intake during prolonged exercise:. A novel concept re-visited. *Eur J Appl Physiol* 1988;57:210-219.

10. Noakes TD, Myburgh KH, duPlessis J, et al: Metabolic rate, not percent dehydration, predicts rectal temperature in marathon runners. *Med Sci Sports Exerc* 1991;23:443-449.

11. Noakes TD: Fluid replacement during exercise. *Exerc Sports Sci Rev* 1993;21:297-330.

12. Coyle EF, Hamilton M: Fluid replacement during exercise: Effects on physiological homeostasis and performance, in Gisolfi CV, Lamb DR (eds): *Perspectives in Exercise Science and Sports Medicine*. Carmel, IN, Brown and Benchmark Press, 1990, vol 3, pp 281-303.

13. Coyle EF, Montain SJ: Carbohydrate and fluid ingestion during exercise: Are there trade-offs? *Med Sci Sports Exerc* 1992;24:671-678.

14. Caldwell JE, Ahonen E, Nousiainen U: Differential effects of sauna-, diuretic-, and exercise-induced hypohydration. *J Appl Physiol* 1984;57:1018-1023.

15. Montain SJ, Coyle EF: Fluid ingestion during exercise increases skin blood flow independent of increases in blood volume. *J Appl Physiol* 1992;73:903-910.

16. Sawka MN, Pandolf KB: Effects of body water loss on physiological function and exercise performance, in Gisolfi CV, Lamb DR (eds): *Perspectives in Exercise Science and Sports Medicine*. Carmel, IN, Brown and Benchmark Press, 1990, vol 3, pp 1-30.

17. Williams C, Nute MG, Broadbank L, et al: Influence of fluid intake on endurance running performance: A comparison between water, glucose and fructose solutions. *Eur J Appl Physiol* 1990;60:112-119.

18. Coggan AR, Coyle EF: Carbohydrate ingestion during prolonged exercise: Effects on metabolism and performance. *Exerc Sports Sci Rev* 1991;19:1-40.

19. Maughan RJ, Fenn CE, Leiper JB: Effects of fluid, electrolyte and substrate ingestion on endurance capacity. *Eur J Appl Physiol* 1989;58:481-486.

20. Walsh RM, Noakes TD: Exercise tolerance is impaired at low levels of dehydration. *Med Sci Sports Exerc* 1992;24(Suppl 5):S43.

21. Hamilton MT, Gonzalez-Alonso J, Montain SJ, et al: Fluid replacement and glucose infusion during exercise prevent cardiovascular drift. *J Appl Physiol* 1991;71:871-877.

22. Candas V, Libert JP, Brandenberger G, et al: Hydration during exercise: Effects on thermal and cardiovascular adjustments. *Eur J Appl Physiol* 1986;55:113-122.

23. Montain SJ, Cole EF: Influence of graded dehydration on hyperthermia and cardiovascular drift during exercise. *J Appl Physiol* 1992;73:1340-1350.

24. Ladell WSS: The effects of water and salt intake upon the performance of men working in hot and humid environments. *J Physiol (Lond)* 1955;127:11-46.

25. Dill DB: *Life, heat and altitude. Physiological effects of hot climates and great heights.* Cambridge, MA, Harvard University Press, 1938.

26. Barr SI, Costill DL, Fink WJ: Fluid replacement during prolonged exercise: Effects of water, saline, or no fluid. *Med Sci Sports Exerc* 1991;23:811-817.

27. Candas V, Libert J-P, Brandenberger G, et al: Thermal and circulatory responses during prolonged exercise at different levels of hydration. *J Physiol (Paris)* 1988;83:11-18.

28. Costill DL, Kammer WF, Fisher A: Fluid ingestion during distance running. *Arch Environ Health* 1970;21:520-525.

29. Ekblom B, Greenleaf CJ, Greenleaf JE, et al: Temperature regulation during exercise dehydration in man. *Acta Physiol Scand* 1970;79:475- 483.

30. Gisolfi CV, Copping JR: Thermal effects of prolonged treadmill exercise in the heat. *Med Sci Sports* 1974;6:108-113.

31. Greenleaf JE, Castle BL: Exercise temperature regulation in man during hypohydration and hyperhydration. *J Appl Physiol* 1971;30:847-853.

32. Moroff SV, Bass DE: Effects of overhydration on man's physiological responses to work in the heat. *J Appl Physiol* 1965;20:267-270.

33. Maughan RJ, Fenn CE, Gleeson M, et al: Metabolic and circulatory responses to the ingestion of glucose polymer and glucose/electrolyte solutions during exercise in man. *Eur J Appl Physiol* 1987;56:356-361.

34. Strydom NB, Holdsworth LD: The effects of different levels of water deficit on physiological responses during heat stress. *Int Z Angew Physiol* 1968;26:95-102.

35. Horstman DH, Horvath SM: Cardiovascular and temperature regulatory changes during progressive dehydration and euhydration. *J Appl Physiol* 1972;33:446-450.

36. Altenkirch HU, Gerzer R, Kirsch KA, et al: Effect of prolonged physical exercise on fluid regulating hormones. *Eur J Appl Physiol* 1990;61:209-213.

37. Brandenberger G, Candas V, Follenius M, et al: The influence of the initial state of hydration on endocrine responses to exercise in the heat. *Eur J Appl Physiol* 1989;58:674-679.

38. Freund BJ, Claybaugh JR, Hashiro GM, et al: Exaggerated ANF response to exercise in middle-aged vs. young runners. *J Appl Physiol* 1990;69:1607-1614.

39. Wade CE, Freund BJ: Hormonal control of blood volume during and following exercise, in Gisolfi CV, Lamb DR (eds): *Perspectives in Exercise Science and Sports Medicine*. Carmel, IN, Brown and Benchmark Press, 1990, vol 3, pp 207-241.

40. Thrasher TN, Nistal-Herrera JF, Keil LC, et al: Satiety and inhibition of vasopressin secretion after drinking in dehydrated dogs. *Am J Physiol* 1981;240:E394-E401.

41. Irving RA, Noakes TD, Buck R, et al: Evaluation of renal function and fluid homeostasis during recovery from exercise-induced hyponatremia. *J Appl Physiol* 1991;70:342-348.

42. Irving RA, Noakes TD, Raine RI, et al: Transient oliguria with renal tubular dysfunction after a 90 km running race. *Med Sci Sports Exerc* 1990;22:756-761.

43. Neufer PD, Young AJ, Sawka MN: Gastric emptying during exercise: Effects of heat stress and hypohydration. *Eur J Appl Physiol* 1989;58:433-439.

44. Sjovall H, Abrahamsson H, Westlander G, et al: Intestinal fluid and electrolyte transport in man during reduced circulating blood volume. *Gut* 1986;27:913-918.

45. Noakes TD, Rehrer NJ, Maughan RJ: The importance of volume in regulating gastric emptying. *Med Sci Sports Exerc* 1991;23:307-313.

46. Costill DL: Sweating: Its composition and effects on body fluids. *Ann N Y Acad Sci* 1977;301:160-174.

47. Davies CT: Influence of skin temperature on sweating and aerobic performance during severe work. *J Appl Physiol* 1979;47:770-777.

48. Davies CT, Brotherhood JR, Zeidifard E: Temperature regulation during severe exercise with some observations on effects of skin wetting. *J Appl Physiol* 1976;41:772-776.

49. Greenhaff PL: Cardiovascular fitness and thermoregulation during prolonged exercise in man. *Br J Sports Med* 1989;23:109-114.

50. Greenhaff PL, Clough PJ: Predictors of sweat loss in man during prolonged exercise. *Eur J Appl Physiol* 1989;58:348-352.

51. Wyndham CH, Strydom NB, van Rensburg AJ, et al: Relation between VO_2 max and body temperature in hot humid air conditions. *J Appl Physiol* 1970;29:45-50.

52. Barr SI, Costill DL: Water: Can the endurance athlete get too much of a good thing? *J Am Diet Assoc* 1989;89:1629-1632,1635.

53. Diamond J: Evolutionary design of intestinal nutrient absorption: Enough but not too much. *NIPS* 1991;6(April):92-96.

54. Moodley D, Noakes TD, Bosch AN, et al: Oxidation of exogenous carbohydrate during prolonged exercise: The effects of the carbohydrate type and its concentration. *Eur J Appl Physiol* 1992;64:328-334.

55. Rehrer NJ: *Limits to fluid availability during exercise*. BV Uitgeverij De Vrieseborch, Haarlem, 1990, pp 1-239.

56. Rehrer NJ, Wagenmakers AJ, Beckers EJ, et al: Gastric emptying, absorption, and carbohydrate oxidation during prolonged exercise. *J Appl Physiol* 1992;72:468-475.

57. Noakes TD: Hyponatremia during endurance running: A physiological and clinical interpretation. *Med Sci Sports Exerc* 1992;24:403-405.

58. Adolph EF, Dill DB: Observations on water metabolism in the desert. *Am J Physiol* 1938;123:369-378.

59. Ladell WSS: Water and salt (sodium chloride) intakes, in Edholm OG, Bacharach AL (eds): *The Physiology of Human Survival*. London, Academic Press, 1 965, pp 235-299.
60. Nose H, Mack GW, Shi XR, et al: Effect of saline infusion during exercise on thermal and circulatory regulations. *J Appl Physiol* 1990;69:609-616.
61. Nose H, Mack GW, Shi XR, et al: Shift in body fluid compartments after dehydration in humans. *J Appl Physiol* 1988;65:318-324.
62. Nose H, Mack GW, Shi XR, et al: Role of osmolality and plasma volume during rehydration in humans. *J Appl Physiol* 1988;65:325-331.
63. Nose H, Mack GW, Shi XR, et al: Involvement of sodium retention hormones during rehydration in humans. *J Appl Physiol* 1988;65:332-336.
64. Okuno T, Yawata T, Nose H, et al: Difference in rehydration process due to salt concentration of drinking water in rats. *J Appl Physiol* 1988;64:2438-2443.
65. Nadel ER, Mack GW, Nose H: Influence of fluid replacement beverages on body fluid homeostasis during exercise and recovery, in Gisolfi CV, Lamb DR (eds): *Perspectives in Exercise Science and Sports Medicine*. Carmel, IN, Brown and Benchmark Press, 1990, vol 3, pp 181-198.
66. Noakes TD: The hyponatremia of exercise. *Int J Sports Nutr* 1992;2:205-228.
67. Costill DL, Sparks KE: Rapid fluid replacement following thermal dehydration. *J Appl Physiol* 1973;34:299-303.
68. Nielsen B, Sjogaard G, Ugelvig J, et al: Fluid balance in exercise dehydration and rehydration with different glucose-electrolyte drinks. *Eur J Appl Physiol* 1986;55:318-325.
69. Powers SK, Lawler J, Dodd S, et al: Fluid replacement drinks during high intensity exercise: Effects on minimizing exercise-induced disturbances in homeostasis. *Eur J Appl Physiol* 1990;60:54-60.
70. Gisolfi CV, Summers RW, Schedl HP, et al: Human intestinal water absorption: Direct vs. indirect measurements. *Am J Physiol* 1990;258:G216-G222.
71. Maron MB, Horvath SM, Wilkerson JE: Acute blood biochemical alterations in response to marathon running. *Eur J Appl Physiol* 1975;34:173-181.
72. Maughan RJ: Thermoregulation in marathon competition at low ambient temperature. *Int J Sports Med* 1985;6:15-19.
73. Pugh LG, Corbett JL, Johnson RH: Rectal temperatures, weight losses, and sweat rates in marathon running. *J Appl Physiol* 1967;23:347-352.

Chapter 8

Muscle Flexibility and Function Under Stretch

William E. Garrett, Jr, MD, PhD

There are many possible approaches in discussing muscular control of movement and changes associated with aging. Characteristics of muscle size, strength, metabolic pathways, trainability, and injury are all addressed in this volume. This chapter will specifically address the characteristics of muscle under stretch. It will start with a brief overview of current psysiologic and pathophysiologic understanding of muscle. Changes in these properties of muscle with aging, specifically at midlife, will then be discussed where data are available. Finally, these characteristics of muscle will be addressed from the standpoint of injury to muscle and tendon.

Normal Muscle-Tendon Structure and Function

Muscles and their attached tendons act as units originating from one bone and attaching to another. They, therefore, are able to influence motion about the joints that they cross, as well as joints above and below in the linked chain of body movements. Although muscle is most often considered to affect joint motion as a result of its ability to shorten, many important functions of muscle involve force production under conditions that do not involve muscle shortening. The length of the activated muscle may not change (an isometric contraction) or the muscle may be lengthened while actively resisting stretch (an eccentric contraction). Muscle that is actively shortening (a concentric contraction) usually causes motion around a joint. Isometric and eccentric contractions often provide control, deceleration, and energy absorption. These coordinated actions are very important in normal physiologic conditions and are especially important when considering the prevention of injury to the musculoskeletal system.

The function of muscle undergoing passive stretch, ie, lengthening while the muscle is not being activated either directly or by neural stimulation, is also important. The range of motion of many joints is limited by the soft tissue around the joint rather than by the osseous structure of the joints. Muscles in normal subjects can limit range of motion in joints under some conditions. For example, with the knees held straight, the hamstring muscles limit the amount of hip flexion as in the sit and reach test. Similarly, the gastrocnemius can limit ankle dorsiflexion when the knee is extended, and the rectus femoris can limit knee flexion when the hip is extended. These limitations in motion occur because muscles have only a limited ability to stretch. Muscles often can limit range of motion when being stretched simultaneously by more than one joint. However, this limiting effect is not restricted to muscles spanning more than one joint. In joints with greater degrees of freedom in movement, such as the hip and shoulder, muscles crossing only one joint can limit motion. For example, the hip adductors and shoulder rotators can limit hip abduction and shoulder rotation.

There are also many other abnormal or pathologic conditions under which passive muscle properties can limit motion. Contractures or motion limitations may occur in the presence of arthritic joints, following joint injury or muscle trauma, or following joint immobilization in which muscles are held in a shortened position.[1,2] Muscle contractures also occur commonly in athletic populations, affecting shoulder rotation in tennis players and adductors and hamstrings in soccer players.[3,4] There is ample evidence that muscle flexibility can limit range of motion.

Flexibility or range of motion of joints can be limited by a number of factors in bone and other soft tissue. This discussion will be concerned primarily with the muscles as limiting factors of motion.

Behavior of Passive Muscle Under Stretch

Muscle behavior under stretch depends on a number of factors, including amount of stretch, the rate of the stretching, and the degree of muscle activation. Consideration of stretching based on the state of activation is helpful for this discussion.

Normal Response

When muscle is stretched without activation, the intrinsic connective tissues of muscle are important in describing its behavior. Muscle behaves as a viscoelastic structure; its response to the application of force or a strain is characterized by viscous and elastic behavior.[5] The force in response to strain is not linear but is stiffening, ie, with more stretch the slope of the stress-strain relationship is steeper and the material acts stiffer. If strain is held constant after a length increase, the force or stress does not remain constant (Fig. 1). Rather, the force or stress relaxes with time, a phenomenon termed stress relaxation. If, on the other hand, a constant force is applied, then the initial length increase is followed by a slow increase in length, a phenome-

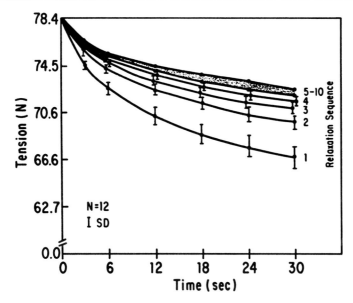

Fig. 1 *The viscoelastic nature of muscle and stress relaxation. Rabbit muscles are stretched to a given length and held while force is measured over time by a force transducer attached to the tendon of the muscle. The first curve shows the relaxaton of force or stress after the first stretch. The muscles are then relaxed and stretched again successfully to the same original tension. For each stretch there is a definite stress relaxation effect. After four stretches, the stress relaxation behavior is quite similar with repeated stretches. (Reproduced with permission from Taylor DC, Dalton JD Jr, Seaber AVE, et al: Viscoelastic properties of muscle-tendon units: The biomechanical effects of stretching. Am J Sports Med 1990;18:300-309.)*

non called creep. The force or stress developed within muscle also characteristically depends on the rate of application of the strain. These viscoelastic properties are common among connective tissues, including bone, ligament, or tendon. Additionally, the biomechanical response of muscle to stretch follows the same quasilinear viscoelastic theory that describes stretch in bone and soft tissue of the body.[6]

Many current descriptions of muscle behavior under stretch are predicated on the assumption that some or most of the tension developed in stretched muscle is due to activation of the muscle and active resistance to stretch. Although this is certainly true in some cases, especially under conditions causing pain, the general response to stretch of muscle under normal testing or stretching maneuvers is a passive response of stretched connective tissue rather than active resistance to stretch.[7,8]

Effect of Aging on Passive Stretch Response of Muscle

Aging affects the response of muscle to passive stretch. Effects of aging are often seen as changes in the flexibility of joints in which movement can be limited by muscles. It is generally felt that flexibility decreases significantly with aging. However, there are relatively few data or published studies in the literature. The relationship of flexibility to age has been evaluated more for the youth and adolescent population than for those of midlife or older. Kendall and Kendall[9] evaluated hamstring and low back flexibility in subjects ranging from preschool to college-age. Female subjects were generally more flexible than male subjects. The flexibility level obtained using the sit and reach test declined yearly until age 12 in males and age 13 in females. After these low points, flexibility increased yearly through the teenage years to college years. These data show that the years of fast skeletal growth are associated with a decrease in flexibility caused by muscle. The muscle, however, does respond with time as the rate of skeletal growth declines.

Obviously, muscle does not have a growth plate or physis like bones. The muscle does, however, have an excellent capacity to adjust its length in response to the length at which it exists in both static (immobilized) or dynamic situations. These properties have been well studied both in normal growth and development and in situations in which muscle is held lengthened or shortened beyond normal as in immobilization of joints in various positions. Muscle from both immature and mature animals is able to adapt to applied length changes. Furthermore, both the active and passive components of muscle can respond. The active force-generating capacity adapts by adding new sarcomeres to the stretched muscle fibers.[10] As muscle grows or is stretched, the sarcomeres are initially stretched beyond their normal or optimal length. With time, the optimal length is restored as new sarcomeres are added to the ends of the stretched fibrils. These additions occur at the myotendinous junctions. With shortening, the muscle sarcomeres initially shorten, but with time they return to normal length as sarcomeres are removed from the muscle.

There are fewer data to document flexibility changes with aging. Standardized fitness tests from a Canadian Government study document the changes in low back and hamstring flexibility by the sit and reach tests.[11] In general, females were more flexible as in the youth population. Flexibility declined after the third decade with steady decreases in each decade for men and women. From the third to the seventh decade, average flexibility for the sit and reach tests declined by approximately 10 cm for men and 60 cm for women.[12]

With the older population there is a widespread belief that flexibility decreases even in the athletic population.[13,14] Certainly, in some sports, diminished flexibility in certain joint range of motion is expected. Tennis players, for example, often or usually have diminished shoulder internal rotation in the dominant arm.[3] Runners often develop tight heelcords and hamstrings. Soccer players often have tight adductors as well as other muscle groups. These changes exist in both the young and the older populations.

Can flexibility training change the extensibility of muscle under passive stretch conditions? A number of studies have shown that stretching exercises can induce both instant and lasting changes in muscle flexibility.[15-17] These studies have generally evaluated flexibility with regard to range of motion involving several joints in which motion can be limited by passive tension in the muscles. In some sports there are associated increases in flexibility of joints that are repeatedly stretched, such as shoulder external rotation in overhead athletes[18] and the hips in gymnasts.[19]

Midlife athletes can also experience increases in flexibility in response to flexibility training.[20] Finger metacarpophalangeal joint flexibility in 19 year olds was compared with that in 63 year olds. At the start of a 6-week training program, the younger group was more flexible. Both groups improved their flexibility with training. However, the discrepancy between young and old persisted, even after the training program. Stretching exercises are successful in increasing muscle extensibility not only in normal subjects, but also in subjects with conditions such as hip osteoarthritis.[1]

The cause of the changes seen in flexibility and other properties of passively stretched muscle remains unclear. There are changes in muscle-tendon units associated with aging that may be inherent properties of the aging process. On the other hand, there are changes that may be related less to aging per se than to the alterations in activity level and physical demands, which often accompany aging. The studies cited above point out that the extensibility of muscle decreases with aging, but that specific exercise and stretching programs allow similar improvements in the young and the aging populations.

The Response of Activated Muscle to Stretch

Normal Response

When activated muscle is stretched, the response is very different from the response of unstimulated or inactive muscle. With activated muscle, the neurally driven contractile apparatus is generating force to provide muscular shortening or to resist lengthening. The mechanical properties of activated muscle are dominated by the muscular contractile apparatus rather than by the connective tissue viscoelastic responses characteristic of passively stretched muscle. The contractile properties of muscle are discussed in chapters 23 and 24 of this volume by Kraemer and Tipton and will not be discussed in much detail here.

Increasing attention has been paid to strength assessment under eccentric loading conditions, ie, to the function of activated muscle while it is being lengthened.[21] This interest is due, in part, to the development of isokinetic testing equipment that can control the angular rotation of a joint at a specified angular velocity and vary the torque of the dynamometer to match that of the exercising limb. The muscle can be exercised under muscular shortening (concentric) or muscular lengthening (eccentric) conditions. To exercise the muscle under eccentric conditions, the dynamometer must be active, ie, it must have the power to move the joint through a range of motion at a given velocity.

For activated muscle, there is a known relationship between force and velocity of shortening. Force reaches a maximum near zero velocity and decreases with increasing velocity. More recently, the relationship of force and negative velocity (lengthening) has been evaluated.[22] Muscle generates significantly more force during eccentric conditions than for concentric conditions. The force exceeds the maximum for concentric or isometric conditions and increases further at higher velocities of lengthening. Thus, for the same degree of activation muscle generates more force resisting lengthening than causing shortening at the same velocity.[23] These facts are especially important when muscles are considered with regard to their functions in physical activity.

Eccentric muscle function is especially important in the deceleration, stabilization, and control of joint motion. For example, during walking and running exercises, the predominant activity of lower extremity muscles, including the quadriceps, hamstrings, and triceps surae, is eccentric. The quadriceps muscles are most active in preventing knee flexion; hamstrings, resisting and controlling knee extension in late swing phase; and the triceps, preventing dorsiflexion of the ankle in mid to late stance phase. Of course, there also are concentric functions, but it is clear that muscles are being used as springs or shock absorbers in the body.[24] The concept of active muscle force in controlling and decelerating joints emphasizes the importance of eccentric muscle force as a protector of the musculoskeletal system rather than simply as a prime mover.

Effect of Aging on Response of Activated Muscle to Stretch

The changes in strength with age are discussed in more detail in this volume by Kraemer and Tipton. Most studies have evaluated the effects of aging on torque measured isometrically or in a concentric fashion. In general, muscle strength is maintained relatively well through the fifth decade with a decline thereafter.[25] Strength loss appears to occur faster with women than with men.[26,27]

Few studies have examined strength and age under eccentric loading conditions. Two studies have evaluated eccentric torque values as a function of age.[28,29] These studies show that concentric and eccentric torque values both decrease with age. However, the differences between age groups were less pronounced with eccentric muscle testing. This was especially true for men at higher angular velocities.

This decline in eccentric torque production with age may affect the ability of muscle to absorb energy and to protect itself and the musculoskeletal system (eg, articular structures) from injury.[30] This effect may be compounded when considered together with changes in passively stretched muscle. If flexibility of muscle is diminished and ability to resist extension is reduced, the ability of muscle to absorb energy and control joint motion is adversely affected in two ways.

Strain Injury to Muscle and Tendon

Muscle Injury

Injury to muscle and tendon frequently occurs under conditions of stretch.[24,31] Very often injuries occur during eccentric loading when tension is increasing as a result of simultaneous stretch and activation. In normal muscle-tendon units, the injury usually occurs at the myotendinous junction,[32] although other locations of injury are possible.

Recent research has characterized injury to the myotendinous junction, showing disruption within the muscle fibers near the junction but not precisely at the histologic junction.[33] Two imaging studies of muscle injury demonstrate that myotendinous junctions are the usual location of injury in clinically significant muscle strains.[34]

Studies have evaluated various risk factors for muscle strain injury. Many of the putative risk factors for muscle injury also affect flexibility and extensibility of muscle and the ability to do negative work (or absorb energy) under stretch. A significant warm-up period can provide some protection.[35] Under some conditions warm muscle can stretch further before injury.[36] Muscle strength and fatigue under stretch conditions affect the energy a muscle can absorb prior to failure.[30,37]

Aging effects on muscle certainly suggest that age might be a significant risk factor for muscle injury; however, sound epidemiologic studies do not exist to prove this point. Some musculotendinous injuries are much more likely in the midlife athlete. Injury to the medial head of the gastrocnemius at the musculotendinous junction is a frequent injury in active midlife people (Fig. 2).[38] The injury occurs in sports such as tennis or basketball in response to an intense eccentric load. Other common muscle injuries prevalent in younger populations are less frequent in midlife athletes, in part because of the nature of the sports. High-intensity athletic bursts and sprints are common in sports injuries, but as athletes approach midlife and beyond they frequently become less involved with sports using explosive bursts of speed. Even so, there are indications that muscle strain injury is more common in midlife as Jokl discusses in Chapter 30. It is possible to get a strong impression of the significance of muscle strain injuries in professional athletes approaching midlife. The injury reports and the sports pages chronicle the importance of muscle strains to the hamstrings, groin, quadriceps, back, and shoulder.

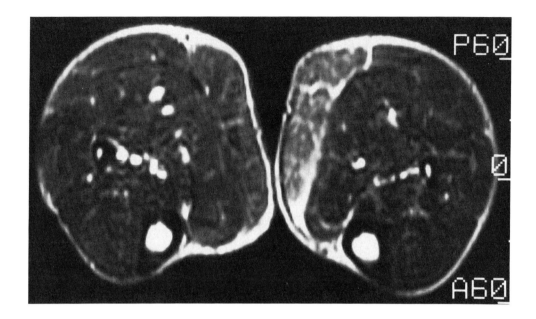

Fig. 2 *Characteristic muscle injury in a middle-aged athlete. The MRI demonstrates a strain injury to the medial head of the gastrocnemius muscle in a 38-year-old recreational athlete. The MRI shows axial (A) and sagittal views through the involved right leg. The MRI images are T2 weighted and therefore show increased fluid (such as edema or bleeding) as an increase in signal or a lighter image. The axial view (A) shows the muscle of the medial head of the gastrocnemius to be the only muscle involved. The axial view (B) shows that the involvement occurs at the junction of the muscle fibers with the tendon of the triceps surae muscle. (Speer KP, Garrett WE Jr: Radiographic imaging of muscle strain injury. Med Sci Sports Exerc 1991;23(suppl):S139.)*

What can be done to prevent these muscle injuries? Once again there are many suggestions based on clinical experience and "common sense," but not on sound epidemiologic studies. Stretching and strengthening programs designed to maintain or improve fitness are routinely prescribed for preventive conditioning in the older athlete and for specific sports common in midlife athletes, such as golf and tennis.[13,14,39]

Basic studies show clearly that muscle-tendon injuries occur in response to stretch. Muscles are less extensible in the aging athlete and might therefore be more prone to injury. Flexibility training is effective in the older populations and might thereby diminish injury. Similarly, aging is associated with diminished strength in muscle, which can significantly decrease the ability of muscle to absorb energy and prevent injury. Because strengthening programs are effective in aging athletes, strengthening might have a protective effect by increasing the ability of muscle to absorb injury.

Tendon Injury

Tendon injuries in clinical practice are characterized by different pathophysiologic processes. As discussed above, normal muscle-tendon units subjected to strain usually disrupt within the muscle near the myotendinous junction. Normal tendon rarely fails when the whole muscle-tendon unit is stretched, because the tensile strength of the tendon is the highest of the entire muscle-tendon unit.[40] There is considerable support for the concept that failure within a tendon in response to stretch occurs only in tendons that are in some way abnormal or diseased.[38] Tendon ruptures were investigated by Kannus and Jozsa,[41] who did biopsy studies on acutely ruptured tendons, including Achilles, biceps brachii, extensor pollicis longus, quadriceps, and patellar tendons. In 891 specimens, no normal tendons were seen. Most of the tendons demonstrated degenerative pathologic processes rather than inflammatory changes. Further, similar processes were found in one third of tendons from healthy individuals without tendon rupture. These findings clearly indicated that a high percentage of people over the age of 35 years have degenerative changes that probably predispose them to injury. Recreational sports have been frequently cited as the causal event of certain tendon injuries, especially those of the Achilles tendon.[42,43]

Again, there is uncertainty regarding whether the changes seen in aging tendon are due to aging processes per se or to the altered physical activity levels that frequently accompany aging. It appears that both processes are important. Aging itself is associated with matrix changes in experimental animals, but exercise produces effects that slow the decline in tendon properties associated with aging.[44] There is also evidence that there must be normal forces on the tendon for the tendon to maintain homeostasis.[45] Factors such as immobilization, deprivation of stresses by nonweightbearing, and disuse might be associated with biochemical and biomechanical changes in tendon. Therefore, there are strong indications that tendons, like other body tissues, undergo changes with aging that may be a combined effect of age per se and altered activity levels. Activity levels can be modified by regular exercise to offset some of these changes.

Summary

This chapter has discussed muscle and its response to lengthening under passive and active conditions, with an emphasis on changes associated with aging. Because muscles and tendons are usually injured during lengthening processes, these data are relevant to the cause and potential prevention of injury to the musculoskeletal system.

In general, muscles and tendons become less extensible with age. Muscles are also able to generate less force while lengthening. Both extensibility and strength can be specifically increased with training and exercise. Deleterious effects are probably due to the aging process and to the relative disuse that accompanies age. Susceptibility to injury might be improved with proper exercise programs in midlife.

References

1. Leivseth G, Torstensson J, Reikeras O: Effect of passive muscle stretching in osteoarthritis of the hip. *Clin Sci* 1989;76:113-117.

2. de la Tour EH, Tabary JC, Tabary C, et al: The respective roles of muscle length and muscle tension in sarcomere number adaptation of guinea-pig soleus muscle. *J Physiol (Paris)* 1979;75:589-592.

3. Chandler TJ, Kibler WB, Uhl TL, et al: Flexibility comparisons of junior elite tennis players to other athletes. *Am J Sports Med* 1990;18:134-136.

4. Ekstrand J, Gillquist J: The frequency of muscle tightness and injuries in soccer players. *Am J Sports Med* 1982;10:75-78.

5. Taylor DC, Dalton JD Jr, Seaber AV, et al: Viscoelastic properties of muscle-tendon units: The biomechanical effects of stretching. *Am J Sports Med* 1990;18:300-309.

6. Best TM, McElhaney J, Garrett WE Jr, et al: Characterization of the passive responses of live skeletal muscle using the quasi-linear theory of viscoelasticity. *J Biomech* 1993, in press.

7. McHugh MP, Magnusson SP, Gleim GW, et al: Poster biomechanics: Gait analysis: The relationship of contractile inhibition to decreased resistance during stretch. *Med Sci Sports Exerc* 1993;25(suppl):S115.

8. Cole E, Malone T, Garrett WE Jr: Passive muscle stretch and the viscoelastic response. *Trans Orthop Res Soc* 1992;17:255.

9. Kendall HO, Kendall FP: Normal flexibility according to age groups. *J Bone Joint Surg* 1948;30A:690-694.

10. Tabary JC, Tabary C, Tardieu C, et al: Physiological and structural changes in the cat's soleus muscle due to immobilization at different lengths by plaster casts. *J Physiol (Lond)* 1972;224:231-244.

11. *Fitness Canada*. Canadian Standardized Text of Fitness Operations Manual (Third Edition). Ottawa. Fitness and Amateur Sport, 1986.

12. Bell RD, Hoshizaki TB: Relationships of age and sex with range of motion of seventeen joint actions in humans. *Can J Appl Sport Sci* 1981;6:202-206.

13. Seto JL, Brewster CE: Musculoskeletal conditioning of the older athlete. *Clin Sports Med* 1991;10:401-429.

14. Leach RE, Abramowitz A: The senior tennis player. *Clin Sports Med* 1991;10:283-290.

15. Fieldman H: Effects of selected extensibility exercises on the flexibility of the hip joint. *Res Quar* 1966;37:326-331.

16. De Vries HA: Evaluation of static stretching procedures for improvement of flexibility. *Res Quar* 1962;33:222-229.

17. Kottke FJ, Pauley DL, Ptak RA: The rationale for prolonged stretching for correction of shortening of connective tissue. *Arch Phys Med Rehabil* 1966;47:345-352.

18. Kibler WB, Chandler TJ, Uhl TL, et al: A musculoskeletal approach to the preparticipation physical examination: Preventing injury and improving performance. *Am J Sports Med* 1989;17:525-531.

19. Sermeev BV: Development of mobility in the hip joint in sportsmen. *Theory and Practice of Physical Culture* 1966;12:25-26.

20. Chapman EA, deVries HA, Swezey R: Joint stiffness: Effects of exercise on young and old men. *J Gerontol* 1972;27:218-221.

21. Davies GJ, Ellenbecker TS: Eccentric isokinetics. *Orthop Phys Therapy Clin North Am* 1992;1:297-336.

22. Westing SH, Seger JY, Karlson E, et al: Eccentric and concentric torque-velocity characteristics of the quadriceps femoris in man. *Eur J Appl Physiol* 1988;58:100-104.

23. Colliander EB, Tesch PA: Bilateral eccentric and concentric torque of quadriceps and hamstring muscles in females and males. *Eur J Appl Physiol* 1989;59:227-232.

24. Garrett WE Jr, Kuester DJ, Best TM: Skeletal muscle and the knee joint, in Finerman GAM, Noyes FR (eds): *Biology and Biomechanics of the Traumatized Synovial Joint: The Knee as a Model*. Rosemont, IL, American Academy of Orthopaedic Surgeons, 1992, pp 289-302.

25. Larsson L, Grimby G, Karlsson J: Muscle strength and speed of movement in relation to age and muscle morphology. *J Appl Physiol* 1979;46:451-456.

26. Freedson PS, Gilliam TB, Mahoney T, et al: Industrial torque levels by age group and gender. *Isokin Exerc Sci* 1993;3:34-42.

27. Graves JM, Ragnarsdottir M, Ellingham CT, et al: Relationship between habitual physical activity and isometric peak torque of knee extensors and plantar flexors of older men and women. *Isokin Exerc Sci* 1992;2:166-174.

28. Poulin MJ, Vandervoort AA, Paterson DH, et al: Eccentric and concentric torques of knee and elbow extension in young and older men. *Can J Sport Sci* 1992;17:3-7.

29. Vandervoort AA, Kramer JF, Wharram ER: Eccentric knee strength of elderly females. *J Gerontol* 1990;45:B125-128.

30. Garrett WE Jr, Safran MR, Seaber AV, et al: Biomechanical comparison of stimulated and nonstimulated skeletal muscle pulled to failure. *Am J Sports Med* 1987;15:448-454.

31. Garrett WE Jr: Muscle strain injuries: Clinical and basic aspects. *Med Sci Sports Exerc* 1990;22:436-443.

32. Garrett WE Jr, Nikolaou PK, Ribbeck BM, et al: The effect of muscle architecture on the biomechanical failure properties of skeletal muscle under passive extension. *Am J Sports Med* 1988;16:7-12.

33. Reddy AS, Reedy MK, Seaber AV, et al: Restriction of the injury response following an acute muscle strain. *Med Sci Sports Exerc* 1993;25:321-327.

34. Speer KP, Garrett WE Jr: Radiographic imaging of muscle strain injury. *Med Sci Sports Exerc* 1991;23(suppl):S139.

35. Safran MR, Garrett WE Jr, Seaber AV, et al: The role of warmup in muscular injury prevention. *Am J Sports Med* 1988;16:123-129.

36. Noonan TJ, Best TM, Reddy AS, et al: Thermal effects on skeletal muscle tensile behavior. *Trans Orthop Res Soc.* 1992;17:515.

37. Mair SD, Seaber AV, Glisson RR, et al: The biomechanical effects of fatigue on muscle-tendon units pulled to failure. *Med Sci Sports Exerc* 1991;23(suppl):S92.

38. Garrett WE Jr: Chapter 237: Traumatic disorders of muscles and tendons, in Chapman MW, Madison M (eds): *Operative Orthopaedics*, ed 2. Philadelphia, PA, JB Lippincott, 1993, vol 4, pp 3411-3418.

39. Jobe FW, Schwab DM: Golf for the mature athlete. *Clin Sports Med* 1991;10:269-282.

40. McMaster PE: Tendon and muscle ruptures: Clinical and experimental studies on the causes and location of subcutaneous ruptures. *J Bone Joint Surg* 1933;15A:705-722.

41. Kannus P, Jozsa L: Histopathological changes preceding spontaneous rupture of a tendon: A controlled study of 891 patients. *J Bone Joint Surg* 1991;73A:1507-1525.

42. Jozsa L, Kvist M, Balint BJ, et al: The role of recreational sport activity in Achilles tendon rupture: A clinical, pathoanatomical, and sociological study of 292 cases. *Amer J Sports Med* 1989;17:338-343.

43. Fox JM, Blazina ME, Jobe FW, et al: Degeneration and rupture of the Achilles tendon. *Clin Orthop* 1975;107:221-224.

44. Vailas AC, Zernicke RF, Matsuda J, et al: Regional biochemical and morphological characteristics of rat knee meniscus. *Comp Biochem Physiol [B]* 1985;82:283-285.

45. Vailas AC, Deluna DM, Lewis LL, et al: Adaptation of bone and tendon to prolonged hindlimb suspension in rats. *J Appl Physiol* 1988;65:373-376.

Chapter 9

Structural Changes in the Tendon: Injury Prevention

J. Nardi, MD, PhD
A. Navarro, MD, PhD

Introduction

Injuries to the tendons and the tendon insertions (the latter are also known as enthesopathies) are currently the most frequently encountered injuries in sports; 80% of all cases of tendinitis occur during the practice of sports.[1,2] In advanced societies, the practice of sports has become a popular social activity, and because sports are frequently performed in a discontinuous and aggressive fashion, the athlete (especially the amateur athlete) is vulnerable to tendon injuries.

Tendons vary structurally throughout the lifetime. Tendinitis occurs rarely in children and adolescents, but its incidence increases during the midlife years, when it can lead to complete destruction of the tendon, as in a spontaneous rupture of the Achilles tendon. This chapter focuses on the structural changes seen in tendons and their role in injury cause and prevention.[3,4]

Incidence and Etiology of Tendon Injuries

Tendon injuries are seen in all sports, including those that begin with a rapid start from the lower extremities, such as jumping, sprinting, and gymnastics on apparatus, and those that primarily involve the upper extremities, such as the javelin throw, shotput, or weightlifting. Tendon injuries also occur in athletes who receive direct blows, such as soccer, basketball, and karate participants, and those who constantly repeat certain movements, such as marathon runners, swimmers, golfers, and tennis players. Acute and chronic injuries to the tendon insertions or to the tendons themselves may occur in all these sports, affecting the athlete's performance and sometimes even making it necessary for the athlete to stop practicing the sport temporarily. One very common example, and perhaps the most important one from the point of view of frequency and seriousness, is injury to the Achilles tendon, which occurs in many sports, principally those where the impetus comes from the foot.

There are several possible etiologies for the injuries to the tendon: vascular disturbances, collagen disturbances, certain genetic factors, and improper training; the latter may be responsible for a lack of muscle motor coordination and strength. Several studies (using different methodologies, including arteriography, radioisotopes, etc.) have been performed to gain an understanding of tendinous vascularization and the microcirculation of the tendon in its various areas: the free tendon and the attachments of the tendon to muscle and bone.[5-8] These studies demonstrated that the tendon is a poorly vascularized structure; a reduction in its arterial supply may initiate the tendinous degeneration and lead to a chronic pathologic state, the end result of which is tearing of the tendon.

An important gap in these studies is an examination of the dynamics of the blood supply during muscular contraction and exercise. It appears that the tendon has limited blood supply during muscular contraction and exercise, although it is difficult to determine the duration of ischemia that can be tolerated without incurring permanent damage. Overtraining may, therefore, lead to an acceleration in the degeneration of the tendon.

Another important factor is a predisposition to tendon injuries from a preexisting disturbance in the tendinous matrix, due to disturbances in collagen,[9-11] in laminin, in fibronectin,[12,13] or in other components of the tendon. Injuries may be caused by previous microtrauma, systemic illnesses, or in situ treatment with corticosteroids.[14] The studies of Kannus and Józsa[15] show that more than 30% of healthy young people who died in accidents displayed pathologic disturbances in the Achilles tendon. These findings suggest that, in an urban population, degenerative disturbances of the tendons are common in individuals over 35 years old and may predispose for injuries to the tendon.

Finally, several authors, including Genety,[16] define "mistaken automatism" as a scheme describing muscular incoordination that would place the tendon under conditions of extreme tension. Inglis and Sculco[17] suggested that a failure may occur in the mechanism that regulates muscular contraction. If a subject is not in optimal physical condition and attempts to perform sports activities requiring speed and coordination, the contraction-inhibiting mechanism may be suppressed or operate incorrectly, which could lead to injury of the tendon.

Therefore, it is important to evaluate the state of the tendon's vascularization, its structure and ultrastructure, and the presence of laminin and fibronectin via immunohistochemical techniques, and to evaluate changes with aging.

Studies on Normal and Injured Tendons

Achilles tendon tissue samples were obtained from patients with spontaneous tears and from cadaver organ donors with normal tendons. The samples were evaluated using intratendinous vascularization with latex injection, structural study with the optical microscope, ultrastructural study with the electron microscope, and immunohistochemistry.

Methods

We studied the vascularization of 40 Achilles tendons from non-embalmed cadavers that were frozen at $-40°C$. The arterial tree was filled with red latex in 30 of these sections and with a radiologic contrast medium in ten sections. These 40 anatomic sections were from the lower limbs of 20 organ donors who were between 32 and 59 years old.

Microangiographic vascularization studies were performed following the injections of latex or radiologic contrast medium. The limbs receiving latex were dissected, the topographic anatomy examined, and the Achilles tendon removed. Three microscopic sections with a thickness of $10\mu m$ each were taken every 2 cm of tendon, up to a length of 12 cm from its insertion in the calcaneus. The sections were stained with Mallory's trichrome stain and examined by optical microscope. Radiographs were taken of the ten tendons that were injected with radiologic contrast medium using a Senographe 500T apparatus.

For the evaluation of the tendon's structure, 73 Achilles tendons from two large groups of patients were studied. Twenty of these tendons belonged to healthy organ donors with no pertinent medical history, who were generally victims of traffic accidents. The 53 remaining samples were from patients with spontaneous tears of the Achilles tendon who underwent surgical treatment. A sample of the tendon was removed at the level of the tear and a second sample 2 to 3 cm above it.

All sections were fixed with 10% formaldehyde, enclosed in paraffin, and sliced transversely to a thickness of $10\mu m$. Alternate sections were stained with hematoxylin-eosin and Mallory's trichrome stain. The tendon samples were sectioned in $1\ mm^3$ blocks for processing in accordance with the classic technique for transmission electron microscopy, creating semifine slices $2\mu m$ thick, and mounting them on 300-mesh grids. The preparations were observed under a Philips EM 301 transmission electron microscope.

Finally, 22 Achilles tendons were processed for the immunohistochemical study, with the goal of detecting the presence of fibronectin and laminin in the tendon. Ten of the 22 Achilles tendon samples were obtained from organ donors and the remaining 12 were from spontaneously torn tendons. The method used was that described by Ekblom and associates,[18] with enzyme digestion according to the guidelines of Burns and associates.[19]

Results of the Intratendinous Vascularization Study

Fine-grained, high-definition radiographs allowed observation of the intratendinous vascularization (Fig. 1). The radiographs of samples of complete tendons, including the paratenon, showed a nearly homogeneous distribution of arterioles that is much denser at the level of the muscle-tendon and bone-tendon attachments and somewhat less dense at the level of the free tendon. The vascularization came almost exclusively from the arterioles that are supplied from their ventral side, as can be seen in the projections of the tendon's profile.

The radiologic studies performed after extraction of the paratenon showed a marked reduction in vascularization, and marked scarcity of intratendinous arterioles at the level of the segment corresponding to the free tendon, at a distance between 2 and 6 cm from the insertion into the calcaneus. This tendinous area with reduced vascularization is of variable length. When the soleus muscle fibers descend more steeply, the free tendon is shorter in length, and the area of reduced vascularization is therefore smaller (Fig. 2). The area of reduced arterial vascularization, corresponding to the segment of free tendon, is the area that is most predisposed to tearing.

An increase in vascularization is observed at the level of insertion into the calcaneus and is caused by arterioles ascending from the calcaneus. Similarly, at the level of the muscle-tendon attachment, there is an increase in vascularization owing to descending arterioles that come from the intramuscular circulation.

In three of the ten samples, we saw the existence of a central and ventral arteriole that runs the length of the tendon in a craniocaudal direction. This arteriole gives rise to segmentary arterioles that are distributed towards the periphery in a perpendicular and dorsal direction and toward both edges of the tendon. A disordered network that followed no homogeneous pattern was seen in the remaining seven cases.

In the transverse sections studied by optical microscope, the number of intratendinous arterioles varied throughout the tendon. The mean number of vessels evaluated was significantly lower and different in configuration in the sections corresponding to a distance between 3 and 5 cm from the insertion of the tendon in the calcaneus. These data are comparable to those obtained from the radiographic study.

Results of the Structural and Ultrastructural Study

We will present separately the results obtained from the study of sections of normal tendons from organ donors and of pathologic sections from spontaneously torn Achilles tendons.

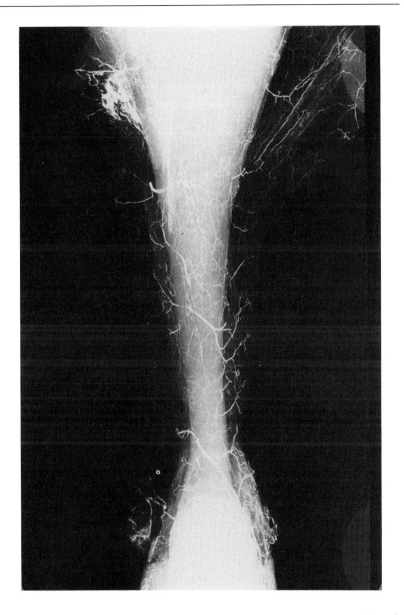

Fig. 1 *High-sensitivity and high-definition radiograph of an anatomic specimen injected with contrast medium. Observe the tendon vascularization and dissected paratenon.*

Normal Tendons   An undulation in the fibers was noted in the tendons studied. In general, the fibrillar constitution of the tendinous fibers is not visible by optical microscope, even when hydrated, because of the density of the fibrils. The elongations of the tendinous cells can be found among the fiber shafts (Fig. 3).

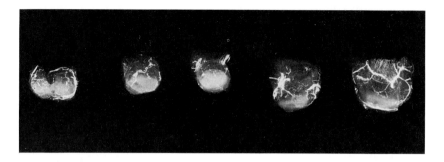

Fig. 2 *Microradiograph of Achilles tendon slices made at 2 cm intervals. From right to left, the slices are ordered proximal to distal. Observe the scarcity of vessels in the central zone of the tendon.*

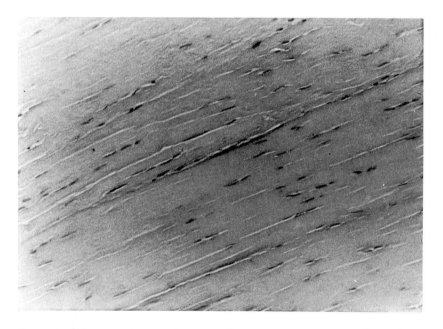

Fig. 3 *Sagittal section of a control tendon. Light microscopy (H&E × 20). Observe the longitudinal arrangement of the collagen fibers and tenocytes.*

The tendinous cells are fibrocytes adapted to the special conditions existing in the tendon, and they are present in long series between the collagen fibers. As seen under the optical microscope, the cells appear as long, flat, triangular, or rectangular formations, with an intensely basophilic cytoplasm and a rounded and slack nucleus.

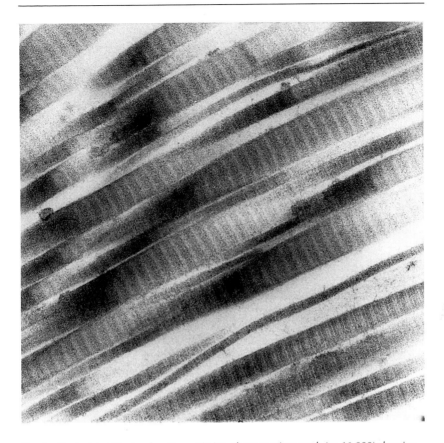

Fig. 4 *Control Achilles tendon. Transmission electron micrograph (× 16,000) showing the longitudinal and homogeneous arrangement of the collagen fibers.*

The cells are sometimes separated from each other only by very small cracks.

The tendons are formed by collagen and elastin embedded in a matrix with proteoglycans and water; the collagen forms 65% of the dry weight of the tendon. These elements are produced inside the fibroblast and are organized extracellularly in a specific three-dimensional structure. The organization of the tendinous fibers in a parallel arrangement in the longitudinal axis can be seen by optical microscope (Fig. 3).

By transmission electron microscope and by scanning electron microscope, the collagen fibers were seen to be oriented not only in a longitudinal orientation, but also horizontally and transversely (Figs. 4 and 5). Additionally, the spiral orientation of the collagen fibers can be seen by scanning electron microscope (Fig. 6). These findings were constant in all the tendons, with no discernible differences due to age or sex.

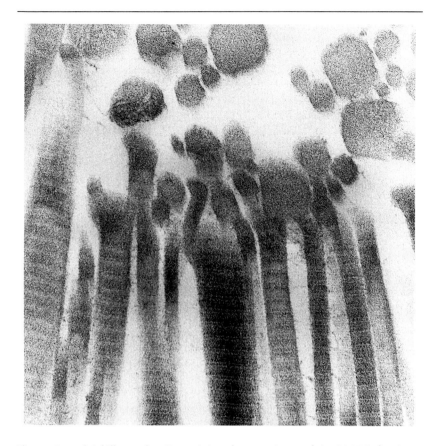

Fig. 5 *Control Achilles tendon. Transmission electron micrograph (× 20,000) showing that collagen fibers are wavy, change direction in a loopy manner, and dispose transversally to their initial course.*

Spontaneous Ruptures of the Achilles Tendon   Of the 53 samples prepared for optical microscopic study, 45 showed clear signs of a degenerative-type disturbance in the connective tissue, consisting of edema and disintegration of the connective tissue with fragmentation and fraying of the collagen fibers. This degeneration brings about an increase in the undulation of the connective tissue structure. Few nuclei were observed in the areas of degeneration. Well-preserved areas were frequently noted, alternating with areas having clearly visible degenerative lesions.

The four types of histologic disturbances found in the structure of the tendon are discussed below.

Hypoxic Degeneration   In the study by conventional optical microscope and under polarized light, as well as in transmission electron microscopy, the changes associated with hypoxic disturbances

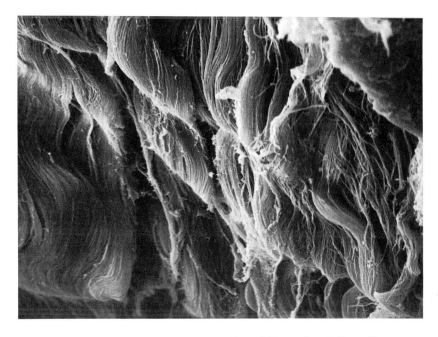

Fig. 6 *Scanning electron micrograph of a healthy Achilles tendon. Collagen fibers are ordered along the longitudinal axis and arranged in thin and regular waves.*

were obvious both in the tenocytes and in the collagen fibers. As seen by optical microscope, the hypoxic degeneration was characterized by the absence of pigmentation in the tenocyte nuclei. Electron microscopy revealed changes in the size and configuration of the tenocyte mitochondria (Fig. 7). The longitudinal disintegration of the collagen fibers was observed along with variations in their diameter and angulation.

Mucoid or Myxoid Degeneration   Some of the collagen fibers were thin and some were fragmented, while others appeared normal. The changes in the tenocytes were similar to those seen in hypoxic degeneration. The cytoplasm was occupied by large vacuoles and degranulation of the endoplasmic reticulum was frequent (Fig. 8).

Lipid Degeneration   The initial phase of fat degeneration was characterized by the appearance of small, isolated groups of adipocytes among the collagen fibers of the tendon. In more advanced phases, the adipose cells interrupted the continuity of the collagen fibers (Fig. 9).

In the initial phases, electron microscopy revealed the disappearance of the normal pattern of the collagen shafts, which were thinner in the areas where there were a greater number of adipo-

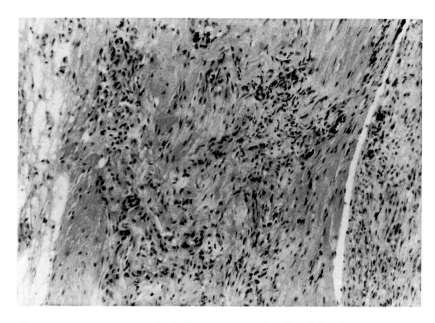

Fig. 7 *Spontaneously ruptured Achilles tendon viewed under a light microscope (H&E × 20). Changes in the collagen fibers orientation and pyknotic nuclei and longitudinal splitting in the collagen fibers are evident.*

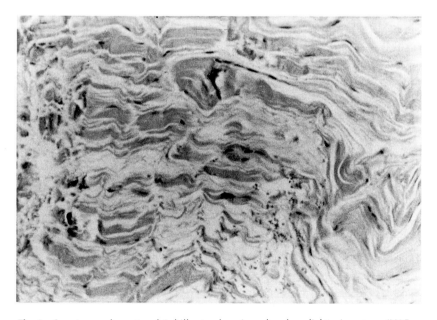

Fig. 8 *Spontaneously ruptured Achilles tendon viewed under a light microscope (H&E × 30). Pattern of myxoid degeneration can be seen.*

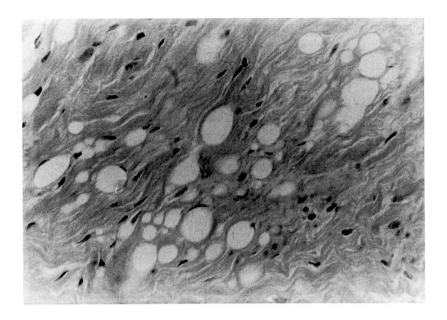

Fig. 9 *Spontaneously ruptured Achilles tendon seen under a light microscope (H&E ×
30). Pattern of lipomatous degeneration can be seen.*

cytes. In advanced phases, chains of adipocytes were formed in
three-dimensional groupings (Fig. 10).

    Tendinous Calcification   In two of our cases, we found calcium
deposits and metaplasia of the tendinous tissue in cartilage and bone
(Fig. 11). Widespread deposits of calcium were observed among the
collagen fibers and were even intimately attached to them.

Results of the Immunohistochemical Study

Laminin and fibronectin were present in the vascular walls of
Achilles tendons that were obtained from healthy subjects. The an-
tilaminin antibodies caused a deep stain in the muscle-tendon attachment. Laminin was also found in the endomysium, but not in
the perimysium, which was, however, stained with antifibronectin
antibodies. The muscle-tendon attachment revealed fibronectin deposits.

    In the sections obtained from patients with torn Achilles ten-
dons, fibronectin could be detected 6 hours after the accident at the
level of the surface of the tear. In other areas of the tendon, fibronectin was detected on the surface of the collagen fibers and on the surface of the tenocytes (Fig. 12).

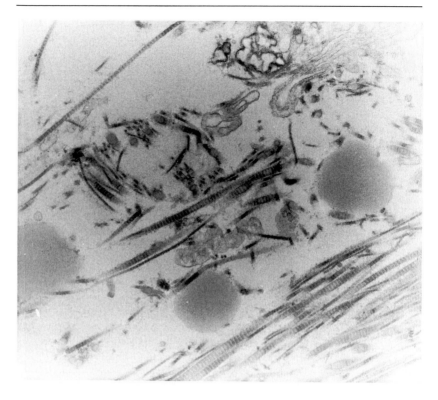

Fig. 10 *Transmission electron micrograph (× 4,200) showing spontaneously ruptured Achilles tendon. An accumulation of lipid cells is evident.*

Discussion

Various causes have been invoked in the pathogenesis of tendinous disturbances in athletes: vascular disturbances that lead to ischemia in the tendon; degenerative disturbances of the tendinous matrix, especially the collagen; genetic factors; and improper training, leading to motor muscle incoordination and lack of strength.

In general, the tendinous tissue appears to be appropriately vascularized, whether it is at the expense of the muscle-tendon attachment, the bone-tendon attachment, or the segmentary arterioles, which in the Achilles tendon proceed from the posterior tibia and the fibula. Nevertheless, we agree with Fischer and associates[20] in that this local circulation is distributed throughout the paratenon and does not generally provide significant vascularization to the inside of the tendon.

On the other hand, in accordance with Carr and Norris[5] and Schmidt-Rohlfing and associates,[8] we can also state that in the middle one third of the Achilles tendon, at a distance between 3 and 5 cm from its insertion in the calcaneus, the vascularization is less than

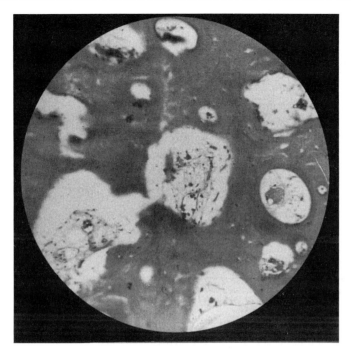

Fig. 11 *Ossification of the Achilles tendon viewed under the light microscope (H&E ×
20). Trabecular bone can be seen inside the tendon.*

in the rest of the tendon. Furthermore, this is the area of the Achilles
tendon where the majority of tears are found in athletes, and as
noted by Kannus and Józsa[15] this is the area of posterior support in
the majority of sports footwear. Tendinous vascularization is decreased in areas of friction, torsion, or compression.

All these findings suggest that when there is a reduction in tendinous vascularization, a certain ischemia of the tendon may occur,
even reaching the point of tissue necrosis, as has been seen in our
results and in those described by Kannus and Józsa.[15] This ischemia
has also been noted in the genesis of other tendon tears, such as in
the posterior tibial tendon[21] or the supraspinous tendon.[22,23]

In the studies by transmission electron microscope and scanning
electron microscope, the collagen fibers were not just arranged in a
longitudinal orientation, but were also oriented horizontally and
transversely. Fibers in a spiral pattern with the formation of loops
were also observed.

This complex three-dimensional structure is best understood if
we consider that the tendon is exposed to multidirectional loads, not
just to longitudinal loads. According to Kannus and Józsa,[15] this
three-dimensional structure forms a framework of fibers that sup-

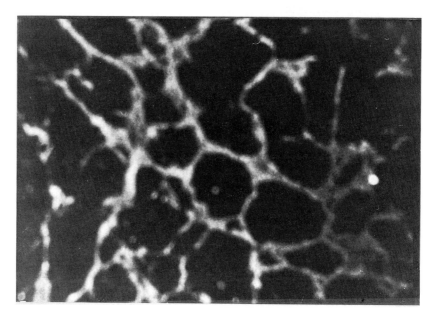

Fig. 12 *Ruptured Achilles tendon. Immunofluorescence detection of fibronectin at different levels: between bundles of fibers, over the fibers' surface, and at the breaking surface.*

ports forces in various directions, preventing the disconnection of these fibers and resultant tearing.

In all the cases of Achilles tendons that had already experienced tearing, we found preexisting pathologic disturbances, which were minimal in number in the control tendons obtained from organ donors. These observations confirm the studies of Arner and associates[24] and Kannus and Józsa,[15] among others, by affirming that the tearing of a tendon is preceded by degenerative disturbances, including degenerative tendinopathy, myxoid degeneration, fatty degeneration, or calcifying degeneration. The presence of fatty degeneration can, itself, lead to the tearing of the tendon without other degenerative changes having occurred in the collagen tissue.[15]

Hypoxic degeneration is the most frequent finding in tendons that have been torn, whether in isolation or in combination with other types of degeneration. Some authors, such as Kannus and Józsa,[15] described the existence of intramitochondrial calcification, within what they call degenerative hypoxic tendinopathy, although we were not able to observe the same condition.

In the control group of this study, with a mean age of 33.7 years, all of whom were presumably healthy at the time of their accidental deaths, slightly more than one fourth demonstrated pathologic disturbances in the Achilles tendon. These findings suggest that in an urban population such as the one studied, degenerative changes in the tendons may be frequent in subjects over 30 years of age, and it appears logical that these disturbances could predispose to tearing.

The reason for the degeneration of the tenocytes and collagen fibers, as well as the differences in the types of degeneration in the various tendons, is unknown. Nevertheless, current evidence suggests that the decrease in arterial oxygen supply, with the consequent tissue hypoxia and the resulting effects on the metabolism and nutrition of the tendon, can be inciting factors.[25]

The presence of laminin, which we found at the level of the muscle-tendon attachment and the endomysium in healthy tendons, is not predictive of a pathologic tendon, while the presence of fibronectin in the surface of the collagen fibers or the tenocytes is an indicator of the degeneration of these structures. We agree with Kvist and associates[12] that the presence of fibronectin confirms the existence of immature collagen tissue that leaves the chronically inflamed tendon vulnerable to tearing.

References

1. Sandelin J, Kiviluoto O, Santavirta S, et al: Outcome of sports injuries treated in a casualty department. *Br J Sports Med* 1985;19:103-106.

2. Józsa L, Kvist M, Balint BJ, et al: The role of recreational sport activity in Achilles tendon rupture: A clinical, pathoanatomical, and sociological study of 292 cases. *Am J Sports Med*, 1989;17:338-343.

3. Williams JG. Achilles tendon lesions in sport. *Sports Med* 1986;3:114-135.

4. Gale DW, Dias JJ, Khokhar AA, et al: Operative or conservative treatment of closed rupture of the Tendo-Achilles? *J Bone Joint Surg* 1992;74B(suppl II):142-143.

5. Carr AJ, Norris SH: The blood supply of the calcaneal tendon. *J Bone Joint Surg* 1989;71B:100-101.

6. Graf J, Schneider U, Niethard FU: Microcirculation of the Achilles tendon and significance of the paratenon: A study with the plastination method. *Handchir Mikrochir Plast Chir* 1990;22:163-166.

7. Backman C, Boquist L, Friden J, et al: Chronic Achilles paratenonitis with tendinosis: An experimental model in the rabbit. *J Orthop Res* 1990;8:541-547.

8. Schmidt-Rohlfing B, Graf J, Schneider U, et al: The blood supply of the Achilles tendon. *Int Orthop* 1992;16:29-31.

9. Di Stefano VJ: Pathogenesis and diagnosis of the ruptured Achilles tendon. *Orthop Rev* 1975,4:17-18.

10. Coombs RRH, Klenerman L, Narcisi P, et al: Collagen typing in Achilles tendon rupture. *J Bone Joint Surg* 1980;62B:258.

11. Holz, U: Achilles tendon rupture and achillodynia: The importance of tissue regeneration. *Fortschr Med* 1980;98:1517-1520.

12. Kvist MH, Lehto MU, Józsa L, et al: Chronic Achilles paratenonitis: An immunohistologic study of fibronectin and fibrinogen. *Am J Sports Med* 1988;16:616-623.

13. Józsa L, Lehto M, Kannus P, et al: Fibronectin and laminin in Achilles tendon. *Acta Orthop Scand* 1989;60:469-471.

14. Newnham DM, Douglas JG, Legge JS, et al: Achilles tendon rupture: An underrated complication of corticosteroid treatment. *Thorax* 1991;46:853-854.

15. Kannus P, Józsa L: Histopathological changes preceding spontaneous rupture of a tendon: A controlled study of 891 patients. *J Bone Joint Surg* 1991;73A:1507-1525.

16. Genety J: La tendinite et la rupture du tendon d'Achille. *Cah Méd Lyon* 1972;48:1639-1644.

17. Inglis AE, Sculco TP: Surgical repair of ruptures of the tendo Achillis. *Clin Orthop* 1981;156:160-169.

18. Ekblom P, Miettinen M, Rapola J, et al: Demonstration of laminin, a basement membrane glycoprotein, in routinely processed formalin-fixed human tissues. *Histochemistry* 1982;75:301-307.

19. Burns J, Dixon AJ, Woods JC: Immunoperoxidase localisation of fibronectin in glomeruli of formalin-fixed paraffin processed renal tissue. *Histochemistry* 1980;67:73-78.

20. Fischer LP, Carret JP, Gonon GP, et al: Vascularisation arterielle du ligament rotulien (ligamentum patellae) et du tendon d'Achille (tendo calcaneus) chez l'homme. (Arterial vascularization of the patellar ligament (ligamentum patellase) and of the Achilles tendon (tendo calcaneous) in man.) *Bull Assoc Anat* 1976;60:323-334.

21. Frey C, Shereff M, Greenidge N: Vascularity of the posterior tibial tendon. *J Bone Joint Surg* 1990;72A:884-888.

22. Ling SC, Chen CF, Wan RX: A study on the vascular supply of the supraspinatus tendon. *Surg Radiol Anat* 1990;12:161-165.

23. Lohr JF, Uhthoff HK: The microvascular pattern of the supraspinatus tendon. *Clin Orthop* 1990;254:35-38.

24. Arner O, Lindholm A, Orell SR: Histologic changes in subcutaneous rupture of the Achilles tendon: A study of 74 cases. *Acta Chir Scand* 1958;116:484-490.

25. Hess GP, Cappiello WL, Poole RM, et al: Prevention and treatment of overuse tendon injuries. *Sports Med* 1989;8:371-384.

Chapter 10

The Response of Ligaments to Exercise

Joseph A. Buckwalter, MD
Savio L-Y. Woo, PhD

Skeletal ligaments and joint capsules help to guide normal joint motion and prevent abnormal motion. They may also have sensory functions, such as providing joint proprioception and initiating protective reflexes.[1,2] The ability to perform the rapid, repetitive joint movements required in sports and other types of vigorous exercise depends on the ability of ligaments and joint capsules to stabilize joints throughout their range of motion. Frequently, recreational or competitive sports result in ligament or joint capsule sprains or tears that cause pain and may compromise joint stability. Compromised joint stability may limit an individual's participation in sports, and significant joint instability may result in degeneration of the affected joint.[3,4]

Ligament strength, and possibly the ability of ligaments to respond to exercise by increasing ligament strength, decreases with age.[5-7] These changes may increase the probability of injury. Understanding age-related changes in ligaments is fundamental for clarifying the effects and roles of exercise and sports for midlife and older individuals and also for directing future investigations into the response of ligaments to exercise.

This chapter first summarizes current information on the structure, composition, and mechanical properties of ligaments. The second section describes the response of ligaments to loading, and the final section addresses age-related changes in ligaments and the response of ligaments to exercise. Joint capsules have not been studied as extensively as ligaments, but because ligaments and joint capsules are similar in structure, composition, and in some instances function, much of the information concerning ligaments may also apply to joint capsules.

Ligament Structure

Skeletal ligaments vary in length, shape, and thickness. Many ligaments, such as the anterior cruciate ligament, form discrete, easily identifiable structures with distinct mechanical functions. Others, such as the hip joint capsular ligaments, blend with the joint capsule, making their exact structure and function difficult to define. Some ligaments cross joints with wide ranges of motion, such as the hip and glenohumeral joints; others cross joints with little or no normal motion, such as the sacroiliac and the proximal tibiofibular joints. Grossly, ligaments appear as firm, white fibrous bands, sheets, or thickened strips of joint capsule securely anchored to bone. They consist of a proximal bone insertion, the substance of the ligament or capsule, and a distal bone insertion.

Ligament Substance

Bundles or sheets of collagen fibrils form the bulk of ligament substance.[2,8-10] Some ligaments, including the anterior cruciate ligament, consist of more than one band of collagen fibril bundles; as the joint moves, different bands become taut.[11] The alignment of collagen-fiber bundles within ligament substance generally follows the lines of tension applied to the ligament during normal activities. However, examination under a light microscope shows that these bundles may also have a wave or "crimp" pattern. The "crimp" pattern of matrix organization may allow for slight elongation of the ligament with minimal tension.[10] In some regions, ligament cells align themselves in rows between collagen-fiber bundles, but in other regions the alignment of the cells appears unrelated to the alignment of the matrix collagen fibers. Scattered blood vessels penetrate the ligament substance to form small-diameter, longitudinal vascular channels that lie parallel to the collagen-fiber bundles. Nerve fibers lie next to some vessels, and nerve endings with the structure of mechanoreceptors have been found in some ligaments.[1,2,8]

Ligament Insertions

Ligament insertions attach the flexible ligament substance to the rigid bone and allow motion between the bone and the ligament without damaging the ligament. Despite their small size, ligament insertions are more variable and elaborate in structure than ligament substance,[2,12-16] and they may also have different mechanical properties than ligament substance. Measurement of ligament-bone complex deformation with tension shows that insertions or ligament regions near insertions deform more than ligament substance.[17]

Ligament insertions vary in size and strength, in the angle of collagen-fiber bundles relative to bone, and in the proportion of collagen fibers that penetrate directly into bone.[2,13-16] Based on the angle between the collagen fibrils and the bone, and the proportion of the collagen fibers that penetrate directly into bone, ligament insertions are classified as either direct or indirect insertions.

Direct Insertions   Direct insertions into bone, such as the femoral insertion of the medial collateral ligament or the tibial insertion of the anterior cruciate ligament of the knee, consist of sharply defined regions where the ligament appears to pass directly into the cortex of the bone.[2,12,13,16,18] The interdigitation of collagen fibrils with bone matrix makes the bond between the ligament and the bone extremely strong. Surgical attempts to separate a ligament with a direct insertion from the bone by applying tension or by elevating the periosteum usually fail unless the ligament substance is cut through the region next to the insertion.

In direct insertions, a thin layer of superficial ligament collagen fibers joins the fibrous layer of the periosteum, but most of the ligament insertion consists of deeper fibers that directly penetrate the cortex, often at right angles to the bone surface. In ligaments that approach the bone surface at a right angle, the collagen fibers follow a straight line into the bone, but in ligaments that approach the bone surface at an oblique angle, the collagen fibers make a sharp turn to enter the insertion. The angle of collagen fibril insertion may not be apparent from gross examination. For example, the medial collateral ligament of the femur approaches the surface of the femur obliquely; grossly it appears to insert at a 50° to 70° angle, but microscopic examination shows that the collagen fibers of the ligament enter the bone at about a 90° angle.

The deeper collagen fibers pass through four zones, each with increasing stiffness[2,12,13,16,18] as follows: ligament substance, fibrocartilage, mineralized fibrocartilage, and bone. In the fibrocartilage zone, the cells become larger and more spherical than the cells in most regions of the ligament substance. A sharp border of mineralized and unmineralized matrix separates the fibrocartilage zone from the mineralized fibrocartilage zone. From this latter zone, the ligament collagen fibers pass into the bone and blend with the bone collagen fibers.

Indirect Insertions   Indirect or oblique ligament insertions into bone,[2,12,13,16,18,19] such as the tibial insertion of the medial collateral ligament or the femoral insertion of the lateral collateral ligament of the knee, are less common than direct insertions. These insertions usually cover more bone surface area than direct insertions, and their boundaries cannot be easily defined because the ligament passes obliquely along the bone surface, rather than directly into the cortex. Ligaments with indirect insertions into bone can often be lifted from the bone by elevating the periosteum, and they may not have a fibrocartilage zone.

Like direct insertions, indirect insertions have both superficial and deep collagen fibers, but the superficial collagen fibers passing into the fibrous layer of the periosteum form most of the substance of indirect insertions. The deeper fibers of indirect insertions approach the bone cortex at oblique angles, and they do not pass through well-defined fibrocartilage zones.

The structure of indirect insertions, particularly the distribution of ligament fibers between bone and periosteum, may change with skeletal development, altering the mechanical properties of the insertions. A study of the maturation of the rabbit medial collateral ligament insertion into the tibia showed that with skeletal growth more of the ligament collagen fibers enter the bone, decreasing the contribution of the periosteal component to the insertion.[19] Aging changes in the periosteum may also alter the structure and mechanical properties of the insertions.[16]

Ligament Composition

Ligaments consist of fibroblasts surrounded by an extracellular matrix, which is formed by two components: a solid, highly ordered arrangement of macromolecules, primarily type I collagen, and water, which fills the macromolecular framework.[2,9] The composition of the matrix, the organization of the matrix macromolecules, and the interaction between the matrix macromolecules and the tissue water determine the mechanical properties of the tissue.

Although the exact composition of many ligaments has not been determined, the available evidence shows that different ligaments and even different regions within the same ligament may vary slightly in matrix composition and in cell shape and density, and that ligament composition may change slightly with age.[2,9,20,21] The matrix composition of ligaments can also change in response to changes in the mechanical environment.

Cells

Fibroblasts form the dominant cells of ligaments, although the endothelial cells of small vessels and nerve cell processes also exist within ligament substance.[2,9,12-15,22] Fibroblasts form and maintain the extracellular matrix. They vary in shape, activity, and density among ligaments, among regions of the same ligament, and with the age of the tissue.[2,9,12-15,22] Many fibroblasts have long, small-diameter cell processes that extend between collagen fibrils and may contact other cells.[9,13]

Ligaments in younger individuals have a higher concentration of cells that synthesize new matrix. These cells frequently have a large volume of cytoplasm, which contains vast amounts of endoplasmic reticulum. With increasing age, the cells become less active; but at any age, they synthesize the matrix macromolecules necessary to maintain the structure and function of the tissue.

Integrins, a specialized group of transmembrane proteins, link actin-containing components of the cell cytoskeleton to the matrix molecules. In addition to mechanically binding the cell to the matrix, these proteins help mediate a variety of cell functions, including migration, proliferation, and possibly the synthetic response of the cell to changes in matrix composition.

Matrix Water

Tissue fluid contributes 60% to 70% of the wet weight of most ligaments. Because many ligament cells lie at some distance from vessels, these cells must depend on diffusion of nutrients and metabolites through the tissue fluid. In addition, the interaction of the tissue fluid and the matrix macromolecules influences the mechanical properties of the tissue.

Matrix Macromolecules

Four classes of molecules (collagens, elastin, proteoglycans, and noncollagenous proteins) form the molecular framework of the ligament matrix and contribute about 30% to 40% of the wet weight of most ligaments.[2,9,12] Elastin and most of the collagens form fibrils. The proteoglycans and noncollagenous proteins assume a variety of forms and lie on or between the collagen and elastin fibrils.

Collagens Collagen fibers, which give ligaments their form and tensile strength, constitute 70% to 80% of ligament dry weight.[2,9,12,23] Type I collagen is the major component of ligament molecular framework, contributing more than 90% of the ligament collagen. Type III collagen contributes about 10% of the ligament collagen, and small amounts of other collagen types may be present as well. Type I collagen is also the primary structural component of the tendon matrix, but tendons have less type III collagen.[21]

Elastin Most ligaments have little elastin (usually less than 5%), but a few ligaments, such as the nuchal ligament and the ligamentum flavum, have high concentrations of elastin.[2,12] Elastin can form fibrils that lie parallel to adjacent collagen fibrils. However, the elastin fibrils lack the cross-banding pattern of collagen fibers and differ in amino acid composition. Elastin contains desmosine and isodesmosine, two amino acids not found in collagens. Also, unlike collagens, the elastin amino acid chains assume random coil conformations when the molecules are not loaded. This conformation of the amino acid chains makes it possible for elastin to undergo some deformation without rupturing or tearing, and then when unloaded, return to its original size and shape.

Proteoglycans Proteoglycans consist of small amounts of protein bound to negatively charged polysaccharide chains referred to as glycosaminoglycans. Unlike articular cartilage, in which proteoglycans form a large part of the macromolecular framework (commonly about 30% to 35% of the cartilage dry weight), they form only a small portion of the ligament macromolecular framework (usually less than 1% of the ligament dry weight).[9] Nonetheless, proteoglycans have an important role in organizing the extracellular matrix and in interacting with the tissue fluid.[2,12,24-30] Most ligaments have a higher concentration of glycosaminoglycans than tendons.[21]

Like tendons, menisci, and articular cartilage, ligaments contain two known classes of proteoglycans: large, articular cartilage-type proteoglycans that have long, negatively charged chains of chondroitin and keratan sulfate and smaller proteoglycans that contain dermatan sulfate.[2,12,23,25,31,32] Because of their long chains of negative charges, the large articular cartilage-type proteoglycans tend to expand in solution until restrained by the collagen fibril network. As a result, they maintain water within the tissue and exert a swelling pressure, which contributes to the mechanical properties of the tissue and fills the regions between collagen fibrils.

Unlike the large, aggregating proteoglycans, the small dermatan sulfate proteoglycans do not appear to contribute directly to the mechanical properties of the tissue. These small proteoglycans usually lie on the surface of the collagen fibrils and appear to affect the formation, organization, and stability of the extracellular matrix, including the formation and diameter of collagen fibrils.[30-32] These molecules may also affect the ability of mesenchymal cells to repair ligament injuries. They can inhibit the adhesion of fibroblasts to other matrix macromolecules (especially the noncollagenous protein fibronectin) and, hence, may limit the ability of the cells to bind to the matrix and form new tissue.[31]

Noncollagenous Proteins   These molecules consist primarily of protein, but many of them also contain a few monosaccharides and oligosaccharides.[2,9,12,31] Although noncollagenous proteins contribute only a few percent to the dry weight of ligaments, they appear to help organize and maintain the macromolecular framework of the matrix, help cells adhere to the matrix molecular framework, and possibly influence cell function.

One noncollagenous protein, fibronectin, has been identified in ligament extracellular matrix. This protein may associate with several matrix component molecules as well as blood vessels. Fibronectins examined by electron microscopy appear as fine filaments or granules coating the surfaces of collagen fibrils or cell membranes. Other noncollagenous proteins undoubtedly exist within the ligament matrix, but their identities and functions have not yet been defined.

Mechanical Properties of Ligaments

Ligaments and joint capsules have specialized mechanical properties, which include tensile strength and stiffness, anisotropy, nonlinear response to loading, and viscoelasticity. The characteristics of these properties depend on the composition and organization of the ligament matrix.[33-35] The high concentration of type I collagen fibrils gives ligaments great tensile stiffness and strength. The anisotropy and nonlinear response to loading of ligaments result from the ordered arrangement of the collagen fibrils. The viscoelasticity of ligaments results from the interaction of the matrix macromolecules with the tissue fluid.

Anisotropy

The alignment of ligament collagen fibrils, usually parallel to the long axis of the ligament and extending from the proximal insertion to the distal insertion, makes the tissue uniquely stiff and strong in resisting loading along this axis compared with other axes (ie, anisotropic).[5,35-37] For example, ligaments have a greater modulus and tensile strength in the direction parallel to the predominant collagen fibril orientation than in the direction perpendicular to the predominant collagen fibril orientation.

Nonlinear Response to Tension Loading

The wave or "crimp" pattern of ligament collagen fibrils contributes to the nonlinear mechanical behavior of the tissue.[5,35-37] Subjecting a ligament to progressively increasing tension first straightens the "crimp" pattern. Because the "crimp" pattern varies among the collagen-fibril bundles, increasing tensile deformation of a ligament "recruits" additional fibrils to resist the stress, thereby increasing the number of loaded collagen fibrils with greater tissue elongation. "Recruiting" more collagen fibrils increases the tissue stiffness and makes the stress-strain curve nonlinear.

Viscoelasticity   Like many biologic soft tissues, ligament tissue is viscoelastic[5,35-37]; that is, its response to loading combines viscosity with elasticity. When loaded, viscoelastic materials respond with "creep" and stress relaxation. "Creep" refers to the increase in ligament deformation with time under constant load. Stress relaxation refers to the decline in ligament stress over time under constant deformation. These behaviors occur as a result of realignment of matrix macromolecules and flow of fluid in the matrix.

Viscoelasticity allows ligaments to change their properties during exercise. For example, during continuous running, the repetitive ligament strains and strain rates are nearly constant. Cyclic stress relaxation softens ligament substance, so that peak stress progressively decreases with exercise. This reduction in peak stress may help to prevent fatigue failure. Ligament deformation also increases slightly during cycles to a constant load. This "creep" behavior may increase the laxity and motion of exercised joints. Once an individual has stopped exercising, the ligaments and joint capsules return to normal stiffness and length.

Response of Ligaments to Exercise

Maintenance of ligament structure, composition, and function depends on the response of the tissue to the repetitive loading that results from exercise. In addition, the structure, composition, and mechanical properties of ligaments change with increased training (exercise), decreased training and immobilization, overuse, and aging.

The type, intensity, and frequency of loading needed to maintain the normal composition, structure, and mechanical properties of most tissues vary widely. Moderate increases or decreases in training generally do not cause detectable alterations in the tissues; however, when the intensity and frequency of training exceeds or falls below the levels necessary to maintain the tissue, the balance between synthesis and degradation changes, causing modifications in the mechanical properties of the tissue.

Changes in the patterns of training can strengthen or weaken normal ligaments, and controlled loading and motion can speed rehabilitation and repair of injured tissues.[38] However, repetitive loading that exceeds the ability of the tissues to adapt may cause "overuse" injuries.[39] Excessive, premature, or uncontrolled loading of repair tissue can inhibit or disrupt repair.[38] Mesenchymal cells, including ligament fibroblasts, respond to persistent changes in tissue stresses and strains from external loadings by changing the balance between their synthetic and degradative activity, and in at least some tissues, their proliferative activity and the organization of the tissue. In general, decreased stresses and strains reduce cell synthetic function and matrix organization, while increased stresses and strains, up to a critical level, enhance cell synthetic function and matrix organization. Stresses and strains above the critical level will disrupt the tissue or cause tissue degeneration.[39]

Mechanisms of Ligament Adaptation to Changes in Loading

For the last 25 years, studies have documented the effects of exercise on bone, tendon, ligament, and cartilage; recent investigations on isolated tissues and cells have shown that various types and intensities of repetitive loading influence cell shape and cell synthetic and proliferative functions.[40-44] Research has further shown that loading alters the alignment of the matrix,[45] that the matrix can transmit loads to cells, and that cells can realign the matrix macromolecules in response to the loads.[44,46] Despite these advances in the ability to show the results of cyclic mechanical forces on cells and tissues, the systemic and local mechanisms of tissue responses to repetitive loading remain poorly understood.

Systemic Mechanisms of Adaptation

Regular exercise causes systemic changes, including alterations in vascular perfusion, metabolism, collagen turnover,[47] and hormonal balance. These changes may influence the adaptive response of specific tissues to repetitive loading, possibly by altering the sensitivity of the tissues to cyclic loads. The influence of systemic changes on local tissue responses to repetitive loading has not been studied, in part due to difficulties in isolating the potential effects of different systemic changes associated with exercise.

Local Mechanisms of Adaptation

One local mechanism of adaptation is that cells detect repetitive tissue stress and strain and respond by modifying the tissue. Studies of the local effects of tissue loading show that cells may detect their own deformation or alterations in the matrix due to deformation. Cyclic stretching or compressing of mesenchymal cells can align intracellular microfilaments along the axis of tension, change cell shape,[48,49] and alter the synthesis of DNA, matrix molecules, and prostaglandins.[41,50-57] Deformation of the matrix can alter matrix macromolecular organization, fluid flow, streaming currents, pressure gradients, and electrical fields. These matrix alterations can also influence cell function.[45,50,53,58-61] Tissue loading can also affect vascular perfusion and diffusion through the matrix, thereby influencing the flow of nutrients and metabolites.[62] Cells may also sense and respond to deformation of or damage to matrix macromolecules that result from repetitive loading.

The Response of Normal Ligaments to Decreased Exercise

Decreased loading and motion changes the composition, morphology, and mechanical properties of ligaments. Unloading dense fibrous tissues that normally resist tensile stresses alters matrix turnover so that with time, matrix degradation exceeds formation. The newly synthesized matrix is less well organized or aligned along the lines of stress, and as a result, tissue stiffness and strength decline. Figure 1 shows the loss of mechanical properties in the medial collateral ligament of a rabbit following 9 weeks of joint immobilization. Other studies show that prolonged immobilization (usually 6 weeks or more) decreases the glycosaminoglycan and water content of ligamentous, capsular, and tendinous tissue, decreases the degree of orientation of the matrix collagen fibrils, and may increase collagen cross-linking.[2,63-75] With prolonged immobilization, total ligament collagen mass and ligament stiffness decline. In a study using rat limbs, decreased use due to denervation increased matrix turnover and caused a net loss of ligament collagen mass. Collagen synthesis and degradation both increased, so the proportion of new collagen to old collagen increased, but collagen

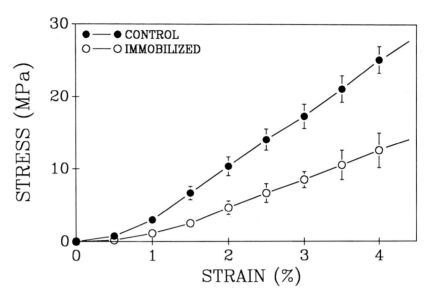

Fig. 1 *Mechanical properties of normal and immobilized rabbit medial collateral ligaments. Notice that immobilization for 9 weeks decreased tensile strength and tangent modulus (measured as the slope between 2% and 4% strain). (Modified with permission from Woo SL-Y, Gomez MA, Sites TJ, et al: The biomechanical and morphological changes in the medial collateral ligament of the rabbit after immobilization and remobilization. J Bone Joint Surg 1987;69A:1200-1211.)*

synthesis did not balance collagen degradation, resulting in a net loss of collagen.[76]

The type of exercise necessary to maintain ligament composition, structure, and function has not been clearly defined. Allowing active joint motion in dogs while preventing weightbearing for 8 weeks decreased bone density, but did not cause resorption or weakening of the knee ligaments.[76] These results suggest that maintaining structural and mechanical properties in bone requires weightbearing. However, maintaining the composition and mechanical properties of ligaments is possible, for at least 2 months, with loading from muscle contractions and active motion.

Decreased loading also alters ligament insertions into bone.[2,16,18,77-79] The extent and severity of the alterations depend to some degree on the type of ligament insertion. Decreased loading due to immobilization usually produces more extensive changes in periosteal or indirect insertions. In these insertions, subperiosteal osteoclasts resorb much of the bony insertion of ligaments during prolonged immobilization. This resorption leaves the ligament attached primarily to periosteum.[12,13,16] In direct insertions, resorption occurs around the insertion site, and relatively little occurs within the insertion. The cruciate ligaments are examples of direct ligament insertions, and the tibial insertion of the medial collateral ligament is an example of the periosteal or indirect insertion. Prolonged immobilization causes bone resorption around the periphery of the cruciate ligament insertions, but only limited resorptive activity beneath the insertion site and in the zone of mineralized fibrocartilage.[77,78] In contrast, prolonged immobilization causes significant diffuse resorption of the bony part of the tibial insertion of the medial collateral ligament.[16,18,79] These changes, particularly those in the periosteal or indirect insertions, weaken the bone ligament junction significantly within 6 to 8 weeks of immobilization.

Following resumption of normal joint loading, the cells in the insertion site begin to form new bone and to restore the structural and mechanical properties of the insertions. Complete restoration of the structure and strength of the insertion site following 9 weeks of immobilization requires an extended period of active loading.[73] The optimal rehabilitation program to restore ligament insertion strength following immobilization has not been defined, but the available evidence suggests that complete restoration of normal ligament insertion structure and mechanical properties may require up to 1 year of activity following 6 weeks or more of immobilization.[18,77-79] Muscle contractions alone probably will not prevent the changes due to decreased ligament loading, since in one experiment isotonic exercises during immobilization did not prevent weakening of ligament insertions.[77]

The Response of Normal Ligaments to Increased Exercise

Ligament insertions, especially periosteal or indirect insertions, become stronger with exercise and may be more responsive to changes in loading than ligament substance.[35,69] However, studies show that exercise can increase the strength, size, matrix organization, and possibly the collagen content of ligaments.[16,38,45,61,67-69,73,74,80-88] These studies cannot separate the systemic effects of exercise from the local effects of repetitive loading on the tissues, yet investigations of the response of dense fibrous tissues to loading show that the tissues respond directly to increased loadings. The application of tension to cultured tendons increased protein and DNA synthesis,[56] and a recent in vivo study showed that increased loading alone can increase ligament strength.[75,89,90] Insertion of a small pin under the medial collateral ligaments in rabbits increased the in situ load of the ligaments at 90° of flexion by 200% to 350%. The presence of the pin for 6 weeks significantly altered the ligament properties; ultimate load increased 26% and ultimate elongation increased 33%.

Changes induced by long-term exercise are equally important, but only limited data are available. One study found that prolonged exercise affected the biomechanical properties of the bone medial collateral ligament complex.[91] One-year-old swine were trained for 12 months on a schedule of 1 h/day at 1.6 m/s plus 0.5 h every other day

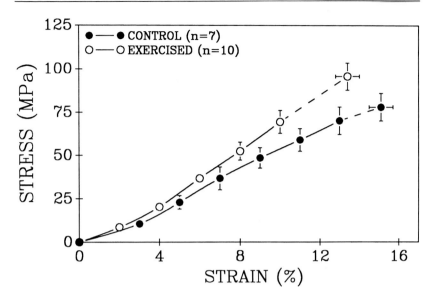

Fig. 2 *Stress-strain curves of control and exercised swine medial collateral ligaments. Exercise for 1 year increased tangent modulus (measured between 4% and 10% strain) slightly, increased tensile strength by 20%, and increased ultimate strain by 10%. (Reproduced with permission from Woo SL-Y, Wang CW, Newton PO, et al: The response of ligaments to stress deprivation and stress enhancement: Biomechanical studies, in Daniel D, Akeson W, O'Connor J (eds): Knee Ligaments: Structure, Function, Injury, and Repair. New York, NY, Raven Press, 1990, pp 337-350.)*

at 2.2 m/s, based on a 5-day/week regimen. Age-matched control swine were allowed ad lib activity in 1.5- × 3-m cages during this time. Tensile testing showed that this long-term exercise program induced increases in the structural properties of the medial collateral ligament bone complex: the ultimate load increased from 945 ± 74 N to 1008 ± 83 N. These values were not significantly different, but when normalized to body weight, a 38% increase was shown. There was also a 14% increase in the linear stiffness, but ultimate deformation remained unaffected. Figure 2 shows the stress-strain characteristics of the medial collateral ligament substance. The long-term exercise program produced slight increases in modulus (the linear slope measured between 4% and 10% strain), a 20% increase in ultimate tensile strength, and a 10% increase in ultimate strain.

These findings provide the basis for a hypothesis that schematically describes the homeostatic responses for connective tissues such as tendons and ligaments (Fig. 3). The relationship between the level and duration of stress and motion, and the resulting changes in tissue properties and tissue mass, can be represented by a series of nonlinear curves. With stress and motion deprivation (immobilization), a rapid reduction in tissue properties and mass may occur. The changes resulting from exercise training are not as pronounced.

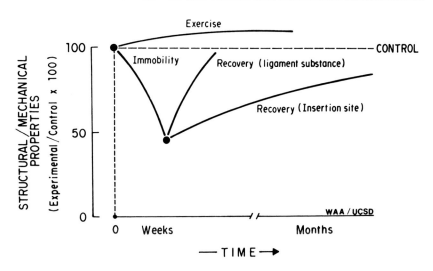

Fig. 3 *Schematic representation of the time course and magnitude of the responses of the bone-ligament-bone complex when subjected to different levels of physical activity. (Reproduced with permission from Woo SL-Y, Gomez MA, Sites TJ, et al: The biomechanical and morphological changes in the medial collateral ligament of the rabbit after immobilization and remobilization. J Bone Joint Surg 1987;69A:1200-1211.)*

In terms of recovery following immobilization, differences have been observed in the response of the individual tissue constituents and the ligament-bone complex as a whole. The functional integrity of the uninjured, immobilized ligament returns to normal characteristics quite rapidly following remobilization. However, the recovery of the ligament-bone insertion is much slower than that of the ligament substance. It takes many months for ligament insertion sites to remodel before returning to their normal properties.

Dense, fibrous tissues respond not only to changes in intensity and frequency of loading, but to changes in the type of loading. This tissue response has been studied most extensively in tendons. Tendon regions regularly subjected to tension during normal activities differ from regions regularly subjected to compression when tissue structure, matrix composition, and cell synthetic activity are compared.[92-94] Tendon regions subjected primarily to tension consist of linearly arranged dense collagen fibrils and elongated cells; they have a lower proteoglycan concentration, different proportions of proteoglycan types, and a higher rate of collagen synthesis than regions subjected to both compression and tension.[93-97] Tendon regions subjected primarily to compression consist of a network of collagen fibrils separated by a proteoglycan-containing matrix and more rounded cells than those found in tension-bearing regions. The cells of these compression regions synthesize larger proteoglycans than the cells of the tension-bearing regions.[94] These differences may be caused, at least in part, by differences in the type of loading. Subjecting tendons to compression increased the hyaluronic acid and chondroitin sulfate content, while applying tension to the same tendon decreased the glycosaminoglycan content.[93] Like tendons, ligaments and even regions of the same ligament vary in thickness, matrix composition, and water content.[9,20] Presumably, at least some of these differences result from adaptation to differences in loading.

The Response of Injured Ligaments to Exercise

Controlled loading applied at the optimal time during healing of ligaments and other dense fibrous tissue structures can promote healing.[12,38,67-69,98-109] Tensile loading of tendon repair tissue appears to align the repair cells and matrix collagen fibrils parallel to the line of tension.[40,110] Without tensile loading, repair tissue cells and matrix collagen fibrils fail to form a discernible pattern.

Loading may also alter the rate of tendon repair.[111] Three weeks following injury, surgically repaired tendons treated with early loading and motion had twice the strength of repaired tendons treated with immobilization.[100] Twelve weeks following injury, repaired tendons treated with early mobilization still had greater strength than repaired tendons treated with an initial period of immobilization. Controlled loading and motion soon after injury can also accelerate ligament repair by increasing the wet and dry weights of injured ligaments, improving matrix organization, and inducing more rapid return of normal tissue DNA content, collagen synthesis, and strength.[101,108,112,113]

Excessive or uncontrolled loading of injured tissues disrupts repair tissue, which may cause further damage and delay or prevent repair.[38] In a study of medial collateral ligament healing in rats, forced exercise increased the strength of ligament repair tissue in stable knees[98]; however, in unstable knees, forced exercise failed to increase the stiffness and strength of the repair tissue, but did increase joint instability. Another study of the effects of anterior cruciate ligament transection showed that temporary immobilization of the knee prevented the development of osteophytes, suggesting that early motion following injury may result in increased instability.[114]

Age-Related Changes in Ligaments

With increasing age, many individuals who participate in regular, vigorous exercise report frequent ligament and joint capsule sprains. Some individuals also notice that sprains remain painful longer. Some of these changes may result from age-related alterations in ligaments and joint capsules.

Age-Related Changes in Ligament Properties

Studies of ligaments have shown age-related deterioration of the mechanical and structural properties of ligaments.[5,6,115,116] In particular, these studies suggest that the strength and stiffness of ligaments decline with age, making ligament injury more likely.

The importance of age-related changes in the properties of the femur-anterior cruciate ligament-tibia complex (FATC) was addressed by Noyes and Grood,[6] who found that tensile stress and strain energy to failure of younger specimens (16 to 26 years) were two to three times greater than those for older specimens (48 to 86 years). Rauch and associates[117] recently tested human FATC from donors ranging in age from 17 to 84 years and reported similar trends with increasing age. In a study investigating the effects of both age and specimen orientation during testing on FATC properties,[5] age was again shown to have a profound effect on the FATC structural properties. For specimens tested in a more physiologic position, the ultimate load at failure of the younger group (22 to 35 years) was approximately 50% higher than that of the middle-aged group (40 to 50 years), and more than three times higher than that of the older group (60-97 years). The linear stiffness and energy absorbed at failure followed similar trends.

Because the anterior cruciate ligament is geometrically complex, the structural response is sensitive to the orientation in which loading is applied.[5] A physiologic orientation, in which the normal angles of ligament insertion to bone were maintained, resulted in significantly higher ultimate load and linear stiffness than a nonphysiologic orientation. This may be because more of the fiber bundles of the anterior cruciate ligament were simultaneously loaded when tested in the physiologic orientation. The mode of failure of the FATC was found to depend on the orientation during testing. For younger specimens, tibial avulsions were found only in the nonphysiologic orientation. With increasing age, more avulsions were found in both orientations, suggesting that although the ligament tissue had deteriorated with age, the bone had become the "weak link."

Age-Related Changes in Ligament Response to Loading

The mechanism responsible for the age-related changes in ligament properties remains uncertain. Because age-related changes resemble those associated with decreased activity, it is possible that decreased exercise leads to the age-related decline in ligament properties. However, it is also possible that the loss of strength results from a decline in the ability of the ligament cells to replace the matrix macromolecules or a decrease in their ability to respond to exercise.

Connective tissues from skeletally immature individuals appear more responsive to repetitive loading than tissues from skeletally mature individuals.[118] For example, during the formation and growth of the musculoskeletal system, repetitive loading may influence not only matrix composition, organization, and tissue volume, but also the type of tissue formed and the shape of tissue structures like bones and joints.[119,120] Following completion of skeletal growth, maintenance of connective tissues like ligaments requires that the cells continually replace matrix macromolecules. This process requires at least some loading of the tissue.[39] If the ability of the tissue to respond to loading declines with age, because of a decrease in cell density, systemic changes, reduced tissue nutrition, or because of a decrease in the ability of the cells to respond to loading, then mechanical properties of the tissue will deteriorate.[121]

The results of a recent study suggest that older ligament cells do not respond to exercise. In this study, one group of dogs, beginning at 12 months of age, ran on a treadmill while wearing a weight vest 5 days a week for 420 to 557 weeks. A matched group of animals remained in cages. The lifelong training program did not improve the mechanical properties of the dogs' medial collateral ligaments or the flexor digitorum profundus tendons.[7] From this work, it appears that age-related changes in ligaments may eventually decrease the potential benefits of exercise.

Summary

The stability of synovial joints during exercise depends in part on ligaments and joint capsules. These structures consist primarily of scattered fibroblasts, surrounded by an abundant extracellular matrix consisting of water and matrix macromolecules. During formation of the musculoskeletal system, fibroblasts create the ligament macromolecular framework from collagens (primarily type I), elastin, proteoglycans, and noncollagenous proteins; then, during growth and throughout life, they maintain and constantly remodel the matrix macromolecular framework. This macromolecular framework and its interaction with the tissue water give ligaments their specialized mechanical properties, including stiffness, tensile strength, anisotropy, nonlinear response to tensile loading, and viscoelasticity. Maintenance of normal ligament composition, and thus, normal ligament mechanical properties, requires repetitive loading of the tissue. Immobilization of joints alters ligament composition and decreases ligament stiffness and strength. Regular vigorous exercise can increase ligament stiffness and strength in young animals, and controlled exercise can facilitate healing of ligament injuries. With age, ligament stiffness and strength decline. Recent evidence suggests that this decline is due at least in part to a decrease in the ability of ligament cells to respond to loading of the tissue. Critical areas for future research include a better definition of age-related changes in normal ligament structure, composition, and mechanical properties; the response of normal and injured ligaments to loading; changes in ligament structure, composition, and mechanical properties with age; and changes in ligament response to exercise with age.

References

1. Barrack RL, Skinner HB: The sensory function of knee ligaments, in Daniel DM, Akeson WH, O'Connor JJ (eds): *Knee Ligaments: Structure, Function, Injury, and Repair*. New York, NY, Raven Press, 1990, chap 6, pp 95-114.

2. Buckwalter JA, Maynard JA, Vailas AC: Skeletal fibrous tissues: Tendon, joint capsule, and ligament, in Albright JA, Brand RA (eds): *The Scientific Basis of Orthopaedics*, ed 2. Norwalk, CT, Appleton & Lange, 1987, chap 14, pp 387-405.

3. Gillquist J: Knee stability: Its effect on articular cartilage, in Ewing JW (ed): *Articular Cartilage and Knee Joint Function: Basic Science and Arthroscopy*. New York, NY, Raven Press, 1990, chap 18, pp 267-271.

4. Mow VC, Bigliani LU, Flatow EL, et al: The role of joint instability in joint inflammation and cartilage deterioration: A study of the glenohumeral joint, in Leadbetter WB, Buckwalter JA, Gordon SL (eds): *Sports-Induced Inflammation: Clinical and Basic Science Concepts*. Park Ridge, IL, American Academy of Orthopaedic Surgeons, 1990, chap 21, pp 337-355.

5. Woo SL-Y, Hollis JM, Adams DJ, et al: Tensile properties of the human femur-anterior cruciate ligament-tibia complex: The effects of specimen age and orientation. *Am J Sports Med* 1991;19:217-225.

6. Noyes FR, Grood ES: The strength of the anterior cruciate ligament in humans and Rhesus monkeys. *J Bone Joint Surg* 1976;58A:1074-1082.

7. Wang CW, Weiss JA, Albright J, et al: Life-long exercise and aging effects on the canine medial collateral ligament. *Trans Orthop Res Soc* 1990;15:518.

8. Burks RT: Gross anatomy, in Daniel DM, Akeson WH, O'Connor JJ (eds): *Knee Ligaments: Structure, Function, Injury, and Repair*. New York, NY, Raven Press, 1990, chap 4, pp 59-76.

9. Frank C, Woo S, Andriacchi T, et al: Normal ligament: Structure, function, and composition, in Woo SL-Y, Buckwalter JA (eds): *Injury and Repair of the Musculoskeletal Soft Tissues*. Park Ridge, IL, American Academy of Orthopaedic Surgeons, 1988, chap 2, pp 45-101.

10. Viidik A: Simultaneous mechanical and light microscopic studies of collagen fibers. *Z Anat Entwickl-Ges* 1972;136:204-212.

11. Butler DL: Kappa Delta Award paper. Anterior cruciate ligament: Its normal response and replacement. *J Orthop Res* 1989;7:910-921.

12. Buckwalter JA, Cooper RR: The cells and matrices of skeletal connective tissue, in Albright JA, Brand RA (eds): *The Scientific Basis of Orthopaedics*, ed 2. Norwalk, CT, Appleton & Lange, 1987, chap 1, pp 1-29.

13. Cooper RR, Misol S: Tendon and ligament insertion: A light and electron microscopic study. *J Bone Joint Surg* 1970;52A:1-20.

14. Cooper RR: Alterations during immobilization and regeneration of skeletal muscle in cats. *J Bone Joint Surg* 1972;54A:919-953.

15. Frank CB, Hart DA: The biology of tendons and ligaments, in Mow VC, Ratcliffe A, Woo SL-Y (eds): *Biomechanics of Diarthrodial Joints*. New York, NY, Springer-Verlag, 1990, vol 1, chap 2, pp 39-62.

16. Woo S, Maynard J, Butler D, et al: Ligament, tendon, and joint capsule insertions to bone, in Woo SL-Y, Buckwalter JA (eds): *Injury and Repair of the Musculoskeletal Soft Tissues*. Park Ridge, IL, American Academy of Orthopaedic Surgeons, 1988, chap 4, pp 133-166.

17. Woo SL-Y, Gomez MA, Seguchi Y, et al: Measurement of mechanical properties of ligament substance from a bone-ligament-bone preparation. *J Orthop Res* 1983;1:22-29.

18. Laros GS, Tipton CM, Cooper RR: Influence of physical activity on ligament insertions in the knees of dogs. *J Bone Joint Surg* 1971;53A:275-286.

19. Matyas JR, Bodie D, Andersen M, et al: The developmental morphology of a "periosteal" ligament insertion: Growth and maturation of the tibial insertion of the rabbit medial collateral ligament. *J Orthop Res* 1990;8:412-424.

20. Frank C, McDonald D, Lieber R, et al: Biochemical heterogeneity within the maturing rabbit medial collateral ligament. *Clin Orthop* 1988;236:279-285.

21. Amiel D, Frank C, Harwood F, et al: Tendons and ligaments: A morphological and biochemical comparison. *J Orthop Res* 1984;1:257-265.

22. Oakes, BW: Experimental studies on the development, structure and properties of elastic fibers and other components of connective tissues. Clayton, Australia, 1978. Thesis.

23. Eyre DR: The collagens of musculoskeletal soft tissues, in Leadbetter WB, Buckwalter JA, Gordon SL (eds): *Sports-Induced Inflammation: Clinical and Basic Science Concepts*. Park Ridge, IL, American Academy of Orthopaedic Surgeons, 1990, chap 8, pp 161-170.

24. Buckwalter JA: Cartilage, in Dulbecco R (ed): *Encyclopedia of Human Biology*. San Diego, CA, Academic Press, 1991, vol 8.

25. Buckwalter JA, Rosenberg LC, Hunziker E: Articular cartilage: Composition, structure, response to injury and methods of facilitating repair, in Ewing JW (ed): *Articular Cartilage and Knee Joint Function: Basic Science and Arthroscopy*. New York, NY, Raven Press, 1990, pp 19-56.

26. Bray DF, Frank CB, Bray RC: Cytochemical evidence for a proteoglycan-associated filamentous network in ligament extracellular matrix. *J Orthop Res* 1990;8:1-12.

27. Hardingham TE: Proteoglycans: Their structure, interactions and molecular organization in cartilage. *Biochem Soc Trans* 1981;9:489-497.

28. Hascall VC: Interaction of cartilage proteoglycans with hyaluronic acid. *J Supramol Structure* 1977;7:101-120.

29. Muir H: Proteoglycans as organizers of the intercellular matrix. *Biochem Soc Trans* 1983;11:613-622.

30. Poole AR, Webber C, Pidoux I, et al: Localization of a dermatan sulfate proteoglycan (DS-PGII) in cartilage and the presence of an immunologically related species in other tissues. *J Histochem Cytochem* 1986;34:619-625.

31. Rosenberg LC, Choi HU, Poole AR, et al: Biological roles of dermatan sulphate proteoglycans. *Ciba Found Symp* 1986;124:47-68.

32. Rosenberg LC, Choi HU, Neame PJ, et al: Proteoglycans of soft connective tissues, in Leadbetter WB, Buckwalter JA, Gordon SL (eds): *Sports-Induced Inflammation: Clinical and Basic Science Concepts*. Park Ridge, IL, American Academy of Orthopaedic Surgeons, 1990, chap 9, pp 171-188.

33. Viidik A: Structure and function of normal and healing tendons and ligaments, in Mow VC, Ratcliffe A, Woo SL-Y (eds): *Biomechanics of Diarthrodial Joints*. New York, NY, Springer-Verlag, 1990, vol 1, chap 1, pp 3-38.

34. Woo SL-Y, Weiss JA, MacKenna DA: Biomechanics and morphology of the medial collateral and anterior cruciate ligaments, in Mow VC, Ratcliffe A, Woo SL-Y (eds): *Biomechanics of Diarthrodial Joints*. New York, NY, Springer-Verlag, 1990, vol 1, chap 3, pp 63-104.

35. Woo SL-Y, Young EP: Structure and function of tendons and ligaments, in Mow VC, Hayes WC (eds): *Basic Orthopaedic Biomechanics*. New York, NY, Raven Press, 1991, chap 5, pp 199-243.

36. Woo SL-Y, Adams DJ: The tensile properties of human anterior cruciate ligament (ACL) and ACL graft tissues, in Daniel DM, Akeson WH, O'Connor JJ (eds): *Knee Ligaments: Structure, Function, Injury, and Repair*. New York, NY, Raven Press, 1990, chap 13, pp 279-289.

37. Woo SL-Y, Young EP, Kwan MK: Fundamental studies in knee ligament mechanics, in Daniel DM, Akeson WH, O'Connor JJ (eds): *Knee Ligaments: Structure, Function, Injury, and Repair.* New York, NY, Raven Press, 1990, chap 7, pp 115-134.

38. Buckwalter JA, Cruess RL: Healing of the musculoskeletal tissues, in Rockwood CA Jr, Green DP, Bucholz RW (eds): *Fractures in Adults,* ed 3. Philadelphia, PA, JB Lippincott, 1991, vol 1, chap 2, pp 181-222.

39. Buckwalter JA: Section 2: Overview: Pathophysiologic mechanisms in sports-inflammation, in Leadbetter WB, Buckwalter JA, Gordon SL (eds): *Sports-Induced Inflammation: Clinical and Basic Science Concepts.* Park Ridge, IL, American Academy of Orthopaedic Surgeons, 1990, pp 125-127.

40. Arem AJ, Madden JW: Effects of stress on healing wounds: I. Intermittent noncyclical tension. *J Surg Res* 1976;20:93-102.

41. Binderman I, Shimshoni Z, Somjen D: Biochemical pathways involved in the translation of physical stimulus into biological message. *Calcif Tissue Int* 1984;36(suppl 1):S82-S85.

42. Brunette DM: Mechanical stretching increases the number of epithelial cells synthesizing DNA in culture. *J Cell Sci* 1984;69:35-45.

43. DeWitt MT, Handley CJ, Oakes BW, et al: In vitro response of chondrocytes to mechanical loading. The effect of short term mechanical tension. *Connect Tissue Res* 1984;12:97-109.

44. Klebe RJ, Caldwell H, Milam S: Cells transmit spatial information by orienting collagen fibers. *Matrix* 1989;9:451-458.

45. Mosler E, Folkhard W, Knorzer E, et al: Stress-induced molecular rearrangement in tendon collagen. *J Mol Biol* 1985;182:589-596.

46. Grinnell F, Lamke CR: Reorganization of hydrated collagen lattices by human skin fibroblasts. *J Cell Sci* 1984;66:51-63.

47. Heikkinen E, Vuori I: Effect of physical activity on the metabolism of collagen in aged mice. *Acta Physiol Scand* 1972;84:543-549.

48. Albrecht-Buehler G: Role of cortical tension in fibroblast shape and movement. *Cell Motil Cytoskeleton* 1987;7:54-67.

49. Kolega J: Effects of mechanical tension on protrusive activity and microfilament and intermediate filament organization in an epidermal epithelium moving in culture. *J Cell Biol* 1986;102:1400-1411.

50. Gray ML, Pizzanelli AM, Godzinsky AJ, et al: Mechanical and physicochemical determinants of the chondrocyte biosynthetic response. *J Orthop Res* 1988;6:777-792.

51. Hall AC, Urban JPG: Responses of articular chondrocytes and cartilage to high hydrostatic pressure. *Trans Orthop Res Soc* 1989;14:49.

52. Leung DY, Glagov S, Mathews MB: A new in vitro system for studying cell response to mechanical stimulation. Different effects of cyclic stretching and agitation on smooth muscle cell biosynthesis. *Exp Cell Res* 1977;109:285-298.

53. Norton LA, Rodan GA, Bourret LA: Epiphyseal cartilage cAMP changes produced by electrical and mechanical perturbations. *Clin Orthop* 1977;124:59-68.

54. Palmoski MJ, Brandt KD: Effects of static and cyclic compressive loading on articular cartilage plugs in vitro. *Arthritis Rheum* 1984;27:675-681.

55. Sah RL, Kim Y-J, Doong J-Y, et al: Biosynthetic response of cartilage explants to dynamic compression. *J Orthop Res* 1989;7:619-636.

56. Slack C, Flint MH, Thompson BM: The effect of tensional load on isolated embryonic chick tendons in organ culture. *Connect Tissue Res* 1984;12:229-247.

57. Yeh C-K, Rodan GA: Tensile forces enhance prostaglandin E synthesis in osteoblastic cells grown on collagen ribbons. *Calcif Tissue Int* 1984;36(suppl 1):S67-S71.

58. Grodzinsky AJ: Electromechanical and physicochemical properties of connective tissue. *Crit Rev Biomed Eng* 1983;9:133-199.

59. Rodan GA, Bourret LA, Norton LA: DNA synthesis in cartilage cells is stimulated by oscillating electric fields. *Science* 1978;199:690-692.

60. Schwartz ER, Kirkpatrick PR, Thompson RC: The effect of environmental pH on glycosaminoglycan metabolism by normal human chondrocytes. *J Lab Clin Med* 1976;87:198-205.

61. Michna H: Morphometric analysis of loading-induced changes in collagen-fibril populations in young tendons. *Cell Tissue Res* 1984;236:465-470.

62. Bader DL, Barnhill RL, Ryan TJ: Effect of externally applied skin surface forces on tissue vasculature. *Arch Phys Med Rehabil* 1986;67:807-811.

63. Akeson WH, Amiel D, LaViolette D: The connective tissue response to immobility: A study of the chondroitin-4 and 6-sulfate and dermatan sulfate changes in periarticular connective tissue of control and immobilized knees of dogs. *Clin Orthop* 1967;51:183-197.

64. Akeson WH, Woo SL-Y, Amiel D, et al: The connective tissue response to immobility: Biochemical changes in periarticular connective tissue of the immobilized rabbit knee. *Clin Orthop* 1973;93:356-362.

65. Akeson WH, Amiel D, Mechanic GL, et al: Collagen cross-linking alterations in joint contractures: Changes in the reducible cross-links in periarticular connective tissue collagen after nine weeks of immobilization. *Connect Tissue Res* 1977;5:15-19.

66. Amiel D, Woo SL-Y, Harwood FL, et al: The effect of immobilization on collagen turnover in connective tissue: A biochemical-biomechanical correlation. *Acta Orthop Scand* 1982;53:325-332.

67. Tipton CM, Tcheng TK, Mergner W: Ligamentous strength measurements from hypophysectomized rats. *Am J Physiol* 1971;221:1144-1150.

68. Tipton CM, James SL, Mergner W, et al: Influence of exercise on strength of medial collateral ligaments of dogs. *Am J Physiol* 1970;218:894-902.

69. Tipton CM, Matthes RD, Maynard JA, et al. The influence of physical activity on ligaments and tendons. *Med Sci Sports* 1975;7:165-175.

70. Tipton CM, Schild RJ, Tomanek RJ: Influence of physical activity on the strength of knee ligaments in rats. *Am J Physiol* 1967;212:783-787.

71. Tipton CM, Matthes RD, Sandage DS: In situ measurement of junction strength and ligament elongation in rats. *J Appl Physiol* 1974;37:758-761.

72. Walsh S, Frank C, Hart D: Immobilization alters cell function in growing rabbit ligaments. *Trans Orthop Res Soc* 1988;13:57.

73. Woo SL-Y, Wang CW, Newton PO, et al: The response of ligaments to stress deprivation and stress enhancement: Biomechanical studies, in Daniel DM, Akeson WH, O'Connor JJ (eds): *Knee Ligaments: Structure, Function, Injury, and Repair*. New York, NY, Raven Press, 1990, chap 17, pp 337-350.

74. Woo SL-Y, Tkach LV: The cellular and matrix response of ligaments and tendons to mechanical injury, in Leadbetter WB, Buckwalter JA, Gordon SL (eds): *Sports-Induced Inflammation: Clinical and Basic Science Concepts*. Park Ridge, IL, American Academy of Orthopaedic Surgeons, 1990, chap 10, pp 189-204.

75. Woo SL-Y, Matthews JV, Akeson WH, et al: Connective tissue response to immobility: Correlative study of biomechanical and biochemical measurements of normal and immobilized rabbit knees. *Arthritis Rheum* 1975;18:257-264.

76. Klein L, Dawson MH, Heiple KG: Turnover of collagen in the adult rat after denervation. *J Bone Joint Surg* 1977;59A:1065-1067.

77. Noyes FR, Torvik PJ, Hyde WB, et al: Biomechanics of ligament failure: II. An analysis of immobilization, exercise, and reconditioning effects in primates. *J Bone Joint Surg* 1974;56A:1406-1418.

78. Noyes FR, DeLucas JL, Torvik PJ: Biomechanics of anterior cruciate ligament failure: An analysis of strain-rate sensitivity and mechanisms of failure in primates. *J Bone Joint Surg* 1974;56A:236-253.

79. Woo SL-Y, Gomez MA, Sites TJ, et al: The biomechanical and morphological changes in the medial collateral ligament of the rabbit after immobilization and remobilization. *J Bone Joint Surg* 1987;69A:1200-1211.

80. Michna H: Tendon injuries induced by exercise and anabolic steroids in experimental mice. *Int Orthop* 1987;11:157-162.

81. Woo SL-Y, Gomez MA, Amiel D, et al: The effects of exercise on the biomechanical and biochemical properties of swine digital flexor tendons. *J Biomech Eng* 1981;103:51-56.

82. Woo SL-Y, Ritter MA, Amiel D, et al: The biomechanical and biochemical properties of swine tendons: Long term effects of exercise on the digital extensors. *Connect Tissue Res* 1980;7:177-183.

83. Viidik A: Elasticity and tensile strength of the anterior cruciate ligament in rabbits as influenced by training. *Acta Physiol Scand* 1968;74:372-380.

84. Viidik A: The effect of training on the tensile strength of isolated rabbit tendons. *Scand J Plast Reconstr Surg* 1967;1:141-147.

85. Viidik A: Tensile strength properties of Achilles tendon systems in trained and untrained rabbits. *Acta Orthop Scand* 1969;40:261-272.

86. Vilarta R, Vidal B de C: Anisotropic and biomechanical properties of tendons modified by exercise and denervation: Aggregation and macromolecular order in collagen bundles. *Matrix* 1989;9:55-61.

87. Zuckerman J, Stull GA: Effects of exercise on knee ligament separation force in rats. *J Appl Physiol* 1969;26:716-719.

88. Zuckerman J, Stull GA: Ligamentous separation force in rats as influenced by training, detraining, and cage restriction. *Med Sci Sports* 1973;5:44-49.

89. Gomez MA, Ishizue KK, Lyon RM, et al: The effects of increased stress on medial collateral ligaments: An experimental and analytical approach. *Trans Orthop Res Soc* 1988;13:194.

90. Gomez MA, Woo SL-Y, Amiel D, et al: The effects of increased tension on healing medial collateral ligaments. *Am J Sports Med* 1991;19:347-354.

91. Woo SL-Y, Kuei SC, Gomez MA, et al: The effect of immobilization and exercise on the strength characteristics of bone-medial collateral ligament-bone complex. *ASME Biomech Symp AMD* 1979;32:67-70.

92. Amadio PC, Berglund LJ, An KN: Tensile properties of biochemically discrete zones of canine flexor tendon. *Trans Orthop Res Soc* 1989;14:251.

93. Gillard GC, Reilly HC, Bell-Booth PG, et al: The influence of mechanical forces on the glycosaminoglycan content of the rabbit flexor digitorum profundus tendon. *Connect Tissue Res* 1979;7:37-46.

94. Merrilees MJ, Flint MH: Ultrastructural study of tension and pressure zones in a rabbit flexor tendon. *Am J Anat* 1980;157:87-106.

95. Koob TJ, Vogel KG: Proteoglycan synthesis in organ cultures from regions of bovine tendon subjected to different mechanical forces. *Biochem J* 1987;246:589-598.

96. Vogel KG, Keller EJ, Lenhoff RJ, et al: Proteoglycan synthesis by fibroblast cultures initiated from regions of adult bovine tendon subjected to different mechanical forces. *Eur J Cell Biol* 1986;41:102-112.

97. Vogel KG, Thonar EJ: Keratan sulfate is a component of proteoglycans in the compressed region of adult bovine flexor tendon. *J Orthop Res* 1988;6:434-442.

98. Burroughs P, Dahners LE: The effect of enforced exercise on the healing of ligament injuries. *Am J Sports Med* 1990;18:376-378.

99. Frank C, Akeson WH, Woo SL-Y, et al: Physiology and therapeutic value of passive joint motion. *Clin Orthop* 1984;185:113-125.

100. Gelberman RH, Woo SL-Y, Lothringer K, et al: Effects of early intermittent passive mobilization on healing canine flexor tendons. *J Hand Surg* 1982;7A:170-175.

101. Andriacchi T, Sabiston P, DeHaven K, et al: Ligament: Injury and repair, in Woo SL-Y, Buckwalter JA (eds): *Injury and Repair of the Musculoskeletal Soft Tissues*. Park Ridge, IL, American Academy of Orthopaedic Surgeons, 1988, chap 3, pp 103-128.

102. Burks R, Daniel D, Losse G: The effect of continuous passive motion on anterior cruciate ligament reconstruction stability. *Am J Sports Med* 1984;12:323-327.

103. Mason ML, Shearon CG: The process of tendon repair: An experimental study of tendon suture and tendon graft. *Arch Surg* 1932;25:615-692.

104. Mason ML, Allen HS: The rate of healing of tendons: An experimental study of tensile strength. *Ann Surg* 1941;113:424-459.

105. Indelicato PA, Hermansdorfer J, Huegel M: Nonoperative management of complete tears of the medial collateral ligament of the knee in intercollegiate football players. *Clin Orthop* 1990;256:174-177.

106. Piper TL, Whiteside LA: Early mobilization after knee ligament repair in dogs: An experimental study. *Clin Orthop* 1980;150:277-282.

107. Urschel JD, Scott PG, Williams HT: The effect of mechanical stress on soft and hard tissue repair: A review. *Br J Plast Surg* 1988;41:182-186.

108. Vailas AC, Tipton CM, Matthes RD, et al: Physical activity and its influence on the repair process of medial collateral ligaments. *Connect Tissue Res* 1981;9:25-31.

109. Woo SL-Y, Horibe S, Ohland KJ, et al: The response of ligaments to injury: Healing of the collateral ligaments, in Daniel DM, Akeson WH, O'Connor JJ (eds): *Knee Ligaments: Structure, Function, Injury, and Repair*. New York, NY, Raven Press, 1990, chap 18, pp 351-364.

110. Bair GR: The effect of early mobilization versus casting on anterior cruciate ligament reconstruction. *Trans Orthop Res Soc* 1980;5:108.

111. Gelberman R, Goldberg V, An KN, et al: Tendon, in Woo SL-Y, Buckwalter JA (eds): *Injury and Repair of the Musculoskeletal Soft Tissues*. Park Ridge, IL, American Academy of Orthopaedic Surgeons, 1988, chap 1, pp 5-40.

112. Fronek J, Frank C, Amiel D, et al: The effect of intermittent passive motion (IPM) in the healing of the medial collateral ligament. *Trans Orthop Res Soc* 1983;8:31.

113. Long ML, Frank C, Schachar NS, et al: The effects of motion on normal and healing ligaments. *Trans Orthop Res Soc* 1982;7:43.

114. Palmoski MJ, Brandt KD: Immobilization of the knee prevents osteoarthritis after anterior cruciate ligament transection. *Arthritis Rheum* 1982;25:1201-1208.

115. Nachemson AL, Evans JH: Some mechanical properties of the third human lumbar interlaminar ligament (ligamentum flavum). *J Biomech* 1968;1:211-220.

116. Tkaczuk H: Tensile properties of human lumbar longitudinal ligaments. *Acta Orthop Scand Supp* 1968;115:8-69.

117. Rauch G, Allzeit B, Gotzen L: Tensile strength of the anterior cruciate ligament in dependence on age, in *Biomechanics of Human Knee Ligaments*. Proceedings of the European Society of Biomechanics. University of Ulm, Ulm, West Germany, 1987.

118. Butler DL, Siegel AJ: Alterations in tissue response: Conditioning effects at different ages, in Leadbetter WB, Buckwalter JA, Gordon SL (eds): *Sports-Induced Inflammation: Clinical and Basic Science Concepts*. Park Ridge, IL, American Academy of Orthopaedic Surgeons, 1990, chap 49, pp 713-730.

119. Carter DR: Mechanical loading histories and cortical bone remodeling. *Calcif Tissue Int* 1984;36(suppl 1):S19-S24.

120. Carter DR, Wong M: The role of mechanical loading histories in the development of diarthrodial joints. *J Orthop Res* 1988;6:804-816.

121. Buckwalter JA, Woo SL-Y, Goldberg VM, et al: Soft tissue aging and musculoskeletal function. *J Bone Joint Surg* 1993;75A:1533-1548.

Chapter 11

Structure and Function of Cartilage: Adult and Age-Related Changes

Stephen L. Gordon, PhD
Andre J. Premen, PhD

Introduction

Articular cartilage covers and protects the contact surfaces of articulating bones. These thin tissues must withstand loads that can be several times body weight, and yet, provide a smooth, lubricating, bearing material that exhibits minimal wear. It is not surprising that most people have radiologic evidence of joint space narrowing as they age; however, in most individuals, articular cartilage remains functional throughout life.

There is a considerable body of literature on healthy, young adult articular cartilage. A moderate science base is available regarding developmental changes in cartilage. A lesser amount is known about cartilage in the elderly, and very little has been reported regarding the structure and function of cartilage in midlife. This literature survey considers the major structural components and biomechanical properties of adult articular cartilage and defines age-related changes. Even though osteoarthritis is a very common result of degenerative changes of articular cartilage, most investigators believe that the disease process may be separate from the slight normal wear that occurs with aging. Therefore, osteoarthritis is intentionally not included in this chapter.

Collagen in Adult Articular Cartilage

Five types of collagen have been identified in articular cartilage: type II (90%-95%), type XI (2%-3%), type IX (1%-2%), type VI (0-2%), and type X (0-1%).[1] Type II collagen molecules are composed of a single, uninterrupted triple helix of alpha 1(II) chains, which are the product of a single gene, COL2A1. The polymeric form appears as fibrils with highly organized, repeated bands on electron microscopy and is

Fig. 1 *Structure of the type II collagen molecule (**top**) and its cross-linked polymer, the 67 nm-periodic fibril (**bottom**). All class I collagens (types I, II, III, V, and XI) have this basic molecular and fibrillar form. (Reproduced with permission from Eyre DR, Wu JJ, Woods P: Cartilage specific collagens: Structural studies, in Kuettner KE, Schleyerbach R, Peyron JG, et al (eds): Articular Cartilage and Osteoarthritis. New York, NY, Raven Press, 1992, pp 119-131.)*

similar to other fibrillar forms of collagen (Fig. 1). The tensile strength of collagen, and therefore cartilage, is based on collagen type II fibrils and their cross-links that establish a strong interwoven network. Type II collagen fibrils are thicker in the deeper layers of cartilage and thinner and arranged horizontally near the surface.[2]

The type XI collagen molecule consists of three distinct alpha chains that appear in several different configurations in the class of fibril-forming collagens (Fig. 2). There is a strong analogy of type XI collagen in cartilage with type V collagen in bone and other type I collagen-based connective tissues. In mature tissues there is a substitution of some α1(V) for α1(XI) chains.[3] Type XI collagen may organize type II collagen by controlling lateral fibril growth and determining the final diameter of collagen fibrils.[4] Another functional role of type XI collagen may be as a core fibril upon which the type II and other collagens are superimposed.[5]

Type IX collagen can be classified as both a collagen and a proteoglycan. The role of its single glycosaminoglycan side chain, which confers the classification as a proteoglycan, is not clear. This short-helix molecule is a heterotrimer of three distinct gene products: α1(IX), α2(IX), and α3(IX). It consists of three triple-helical domains: COL 1, COL 2, and COL 3.[3] All three chains can form cross-links with type II collagen (Fig. 3). On electron microscopy, type IX collagen has been found on the surface of type II collagen fibrils, to which it appears to be cross-linked at one or more molecular sites. The role of type IX collagen is to enhance the mechanical stability of the fibril network and to help resist the swelling pressure of entrapped proteoglycans.

N-PROPEPTIDE

Fig. 2 *Top*, *Structure of the type XI collagen molecule.* **Bottom**, Current extent of knowledge of its polymeric form based on cross-linking data. Unlike type I or II collagen molecules, the N-propeptide domain is retained in the functioning molecule in the extracellular matrix. (Reproduced with permission from Eyre DR, Wu JJ, Woods P: Cartilage specific collagens: Structural studies, in Kuettner KE, Schleyerbach R, Peyron JG, et al (eds): *Articular Cartilage and Osteoarthritis. New York, NY, Raven Press, 1992, chap 9, pp 119-131.)*

The cross-linking chemical bonds are facilitated by the amino acid hydroxylysine, which acts as a precursor to the stable and unstable cross-links in various collagens. The unstable cross-links are intermediate, divalent bonds that are reducible on chemical analysis by borohydride. The stable cross-links in cartilage are trivalent bonds that contain pyridinoline residues. This stable cross link has two forms, which are both present in type IX collagen. Only one form (hydroxylysyl pyridinoline) is present in type II collagen, the principal source of these cross-links in cartilage.[6] This cross-linking plays a major role in providing tensile strength for the collagen network.[7]

Two other short-helical types of collagen are present in cartilage: type VI and type X. Type VI seems to be more concentrated in the pericellular space around chondrocytes.[8] Type X appears to be restricted to metabolically active hypertrophic chondrocytes within the zone of calcified cartilage.[9] There are as yet few definitive data on the precise functions of these two collagen types.

Changes in Age-Related Articular Collagen

Most of the age-related changes in cartilage collagen are documented as the difference between fetal (or very young) and skeletally mature tissue samples. Therefore, it is not clear to what degree the documented changes represent developmental stages or modifications of mature tissues with progressing age.

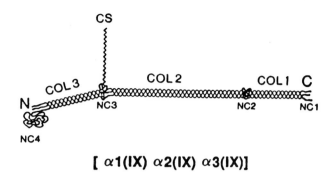

$$[\alpha1(IX) \ \alpha2(IX) \ \alpha3(IX)]$$

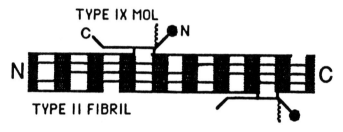

Fig. 3 *Type IX collagen.* **Top,** *Domain structure of the type IX collagen molecule showing the three collagenous domains and glycosaminoglycan attachment site in the NC3 domain of α2(IX).* **Bottom,** *Most molecules function in the extracellular matrix in covalent linkage to the surface of type II collagen fibrils. The lateral interrelationship is antiparallel based on the spacing of α1(II) N-telopeptide and α1(II) C-telopeptide cross-linking sites in the COL2 domain. (Reproduced with permission from Eyre DR, Wu JJ, Woods P: Cartilage specific collagens: Structural studies, in Kuettner KE, Schleyerbach R, Peyron JG, et al (eds): Articular Cartilage and Osteoarthritis. New York, NY, Raven Press, 1992, pp 125.)*

Type II collagen fibrils increase in diameter from as little as 20 nm in fetal human cartilage to 50 to 100 nm in adult human cartilage. This change appears to progress continuously with aging.[3] In pre-chondrogenic, but not mature type II procollagen, a new exon was recently discovered that produces a larger molecule.[10] Table 1 displays the percentage of collagen types from fetal and adult bovine cartilage. The functional significance of these differences is not yet defined, although it appears to be related to the gradual increase in type II collagen fibril diameters with advancing tissue age. As mentioned above, in type XI collagen there is a ratio of α1(XI) to α1(V) chains of about 2:1 in mature tissue, whereas there are very few α1 chains in fetal samples. A large scientific base of knowledge on age-

Table 1 Collagen types in bovine cartilage

| | Percentage of Total Collagen | |
	Fetal	Adult
Type II	80	95
Type XI	10	3
Type IX	10	1
Type VI	<1	<1
Type X	<1	<1

(Reproduced with permission from David R. Eyre, PhD.)

related changes in cartilage (either human or animal samples) from adult tissues in midlife is currently lacking.

Many of the changes that occur in cartilage with aging are related to cross-linking, and this cross-linking has a profound effect on collagen network tensile properties.[11] In general, stable pyridinoline cross-links increase in concentration with developmental age.[2] Both type IX and type II collagen show a decrease in the ratio of reducible to mature cross-links with tissue maturity. The largest difference is in the type II collagen ratio of reducible to mature cross-links in fetal tissue (1:1) compared to adult tissue (1:10).[12]

Proteoglycans in Adult Articular Cartilage

The extracellular matrix (ECM) of adult articular cartilage is abundant in proteoglycans, which are complex biologic glycoconjugates serving as binding or cementing material in connective tissues. These large viscoelastic substances, the major space-filling molecules of the ECM, are negatively charged, hydrophilic, and entangled in a network of type II collagen fibrils.[11] These biologic macromolecules play an important role in maintaining the structure and function of the ECM, including important influences on hydraulic permeability, nutrient delivery through the synovial space, and disposal of metabolites. Importantly, the special properties of proteoglycans provide cartilage with its ability to undergo reversible deformation during loading, and thus, play a key role in maintaining cartilage homeostasis.[2,13,14]

The predominant proteoglycans in articular cartilage are those that contain aggrecan monomers attached to a single strand of hyaluronic acid (hyaluronan or HA), which is an extracellular, linear, high-molecular-weight glycosaminoglycan. These proteoglycans represent approximately 90% of the total tissue proteoglycan mass.[2,15] To aggrecan's large protein core (molecular weight of 230 kd) are attached N-linked and O-linked oligosaccharides and numerous glycosaminoglycan side chains of chondroitin sulfate (CS) and keratan sulfate (KS). The core protein contains three globular regions (G1, G2, and G3) and two extended interglobular regions (E1 and E2). The

G1 and G3 domains are found at the amino and carboxyl terminal ends of the core protein, respectively. The regions G1 and G2 are separated by E1, the domain of which contains KS side chains. N-linked oligosaccharides are concentrated within the G1-E1-G2 region and near the G3 domain.[16] The E2 domain is the major functional segment because of its glycosaminoglycan-rich bearing region (Fig. 4).[15] The E2 domain carries over 100 CS side chains, numerous KS side chains (located adjacent to the G2 domain), and O-linked oligosaccharides.[17,18] Monomeric aggrecan molecules in adult cartilage can be subdivided, reflecting a maturation process, into two populations: CS-rich and CS-poor (KS-rich) molecules, based on their protein/glycosaminoglycan ratios. CS-poor molecules are most likely the result of proteolytic cleavage of intact aggrecan (within the CS-rich region) and have been found to accumulate with time. Proteolytic digestion of aggrecan near the carboxyl terminal region apparently occurs, because it has been found that only about 33% of aggrecan contains an intact G3 domain. The importance of the reduced aggrecan size as well as the significance of the released fragments remains an area of active investigation.[2]

The G1 domain of aggrecan is involved in aggregate formation while G3, containing a lectin-binding region, is thought to facilitate aggrecan binding within the ECM through its ability to bind to select carbohydrate entities.[16,19] Little, however, is known about the function of the G2 domain. Both G1 and G2 domains contain a double loop structure known as the "proteoglycan tandem repeat" (PTR). The PTR is also found in the link protein (LP). Further, both G1 and LP have a loop structure (immunoglobulin fold), which is important for binding to HA during aggregate formation (Table 2).[2,19]

Most aggrecan molecules do not exist as single monomers in the ECM. Following synthesis and secretion by chondrocytes, monomers form multimolecular aggregates in the ECM. The G1 domain of individual aggrecan monomers interacts reversibly (noncovalently) with a single strand of HA. One LP interacts with HA and G1 to stabilize the aggregate. This tripartite arrangement forms a highly stable, immobilized complex in which LP and G1 are relatively protected from proteolytic digestion. The composition and size of individual aggregates can vary widely. Up to 200 aggrecan molecules can bind to one HA molecule (1×10^6 molecular weight) to form large aggregates with a molecular weight between 5×10^7 and 5×10^8. Aggregate formation is a time-dependent phenomenon, because freshly secreted monomers in the adult have a low affinity for HA, and time is therefore necessary for conversion of monomers into a higher-affinity form. This conversion is also both temperature- and pH-dependent, and the process is inhibited by N-ethylmaleimide. Monomers diffuse through the ECM, away from their site of secretion, before becoming immobilized as aggregates. An assessment of the time-rate of binding was provided by viscometric measurements of aggrecan and HA solutions by observing increases in solution viscosities.[20] This process, together with the availability of HA and LP,

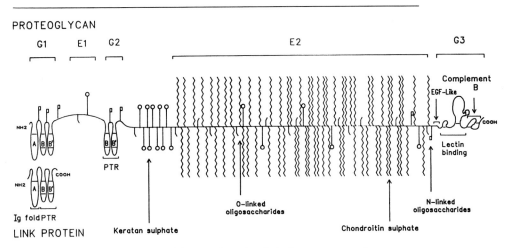

Fig. 4 *Schematic representation of the protein and carbohydrate structures of aggrecan and link protein from cartilage. (Reproduced with permission from Hardingham TE, Fosang AJ, Dudhia J: Aggrecan, the chondroitin sulfate/keratan sulfate proteoglycan from cartilage, in Kuettner KE, Schleyerbach R, Peyron JG, et al (eds):* Articular Cartilage and Osteoarthritis. *New York, NY, Raven Press, 1992, p 6.)*

Table 2 Domain structure of cartilage aggregating proteoglycan and link protein

Protein domain	Protein mol. mass (kDa)	Carbohydrate	Structural motifs	Functions
Link protein	39	N-linked	Ig fold PTR	G1 binding HA binding
Proteoglycan				
G1	38	N- and O-linked KS chains	Ig fold PTR	LP binding HA binding
E1	12	KS chains	—	No HA
G2	25	N- and O-linked	PTR	binding?
KS ⎰ E2	5-10	KS chains		
CS ⎱	125	CS chains		GAG
	~110	KS chains O-linked		attachment
G3	25	N-linked	(EGF) Lectin Complement B	Gal/Fuc binding Protein interaction?

KS chains, keratan sulfate chains; CS chains, chondroitin sulfate chains; N-, O-, N- or O-linked oligosaccharides; LP, link protein; Lectin, hepatocyte cell surface glycoprotein receptor-like domain; GAG, glycosaminoglycan; PTR, proteoglycan tandem repeat; HA, hyaluronan; Gal, galactose; Fuc, fucose. (Reproduced with permission from Hardingham TE, Fosang AJ, Dudhia J: Aggrecan, the chondroitin sulfate/ keratan sulfate proteoglycan from cartilage, in Kuettner KE, Schleyerbach R, Peyron JG, et al (eds): *Articular Cartilage and Osteoarthritis.* New York, NY, Raven Press, 1992, p 14.)

may determine the overall size, rate, and site of aggregate formation in the ECM. The structure of and modifications to aggrecan monomers are a consequence of numerous synthetic and catabolic activities regulated by both cellular and extracellular factors.[2,13,21]

Along with aggrecan, other smaller proteoglycans are found in the ECM. They include decorin, biglycan, and fibromodulin. These "minor" proteoglycans have been known to associate with other ECM constituents, such as collagen, fibronectin, and various growth factors.[2,17,22]

Biglycan and decorin are dermatan sulfate (DS)-containing proteoglycans that have core proteins (30 kd) that are similar (leucine-rich), but not identical to, one another. Both proteoglycans show a significant homology to heavily glycosylated fibromodulin molecules. Biglycan, also known as dermatan sulfate proteoglycan-I (DSPG-I), has a molecular weight of 100 kd and carries two DS chains. Decorin (DSPG-II) has a molecular weight of 70 kd and carries only one DS chain. Biglycan is located primarily around chondrocytes and may inhibit processes involved in tissue repair, because the molecule binds to fibronectin and also restricts cell adhesion and migration and clot formation.[23] Decorin has a strong binding affinity for type I and type II collagen and inhibits collagen fibrillogenesis in vitro.[24-27] Decorin also has been implicated in inhibiting tissue repair processes.

Fibromodulin (molecular weight of 50 to 65 kd) is located on the surface of type II collagen fibrils (like decorin) and may regulate the assembly and maintenance of collagen. Its precise role within the ECM seems to be related to the extent of glycosylation, KS chain length, and degree of sulfation.[28,29] Type IX collagen may also be regarded as a proteoglycan because the $\alpha2$ IX chain is glycosylated with CS. Because of the apparent regulatory roles for these small proteoglycans in cartilage ECM, growth in the diameter of type II collagen fibers depends on the removal of both fibromodulin and decorin from the surfaces of type II collagen fibers and of type IX collagen fibers bound alongside of the type II collagen.[2] A composite of articular cartilage ECM, including proteoglycans, collagen, and a chondrocyte is illustrated in Figure 5.

Age-Related Changes in Articular Proteoglycans

Data suggest that age has a pronounced effect on the composition and stability of human proteoglycans, especially aggrecan monomers.[13] In embryonic and immature cartilage, aggrecan contains a high proportion of O-linked oligosaccharides. As the tissue matures and ages, a larger number of these oligosaccharides are substituted by KS. The degree of sulfation of KS and the length of glycosaminoglycan side chains are clearly age-related. The KS content of monomers in young cartilage is only about 7% of the total glycosaminoglycan concentration. This amount is approximately half as much as is found in adult cartilage.[2] It is generally agreed that as cartilage ages, the half-life of aggrecan increases, especially in humans. Yet, there continues to be disagreement concerning the average half-life, with

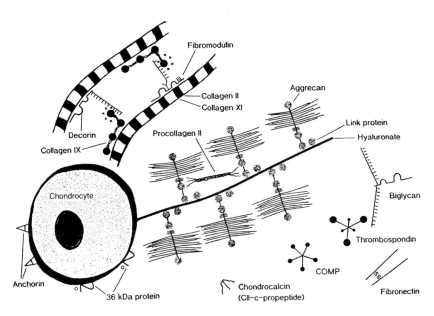

Fig. 5 *Schematic illustration of major constituents in cartilage matrix. The various constituents are involved in multiple interactions and the matrix can be viewed as a composite with a network of linked matrix constituents. (Reproduced with permission from Heinegard D, Oldberg A: Structure and biology of cartilage and bone matrix noncollagenous macromolecules. FASEB J 1989;3:2046.)*

values ranging from a few weeks to a year.[30] Proteoglycan synthesis may be significantly decreased by changes in tissue hydration and ionic concentration, among other factors. Interestingly, it has been reported that adult articular cartilage is less sensitive, as compared to immature cartilage, to these changes, a finding that may be related to the changing ECM environment in aging cartilage.[13]

With advancing age, newly synthesized aggrecan monomers take longer to mature and to bind, with high affinity, to HA as compared to younger cartilage. Yet, for both young and old cartilage, transformation of aggrecan to a high-affinity binding form is enhanced by a mild alkaline environment. Moreover, the overall rate of proteoglycan synthesis is diminished for both young and old in an alkaline environment. In aging articular cartilage, monomers become smaller, contain a shorter core protein, are substituted with fewer and smaller CS-rich side chains, demonstrate an increase in 6-sulfation relative to 4-sulfation, and contain more KS-rich side chains. Some of these changes can be seen in electron micrographs (Fig. 6). The conversion rate of CS-rich to CS-poor (ie, KS-rich) proteoglycans shows a marked age-dependent increase in both human and bovine adult articular cartilage. The increasing concentration of small, KS-rich monomers in aging articular cartilage maintains the fixed charge

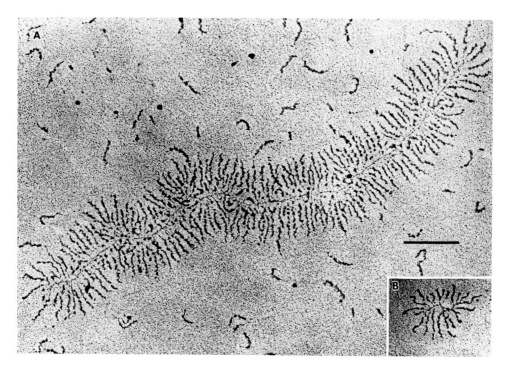

Fig. 6 *Electron micrographs of bovine articular cartilage proteoglycans.* **Top,** *A large proteoglycan aggregate from a calf consists of a central hyaluronic acid filament and multiple aggregated monomers surrounded by nonaggregated monomers. Most calf proteoglycan aggregates were approximately one-half this size. The aggregated monomers did not vary greatly in length. Bar equals 500 nm.* **Insert,** *A typical steer proteoglycan aggregate × 33,150. (Reproduced with permission from Buckwalter JA, Kuettner KE, Thonar EJ: Age-related changes in articular cartilage proteoglycans: Electron microscopic studies. J Orthop Res 1985;3:251-259.)*

density, viscoelastic properties, and osmotic swelling pressure of the tissue.[2,13,16,17,31]

Other age-related changes in cartilage include a decrease in the size of the aggrecan chains by an order of magnitude, as evidenced by a five- to tenfold decrease in the average chain length of HA and a twofold decrease in the size of individual monomers. Overall HA concentration, however, continues to increase in the ECM (a three- to fourfold increase has been reported from birth to age 90). The G1 domain (HA-binding region), although becoming poorly glycosylated with aging, remains functional.[13] The ECM becomes enriched with numerous monomer-derived fragments lacking CS-rich side chains (smaller monomers). Together with the slow accumulation of smaller-chained HA, which may be insufficient to accommodate binding for both fragments and intact aggrecan monomers, aggregate molecular weight is significantly reduced in older as compared to younger cartilage. Additionally, there appear to be important age-related changes to LP. Although the concentration of LP increases with age (as expected), its concentration still lags behind that of the HA-binding region (G1 domain), and thus, a 1:1 molar ratio cannot be maintained. Together with the finding of an age-related increase in LP heterogeneity and tendency to fragment more readily, there may be an insufficient amount of LP to stabilize sufficiently the G1-HA noncovalent interaction in the ECM.[2,13,17]

These age-related changes to proteoglycans may encourage multimolecular aggregate destabilization in the ECM, which raises important questions on the quality of aging aggregates and their functional integrity in articular cartilage. The major changes occurring within aging articular cartilage have been suggested to result mainly from alterations in cellular synthetic and catabolic processes and other ECM processes. At least two mechanisms have been invoked recently to account for age-related heterogeneity in aggrecan monomers: a variation in post-translational glycosylation and sulfation and proteolytic modification of the core protein, both mediated by specific enzymes.[2,13] Figure 7 illustrates the major age-related changes to aggrecan-containing proteoglycans in articular cartilage.

Considerably less is known about specific age-related changes to the "minor" proteoglycans. For example, there exist little quantitative data on the half-life of biglycan, decorin, and fibromodulin in young, mature, and aging articular cartilage.[2] In young cartilage, there is an equimolar concentration of biglycan and decorin.[29] Yet, as articular cartilage ages, although the concentration of both biglycan and decorin increases in the ECM, the predominant rise has been ascribed to decorin. Interestingly, biglycan appears to be most concentrated in the superficial layer of articular cartilage. These age-related changes most likely have an important impact on both tissue repair and regulation of type II collagen fibrillogenesis.[29]

Data suggest that for all proteoglycans in the ECM, the ability of local regulatory factors (eg, insulin-like growth factor-I, transforming growth factor-β, and interleukin-1) to affect in vitro proteoglycan synthesis and catabolism is reduced in aging articular cartilage.[2,13,32]

Cartilage Biomechanics

The intrinsic material characteristics of articular cartilage vary in both homogeneity (site-specific differences) and anisotropy (directional differences). Therefore, while average properties are often presented, specific test results may depend on the anatomic site and depth of tissue sample below the articular surface, as well as the orientation of the sample in the testing apparatus. The most commonly reported biomechanical data include tensile, compressive, shear, and swelling properties.

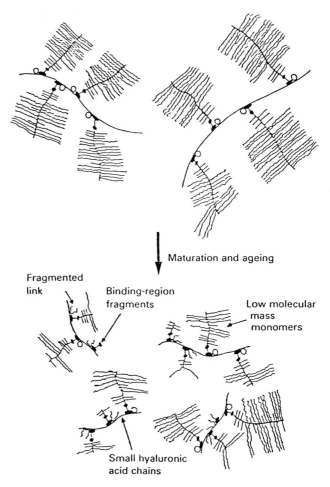

Fig. 7 *Scheme showing the major age-related changes in aggregating proteoglycan structure in human articular cartilage. (Reproduced with permission from Bayliss MT: Proteoglycan structure and metabolism during maturation and ageing of human articular cartilage. Biochem Soc Trans 1990;18:799-802.)*

When cartilage is exposed to tensile stresses and strains, the randomly oriented fibrils and entangled proteoglycan molecules are stretched and become aligned with the axis of loading. If the tensile load is applied slowly, fluid movement in the extracellular matrix occurs without significant resistance, and the results represent a flow-independent or intrinsic tensile behavior of the solid matrix. As with most soft connective tissue, the orienting of fibers produces a non-linear toe region of the stress-strain curve. After the collagen fibers align, the linear portion of the curve is the tensile modulus, which reflects the stiffness of the collagen network in tension. The tensile modulus for normal cartilage varies from 0.193 MPa to 10.13 MPa, depending on the location, depth, and orientation of the test specimen.[33]

In testing the surface zone, subsurface zone, and middle zone of normal human cartilage, the tensile modulus was shown to be 10.1, 5.9, and 4.5 MPa, respectively. The "split-line" of cartilage is the tear line that occurs when the cartilage is pierced with a sharp object. The tensile modulus is higher when the specimen is aligned parallel to the split-line, as compared to perpendicular to it. Specimens from high weightbearing areas are less stiff than those from low weightbearing areas.[34]

The biochemical structure of ECM determines the material properties described above. There is a highly significant relationship between the tensile modulus of normal human cartilage and the ratio of collagen to proteoglycan ($r = 0.714$, $p < 0.001$).[34] Extraction of proteoglycan from cartilage has had little effect on the tensile properties of the remaining collagen network.[35] Leukocyte elastase, which disrupts intermolecular collagen cross-links, was used on human cadaver cartilage test specimens and yielded a significantly reduced modulus on tensile testing.[36] In all these tests, collagen is the dominant determinant of tensile stiffness and strength.

At higher rates of tensile loading, there is a substantial amount of resistance to fluid movement, and frictional drag is exerted on the solid matrix. In this case, the interaction between collagen, proteoglycan, and interstitial fluid is key to determining material properties. Cartilage effectively stiffens with increasing strain rate. At high strain rates, the modulus can approach 300 MPa.[34] These values were again found to depend on location, depth, and orientation.

The equilibrium compressive properties of cartilage matrix are determined from confined compression and indentation experiments when all fluid flow effects have subsided. The aggregate modulus is computed at creep equilibrium. For small strain (less than 20%), human and bovine cartilage have a linear stress-strain relationship.[34] Detailed mapping of the spatial distribution of the equilibrium compressive aggregate modulus in human femoral head articular cartilage shows the highest values on the superior medial surface (1.816 MPa) and the lowest values on the inferior lateral surface (0.679 MPa).[37] In general, the compressive modulus varies with location, species, biochemical composition, and pathology. Compressive properties are determined primarily by proteoglycan structures and fixed charge density, and tensile properties by collagen.[34,38]

One theoretical model used to mathematically describe the physical structure of cartilage is the biphasic theory of Mow and associates.[34] Solid and liquid phases are defined to perform under the following assumptions: (1) the solid matrix is linearly elastic and isotropic; (2) there is incompressibility of the solid matrix and interstitial fluid; (3) there is viscous dissipation from relative fluid flow; and (4) frictional drag is directly proportional to relative velocity. The biphasic theory accurately describes compressive creep and stress-relaxation behaviors of cartilage. The model predicts that even at very small flow speeds, very large drag forces are exerted on the solid matrix. In a simple case of cartilage compression by 25%, the ratio of stress due to fluid drag versus the stress required to compress the matrix alone is 30:1.[34] Therefore, interstitial fluid drag is the major mechanism for joint support during normal loading patterns.

Recently, dynamic compression experiments were performed on human cartilage in which the extracellular matrix had been altered to reduce proteoglycan content, and separately, collagen cross-links. Proteoglycan digestion reduced viscous damping, but not dynamic elastic stiffness. Diminished collagen cross-links reduced both viscous damping and dynamic elastic stiffness.[39]

Another perspective on the interaction of structure and function is the effect of dynamic compressive loading on the synthesis of matrix proteins. Oscillatory loading can produce changes in the synthesis of extracellular proteins as measured by labelled proline and sulfate. However, the response is strongly dependent on the frequency and amplitude of loading.[40] Both mechanical and osmotic compression produce equivalent reductions in sulfate uptake. This reduction in sulfate uptake is hypothesized to be the result of increased pressure on the chondrocytes and not changes in solute transport.[41]

Under conditions of small strain and pure shear, no hydrodynamic pressures are produced and there is no interstitial flow of fluid. Therefore, the intrinsic properties of the cartilage matrix can be measured. In one type of experiment, shear on a small circular sample of cartilage between two platens is instantaneously increased and decay is monitored until equilibrium is reached. The range of equilibrium moduli for human and bovine articular cartilage is 0.05 to 0.25 MPa. Dynamic shear properties can be determined with sinusoidal torsional strains applied over varying frequencies. The dynamic modulus depends on applied frequency and varies from 0.2 to 2.5 MPa.[34]

Several studies have examined the role of proteoglycans and collagen, separately and together, in determining the shear properties of cartilage. An increase in aggregation of proteoglycan monomers from 0 to 100% increased by fivefold the zero shear-rate viscosity.[42] The addition of link proteins in proteoglycan solutions produced more elastic and stiffer networks than link-free aggregates.[43] In another experiment, a threefold increase in hyaluronic acid molecular weight caused about a 40% increase in dynamic shear modulus.[44] Finally, the proteoglycan network was shown to play a greater role in viscoelastic effects than the collagen network and a lesser role in stiffness.[45]

Cartilage swelling is another biomechanical ramification of the complex interactions between the extracellular matrix components and the interstitial fluid. The glycosaminoglycan chains of proteoglycan are negatively charged, with a fixed charge density that ranges from 0.04 to 0.18 mEq/g wet tissue at physiologic pH. The total ion concentration inside the tissue is greater than that of the external bathing solution. This ionic imbalance gives rise to a higher interstitial fluid pressure, called Donnan osmotic pressure, which is one of the causes of swelling.[46] In the extracellular matrix, proteoglycans interspersed with collagen are restrained to one fifth of their volume in a free solution. The fixed charges are constrained close together, causing large charge-to-charge repulsive forces, which also contribute to swelling.[34] One of the important implications of swelling and water content is the strong negative linear correlation between water content and equilibrium compressive modulus.[47]

Extensive studies have described the intra- and extrafibrillar compartments and the effect of ionic contributions on the swelling of cartilage.[48] Swelling consists of an increase in water content, with related physical increase in size and a decrease in modulus or softening. Kinetic swelling studies have shown significant variation with regard to location and biochemical composition. Measured parameters correlated well with normal, fibrillated, and degenerative tissue samples.[49]

Age-Related Changes in Cartilage Biomechanics

Although many publications describe studies of cartilage biochemical changes with age, relatively few investigations have directly measured cartilage mechanical properties as a function of age. In addition to the studies described below, other authors have drawn indirect conclusions using the following methods: (1) observing the structural biochemical changes with age; (2) noting the changes in mechanical properties that result from disrupting proteoglycan or collagen components in normal tissue; and (3) combining these findings to predict what the properties might be with changes in age. While these methods may produce a reasonable approximation of age-related changes in cartilage properties, direct measurements are necessary.

In one study, bovine cartilage samples from immature and mature animals were compared. The tensile strength properties of the middle and deep zones of cartilage decreased significantly, whereas the superficial tangential zone remained unchanged.[50] In a study of cadaver knee cartilage, the tensile fracture strength in the superficial zone showed a peak (40 MN/m^2) at age 25 and a steady decline thereafter. The tensile fracture strength in the deeper zones decreased from youth. Tensile stiffness tended to peak at age 25, but demonstrated a smaller rate of decline than that observed for strength.[51] Results of another study[52] agreed with the age-related decline in tensile strength, but found a trend (not significant) toward increased tensile stiffness. Methodologic differences may account for the opposing results.

A recent study by Kempson[53] provided extensive data on changes in tensile properties in hip and ankle cartilage from cadavers. Figure 8 displays the primary results from this extensive investi-

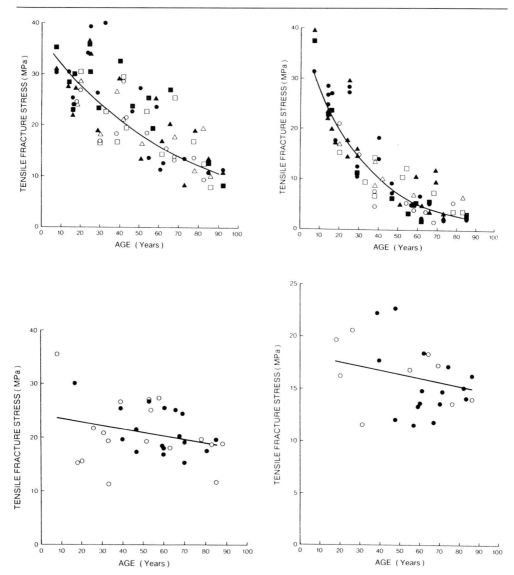

Fig. 8 *Tensile fracture stress versus age.* **Top left**, *Femoral head: Superficial layer.* **Top right**, *Femoral head: Middepth layer.* **Bottom left**, *Talus: Superficial layer.* **Bottom right**, *Talus: mid-depth layer. Squares, anterior; dots, posterior; and triangles, superior. Solid symbols, males; and open symbols, females. (Reproduced with permission from Kempson GE: Age-related changes in the tensile properties of human articular cartilage: A comparative study between the femoral head of the hip joint and the talus of the ankle joint. Biochim Biophys Acta 1991;1075:226.)*

gation. In hip cartilage, fracture stress and tensile stiffness at 10 MPa decrease markedly with age. In ankle cartilage, changes with age are mild. This important finding may help to explain the relatively high rate of occurrence of osteoarthritis in the hip versus the ankle. At lower stress levels (1 MPa), when proteoglycan and fluid resistance may be dominant factors rather than collagen, there is a reduced effect of tensile stiffness changes with age.

Studies of patellar and tibial plateau cadaver cartilage have shown that the compressive equilibrium modulus decreases and water content increases with increasing age. Also, these changes have correlated with histologic grading of the degradative condition of the cartilage surface.[17,54]

Effects of Exercise on Cartilage

The largest body of literature regarding the effects of exercise on cartilage is directed toward conditions of disuse or lack of exercise. Immobilization of joints by casting produces rapid deterioration of articular cartilage. In one study,[55] 6 weeks of casting in dogs led to decreased cartilage thickness, reduced uronic acid content, and lessened proteoglycan synthesis, as well as diminished aggregation. Three weeks of normal ambulation reversed these changes, whereas vigorous exercise prevented reversal. In another study,[56] cast immobilization allowing 8° to 15° of motion was compared to rigid external fixation. In the case of the more rigid fixator, there was greater cartilage damage and lack of recovery on remobilization. It is clear that excessive inactivity is detrimental to maintaining healthy cartilage.

Joint disuse has also been shown to produce altered material properties, as in one study of Greyhound dog knee cartilage after 4 and 8 weeks of cast immobilization.[57,58] The articular cartilage responded to periods of reduced joint loading in a site-specific manner, with a decrease of between 25% and 40% of control values in the tensile stiffness of surface zone cartilage in the femoral condyle, and no change from control values in cartilage from the patellofemoral groove. Also, an apparent stiffening effect in shear was observed, in that the equilibrium shear modulus of cartilage after 4 weeks of joint disuse was significantly elevated above control values.[59] For the same samples, a reduction in the ratio of proteoglycan to collagen was also noted.[58] Therefore, the metabolic changes in response to periods of joint disuse, particularly with respect to the conformation and composition of proteoglycans, appear to have a profound effect on the mechanical behavior of articular cartilage. The response of condylar cartilage to altered joint loading in this study as opposed to the lack of response from patellofemoral groove cartilage, likely reflects the maintenance of joint contact across the patellofemoral joint during cast immobilization.

In one extensive study[60] of 15 weeks of running exercise (4 km/day) in young beagle dogs, running increased the levels of proteoglycans in cartilage from several weightbearing anatomic sites. There was no change in the content of aggregating proteoglycans. There was an increase in chondroitin-6-sulfate as compared to chondroitin-

4-sulfate levels. This indicates the physiologic adjustment to more mature tissue as a result of increased loading. In another study,[61] investigators used microspheres in exercising dogs to determine blood flow to articular tissues. While soft tissues, such as synovia, ligaments, and menisci, showed increased blood flow, the femoral condyle and tibial plateau had decreased blood flow. In a relatively avascular tissue, it is not clear if the lower blood flow will have a deleterious effect on cartilage metabolism.

Experimental animal models have demonstrated that articular cartilage responds to periods of joint instability with increased hydration and altered mechanical behavior.[62] In one study of Greyhound dog knees, there was a significant decrease in the tensile stiffness of articular cartilage from both the femoral condyle and the patellofemoral groove at 6 and 12 weeks after transection of the anterior cruciate ligament.[58,63] The results of this and a previous study[64] suggest that these changes are progressive with time and begin at the surface zone. Analyses of the biochemical composition indicated that there was little change in either collagen or proteoglycan composition after joint instability, as compared to periods of joint disuse. These findings suggest that structural factors, such as alterations in the conformation of the proteoglycan and collagen molecule, rather than compositional factors, may be of primary importance in determining the cartilage response to altered joint loading produced by instability.

Joint instability produces abnormally high levels of local forces and force gradients in cartilage. This principle is used as a model to induce osteoarthritis in animals. Therefore, high local stress levels are damaging to cartilage. It is not clear at what load levels the benefits of motion are outweighed by excessive force causing tissue damage. Also, complete documentation of the local loads produced in exercising individuals is not available. There is no clinical study clearly linking a pounding exercise, such as jogging, and deterioration of cartilage. On the other hand, some studies[65,66] have indicated that low-impact exercise over time periods up to 12 weeks may be beneficial for patients with mild to moderate osteoarthritis.

Summary

Cartilage changes with age. The details of many of the changes in cartilage properties at midlife are not presently available. With increased age, collagen shows an increase in fibrillar size, redistribution of types, and an increase in stable cross-links. Proteoglycans become smaller, with shorter and less-aggregated structures that contain more KS-rich monomers. Increased tissue swelling is uniformly reported in the literature. In some studies, cartilage properties were found to diminish with increasing age, but these results are highly dependent on the anatomic site (knee versus ankle) and location within the tissue (superficial versus deep).

At this time, it cannot be determined if exercise is beneficial or harmful to cartilage. There are no known data on the effects of exercise on cartilage in midlife. In patients with moderate osteoarthritis, low-impact exercise (eg, swimming and walking) appears to be beneficial. Based on an overriding principle of "all things in moderation," it seems that midlife individuals can adopt exercise programs, based on their current physical condition and medical history of joint pain, that meet their general needs for physical activity and do not injure cartilage.

References

1. Eyre DR, Wu J, Apone S: A growing family of collagens in articular cartilage: Identification of 5 genetically disinct types. *J Rheumatol* 1987;14:25-27.

2. Kuettner KE: Cartilage integrity and homeostasis, in Klippei JH, Dieppe P (eds): *Rheumatology*, in press.

3. Eyre DR, Wu JJ, Woods P: Cartilage specific collagens: Structural studies, in Kuettner KE, Schleyerbach R, Peyron JG, et al (eds): *Articular Cartilage and Osteoarthritis*. New York, NY, Raven Press, 1992, pp 119-131.

4. Eikenberry EF, Mendler M, Brgin R, et al: Fibrillar organization in cartilage, in Keuttner KE, Schleyerbach R, Peyron JG, et al (eds): *Articular Cartilage and Osteoarthritis*. New York, NY, Raven Press, 1992, pp 133-149.

5. van der Rest M: Part III. Structural components of cartilage: Collagens: Introduction, in Kuettner KE, Schleyerbach R, Peyron JG, et al (eds): *Articular Cartilage and Osteoarthritis*. New York, NY, Raven Press, 1992, pp 115-117.

6. Eyre DR, Wu JJ, Woods PE: The cartilage collagens: Structural and metabolic studies. *J Rheumatol Suppl* 1991;27:49-51.

7. Schmidt MB, Schoonbeck JM, Mow VC, et al: The relationship between collagn crosslinking and the tensile properties of articular cartilage. *Trans Orthop Res Soc* 1987;12:134.

8. Poole CA, Ayaad S, Schofield JR: Chondrons from articular cartilage: I. Immunolocaliation of type VI collagen in the pericellular capsule of isolated canine tibial chondrons. *J Cell Sci* 1988;90:635-643.

9. Gannon JM, Walker G, Fischer M, et al: Localization of type X collagen in canine growth plate and adult articular cartilage. *J Orthop Res* 1991;9:485-494.

10. Ryan MC, Sandell LJ: Differential expression of a cysteine-rich domain in the amino-terminal propeptide of type II (cartilage) procollagen by alternative splicing of mRNA. *J Biol Chem* 1990;265:10334-10339.

11. Zhu W, Lai WM, Mow VC: The density and strength of proteoglycan-proteoglycan interaction sites in concentrated solutions. *J Biomech* 1991;24:1007-1018.

12. Eyre DR, Wu J, Niyibizi C: The collagens of bone and cartilage: Molecular diversity and supramolecular assembly, in Cohn DV, Glorieux FH, Martin TJ (eds): *Calcium Regulation and Bone Metabolism: Basic and Clinical Aspects*. Amsterdam, Excerpta Medica, 1990, pp 188-194.

13. Bayliss MT: Proteoglycan structure and metabolism during maturation and ageing of human articular cartilage. *Biochem Soc Trans* 1990;18:799-802.

14. Mow VC, Setton LA, Ratcliffe A, et al: Structure-function relationships of articular cartilage, in Brandt KE (ed): *Cartilage Changes in Osteoarthritis*, Indianapolis, IN, Indiana University School of Medicine, 1990, pp 22-42.

15. Hardingham TE, Fosang AJ, Dudhia J: Aggrecan, the chondroitin sulfate/keratan sulfate proteoglycan from cartilage, in Kuettner KE, Schleyerbach R, Peyron JG, et al (eds): *Articular Cartilage and Osteoarthritis*. New York, NY, Raven Press, 1992, pp 5-20.

16. Doege KJ, Sasaki M, Kimura T, et al: Complete coding sequence and deduced primary structure of the human cartilage large aggregating proteoglycan, aggrecan: Human-specific repeats, and additional alternatively spliced forms. *J Biol Chem* 1991;266:894-902.

17. Thonar EJ, Kuettner KE: Biochemical basis of age-related changes in proteoglycans, in Wight TN, Mecham RP (eds): *Biology of Proteoglycans*. Orlando, FL, Academic Press, 1987, pp 211-246.

18. Heinegard D, Paulsson M: Structure and metabolism of proteoglycans, in Piez KA, Reddi AH (eds): *Extracellular Matrix Biochemistry*. New York, Elsevier, 1984, pp 277-328.

19. Hardingham T, Bayliss M: Proteoglycans of articular cartilage: Changes in aging and in joint disease. *Semin Arthritis Rheum* 1990;20(suppl 1):12-33.

20. Zhu WB, Mow VC: Viscometric properties of proteoglycan solutions at physiological concentrations, in Mow VC, Ratcliffe A, Woo SLY (eds): *Biomechanics of Diarthrodial Joints*. New York, NY, Springer-Verlag, 1990, pp 313-344.

21. Sandy JD, Plaaas AH: Studies on the hyaluronate binding properties of newly synthesized proteoglycans purified from articular chondrocyte cultures. *Arch Biochem Biophys* 1989;271:300-314.

22. Heinegård D, Oldberg A: Structure and biology of cartilage and bone matrix noncollagenous macromolecules. *FASEB J* 1989;3:2042-2051.

23. Rosenberg LC: Structure and function of dermatan sulfate proteoglycans in articular cartilage, in Kuettner KE, Schleyerbach R, Peyron JG, et al (eds): *Articular Cartilage and Osteoarthritis*, New York, NY, Raven Press, 1992, pp 45-63.

24. Hedbom E, Heinegård D: Interaction of a 59-kDa connective tissue matrix protein with collagen I and collagen II. *J Biol Chem* 1989;264:6898-6905.

25. Scott JE: Proteoglycan: Collagen interactions and subfibrillar structure in collagen fibrils: Implications in the development and ageing of connective tissues. *J Anat* 1990;169:23-35.

26. Vogel KG, Paulsson M, Heinegård D: Specific inhibition of type I and type II collagen fibrillogenesis by the small proteoglycan of tendon. *Biochem J* 1984;223:587-597.

27. Poole AR, Webber C, Pidoux I, et al: Localization of a dermatan sulfate proteoglycan (DS-PGII) in cartilage and the presence of an immunologically related species in other tissues. *J Histochem Cytochem* 1986;34:618-625.

28. Oldberg A, Antonsson P, Lindblom K, et al: A collagen-binding 59-kd protein (fibromodulin) is structurally related to the small interstitial proteoglycans PG-S1 and PG-S2 (decorin). *EMBO-J* 1989;8:2601-2604.

29. Plaas AHK, Barry F, Wong-Palms S: Keratan sulfate substitution on cartilage matrix molecules, in Kuettner KE, Schleyerbach R, Peyron JG, et al (eds): *Articular Cartilage and Osteoarthritis*. New York, NY, Raven Press, 1992, pp 69-79.

30. Thonar EJ-MA; Bjornsson S, Kuettner KE: Age-related changes in cartilage proteoglycans, in Kuettner KE, Schleyerbach R, Hascall VC (eds): *Articular Cartilage Biochemistry*. New York, NY, Raven Press, 1986, pp 273-288.

31. Buckwalter JA, Kuettner KE, Thorar EJ: Age-related changes in articular cartilage proteoglycans: Electron microscopic studies. *J Orthop Res* 1985;3:251-257.

32. Barone-Varelas J, Schnitzer TJ, Meng Q, et al: Age-related differences in the metabolism of proteoglycans in bovine articular cartilage explants maintained in the presence of insulin-like growth factor I. *Connect Tissue Res* 1991;26:101-120.

33. Akizuk S, Mow VC, Muller F, et al: Tensile properties of human knee joint cartilage: I. Influence of ionic conditions, weight bearing, and fibrillation on the tensile modulus. *J Orthop Res* 1986;4:379-392.

34. Mow VC, Zhu W, Ratcliffe A: Structure and function of articular cartgilage and meniscus, in Mow VC, Hayes WC (eds): *Basic Orthopaedic Biomechanics*. New York, NY, Raven Press, 1991, pp 143-198.

35. Schmidt MB, Mow VC, Chun LE, et al: Effects of proteoglycan extraction on the tensile behavior of human articular cartilage. *J Orthop Res* 1990;8:353-363.

36. Bader DL, Kempson GE, Barrett AJ, et al: The effects of leucocyte elastase on the mechanical properties of adult human articular cartilage in tension. *Biochim Biophys Acta* 1981;677:103-108.

37. Athanasiou KA, Agarwal A, Dzida FJ: Variations in the material properties of human hip cartilage. *Trans Orthop Res Soc* 1992;17:612.

38. Broom ND, Silyn-Roberts H: Collagen-collagen versus collagen-proteoglycan interactions in the determination of cartilage strength. *Arthritis Rheum* 1990; 33:1512-1517.

39. Bader DL, Kempson GE, Egan J, et al: The effects of selective matrix degradation on the short-term compressive properties of adult human articular cartilage. *Biochim Biophys Acta* 1992;1116:147-154.

40. Sah RL, Kim YJ, Doong JY, et al: Biosynthetic response of cartilage explants to dynamic compression. *J Orthop Res* 1989;7:619-636.

41. Schneiderman R, Keret D, Maroudas A: Effects of mechanical and osmotic pressure on the rate of glycosaminoglycan synthesis in the human adult femoral head cartilage: An in vitro study. *J Orthop Res* 1986;4:393-408.

42. Hardingham TE, Muir H, Kwan MK, et al: Viscoelastic properties of proteoglycan solutions with varying proportions present as aggregates. *J Orthop Res* 1987;5:36-46.

43. Mow VC, Zhu W, Lai WM, et al: The influence of link protein stabilization on the viscometric properties of proteoglycan aggregate solutions. *Biochim Biophys Acta* 1989;992:201-208.

44. Zhu WB, Iatridis JC, Hardingham TE, et al: Effect of hyaluronan size on shear flow properties of proteoglycan aggregate solutions. *Trans Orthop Res Soc* 1992;17:30.

45. Zhu WB, Iatridis JC, Hlibczuk V, et al: Proteoglycan-collagen interactions in vitro. *Trans Orthop Res Soc* 1992;17:129.

46. Maroudas A: Physicochemical properties of articular cartilage, in Freeman MAR (ed): *Adult Articular Cargilage*, ed 2. Kent, England, Pitman Medical, 1979, pp 215-290.

47. Armstrong CG, Mow VC: Variations in the intrinsic mechanical prperties of human articular cartilage with age, degeneration, and water content. *J Bone Joint Surg* 1982;64A:88-94.

48. Maroudas A, Schneiderman R, Popper O: The role of water, proteoglycan, and collagen in solute transport in cartilage, in Kuettner KE, Schleyerbach R, Peyron JG, et al (eds): *Articular Cartilage and Osteoarthritis*. New York, NY, Raven Press, 1992, pp 355-371.

49. Akizuki S, Mow VC, Muller F, et al: Tensile properties of human knee joint cartilage: II. Correlations between weight bearing and tissue pathology and the kinetics of swelling. *J Orthop Res* 1987;5:173-186.

50. Roth V, Mow VC: The intrinsic tensile behavior of the matrix of bovine articular cartilage and its variation with age. *J Bone Joint Surg* 1980;62A:1102-1117.

51. Kempson GE: Relationship between the tensile properties of articular cartilage from the human knee and age. *Ann Rheum Dis* 1982;41:508-511.

52. Roberts S, Weightman B, Urban J, et al: Mechanical and biochemical properties of human articular cartilage in osteoarthritic femoral heads and in autopsy specimens. *J Bone Joint Surg* 1986;68B:278-288.

53. Kempson GE: Age-related changes in the tensile properties of human articular cartilage: A comparative study between the femoral head of the hip joint and the talus of the ankle joint. *Biochim Biophys Acta* 1991;1075:223-230.

54. Akizuki S, Wada T, Yasukawa Y, et al: Topographical variations of osteoarthritic changes and mechanical properties on human tibial plateau cartilage in different age. *Transactions of the Combined Meeting of the Orthopaedic Research Societies of U.S.A., Japan and Canada, Oct. 21-23, 1991, Banff, Alberta, Canada.* Calgary, Alberta, Canada, Organizing Committee of the Orthopaedic Research Societies, 1991, p 84.

55. Palmoski MJ, Brandt KD: Immobilization of the knee prevents osteoarthritis after anterior cruciate ligament transection. *Arthritis Rheum* 182;25:1201-1208.

56. Behrens F, Kraft EL, Oegema TR Jr: Biochemical changes in articular cartilage after joint immobilization by casting or external fixation. *J Orthop Res* 1989;7:335-343.

57. Setton LA, Zimmerman JR, Mow VC, et al: Effects of disuse on the tensile properties and composition of canine knee joint cartilage. *Trans Orthop Res Soc* 1990;15:155.

58. Setton LA, Mow VC, Muller FJ, et al: Comparison of tensile and swelling properties of disuse and Pond-Nuki osteoarthritic knee cartilage. *Trans Orthop Res Soc* 1991;16:358.

59. Setton LA, Gu WY, Muller FJ, et al: Changes in the intrinsic shear behavior of articular cartilage with joint disuse. *Trans Orthop Res Soc* 1992;17:209.

60. Saamanen AM, Tammi M, Kiviranta I, et al: Levels of chondroitin-6-sulfate and nonaggregating proteoglycans at articular cartilage contact sites in the knees of young dogs subjected to moderate running exercise. *Arthritis Rheum* 1989;32:1282-1292.

61. Simkin PA, Huang A, Benedict RS: Effects of exercise on blood flow to canine articular tissues. *J Orthop Res* 1990;8:297-303.

62. Moskowitz RW: Experimental models of osteoarthritis, in Moskowitz RW, Howell DS, Goldberg VM, et al (eds): *Osteoarthritis: Diagnosis and Medical/Surgical Management*, ed 2. Philadelphia, PA, WB Saunders, 1992, pp 213-232.

63. Setton LA, Mow VC, Muller FJ, et al: Progressive changes in the mechanical properties of articular cartilage in an experimental model of osteoarthrits. *Transactions of the Combined Meeting of the Orthopaedic Research Societies of U.S.A., Japan and Canada, Oct. 21-23, 1991, Banff, Alberta, Canada.* Calgary, Alberta, Canada, Organizing Committee of the Orthopaedic Research Societies, 1991, p 171.

64. Myers ER, Hardingham TE, Billingham MEJ, et al: Changes in the tensile and compressive properties of articular cartilage in a canine model of osteoarthritis. *Trans Orthop Res Soc* 1986;11:231.

65. Minor MA, Hewett JE, Webel RR, et al: Efficacy of physical conditioning exercise in patients with rheumatoid arthritis and osteoarthritis. *Arthritis Rheum* 1989;32:1396-1405.

66. Kovar PA, Allegrante JP, MacKenzie CR, et al: Supervised fitness walking in patients with osteoarthritis of the knee: A randomized, controlled trial. *Ann Intern Med* 1992;116:529-534.

Chapter 12

Aging Effects Upon the Repair and Healing of Athletic Injury

Wayne B. Leadbetter, MD

Introduction

The process of aging implies a decline not only in athletic performance but also in potential to recover from sports-induced injury. While current evidence would suggest some individual variability in the rate of progression in both physiologic as well as structural aging, aging will affect all athletes eventually.[1] How significant these aging effects will prove to be upon the healing of a specific tissue injury depends on a variety of intrinsic and extrinsic factors.[2] In addition, the type of injury (ie, acute macrotrauma versus chronic microtrauma), the nature of the tissue involved, the presence or absence of pre-existing tissue degeneration, and the rate at which healing tissues are re-exposed to both load and use, play an important role in determining the outcome of treatment.[3]

This chapter will define relevant aspects of soft-tissue cell-matrix biology, inflammation, and wound repair; and known cellular tissue and clinical evidence will be reviewed to suggest possible effects of aging on the various stages of these events. While these observations may be applied to a variety of tissues, particular reference will be made to the most commonly athletically injured tissues; that is, dense connective tissue such as ligament and tendon.[4]

The Concept of Aging

Aging is probably a multifactorial biologic process with respect to both its causes and regulation, occurring over the life span of an organism.[5] Maturation is defined as that span of growth of the organism culminating in sexual maturity; epiphyseal closure is an accepted end point for maturation in mammalian growth.[5,6] Aging is the general term used to include all periods of the life span, while the term senescence is reserved for the postmaturation accumulative physiologic decrements in members of a species that increase the probability of death.[7] Both terms are imprecise. At the cellular level, senes-

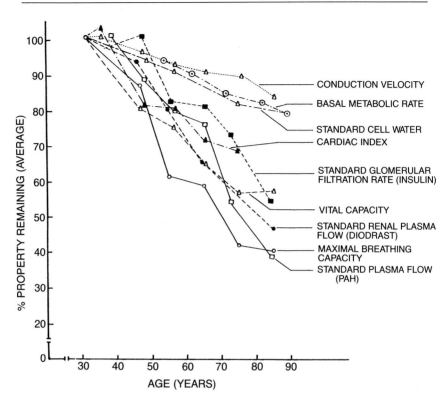

Fig. 1 *Decrease with age in some physiological functions in humans expressed as percent of mean value at age 30. (Reproduced with permission from Shock NW, in* Program and Papers of the Conference on Gerontology. *Durham, NC, Duke University Press, Durham, NC, 1959, pp 123-140.)*

cence is defined as a decreased capacity of diploid cells to proliferate during prolonged periods of culture.[8] Age-related changes in structure and function occur at all levels of tissue organization during the life span of an individual.[9] The rate constants for this linear loss are estimated to decline about 0.8% to 0.9% per year for many functional capacities present at 30 years of age (Fig. 1).

In mammals, aging is identified by a predictable set of characteristics.[5] First, mortality is increased with age after maturation.[10] Second, there are changes in both the cellular and extracellular matrix components of connective tissues; for example, decreased cellularity at ligament insertions;[6] diminished proteoglycan and water content in tendon;[6] accumulation of lipofuscin pigment (age pigment) in various tissues, including brain, heart, muscle, and tendon;[11,12] and a generalized increase in stabilized cross-linking of matrix molecules such as collagen.[13] Third, there is a wide spectrum of progressive deteriorative physiologic changes, including changes in glomerular

Table 1 Effects of aging on body composition and major organ systems

Organ System	Anatomic Changes	Functional Changes
Body composition	Increased lipid fraction Loss of skeletal mass	Increased half-life for lipid-soluble drugs Decreased O_2 consumption, heat production, and cardiac output
Nervous system	Attrition of neurons Decreased neurotransmitter activity	Deafferentation, neurogenic atrophy, and decreased anesthetic requirement Impaired autonomic homeostasis
Cardiovascular system	Decreased arterial elasticity Ventricular hypertrophy Reduced adrenergic responsiveness	Increased impedance to ejection, widened pulse pressure Decreased maximal cardiac output
Pulmonary system	Loss of lung elastin Increased thoracic stiffness Reduced alveolar surface area	Increased residual volume Loss of vital capacity Impaired efficiency of gas exchange Increased work of breathing
Renal system	Reduced vascularity Tissue atrophy	Decreased plasma flow, glomerular filtration rate, drug clearance, and ability to handle salt and water loads
Hepatic system	Reduced tissue mass	Reduced hepatic blood flow and drug clearance

(Reproduced with permission from Muravchick S: Anesthesia for the elderly, in Miller RD, Cucchiara RF, Miller ED Jr, et al (eds): *Anesthesia*, ed 3. New York, NY, Churchill Livingstone, 1990, Vol 2. p 1970.)

filtration rate, maximum heart rate, vital capacity, aerobic capacity and other measures of functional capacity, and body composition.[1,10,14-16] Many of those functions have potential effects on wound healing (Table 1). Fourth, the reasons why there is an increased vulnerability to many diseases with age is not completely understood.[10] Fifth, the ability to respond adaptively to environmental change is reduced.

In the aging athlete, it is this last characteristic that is most salient; for it is not so much a decrease in basal functional capacity as it is a reduced ability to adapt to environmental stress that characterizes the aging process.[17] The maintenance of tissue homeostasis or continued connective tissue renewal under conditions of physiologic stress (ie, morphostasis) depends on the ability to generate these adaptive responses.[18] It is the maintenance or disruption of this balance that lies at the crux of differentiating the healthy, noninjured, or "normal," from the injured, diseased, or "pathologic."[17] Evidence for the influence of aging on such adaptation as well as its potential adequacy and rate exists at the tissue and cell-matrix levels, and will be discussed later in the chapter.

Woo and Tkach[19] have described a hypothetical model of the nonlinear effects of stress and motion on the homeostatic responses in soft connective tissues (Fig. 2). While the effect of aging on such parameters has not been well documented, clinical experience in the rehabilitation of athletic injury would tend to support the speculation that recovery from immobilization would be slowed and tolerance to increased stress would be more sensitive to rate. Thus, the older athlete should expect that rehabilitation for any injury

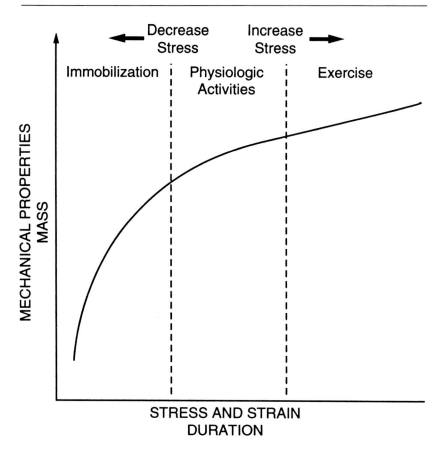

Fig. 2 *Hypothetical curve describing the nonlinear effects of stress and motion on the homeostatic responses of soft connective tissues. (Reproduced with permission from Woo SL, Gomez MA, Woo YK, et al: Mechanical properties of tendons and ligaments: II. The relationships of immobilization and exercise on tissue remodeling. Biorheology 1982;19:397-408.)*

would take longer[20] and that return to activity would proceed with moderation.[21]

Implicit in the concept of tissue morphostasis is the existence of a "homeostatic stress window." The existence of such a window is implied by the marked adverse tissue effects that result from inactivity or disuse of musculoskeletal tissues. Such effects include a decreased rate of collagen turnover in tendon and ligament with resultant increased tissue stiffness, osseous resorption occurring at ligamentous attachment sites with increased vulnerability to disruption of tendon or ligament from its bony insertion, decreased cellularity of ligament and tendon, decreased collagen fiber bundle thickness, reduced capillarization, increased extensibility per unit length, and decreased glycosaminoglycans and reduced water content.[22]

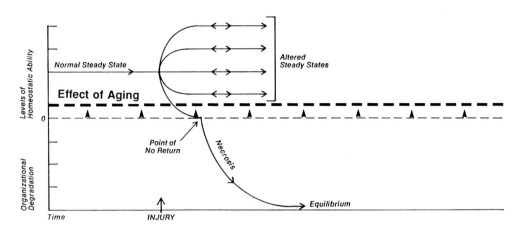

Fig. 3 *Model of various reactions a cell is capable of performing after an alteration in its environment. The cell in the normal steady state is able to maintain a homeostasis compatible with optimal function. Once injury occurs, the cell either alters steady state and its function or, if injury is of sufficient severity, reaches a steady state such that it is unable to maintain its homeostatic mechanisms at the level required for life (point of no return) and dies. Aging would appear to alter the threshold for cell necrosis. (Adapted with permission from Scarpelli DG, Trump BF:* Cell Injury. *Kalamazoo, MI, Upjohn Company, 1971, p 8.)*

However, these changes appear to be distinct from aging because these biochemical and biomechanical alterations are fully reversible in response to a consistent training program.[23] Thus, disuse produces an atrophic cellular response, which is a reversible energy-conserving shutdown of differentiated cellular functions, presumably with the effect of conserving energy.[17] When appropriately stimulated, atrophic cells are fully capable of resuming their differentiated functions, such as protein synthesis or contractile force.[17] The histologic hallmark of aging is cell atrophy; eg, the size of all parenchymal organs in the body decrease with age.[17] Aging and degeneration may represent successive stages within a single process.[24] In the concept of cell injury as proposed by Scarpelli and Trump,[25] aging theoretically alters the threshold at which a given cell reaches the "point of no return"; that is, loss of viability (Fig. 3).

While there is no single adequate theory of aging,[26,27] a working definition of the aging process might be developed in view of previous observations in the literature[5,17,27] and in keeping with accepted precepts of Strehler.[28] Aging may be defined as universal, intrinsic, progressive, and decremental cell-matrix adaptive failure to maintain homeostasis under changing conditions of physiologic stress. Although any valid aging phenomenon should be observable in all older members of the species, the rate of aging does not appear to be a universal characteristic of all animals, but rather of individual species.[28] An appreciation of the biological mechanisms of aging requires a tissue by tissue, and even cell by cell, analysis.

The Evidence for Cellular Aging

Indirect evidence for an aging effect on inflammation and wound repair has been derived from the field of cellular senescence (cytogerontology).[8] The cell type that is most capable of sustained proliferation with the usual methods of tissue culture is the spindle-shaped cell, commonly called a "fibroblast." It has been extensively used for the study of cellular senescence in vitro.[29] There is evidence that fibroblasts from different anatomic sites in the same organism may vary in vitro in proliferative capacity as well as other attributes.[8] It is unreasonable a priori to assume that a dermal fibroblast would possess the same biologic characteristics in culture, as, for example, tendon fibroblast. It is now known that fibroblasts from similar structures, such as the anterior cruciate ligament and medial collateral ligament, as well as cells from different sites within the same ligament structure, display variable biologic capabilities (Fig. 4).[30,31]

In the absence of specific cell markers, the precise origin of a given cultured cell type may be uncertain.[8] Another limitation of cytogerontology is that despite the accepted widespread use throughout the world of established cell lines, such as the W-18 fibroblast, there is concern that such cells may not be characteristic of any specific cell type found in human or animal tissue.[7] Also, the environmental conditions of in vitro cell growth may significantly alter the genetic expression of a cell. For instance, fibroblasts reduce dramatically the gene expression and biosynthesis of interstitial collagens when grown in a three-dimensional collagen gel compared to a regular monolayer.[32] Therefore, the term "fibroblast like cell" is often more appropriate when referring to cell senescence data.

Cellular aging in vitro is not specific to fibroblasts, but has also been demonstrated in smooth muscle cells, endothelial cells, glial cells, and lymphocytes.[5] While it is generally assumed that cells aging in vitro and cells from aging organisms have many attributes in common,[8] it is likely that the aging of proliferating mesenchymal cells may be different from that of fixed postmitotic cells (eg, neurons) or reverting postmitotic cells (Fig. 5). Decreased proliferative ability of the aging cultured fibroblast-like cell remains one of the most compelling arguments for its validity as a model in the study of cellular aging. Cellular life spans may be under genetic control and limited by the number of population doublings in vitro rather than sidereal, or clock time.[8] Embryonic cells double an average of 48 times in culture, but adult fibroblasts only average 20 to 30 times.[7,29]

The loss of proliferative capacity observed in human fibroblast cultures, however, does not unequivocally imply senescence, because terminal differentiation of the cell also results in postmitotic

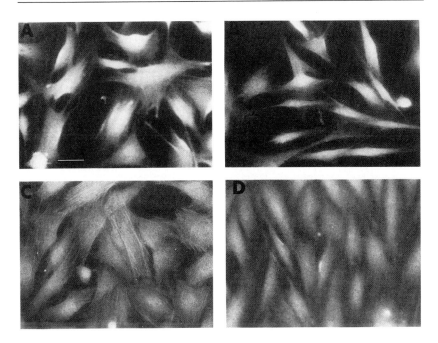

Fig. 4 *Representative fluorescent images of cells of the anterior cruciate ligament (ACL) and medial collateral ligament (MCL) (passage 4) stained with FITC-phalloidin.* **Top left,** *ACL and* **top right,** *MCL cultures 1 day after plating.* **Bottom left,** *ACL and* **bottom right,** *MCL cultures 6 days after plating. Note spread-out morphology and more prominent stress fibers in ACL cells. Bar (**top left**) represents 50 μm. All pictures are at the same magnification. (Reproduced with permission from Nagineni CN, Amiel D, Green MH, et al: Characterization of the intrinsic properties of the anterior cruciate and medial collateral ligament cells: An in vitro cell culture study. J Orthop Res 1992;10:465-475.)*

inactivity.[33] Senescent fibroblasts display a number of differences from younger cells, including a different set of surface glycoproteins and reduced amounts of fibronectin, increased membrane permeability and altered lipid composition of the fibroblast membrane, larger bundles of more prominent actin filaments (so-called aging fibers), increased mitochondrial mass, and changes in cell morphology.[14] Because of their role in synthesizing the fibers that provide form and function to the extracellular matrix, the regulation of fibroblast-like cells would seem critical to the success of wound repair.

In discussing age-related cellular dysfunction, it is helpful to review the basic informational flow pattern in eukaryotes, as outlined by Kanungo.[9] Cell informational flow follows the pattern of DNA → RNA → synthesized protein.[9] The rates of protein synthesis and the amounts of various proteins necessary for specific functions may be regulated at one or more of the following steps: (1) transcription of precursor heterogeneous nuclear RNAs (HnRNA) from chromatin; (2) processing of HnRNAs to mature translatable messenger RNAs

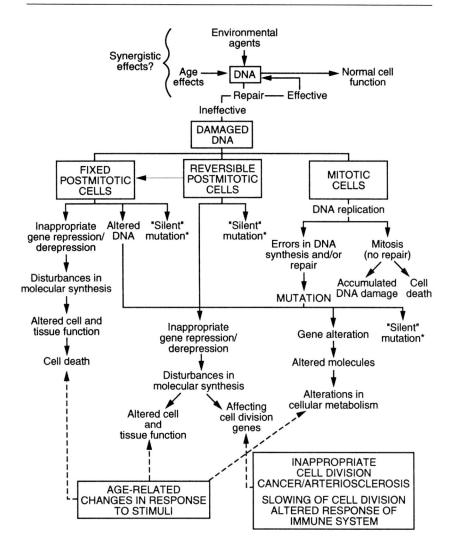

Fig. 5 *A diagrammatic view of the possible forms of damage to DNA and subsequent cellular responses. *These changes are only of consequence during redifferentiation and/ or stimulation of further mitoses. (Modified with permission from Davies I: Biology of aging: General principles, in Brocklehurst JC (ed): Textbook of Geriatric Medicine and Gerontology, ed 3. Edinburgh, Churchill Livingstone, 1985, p 41.)*

(mRNAs); (3) translation of mRNA on ribosomes; and (4) degradation of the proteins by various factors. Direct modulation of the activities of proteins (for example, phosphorylation and adenylation) also may govern the amount of active and inactive proteins available for activity.

Transcription, which is the first and primary step in this sequence of events, may be modulated by alterations in the structural organization of the chromatin. These alterations may include proper confirmation of the DNA, availability of DNA for RNA polymerase, the extent of association of histones in non-histone chromosomal (NHC) proteins to DNA, and (4) modifications of histones in NHC proteins that alter their association with DNA.[9] However, while evidence exists for decremental age-related alterations in this informational flow at practically every site, the significance of these findings remains controversial.[8,17,29,33,34] In addition, no marked accumulation of altered proteins with age has been found in most human tissues.[27] A general pattern of decreased RNA synthesis and degradation with age has been noted.[9,35] Paralleling the diminished activity of mRNA, there is a generalized decrease in all protein synthesis and proteolysis. Decreased collagen synthesis is characterized by reversibility with ascorbic acid, possibly through the induction of polyADP-ribose synthetase enzyme.[36,37] Collagen synthesis declines with aging, which also may alter this reversibility. Paz and Gallop[38] found little response by in vitro senescent fibroblasts to ascorbic acid with respect to the amount of collagen and no change in hydroxylation.

Age-related accumulation of altered enzymes in the aging human fibroblast has been postulated and in some cases found.[9,35,39] After an extensive review, however, pitfalls in most present research design had led Kanungo,[9] to conclude that "in the enzyme studies, no comparable data on all enzymes of even one metabolic pathway are available for any organism as a function of its age. We also have no detailed information on the key regulatory enzymes of different metabolic paths whose levels are critical for the rates at which the paths operate."[9] Because enzymes are the polypeptide catalysts of various chemical reactions in the body, it is strongly suspected that pretranslational errors in the genetic coding and synthesis or post-translational modification of such enzymes in old age would have significant effects on function, particularly on response to injury. Such reasoning has led to the hypothesis of age-related changes in enzymatic function during collagen synthesis (Fig. 6). However, evidence for altered intracellular enzymatic activity—such as the hydroxylation of prolyl and lysyl residues by the enzymes prolyl and lysyl hydroxylase, leading to stabilization of the collagen triple helix and intermolecular cross-linking during collagen synthesis to form hydroxyproline and hydroxylysine in procollagen—is inconclusive.[35] While progressive decrease in collagen content has been observed in both epidermal and mesenchymal tissues, it is still not fully resolved as to whether this is a result of a decreased synthesis or increased degradation of collagen. Such findings as the decreased level of activity of type I collagen mRNA in senescent fibroblasts[40] would tend to support the former, whereas, evidence of increased stability of the collagen message and increased collagenase activity in senescent fibroblasts would tend to support the latter.[40,41]

Hormones are an important regulator of wound repair.[42-44] Growth hormone, insulin, thyroxine, and adrenal corticosteroids

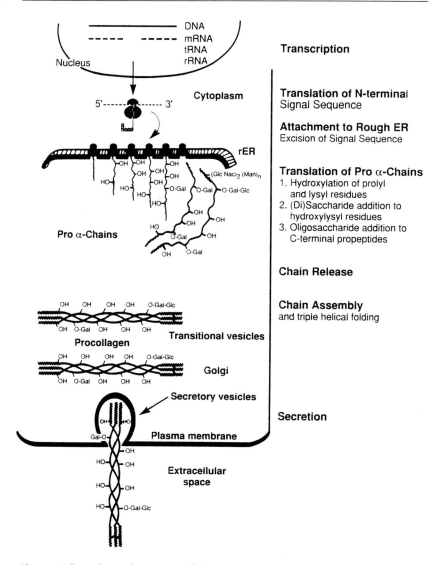

Fig. 6 *Collagen biosynthesis: intracellular events and secretion. (Reproduced with permission from Goldberg B, Rabinovitch M: Connective tissue, in Weiss L: Cell and Tissue Biology: A Textbook of Histology, ed 6. Baltimore, MD, Urban & Schwarzenberg, 1988, p 164.)*

have been shown to influence healing.[9,17,45] There are three categories of hormones: steroids of the gonads and adrenal cortex; amino acid derivatives of the thyroid and adrenal medulla; and peptides of the hypothalamus, pituitary, thyroid, parathyroid, and islets of Langerhans.[17] Hormones effect replication of DNA, transcription and translation, cell division and growth, enzyme levels, and homeostatic control of metabolites.[9] Wound mediators, such as cytokines or growth factors, may be considered as an additional category of local protein hormone messengers that represent the most prevalent and universal method of cell-to-cell and cell-to-matrix regulation throughout the body.[44,46] There are several subcategories of cytokines, which include monokines, so named for their derivation from mononuclear phagocytes; lymphokines, produced by activated T lymphocytes; colony-stimulating factors, produced by lymphocytes and mononuclear phagocytes; interleukins, principally synthesized by leukocytes; and growth factors, such as transforming growth factor-beta, platelet-derived growth factor, fibroblast growth factor, and epidermal growth factor, produced by a variety of sources, such as platelets, fibroblasts, and particularly, tissue macrophages.[46,47] Such biologic response modifiers are not limited to cell-synthesized protein molecules. For example, the degradation products of such structures as cell wall lipoproteins (eg, prostaglandins) are traumatically induced fragments of proteoglycan molecules (eg, from muscle or cartilage) that act as potent cell stimuli in tissue trauma responses.[17,48] All of these molecules may be thought to interact like letters of an alphabet to create words, sentences, and whole messages. Taken out of context, it is likely that the meaning of any one is often lost. Individual cell signaling or activation during the complex chemical events of wound healing depend on the integrity and efficiency of cell membrane receptors as well as the accurate transduction of information into the nucleus.[9,45,49]

Age-related decline in hormonal target tissue response is well documented.[27,48] This lack of responsiveness has been attributed to both receptor changes at the cell membrane level and postreceptor changes with respect to the role of so-called "second messenger" molecules and, in particular, intracellular calcium ion flux (Fig. 7).[49] Several studies have shown cell senescence in culture or that cells from donors of different ages progressively lose their responsiveness to growth factors with age.[8] The reasons for this loss of responsiveness are controversial and complex and represent not only senescent changes in receptor function, but also more complex changes in cellular phenotype associated with terminal cell differentiation.[49,50]

Proliferative capacity is another important feature of human diploid fibroblasts that is progressively lost with senescence.[8] Proliferation is regulated by extracellular factors and the state of cellular differentiation.[50] In addition to changes in responsiveness to polypeptide growth factors and growth inhibition, there also appears to be a down regulation of growth-related gene function, particularly as evidenced in the c-myc and c-fos proto-oncogenes.[45,50] The c-myc and c-fos proto-oncogenes and coproteins are localized to the cell nucleus.[45] Although the precise functions of the c-myc and the c-fos proteins are unknown, indirect evidence suggests that they may regulate secondary nuclear events that occur in response to growth factors. Both genes are expressed in very low levels in senescent fibroblasts, but are inducible in the nonsenescent human fibroblast.[50]

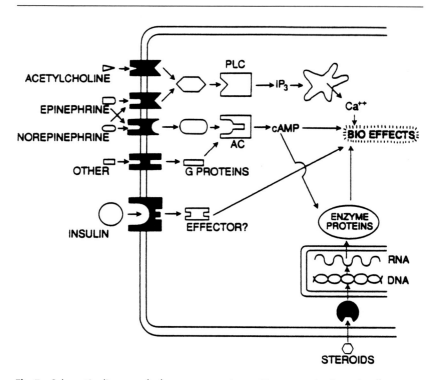

Fig. 7 *Schematic diagram of a hormone-neurotransmitter responsive (target) cell. Essentially all hormones and neurotransmitters initiate their biologic effects (BIO EFFECTS) by binding to specific receptor proteins (shaded). Most of these agents attach to receptors on the surface of the cell; steroid hormones have intracellular receptors. Acetylcholine and epinephrine bind to a receptor, initiating the coupling of regulatory elements called "G PROTEINS" to the enzyme phospholipase C (PLC). PLC catalyzes the production of IP_3, which releases calcium (Ca^{++}) ions from intracellular stores. Ca^{++} flux causes certain specific biologic effects. Norepinephrine also may stimulate IP_3 production. Both norepinephrine and epinephrine can bind to another receptor that uses a different G protein to activate the enzyme adenylate cyclase (AC). AC catalyzes the production of cyclic AMP (cAMP), which either activates certain enzyme proteins by phosphorylation or elicits particular BIO EFFECTS. Other hormones activate G proteins, which are actually inhibitory (eg, reduce AC activity). Insulin exerts biologic actions through pathways that are not well defined. Steroid hormones bind to intracellular receptors in the cytoplasm or nucleus, which directly activate genes by binding to the DNA. Specific mRNAs are transcribed and translated in enzyme proteins, which elicit characteristic, steroid-dependent BIO EFFECTS. (Reproduced with permission from Roth GS: Mechanisms of altered hormone-neurotransmitter action during aging: From receptors to calcium mobilization. Ann Rev Gerontol Geriatr 1990;10:134.)*

Aging effects on immunologic cell populations also occur, but are not uniform.[51] The lymphocyte is a primary cellular component in chronic inflammation and is represented by two subtypes; B lymphocytes and T lymphocytes. The B lymphocytes, referring to their bursal or bone marrow derivation, are the only cells capable of producing antibodies; hence, they are characterized by a prominent rough endoplasmic reticulum. This cell often differentiates into a specialized form called the plasma cell. The T lymphocyte, which is derived from the thymus, is cytotoxic.[17,52] In response to antigenic simulation, a subset of T cells, the helper cells, secrete cytokines, which promote the proliferation and differentiation of the T cells as well as other cells, including B cells and macrophages.[53] Cytolytic T cells are a second subset of T cells that lyse cells which produce foreign proteins and participate in allograft rejection.[53] Natural killer cells, also called large granulolymphocytes, are circulating cells derived mainly from the spleen.[53] They attack tissue cells and have been implicated in chronic muscle injury.[54] Lymphocytes and derived plasma cells are important in humeral and cell-mediated immune responses.[17] Aging profoundly affects most T cell functions.[55] T cells produce an important class of lymphokines known as the interleukins, which stimulate growth and maturation of parenchymal target cells. With aging, the ability of T cells to express receptors to interleukin 2 also declines.[51] While specific immune response is designed to protect the host in infectious disease, nonspecific tissue damage in sports-induced injury may theoretically be promoted by the age-related T cell loss of fidelity in recognition of self (Fig. 8).[56] Age-related defects in the phagocytic ability of the polymorphonuclear leukocyte has been demonstrated; both fetal and senescent neutrophils have decreased function; this correlates with the vulnerability of the very young and very old to infectious disease.[55,54]

The tissue macrophage is a circulating monocyte from the peripheral blood that has migrated into the extracellular space.[17] Macrophages appear to be relatively unaffected by aging.[51,55] The number of circulating monocytes in the peripheral blood does not appear to change with increasing age, nor does aging affect the function or production of cellular mediators by macrophages.[51] Alterations in cell membrane receptors among immune cell populations have been reported.[51,57]

Hayflick[7] has provided an extensive review of the changes occurring in cellular senescence, which is summarized in Tables 2-4.

Evidence for Tissue Aging Effects

As with cell culture research, efforts to document cell matrix tissue aging effects are fraught with unique problems, which include efforts to distinguish disuse from true aging effects,[22] inability to accurately establish the evolutionary stages of microtraumatic injury because of the inherent nonsurgical nature of the early stages of the lesion,[2,3,58] and the lack of adequate animal models for cumulative traumatic injury.[59] Despite these constraints, present evidence for aging cell matrix change exists from biomechanical, morphologic, histologic, and biochemical tissue study.

The variation in biology and biomechanical properties of tendons and ligaments with postmaturational aging has been well docu-

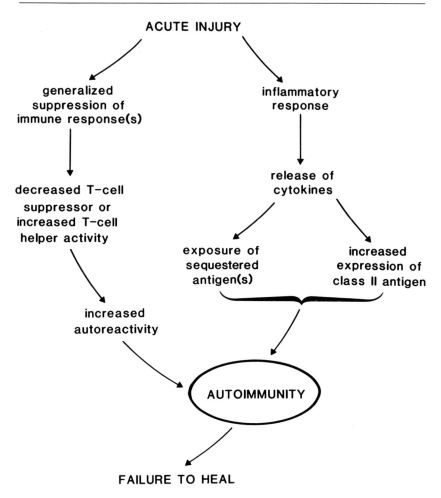

Fig. 8 *Hypothetical pathway for an autoimmune contribution to the response after acute trauma. (Reproduced with permission from Friedlaender GE, Jokl P, Horowitz MC: The autoimmune nature of sports-induced injury: A hypothesis, in Leadbetter WB, Buckwalter JA, Gordon SL (eds): Sports-Induced Inflammation: Clinical and Basic Science Concepts. Park Ridge, IL, American Academy of Orthopaedic Surgeons, 1990, p 625.)*

mented.[60] Generally, there are large decreases in linear stiffness and ultimate load as well as energy-absorbed failure in primate and human models, such as the femur-anterior cruciate ligament (ACL)-tibial complex demonstrated by tensile testing.[61] As Woo and associates[61] note, in human cadaveric studies where types and level of physical activity and physical condition of the donors is largely unknown, the contribution of disuse to these observations is difficult to quantify.[61] In a study of the aging effects of the medial collateral ligament and ACL in the rabbit, Amiel and associates[62] established ultrastructural changes of fibroblast degeneration with a substantial

Table 2 Properties that increase as normal human diploid cells approach the end of their in vitro lifespan (Phase III)

Lipids
  Lipid content
  Lipid synthesis
  Requirement for delipidized serum protein
    for stimulation of lipid synthesis

Carbohydrates
  Glucose utilization
  Glycogen content

Proteins and Amino Acids
  Protein content
  Proteins with increased proteolytic
    susceptibility (only at last PDL)
  Protein component P8
  Breakdown rate of proteins when treated
    with an amino acid analog
  Albumin uptake
  Stimulatory activity of polyornithine on
    protein uptake
  Proportion of rapidly degradable proteins
  Amino acid efflux
  Error level for misincorporation of
    methionine into histone H1
  Number of methionine residues
  Complexity of H1 polypeptide chains

RNA
  RNA content
  RNA turnover
  Proportion of RNA and histone in
    chromatin

Enzymes
  Lysosomes and lysosomal enzymes
  Heat liability and activity of G6PD and 6-
    phosphogluconate dehydrogenase
  Activity of "chromatin-associated enzymes"
    (RNAase, DNAase, protease, nucleoside
    triphosphatase, DPN pyrophosphorylase)
  5' MNase activity
  Esterase activity
  Acid phosphatase band 3
  Acid phosphatase
  B-glucuronidase activity
  Membrane associated ATPase activity
  pH 3,4 protease activity (decreased in
    middle population doublings)
  N-acetyl-β-glucosaminidase
  5'-nucleotidase
  Cytochrome oxidase
  Tyrosine aminotransferase activity

Acid hydrolases:
  a-D-mannosidase
  N-acetyl-β-galactosaminidase
  N-acetyl-β-glucosaminidase
  β-L-fucosidase
  β-D-galactosidase
  γ-glutamyltransferase (5-glutamyl)-peptide:
    amino-acid 5-glutamyltransferase activity
Monoamine oxidase activity

Morphology
  Cell size and volume
  Number and size of lysosomes
  Number of residual bodies
  Cytoplasmic microfibrils
  Endoplasmic reticulum, constricted and
    "empty"
  Particulate intracellular fluorescence
  Nuclear size of the slow or nonreplicating
    cell component
  Mean nuclear area in cells from donors
    aged 8, 40, and 84 years
  Cell sizes in both G1 and G2 + M
  Particles on freeze fracture face E
  Microvilli on cell surfaces, chromatin
    condensation and dense bodies
  Cells containing long, thin, dense
    mitochondria and bizarre shapes, cells
    exhibiting filamentous degeneration
  Blebs and marginal ruffling
  Fraction of cells with one large nucleolus
    per nucleus
  Mean nucleolar dry mass and area

Cell Cycle
  Prolongation of doubling time
  Heterogeneity in length of division cycle
  Slow or nonreplicating cells
  Mitotic Cycle
  Cell longevity with certain fractions of
    cigarette smoke condensate

Unclassified
  Cyclic AMP level/mg protein
  Tolerance to sublethal radiation damage
  Time needed to respond to proliferative
    stimulus by medium change
  Reversion rate of herpesvirus temperature
    sensitive mutant E
  DNA repair in cells arrested by low serum
    concentration
  Rate of uridine transport
  Cyclic AMP levels

(Reproduced with permission from Hayflick L: Origins of aging, in Horvath SM, Yousef MK (eds): *Environmental Physiology: Aging, Heat and Altitude.* New York, NY, Elsevier Science Pub, pp 399-414.)

Table 3 Properties that decrease as normal human diploid cells approach the end of their in vitro lifespan (Phase III)

Proteins
  Collagen synthesis
  Collagen synthesis and collagenolytic
    activity
  Rate of histone acetylation
  Total protein and hydroxyproline
  Proteolytic capacity
  Incorporation of isotope into histone
RNA
  Rate of RNA synthesis
  Ribosomal RNA content
  RNA synthesizing activity of chromatin
  Chromatin template activity
  Incorporation of tritiated uridine into
    cellular RNA
  Nucleolar synthesis of RNA
  Template activity of isolated nuclei (only in
    late Phase III)
DNA
  DNA synthesis
  Nucleic acid synthesis
  Rate of DNA chain elongation
  Rate of DNA strand rejoining and repair
    rate
  Induced sister chromatid exchanges
  DNA polymerase activity
Enzymes
  Lactic dehydrogenase isoenzyme pattern
  Glycolytic enzymes
  Transaminases
  Alkaline phosphatase
  Specific activity of lactic dehydrogenase
  Response to induction of ornithine
    decarboxylase
  pH 7.8 neutral protease activity
  Prolyl hydroxylase activity
  Ascorbate dependence of the prolyl
    hydroxylase system
  Glutamine synthetase specific activity and
    heat lability
Cell Cycle
  Numbers of cells in proliferating pool
  Cell saturation density

Population doubling potential as a function
    of donor age
  Incorporation of tritiated thymidine
  Synchronous division, constancy of
    interdivision time and motility
  Growth potential
  Percent of colonies exceeding a given
    colony size
  Cell longevity decreased by one fraction of
    cigarette smoke condensate
Morphology
  Proportion of mitochondria with completely
    transverse cristae
  Distribution and development of specialized
    structures for intercellular contact and
    communication
  Particles on freeze fracture face P
  Number of mitochondria and granular
    endoplasmic reticulum
Synthesis, Incorporation, and Stimulation
  Mucopolysaccharide synthesis
  Pentose phosphate shunt
  Cyclic AMP level (molar values)
  Stimulation of growth with putrescine
  Radioactive uridine, thymidine, protein-
    hydrolysate, acetate, oleic acid,
    cholesterol
  Synthesis of glycosaminoglycans
  Interferon production
  Number of cells responding to proliferative
    stimulus by medium change
  Ability to synthesize proteins and amino
    acids
Unclassified
  HLA specificities (cloned cells)
  Adherence to polymerizing fibrin and
    influence on fibrin retraction
  Electrophoretic mobility (net negative cell
    surface change)
  Lifespan after chronic exposure to elevated
    partial pressures of oxygen
  Reversion rate of herpesvirus temperature-
    sensitive mutant G

(Reproduced with permission from Hayflick L: Origins of aging, in Horvath SM, Yousef MK (eds): *Environmental Physiology: Aging, Heat and Altitude.* New York, NY, Elsevier Science Pub, pp 399-414.)

decrease in collagen synthesis observed with both maturation and aging correlated with a lack of rough endoplasmic reticulum.

Morphologically, aging connective tissue at the ultrastructural level demonstrates decreased organelles, decreased rough endoplasmic reticulum, and increased actin (ie, stress or aging filaments).[7,30,62] Aging changes in the extracellular matrix have been documented in such connective tissues as the meniscus[63] and tendon.[12] These include marginal fraying, cleavage lesions, and collagen disarray in

Table 4 Properties that do not change as normal human diploid cells approach the end of their in vitro lifespan (Phase III)

DNA and RNA
 Soluble RNAase, soluble DNAse, soluble seryl T-RNA synthetase, soluble and chromatin-associated DNA polymerase
 Mean temperature of denaturation of DNA and chromatin
 Histone/DNA ratio
 Rate of DNA strand rejoining and ability to perform repair replication
 Chromatin template activity
 Nucleoplasmic synthesis of RNA
 Heat lability in relative profiles of DNA, RNA, and protein precursors (minor increase at last doubling)
 Level of unscheduled DNA synthesis in confluent cultures

Enzymes
 Respiratory enzymes
 Glutamic dehydrogenase
 Alkaline phosphatase
 Superoxide dismutase activity
 Heat stability of G6PD
 Catalase activity
 Lysyl hydroxylase activity
 Enzymes of the "γ-glutamyl cycle"
 Specific activity or thermostability of phosphoglucose isomerase
 G6PD alterations
 N-acetyl-α-D-galactosaminidase
 N-acetyl-β-D-glucosaminidase-β-D-glucosidase
 Sulphite cytochrome C reductase

Cell Cycle
 S phase of cell cycle
 Generation time of selected mitotic cells

Karyology
 Diploidy (only changes in late phase III)
 Prematurely condensed chromosomes
 Proportion of colchicine induced polyploid cells

Synthesis and Degradation

Glycolysis
 Mis-synthesized or post-translationally modified proteins
 Conversion of glutamate to proline or hydroxyproline
 Hydralazine inhibition of hydroxylation
 Increase in V_{max} of uridine transport with serum stimulation
 Ability to degrade normal or analogue-containing proteins

Cyclic AMP, GMP
 Cyclic AMP concentration
 cAMP-cAMP phosphodiesterase activity
 Decrease in kg of cyclic AMP phosphodiesterase with serum stimulation
 Levels of cAMP and cGMP

Virology
 Virus susceptibility
 Poliovirus and herpesvirus titer, mutation rate and protein chemistry
 Chromosome 21-directed antiviral gene(s)
 Reversion rate of herpesvirus temperature sensitive mutant D
 Synthesis of vesicular stomatitis virus RNA
 Susceptibility to interferon

Morphology
 Numbers of mitochondria
 Number of intramembrane particles

Unclassified
 Irreversible absorption/uptake of foreign macromolecules
 Membrane fluidity
 Phospholipid and neutral fat content
 Effect of nicotine
 Effect of polynuclear hydrocarbon carcinogens
 Cell viability at subzero temperatures (17 years)
 Respiration
 HLA specificities (mass cultures)

(Reproduced with permission from Hayflick L: Origins of aging, in Horvath SM, Yousef MK (eds): *Environmental Physiology: Aging, Heat and Altitude.* New York, NY, Elsevier Science Pub, pp 399-414.)

meniscal tissue and longitudinal splitting, disintegration, collagen fiber angulation, and abnormal variation in diameter of collagen fibers in tendon.[12] At what point these findings are considered degenerative rather than aging, appears arbitrary. Kannus and Jozsa[12] provided extensive age- and sex-match control specimens in a study of histopathologic changes preceding spontaneous rupture in multiple tendon sites, finding that two thirds (66%) of the control tendons were "structurally healthy,"[12] while 34% of the control tendons did show abnormal change of less intensity than injured tendons. The study implied that in an urban population, silent degenerative changes are common in tendons of people who are older than 35 years, and that these changes are associated with spontaneous rupture.[12] In my opinion, the study also tends to support the concept of a continuum of aging and degeneration.

Histologically, aging tissues reveal decreased cellularity,[62] as well as lipofuscin deposition.[9,12,64] Dystrophic calcium pyrophosphate dihydrate crystal deposition increases in connective tissue such as meniscus and tendon.[3,65] Such changes are the figurative "tombstones" of age-related degeneration.[2] Similar changes have been documented in the lumbar disc and include loss of distinction between the inner annulus and nucleus, some loss of hydration in proteoglycan, accumulation of proteoglycan fragments, the accumulation of lipid oxidation products with both lipofuscin and amyloid deposition, and merging of the annulus fibrils.[24,66]

In addition to increasing the percentage of stable collagen cross-links, there is an aging trend in connective tissue in cartilage and tendon of increased fibril diameter.[19] These findings may contribute to the "stiffness factor" experienced at all ages,[11] however, increased collagen cross-linking stability is not believed to be the cause of aging.[5] In contradistinction to the intervertebral disc, proteoglycan synthesis may increase in degenerative meniscal tissue.[63] Such findings are also documented in spontaneous osteoarthritis;[24,63] however, there is a distortion of the normal profile of proteoglycan aggregan monomers with a significant trend toward molecules deficient in chondroitin-6-sulfate or rich in keratin sulfate. Proteoglycans and glycosaminoglycans molecules are important in the initial stages of adult wound healing by forming an interaction with hyaluronic acid and fibrin to create the initial scaffold for cell migration into the wound.[48] Therefore, these documented age-related molecular changes are presumed to have significance in wound repair.

Free Radicals, Lipid Peroxidation, and Age Pigment

All aging theories can be classified into two broad categories: those proposing that aging is a direct result of the accumulation of random injurious events, and those proposing that aging and longevity are under direct genetic control.[5,29] One theory in particular, the free radical or lipid peroxidation theory of aging, first introduced in 1956,[67] deserves particular mention because of the resurgent evidence that lipid peroxidation may be a common pathway for inflammatory induced tissue damage,[48] postischemic reperfusion injury,[17,68] as well as connective tissue damage secondary to cumulative microtrauma.[3,12]

Free radicals are highly reactive cellular components derived from atoms or molecules in which an electron pair has been transiently separated into two electrons that inhibit independence of motion.[64] The most common source for free radical generation is the incomplete reduction of oxygen (O_2 to H_2O) under such conditions as postischemic reperfusion or inflammation.[69] Free radicals are extremely reactive, chemically unstable, and therefore short-lived, and usually occur in low concentrations.[17] They may chemically attack phospholipid structure of the cell membrane by the process of lipid peroxidation, forming unstable lipid peroxide radicals, which break down into smaller molecules, leading eventually to the dissolution of cell walls as well as to the walls of critical organelles such as mitochondria that are exposed to free radicals more readily because they are the sites of intracellular oxygen metabolism.[17,64] Free radical activity is also presumed harmful in that it does not appear to contain or reflect any useful biologic information. In theory, free radicals may replace the genetically determined order of the membranes by randomness. The result is the generation of cell wall structure that is increasingly less able to transmit biologic information through the cell substrate and across cell interfaces. As a consequence of this random destructiveness, even correctly programmed protein enzymes, endocrine receptors, or modulators of facilitated transport that are adjacent to a damaged site may be rendered nonfunctional.[64] Phagocytic cells (such as the neutrophil) generate high volumes of oxygen-free radicals during inflammatory and repair processes (Fig. 9).[69] These byproducts of the so-called neutrophil respiratory burst account, in part, for the additional tissue injury that becomes a focus of acute athletic treatment. While acute cell injury and cell death always stimulate inflammation;[17] theoretically, microtraumatic sports injury, tissue hypoxia, and sublethal cell matrix insults may alter cell metabolic activity with the release of increased harmful metabolic products, including free radicals. Support for this hypothesis exists in the observed deposition of lipofuscin pigments. First described by Hodge[70] in 1894 in the cytoplasm of neurons of senile individuals, lipofuscin is thought to be the residual of lipid peroxidation effects.[64]

Antioxidants are chemical scavenger molecules that buffer excessive production of oxygen free radicals, themselves byproducts of oxidative damage and exercise-induced lipid peroxidation of cell membranes.[71,72] Antioxidants are normally present in the body to help reduce the activities of these radical-induced reactions. Such oxidative distress also can be a byproduct of intensive aerobic exercise.[73] Normal tissue sources of antioxidant defenses include the enzymes superoxide dismutase, catalase, glutathione peroxidase, and the antioxidant vitamins.[71] Vitamins E and C and beta carotene (a metabolic precursor of vitamin A) are powerful antioxidants implicated in the treatment of cancer, aging, arthritis, and exercise-induced oxidative stress.[72] As a metabolic byproduct, it is estimated that oxygen free radicals produce in excess of 1,000 oxidative hits per cell, per day, on DNA in the human body.[67] It is postulated that even if 99.9% of normal radical generation is scavenged by protective mechanisms, there may be very slow progressively cumulative damage. The observed

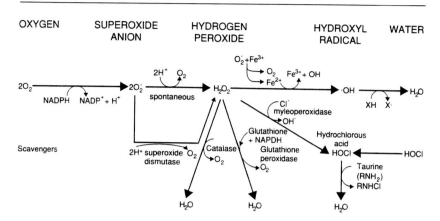

Fig. 9 *Pathway for the production of various activated oxygen species. (Reproduced with permission from Wahl SM, Wahl LM: Inflammation, in Cohen IK, Diegelmann RF, Lindblad WJ (eds): Wound Healing: Biochemical and Clinical Aspects. Philadelphia, PA, WB Saunders, 1992, p 43.)*

age-associated increase in autoantibodies in humans has also been attributed to this mechanism.[67]

Basic Aspects of Soft-Tissue Sports Injury

Sports-induced soft-tissue injuries are characterized by a spectrum of interrelated cell matrix responses—the processes of inflammation repair and degeneration.[74] Trauma implies an injury from a mechanical force applied external to the involved tissue, causing structural stress or strain that results in a cellular or tissue response. Load is a measure of external mechanical force. Use implies the accumulation of load over time (ie, a rate). Such repetition is seen in endurance sports in the form of cyclic loading and overuse. The effect of load on tissues is described by the term "strain and stress." Strain is the deformation of a structure in response to external load, whereas stress is the internal resistance to deformation when a load per unit area is applied. Sports trauma may be thought of as a mechanism by which injury occurs.

Sports injury is the loss of cells or extracellular matrix resulting from sports-induced trauma.[3,19] As in other wounds, an athletic wound is a disruption of normal anatomic structure and function. All wounds result from pathologic processes beginning internal or external to the involved part.[75] Injuries are acute or chronic, depending on the rate of onset and the mechanism. Acute wounds are characterized by generating an orderly and timely repair process that results in a sustained restoration of anatomic and functional integrity. Chronic wounds have failed to proceed through an orderly and timely process to produce anatomic and functional integrity or have proceeded through the repair process without establishing a sustained anatomic and functional result. Chronic injury often represents a failure of cell matrix adaptation to load exposure.[3]

The mechanism of injury has much to do with the subsequent pathohistologic pattern. "Overuse" and "overload" are not synonymous terms because injury can result from excessive and rapid change in use without significant change in resistance; hence, the origin of the term "accumulative trauma disorder," or "accumulative cell-matrix failed adaptive response."[3] Synovial structures, such as the tendon sheath and the peritenon structures, are prone to this form of stress response.[3] Injuries can further be divided into acute and chronic patterns according to rate of onset. Acute injuries are typified by sudden crises followed by a predictable although often lengthy resolution. Acute disruptions of structures accompanied by bleeding produce a predictable classic acute phase reaction typical of human postnatal wound healing. In tendon, an acute injury often consists of midsubstance rupture occurring either through aberrant tissue or as the result of high strain rates.[76] Chronic injury is characterized by a slow, insidious onset, implying an antecedent subthreshold spectrum of structural damage. Eventually this leads to a crisis episode that is often heralded by pain and/or signs of inflammation. Chronic injury may last months or even years and is distinguished by a persistence of symptoms without resolution. Synovitis, bursitis, paratendinitis, and tendinitis are typical of such complaints.

It is now known that pertubation of in vivo or in vitro cell populations induces the release of chemical mediators and initiates cascades of inflammatory products.[77] Aging does not appear to retard such responses. How these events lead to further change in matrix integrity of connective tissue is only becoming understood. Furthermore, it is not clear whether microdamage due to tensile overload and formed element separation with tissue fatigue is the initiating event or whether some type of stress-induced failure of cell metabolism occurs first, resulting in the loss of the ability of cells to maintain tissue integrity by increasing cell synthesis. It is likely that both processes may occur under different circumstances.[3] There appears to be some overlap between acute and chronic injuries, with the bridging stage at 4 to 6 weeks conventionally termed the subacute stage of injury. Another perspective on the acute versus chronic process would define a chronic injury as an acute injury occurring in association with some impairment to healing (Thomas K. Hunt, MD, personal communication, 1993). In the older athlete, the clinically observed tendency toward chronic injury may partially be explained on the basis of aging-impaired rate and quality of healing. Also, at any age, there are additional intrinsic and extrinsic factors that can impair the healing of sports injury (Outline 1).[2]

Sports-induced inflammation is a localized tissue response initiated by injury or destruction of vascularized tissue exposed to exces-

Outline 1 Factors leading to failed soft-tissue healing

Intrinsic
    Vascular vulnerability
    Limited cell function potential
    Limited cellularity
    Aging
    Genetic predisposition (mesenchymal syndrome, structural variability, etc)
    Degeneration
    Hormonal
    Other (autoimmunity, etc)
Extrinsic
    Overt
        Incorrect diagnosis
        Continued self-abuse
        Improper training (excessive stimulus or inadequate stimulus)
        Improper technique
        Improper equipment
        Inappropriate treatment
        Inadequate treatment
        Harsh environment
    Covert
        Joint instability
        Extrinsic pressure
        Biomechanical fault

sive mechanical load or use.[3,74] It is a time-dependent evolving process characterized by vascular chemical and cellular events leading to tissue repair, regeneration, or scar formation. Clinically observed pathways of sports-induced soft-tissue inflammation include spontaneous resolution, fibro-productive healing, regeneration, or chronic inflammatory response (Fig. 10).[74] Not all sports injuries produce a classic inflammatory pattern of response, nor are all tissues capable of generating such a response.[74] Articular cartilage is the prototypical example of an avascular tissue that does not generate an adequate healing response.[78]

Repair of soft-tissue injury has been defined as replacement of damaged or lost cells or extracellular matrices with new cells or matrices.[19] Regeneration is a form of repair that produces new tissue that is structurally and functionally identical to normal tissue.[19,42] Repair by scar is the most prevalent postnatal mammalian response to injury, unlike in the fetal wound, which is uniquely capable of healing without exuberant scar formation.[40] The observation that the midgestational human fetus heals by mesenchymal proliferation and without scar formation remains poorly understood, with recent evidence suggesting differences in the regulation of collagen synthesis, in particular the activity of polyADP-ribose synthetase enzyme, which is elevated in tissues undergoing development and differentiation.[40] This enzyme unmasks and increases the expression of collagen and related genes in utero and is down-regulated as a function of age.[40] Such age-related alterations in enzymatic function are common and may explain diminished functional capacity.[9] Acutely injured tis-

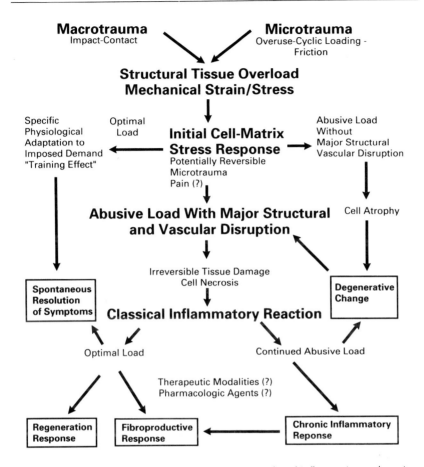

Fig. 10 *Schema of the theoretical pathways of sports-induced inflammation and repair.*

sue such as tendon or ligament is repaired by scarred deposition that never actually replicates the histologic or biomechanical properties of the original structures.[19,33] Regeneration is often seen as the ideal wound-healing response. The response in soft-tissue healing may result in an adequate response or inadequate response depending on the athlete's demands.

Healing is a complex dynamic tissue process that results in the restoration of anatomic continuity and function as a result of an orderly, biologic repair process.[75] Several qualities of wound healing have been defined (Outline 2). An ideally healed wound is one that has returned to normal anatomic structure, function, and appearance. A complete failure of wound healing restores none of the former characteristics. Between these two extremes is an acceptably healed wound, which is characterized by restoration of sustained functional and anatomic continuity.[75] A minimally healed wound is

Outline 2 Adequacy of wound healing

Ideal	Normal anatomic structure, function, and appearance
Acceptable	Restoration of sustained functional and anatomic continuity
Minimal	Restoration of anatomic continuity, without sustained functional result
Failed	No restoration of anatomic or functional continuity

(Adapted with permission from Lazarus GS, Cooper DM, Knighton DR, et al (eds): *The Newsletter of the Wound Healing Society* 1992;2:7-14.)

characterized by restoration of anatomic continuity but without a sustained functional result and, hence, the wound may recur. In the treatment of soft-tissue athletic injury, ideal wound healing is rarely if ever obtained and acceptable wound healing is common. Aging appears to bias healing in the direction of minimal or failed results. It is the challenge of the treating physician to avoid returning the athlete to play with a minimally healed condition.

Degeneration describes a change in tissue from a higher to a lower less functionally active form. Such weakened structures are then more vulnerable to sudden dynamic overload or cyclic overloading, leading to mechanical fatigue and failure.[74] A prominent source of degeneration is cell atrophy, which is the decrease in size or function of a cell in response to the presence (or lack of) an environmental signal.[17] Such down regulation involves decreased protein synthesis and decrease in such activities as energy production, application, storage, and contractility. In sports injury, immobilization is a prominent cause of cell atrophy in connective tissues.[17] Additional causes include decreased nutrition, diminished endocrine, hormonal influence, persistent inflammation, aging, and denervation (Fig. 11).[3] A reversal of the degenerative process is not a typical feature in degenerative conditions beyond an undefined cell-matrix limit. Ultimately, degeneration represents a profound imbalance in cell-matrix homeostasis.

A differentiation of aging and degeneration may prove difficult. It has been suggested that degeneration is an end result of the aging process.[24] In studies of degenerative disc disease and aging, the finding that discs of different morphologic degenerative grade within the same spine do not necessarily show marked biochemical differences, favors a successive stage theory. Both normal and degenerative discs have decreased water and proteoglycan content.[24] Findings that contrast degeneration and aging include the observation that the normal human disc tissue contains collagenolytic enzymes specific for collagen type II with little or no activity against type I collagen, whereas a prolapsed disc reveals significant elastolytic and type I collagen-degrading potential with little enzymatic activity against collagen type II. No variance in these observations with respect to age has been noted.[79] Decreased proteoglycan concentration has been associated with disc degeneration. It appears relatively independent from normal aging.[80] Other evidence to suggest that aging is not synonymous

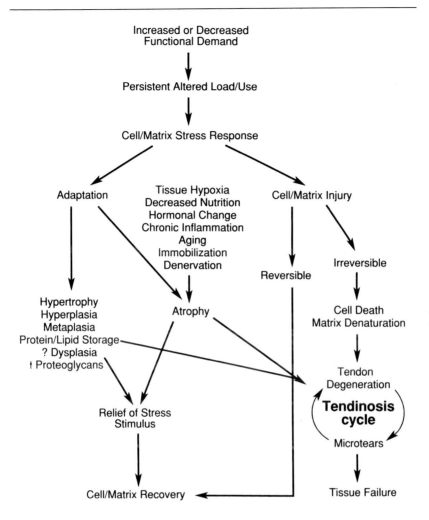

Fig. 11 *Cell matrix response to change in functional level. In this model, a degenerative tendon injury, tendinosis, results from a failed cell matrix adaptation to excessive changes in load use. Such failure is modified by both intrinsic and extrinsic factors. (Reproduced with permission from Leadbetter WB: Cell-matrix response in tendon injury.* Clin Sports Med *1992;11:537-547.)*

with degeneration is deduced from studies of osteoarthritic cartilage. Whereas there is an age-dependent selective loss of proteoglycans with a high chondroitin sulfate content in aging cartilage, osteoarthritic cartilage demonstrates selective accumulation of the same proteoglycan.[81] In the previously cited findings of Kannus and Jozsa[12] on age- and sex-matched control tendon specimens harvested at the time of death from cadavers of previously healthy individuals who died by accident, evidence of degenerative tendonopathy, tendolipomatosis, mucoid degeneration, and calcifying tendonopathy were found in 34% of the control tendons, but such findings were present in 97% of spontaneously ruptured tendons. The average age of the affected patients was 49 ± 9 years; and that of the controls, 48 ± 11 years. Two thirds of the control tendons were structurally healthy.[12] One interpretation of the aforementioned studies is that aging combined with other variables, such as overuse or disuse, promotes the evolution of events that leads to tissue degeneration.

Necrosis is the biologic deterioration in a cell occurring subsequent to tissue death in a living organism.[82,83] This is a focal process resulting from the presence of both extracellular enzymes and the release within the cell of selfdegradating lysosomal hydrolytic enzymes in response to a rising acid pH of a hypoxic or anoxic metabolism, a process known as autolysis.[83] The process of this enzymatic degradation of the cell membrane, lipids, and intracellular organelles, along with the breakdown of tissue macromolecules provide the prime stimulus for the mobilization of inflammatory cells from the blood and nonnecrotic tissues surrounding an area of necrotic injury.[82] As Robbins and Cotran[83] have noted, "necrotic cells are dead cells, but dead cells are not necessarily necrotic." This refers to the fact that cell necrosis by definition cannot occur suddenly. Hence, viable cells that are placed in a tissue fixative, such as formalin, do not demonstrate necrosis, but do experience cell death. Furthermore, while initiation of inflammation does not require necrosis (eg, immune response), necrosis always stimulates inflammation if there is an adequate tissue vascularity.[17] At any age, the severity of sports injury depends on the extent of cell necrosis. The effect of aging on cell necrosis needs further study.

Chronic inflammation involves the replacement of leukocytes by macrophages, plasma cells, and lymphocytes in a highly vascularized and innervated loose connective tissue milieu at the site of injury.[17] Although findings of chronic inflammation are typical in sites such as the lateral epicondyle lesions of the elbow,[84] these responses are not found in all chronic sports injuries.[12,85] The mechanism that converts an acute inflammation to a chronic inflammatory process is not known. Continued abuse of load and irritation may stimulate the local release of cytokines, resulting in both autocrine (cell selfstimulation) and paracrine (stimulation of adjacent cells) modulation of further cell activity.[48,77] Alternatively, activation of T-cell mediated autoimmunity has been hypothesized.[56] Supporting this hypothesis is the existing evidence for the declining fidelity of the immune system with age and concomitant marked increase in age-associated autoimmune disease.[5,86] There is further evidence that genes coding for the major histocompatibility complex (MHC) class II antigens comprise an important group whose expression is regulated by appropriate cell types, such as the tissue macrophage. These proteins "present" antigenic peptides (epitopes) representing hydrolytic breakdown products of connective tissue, such as collagen or proteoglycans to T lymphocytes for recognition by T-cell receptor complex.

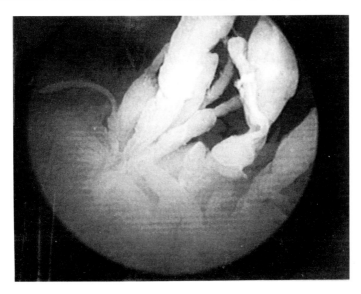

Fig. 12 *Arthroscopic view of chronic synovitis. Matrix degradation products from articular cartilage (epitopes) may generate age-related autoimmune synovial inflammatory response.*

It is through the MHC antigens that the immune system distinguishes between self and nonself antigens. Such systems are suspected to be active in chronic nonhealing wounds and in chronic synovitis (Fig. 12).[56,87]

Overview of the Normal Wound Healing Response to Athletic Injury

All sports-related connective tissue injury responses occur in the context of two interrelated categories: (1) macrotraumatic, or acute tissue destruction, and (2) microtraumatic, or chronic abusive load or use.[74]

Acute Macrotraumatic Tissue Response

Acute tissue loss or damage may result from sudden compression, laceration, extreme tensile load, or shear. Hemorrhage and necrosis are distinguishing features of acute injury. The moment of tissue injury is defined by the onset of vascular disruption and the initiation of the clotting mechanism with platelet activation. A cascade of overlapping processes then follows: (1) inflammation, (2) cell replication, (3) angiogenesis, (4) matrix deposition, (5) collagen protein formation, (6) contraction (ie, remodeling), and, in the case of exposed

Outline 3 Phases of acute injury tissue response

Phase I
  Acute vascular—Inflammatory
    Bleeding ⎫   Hemostasis
    Coagulation ⎬   Wound debridement
    Inflammation ⎭

Phase II
  Repair—Regeneration
    Cell proliferation ⎫   Tissue
    Angiogenesis ⎬   reconstruction
    Matrix synthesis ⎭

Phase III
  Maturation:
    Remodeling ⎫   Functional
    Epithelialization ⎭   restoration

---

wounds, (7) epithelialization. These highly interdependent events are summarized in Outline 3.

With respect to time, there is great disparity between the phases. While phase one subsides in a few days, phase three may extend indefinitely (Fig. 13). A severe muscle strain, a spontaneous Achilles tendon rupture, or a surgical wound typically generates this type of response (Figs. 14 and 15). In fact, this represents an ideal sequence of events influenced not only by the type of insult but also by such factors as age, vascularity, nutrition, genetics, hormonal changes, innervation, and activity level. The literature contains many excellent and exhaustive reviews of the vascular, cellular, and biochemical events in this process.[3,18,37,42,48,69,88-90] What follows is a summary of some of this literature.

Phase I: Acute Vascular-Inflammatory Response   After wounding, the first reparative "cells" to appear in most vascularized wounds are platelets. Platelets are a prominent source of cell mediators, such as platelet-derived growth factor, platelet factor IV, insulin-like growth factor I, transforming growth factor-beta I and -beta II, and an uncharacterized chemoattractant to endothelial cells.[91] Activation of the coagulation cascade and formation of a fibrin clot containing fibronectin with cross-linking to collagen and hyaluronic acid are vital to facilitate reparative cell activity.[48] Also known as the reaction phase, phase I is characterized by inflammatory cell mobilization aided by an acute vascular response that begins within moments of injury and lasts for a few minutes to several days. Alterations in the anatomy and function of microvasculature are among the earliest responses to injury. An acute vasoconstriction lasts a few minutes and is followed by vasodilatation, primarily of precapillary arterioles that bring increased blood flow to the injured area, which with increased vascular permiability contributes to swelling. Blood from the disrupted vessels collects locally and with cellular debris and early ne-

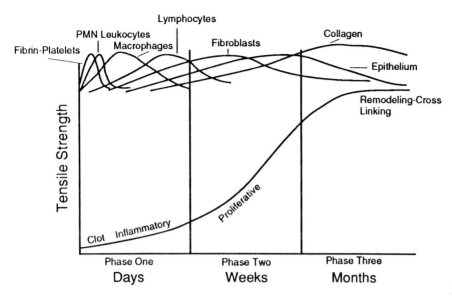

Fig. 13 *Ideal wound healing model. A variety of factors may distort the actual healing sequence in tendon. The temporal relationship of the various phases is such that the duration of phase one is measured in hours or a few days, but phase three may extend indefinitely. Normal tendon is not regenerated, however. PMN, polymorphonuclear cell. (Adapted with permission from Gamble JG: The musculoskeletal system: Physiological basics, in Hunter-Griffin L (ed): Athletic Training and Sports Medicine, ed 2. New York, NY, Raven Press, 1988, p 105.)*

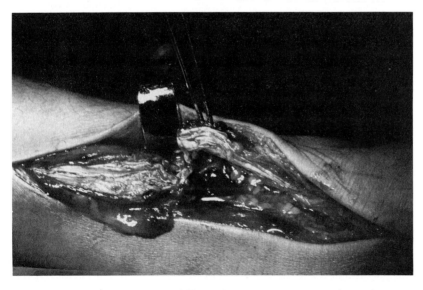

Fig. 14 *Macrotraumatic injury of Achilles tendon; traumatic rupture with prominent hemorrhage.*

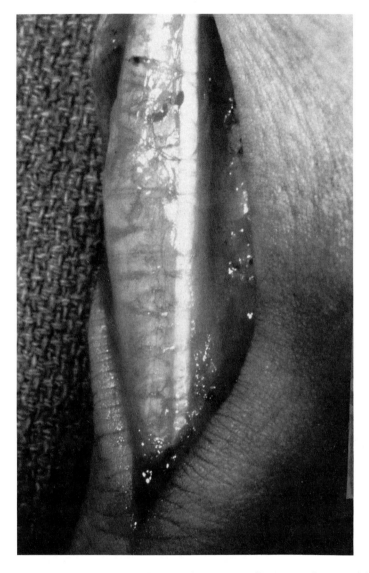

Fig. 15 *Microtraumatic injury of Achilles tendon. Note swollen intratendinous nodule evidencing failed adaptation or tendinosis. Thus, the same structure displays varying patterns of response according to mechanism of injury.*

crotic tissue forms a hematoma. The extent of the initial hematoma in the area of devitalized tissue defines the zone of primary injury.[88] A humoral response is nearly coincident with the neurovascular events and centers on the activation of Hageman factor (clotting factor 12) in the plasma, resulting in four subsystems of mediator production that have the following functions: (1) The coagulation systems reduce blood loss by local clot formation, a process activated in part by collagen exposed in the walls of damaged blood vessels. (2) Fibrinolysis discourages widespread blood clotting by fibrin degradation. (3) Kallikrein produces the strong vasodilator bradykinin, which increases capillary permeability and edema. (4) Compliment activation produces anaphylatoxin which activates chemotaxis (the attraction of inflammatory cells in the activation of phagocytoses in wound debridement).[90]

Stimulated by the compliment system, mast cells and basophils release histamine. Platelets, in addition to providing clot formation, are primary sources of serotonin. Histamine and serotonin work to increase vascular permeability.[89]

Fibronectins are a class of noncartilaginous glycoproteins that act as adhesive molecules, integrating the extracellular matrix.[18] Hyaluronic acid, a high-molecular-weight matrix glycosaminoglycan, interacts with fibronectin to create a scaffold for cell migration; later, its degradation by neutrophil hyaluronidases to a smaller molecular form stimulates the angiogenesis that will support fibroblast activity.[48]

There are three major consequences of the inflammatory phase: (1) some initial wound strength is provided by the cross-linking of fibronectin and collagen, (2) damaged tissue from the initial trauma is removed, and (3) endothelial cells and fibroblasts are recruited and stimulated to divide.[91] During this phase, release of compliment activates polymorphonuclear cell migration into the extravascular space providing for the removal of cellular debris and initiating chemotaxis of additional inflammatory cells, including the tissue macrophage. Granules within leukocytes are a source of hydrolytic enzymes that hydrolyze cell membranes and cell membrane phospholipids, producing arachidonic acid metabolites, cytokines, proteases, and oxidants.[89] The resulting arachidonic acid cascade is an enzymatically driven sequence leading to the marked increased production of prostaglandins, thromboxanes, leukotrienes, eicosanoids, and slow-reacting substance of anaphylaxis (Fig. 16).[89,92] Collectively, these polypeptide proteins activate further inflammatory cellular behavior. For this reason, they are the targets of modern day anti-inflammatory drug therapy. The intense chemical activity and exudation of this phase produce the initial clinical signs of inflammation, edema, and hypoxia and create the zone of secondary injury (Fig. 17).[90] This cascade is the primary chemical event producing the cardinal signs of inflammation (redness, swelling, heat, pain, and loss of function).[74] Initiating in minutes, this phase lasts for essentially as long as the body requires and is the ignition for subsequent repair. Assuming no coincident infection or repetitive disturbance to the wound, this usually is a matter of 3 to 5 days.

Phase II: Repair-Regeneration This phase begins at 48 hours and lasts up to 6 to 8 weeks. Phase II is characterized by the presence of the tissue macrophage, formally a circulating monocyte. This pluri-

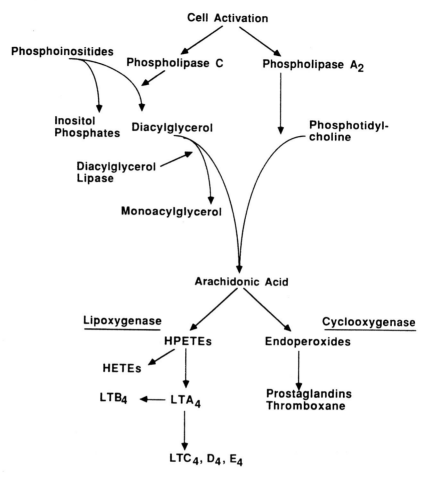

Fig. 16 *Generation of arachidonic acid metabolites. HETEs = hydro-oxyecoia tetranoic acids; HPETEs = hydroperoxecoiatetranoic acid compounds; LT = leukotriene.*

potential cell is the "starship" of wound repair and is capable of directing essentially the complete sequence of events in this proliferative phase.[48,91] The macrophage is characteristically mobile, capable of releasing a wide menu of growth factors, chemoattractants, and proteolytic enzymes when appropriate or necessary for the activation of fibroblasts and wound repair. The reparative connective tissue cell, in this phase, is the modified fibroblast, chondroblast, or myofibroblast. This cell is the source of collagen production, protein mediators of repair, and matrix proteoglycans. The fibroblast cell populations of dense connective tissue are typically classified as stable cells, meaning less than 1.5% are mitotically active at any one time.[18] The cells have a characteristic low respiratory quotient and a low rate of collagen turnover.[93,94] Found normally within a dense linearly ori-

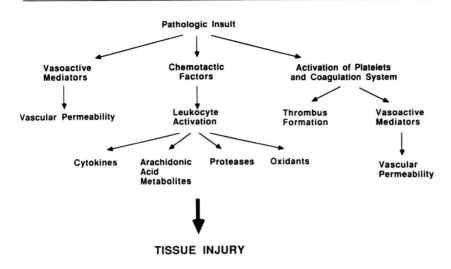

Fig. 17 *Mediators of the inflammatory response.*

ented collagenous matrix, these cells take on a distinct activated behavior and a fibroproductive phenotypic expression that can be further altered by deformation or changes in cell shape. In acute wounding, type III collagen is rapidly deposited in a woven pattern initially.[18,48] Type III collagen is characterized by a small fibril that is deficient in cross-linking. The remainder of the repair process is characterized by a shift to the deposition of type I collagen, which continues for an indeterminate period in the final maturation phase.[18] The critical driving force in this stage of the wounding response is a relative hypoxia in the wound microenvironment and rising lactate levels contributed in part by the release of large amounts of lactate by the tissue macrophage.[91] At the same time, a process of vascular proliferation and ingrowth (angiogenesis) occurs; tiny blood vessels grow and anastomose with each other to form a new capillary bed. Granulation tissue is the visible evidence of this process.[48] Various growth factors that promote this activity are prevalent in the wound.[18,48,89]

Phase III: The Remodeling Maturation Phase   This phase is characterized by a trend toward decreased cellularity and an accompanying decrease in synthetic activity, increased organization of extracellular matrix, and a more normal biochemical profile.[19] Collagen maturation and functional linear realignment are usually seen by 2 months after injury in ligament and tendon.[33,61] By approximately 4 months after the flexor tendon is lacerated, maturation of the repair site appears to be complete and the fibroblasts revert to quiescent tenocytes. However, final biomechanical properties can be reduced by as much as 30% despite this remodeling effort.[95] The point at which remodeling ceases in soft-tissue injury response has not been determined.[95,96] Biochemical differences in collagen type and arrangement, water content, DNA content, and glycosaminoglycan content persist indefinitely and the material properties of these scars never equal those of the intact tissue.[33,76]

Clinically, it should be appreciated that the human inflammatory repair response to acute injury is not so much purposeful as it is simply an example of the way things work. What factors initiate healing, control its rate, and eventually signal its completeness are not fully understood.[42] Whatever relative benefit of expediency in initial healing must be balanced against the costs of early loss of function due primarily to inflammatory pain and late functional deficit due to scar. If the "purpose" of inflammation is healing,[97] then the body's "good intentions" pave the way to pain and performance loss. This system works well enough for survival; but for the injured athlete with an urgent competitive goal, well enough is seldom soon enough. These events are summarized in Figure 18.

Chronic Microtraumatic Injury Response

Microtraumatic soft-tissue injury, as typically occurs in tendon, is distinguished by the observation that degenerative changes are a prominent histologic feature, especially in cases of spontaneous tendon rupture.[3,12,85,93] This degenerative tendinopathy is much less understood but is thought to be the result of a hypoxic degenerative process involving both tenocyte and matrix components. Inflammatory cell infiltration and an orderly phased wound repair as seen in macrotrauma seem to be absent or aborted.

The microtraumatic response to load and use is best understood within the context of a failed adaptation to physical load and use.[3] The histologic picture includes a range from synovial inflammation to tissue degeneration. Leadbetter[3,98] has reported similar findings in the adult athlete with overuse tendon injury requiring surgical treatment prior to rupture. Specimens included Achilles tendon, posterior tibial tendon, digital flexor finger flexor tendon, lateral elbow extensor, medial elbow flexor, patella tendon, and triceps tendon. All specimens displayed varying degrees of the following: (1) tenocyte hyperplasia; (2) blastlike change in morphology from normal resting tenocyte appearance; (3) prominent small vessel ingrowth with accompanying mesenchymal cells; (4) paravascular collections of histiocytic or macrophage-like cells; (5) endothelial hyperplasia and microvascular thrombosis; (6) collagen fiber disorganization with mixed reparation and degenerative change; and (7) microtears in collagen fiber separations (Figs. 19-21).[3,12,98] Statistically, these findings have a strong correlation with aging and with sedentary tissue disuse.[99] In one author's experience, these changes have not been seen prior to maturation in the athlete.

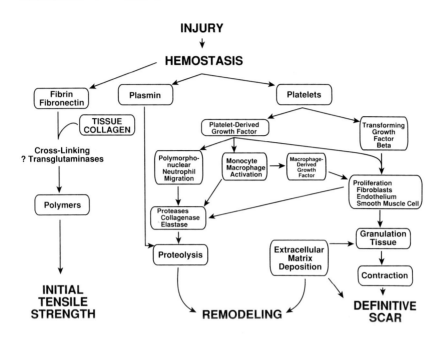

Fig. 18 *Summary of events in macrotraumatic wound response.*

The synovial sheath and peritenon are also involved in microtraumatic injury, especially as a result of friction with excitation of the synovial cells. The synovial A cell, in particular, is an immunologically competent cell with potential for pronounced cytokine production.[100] Kvist and associates[101] studied 16 athletes presenting with peritenonitis. Increased enzyme activity was mainly found in the fibroblast, inflammatory cells, and vascular walls in the peritenon. The results indicated that marked metabolic changes occur with an increased catabolism, lowered pH, and decreased oxygenation of the inflamed areas. Typical findings included fibroexudation with deposition of fibronectin and fibrinogen, proliferation of blood vessels, and, in some cases, marked endothelial hyperplasia with obliteration of microarterials.[101,102] Growth factors have been substantiated to modulate this process.[103] Almekinders and associates[77] have demonstrated an in vitro capacity of human tendon tenofibroblast to produce inflammatory mediators, including prostaglandin E2 and leukotriene (LTB 4) in response to repetitive motion.

In flat tendons, such as the extensor carpi radialis brevis of the lateral elbow, there are findings of intratendinous degeneration with dull, immature, edematous and gross appearance, as well as paratendinous granulation tissue.[3,84,98] The electron microscopic appearance of microtraumatic injury response is typified in tendon by de-

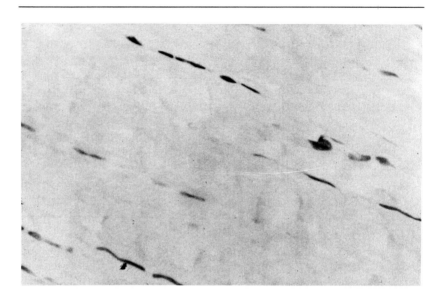

Fig. 19 *Normal Achilles tendon; note the linear cell shape and orientation. Hematoxylin-eosin, x162.5. (Reproduced with permission from Leadbetter WB: Cell matrix response in tendon injury. Clin Sports Med 1992;11:537-547.)*

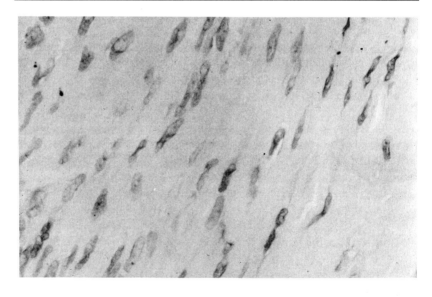

Fig. 20 *Achilles tendinosis. Note the tenocyte hyperplasia, cell vacuolation, and blast-like change in morphology characteristic of the stress-responsive tenocyte (ie, tendon fibroblast). Hematoxylin-eosin, x260. (Reproduced with permission from Leadbetter WB: Cell matrix response in tendon injury. Clin Sports Med 1992;11:537-547.)*

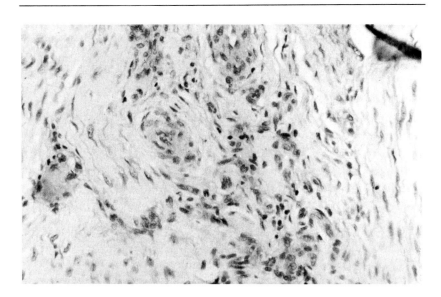

Fig. 21 *Achilles tendinosis. Endothelial hyperplasia and microvascular thrombosis hematoxylin-eosin, x162.5. (Reproduced with permission from Leadbetter WB: Cell matrix response in tendon injury. Clin Sports Med 1992;11:537-547.)*

generative findings, as reflected in the alterations in size and shape of mitochondria in the nuclei of the internal fibroblast or tenocyte. Intracytoplasmic or mitochondrial calcification may be seen. Cytoplasmic vacuoles, lipid deposition, and cell necrosis changes are thought to result from relative tissue hypoxia (Fig. 22).[3,12,98]

Effects of Aging On Wound Repair

The state of knowledge regarding the effect of aging on postnatal human inflammation and wound repair could be summed up in the casual observation that wounds in adults heal slower than in children and that wound healing generally slows with age. Such conclusions stem from the earliest scientific work on the effects of aging on wound healing by Carrel and duNovy[104] during World War I, with findings of slower rates of contracture and closure of open traumatic wounds; 20-year-old patients close their wounds in an average of 40 days, compared to 76 days for 40 year olds. In linear closed wounds, wounds in young animals are associated with earlier monocyte and macrophage infiltration, more-active fibroblast activity, higher rate of collagen synthesis, with greater breaking strength.[105] There are both qualitative and quantitative differences in the healing pattern of young versus old animals.[106,107] Generally, these differences are not so much in the ability to initiate inflammation as they are alterations

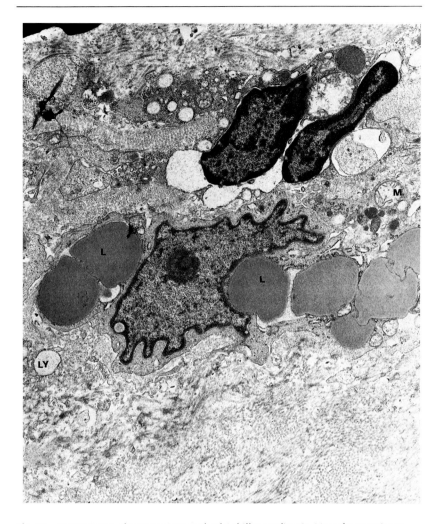

Fig. 22 *Transmission electron micrograph of Achilles tendinosis. Note the prominent lipid storage (L), enlarged lysosomal cavities (LY), and swollen disrupted mitochondria (M) consistent with severe cell stress response and impending cell necrosis. Osmium stain, original magnification ×17,500.*

in the reparative and maturation stages of healing. From a functional point of view, the healing of any wound requires the reestablishment of cell matrix disruption by the synthetic efforts of new cells that must migrate to the site, replicate, and modulate their function.[78] In the acute vascular and inflammatory response phase, in the absence of disease, aging produces little effect on circulating red cell mass, white cell count, the number or function of platelets, or coagulation.[108] While there are age-related changes in neutrophil function, the presence of the neutrophil is not essential for the progression of wound healing.[48] This seems reasonable teleologically because the neutrophil's primary function is to resist foreign invasion or infection.[69]

The macrophage is the vital cell in wound healing.[42,45,48] Macrophages play four major roles in matrix remodeling: they degrade matrix directly by secreting UPA and metalloproteinases; they participate in the activation of proteinases made by other cells; they produce cytokines (eg, interleukin-1 and tumor necrosis factor alpha) that can stimulate fibroblasts and endothelial cells to express metalloproteinases; and they are phagocytic, ingesting and digesting fragments of matrix produced by proteolytic attack or by injury.[109] The tissue macrophage is a multi-potential cell capable of generating almost any known mediator.[48] It is the cell ultimately responsible for matrix degradation, remodeling and regulation.[48,109] Macrophage function is not affected by age.[11,86] In older animals, macrophages may be activated and increase their phagocytic capacity.[86]

In contrast to the macrophage, the fibroblast is a cell prone to exhibit signs of senescence.[8] As the critical cellular component of both the repair regenerative and remodeling maturation phases of wound healing, fibroblast dysfunction directly impacts on the quality of collagen formation. Peacock[110] has stated that wound repair is essentially synonymous with the adequacy of collagen synthesis, collagen degradation, and the equilibrium between the two. Collagen synthesis is crucial for adequate wound repair because collagen: (1) modulates cell behavior, including proliferation, migration, and specific gene expression; (2) is a major determinant of tissue biomechanical properties; (3) is important in the wound contraction process; and (4) promotes reepithelialization by constituting the substratum along with fibrin and fibronectin for the migration of epidermal cells in open wounds.[37,111]

The highest rates of collagen synthesis are observed in fetal skin and decrease with age up to about 30 to 40 years.[111] The functioning of the immunologic system also impacts directly on wound healing by effecting the proliferative activity of the fibroblast.[112] Fibroblasts migrate to an injury site from neighboring connective tissue in response to chemotactic products of platelets, neutrophils, T lymphocytes, and monocytes. Transforming growth factor-beta is a potent chemotactic signal for leukocyte recruitment released by platelets as well as tissue macrophages. It is also a potent inducer of growth factor gene expression,[112] leading to possible pathologic fibrosis.[112,113] As emphasized by Hasslet and Henson,[114] there is significant overlap and interdependency of the various stages in inflammation and wound healing. It is probably inaccurate to overlook the contribution of tissue signaling cells (eg, mast cells, resident tissue macrophages), and the importance of the complex series of lymphocytic effects on resident reparative cells.

From the surgeon's point of view, all of the morphologic and chemical events of wound healing must lead to a single important end point. Wounds must become stronger with time.[43] In the absence of disease, this phenomenon occurs in both the young and the old athlete by three mechanisms: (1) increasing scar collagen volume, (2) increasing chemical bond stability of collagen, and (3) selective aggregation of collagen fibers along stress lines.[115] In the remodeling maturation phase, remodeling proceeds at rates that are characteristic of the tissue, age, and the species of animal.[116] Knowledge regarding the duration and extent of remodeling during a rematuration phase of wound repair is poorly understood but appears to extend indefinitely.[19,33] With the exception of the nonvascularized portion of the meniscus, articular cartilage, and unique intrasynovial structures, such as the ACL, surgical repair of ligament and tendon disruptions heal in the older athlete, albeit more slowly and with less predictability.

Factors Further Modifying Soft-Tissue Healing

There are epigenetic and genetic influences on connective tissue healing.[3] Epigenetic factors are defined as those factors that can influence the phenotypic expression (ie, protein production) of the cell without altering the genome. Vascularity, hormonal influence, and rest may exert epigenetic influence on tissue injury healing. Genetic factors are intrinsic to the individual but may be variably expressed. In theory, such poorly understood phenomenon as the "quality" of collagen synthesis, the rate of healing, the propensity to inflame after injury, and the rate of recovery are to some degree under genetic control. Aging may be considered to have both epigenetic and genetic roles in injury response.

Vascularity

Vascularity has long been thought to play a prominent role in tendon degeneration, especially in the supraspinatus portion of the rotator cuff, in the Achilles tendon, and at sites of extrinsic bone pressure.[117] In addition to new cells, there must be a vascular supply for tissues to heal.[17,42,48] Vascularity implies a source of nutrition (namely oxygen), a clearance of metabolic waste, and an avenue by which reparative cells may access the wounding site. For instance, the observed faster healing rate of facial versus lower extremity wounds has been largely explained on the basis of vascularity.[43] Aging tissues may vary in their vascularization. At one extreme, articular cartilage is devoid of a vascular supply and fails to heal.[78] At the other extreme, muscle is well vascularized and may heal with excessive scar formation.[118] The vascular supply of tendon has been a source of recent controversy with existing evidence suggesting that a watershed hypovascularity zone may be present in round tendons (such as the Achilles tendon).[119] There seems to be a preponderance of support for a diminished microvascular supply in the central core of a round tendon such as the distal third of the Achilles tendon.[118] Since the injection studies of Rathbun and Mcnab,[120] a watershed area in the distal supraspinatus tendon had been offered as an explanation of the etiology of rotator cuff degeneration. More recent studies of the microvascular supply of the supraspinatus tendon in symptomatic patients with impingement syndrome suggests that, in the area of greatest impingement (ie, the critical zone), there is actually hypervascularity. These findings are explained on the basis of low-grade inflammation and neurovascularizations incited after mechanical irritations.[58] While vascular penetration is slightly greater in children, the pattern of vascularity in the adult meniscus has not been found to deteriorate significantly with age.[121] Brooks and associates[122] likewise came to the conclusion that no significant difference existed between the vascularity of the supraspinatus portion of the rotator cuff, and that factors other than vascularity were important in the pathogenesis of supraspinatus tendon rupture. These assertions tend to shed a different light on the theory of hypoxic intratendinous degeneration and the etiology of tendinosis. Because focal load influences on cell matrix metabolism may play as great a role as any proposed diminished vascularity, the contribution of hypovascularity to the onset of degeneration as well as failed repair remains an active area of investigation.[58]

Hormones

Hormonal influence on wound healing has been thought to be important.[42,43] It has been suggested that diminished estrogen levels, premature menopause, or premenopausal hysterectomy may be associated with incidence of tendinosis in women.[123] Diabetics are known to heal with some difficulty.[18] Elderly patients have a virtually universal, progressive decrease in their ability to handle a glucose load. Healthy persons older than 40 years of age require 90 to 95 minutes for return to fasting glucose levels after a 25-g intravenous glucose challenge; their younger counterparts require, on average, only 65 minutes.[124]

Rest

Rest has long been clinically recognized to aid the patient with a soft-tissue injury. Yet, the beneficial role of rest in the therapeutic intervention of the inflammation repair process remains empirical and undefined. Although it may be said that rest does not heal;[125] theoretically, cell reparative efforts may catch up in the face of rest. The effects of rest are probably multifactorial and may include improved vascularity in the tendon at rest or represent an improved morphostatic balance between matrix degradation and production. Different forms of rest include total abstinence, protected activity, or altered activity.[2] Such classifications imply an attempt to control both cell matrix load signal and the recovery from cell loading. There is evidence that repetitive motion and variation of frequency (ie, cycles) may create a positive reparative signal after injury.[95] Absolute rest or abstinence does not de facto increase the athlete's potential to tolerate renewed load during participation.[2,3,125] Modifying load through rehabilitative exercise prescription has been shown to be important to any successful return to sports performance.[21,126,127]

Genetic Influences

Genetic influences are implicated in the modulation of soft-tissue cell matrix response based primarily on clinical observations. The mesenchymal syndrome is a theoretical, genetically determined cause of failed healing.[125] Tendinosis appears in multiple sites in approximately 15% of such patients and in sites not necessarily subjected to obvious overuse.[84] An association among lateral epicondyle extensor carpi radialis brevis tendinosis, rotator cuff degeneration, carpal tunnel syndrome, cervical and lumbar disk degeneration, plantar fasciosis, de Quervain's syndrome, and triggerfinger tendinosis has been observed.[3,84] Blood type O has been statistically related to tendon rupture.[128] It is interesting that Achilles tendon rupture in children is uncommon and has been encountered only in children whose parents have experienced tendon rupture.[129] My personal experience has been that young adult herniated disk syndrome is often seen in the presence of a familial history. An underlying collagen diathesis can be theorized. The clinical significance of the mesenchymal theory is in the early recognition of the patient who presents with frequent tendon complaints disproportionate to the level of activity. In addition to ruling out systemic disease, these patients are unusually vulnerable and must be counseled as to proper participation and moderation in their activity.

Structural Variability

Structural variability in connective tissues may explain alterations in response to injury and adaptive capability that are observed, both in the animal model and clinically.[6] Recent work by Lyon and associates[130] has called attention to the inherent differences between the medial collateral ligament (MCL) and the ACL structures that would superficially appear similar but behave biologically differently with respect to healing. These differences include alterations in basic crimp pattern, a more cartiloid and plumper cellular appearance to the fibroblast in the ACL, a more spindle-shaped linear cellular phenotype of the fibroblast in the MCL, and differences in the cytoplasmic processes between these two structures.[130] Nagineni and associates[30] performed an in vivo cell culture study to characterize the intrinsic properties of the ACL and the MCL cells. They discovered a slower rate of proliferation of ACL cells than MCL cells, a spread-out phenotypical appearance of ACL cells versus elongated appearance of MCL cells, relatively more stress fibers, and higher actin content in ACL cells. The implication from these results is a possible earlier senescence, a greater tendency toward confluence in cell culture of the MCL cell, ultimately suggesting a lowered proliferation and migration potential for ACL cells compared with MCL cells.[30] Nagineni and associates concluded that these factors may contribute to the differential healing potentials of these ligaments seen in vivo.[30] The observed differences in ligaments and tendons in their structure and biochemistry is likely due to different mechanical demands and local nutritional supply.[6] Furthermore, ligaments are nonuniform structures. For instance, differences have been found in the thickness, collagen content, hexosamine, and percentage of total water in different areas of the same rabbit MCL.[31] In the past, ligaments and tendons have been thought to be structurally distinct with ligaments composed of densely packed collagen bundles arranged in less linear orientation than tendon.[131] However, recent cadaver studies of the rotator cuff tendons have revealed a complex interwoven multilayered orientation combining microscopic features of both ligament and tendon.[132] These characteristics impact directly on the potential evolution of injury as well as the location of initial degenerative lesions in such injured tissues.

Muscle structure also displays great variability. There are fusiform, parallel, unipennate, bipennate, and multipennate muscle forms. Because of their larger number of parallel fibers, pennate muscles are more powerful, whereas fusiform muscles allow for greater range of motion.[117] Muscle and ligaments display different failure patterns. Muscles injure primarily at the myotendinous junction or at bony attachment sites,[117,133] whereas ligaments vary in failure pattern from osseous detachment to intrasubstance disruption, depending on strain rate.[134]

Thus, it is clear that all connective tissues are not the same. Not only do dissimilar structures possess different biomechanical and biologic properties, but similar structures also differ. It is likely that no two ligaments are the same, and that any one ligament may vary from day-to-day and even site-to-site within its structure.

Based on such findings, it is necessary to temper generalizations regarding the adequacy and predictability of connective tissue healing response unless the wounding mechanism, the biologic nature of the involved tissue, and the environmental conditions are carefully defined. How aging further influences these factors is largely unknown.

Sports Injury—The Midlife Experience

Despite theoretical concerns, a review of the clinical experience in the treatment of the midlife and older athlete reveals a relatively high rate of success both with nonsurgical and surgical treatment. Injury to the extensor mechanism origin at the lateral epicondyle of the elbow, particularly tendinosis of the extensor carpi radialis brevis origin "tennis elbow," is a relatively common midlife malady. In a review of 1,213 cases, Nirschl and Pettrone[84] noted that the vast majority responded to nonsurgical treatment. In a review of 200 patients, 73 of whom were older than 36 years, Curwin and Stanish[127] found that an eccentric rehabilitation program for multiple sites of tendinitis had a rate of success which approached 90%. A difference in success in different sites was noted, with patella tendinitis being treated with the least success, having only 30% relief with rehabilitative therapy. Clinical experience would imply that acute traumatic lesions occurring in vascularized tissues will heal adequately in the midlife athlete (eg, an isolated partial or complete sprain of the MCL, an acute muscle strain, or a partial rotator cuff strain). However, any conclusions regarding the success of present day nonsurgical treatment is fraught with lack of definition as to the exact extent of injury. This is especially true in overuse injuries.

The controversies underlying the efficacy of nonsurgical treatment of athletic injury was underlined in an exhaustive meta-analysis by Labelle and associates[135] regarding the lack of scientific evidence for the treatment of epicondylitis of the elbow. Of 185 published articles since 1966, only 18 were randomized controlled studies. The remaining papers were reviewed with respect to therapy used: ultrasound, iontophoresis, oral nonsteroidal anti-inflammatory drug, and steroid injection, usually in combination with some form of rehabilitation. It was noted that these studies were characterized by (1) poor methodological design, (2) prominent placebo effect, (3) small sample size, and (4) significant improvements from baseline, which confirmed either that all treatments had therapeutic effect or that the condition improved spontaneously with time. Labelle and associates[135] concluded that there was not enough scientific evidence to favor any particular treatment for acute lateral epicondylitis. Well designed outcome studies regarding the prognosis of nonsurgical treatment of athletic injury in the aging athlete are needed.

Because of its prevalence, surgical experience with arthroscopic surgery in patients aged 40 years and older, has been frequently reported. Wouters and associates[136] studied the patients requiring knee arthroscopy with an age range of 50 to 70 years and an average age of 62 years. Age was not found to be a factor in outcome and a radiograph that showed preexisting degenerative disease had the greatest negative impact on successful results. In other words, success of surgical treatment was limited by preexisting or existing irreversible structural damage, and not by age-dependent reparative capacity. Favorable outcome criteria were symptoms of less than 3 months duration, a history of locking (ie, mechanical, rather than degenerative inflammatory symptoms), a history of twisting injury, and a negative radiograph with minimal clinical signs of inflammation. Negative factors were pending litigation, pain of duration greater than 1 year preoperatively, prominent effusion, history of previous surgery, advanced radiologic disease, and static malalignment (varus or valgus).[136] Of interest is the negative correlation with prominent effusion and inflammatory signs.

In my experience, articular cartilage fragmentation is often associated with demonstrable hypertrophic synovitis and what appears to be the clinical manifestations of an autoimmune synovitis. Histologic study has suggested chronic inflammatory cell populations, lymphocytes, and macrophages capable of generating such a response (Wayne B. Leadbetter, MD, unpublished data, 1993). In a review of arthroscopic meniscectomy in patients with an average age of 57 years (range 40 to 78 years), Bonamo and associates[137] found a 60% significant improvement rate but a 75% resumption and continued recreational activity. Again, coexisting grades III and IV degenerative arthritis demonstrated a poorer prognosis, as would be expected in this relatively poorly healing lesion. In a study of patients 45 years old or older, Lotke and associates[138] found that an isolated medial meniscectomy performed nonarthroscopically produced a 90% chance of an excellent or good result in the absence of degenerative change, but only a 21% chance of a good or excellent result if arthritis was present. Jackson and associates[139] reported the results of partial arthroscopic meniscectomy in patients older than 40 years of age who had a 95% good to excellent result, an average of 2 1/2 years postoperatively in the absence of degenerative disease. It is not clear that these types of results would not deteriorate over time, because the follow-up was 3 years or less in all but one study.

Meniscal salvage and repair remains a goal of surgical technique.[121] Vander Schilden and associates[140] performed a study to determine whether human fibrochondrocytes possess the same biologic potential for initiating reparative response in a meniscal defect, as that found in lower vertebrates. The authors found that the aging human meniscal fibrochondrocyte, while able to initiate a reparative response, displayed an age-dependent rate of healing. Meniscal fibrochondrocytes harvested from the second decade of life began migration into the fibrin clot at 1 week, whereas in the eighth decade of life, no cellular migration had begun in a 72-year-old meniscus. Cellular proliferation, likewise, was not noted until 3 weeks. Diminished cell migration in the first week was noted in specimens in the third decade of life and older.[140] It has been established using DNA probe techniques that cell survival after transplantation of fresh meniscal allografts does not occur, but rather host fibrochondrocytes and undifferentiated mesenchymal cells repopulate the meniscal graft.[139] It is presumed that aging would have a slowing effect on this process, but this has not been well studied.

Anterior cruciate ligament reconstruction of the knee is becoming more commonplace in the midlife athlete older than 40 years of age because of the increased availability of arthroscopically assisted ligament reconstruction.[141] Commonly used autograft and allograft intra-articular reconstruction techniques require a standard three-phase inflammation and repair response leading to incorporation of the graft by the host.[142] MacKinlay and associates[143] studied the results of arthroscopically assisted anterior cruciate reconstructions using an autogenous central third patella tendon technique. They demonstrated that 57% felt they were as active in sports as they were before their injury, and the remaining patients had only dropped one or two levels in their preinjury sports, despite advancing age. In addition, 95% of the patients thought they were as active with their activities of daily living as before their injury, and 95% performed a battery of six functional tests with no, or only mild, limitation.[143] Interestingly, there appeared to be a tendency to develop arthrofibrosis in the open arthrotomy technique group. One might speculate that this could in some way be related to the previously described regulation of fibrosis by the T lymphocyte and aging immunologic potential of synovial cells. In any case, age does not preclude obtaining a good to excellent result in the aging athlete who requires ACL surgery. My experience extends to several patients in the fifth decade and one in the seventh decade who have done well without complication with such surgery. In understanding successful wound healing in this age group, it is possible that these patients are self-selected by their vigorous lifestyle and possess other healthy attributes that potentiate the outcome of surgical intervention.

The surgical treatment of tendinitis in the aging athlete may be helpful, but there are many inherent limitations to present surgical approaches. The crux of the difficulty in the diagnosis of sports-induced soft-tissue overuse injury of tendon and tendonopathy is that the exact nature and extent of the pathology is difficult to assess until the time of surgery.[2] Ideally, aberrant pathologic tissues are eradicated and the environment of the tendon improved. However, the process of inflammation in scar repair after surgical wounding tends to be a poorly regulated scar response and is not a true regeneration.

Surgery necessitates the disruption of normal tissue as an avenue by which to access the abnormal tissue. The creation of surgical adhesions is a common undesired risk. It is simplistic to claim that "bad scar" is replaced by "good scar" as a result of surgical intervention. More often, structurally inadequate or excessively inflamed tissue is replaced by woven, immature, and disorganized collagen fabric that demonstrates prolonged remodeling and increased volume in compensation for quality of repair. This tissue may be adequate, but is not normal.[2] Placed under the repetitive demands of sports performance, such tissue may be very sensitive to transitional stress and of vulnerable durability.[144] In the chronically injured tendon, the surgeon is often operating on a pathologic tissue affected not only by sports-induced trauma, but also by the aging process.

As further confirmation of the multifactorial nature of injury and surgical treatment response, Eaton,[145] in reviewing prognostic factors for outcome of carpal tunnel syndrome surgery, noted that the presence of a stenosing paratenonitis (ie, triggerfinger) contributed significantly to a poorer outcome, as did age above 50 years. Some type of abnormality in cellular biology or fibrogenesis is theorized to exist in these subgroups of patients. Repair and functional improvement under such conditions can be unpredictable.

Therapeutic Implications

In light of the previous discussion, a statement that wound healing progresses in an orderly manner regardless of the injury is untenable.[88] Statements that the body's immediate and long-term responses to physical trauma are essentially the same for all types of athletic injuries,[146] or that a tissue's response to injury is inflammation, no matter what the cause or type,[4] must be qualified. Aging figures prominently among the many factors that may influence individual wound healing. In overall treatment, there is a distinction to be made between tissue healing and functional recovery after injury. Healing implies a process of structural restoration, whereas functional recovery encompasses the successful return to athletic performance. The disuse and immobilization imposed by initial inflammation after injury may prolong functional recovery long after tissue healing is complete. Alternatively, too rapid a return to performance may frustrate wound repair or lead to immediate re-injury. Brown[20] proposed a safe, best estimate for treatment duration of twice as long for the athlete 60 years or older as that required for a 20 year old, and three times as long for the athlete older than 75 years.[20] Aging makes the athlete particularly sensitive to such transition in activity. The principle of transition states that sports injury is most likely to occur when the athlete experiences any change in mode or use of the involved part (Fig. 23).[74] In addition to aging, examples of transitional risks include: any increase in performance level; a change in position played; training improperly; a change in equipment; a change in playing environment, including new shoes, new surfaces, or different altitudes; an alteration in the frequency, intensity, or duration of training; an attempt to master new techniques; or too rapid a return to activity after injury.[3] This can best be summarized by the "Rule of Too's"—too often, too hard, too soon, too much, too little, too late, etc.[2]

While appropriate for the reduction of inflammation, there is no convincing evidence that medication, such as nonsteroidal antiinflammatory drugs,[147] or physical therapy modalities will significantly increase the quality or rate of healing.[148] Yet, despite a wide variety of cell senescence and tissue aging effects, the clinical success that exists in achieving wound repair in the aging athlete implies that

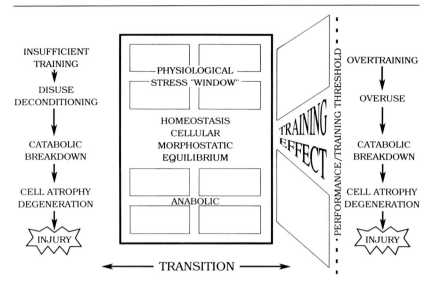

Fig. 23 *Principle of transition: the more rapid the transition, the greater the risk. Aging is associated with a decreased tolerance to transition stress. (Reproduced with permission from Physiology of tissue repair, in Hunter-Griffin LY (ed): Athletic Training and Sports Medicine, ed 2. Park Ridge, IL, American Academy of Orthopaedic Surgeons, 1991, pp 96-123.)*

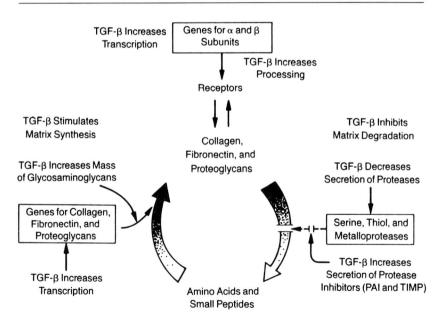

Fig. 24 *The role of TGF-β in the stimulation of extracellular matrix. (Reproduced with permission from Sporn MB, Roberts AB: Transforming growth factor-beta: Multiple actions and potential clinical applications. JAMA 1989;262:938-941.)*

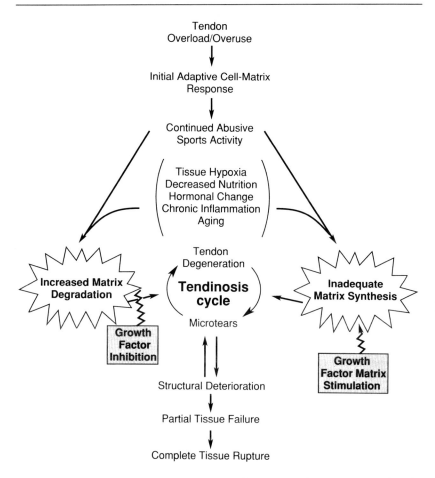

Fig. 25 *Theoretical application of growth factor therapy in tendon injury. (Reproduced with permission from Sporn MB, Roberts AB: Transforming growth factor-beta: Multiple actions and potential clinical applications. JAMA 1989;262:938-941.)*

such capability still resides within the genome and, therefore, therapeutic efforts can possibly target its potentiation. In the open system of connective tissue metabolism, clinical attempts to modulate wound healing have been challenging. Various cytokines and growth factors, such as transforming growth factor-beta offer a promising avenue for future therapeutic intervention (Figs. 24 and 25).[149] However, the definition of proper dosing, sequencing, timing, and combinations of these factors remains a formidable obstacle to their practical clinical application.

Conclusions

Aging effects on the healing and repair of athletic injury are complex and poorly understood. In general, healing slows with age, but there is considerable individual variation. Chronological age is not a singular deterrent to biologic response. This was eloquently implied by the legendary baseball pitcher, Satchel Paige, who, when queried as to his exact age, reputed to be between 40 and 50 years, answered rhetorically, "How old would you be if you didn't know how old you was?".[150]

An inflammatory repair response occurs at all ages. With wounding, aging appears to affect both quantitative and qualitative changes in the body's response but the basic phasic pattern in acute injury does not greatly change. Observed aging changes are consistent with the known biological spectrum of diminished cell matrix adaptive capabilities. Transition plays an important role in sports-induced injury in the aging athlete. The adequacy and rate of healing and wound repair implies regulation by both genetic and epigenetic factors. At all ages, the mechanism of injury has much to do with the observed inflammatory repair response; not all sports-related injury is inflammatory dominant. The acute macrotraumatic healing response differs significantly from the microtraumatic process.

The population of the world is aging at an accelerating rate. In 1900, there were 10 million to 17 million people age 65 or older, constituting less than 1% of the total population. By 1992, there were 342 million people in that age group, making up 6.2% of the population. By 2050, the number of people 65 years or older will expand to at least 2.5 billion people, about one fifth of the world's projected population.[26] Assuming even a limited participation in exercise and athletic activity, such a demographic trend assures that the challenge of improving the healing and recovery of the aging athlete will be a continuing responsibility for sports medicine. While such efforts are presently limited by our present knowledge, future success promises to be limited only by our imagination.

References

1. Sutton JR, Brock RM: *Sports-medicine for the Mature Athlete*. Indianapolis, IN, Benchmark Press, 1986.

2. Leadbetter WB, Mooar PA, Lane GJ, et al: The surgical treatment of tendinitis: Clinical rationale and biologic basis. *Clin Sports Med* 1992;11:679-712.

3. Leadbetter WB: Cell-matrix response in tendon injury. *Clin Sports Med* 1992;11:533-578.

4. Herring SA, Nilson KL: Introduction to overuse injuries. *Clin Sports Med* 1987;6:225-239.

5. Cristofalo VJ: Biological mechanisms of aging: An overview, in Hazzard WR, Andres R, Bierman EL, et al (eds): *Principles of Geriatric Medicine and Gerontology*, ed 2. New York, NY, McGraw Hill, 1990, pp 3-14.

6. Woo SL-Y, Buckwalter JA (eds): *Injury and Repair of the Musculoskeletal Soft Tissues*, Park Ridge, IL, American Academy of Orthopaedic Surgeons, 1988.

7. Hayflick L: Origins of aging, in Horvath SM, Yousef MK (eds): *Environmental Physiology: Aging, Heat and Altitude*. New York, NY, Elsevier/North-Holland, 1980, pp 399-414.

8. Stanulis-Praeger BM: Cellular senescence revisited: A review. *Mech Aging Dev* 1987;38:1-48.

9. Kanungo MS: *Biochemistry of Ageing*. London, Academic Press, 1980.

10. Shock NW: Longitudinal studies of aging in humans, in Finch CE, Schneider EL, Adelman RC, et al (eds): *Handbook of the Biology of Aging*, ed 2. New York, NY, Van Nostrand Reinhold, 1984, p 721.

11. Hall DA: Biology of aging: Structural and metabolic aspects, in Brocklehurst JC (ed): *Textbook of Geriatric Medicine and Gerontology*. Edinburgh, Churchill Livingstone, 1985, pp 46-61.

12. Kannus P, Jozsa L: Histopathological changes preceding spontaneous rupture of a tendon: A controlled study of 891 patients. *J Bone Joint Surg* 1991;73A:1507-1525.

13. Nimni ME: Collagen: Structure, function and metabolism in normal and fibrotic tissues. *Semin Arthritis Rheum* 1983;13:1-86.

14. Butler DL, Siegel AJ: Alterations in tissue response: Conditioning effects at different ages, in Leadbetter WB, Buckwalter JA, Gordon SL (eds): *Sports-Induced Inflammation: Clinical and Basic Science Concepts*. Park Ridge, IL, American Academy of Orthopaedic Surgeons, 1990, pp 713-730.

15. Asmussen E: Aging and exercise, in Horvath SM, Yousef MK (eds): *Environmental Physiology: Aging, Heat and Altitude*. New York, NY, Elsevier/North Holland, 1980, pp 419-428.

16. Burns TP, Steadman JR, Rodkey WG: Alpine skiing and the mature athlete. *Clin Sports Med* 1991;10:327-342.

17. Rubin E, Farber JL (eds): *Pathology*. Philadelphia, PA, JB Lippincott, 1988.

18. Martinez-Hernandez A, Amenta PS: Basic concepts in wound healing, in Leadbetter WB, Buckwalter JA, Gordon SL (eds): *Sports-Induced Inflammation: Clinical and Basic Science Concepts*. Park Ridge, IL, American Academy of Orthopaedic Surgeons, 1990, pp 55-101.

19. Woo SLY, Tkach LV: The cellular and matrix response of ligaments and tendons to mechanical injury, in Leadbetter WB, Buckwalter JA, Gordon SL (eds): *Sports-Induced Inflammation: Clinical and Basic Science Concepts*. Park Ridge, IL, American Academy of Orthopaedic Surgeons, 1990, pp 189-204.

20. Brown M: Special considerations during rehabilitation of the aged athlete. *Clin Sports Med* 1989;8:893-901.

21. Clement DB, Taunton JE, Smart GW: Achilles tendinitis and peritendinitis: Etiology and treatment. *Am J Sports Med* 1984;12:179-184.

22. Menard D, Stanish WD: The aging athlete. *Am J Sports Med* 1989;17:187-196.

23. Vailas AC, Pedrini VA, Pedrina-Mille A, et al: Patellar tendon matrix changes associated with aging and voluntary exercise. *J Appl Physiol* 1985;58:1572-1576.

24. Ballard WT, Weinstein JN: Biochemical aspects of aging and degeneration in the intervertebral disc. *Contemp Orthop* 1992;24:453-458.

25. Scarpelli DG, Trump BF (eds): *Cell Injury*. Kalamazoo, MI, Published by the UpJohn Company for Universities Associated for Research and Education in Pathology, Inc, Bethesda, Maryland, 1971.

26. Rusting RL: Why do we age? *Sci Am* 1992;267:130-141.

27. Davies I: Biology of aging: Theories of aging, in Brocklehurst JC (ed): *Textbook of Geriatric Medicine and Gerontology*, ed 3. Edinburgh, Churchill Livingstone, 1985, pp 62-81.

28. Strehler BL (ed): Definitions, criteria, categories, and origins of age changes, in *Time, Cells, and Aging*, ed 2. New York, NY, Academic Press, 1977, pp 4-32.

29. Norwood TH, Smith JR, Stein GH: Aging at the cellular level: The human fibroblastlike cell model, in Schneider EL, Rowe JW (eds): *Handbook of the Biology of Aging*, ed 3. San Diego, CA, Academic Press, 1990, pp 131-154.

30. Nagineni CN, Amiel D, Green MH, et al: Characterization of the intrinsic properties of the anterior cruciate and medial collateral ligament cells: An in vitro cell culture study. *J Orthop Res* 1992;10:465-475.

31. Frank C, McDonald D, Lieber R, et al: Biochemical heterogeneity within the maturing rabbit medial collateral ligament. *Clin Orthop* 1988;236:279-285.

32. Mauch C, Hatamochi A; Scharffetter K, et al: Regulation of collage synthesis in fibroblasts within a three-dimensional collagen gel. *Exp Cell Res* 1988;178:493-503.

33. Frank C, Amiel D, Woo SL, et al: Normal ligament properties and ligament healing. *Clin Orthop* 1985;196:15-25.

34. Davies I: Biology of aging: General principles, in Brocklehurst JC (ed): *Textbook of Geriatric Medicine and Gerontology*, ed 3. Edinburgh, Churchill Livingstone, 1985, pp 29-45.

35. Danner DB, Holbrook NJ: Alterations in gene expression with aging, in Schneider EL, Rowe JW (eds): *Handbook of the Biology of Aging*. San Diego, CA, Academic Press, 1990, pp 97-115.

36. Furth JJ: The steady-state levels of type I collagen mRNA are reduced in senescent fibroblasts. *J Gerontol* 1991;46:B122-B124.

37. Adzick NS, Longaker MT: *Fetal Wound Healing*. New York, NY, Elsevier, 1992.

38. Paz MA, Gallop PM: Collagen synthesized and modified by aging fibroblasts in culture. *In-Vitro* 1975;11:302-312.

39. Houben A, Raes M, Houbion A, et al: Alteration of enzymes in ageing human fibroblasts in culture: I. Conditions for the appearance of an alteration in glucose 6-phosphate dehydrogenase. *Mech Ageing Dev* 1984;25:23-34.

40. Houben A, Raes M, Houbion A, et al: Alteratiaon of enzymes in ageing human fibroblasts in culture: II. Conditions for the reversibility and the mechanism of the alteration of glucose 6-phosphate dehydrogenase. *Mech Ageing Dev* 1984;25:35-45.

41. Murad S, Sivarajah A, Pinnell SR: Prolyl and lysyl hydroxylase activities of human skin fibroblasts: Effect of donor age and ascorbate. *J Invest Derm* 1980;75:404-407.

42. Hunt TK, Dunphy JE (eds): *Fundamentals of Wound Management*. New York, NY, Appleton-Century-Crofts, 1979.

43. Madden JW, Arem AJ: Wound healing: Biologic and clinical features, in Sabiston DC Jr (ed): *Textbook of Surgery: The Biological Basis of Modern Surgical Practice*, ed 14. Philadelphia, PA, WB Saunders, 1991, pp 164-177.

44. Castor CW: Regulation of connective tissue metabolism, in McCarty DJ (ed): *Arthritis and Allied Conditions: A Textbook of Rheumatology*, ed 11. Philadelphia, PA, Lea & Febiger, 1989, pp 256-272.

45. Cohen IK, Diegelmann RF, Lindblad WJ (eds): *Wound Healing: Biochemical and Clinical Aspects*. Philadelphia, PA, WB Saunders, 1992, pp 384-395.

46. Fong Y, Moldawer LL, Shires GT, et al: The biologic characteristics of cytokines and their implication in surgical injury. *Surg Gynecol Obstet* 1990;170:363-378.

47. Goldring MB, Goldring SR: Skeletal tissue response to cytokines. *Clin Orthop* 1990;258:245-278.

48. Clark RAF, Henson PM (eds): *The Molecular and Cellular Biology of Wound Repair*. New York, NY, Plenum Press, 1988.

49. Roth GS: Mechanisms of altered hormone-neurotransmitter action during aging: From receptors to calicum mobilization. *Ann Rev Gerentol Geriatr* 1990;10:132-146.

50. Seshadri T, Campisi J: Growth-factor-inducible gene expression in senescent human fibroblasts. *Exp Gerontol* 1989;24:515-522.

51. Miller RA: Aging and the immune response, in Schneider EL, Rowe JW (eds): *Handbook of the Biology of Aging*, ed 3. San Diego, CA, Academic Press, 1990, pp 157-180.

52. Gallin JI, Goldstein IM, Snyderman R (eds): *Inflammation: Basic Principles and Clinical Correlates*. New York, NY, Raven Press, 1988.

53. Abbas AK, Lichtman AH, Pober JS: *Cellular and Molecular Immunology*. Philadelphia, PA, WB Saunders, 1991.

54. Stauber WT, Fritz VK, Vogelbach DW, et al: Characterization of muscles injured by forced lengthening: I. Cellular infiltrates. *Med Sci Sports Exerc* 1988;20:345-353.

55. Fox RA: Immunology of aging, in Brocklehurst JC (ed): *Textbook of Geriatric Medicine and Gerontology*, ed 3. Edinburgh, Churchill Livingstone, 1985, pp 82-104.

56. Friedlaender GE, Jokl P, Horowitz MC: The autoimmune nature of sports-induced injury: A hypothesis, in Leadbetter WB, Buckwalter JA, Gordon SL (eds): *Sports-Induced Inflammation: Clinical and Basic Science Concepts*. Park Ridge, IL, American Academy of Orthopaedic Surgeons, 1990, pp 619-627.

57. Zahniser NR, Parker DC, Bier-Laning CM, et al: Comparison between the effects of aging on antagonist and agonist interactions with beta-adrenergic receptors on human mononuclear and polymorphonuclear leukocyte membranes. *J Gerontol* 1988;43:M151-M157.

58. Chansky HA, Iannotti JP: The vascularity of the rotator cuff. *Clin Sports Med* 1991;10:807-822.

59. Curwin SL: Models for use in studying sports-induced soft-tissue inflammation, in Leadbetter WB, Buckwalter JA, Gordon SL (eds): *Sports-Induced Inflammation: Clinical and Basic Science Concepts*. Park Ridge, IL, American Academy of Orthopaedic Surgeons, 1990, pp 103-121.

60. Noyes FR, Grood ES: The strength of the anterior cruciate ligament in humans and Rhesus monkeys. *J Bone Joint Surg* 1976;58A:1074-1082.

61. Woo SLY, Hollis JM, Adams DJ, et al: Tensile properties of the human femur-anterior cruciate ligament-tibia complex: The effects of specimen age and orientation. *Am J Sports Med* 1991;19:217-225.

62. Amiel D, Kuiper SD, Wallace CD, et al: Age-related properties of medial collateral ligament and anterior cruciate ligament: A morphologic and collagen maturation study in the rabbit. *J Gerontol* 1991;46:B159-B165.

63. Arnoczky S, Adams M, DeHaven K, et al: Meniscus, in Woo SL-Y, Buckwalter JA (eds): *Injury and Repair of the Musculoskeletal Soft Tissues*. Park Ridge, IL, American Academy of Orthopaedic Surgeons, 1988, pp 487-537.

64. Gordon P: Free radicals and the aging process, in Rockstein M, Sussman ML, Chesky J (eds): *Theoretical Aspects of Aging*. New York, Academic Press, 1974, pp 61-81.

65. Finerman GAM, Shapiro MS: Sports-induced soft-tissue calcification, in Leadbetter WB, Buckwalter JA, Gordon SL (eds): *Sports-Induced Inflammation: Clinical and Basic Science Concepts*. Park Ridge, IL, American Academy of Orthopaedic Surgeons, 1990, pp 257-275.

66. Oegema TR Jr: Biochemistry of the intervertebral disc. *Clin Sports Med* 1993;12:419-439.

67. Halliwell B, Gutteridge JMC (eds): *Free Radicals in Biology and Medicine*, ed 2. Oxford, Clarendon Press, 1989, pp 450-466.

68. Trump BF, Berezesky IK, Smith MW, et al: The role of ionized cytosolic calcium ($[Ca2+]i$) in injury and recovery from anoxia and ischemia. *Maryland Med J* 1992;41:505-508.

69. Wahl SM, Wahl LM: Inflammation, in Cohen IK, Diegelmann RF, Lindblad WJ (eds): *Wound Healing: Biochemical and Clinical Aspects*. Philadephia, PA, WB Saunders, 1992, pp 40-62.

70. Hodge CF: Changes in ganglion cells from birth to senile death: Observations on man and the honeybee. *J Physiol* 1894;17:129-134.

71. Ward PA, Till GO, Johnson KJ: Oxygen derived free radicals and inflammation, in Leadbetter WB, Buckwalter JA, Gordon SL (eds): *Sports-Induced Inflammation: Clinical and Basic Science Concepts*. Park Ridge, IL, American Academy of Orthopaedic Surgeons, 1990, pp 315-324.

72. Packer L: Protective role of vitamin E in biological systems. *Am J Clin Nutr* 1991;153(suppl):1050S-1055S.

73. Alessio HM: Exercise-induced oxidative stress. *Med Sci Sports Exerc* 1993;25:218-224.

74. Leadbetter WB: An introduction to sports-induced soft-tissue inflammation, in Leadbetter WB, Buckwalter JA, Gordon SL (eds): *Sports-Induced Inflammation: Clinical and Basic Science Concepts.* Park Ridge, IL, American Academy of Orthopaedic Surgeons, 1990, pp 3-23.

75. Lazarus GS, Cooper DM, Knighton DR, et al (eds): Definitions and guidelines for assessment of wounds and evaluaiton of healing in "Scars and Stripes," *The Newsletter of the Wound Healing Society* 1992, vol 2, pp 7-14.

76. Amadio PC: Tendon and ligament, in Cohen IK, Diegelmann RF, Lindblad WJ (eds): *Wound Healng: Biochemical and Clinical Aspects.* Philadelphia, PA, WB Saunders, 1992, p 384.

77. Almekinders LC, Banes AJ, Ballenger CA: Inflammatory response of fibroblasts to repetitive motion. *Trans Orthop Res Soc* 1992;17:678.

78. Mankin HJ: The response of articular cartilage to mechanical injury. *J Bone Joint Surg* 1982;64A:460-466.

79. Ng SC, Weiss JB, Quennel R, et al: Abnormal connective tissue degrading enzyme patterns in prolapsed intervertebral discs. *Spine* 1986;11:695-701.

80. Pearce RH, Grimmer BJ, Adams ME: Degeneration and the chemical composition of the human lumbar intervertebral disc. *J Orthop Res* 1987;5:198-205.

81. Inerot S, Heinegård D, Audell L, et al: Articular-cartilage proteoglycans in aging and osteoarthritis. *Biochem J* 1978;169:143-156.

82. Grisham JW, Nopanitaya W: Cellular basis of disease, in Kissane JM (ed): *Anderson's Pathology,* ed 9. St. Louis, MO, CV Mosby, 1990.

83. Robbins SL, Cotran RS: *Pathologic Basis of Disease,* ed 2. Philadelphia, PA, WB Saunders, 1979.

84. Nirschl RP, Pettrone FA: Tennis elbow: The surgical treatment of lateral epicondylitis. *J Bone Joint Surg* 1979;61A:832-839.

85. Puddu G, Ippolito E, Postacchini F: A classification of Achilles tendon disease. *Am J Sports Med* 1976;4:145-150.

86. Miller RA: Aging and the immue response, in Schneider EL, Rowe JW (eds): *Handbook of the Biology of Aging,* ed 3. San Diego, CA, Academic Press, 1990, pp 157-180.

87. Rodosky MW, Fu FH: Induction of synovial inflammation by matrix molecules, implant particles, and chemical agents, in Leadbetter WB, Buckwalter JA, Gordon SL (eds): *Sports-Induced Inflammation: Clinical and Basic Science Concepts.* Park Ridge, IL, American Academy of Orthopaedic Surgeons, 1990, pp 357-381.

88. Arnheim DD: *Modern Principles of Athletic Training.* St. Louis, MO, Times Mirror/Mosby College Pub. 1989, p 230.

89. Fantone JC: Basic concepts in inflammation, in Leadbetter WB, Buckwalter JA, Gordon SL (eds): *Sports-Induced Inflammation: Clinical and Basic Science Concepts.* Park Ridge, IL, American Academy of Orthopaedic Surgeons, 1990, pp 25-53.

90. van der Meulen JC: Present state of knowledge on processes of healing in collagen structures. *Int J Sports Med* 1982;3(suppl 1):4-8.

91. Jennings RW, Hunt TK: Overview of post-natal wound healing, in Adzick NS, Longaker MT (eds): *Fetal Wound Healing.* New York, NY, Elsevier, 1992, pp 25-52.

92. Physiology of tissue repair, in Hunter-Griffin L (ed): *Athletic Training and Sports Medicine,* ed 2. Park Ridge, IL, American Academy of Orthopaedic Surgeons. 1991, pp 96-123.

93. Clancy WG Jr: Tendon trauma and overuses injuries, in Leadbetter WB, Buckwalter JA, Gordon SL (eds): *Sports-Induced Inflammation: Clinical and Basic Science Concepts.* Park Ridge, IL, American Academy of Orthopaedic Surgeons, 1990, pp 609-618.

94. Gerber G, Gerber G, Altman KI: Studies on the metabolism of tisue proteins: I. Turnover of collagen labeled with proline U-C14 in young rats. *J Biol Chem* 1960;235:2653-2656.

95. Gelberman R, Goldberg V, An KN, et al: Tendon, in Woo SLY, Buckwalter JA (eds): *Injury and Repair of the Musculoskeletal Soft Tissues.* Park Ridge, IL, American Academy of Orthopaedic Surgeons, 1988, pp 5-40.

96. Laurent TC: Structure, function and turnover of the extracelllar matrix. *Adv Microcirc* 1987;13:15-34.

97. Smith LL: Acute inflammation: The underlying mechanism in delayed onset muscle soreness? *Med Sci Sports Exerc* 1991;23:542-551.

98. Leadbetter WB: Histologic characteristics of overuse tendon injury in sports. *J Cell Biochem Suppl* 1991;15:195.

99. Jozsa L, Kvist M, Balint BJ, et al: The role of recreational sport activity in Achilles tendon rupture: A clinical, pathoanatomical, and sociological study of 292 cases. *Am J Sports Med* 1989;17:338-343.

100. Fox RI, Lotz M, Carson DA: Stucture and function of synoviocytes, in McCarty MJ (ed): *Arthritis and Allied Conditions: A Textbook of Rheumatology,* ed 11. Philadelphia, PA, Lea & Febiger, 1989, pp 273-288.

101. Kvist M, Jozsa L, Jarvinen MJ, et al: Chronic Achilles paratenonitis in athletes: A histological and histochemical study. *Pathology* 1987;19:1-11.

102. Kvist MH, Lehto MU, Jozsa L, et al: Chronic Achilles paratenonitis: An immunohistologic study of fibronectin and fibrinogen. *Am J Sports Med* 1988;16:616-623.

103. Harper J, Amiel D, Harper E: Changes in collagenase and inhibitor in ligaments and tendon during early development of stress deprivation. *Trans Orthop Res Soc* 1991;16:114.

104. Carrel A, Lecomte du Novy P: Cicatrization of wound: XI. Latent period. *J Exp Med* 1921;34:339-348.

105. Mast B: The skin, in Cohen IK, Diegelmann RF, Lindblad WJ (eds): *Wound Healing: Biochemical and Clinical Aspects.* Philadelphia, PA, WB Saunders, 1992, pp 344-355.

106. Heikkinen E, Aalto M, Vihersaari T, et al: Age factor in the formation and metabolism of experimental granulation tissue. *J Gerontol* 1971;26:294-298.

107. Forscher BK, Cecil HC: Some effects of age on the biochemistry of acute inflammation. *Gerontologia* 1958;2:174-182.

108. Hussain S: Disorders of hemostasis and thrombosis in the aged. *Med Clin North Am* 1976;60:1273-1287.

109. Alexander CM, Werb Z: Extracellular matrix degradation, in Hay ED (ed): *Cell Biology of Extracellular Matrix,* ed 2. New York, NY, Plenum Press, 1991, pp 255-302.

110. Peacock EE: Wound healing and wound care, in Schwartz SI, Shires TG, Spencer F (eds): *Principles of Surgery,* ed 5. New York, NY, McGraw-Hill, 1989, pp 307-330.

111. Duncan BW, Qian J, Liu X: Regulation of prolyl hydroxylase activity in fetal and adult fibroblasts, in Adzick NS, Longaker MT (eds): *Fetal Wound Healing.* New York, NY, Elsevier, 1992, pp 303-315.

112. Wahl SM, Renström P: Fibrosis in soft-tissue injuries, in Leadbetter WB, Buckwalter JA, Gordon SL (eds): *Sports-Induced Inflammation: Clinical and Basic Science Concepts.* Park Ridge, IL, American Academy of Orthopaedic Surgeons, 1990, pp 637-647.

113. Heckmann M, Kreig T: Biological and pharmacological modulations of fibroblast functions. *Skin Pharmacol* 1989;2:125-137.

114. Hasslet C, Henson PM: Resolution of inflammation, in Clark RAF, Henson PM (eds): *The Molecular and Cellular Biology of Wound Repair.* New York, NY, Plenum Press, 1988, pp 185-211.

115. Tillman LJ, Cummings GS: Biologic mechanisms of connective tissue mutability, in Currier DP, Nelson RM (eds): *Dynamics of Human Biologic Tissues*. Philadelphia, PA, FA Davis, 1992, pp 1-44.

116. Cummings GS, Tillman LJ: Remodeling of dense connective tissue in normal adult tissue, in Currier DP, Nelson RM (eds): *Dynamics of Human Biologic Tissues*. Philadelphia, PA, FA Davis, 1992, pp 45-73.

117. Uhthoff HK, Sarkar K: Classification and definition of tendinopathies. *Clin Sports Med* 1991;10:707-720.

118. Garrett WE Jr: Muscle strain injuries: Clinical and basic aspects. *Med Sci Sports Exerc* 1990;22:436-443.

119. Schatzker J, Branemark PI: Intravital observations on the microvascular anatomy and microcirculation of the tendon. *Acta Orthop Scand Suppl* 1969;126:1-23.

120. Rathbun JB, Mcnab I: The microvascular pattern of the rotator cuff. *J Bone Joint Surg* 1970;52B:540-553.

121. DeHaven KE, Arnoczky SP: Meniscal repair, in Finerman GAM, Noyes FR (eds): *Biology and Biomechanics of the Traumatized Synovial Joint: The Knee as a Model*. Rosemont, IL, American Academy of Orthopaedic Surgeons, 1992, pp 185-202.

122. Brooks CH, Revell WJ, Heatley FW: A quantitative histological study of the vascularity of the rotator cuff tendon. *J Bone Joint Surg* 1992;74B:151-153.

123. Nirschl RP: Mesenchymal syndrome. *Virginia Med Monthly* 1969;96:659-662.

124. Muravchick S: Anesthesia for the elderly, in Miller RD, Cucchiara RF, Miller ED Jr, et al (eds): *Anesthesia*, ed 3. New York, NY, Churchill Livingstone, 1990, vol 2, pp 1969-1983.

125. Nirschl RP, Pettrone FA: Tennis elbow: The surgical treatment of lateral epicondylitis. *J Bone Joint Surg* 1979;61A:832-839.

126. Teitz CC: Overuse injuries, in Teitz CC (ed): *Scientific Foundations of Sports Medicine*. Toronto, BC Decker, 1989, p 299.

127. Curwin S, Stanish WD: *Tendinitis: Its Etiology and Treatment*. Lexington, MA, Collamore Press, 1984.

128. Jozsa L, Balint JB, Kannus P, et al: Distribution of blood groups in patients with tendon rupture: An analysis of 832 cases. *J Bone Joint Surg* 1989;71B:272-274.

129. Singer KM, Jones DC: Soft tissue conditions of the ankle and foot, in Nicholas JA, Hershman EB (eds): *The Lower Extremity and Spine in Sports Medicine*. St. Louis, MO, CV Mosby, 1986, p 148.

130. Lyon RM, Akeson WH, Amiel D, et al: Ultrastructural differences between the cells of the medial collateral and the anterior cruciate ligaments. *Clin Orthop* 1991;272:279-286.

131. Williams PL, Warwick R, Dyson M, et al: *Gray's Anatomy*, ed 36. Edinburgh, Churchill Livingstone, 1980.

132. Clark JM, Harryman DT II: Tendons, ligaments, and capsule of the rotator cuff: Gross and microscopic anatomy. *J Bone Joint Surg* 1992;74A:713-725.

133. Caplan A, Carlson B, Faulkner J, et al: Skeletal muscle, in Woo SL-Y, Buckwalter JA (eds): *Injury and Repair of the Musculoskeletal Soft Tissues*. Park Ridge, IL, American Academy of Orthopaedic Surgeons, 1988, pp 213-291.

134. Butler DL, Grood ES, Noyes FR, et al: Biomechanics of ligaments and tendons. *Exerc Sports Sci Rev* 1978;6:125-181.

135. Labelle H, Guibert R, Joncas J, et al: Lack of scientific evidence for the treatment of lateral epicondylitis of the elbow: An attempted meta-analysis. *J Bone Joint Surg* 1992;74B:646-651.

136. Wouters E, Bassett FH III, Hardaker WT Jr, et al: An algorithm for arthroscopy in the over-50 age group. *Am J Sports Med* 1992;20:141-145.

137. Bonamo JJ, Kessler KJ, Noah J: Arthroscopic meniscectomy in patients over the age of 40. *Am J Sports Med* 1992;20:422-429.

138. Lotke PA, Lefkoe RT, Ecker ML: Later results following medial meniscectomy in an older population. *J Bone Joint Surg* 1981;63A:115-119.

139. Jackson DW, Whelan J, Simon TM: Cell survival after transplantation of fresh meniscal allografts: DNA probe analysis in a goat model. *Am J Sports Med* 1993;21:540-550.

140. Vander Schilden JL, York JL, Webber RJ: Age dependent fibrin clot invasion by human meniscal fibrochondrocytes: A preliminary report. *Orthop Rev* 1991;20:1089-1097.

141. Johnson RJ, Beynnon BD, Nichols CE, et al: The treatment of injuries of the anterior cruciate ligament. *J Bone Joint Surg* 1992;74A:140-151.

142. McFarland EG: The biology of anterior cruciate ligament reconstructions. *Orthopedics* 1993;16:403-410.

143. MacKinley D, Steadman JR, Devine SD, et al: ACL reconstruction in patients ≥ 40 years. Presented at the Combined Congress of the International Arthroscopy Association and the International Society of the Knee, Toronto, May 13-17, 1991.

144. Chaytor R, Stanish WD: Clinical treatment of tendinitis. *Sports Med Digest* 1992;14:2.

145. Eaton RG: Ruling out surgery for carpal tunnel syndrome, in Jaffee WL (ed): *Mediguide to Orthopaedics*. 1992, vol 11, p 4.

146. Amheim DD: Modern principles of athletic training. St. Louis, MO, Times Mirror/Mosby, 1989, vol 230.

147. Weiler JM: Medical modifiers of sports injury: The use of nonsteroidal anti-inflammatory drugs (NSAIDS) in sports soft-tissue injury. *Clin Sports Med* 1992;11:625-644.

148. Rivenburgh DW: Physical modalities in the treatment of tendon injuries. *Clin Sports Med* 1992;11:645-659.

149. Sporn MB, Roberts AB: Transforming growth factor-beta: Multiple actions and potential clinical applications. *JAMA* 1989;262:938-941.

150. Bartlett's Quotations, 1992.

Chapter 13

Exercise Fitness and Sports for Individuals With Neurologic Disability

Bruce H. Dobkin, MD

The Significance of Neurologic Disability

More people are surviving diseases and injuries that happen before and during midlife. As a result, there is increased interest in how to optimize their physical abilities and how to prevent the consequences of a sedentary lifestyle induced by disability. The significance of these problems is reflected in the remarkable number of people who are limited in their ability to perform daily activities.

According to the US Bureau of the Census' Survey of Income and Program Participation,[1] disabilities alter the activities of 37 million Americans aged 15 years and older. Limitations were defined by difficulty in performing common tasks. For example, 2.5 million people have difficulty getting around in their homes; 18 million people have trouble climbing a flight of stairs; and 19 million people cannot walk a quarter of a mile.[1]

In 1983, the National Health Interview Surveys (NHIS) began a study on disability and life activities using the World Health Organization (WHO) definition of disability: any restriction or lack of ability to perform an activity in the manner or within the range considered normal for a human being. The NHIS study found that 22 million Americans were restricted or unable to perform the major activity for their age group.[2] For individuals aged 18 to 69, major activities were employment and housekeeping.

The NHIS study also found that cerebrovascular disease and other nervous system diseases listed in Outline 1 are among the leading causes of disability in noninstitutionalized people.[2] Between ages 18 to 69, 645,000 people are paralyzed in one or more extremities and 464,000 people are disabled by stroke, 200,000 people by spinal cord injuries, 120,000 people by multiple sclerosis, and 75,000 people by Parkinson's disease.[2] Many others are disabled due to polyneuropathies, muscular dystrophies, postpolio syndrome, and

Outline 1 Neurologic diseases

Stroke
Spinal cord injury
Traumatic brain injury
Multiple sclerosis
Parkinson's disease
Polyneuropathies
Postpolio syndrome
Motoneuron disease
Ataxias
Neuromuscular diseases

ataxias. In addition, the costs of disability are high. The National Foundation for Brain Research showed that in 1990, the direct and indirect costs of neurologic disorders, excluding alcohol and substance abuse, totaled $107 billion.

The prevalence of neurologic disability will probably continue to rise in midlife. Each year, nearly one third of the 400,000 Americans who experience a stroke are in midlife or even younger. Half of all survivors of stroke have a hemiparesis 6 months after the stroke; more than 20% of the survivors are unable to walk; and 33% need much assistance in activities of daily living. In addition, over 60% of survivors are limited in their social and recreational activities because of disabilities.[3]

Each year about 85,000 people aged 15 to 35 become disabled as a result of a spinal cord injury (10,000 people) or a serious traumatic brain injury (75,000 people). Approximately 640,000 people who survived polio in childhood become susceptible to disability during midlife as a result of decompensation from aging, overuse of muscles, and an exacerbation of their neuromuscular disease.[4]

The goals of short-term inpatient and outpatient rehabilitation for individuals who have varying levels of disability as a result of acute neurologic disease are to enhance mobility, self-care skills, and social and avocational skills. However, organized, long-term efforts to maintain or improve physical function and to improve endurance and strength are a recent and still uncommon undertaking.[5]

The Meanings of Fitness

Definitions of fitness for individuals with diseases of the central or peripheral nervous system will vary. Fitness for some may include balance, coordination of fine and gross motor skills, flexibility, and the skills needed to don or use orthoses and assistive devices. For others, fitness may also include the more traditional concepts of isometric and isokinetic strengthening, muscular endurance training, and cardiovascular conditioning. A growing body of evidence suggests that mechanical loading, such as weightbearing at some minimum amount and frequency every day, can improve many of the negative changes in muscle mass, metabolism, and physiology associated with atrophy that accompanies paresis.[3] Techniques to assist weightbearing might, then, be a reasonable approach to increase lower limb fitness in a person with paraplegia. Even though people with physical impairments often use more energy to perform ordinary activities, the extra effort usually does not improve fitness levels or increase strength in the functioning muscles. Instead, these individuals often restrict or slow their activities. Therefore, a reasonable goal for an exercise program would be to increase the level of conditioning over the aerobic demand of a typical activity, perhaps to twice what is required for daily wheelchair mobility or for 15 minutes of continuous walking.

Muscle fatigability, defined as the inability to sustain a constant or repetitive force at the desired level, often accompanies weakness with diseases of the central and peripheral motor pathways. In a study of 15 individuals with peripheral neurogenic diseases (neuropathies and spinal muscular atrophy), one mechanism of fatigue involved an accelerated reduction in muscle membrane excitation and propagation during a sustained contraction.[6] In central nervous system disorders, such as spinal cord injury and multiple sclerosis, muscle plasticity may contribute to fatigability, because with these disorders fatigue-resistant type I fibers change to fatigable fibers.[7]

Miller and associates[8] have suggested that biochemical changes in the muscles of patients with spastic paraparesis contribute to the greater than normal level of muscle fatigability. With repetitive electrical stimulation of the peroneal nerve, the tetanic decline in tension of the tibialis anterior muscle, as well as the decline in phosphocreatine and intracellular pH, were greater than in normal controls. Also, the half-relaxation time, defined as the number of milliseconds from the time of the last stimulus to the time at which the peak tension had decayed by half, was prolonged. They believed that these findings reflected a reduced rate of ATP production and slowed calcium ATPase activity in the membrane of the sarcoplasmic reticulum. This hypothesis suggests that at least some of the fatigability with central nervous system lesions may arise from secondary changes in the muscle fibers as a result of altered metabolism.[8] Secondary changes in the muscle fibers may also contribute to spasticity. Exercise may have the potential to limit these changes, but when planning an exercise program that involves sustained or repetitive muscle contractions, the limitations of greater than normal muscle fatigability must be considered.

Studies have shown that many individuals with neurologic disabilities can achieve a conditioning and strengthening effect from exercise. These studies also suggest that their sense of physical, social, and psychological well-being might improve with regular participation in exercise and recreational sports. However, fitness testing and training pose special problems, depending on the specific disease, neurologic impairments, and functional disabilities. Recent research findings can help in the design of adaptive procedures for strengthening and aerobic conditioning.

Disease-Specific Exercise Studies

Spinal Cord Injuries

Much of the research on the benefits and limitations of fitness testing and training in individuals with neurologic deficits has focused on those with paraplegia and quadriplegia due to spinal cord injuries. (Glaser and Davis[9] present a detailed discussion on people who are wheelchair-dependent as a result of spinal cord injuries.) Fitness is often difficult to achieve due to the muscle weakness, sensory loss, muscle spasticity, dysautonomia, muscle contractures, and pain that accompany spinal cord injuries.

With training, individuals who have residual voluntary movement in the upper body may attain enough strength and endurance for repetitive activities. However, cardiovascular conditioning can be limited because the individual uses only the small muscle mass of the upper body. Reduced cardiac preloading as a result of pooling of blood in the leg muscles, and impaired cardiovascular reflexes also preclude the training responses of able-bodied persons.

Although walking is commonly used as a conditioning exercise for cardiovascular fitness, the amount of energy required for locomotion is generally too great for people with paraplegia. In addition, strengthening severely paretic or paralyzed muscles with electrical stimulation is complicated both mechanically and physiologically.

An individual with paraplegia must use a knee-ankle-foot orthosis and crutches with a swing-through gait. This achieves an average speed of 30 m/min and oxygen consumption rate of 16 ml/kg-min.[10] By comparison, a nondisabled person aged 20 to 59 consumes oxygen at an average rate of 12 ml/kg-min at a casual walking velocity of 80 m/min. The energy expenditure for an individual with paraplegia is 160% higher than a nondisabled person would use at that speed, and the oxygen cost per meter walked is six times higher than normal. However, the energy required for ambulation may be reduced by combining functional electrical stimulation (FES) of leg muscles with surface or implanted electrodes and use of a reciprocal gait orthosis (RGO).

A more functional approach is to exercise in a way that will enhance muscular and cardiovascular fitness for wheelchair activities. The need for greater fitness becomes apparent by midlife. Routine wheelchair activities use 18% of the peak oxygen intake of paraplegic athletes in their mid-20s, which is about 30% less than their sedentary counterparts. As sedentary individuals with paraplegia approach their 50s, routine wheelchair activities use over 50% of their peak oxygen intake.

Future research will likely reveal additional methods of voluntary arm cranking and wheelchair ergometry, perhaps combining voluntary arm activity with electrical stimulation of leg muscles to allow for more central cardiovascular conditioning after spinal cord injury.[11]

Many neurologic diseases impair stance and ambulation, so fitness regimens must be designed for individuals who are wheelchair bound. Studies of paraplegics that show a conditioning effect as a result of exercise in midlife are evidence that similar effects are possible in individuals with any neurologic disease, especially if the disease largely spares the upper extremities, and if venous pooling in the legs and cardiovascular reflexes are less impaired when compared with a spinal cord injury. For example, cardiovascular fitness improved in sedentary paraplegics with arm crank training at 50% of peak oxygen intake done three times a week for 40 minutes (though not for only 20 minutes) over both 8- and 24-week periods.[12] A similar exercise program might work for a sedentary, wheelchair-bound person with weakness of the lower extremities from any cause.

In nondisabled individuals, the work load for the upper extremities should be about 50% of that for the legs, and the target heart rate should be 10 beats per minute lower. These parameters were suggested because at a given submaximal work load, exercise of the upper extremities requires more energy, while maximal physiologic responses are lower.[13] Using these guidelines, a cardiovascular conditioning effect can be achieved, especially in individuals who have not exercised previously.

A pars course or other series of wheelchair exercise stations, including propelling a wheelchair over a rising power ramp or a ramp of uneven platforms, and doing chin-ups from the wheelchair, produce heart rates and peak oxygen uptake rates from arm exercises alone that are comparable to techniques producing a training effect in both individuals with paraplegia and those without impairment.[14] In paraplegics with adequate motor control and strength, it may be possible to reduce the energy cost of ambulation with interventions that decrease hypertonicity in the legs, including antispasticity medications and physical therapies such as stretching spastic hip adductors.[15] Such interventions might encourage individuals with paraparesis to exercise or participate in recreational activities.

Multiple Sclerosis

Multiple sclerosis is an immune-mediated demyelinating disease that often worsens and then partially remits in middle-aged individuals, leaving about 20% wheelchair bound 10 years after the onset. Hypertonicity, spasms in the reflexive extensor and flexor muscles, ataxia, and exertion-related and heat-induced fatigability may exacerbate lower extremity weakness. These conditions typically interfere with mobility and exercise tolerance in people who have multiple sclerosis.

The energy cost of ambulation in people with multiple sclerosis may be twice normal. In a study of 33 subjects aged 21 to 56, the energy cost of ambulation correlated best with hypertonicity of the lower extremities.[16] The high energy cost of ambulation is likely to result in and intensify the effects of deconditioning.

In a randomized study of 50 subjects with multiple sclerosis, 25 were assigned usual activities, and 25 were assigned unspecified home exercise for 15 to 30 minutes, four to five times a week for 16 weeks.[17] By bicycle ergometry, the home exercise group achieved a 20% to 30% increase in posttest work load, which was contributed largely by the subgroup with the least disability. Exercise did not increase disability, but rather, it resulted in a 10% gain in fitness. As might be expected, individuals with less disability who can exercise their large muscles are capable of the greatest gains.

Stroke

Cardiovascular disease is common in individuals who have had a stroke, as are the risk factors of hypertension (65%), cigarette smoking (40%), diabetes mellitus (20%), and claudication (15%). These factors complicate exercise training and fitness measures with their cardiopulmonary and peripheral neurovascular effects and with the side effects of the medications used for treatment. Decreased range of motion and joint pain in individuals with hemiparesis can limit exercise options. Loss of proprioception makes it difficult for the individual to know where a limb is in space without constant visual tracking. Impairments in speaking ability, vision, perception, learning ability, and verbal or nonverbal memory can interfere with the comprehension of and compliance with an exercise regimen. Because approximately one in three survivors of a stroke become depressed, it may be difficult to maintain a high level of motivation to work at physical activities.

Individuals with a hemiplegic gait often become deconditioned from bed rest early after the stroke and remain so because of their limited mobility. Despite the inefficiency and high energy cost of the hemiplegic gait pattern, the rate of oxygen consumption for an individual with hemiplegia during casual walking at 30 m/min tends to be less than the rate for nondisabled persons whose customary walking speed is 80 m/min.[10] Although the total oxygen cost and heart rate will be significantly greater than that of an able-bodied person, slowing their speed prevents individuals with hemiplegia from experiencing physical exertion and fatigue.

Monitored exercise in the hemiparetic patient without angina or serious hemodynamic compromise or arrhythmias may be safe and result in improved strength and fitness, enhanced locomotion, and perhaps increased participation in associated activities. However, no adequately designed clinical trials have been reported.

In a study of 16 stroke and 16 matched control subjects (mean age = 66 years), there was no significant difference in mean heart rate and blood pressure or in symptoms following isometric hand grip exercises or arm and bicycle ergometry. The control subjects, however, performed more leg work.[18] These results suggest that exercise can be safe for some stroke patients.

Stationary bicycling, with the unaffected leg doing most of the work, is often recommended for patients with hemiparesis. We have successfully increased the force exerted by the paretic leg by placing a strain gauge on each pedal and then giving the patient feedback about performance.

Hemiplegic individuals who walk slowly can also be trained on a treadmill. We have supported up to 50% of an individual's body weight with an overhead harness held by a hydraulic lift (Fig. 1). Partial weight support limits the gait deviations that occur with full weightbearing on the paretic limb until training helps it to function more efficiently. Treadmill velocity was then increased incrementally each time the individual achieved an efficient gait pattern without body weight support.[19] A group of six subjects who were 1 year post-stroke began at 12 m/min with weight support and advanced to over 60 m/min with no support in 12 to 30 sessions. Training was done initially in 5-minute intervals, and the heart rate was kept below 100 beats per minute. Treadmill walking for 20 consecutive minutes led to an increase in the over ground velocity of 30% to 90%. The temporal and kinematic features of their gait cycles also improved. Figure 2 shows the relationship of gains in velocity of treadmill and over ground walking for an individual in the study who had a right hemiplegia and hemisensory loss from a deep intracerebral hemorrhage. As a result of this training, the subjects of this study became community ambulators, were able to socialize more, and covered greater distances without fatigue. Studies to assess associated changes in strength and fitness are underway.

An effective home-based exercise training program, such as the program described by King and associates,[20] is needed for individuals with hemiplegia. Sedentary men and women, aged 50 to 65, with no history of cardiovascular disease were randomly assigned to one of the following groups: (1) a high-intensity group or individual home-based exercise program that consisted of 40 minutes of training three times a week in an attempt to achieve 73% to 88% of peak treadmill heart rate; (2) a low-intensity home-based exercise program that consisted of 30 minutes of training five times a week in an attempt to achieve 60% to 73% of peak treadmill heart rate; or (3) no exercise program. The treated groups walked, jogged, or rode a stationary bicycle. Treadmill endurance increased by 16%, and maximum oxygen consumption by 5% to 8% after 6 and 12 months. The results suggested that home-based exercise programs were as effective as group training and that low-intensity exercise was as beneficial as high-intensity exercise. A monitored program of bicycling, and treadmill or over ground walking may improve the exercise fitness and functional mobility of stroke patients. An exercise program may

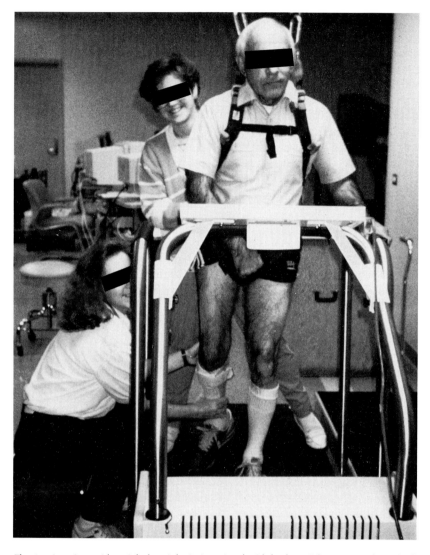

Fig. 1 *A patient with a right hemiplegia is assisted with body weight-supported treadmill training 1 year after a stroke.*

also reduce the risk for recurrent stroke, which is 8% to 11% per year, myocardial infarction, and symptomatic peripheral vascular disease.

Traumatic Brain Injury

Beyond the first year following a serious traumatic brain injury, patients often have residual attention and memory impairments. Perhaps half of these patients will have paresis or ataxia, which adds to disability.

WALKING SPEED (RR)

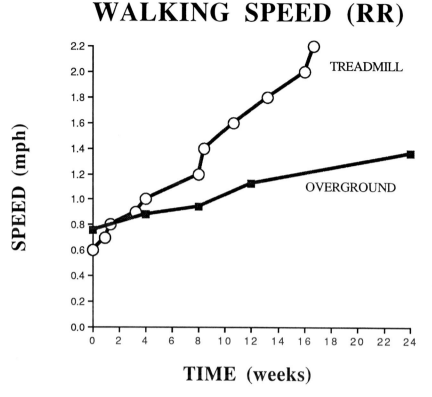

Fig. 2 *Treadmill walking speed gradually improved in the patient and was accompanied by functionally important gains in the speed of over ground locomotion.*

In a study of 14 sedentary adults (mean age = 30 years) who had completed rehabilitation following a traumatic brain injury, an exercise program was developed that included aerobic training stations for cycling, rope skipping, jogging, and stair climbing. Neuromuscular adaptation, strength, and coordination were stimulated by activities such as shooting and dribbling a basketball, three-pin bowling, weightlifting, and calisthenics.[21] The subjects began with 2 minutes at each of ten stations, and they built up to 9 minutes at each station, for a total of approximately 2 hours of exercise three times a week for 16 weeks. Because of their impairments, most of the subjects were unable to exercise at 70% of their maximum rate of oxygen consumption or a minimum target heart rate of 150 beats per minute. Their above-average oxygen cost for locomotion at 80 m/min remained unchanged. Enhanced gross motor coordination and strength are presumably also needed to improve efficiency for locomotion. However, their oxidative capacity improved 15% and abdominal muscular endurance improved 90%.

Ataxia

A 38-year-old man with Friedreich's ataxia, a combined central and peripheral neurologic disorder, who was free of the hypertrophic cardiomyopathy that sometimes accompanies this genetic disease, exercised using bicycle ergometry for 20 minutes over 27 sessions at 70% to 85% of his pretest maximum peak oxygen intake.[22] His peak oxygen consumption increased 27%. In a pilot study at the University of California, Los Angeles (personal communication, S. Perlman, MD, 1986-1988), a twice-a-day home-based exercise program for 20 subjects with spinocerebellar degeneration, ten of whom used a wheelchair, led to gains in strength and walking mobility in 6 weeks. Twelve of the subjects maintained this gain over the next 2 years. Repetitive sit to stand, stepping up onto an 8-inch high stool, and heel-raising exercises contributed most to the gains. While truncal instability, lack of limb coordination, spasticity, and paresis can limit mobility in some individuals with ataxia, many can participate in fitness activities and recreational sports, if given the opportunity.

Postpolio Syndrome

Polio is a viral disease of the anterior horn cells that causes weakness and muscle atrophy, which may result in biomechanical inefficiency and muscle and joint strain. Aging and deconditioning can cause further declines in performance of activities of daily living. Many survivors of childhood polio have new symptoms as they reach midlife, including fatigability and progressive weakness in previously affected and clinically unaffected muscles. Nonfatiguing exercises for strengthening have been suggested to allay concerns about injuring reinnervated muscles, but few studies exist that address this issue.

In a study examining fatigability in postpolio syndrome patients, rest breaks were interspersed with sustained isometric muscle contractions in a work-rest ratio of 1:6. This program design helped subjects increase their isometric work with less local muscle fatigue.[23] To avoid muscle fatigue and overuse of small muscle groups, other investigators[4] designed a training program for postpolio syndrome patients that consisted of 2- to 5-minute sessions of aerobic exercise, separated by 1-minute rest breaks, up to 30 minutes a day, 3 days a week. The subjects in this study achieved an aerobic conditioning effect and increased knee extensor strength when compared with the control group. These protocols might be a useful basis for a training program for any individual with a neurologic disability.

Most individuals with postpolio syndrome probably do not experience progressive paresis during midlife. However, those individuals with symptoms were found to be weaker, able to perform less work at 40% of maximum isometric torque in knee extension, and less likely to recover mean relative strength than asymptomatic persons with polio.[24]

In another study, 12 subjects (mean age = 54 years) were able to increase both isometric (mean 29%) and isokinetic (mean 24%) strength and maintain that increase for a year. These subjects participated in a training program that consisted of 12 sets of eight maximal isokinetic contractions and 12 sets of isolated 4-second isometric contractions of the knee extensors completed in 18 sessions over a 6-week period.[24] A comparison of muscle biopsy specimens before and after the training program revealed no new histopathologic change to suggest fiber damage. In addition, their gains in strength did not correlate with a change in muscle fiber size or oxidative enzyme activity. However, many of the subjects reported greater ease in standing, walking, and climbing.

In an anecdotal report, two subjects with postpolio syndrome were trained on a treadmill 20 times over 8 weeks to the point of perceiving moderate exertion or musculoskeletal discomfort at each session.[25] Treadmill velocity and duration were gradually increased over the 8-week period. After the training program, maximum oxygen cost decreased about 25% and both heart rate and blood pressure levels decreased in the test subjects, compared with the same measurements in a single control subject with postpolio syndrome. The subjects also reported less fatigue in their daily activities. As a result, the investigators suggested that both biomechanical efficiency and oxygen delivery may increase with a modified aerobic walking program.

Amyotrophic Lateral Sclerosis

Amyotrophic lateral sclerosis (ALS) or Lou Gehrig's disease is a progressive disorder that destroys primarily the motor neurons of the cerebral cortex, the brainstem, and the spinal cord. It often begins during midlife and is characterized by muscle weakness, atrophy, spasticity, and reduced motor control that may progress to respiratory insufficiency and aphagia in a period of 2 to 5 years.

Maximum oxygen consumption and work capacity decline as motor function decreases, probably as a consequence of both the inability to recruit muscle fibers and deconditioning.[26] The oxygen cost of submaximal exercise also increases.

In individuals who have ALS, as in those with a variety of metabolic and nonmetabolic neuromuscular diseases, derangements in the production of free fatty acids, ketones, esterified carnitine, and other carbohydrate and lipid metabolic abnormalities have been documented. Alterations in energy production and in substrate utilization require consideration when planning an exercise program for those with ALS.

Polyneuropathies

Individuals with chronic, severe peripheral neuropathies experience muscle wasting (predominantly distally), weakness, and sensory impairment—all factors that could place limitations on exercise. Exercise and fitness in midlife are especially important for individuals with diabetes, because this may reduce the risk for coronary heart disease, stroke, and symptomatic peripheral vascular disease.

Individuals with diabetes commonly have a polyneuropathy, and nearly 20% of individuals with diabetes have an autonomic neuropathy that often includes a baroreceptor defect. Despite the limitations associated with polyneuropathy, 29 subjects, who also had retinopathy, were able to train at 60% of predicted heart rate on a bicycle or by walking. The subjects achieved 3 MET for 28 minutes, and their blood glucose levels decreased 76 mg/dl during their modest exertion.[27]

Neuromuscular Diseases

Concern about overwork-induced weakness, fatigue, and muscle injury has led to disagreement about the use of resistive exercises in individuals with a range of neuromuscular diseases. Many of the diseases that start in adolescence and midlife are hereditary. The growing literature on the metabolic and physiologic factors that set an upper limit to exercise performance in individuals with neuromuscular disorders (including myasthenia gravis, inflammatory, lipid, and carbohydrate metabolic, mitochondrial, and other congenital and dystrophic myopathies) has recently been summarized.[28]

Testing maximal voluntary muscle contraction in individuals with a neuromuscular disease may be complicated by many factors: the ability to cooperate with the procedure; pain and contractures; difficulty in isolating a particular muscle and activating its motor units; and abnormalities of neuromuscular transmission, excitation-contraction coupling, energy metabolism, and contractile efficiency.

In a study of 12 subjects, aged 20 to 53, some with chronically progressive facioscapulohumeral, myotonic, and Becker's and limb-girdle dystrophies, and others with spinal muscular atrophy or an idiopathic polyneuropathy, some improvement in elbow flexion and knee extension was seen with high-resistance weight training. Initially, these muscle groups had no greater than 10% of normal force. Exercise led to significantly increased maximum force sustained for 5 seconds. It decreased the fall in maximum force over 60 seconds.[29] Subjects began with a weight that could be lifted for a maximum of 15 repetitions, and then trained over the next 3 months to reach a maximum of five sets, four times a week. The weight was increased whenever more than ten repetitions were achieved.

Incremental exercise testing of work load by bicycle ergometry and maximum oxygen consumption can also be used in those who have the leg strength equivalent to that needed to climb a few steps.[30] In another study, a 36-year-old man with a nonprogressive, congenital central core myopathy and generalized weakness trained with bicycle ergometry for 3 months. This exercise program improved his work capacity and maximum oxygen consumption by 50% and produced a maximum heart rate of 140 beats per minute.[31] Similar gains have been seen in individuals in their late 30s who have juvenile-onset spinal muscular atrophy and Becker's dystrophy. The proximal weakness associated with steroid-induced myopathy improves after withdrawal of the drug, but also seems to improve with a light resistive exercise program.

Recommendations

Strengthening and Conditioning

It is possible to devise a strategy to increase muscle strength through exercise training for all but the most severely paretic, unmotivated, or cognitively impaired disabled persons. The primary goals of exercise training are to improve performance in daily self-care, social, work, and recreational activities. Although close initial monitoring in the weak and deconditioned individual is required, isolated muscle strengthening may be accomplished using manual resistance near the patient's maximum strength capacity and is adjusted throughout the joint's range of motion. The goal is to complete two to three sets of six repetitions at least three times a week for a minimum of 4 to 6 weeks.[32] The training effect can, perhaps, be maintained or even improved with a home-based program of resistive exercises at about 60% of the ten-repetition maximum or by daily recreational activities. Tasks for strengthening should emphasize lifting, walking, climbing, and achieving respiratory control. Aerobic conditioning is also possible through an individual exercise prescription and thoughtful strategy, preferably one using an exercise regimen that will also improve motor skills and dynamic activities.

The activities described above might benefit disabled persons by increasing balance, mobility, and flexibility; decreasing hypertonicity, fatigability, and lifestyle restrictions; enhancing immune function; and ultimately, improving cognition[33] and mood. The effect of these activities may also diminish long-term health risk factors, such as coronary heart disease, hypertension, hyperlipidemia, non-insulin-dependent diabetes, osteoporosis, and obesity. However, few empiric data support this range of potential benefits.

It is relevant, however, that in a study of sedentary premenopausal women who participated in a modest exercise program, subjects achieved significant increases in high-density lipoprotein cholesterol concentration without vigorous exercise, and increased maximum uptake with walking alone. Subjects considered "aerobic" walkers gained more than "brisk" walkers, and "brisk" walkers gained more than "strollers."[34] These findings suggest that at least one major cardiovascular risk factor might be managed with a modest exercise or recreational program in midlife in individuals who cannot participate in regular aerobic conditioning.

Outline 2 Sports and recreation for individuals with neurologic disability

aerobics	martial arts
aerobic dance	motor soccer
all terrain vehicles	powerlifting
archery	quad rugby
basketball	racquetball
beep baseball	road racing
blowdarts	roller skating
boating	ropes
boccia	rugball
bowling	scuba diving
canoeing	shooting
cross country	showdown
cycling	skiing
fencing	sky diving
equestrian	slalom
fencing	sledge hockey
field events	snowmobiling
fishing	soccer
fitness programs	softball
floor hockey	swimming
flying	table tennis
football	team handball
goalball	tennis
golf	track
gymnastics	volleyball
horseback riding	water skiing
hunting	weightlifting
ice skating	wilderness experiences
ice sledding	wrestling
lawn bowling	

From a basic science point of view, people with neurologic diseases that selectively affect the upper or lower motoneurons or motor units are potentially important to studies of neuromuscular plasticity. For example, exercise, functional overload, the activity of androgens and thyroid and growth hormones, immobilization, starvation, spinal transection, and electrical stimulation cause rather unique muscle adaptations, including the modulation of the expression of specific myosin proteins.[35] By using physiologic, metabolic, biochemical, and imaging techniques for muscle studies in individuals with lesions along the motor pathways, we can learn much more about neural and systemic influences on muscle and motor functions. In turn, these data would help in developing more beneficial treatment plans for improving muscle strength, fitness, and overall activity levels in individuals who are disabled.

Sports

Participation in sports and recreational activities can result in more rapid increases in upper body strength than routine physical therapy alone, as well as fuller reintegration into the work force and enhanced self-esteem in individuals with paraplegia.[36] Depression has been associated with low levels of physical and recreational activities in nondisabled women,[37] and it may be an even more important risk factor among disabled individuals. Increased participation in physical activities through physical therapy, a fitness program, and recreational and competitive sports seems likely to improve a disabled person's perceived quality of life.[38] Sports and exercise activities are easily incorporated into both short-term and long-term rehabilitation programs for individuals with neurologic disability to enhance and maintain functional recovery and build self-esteem. Remarkable advances in equipment design for wheelchair racing and snow skiing have allowed many disabled people to participate in recreational and competitive sports in midlife.[39,40] To date, over 200 local, national, and international organizations have developed rules and equipment that allow disabled persons to participate in sports activities, as shown in Outline 2.[41]

References

1. DeJong G, Batavia A, Griss R: America's neglected health minority: Working age persons with disabilities. *Millbank Q* 1989;67(suppl 2):311-351.

2. LaPlante MP (ed): *Data on Disability From the National Health Interview Survey, 1983-1985: An InfoUse Report*. Washington, DC: U.S. National Institute on Disability and Rehabilitation Research, 1988.

3. Gresham G, Phillips T, Wolf P, et al: Epidemiologic profile of long-term stroke disability: The Framingham study. *Arch Phys Med Rehabil* 1979;61:487-491.

4. Agre JC, Rodriquez AA: Neuromuscular function: Comparison of symptomatic and asymptomatic polio subjects to control subjects. *Arch Phys Med Rehabil* 1990;71:545-551.

5. Hjeltnes N: Capacity for physical work and training after spinal injuries and strokes. *Scand J Soc Med* 1982;29(suppl):245-251.

6. Milner-Brown HS, Miller RG: Increased muscular fatigue in patients with neurogenic muscle weakness: Quantification and pathophysiology. *Arch Phys Med Rehabil* 1989;70:361-366.

7. Lenman AJ, Tulley FM, Vrbova G, et al: Muscle fatigue in some neurological disorders. *Muscle Nerve* 1989;12:938-942.

8. Miller RG, Green AT, Moussavi RS, et al: Excessive muscular fatigue in patients with spastic paraparesis. *Neurology* 1990;40:1271-1274.

9. Glaser RM, Davis GM: Wheelchair-dependent individuals, in Franklin BA, Gordon S, Timmis GC (eds): *Exercise in Modern Medicine*. Baltimore, MD, Williams & Wilkins, 1989, chap 13, pp 237-267.

10. Waters R, Yakura J: The energy expenditure of normal and pathological gait. *Crit Rev Phys Rehab Med* 1989;1:183-192.

11. Figoni SF: Perspectives on cardiovascular fitness and SCI. *J Am Paraplegia Soc* 1990;13:63-71.

12. Davis G, Plyley MJ, Shephard RJ: Gains of cardiorespiratory fitness with arm-crank training in spinally disabled men. *Can J Sport Sci* 1991;16:64-72.

13. Franklin BA: Aerobic exercise training programs for the upper body. *Med Sci Sports Exerc* 1989;21(suppl 5):S141-S148.

14. Cardus D, McTaggart WG, Ribas-Cardus F, et al: Energy requirements of gamefield exercises designed for wheelchair-bound persons. *Arch Phys Med Rehabil* 1989;70:124-127.

15. Mattsson E, Brostrom LA, Borg J, et al: Walking efficiency before and after long-term muscle stretch in patients with spastic paraparesis. *Scand J Rehab Med* 1990;22:55-59.

16. Olgiati R, Burgunder JM, Mumenthaler M: Increased energy cost of walking in multiple sclerosis: Effect of spasticity, ataxia, and weakness. *Arch Phys Med Rehabil* 1988;69:846-849.

17. Shapiro R, Petajan J, Kosich D, et al: Role of cardiovascular fitness in multiple sclerosis: A pilot study. *J Neuro Rehab* 1988;2:43-49.

18. Monga TN, Deforge DA, Williams J, et al: Cardiovascular responses to acute exercise in patients with cerebrovascular accidents. *Arch Phys Med Rehabil* 1988;69:937-940.

19. Dobkin BH, Gregor R, Fowler E: A strategy to train locomotion in patients with chronic hemiplegic stroke. *Ann Neurol* 1991;30:278.

20. King AC, Haskell WL, Taylor CB, et al: Group- vs home-based exercise training in healthy older men and women: A community-based clinical trial. *JAMA* 1991;266:1535-1542.

21. Jankowski LW, Sullivan SJ: Aerobic and neuromuscular training: Effect on the capacity, efficiency, and fatigability of patients with traumatic brain injuries. *Arch Phys Med Rehabil* 1990;71:500-504.

22. Fillyaw MJ, Ades PA: Endurance exercise training in Friedreich ataxia. *Arch Phys Med Rehabil* 1989;70:786-788.

23. Agre JC, Rodriquez AA: Intermittent isometric activity: Its effect on muscle fatigue in postpolio subjects. *Arch Phys Med Rehabil* 1991;72:971-975.

24. Einarsson G: Muscle conditioning in late poliomyelitis. *Arch Phys Med Rehabil* 1991;72:11-14.

25. Dean E, Ross J: Modified aerobic walking program: Effect on patients with postpolio syndrome symptoms. *Arch Phys Med Rehabil* 1988;69:1033-1038.

26. Sanjak M, Paulson D, Sufit R, et al: Physiologic and metabolic response to progressive and prolonged exercise in amyotrophic lateral sclerosis. *Neurology* 1987;37:1217-1220.

27. Bernbaum M, Albert SG, Cohen JD: Exercise training in individuals with diabetic retinopathy and blindness. *Arch Phys Med Rehabil* 1989;70:605-611.

28. Lewis SF, Haller RG: Skeletal muscle disorders and associated factors that limit exercise performance. *Exerc Sport Sci Rev* 1989;17:67-113.

29. Milner-Brown HS, Miller RG: Muscle strengthening through high-resistance weight training in patients with neuromuscular disorders. *Arch Phys Med Rehabil* 1988;69:14-19.

30. Carroll JE, Hagberg JM, Brooke MH, et al: Bicycle ergometry and gas exchange measurements in neuromuscular diseases. *Arch Neurol* 1979;36:457-461.

31. Hagberg JM, Carroll JE, Brooke MH: Endurance exercise training in a patient with central core disease. *Neurology* 1980;30:1242-1244.

32. Bohannon R: Exercise training variables influencing the enhancement of voluntary muscle strength. *Clin Rehabil* 1990;4:325-331.

33. Dustman R, Emmerson R, Shearer D: Aerobic fitness may contribute to CNS health: Electrophysiological, visual and neurocognitive evidence. *J Neuro Rehab* 1990;4:241-254.

34. Duncan JJ, Gordon NF, Scott CB: Women walking for health and fitness: How much is enough? *JAMA* 1991;266:3295-3299.

35. Edgerton VR, Roy RR: Regulation of skeletal muscle fiber size, shape and function. *J Biomech* 1991;24(suppl 1):123-133.

36. Jackson RW, Davis GM: The value of sports and recreation for the physically disabled. *Orthop Clin North Am* 1983;14:301-315.

37. Farmer ME, Locke BZ, Moscicki EK, et al: Physical activity and depressive symptoms: The NHANES 1 Epidemiologic Follow-up Study. *Am J Epidemiol* 1988;128:1340-1351.

38. Shephard RJ: Benefits of sport and physical activity for the disabled: Implications for the individual and for society. *Scand J Rehabil Med* 1991;23:51-59.

39. Laskowski ER: Snow skiing for the physically disabled. *Mayo Clin Proc* 1991;66:160-172.

40. Cooper RA: Wheelchair racing sports science: A review. *J Rehabil Res Dev* 1990;27:295-312.

41. Paciorek MJ, Jones JA (eds): *Sports and Recreation For the Disabled: A Resource Handbook*. Indianapolis, IN, Benchmark Press, 1989.

Chapter 14

Exercise Testing and Training Techniques for the Spinal Cord Injuries

Roger M. Glaser, PhD

Introduction

Muscle paralysis, which may be due to various neuromuscular disorders such as spinal cord injury (SCI), head trauma, stroke, and multiple sclerosis, limits a person's ability to exercise voluntarily and can result in a marked loss of physical fitness, functional independence, and psychosocial status. Aging tends to exacerbate these problems by progressively reducing exercise capacity and further decreasing the ability to perform activities of daily living (ADL). Therefore, a major focus of research at the Institute for Rehabilitation Research and Medicine has been to develop specialized exercise training techniques by which wheelchair users with paralyzed lower limbs can improve physical fitness and potentially alleviate multiple secondary problems. Arm exercises have traditionally been used for the testing and training of wheelchair users. However, physiologic responses to arm exercise performed by neurologically impaired individuals of various ages can be quite different from physiologic responses to leg exercise by their nondisabled cohorts. Therefore, this paper addresses research related to (1) the exercise capability and physiologic responses of wheelchair users of various ages who have SCIs, (2) the use of the arm exercise techniques for physical fitness testing and training, and (3) the use of recently developed training techniques that incorporate functional electrical stimulation (FES)-induced exercise of paralyzed leg muscles. Although most of the subjects used for the described research had SCIs, many of the principles and data presented are applicable to wheelchair users who have other neuromuscular disorders.

The Role of Exercise and Wheelchair Sports in Rehabilitation

Participation in exercise and wheelchair sports programs can have a profound impact on rehabilitation outcome. Such therapeutic practices can challenge the individual with an SCI to overcome physical obstacles and expand functional independence. Indeed, sports competition provides many opportunities for the pursuit of excellence from the novice to the Olympic levels depending upon the particular needs and abilities of the individual. Regardless of an individual's motivation to begin exercise training and to participate in wheelchair sports, clinicians should consider prescribing such programs early in the posttraumatic rehabilitation process to optimize outcome.[1]

Regardless of age, gender, and medical history, most wheelchair users can derive benefits from appropriately designed exercise programs. Well established principles of specificity and overload should be followed to obtain the desired results in an efficient manner.[2,3] Thus, specific exercise regimes (ie, modes and protocols) are used to achieve the goals of muscle strengthening, endurance training, and cardiopulmonary (ie, aerobic) training. Exercise training has resulted in significant improvements in fitness, which can lead to greater physical capability and functional independence, and reduced relative stresses for performing given ADL.[1-3] Appropriate exercise training may also lower the risk for occurrence of secondary medical complications associated with wheelchair confinement and sedentary lifestyles.[4] These complications include muscle atrophy, osteoporosis, decubitus ulcers, and a host of cardiopulmonary disorders.

If exercise and sports participation can enhance health and fitness, as well as societal interactions for wheelchair users, it seems reasonable to assume that there are psychological benefits in terms of self-esteem and body image. Indeed, several studies have indicated that wheelchair users who engaged in sports and recreation programs experienced significant increases in skill performance, self-concept, and self-acceptance.[5,6] However, these results are most likely influenced by inherent differences in pre-existing exercise habits, attitudes, beliefs, and personality. It is also apparent that psychosocial outcome of the individual with SCI is highly influenced by societal attitudes. In this regard, wheelchair sports can have a positive effect in reducing stigmatization, stereotyping, and discrimination, and in improving acceptance of these individuals as fully functioning members of society.[1,7]

Spinal Cord Injury (SCI)

Epidemiology

SCI is a trauma-induced disability that can cause complete paraplegia or quadriplegia (quadriplegia is also known as tetraplegia). This injury typically results in sudden and drastic changes in lifestyle, including a marked decrease in physical activity. Krause and Crewe[8] found that physical activity in individuals with SCI tended to be lower with higher chronologic age and shorter time since injury. These variables were also related to a less rewarding life and a decline in psychological adjustments. Major causes of SCI in the United States are motor vehicle accidents (about 48%), accidents that occur during sports or physical activities (about 14%), and trauma during violent crimes (about 15%).[9,10] There are currently more than 200,000 individuals with SCI in the United States, and each year approximately 8,000 new individuals survive to join this population.[10] Prior to World War II, 80% of those with SCI died within 3 years of injury,[11] primarily as a result of kidney and pulmonary infections.[12] However, with the advent of antibiotic drugs and advances in surgical techniques, individuals with paraplegia can have a near-normal life expectancy, whereas individuals with quadriplegia tend to have a life expectancy that is about 10% lower than that of nondisabled individuals.[12] Generally, the higher the age at the time of SCI, the higher the level of injury, and the more complete the injury, the lower will be the life expectancy.[13,14] Currently, the leading causes of death in the population with long-term SCI (and lower-limb amputees) are related to a variety of cardiovascular and respiratory disorders.[10,15-17]

Le and Price[16] reported that the death rate of their SCI group was 228% greater than that of their age-and gender-matched nondisabled control group. This higher death rate apparently is due in part to a sedentary lifestyle and the ensuing degenerative changes in the cardiovascular system.[17-20] Sedentary individuals with SCI have significantly lower blood high-density lipoprotein-cholesterol (HDL-C) concentrations in comparison to athletes with SCI, as well as sedentary and active nondisabled individuals,[18-21] and consequently, their risk of heart disease is greater. Thus, arm exercise training may increase the health status and reduce the cardiovascular risks of individuals with SCI similarly to the way leg exercise training benefits nondisabled individuals.[21,22]

Pathophysiology

In general, the higher the level and the more complete the SCI, the more widespread will be the loss of somatic and autonomic nervous system function. Figure 1 illustrates the central nervous system (CNS) and neural outflows of the somatic nervous system, which innervates skeletal muscles, and the autonomic nervous system, which innervates internal organs.[2] With respect to somatic function, lesions in the cervical region typically result in quadriplegia, whereas lesions in the thoracic and lumbar regions typically result in paraplegia. The more skeletal muscles that are paralyzed, the lower will be the voluntary exercise capability, and the lower will be the absolute cardiopulmonary (aerobic) fitness level that may be achieved through exercise training. In patients with higher-level SCI, paralysis of intercostal muscles can severely limit pulmonary ventilation, which can further reduce exercise capability and lead to secondary pulmonary problems. Furthermore, paralysis of the leg muscles usually results in marked atrophy of these muscles and osteoporosis of

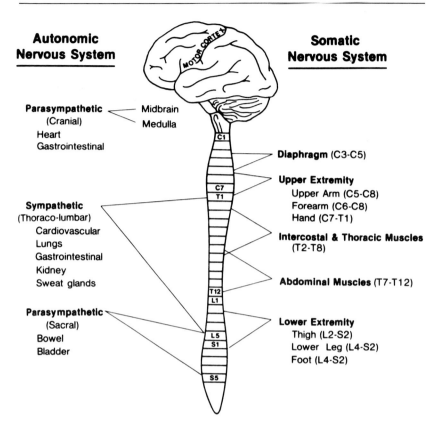

Fig. 1 *Schematic diagram of the central nervous system and the neural outflows from the somatic nervous system (providing skeletal muscle innervation) and autonomic nervous system (providing internal organ innervation). General innervations from each spinal cord level are indicated. (Reproduced with permission from Glaser RM: Exercise and locomotion for the spinal cord injured. Exerc Sports Sci Rev 1985;13:263-303).*

the bones. Immobilization of the lower limbs may also precipitate venous stasis, blood pooling, and edema due to inactivity of the venous muscle pump, which may lead to deep venous thrombosis and subsequent pulmonary embolism. Decubitus ulcers are frequently the result of prolonged pressure on supporting tissues and inadequate local circulation.[4]

In addition to skeletal muscle paralysis, the aerobic exercise capability of individuals with SCI can be limited by diminished sympathetic outflow (Fig. 1), because sympathetic stimulation is required for normal cardiovascular reflex responses to exercise. These reflexes normally augment blood flow to metabolically active skeletal muscles to provide more oxygen and fuel substrates, while increasing the rate of metabolic end-product removal. Such responses include vasoconstriction in relatively inactive tissues (eg, intestines, kidneys, skin);

vasodilation of skeletal muscle arterioles; venoconstriction, which facilitates venous return; and increases in heart rate, myocardial contractility, stroke volume, and cardiac output.[2,3,22] Although these reflexes are absent to varying degrees in most individuals with SCI, interruption of all sympathetic nerves that innervate the heart (from T-4 to T-1), in those with complete lesions above T-1, markedly limits cardioacceleration, myocardial contractility, stroke volume, and cardiac output.[23] In individuals with complete lesions above T-1, any cardioacceleration that occurs with exercise may be due primarily to withdrawal of vagal parasympathetic tone to the sinoatrial node. It is also likely that reduced sympathetic outflow in SCI impairs thermoregulatory capacity because of inappropriate blood flow distribution and insufficient sweating response below the lesion level.

Limitations in Arm Exercise Capability

Thus, the loss of functional skeletal muscle mass with SCI, as well as inactivity of the venous muscle pump in the lower extremities, are compounded with diminished or nonexistent cardiovascular reflexes during exercise. These factors can result in easy fatigability of active arm muscles due to their relatively small mass, inadequate blood flow due to hypokinetic circulation, and limited aerobic energy supply, as well as a greater anaerobic component and the accumulation of metabolites in the muscles.[2,3,24,25] Easy fatigability of arm muscles during wheelchair locomotion and exercise training discourages many wheelchair users from leading active lives. Unfortunately, a sedentary lifestyle can lead to a greater decrement in physical fitness and an even larger reduction in functional capability. Further decreases in cardiovascular, pulmonary, and muscular function due to aging can eventually lead to a loss of independence and an increase in medical complications.[14] Specific exercise training programs are needed to break this vicious cycle of sedentary lifestyle → loss of fitness and to enhance rehabilitation outcome.[2,3]

Special Exercise Precautions and Considerations

Athletes with SCI performing strenuous exercise are exposed to the usual risks for nondisabled individuals, as well as additional risks due to their CNS damage and the resulting motor, sensory, and autonomic dysfunction. Because of the potential for numerous health risks, it is prudent for wheelchair users to have a thorough medical examination (including an electrocardiogram) before beginning a strenuous exercise program. A medical examination is especially important for older individuals who have been sedentary for many years. Unique risks that should be anticipated for individuals with SCI during exercise include exercise hypotension, orthostatic hypotension, autonomic dysreflexia (ie, sudden and inappropriate blood pressure responses), trunk instability, pressure sores, and muscle spasms.[26-29] As previously indicated, thermoregulation may be a problem for some athletes. Therefore, health care professionals supervising exercise for individuals with SCI should be aware of the known risks and take appropriate safety precautions.

Blood pressure responses of patients with SCI during exercise may be quite different and inconsistent in comparison to those elicited from nondisabled individuals. This finding is particularly true for patients with high-level SCI, who may exhibit a paradoxical drop in blood pressure as exercise progresses. This exercise hypotension may result from a lowering of total peripheral resistance, as blood vessels in active muscles dilate in response to hypoxia and increased concentrations of local metabolites, without a corresponding increase in cardiac output. On the other hand, exercise in an upright posture may cause blood pooling in the lower extremities with inadequate venous return and cardiac output, which can result in orthostatic hypotension with dizziness or possible loss of consciousness. This risk may be reduced by regular orthostatic training (eg, head-up tilt, standing, brace ambulation), proper hydration, compression stockings, abdominal binder, and physical conditioning.

Occasionally, some athletes with high-level SCI may exhibit a sudden episode of extremely high blood pressure (hypertension) due to autonomic dysreflexia (hyperreflexia). Autonomic dysreflexia can be quite hazardous and may lead to death if it is not corrected immediately. To help avoid autonomic dysreflexia, proper health practices should be observed and indicated medical treatment should be obtained to eliminate noxious stimuli resulting from bowel impaction, bladder overdistension, and skin tissue trauma. Thus, the bladder should be emptied just prior to exercise and during prolonged exercise sessions, and blood pressure should be monitored at regular intervals (at least during initial exercise sessions).[28] Of course, if any response occurs that places the participant at risk, exercise should be discontinued immediately, and appropriate action should be taken to alleviate the problem (eg, tilting up for hypertension, reclining for hypotension and fainting).

A security belt should be placed around the upper trunk of the individuals with SCI during arm exercise to prevent falls resulting from trunk instability and poor sitting balance. In addition, measures must be taken to minimize pressure on weightbearing tissues to prevent decubitus ulcers. To accomplish this goal, effective cushioning should be incorporated under the ischial tuberosities and other weightbearing areas, and the athlete should perform periodic pressure relief (ie, raising the body off the cushion every 20 to 30 minutes for 30 to 60 seconds).

Furthermore, many individuals with SCI experience occasional spasms in the paralyzed lower-limb muscles, ranging from mild to severe. Care must be taken to avoid damage to the lower limbs in the event of strong spasms and rapid limb movements. Pharmacotherapy is often employed to help control muscle spasms. This treatment may involve the use of oral antispasmodic and muscle relaxant drugs. However, these drugs may further limit exercise capability by reducing skeletal muscle excitability. In addition, there can be detrimental side effects including dizziness, ataxia, and depression.[12]

Careful consideration also should be given to ambient temperature, relative humidity, and clothing worn, as well as exercise intensity and duration. Because many individuals with SCI have limited thermoregulatory capacity due to inadequate secretion by sweat glands and impaired cardiovascular system control, overheating can occur more easily in this population than in nondisabled individuals. Conversely, exercise in cold environments may result in excessive heat loss from the body. Therefore, if there are symptoms of hyperthermia or hypothermia, exercise should be discontinued, and clothing and environmental conditions should be adjusted appropriately.

Problems Associated With Wheelchair Confinement and Use

Individuals who depend upon manual wheelchairs for locomotion are required to rely on their relatively small and weak upper-body musculature. This dependence places them at a marked disadvantage due to the limited maximal (peak) oxygen uptake ($\dot{V}O_2$) and power output capability for arm exercise, which has been reported to be approximately two-thirds of values for leg exercise in nondisabled individuals who are not arm-exercise trained.[30-33] Arm exercise capability may be further reduced because of factors related to the disability (as indicated above), as well as diminished muscular and cardiopulmonary fitness resulting from aging and a sedentary lifestyle. In addition, arm exercise has been reported to be rather inefficient (energy wasteful) and stressful to the muscles involved, as well as to the cardiovascular and pulmonary systems in comparison to the same intensities of leg exercise.[31,34-36] Indeed, when comparing wheelchair propulsion with walking and leg cycling, greater magnitudes of physiologic stresses were generally elicited for handrim stroking.[37-41] These stresses tended to be more pronounced at the greater exercise intensities that occurred at higher locomotive velocities and when negotiating architectural barriers such as carpeting and upward grades. Because self-selected locomotive velocities appear to be directly related to peak $\dot{V}O_2$, they tend to decrease with age.[41]

In studies comparing arm and leg exercise (eg, arm-crank and wheelchair ergometry versus leg cycle ergometry) for nondisabled subjects at matched submaximal power output levels, arm exercise elicited greater metabolic stress, as indicated by the higher $\dot{V}O_2$ and blood lactate values; heavier cardiac load, as indicated by higher heart rate, greater peripheral vascular resistance, increased intra-arterial blood pressure, and elevated stroke work; and greater demand on the pulmonary system, as indicated by higher pulmonary ventilation. Arm exercise also tended to elicit lower cardiac output and ventricular stroke volume.[31,34,39,42-45] Lower cardiac output and stroke volume may be due to a greater afterload on the heart because of the higher peripheral vascular resistance, and a lower end-diastolic volume resulting from attenuated venous return of blood to the heart. During wheelchair propulsion by individuals with SCI, venous return may be restricted by inactivity of the venous muscle pump in the paralyzed legs.[2,3,22] Furthermore, elevated intrathoracic pressure during handrim stroking may decrease thoracic pump effectiveness.[39] These combined factors may reduce the effective blood volume during wheelchair activity and limit peak $\dot{V}O_2$ and maximal power output. Therefore, wheelchair locomotion, even at low power output levels, can represent relatively high exercise loads that may lead to the rapid onset of fatigue. Excessive cardiovascular and pulmonary stresses can hinder rehabilitation efforts and impose risks upon certain patients, such as those with cardiovascular or pulmonary impairments, and the elderly.[2,3,39]

Stress Testing Techniques for Physical Fitness Assessment

With nondisabled individuals, leg exercise modes (eg, treadmill walking/running, bench stepping, cycle ergometry) are typically used for stress testing. Here, a large muscle mass is rhythmically contracted, which stimulates optimal (maximal) metabolic, cardiovascular, and pulmonary responses to permit valid functional evaluation of these systems. Many exercise scientists believe that the primary factor limiting maximal power output and $\dot{V}O_2$ during these tests is central circulatory in nature, and the cardiovascular system is not able to deliver sufficient blood and oxygen to the large exercising muscle mass.[46-49] In contrast, use of arm exercise modes (eg, wheelchair locomotion, arm-crank, and wheelchair ergometry) to stress test wheelchair users incorporates a relatively small muscle mass. The primary factors that limit performance during these tests may be peripheral in nature, and local fatigue of the relatively stressed arm musculature can occur despite the delivery of sufficient blood and oxygen.[24,50-53] Another peripheral factor that may limit arm exercise performance is inadequate venous return of blood to the heart due to deficient skeletal muscle pump activity.[24] This can, in turn, limit cardiac output and the delivery of blood and oxygen to the arm musculature. Thus, due to lower power output capability and the early onset of fatigue, arm exercise may not provide sufficient stimulus to drive the metabolic, cardiovascular, and pulmonary systems to full output, which makes valid functional evaluation of these systems difficult. Because the highest level of $\dot{V}O_2$ that can be obtained for maximal effort arm exercise is somewhat lower than the true physiologic maximum that is expected for leg exercise in nondisabled individuals, the term "peak $\dot{V}O_2$", rather than maximal $\dot{V}O_2$, is typically used.

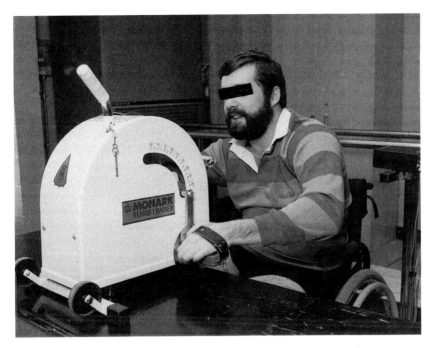

Fig. 2 *Arm crank ergometer exercise being performed by an individual with quadriplegia.*

Arm Exercise Modes

Clinical exercise stress testing, as well as the training of wheelchair users, has typically involved arm-crank ergometers, because they are commercially available and the exercise intensity can be accurately set to desired levels. Figure 2 illustrates an individual with SCI operating a Monark Rehab Trainer ACE. Wheelchair ergometers, which are stationary devices that closely simulate wheelchair locomotion, have also served these purposes.[45,52,54-57] However, most wheelchair ergometers are custom designed and constructed, and they are typically located in research laboratories. Figure 3 illustrates an exercise stress test being performed on a wheelchair ergometer.[58] Such testing enables exercise capacity and metabolic and cardiopulmonary responses to be evaluated. Repeating this test periodically can permit fitness changes to be tracked objectively. A combination wheelchair-arm-crank ergometer has been designed and constructed by Glaser and associates.[58] A conventional Monark leg cycle ergometer serves as the basis of this device, making it relatively easy to construct and calibrate.

Other wheelchair exercise modes that can be useful for stress testing and training include operating a wheelchair on a motor-driven treadmill,[59-62] and actual wheelchair locomotion over a prede-

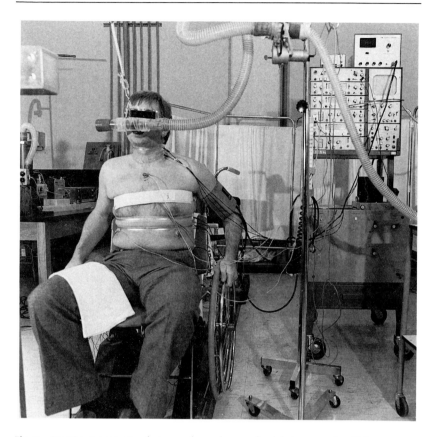

Fig. 3 *Exercise stress testing being performed on a wheelchair ergometer. Data pertaining to exercise capacity and metabolic and cardiopulmonary responses are being collected.*

termined course at specific velocities.[40,41,63,64] To establish verifiable testing and training protocols, it is important to quantify the exercise power output. To estimate power output requirements for actual wheelchair locomotion, Glaser and associates[64] used a strain-gauge transducer, which fed into a Wheatstone bridge and an electronic integrator, to measure the average applied force needed to push a standard medical wheelchair and its occupant over various terrains at a constant velocity. Figure 4 provides the linear regression equations that they derived to permit calculation of the estimated power output required for wheelchair propulsion by entering data concerning body weight, floor surface and grade, and velocity.[64] For example, a 70-kg person operating a wheelchair on a level tile surface at 3 km/h would require a power output of approximately 7 W. The validity of this technique was established by the similar magnitudes of metabolic and cardiopulmonary responses obtained during actual

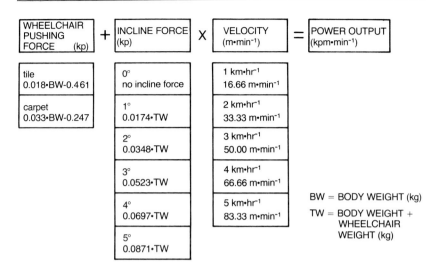

Fig. 4 *Composite summary of linear regression equations used for the prediction of power output requirements (kpm/min) for wheelchair locomotion over given terrains (floor surface and incline) at various velocities. (Reproduced with permission from Glaser RM, Collins SR, Wilde SW: Power output requirements for manual wheelchair locomotion.* Proc IEEE Nat Aerospace Elect Conf *1980;2:502-509.)*

wheelchair locomotion at given power output levels and exercise on a wheelchair ergometer that was set to the same power output levels.[65]

Sawka and associates[66] compared wheelchair ergometer to arm-crank ergometer exercise at the same submaximal power output levels of 30, 90, 150, and 210 kpm/min (5, 15, 25 and 35 W; power output in units of kilopond-meters per minute may be converted to units of watts by dividing by a factor of 6.12; 1 kp = 1 kg·g), and found that wheelchair ergometer exercise generally elicited significantly higher $\dot{V}O_2$, pulmonary ventilation, cardiac output, stroke volume, systolic blood pressure, and heart rate. Figure 5 graphically illustrates these data. In another study, Glaser and associates[58] found that maximal effort wheelchair and arm-crank ergometer exercise elicited similar peak $\dot{V}O_2$ and pulmonary ventilation. However, significantly lower maximal power output, peak heart rate, and blood lactate concentration were elicited for wheelchair ergometer exercise. Table 1 presents these maximal effort wheelchair and arm-crank ergometer data, along with the correlation coefficients between the modes of exercise. Due to similar maximal aerobic metabolic rates, it appears that wheelchair and arm-crank ergometers can be used with similar results for exercise testing and training of wheelchair users, but lower submaximal and maximal power output levels are employed for wheelchair ergometer exercise. Furthermore, the concept of exercise specificity suggests that wheelchair ergometer exercise

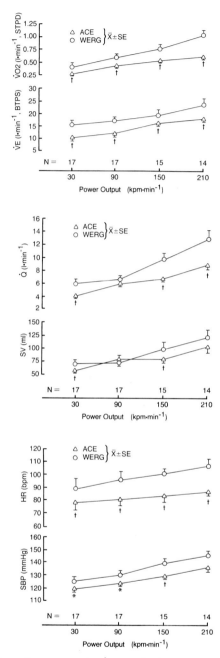

Fig. 5 *Top*, *Comparison of oxygen uptake ($\dot{V}O_2$) and pulmonary ventilation ($\dot{V}E$);* **Center**, *Comparison of cardiac output ($\dot{Q}$) and stroke volume (SV); and,* **Bottom**, *Comparison of heart rate (HR) and systolic blood pressure (SBP) data between wheelchair (WERG) and arm crank (ACE) ergometer exercise at equal power output levels. *P <0.05, +P <0.01. (Reproduced with permission from Sawka MN, Glaser RM, Wilde SW, et al: Metabolic and circulatory responses to wheelchair and arm crank exercise. J Appl Physiol 1980;49:784-788.)*

Table 1 Maximal Effort Wheelchair (WERG) and Arm-Crank (ACE) Ergometer Exercise

	$PO_{max}(W)$		Peak $\dot{V}O_2$(l/min)		VE_{max}(l/min)		HR_{max}(beats/min)		LA_{max}(mmol/l)	
	ACE	WERG	ACE	WERG	ACE	WERG	ACE	WERG	ACE	WERG
X	93	59	1.77	1.73	71.8	71.5	169	158	8.4	6.2
± SE	7	5	0.14	0.14	5.7	6.5	4	4	0.6	0.5
p<		0.01		NS		NS		0.01		0.01
%δ		−36		−2		0		−7		−26
r		0.86		0.92		0.78		0.72		0.52

n = 16; p, probability level; NS, not significantly different; % δ, percent by which WERG exercise values differed from ACE exercise values; r, correlation coefficient between values for WERG and ACE exercise. PO_{max}, maximal power output; Peak $\dot{V}O_2$, peak oxygen uptake; VE_{max}, maximal pulmonary ventilation; HR_{max}, maximal heart rate; LA_{max}, maximal blood lactate concentrations. (Reproduced with permission from Glaser RM, Sawka MN, Brune MF, et al: Physiological responses to maximal effort wheelchair and arm crank ergometry. *J Appl Physiol* 1980;48:1060-1064.)

may be more appropriate than arm-crank ergometer exercise in wheelchair-dependent populations because it more closely resembles actual wheelchair locomotion.[58,67] The lower metabolic rate (greater efficiency) and cardiopulmonary responses found for submaximal arm-crank ergometer exercise, as well as the greater maximal power output achieved, suggest that arm cranking may be superior to handrim stroking for actual wheelchair locomotion. Indeed, Smith and associates[68] found significant reductions in $\dot{V}O_2$ (−32%), pulmonary ventilation (−30%), and heart rate (-19%) for operating an arm crank-propelled wheelchair in comparison to operating a conventional handrim propelled wheelchair under the same locomotive conditions.

Stress Testing Protocols

The fundamental principles followed for lower-limb stress testing of nondisabled individuals may be used for upper-limb stress testing of wheelchair-dependent individuals. These tests are usually progressive with respect to exercise intensity, and have well-defined submaximal or maximal effort end-point criteria. Protocol design may utilize either continuous or discontinuous (alternating exercise and recovery periods) exercise. Discontinuous, submaximal protocols on a wheelchair ergometer may be preferable for stress testing of wheelchair populations because they are relatively safe, and task specific in relation to stresses encountered during daily locomotive activity. Criteria for exercise stress test termination include the following: (1) voluntary cessation, (2) symptoms of cardiovascular or pulmonary abnormalities (eg, chest discomfort, electrocardiogram changes, marked hypertension or hypotension, dyspnea), (3) achievement of the maximal power output level required for the test, and (4) attainment of a predetermined heart rate (eg, 75% of age-adjusted heart rate reserve).[2,52] However, for patients with high-level SCI, use of the heart rate criterion may not be feasible because of the interruption of sympathetic pathways to the heart and limited cardioacceleration.

Basic exercise testing may be achieved by having the patient propel his or her own wheelchair over an established test course at paced or self-selected velocities.[40,41,64] A suitable submaximal protocol consists of locomotive tasks that are 4 to 6 minutes in duration, separated by 5 to 10 minutes of rest. Steady rate physiologic responses can be determined during the last minute of each exercise set by using portable or radiotelemetry monitoring instrumentation. Wheelchair velocity progression increments of 0.5 to 1.0 km/h may be appropriate.

For wheelchair and arm-crank ergometer exercise stress tests, the propulsion velocity is typically held constant (eg, wheel velocity of 3 km/h and crank rate of 50 RPM, respectively) while the braking force (resistance) is incrementally increased to elevate the power output level. The discontinuous, submaximal protocol described in the preceding paragraph can most likely be used for these stress tests. With wheelchair ergometry, 5 W (30 kpm/min) appears to be an appropriate initial power output, because this level is frequently encountered during daily wheelchair locomotion.[64] Power output progression increments of 5 to 10 W may be suitable for many patients, and power output can be limited to 25 to 35 W for submaximal tests.[39,52,66,69] For athletes in better condition, the power output increment and maximal power output permitted can be greater. With arm-crank ergometry, the protocol can be the same, but the power output levels used should be about two times those for wheelchair ergometry. Figure 6 illustrates the $\dot{V}O_2$, pulmonary ventilation, and heart rate data of Glaser and associates[52] for a graded wheelchair ergometer test employing up to five 4-minute exercise sets, each followed by 5 minutes of rest. Because the subjects used for the development of this test protocol were not disabled, heart rate response was linear with respect to power output and $\dot{V}O_2$. To predict maximal power output capability and peak $\dot{V}O_2$ by extrapolating the submaximal data to the predicted maximal heart rate level would only be appropriate with patients who have lower-level SCI and whose cardioacceleration is not impaired. It should be noted that the maximal heart rate for arm exercise may be 10 to 20 beats per minute (bpm) lower than for leg exercise by nondisabled individuals. Thus, values obtained by using the formula 220 bpm minus age should be reduced by 10 to 20 bpm to predict maximal heart rate for wheelchair and arm-crank ergometer exercise.[31,70,71]

To determine actual maximal power output and peak $\dot{V}O_2$, the discontinuous, submaximal test can be extended to a maximal effort test by increasing the number of exercise sets. However, drawbacks to this protocol are the significant amount of time required to complete the test, and the fatiguing effects of multiple exercise sets, which may result in reduced maximal power output and peak $\dot{V}O_2$ values being obtained. Therefore, if maximal effort physiologic responses are desired, and data at several submaximal power output levels are not needed, a continuous, maximal exercise protocol can

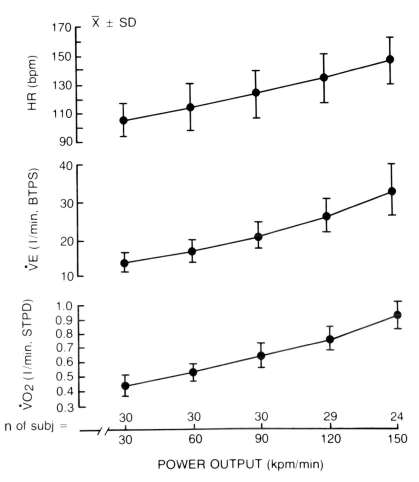

Fig. 6 *Steady-state relationships between wheelchair ergometer power output and oxygen uptake (V̇O₂), pulmonary ventilation (V̇E), and heart rate (HR) for 30 nondisabled female subjects. (Reproduced with permission from Glaser RM, Foley DM, Laubach LL, et al: An exercise test to evaluate fitness for wheelchair activity. Paraplegia 1979;16:341-349.)*

be used. This shorter protocol would usually begin at a low to moderate power output to serve as a warm-up. Power output is then increased by a certain increment every 1 to 2 minutes until maximal effort is reached. By estimating fitness with previous submaximal testing, the initial power output level and the magnitude of the power output increments can be set so that the individual will complete the test in several minutes.[50,72-78]

Stress testing fitness criteria are usually based on the magnitudes of metabolic and cardiopulmonary responses elicited at given power output levels, as well as the maximal power output level achieved.[52.] At submaximal power output levels, better-conditioned individuals may exhibit lower $\dot{V}O_2$, pulmonary ventilation, and heart rate responses. The lower $\dot{V}O_2$ usually indicates lower aerobic energy expenditure and higher efficiency, whereas lower pulmonary ventilation and heart rate usually indicate higher cardiopulmonary fitness and lower relative stress. However, care must be taken not to interpret low exercise heart rate responses of patients with high-level SCI as superior cardiovascular fitness. As previously indicated, cardioacceleration in these individuals is limited by insufficient sympathetic stimulation, and most observed increases in heart rate are probably due to vagal (parasympathetic) withdrawal. Maximal power output, $\dot{V}O_2$, pulmonary ventilation, as well as cardiac output and stroke volume would be expected to be higher for conditioned individuals. However, maximal heart rate may not be markedly different between more and less conditioned individuals. Therefore, better-conditioned individuals would possess greater metabolic and cardiopulmonary reserve, and given submaximal tasks would be less stressful because they would be performed at a lower percentage of maximal power output and peak $\dot{V}O_2$.

Maximal Performance for Wheelchair Users of Different Age Groups

Sawka and associates[69] used maximal effort wheelchair ergometer testing to determine maximal power output, maximal heart rate, and peak $\dot{V}O_2$ of young (20 to 30 years old), midlife (50 to 60 years old), and elderly (80 to 90 years old) wheelchair users. Figure 7 illustrates the data obtained and the decrements with the older age groups. These decrements were best described by parabolic models for maximal power output and maximal heart rate, and a linear model for peak $\dot{V}O_2$. It is interesting to note that maximal power output for the young adults was 83 W, while it was only 16 W for the midlife group and 7 W for the elderly adults.

Figure 8 illustrates data from Sawka and associates[69] and data from other investigators[32,51,72,74,79-82] concerning peak $\dot{V}O_2$ of wheelchair users plotted with respect to age. Using the linear regression equation, it was found that peak $\dot{V}O_2$ tended to decrease by 0.19 l/min for each decade of life. Thus, in comparison to the 20- to 30-year-old subjects, lower peak $\dot{V}O_2$ values of 34% and 68% were found for 50- to 60-year-old subjects and 80- to 90-year-old subjects, respectively.

Exercise Training Techniques for Improving Physical Fitness

It has been stated that normal daily wheelchair activity may not provide sufficient exercise to train the cardiopulmonary system, and that supplemental arm exercise training is necessary to stimulate fitness improvement.[28,60] Enhancing exercise capability and cardiopul-

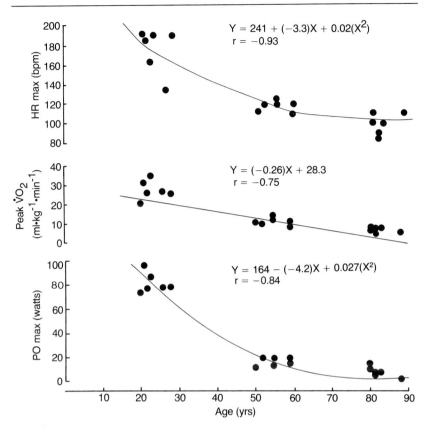

Fig. 7 *Individual subject maximal power output (PO$_{max}$), peak oxygen uptake (peak V̇O$_2$), and maximal heart rate (HR$_{max}$) values for maximal effort wheelchair ergometer exercise plotted with respect to age. (Reproduced with permission from Sawka MN, Glaser RM, Lambach LL, et al: Wheelchair exercise performance of the young, middle-aged, and elderly. J Appl Physiol 1981;50:824-828.)*

monary fitness with specific arm exercise training programs could increase organ system reserve and make ADL (eg, wheelchair locomotion) less stressful, because they would be performed at lower percentages of maximal power output and peak V̇O$_2$. Facilitated performance of ADL may contribute to improved functional independence and rehabilitation outcome.[83] Indeed, with wheelchair locomotion at 7 W, well-trained wheelchair athletes (mean age = 25 years) are estimated to use less than 7% of their maximal power output and 18% of peak V̇O$_2$. These numbers are in contrast to 9% of maximal power output and 29% of peak V̇O$_2$ for their sedentary cohorts. Older, sedentary wheelchair users have a more difficult plight in that 50- to 60-year-olds use 44% of maximal power output and 51% of peak V̇O$_2$, whereas 80- to 90-year-olds may be required to use 100% of their maximal power output and peak V̇O$_2$ for this routine loco-

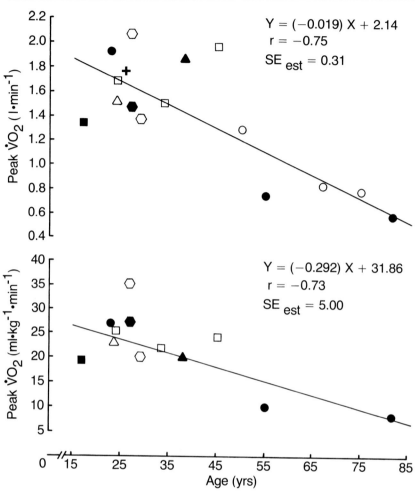

Fig. 8 *Peak oxygen uptake (peak $\dot{V}O_2$) values plotted with respect to age for the wheelchair ergometer study of Sawka and associates[69] and studies previously reported in the literature for males with disabilities during arm-crank ergometer exercise. Previous studies are those of Ekblom and Lundberg (■),[79] Hjeltnes (●),[51] Kavanaugh and Shephard (○),[80] Marincek and Valencic (△),[81] Nilsson and associates (□),[72] Pollock and associates (▲),[82] Wicks and associates (+),[74] and Zwiren and Bar-Or (○).[32] (Reproduced with permission from Sawka MN, Glaser RM, Lambach LL, et al: Wheelchair exercise performance of the young, middle-aged, and elderly. J Appl Physiol 1981;50:824-828.)*

motive task.[41,69] Regular exercise training may reduce the stresses of wheelchair locomotion and lower some of the risks associated with secondary cardiovascular disabilities.

Arm Exercise Protocols

To promote improved muscular and cardiopulmonary fitness, as well as enhanced performance, arm exercise training protocols for wheelchair users should, like leg exercise training protocols, follow the fundamental principle of overload.[2,3,84] To achieve overload, exercise should be performed at intensities (and/or durations) that are beyond those normally encountered during ADL. In addition, exercise intensity and/or duration should be progressively increased as performance improves until fitness goals are reached. Maintenance of this fitness status involves periodic exercise at the final intensity and duration levels achieved. If exercise is discontinued, detraining will occur, and fitness level will diminish in a matter of several weeks.[85,86]

Traditionally, arm-crank ergometer exercise has been used for endurance training of wheelchair users. However, wheelchair ergometer exercise may be advantageous because of the similar peak $\dot{V}O_2$ that can be elicited, and because it more closely resembles actual wheelchair activity, it may enhance locomotive performance.[58,83] Arm exercise training protocols may be either continuous or discontinuous in design. If enhancing cardiopulmonary fitness is the primary goal, power output should be adjusted to moderate levels that enable exercise sessions of relatively long durations (eg, 15 to 60 min for continuous protocols and 3 to 5 min for each of the discontinuous protocols) without excessive fatigue or respiratory distress (ie, marked accumulation of lactate in the blood). Exercise sessions should take place two to five times per week.[87,84]

When prescribing aerobic leg exercise for nondisabled individuals, the appropriate training intensity is typically established by having them exercise at 60% to 90% of their maximal heart rate reserve, which usually corresponds to 50% to 85% of peak $\dot{V}O_2$. The critical factor is that marked anaerobiosis and metabolic acidosis are avoided; both of these can severely limit exercise duration. However, as stated previously, heart rate may not be an adequate indicator of exercise stress in individuals with SCI because cardioacceleration may be insufficient for the increases in metabolic rate. Therefore, to set exercise intensity with this population, direct determination of $\dot{V}O_2$, pulmonary ventilation, and blood lactate concentration during stress testing would be desirable if the instrumentation is available. Otherwise, the subjective feeling of stress and the actual exercise duration capability may be used. It is likely that several trials will be needed for each athlete to effectively set training power output.

Physiologic Adaptations to Arm Exercise Training

Studies on individuals with disabled lower limbs indicated that endurance-type arm exercise training for several weeks can significantly increase power output capability, peak $\dot{V}O_2$, and cardiopulmonary performance.[28,72,82,88,89] Arm-crank ergometer training of active wheelchair users increased their peak $\dot{V}O_2$ by 12% to 19% in 7 to 20 weeks.[72,82] Individuals with quadriplegia who had relatively low initial fitness levels obtained even greater gains in cardiopulmonary fitness in only 5 weeks of training.[89] Miles and associates[88] re-

Table 2 Individual and mean ($\pm$ SD) values attained during maximal wheelchair ergometer exercise before (B) and after (A) 6 weeks of interval training by eight wheelchair athletes with SCI

Subject	$\dot{V}_E$ B	$\dot{V}_E$ A	V_T B	V_T A	R_f B	R_f A	Power output B	Power output A	Peak $\dot{V}O_2$ B	Peak $\dot{V}O_2$ A
1	74.7	111.2	2.49	3.09	30	36	70	96	2.05	2.41
2	136.9	180.8	4.56	3.12	30	58	100	140	3.34	3.73
3	115.2	145.1	1.92	2.20	60	66	72	100	2.41	2.98
4	99.2	116.3	2.20	1.87	45	62	80	90	1.89	2.18
5	103.3	143.7	1.72	2.40	60	60	90	105	2.00	2.65
6	68.2	109.2	1.71	1.82	40	60	52	83	1.57	2.31
7	80.4	106.7	1.61	2.05	50	52	83	95	2.04	2.60
8	119.0	137.3	2.77	2.54	43	54	81	110	219	326
Mean	99.6	131.3	2.37	2.38	44.8	56.0	78.3	102.3	2.19	2.76
SD	22.4	23.8	0.91	0.47	10.9	8.6	14	16	0.49	
	$P<0.05$		NS		$P<0.05$		$P<0.05$		$P<0.05$	

(Reproduced with permission from Miles DS, Sawka MN, Wilde SW, et al; Pulmonary function changes in wheelchair athletes subsequent to exercise training. *Ergonomics* 1982;25:239-246.)

ported a study in which eight wheelchair athletes used wheelchair ergometer exercise during 6 weeks (three times per week) of interval training. This training resulted in increases of 31% for maximal power output capability, 26% for peak $\dot{V}O_2$, and 32% for peak pulmonary ventilation (Table 2). These gains were sizable considering that the subjects had relatively high levels of fitness prior to participating in the training program.

Although arm exercise training imposes a lower limit to the aerobic fitness that can be achieved (as indicated above), some cardiopulmonary benefits can be expected for most participants. However, the magnitudes by which aerobic fitness and exercise performance can be increased with training appear to depend on the initial fitness level and the size of the muscle mass available for exercise. For instance, several studies on wheelchair athletes performing maximal effort arm-crank and wheelchair ergometer exercise indicated that their peak $\dot{V}O_2$ is in the 2 to 3 l/min range.[2] This is approximately half of the maximal $\dot{V}O_2$ that would be expected for healthy nondisabled athletes performing maximal effort leg exercise (eg, cycling, running). Generally, greater gains in fitness may be expected from individuals who initiate training programs at relatively low fitness levels (depending on pathologic limitations).[2,3] Many of the observed gains in arm exercise performance may be due to peripheral adaptations, such as improved capillary density and metabolic capability within muscles (which would increase arteriovenous oxygen difference) rather than central circulatory adaptations.[24,83,90,91] Nevertheless, regular arm exercise training appears to increase maximal power output capability and peak $\dot{V}O_2$, and it may also decrease levels of physiologic responses for given submaximal exercise tasks such as wheelchair locomotion.[83]

In a recent study, Hooker and Wells[92] reported a significant increase in the high-density lipoprotein-cholesterol (HDL-C) level (+20%) and decreases in total cholesterol (−8%) and low-density lipoprotein-cholesterol (LDL-C) levels (−15%) in subjects with SCI following 8 weeks of moderate intensity wheelchair ergometry training (60% to 70% peak $\dot{V}O_2$; 20 minutes per day, three times per week). These beneficial alterations in the blood lipid profile extrapolated to a mean decrease of 20% in the group's future risk for coronary artery disease. Thus, if HDL-C has a protective effect against coronary heart disease, and if LDL-C increases the risk thereof, the risk of coronary heart disease in the wheelchair user population may be decreased with arm exercise intervention in a fashion similar to the way leg exercise training benefits nondisabled individuals. More research is necessary to develop appropriate exercise modes and protocols and to document their efficacy for reducing the risk of cardiovascular disease in this population.

Body Position and Arm Exercise Capability

In some individuals with lower-limb paralysis, the etiology of upper body muscle fatigue may be due to a central factor that is secondary to a peripheral factor. Inactivity of the venous muscle pump caused by paralysis may restrict venous return of blood from the legs to the heart (peripheral factor), and thereby restrict cardiac output capability during arm exercise (central factor). Thus, pooling of blood in the leg veins can lead to a hypokinetic circulation that reduces the availability of blood to the active upper-body musculature and consequently decreases its exercise capability.[2,3,24] The upright, sitting position in which individuals with SCI typically perform arm exercise can elevate hydrostatic pressure and accentuate blood pooling in the leg veins. Arm exercise capability may be enhanced by placing the individual in a supine position, which may minimize the gravitational effects on blood, facilitate venous return, elevate cardiac output, and increase arm muscle blood flow to boost fatigue resistance.

In a preliminary study by Figoni and associates,[93] subjects with quadriplegia performed maximal effort arm-crank ergometry in sitting and supine positions on separate occasions. Maximal effort exercise in the supine position elicited significantly higher maximal power output, peak $\dot{V}O_2$, pulmonary ventilation, heart rate, stroke volume, and cardiac output. The greater magnitudes of these responses suggest that cardiopulmonary training capability in this population may be enhanced by using the supine position. Although these preliminary data appear to be encouraging, there are no data available to determine if prolonged exercise training programs that use this supine body position technique are superior for improving the aerobic fitness of individuals with paralyzed lower limbs.

Use of Functional Electrical Stimulation (FES)-Induced Exercise of the Paralyzed Lower-Limb Musculature

During the past 12 years, functional electrical stimulation (FES; sometimes referred to as functional neuromuscular stimulation, FNS) research has been conducted with the goal of inducing exercise in paralyzed lower-limb muscles.[94-97] This technique typically uses electrical impulses from a stimulator, in conjunction with skin surface electrodes placed over motor points, to directly induce tetanic contractions of controlled intensity. Thus, FES-induced exercise of the paralyzed legs has the potential of using a large muscle mass that otherwise would be dormant. In addition, FES-induced exercise appears to augment the circulation of blood by activating the venous muscle pump. Ultimately, FES may lead to exercise modes that can improve the health, cardiopulmonary fitness, and rehabilitation potential of patients with SCI to levels higher than can be attained with arm exercise alone. Individuals with quadriplegia will probably find this involuntary exercise mode to be particularly advantageous due to the small amount of muscle mass that is under their voluntary control.

Special Considerations and Precautions

The foremost requirement for FES use is that the muscles to be exercised are paralyzed due to upper motor neuron damage, and that the motor units (the lower motor neurons and the skeletal muscle fibers they innervate) are intact and functional. The existence of stretch reflex activity and spasticity indicate that the individual is a potential candidate for FES-induced exercise. However, if the patient retains some degree of sensate skin (which is common with incomplete SCI), FES may cause discomfort or pain and the high stimulation current that is required to induce forceful contractions may not be tolerated. Although much of the instrumentation for FES-induced exercise described in the research literature was specially designed and constructed, the availability of commercial stimulators and exercise devices for clinical and home use is increasing.

Prior to initiating an FES-induced exercise program, a thorough medical examination is essential. This examination should include radiographs of the paralyzed limbs, range of motion testing, neurological examination, an electrocardiogram, and preferably, evaluation of psychological status. The patient should be informed of the potential benefits and risks of FES-induced exercise, and clearly understand that FES will not regenerate damaged neurons and cure paralysis. The athlete should also understand that, as with voluntary exercise training, any health and fitness benefits derived from FES-induced exercise training will be lost several weeks after this activity is discontinued.

Because the muscles, bones, and joints of paralyzed lower limbs tend to be deteriorated, FES-induced contractions should be kept as smooth as possible, and the contraction force generated should be limited to a safe level to prevent injury. Although FES-induced exercise training can improve the strength and endurance of the paralyzed muscles, there is currently no evidence that osteoporosis can be reversed with this activity.[97] Therefore, it is conceivable that the muscles can ultimately generate more force than the bones can withstand. In addition, FES may trigger severe spasms in some muscles, so it is important to observe the quality of the contractions to be certain that they are not harmful.[97,87] In some patients (especially those with quadriplegia), FES-induced exercise may provoke autonomic dysreflexia, which can result in dangerously high blood pressure.[97,98] Therefore, it is essential that blood pressure be monitored periodically, especially during initial FES-induced exercise sessions. Of course, exercise should be discontinued immediately if any response is observed that places the patient at risk.

Promoting Venous Return with FES During Voluntary Arm Exercise

As previously indicated, arm exercise performance and the capability of developing high levels of cardiopulmonary fitness may be limited by hypokinetic circulation caused by inadequate venous muscle pump activity. Although arm exercise in a supine position may help to alleviate this situation, FES-induced contractions of the paralyzed leg muscles may be another viable approach. Here, rhythmic contractions may promote the venous return of blood and enhance cardiac output and blood flow to the upper-body musculature.

It was demonstrated by Glaser and associates[99] that rhythmic patterns of FES-induced isometric contractions (1.5 to 2.5 seconds on-off duty cycle) of calf and thigh muscles can significantly increase the stroke volume (12% to 20%) and cardiac output (12% to 30%) of nondisabled persons and those with SCI at rest in a sitting position. Subsequently, Davis and associates[100,101] and Figoni and associates[102] showed that this FES technique can significantly augment stroke volume and cardiac output during rest and arm-crank ergometer exercise at various gravitational loads (sitting, supine, and head-up tilt body positions). Thus, it appears that this technique can diminish venous stasis and pooling in the legs by activating the venous muscle pump, which may alleviate hypokinetic circulation in patients with SCI and enhance arm exercise capability by increasing blood availability. Indeed, data (unpublished) from our Institute for Rehabilitation Research and Medicine demonstrated an approximate 15% increase in maximal power output by subjects with SCI when using this FES technique during arm-crank ergometer exercise. Thus far, however, long-term exercise training adaptations have not been determined. It is feasible that this FES technique may also have several other clinical applications, including prophylaxis of deep venous thrombus, reduction of excessive edema, and alleviation of orthostatic hypotension.[99] Again, research is needed to document the efficacy of FES for these applications.

FES-Induced Weight Training Exercise

Several studies demonstrated that the same principles known to be effective for voluntary weight (ie, high resistance) training can be adapted for FES-induced weight training. These include dynamic contractions through a specific range of motion, progressive overload, and multiple sets of relatively low numbers of repetitions at relatively high load resistance.[98,103-106] Stimulator designs that enable the setting of the contraction threshold current, initiating stimulation at this level, and providing a gradual ramped output current to a maximum of at least 150 milliamperes (mA) would be most effective for this mode of exercise. Ideally, the stimulator would use limb position feedback (from sensors) to maintain the desired range of motion, and adapt FES current parameters (ie, increasing threshold level and output ramp) as the muscles fatigue in order to retain performance through the recruitment of additional muscle fibers.[107]

Several research studies clearly indicate that FES-induced weight training exercise can markedly increase muscle strength and endurance for this involuntary activity.[98,103-106] Physiologic mechanisms that may account for this enhanced performance are apparently localized within the muscles, and therefore are peripheral, rather than central circulatory in nature.[97,105] Possible adaptations include muscle hypertrophy, conversion of fast- to slow-twitch fiber characteristics, increased concentration of metabolic enzymes, and enhanced capillary density. The relatively low magnitudes of metabolic and cardiopulmonary responses elicited for this mode of FES-induced exercise appear insufficient to stimulate marked central circulatory fitness development.[108,109]

Figure 9 illustrates operation of a knee extension FES-induced weight training device that was laboratory constructed.[107,109] It consists of an exercise chair with laterally mounted hinged levers to support the load weights (at ankle level), and a two-channel, battery-powered stimulator using skin surface electrodes that are placed over motor points of the quadriceps muscles. This configuration permits alternating (asynchronous) right-left FES-induced knee extension exercise. As an alternative, commercially available stimulators that are battery-powered and provide ramped output current may be used in conjunction with ankle weights.

Protocols designed for FES-induced weight training exercise typically incorporate 10 to 30 repetitions per set at a rate of three to five lifts per minute, two to three sets per session, and two to four sessions per week.[98,103,104,106,110] Initial load resistance should be relatively low (eg, 0 to 2 kg) to assure safety and permit adequate habituation to FES. With improved muscle performance, a load resistance progression of 0.5 kg appears to be suitable for most individuals. A

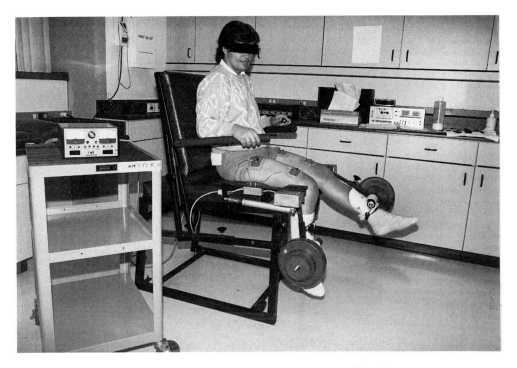

Fig. 9 *Functional electrical stimulation (FES)-induced knee extension weight training exercise being performed by an individual with spinal cord injury. The instrumentation illustrated was especially designed and constructed for this purpose.*

load limit of 15 kg has been used successfully with no adverse effects.[110] When this performance goal is achieved, the number of repetitions may be increased to further enhance endurance.

Training with FES-induced exercise for several weeks has resulted in significant increases in quadriceps muscle strength, endurance, and mass.[98,103,104,106,110] For instance, Rodgers and associates[110] found quadriceps muscle performance (ie, kg x repetitions) of 12 subjects with SCI to increase 47% after 36 sessions (12 to 18 weeks) of training. Faghri and associates[103] reported resistance load increased from 1.5 to 6.0 kg during 7 weeks of training by seven SCI subjects. Figure 10 shows their mean load weight progression and muscle performance. Similar FES techniques and protocols can most likely be used to train other paralyzed and weakened muscles.

FES-Induced Leg Cycle Ergometry

In an effort to develop higher levels of cardiopulmonary fitness in patients in SCI, a leg cycle ergometer that is propelled by the paralyzed lower-limb muscles was designed and constructed by Petrof-

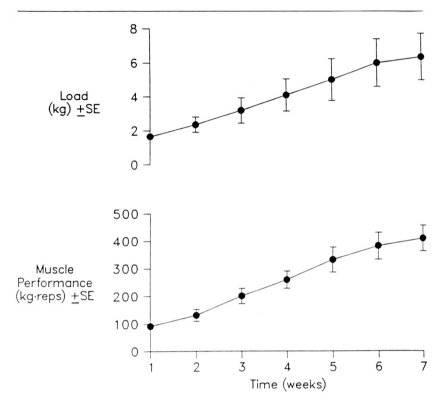

Fig. 10 *Mean resistive load and muscle performance during 7 weeks of FNS-induced knee extension exercise training. (Reproduced with permission from Faghri PD, Glaser RM, Figoni SF, et al: Feasibility of using two FNS exercise modes for spinal cord injured patients.* Clin Kinesiol *1989;43:62-68.)*

sky and associates.[111] In 1984, Therapeutic Technologies Inc. (Tampa, FL) began manufacturing sophisticated versions of this FES-induced leg cycle ergometer for clinical and home use. (The home model is currently available from Therapeutic Alliances, Inc., Fairborn, OH.) Computer-controlled FES of the quadriceps, hamstrings, and gluteus maximus muscle groups is used to induce contractions during appropriate angle ranges of the pedals. Figure 11 illustrates operation of the ERGYS I, which was designed for home use. When pedaling at the 50 RPM target rate, these leg cycle ergometers induce 50 contractions per minute of each contralateral muscle group (a total of 300 muscle contractions per minute), with the cyclic stimulation pattern and current intensity controlled by a microprocessor that receives appropriate feedback information from sensors. As the muscles fatigue, FES current increases automatically to a maximum of about 140 mA in an attempt to maintain RPM by recruitment of additional muscle fibers. Exercise is automatically terminated when the pedal rate falls below 35 RPM. FES leg cycle ergometry appears to be well suited for

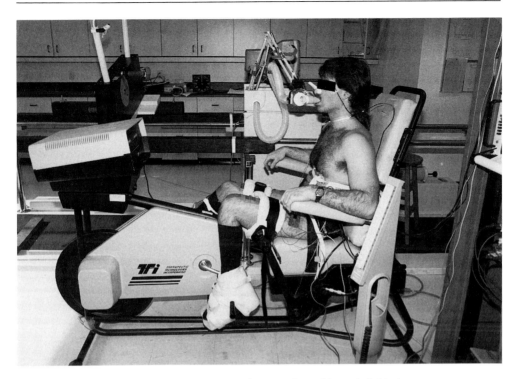

Fig. 11 *FES-induced leg cycle ergometer exercise being performed by an individual with spinal cord injury on an ERGYS I. Aerobic metabolic and cardiopulmonary responses are being monitored.*

endurance training, as many SCI patients can pedal continuously for 30 minutes.

The typical training protocol consists of exercise that is scheduled three times per week. Initially, the patient pedals the FES-induced leg cycle ergometer at a power output of 0 watts (0 kiloponds load resistance; 1 kp = 1 kg·g) for up to 30 minutes. If fatigue occurs, three trials are permitted in an attempt to achieve a total of 30 minutes of exercise. Each exercise set is followed by 10 minutes of rest. When 30 minutes of continuous exercise can be achieved at 0 W, subsequent sessions are conducted at a power output of 6.1 W (1/8 kp increase in load resistance). When 30 minutes of continuous pedaling at this higher power output can be achieved, the power output is further increased by 6.1 watts for subsequent sessions. As performance improves with training, this progressive intensity protocol is increased to a power output limit of 42.7 W.

Physiologic studies conducted on individuals with SCI indicate that this FES-induced exercise mode elicits relatively high magnitudes of aerobic and cardiopulmonary responses, as well as quite favorable central and peripheral hemodynamic responses.[106,112-115]

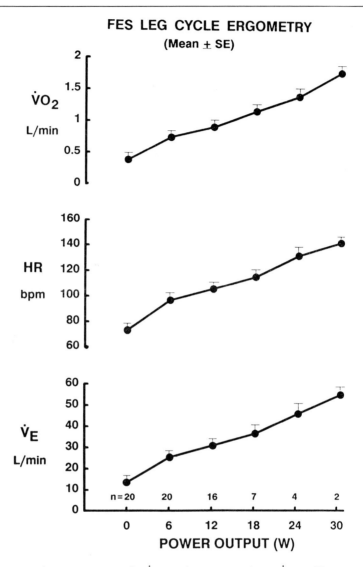

Fig. 12 *Steady-state oxygen uptake ($\dot{V}O_2$), pulmonary ventilation ($\dot{V}E$), and heart rate (HR) responses of individuals with spinal cord injury in relationship to power output for FES-induced leg cycle ergometry. (Modified with permission from Glaser RM, Figoni SF, Collins SR, et al: Physiologic responses of SCI subjects to electrically induced leg cycle ergometry. 1988 IEEE Engineering in Medicine and Biology Tenth Annual Conference. 1988, vol 4, pp 1638-1640.)*

These findings suggest that FES may provide more effective cardio-pulmonary fitness training than arm exercise modes, especially for individuals with quadriplegia who have weakened arm musculature. Figure 12 provides modified data from Glaser and associates[112] depicting steady-rate $\dot{V}O_2$, pulmonary ventilation, and heart rate responses of 20 patients with SCI during progressive intensity FES-induced leg cycling. The relationships between power output and $\dot{V}O_2$, pulmonary ventilation and heart rate were quite linear. Power output for this relatively untrained group ranged from 0 to 30 W. Only two patients could pedal at 30 W, with average peak $\dot{V}O_2$ of 1.80 l/min, pulmonary ventilation of 55 l/min, and heart rate of 144 beats/min. It is predicted from these data that a well-trained individual who could pedal at the power output limit of 42.7 W would have a peak $\dot{V}O_2$ of about 2.0 l/min, with correspondingly high pulmonary ventilation and heart rate responses. For comparison purposes, many nondisabled individuals jog at $\dot{V}O_2$ levels of 1.5 to 2.0 l/min (ie, 50% to 60% of their maximal $\dot{V}O_2$). Therefore, FES-induced leg cycling offers patients with SCI a potential means for training at a similar aerobic metabolic rate. It is unlikely that arm exercise can elicit this magnitude of $\dot{V}O_2$ for a sufficient duration (eg, 30 minutes) to stimulate marked cardiopulmonary adaptations. However, patients would have to be highly trained to achieve such high power output and $\dot{V}O_2$ levels for long durations. Most individuals with SCI perform FES-induced leg cycle ergometry at power output levels that provide $\dot{V}O_2$ magnitudes that are equivalent to walking (eg, about 1.0 l/min; 4 met).

Those familiar with voluntary leg cycle ergometry by nondisabled individuals will note that the power output levels used by individuals with SCI to elicit the relatively high $\dot{V}O_2$ levels for FES-induced leg cycle ergometry are quite low. For example, if a patient with SCI can perform FES-induced leg cycling at 42.7 W, $\dot{V}O_2$ may be about 2.0 l/min. In contrast, a nondisabled individual pedaling voluntarily at this same power output would typically have a $\dot{V}O_2$ of less than 0.9 l/min. This indicates that FES-induced exercise is mechanically inefficient. Such inefficiency may be due to the nonphysiologic activation of the paralyzed muscles, histochemical changes in these muscles, and inappropriate joint biomechanics.[112,116] However, for exercise applications, this inefficiency appears to be desirable because higher magnitudes of metabolic and cardiopulmonary responses can be elicited from patients with SCI who have lower mechanical stress to their paralyzed muscles, bones, and joints.

It also appears that FES-induced leg cycle ergometry may offer superior central hemodynamic responses in patients with SCI compared to voluntary arm cranking. Figoni and associates[113] had six men with quadriplegia perform FES-induced leg cycle ergometer exercise, and on another occasion, arm cranking exercise at power outputs that elicited a $\dot{V}O_2$ level of approximately 1.0 l/min (11 and 38 W, respectively). At this same aerobic metabolic rate, the FES-induced cycling was found to elicit a 59% greater stroke volume (92 versus 58 ml/beat), and a 20% greater cardiac output (8.01 versus 6.66 l/min). Figure 13 illustrates individual data for cardiac output versus $\dot{V}O_2$ of 17 persons with quadriplegia during voluntary arm-

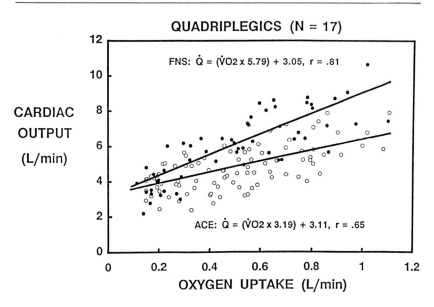

Fig. 13 *Individual data for cardiac output vs oxygen uptake of 17 individuals with quadriplegia during voluntary arm-crank ergometer (ACE) and FES-induced leg cycle ergometer exercise using progressive intensity power output levels. Linear regression equations and lines of best fit for ACE and FES-induced cycling are provided. (Reproduced with permission from Figoni SF, Hooker SP, Glaser RM, et al: Physiologic responses to arm cranking and electrical stimulation leg cycling, part II: quadriplegics (Abstract). Med Sci Sports Exerc 1990;22(suppl):S43.)*

crank ergometer and FES-induced leg cycling exercise using progressive intensity power output levels.[117] The lines of best fit demonstrated a higher cardiac output for FES-induced leg cycling at given levels of $\dot{V}O_2$. It is likely that the mechanism for these responses is that FES-induced contractions of the paralyzed leg muscles activated the venous muscle pump and promoted the return of venous blood to the heart to increase its preload (Frank-Starling mechanism). Figoni and associates,[113] found a 25% lower heart rate (87 versus 116 beats/min) and 19% lower rate-pressure product during FES-induced cycling, which suggested that the higher cardiac volume load was achieved with lower myocardial oxygen demands (ie, greater cardiac efficiency). Therefore, FES-induced leg cycling may potentially be more effective than arm cranking for cardiopulmonary training of individuals with paraplegia, and cause lower cardiovascular risk.

Training studies on FES-induced leg cycling revealed several physiologic adaptations that probably reflect both peripheral (muscle) and central circulatory benefits to individuals with SCI. Following 7 to 24 weeks of training, power output capability and endurance increased by 6 to 15 W.[103,106,115,118,119] At the higher power output levels achieved, peak $\dot{V}O_2$ for this activity increased 22% to

60%.[106,115,118,119] These aerobic metabolic data suggest that peripheral adaptations enabled better FES-induced muscle performance, which in turn may have been further augmented by improved cardiopulmonary fitness and the delivery of more oxygen and fuel substrates to the muscles. Furthermore, there were significant increases in post-training heart rate, pulmonary ventilation, stroke volume, and cardiac output, which should enhance capability for subsequent cardiopulmonary training.

Simultaneous FES-Induced Leg Cycling and Voluntary Arm Cranking Exercise

It appears likely that cardiopulmonary fitness training capability for patients with SCI can be further enhanced by using a hybrid form of exercise consisting of simultaneous FES-induced leg cycling and voluntary arm cranking. The design for this combination mode of exercise is illustrated in Figure 14. Recent studies on physiologic responses to this hybrid exercise (and other combination FES-voluntary exercise modes) suggest that they would provide cardiopulmonary training superior to either mode of exercise performed alone.[100,120,121] This superior cardiopulmonary training is anticipated because of the larger muscle mass used, the greater magnitudes of metabolic and cardiopulmonary responses elicited, and possibly better circulation of blood to both the upper- and lower-body muscles.

Glaser[122] reported additive effects on aerobic metabolism when combining the arm-crank ergometer and FES-induced leg cycling exercise modes. The $\dot{V}O_2$ of a T-8 male with paraplegia was 0.25 l/min at rest; 0.75 l/min during FES-induced leg cycling alone at 6.1 W; 0.75 l/min during voluntary arm cranking alone at 25 W; and 1.25 l/min during hybrid exercise at a total of 31.1 W. Thus, a 0.5 l/min higher $\dot{V}O_2$ was achieved with this combined exercise mode. Hooker and associates[123] studied eight individuals with quadriplegia while performing this hybrid exercise and found significantly higher peak $\dot{V}O_2$, pulmonary ventilation, heart rate, and cardiac output, and significantly lower total peripheral resistance than for performing either arm cranking or FES-induced leg cycling individually. The similar stroke volume values obtained for FES-induced leg cycling and hybrid exercise were significantly higher than for arm-crank ergometry. These data are illustrated graphically in Figure 15. Figoni and associates[124] combined unloaded (0 W) FES-induced leg cycling with maximal effort arm cranking for nine subjects with quadriplegia and found significant increases in peak levels of $\dot{V}O_2$ (by 0.3 l/min, + 35%), stroke volume (by 11 ml/beat, + 26%), cardiac output (by 2.7 l/min, + 46%) and heart rate (by 11 beats/min, + 18%). The higher magnitudes of responses during the hybrid exercise indicated that maximal effort arm cranking by itself was not a sufficient stimulus to drive the central circulation to full output. Full output can apparently be accomplished with the hybrid exercise because of the substan-

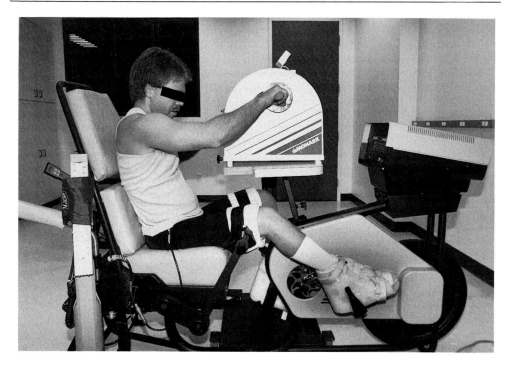

Fig. 14 *Hybrid (simultaneous FES-induced leg cycle ergometer and voluntary arm-crank ergometer) exercise being performed by an individual with spinal cord injury. The adjustable stand supporting the arm-crank ergometer was specially designed and constructed.*

tially larger muscle mass used and the enhanced venous return and cardiac output that occur with lower-limb FES.

Special attention needs to be given to the setting of arm and leg power output levels in order to attain the best compromise between obtaining the highest $\dot{V}O_2$ for the desired exercise duration (eg, 30 min). In administering this hybrid exercise to a number of individuals with paraplegia and quadriplegia, it is interesting to note that there tends to be an interaction between the arm and leg exercises. That is, if the arm exercise intensity is increased beyond a certain level, the exercise capacity of the legs is markedly decreased (ie, exercise time at a given leg power output is shortened), and vice versa. This interaction may be the result of competition between the arms and legs for the available blood. It is thus probable that central circulatory factors, rather than peripheral factors, limit the capacity for this hybrid exercise. Therefore, hybrid exercise appears to provide the optimal levels of metabolic and cardiopulmonary responses for aerobic conditioning of individuals with SCI, while providing training benefits to both the upper- and lower-body musculature.

We find that this hybrid exercise frequently results in peak $\dot{V}O_2$ levels of over 1.5 and 2.0 l/min in nonathletic individuals with quad-

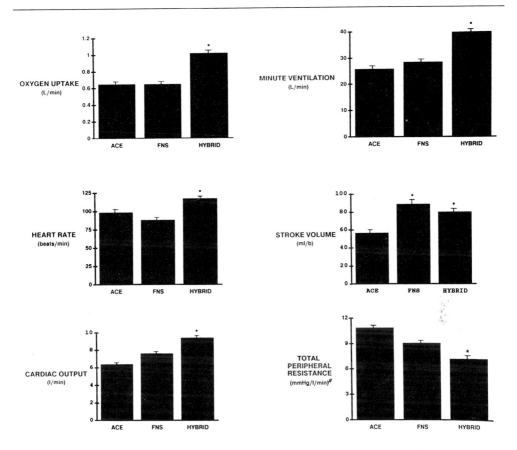

Fig. 15 *Oxgen uptake, minute ventilation, heart rate, stroke volume, cardiac output, and total peripheral resistance of 8 individuals with quadriplegia during voluntary arm cranking alone (ACE x̄ PO = 19.4 W), FES-induced cycling alone (x̄ PO = 3.0 W), and hybrid exercise (x̄ PO = 22.4 W). Values are x̄ + SE. *Denotes significant difference from arm-crank ergometer (p <0.05). (Reproduced with permission from Hooker SP, Figoni SF, Rodgers MM, et al: Metabolic and hemodynamic responses to concurrent voluntary arm crank and electrical stimulation leg cycle exercise in quadriplegics. J Rehabil Res Dev 1992;29:1-11.)*

quadriplegia and paraplegia, respectively. Considering that maximal effort arm exercise in aerobically trained wheelchair athletes had been reported to elicit peak $\dot{V}O_2$ values in the 2 to 3 l/min range,[2] this hybrid exercise mode appears to be superior, because similar peak $\dot{V}O_2$ values can be obtained from the general population of paraplegics with SCI. Additionally, it is unlikely that arm exercise training by itself provides any marked improvements with respect to lower-limb circulation or integrity of the musculature. More research is needed to establish optimal protocols for hybrid exercise training and to document the extent to which cardiopulmonary fitness can be improved with long-term training.

Conclusion

Following SCI, sedentary lifestyle and aging can result in the progressive loss of fitness, work capability, functional independence, and rehabilitation potential, as well as greater risks for secondary disabilities. It is apparent that individuals with SCI who participate in regular physical activity and wheelchair sports are more able to perform ADL, adjust more successfully to societal activities, and possess physical characteristics that may rival those of their counterparts who are 10 to 15 years younger. During the past 25 years, much research had been conducted on developing specialized exercise techniques that can be used to evaluate physical performance and cardiopulmonary function via stress testing and to improve fitness via training programs. Due to lower-limb paralysis, arm exercise modes (eg, arm-crank ergometry, wheelchair ergometry) have been traditionally used for these purposes. Yet, the relatively small muscle mass available and deficient cardiopulmonary responses limit the individual's fitness development capability. However, recent innovations in FES techniques appear to be opening new avenues for more effective training. By using FES to exercise paralyzed leg muscles, greater muscle mass can be utilized and peripheral and central hemodynamic responses may be improved. Recent studies demonstrate that FES-induced weight training can increase the performance characteristics of specific muscle groups, and that FES-induced leg cycle ergometer exercise can elicit aerobic metabolic and cardiopulmonary responses of sufficient magnitudes and durations to stimulate cardiopulmonary training effects. These cardiopulmonary responses may be superior to those elicited by voluntary arm-crank ergometer exercise, especially for those with quadriplegia. But, it is apparent that FES-induced leg exercise should be used in conjunction with arm exercise (separately and combined) to optimize upper-body, lower-body, and cardiovascular fitness. Thus, hybrid exercise (FES-induced leg cycling and voluntary arm cranking) may currently be the most effective and efficient exercise technique for enhancing physical performance and cardiopulmonary function in individuals with paraplegia and quadriplegia. Ultimately, individuals with SCI who incorporate these specialized exercise techniques into their lifestyles may experience improved quality of life and fewer medical problems, as well as enhanced sports performances. It is not yet known how the benefits of these new and highly promising exercise programs for individuals with SCI can be specifically applied to people in their midlife and beyond.

Acknowledgments

The author wishes to thank the Dayton Veterans Affairs Medical Center and the Rehabilitation Institute of Ohio at Miami Valley Hospital for enabling implementation of his research projects on wheelchair users. Most of the research projects from the author's laboratory were supported by the Rehabilitation Research and Development Service of the US Department of Veterans Affairs.

References

1. Davis GM, Glaser RM: Cardiorespiratory fitness following spinal cord injury, in Ada L, Canning C (eds): *Physiotherapy: Key Issues in Neurological Physiotherapy*. London, Heinemann Medical Books, 1991, pp 155-195.

2. Glaser RM: Exercise and locomotion for the spinal cord injured. *Exerc Sports Sci Rev* 1985;13:263-303.

3. Glaser RM, Davis GM: Wheelchair-dependent individuals, in Franklin BA, Gordon S, Timmis GC (eds.): *Exercise in Modern Medicine*. Baltimore, MD, Williams & Wilkins, 1989, chap 13, pp 237-267.

4. Graicter PL, Maynard FW (eds): *Proceedings of the First Colloquium on Preventing Secondary Disabilities Among People with Spinal Cord Injuries*. Atlanta, GA, Centers for Disease Control, 1990.

5. Davis GM, Kofsky PR, Shephard RJ, et al: Classification of psychophysiological variables in the lower limb disabled. *Can J Appl Sport Sci* 1981;6:141.

6. Shephard RJ, Davis GM, Kofsky PR, et al: Interactions between attitudes, personality and physical activity in the lower-limb disabled. *Can J Appl Sport Sci* 1983;8:223.

7. Sherrill C: Social and psychological dimensions of sport for disabled athletes, in Sherrill C (ed): *Olympic Scientific Congress 1984: Eugene, OR. Sport and Disabled Athletes*. Champaign, IL, Human Kinetics, 1986, pp 21-34.

8. Krause JS, Crewe NM: Chronologic age, time since injury, and time of measurement: Effect on adjustment after spinal cord injury. *Arch Phys Med Rehabil* 1991;72:91-100.

9. Bruce DA, Schut L, Sutton LN: Brain and cervical spine injuries occurring during organized sports activities in children and adolescents. *Primary Care* 1984;11:175-194.

10. Stover SL, Fine PR (eds): *Spinal Cord Injury: The Facts and Figures*. Birmingham, AL, The University of Alabama, 1986.

11. Jackson RW, Fredrickson A: Sports for the physically disabled: The 1976 Olympiad (Toronto). *Am J Sports Med* 1979;7:293-296.

12. Stauffer ES: Long-term management of traumatic quadriplegia, in Pierce DS, Nickel VH (eds): *The Total Care of Spinal Cord Injuries*. Boston, MA, Little Brown & Co, 1977, pp 81-102.

13. DeVivo MJ, Fine PR, Maetz HM, et al: Prevalence of spinal cord injury: A reestimation employing life table techniques. *Arch Neurol* 1980;37:707-708.

14. Lammertse DP, Yarkony GM: Rehabilitation in spinal cord disorders: 4. Outcomes and issues of aging after spinal cord injury. *Arch Phys Med Rehabil* 1991;72(4 suppl):S309-S311.

15. Hrubec Z, Ryder RA: Traumatic limb amputations and subsequent mortality from cardiovascular disease and other causes. *J Chron Dis* 1980;33:239-250.

16. Le CT, Price M: Survival from spinal cord injury. *J Chron Dis* 1982;35:487-492.

17. Yekutiel M, Brooks ME, Ohry A, et al: The prevalence of hypertension, ischaemic heart disease and diabetes in traumatic spinal cord injured patients and amputees. *Paraplegia* 1989;27:58-62.

18. Heldenberg D, Rubinstein A, Levtov O, et al: Serum lipids and lipoprotein concentrations in young quadriplegic patients. *Atherosclerosis* 1981;39:163-167.

19. LaPorte RE, Adams LL, Savage DD, et al: The spectrum of physical activity, cardiovascular disease and health: An epidemiologic perspective. *Am J Epidemiol* 1984;120:507-517.

20. Dearwater SR, LaPorte RE, Robertson RJ, et al: Activity in the spinal cord-injured patient: An epidemiologic analysis of metabolic parameters. *Med Sci Sports Exerc* 1986;18:541-544.

21. Bostom AG, Toner MM, McArdle WD, et al: Lipid and lipoprotein profiles relate to peak aerobic power in spinal cord injured men. *Med Sci Sports Exerc* 1991;23:409-414.

22. Glaser RM: Cardiovascular problems of the wheelchair disabled, in Shephard RJ, Miller HS Jr (eds): *Exercise and the Heart in Health and Disease*. New York, NY, Marcel Dekker, 1992, chap 15, pp 467-499.

23. Freyschuss U, Knuttson E: Cardiovascular control in man with transverse cervical cord lesions. *Life Sci* 1969;8:421-424.

24. Glaser RM: Central and peripheral etiology of fatigue for the disabled, in *1988 Am Assoc EMG Electrodiag Didactic Prog*. 1988, pp 21-26.

25. Glaser RM: Arm exercise training for wheelchair users. *Med Sci Sports Exerc* 1989;21(suppl):S149-S157.

26. Cole TM, Kottke FJ, Olson M, et al: Alterations of cardiovascular control in high spinal myelomalacia. *Arch Phys Med Rehabil* 1967;48:359-368.

27. Corbett JL, Frankel HL, Harris PJ: Cardiovascular reflexes in tetraplegia. *Paraplegia* 1971;9:113-122.

28. Knutsson E, Lewenhaupt-Olsson E, Thorsen M: Physical work capacity and physical conditioning in paraplegic patients. *Paraplegia* 1973;11:205-216.

29. Pierce DS, Nickel VH (eds): *The Total Care of Spinal Cord Injuries*. Boston, MA, Little Brown & Co, 1977.

30. Åstrand P-O, Saltin B: Maximal oxygen uptake and heart rate in various types of muscular activity. *J Appl Physiol* 1961;16:977-981.

31. Stenberg J, Åstrand P-O, Ekblom B, et al: Hemodynamic response to work with different muscle groups, sitting and supine. *J Appl Physiol* 1967;22:61-70.

32. Zwiren LD, Bar-Or O: Responses to exercise of paraplegics who differ in conditioning level. *Med Sci Sports* 1975;7:94-98.

33. Bergh U, Kanstrup I-L, Ekblom B: Maximal oxygen uptake during exercise with various combinations of arm and leg work. *J Appl Physiol* 1976;41:191-196.

34. Bobbert AC: Physiological comparison of three types of ergometry. *J Appl Physiol* 1960;15:1007-1014.

35. Vokac Z, Bell H, Bautz-Holter E, et al: Oxygen uptake/heart rate relationship in leg and arm exercise, sitting and standing. *J Appl Physiol* 1975;39:54-59.

36. Glaser RM, Sawka MN, Miles DS: Efficiency of wheelchair and low power bicycle ergometry. *Proc IEEE Nat Aerospace Elect Conf* 1984;2:946-953.

37. Traugh GH, Corcoran PJ, Reyes RL: Energy expenditure of ambulation in patients with above-knee amputations. *Arch Phys Med Rehabil* 1975;56:67-71.

38. Wolfe GA, Waters R, Hislop HJ: Influence of floor surface on the energy cost of wheelchair propulsion. *Phys Ther* 1977;57:1022-1027.

39. Glaser RM, Laubach LL, Sawka MN, et al: Exercise stress, fitness evaluation and training of wheelchair users, in Leon AS, Amundson GJ (eds): *Proceedings -International Conference on Lifestyle and Health, 1978: Optimal Health and Fitness for People with Physical Disabilities*. Minneapolis, MN, University of Minnesota Press, 1979, pp 167-194.

40. Glaser RM, Sawka MN, Wilde SW, et al: Energy cost and cardiopulmonary responses for wheelchair locomotion and walking on tile and on carpet. *Paraplegia* 1981;19:220-226.

41. Glaser RM, Simsen-Harold CA, Petrofsky JS, et al: Metabolic and cardiopulmonary responses of older wheelchair-dependent and ambulatory patients during locomotion. *Ergonomics* 1983;26:687-697.

42. Åstrand P-O, Ekblom B, Messin R, et al: Intra-arterial blood pressure during exercise with different muscle groups. *J Appl Physiol* 1965;20:253-256.

43. Bevegård S, Freyschuss U, Strandell T: Circulatory adaptation to arm and leg exercise in supine and sitting position. *J Appl Physiol* 1966;21:37-46.
44. Schwade J, Blomqvist CG, Shapiro W: A comparison of the response to arm and leg work in patients with ischemic heart disease. *Am Heart J* 1977;94:203-208.
45. Glaser RM, Sawka MN, Laubach LL, et al: Metabolic and cardiopulmonary responses to wheelchair and bicycle ergometry. *J Appl Physiol* 1979;46:1066-1070.
46. McArdle WD, Glaser RM, Magel JR: Metabolic and cardiorespiratory response during free swimming and treadmill walking. *J Appl Physiol* 1971;30:733-738.
47. Clausen JP, Klausen K, Rasmussen B, et al: Central and peripheral circulatory changes after training of the arms or legs. *Am J Physiol* 1973;225:675-682.
48. Reybrouck T, Heigenhauser GF, Faulkner JA: Limitations to maximum oxygen uptake in arms, leg, and combined arm-leg ergometry. *J Appl Physiol* 1975;38:774-779.
49. American College of Sports Medicine. *Guidelines for Graded Exercise Testing and Exercise Prescription*, ed 2. Philadelphia, PA, Lea & Febiger, 1980.
50. Bar-Or O, Zwiren LD: Maximal oxygen consumption test during arm exercise: Reliability and validity. *J Appl Physiol* 1975;38:424-426.
51. Hjeltnes N: Oxygen uptake and cardiac output in graded arm exercise in paraplegics with low level spinal lesions. *Scand J Rehabil Med* 1977;9:107-113.
52. Glaser RM, Foley DM, Laubach LL, et al: An exercise test to evaluate fitness for wheelchair activity. *Paraplegia* 1979;16:341-349.
53. Sawka MN: Physiology of upper body exercise. *Exerc Sport Sci Rev* 1986;14:175-211.
54. Brattgård S-O, Grimby G, Höök O: Energy expenditure and heart rate in driving a wheelchair ergometer. *Scand J Rehabil Med* 1970;2:143-148.
55. Glaser RM, Sawka MN, Young RE, et al: Applied physiology for wheelchair design. *J Appl Physiol* 1980;48:41-44.
56. Wilde SW, Miles DS, Durbin RJ, et al: Evaluation of myocardial performance during wheelchair ergometer exercise. *Am J Phys Med* 1981;60:277- 291.
57. Wicks JR, Oldridge NB, Cameron BJ, et al: Arm cranking and wheelchair ergometry in elite spinal cord-injured athletes. *Med Sci Sports Exerc* 1983;15:224-231.
58. Glaser RM, Sawka MN, Brune MF, et al: Physiological responses to maximal effort wheelchair and arm crank ergometry. *J Appl Physiol* 1980;48:1060-1064.
59. Voigt E-D, Bahn D: Metabolism and pulse rate in physically handicapped when propelling a wheelchair up an incline. *Scand J Rehabil Med* 1969;1:101-106.
60. Hildebrandt G, Voigt E-D, Bahn D, et al: Energy costs of propelling wheelchair at various speeds: Cardiac response and effect on steering accuracy. *Arch Phys Med Rehabil* 1970;51:131-136.
61. Engel P, Hildebrandt G: Long-term spiroergometric studies of paraplegics during the clinical period of rehabilitation. *Paraplegia* 1973;11:105-110.
62. Gass GC, Camp EM: Physiological characteristics of trained Australian paraplegic and tetraplegic subjects. *Med Sci Sports* 1979;11:256-259.
63. Clarke KS: Caloric costs of activity in paraplegic persons. *Arch Phys Med Rehabil* 1966;47:427-435.
64. Glaser RM, Collins SR, Wilde SW: Power output requirements for manual wheelchair locomotion. *Proc IEEE Nat Aerospace Elect Conf* 1980;2:502-509.
65. Glaser RM, Collins SR: Validity of power output estimation for wheelchair locomotion. *Am J Phys Med* 1981;60:180-189.
66. Sawka MN, Glaser RM, Wilde SW, et al: Metabolic and circulatory responses to wheelchair and arm crank exercise. *J Appl Physiol* 1980;49:784-788.
67. McCafferty WB, Horvath SM: Specificity of exercise and specificity of training: A subcellular response. *Res Q* 1977;48:358-371.
68. Smith PA, Glaser RM, Petrofsky JS, et al: Arm crank vs handrim wheelchair propulsion: Metabolic and cardiopulmonary responses. *Arch Phys Med Rehabil* 1983;64:249-254.

69. Sawka MN, Glaser RM, Laubach LL, et al: Wheelchair exercise performance of the young, middle-aged, and elderly. *J Appl Physiol* 1981;50:824-828.

70. Wilde SW, Glaser RM, Sawka MN, et al: Prediction of peak oxygen uptake from submaximal arm crank exercise. *Fed Proc* 1980;39:289.

71. Sawka MN, Glaser RM, Wilde SW, et al: Submaximal test to predict peak oxygen uptake for wheelchair exercise. *Fed Proc* 1980;39:287.

72. Nilsson S, Staff PH, Pruett ED: Physical work capacity and the effect of training on subjects with long-standing paraplegia. *Scand J Rehabil Med* 1975;7:51-56.

73. Emes C: Physical work capacity of wheelchair athletes. *Res Q* 1977;48:209-212.

74. Wicks JR, Lymburner K, Dinsdale SM, et al: The use of multistage exercise testing with wheelchair ergometry and arm cranking in subjects with spinal cord lesions. *Paraplegia* 1977;15:252-261.

75. Coutts KD, Rhodes EC, McKenzie DC: Maximal exercise responses of tetraplegics and paraplegics. *J Appl Physiol* 1983;55:479-482.

76. Huang C-T, McEachran AB, Kuhlemeier KV, et al: Prescriptive arm ergometry to optimize muscular endurance in acutely injured paraplegic patients. *Arch Phys Med Rehabil* 1983;64:578-582.

77. Kofsky PR, Davis GM, Shephard RJ, et al: Field testing: Assessment of physical fitness of disabled adults. *Eur J Appl Physiol* 1983;51:109-120.

78. Whiting RB, Dreisinger TE, Abbott C: Clinical value of exercise testing in handicapped subjects. *South Med J* 1983;76:1225-1227.

79. Ekblom B, Lundberg A: Effect of physical training on adolescents with severe motor handicaps. *Acta Paediatr Scand* 1968;57:17-23.

80. Kavanagh T, Shephard RJ: The application of exercise testing to the elderly amputee. *Can Med Assoc J* 1973;108:314-317.

81. Marincek CR, Valencic V: Arm cycloergometry and kinetics of oxygen consumption in paraplegics. *Paraplegia* 1977;15:178-185.

82. Pollock ML, Miller HS, Linnerud AC, et al: Arm pedaling as an endurance training regimen for the disabled. *Arch Phys Med Rehabil* 1974;55:418-424.

83. Glaser RM, Sawka MN, Durbin RJ, et al: Exercise program for wheelchair activity. *Am J Phys Med* 1981;60:67-75.

84. McArdle WD, Katch FI, Katch VL (eds): *Exercise Physiology: Energy, Nutrition, and Human Performance*, ed 3. Philadelphia, PA, Lea and Febiger, 1991.

85. Thorstensson A: Observations on strength training and detraining. *Acta Physiol Scand* 1977;100:491-493.

86. Pollock ML, Wilmore JH, Fox SM III (eds): *Exercise in Health and Disease: Evaluation and Prescription for Prevention and Rehabilitation*. Philadelphia, PA, WB Saunders, 1984.

87. Fox EL, Mathews DK: *Interval Training: Conditioning for Sports and General Fitness*. Philadelphia, PA, WB Saunders, 1974.

88. Miles DS, Sawka MN, Wilde SW, et al: Pulmonary function changes in wheelchair athletes subsequent to exercise training. *Ergonomics* 1982;25:239-246.

89. DiCarlo SE, Supp MD, Taylor HC: Effect of arm ergometry training on physical work capacity of individuals with spinal cord injuries. *Phys Ther* 1983;63:1104-1107.

90. Simmons R, Shephard RJ: Effects of physical conditioning upon the central and peripheral circulatory responses to arm work. *Int Z Angew Physiol* 1971;30:73-84.

91. Magel JR, McArdle WD, Toner M, et al: Metabolic and cardiovascular adjustment to arm training. *J Appl Physiol* 1978;45:75-79.

92. Hooker SP, Wells CL: Effects of low- and moderate-intensity training in spinal cord-injured persons. *Med Sci Sports Exerc* 1989;21:18-22.

93. Figoni SF, Gupta SC, Glaser RM, et al: Exercise hemodynamics of quadriplegics: A pilot study. *Rehabil R & D Prog Rep Suppl* 1988;25:108.

94. Mortimer JT: Motor prostheses, in Brookhart JM, Mountcastle VB, Brooks VB, et al (eds): *Handbook of Physiology: Section 1. The Nervous System: Vol II. Motor Control Part 1*. Bethesda, MD, American Physiological Society, 1981, pp 155-187.

95. Benton LA, Baker LL, Bowman BR, et al: *Functional Electrical Stimulation: A Practical Clinical Guide*. Downey, CA, Rancho Los Amigos Rehabilitation Engineering Center, Rancho Los Amigos Hospital, 1981.

96. Cybulski GR, Penn RD, Jaeger RJ: Lower extremity functional neuromuscular stimulation in cases of spinal cord injury. *Neurosurgery* 1984;15:132-146.

97. Glaser RM: Physiologic aspects of spinal cord injury and functional neuromuscular stimulation. *Cent Nerv Syst Trauma* 1986;3:49-62.

98. Gruner JA, Glaser RM, Feinberg SD, et al: A system for evaluation and exercise-conditioning of paralyzed leg muscles. *J Rehabil R & D* 1983;20:21-30.

99. Glaser RM, Rattan SN, Davis GM, et al: Central hemodynamic responses to lower-limb FNS. *Proceedings of the Ninth Annual Conference of the IEEE Engineering in Medicine and Biology Society*. 1987;2:615-617.

100. Davis GM, Servedio FJ, Glaser RM, et al: Cardiovascular responses to arm cranking and FNS-induced leg exercise in paraplegics. *J Appl Physiol* 1990;69:671-677.

101. Davis GM, Figoni SF, Glaser RM, et al: Cardiovascular responses to FNS-induced isometric leg exercise during orthostatic stress in paraplegics. *Proc Intl Conf Assoc Adv Rehabil Tech* 1988;326-327.

102. Figoni SF, Davis GM, Glaser RM, et al: FNS-assisted venous return in exercising SCI men. *Proc Intl Conf Assoc Adv Rehabil Tech* 1988;328-329.

103. Faghri PD, Glaser RM, Figoni SF, et al: Feasibility of using two FNS exercise modes for spinal cord injured patients. *Clin Kinesiol* 1989;43:62-68.

104. Petrofsky JS, Phillips CA: Active physical therapy: A modern approach to rehabilitation therapy. *J Neuro Orthop Surg* 1983;4:165-173.

105. Glaser RM: Physiology of functional electrical stimulation-induced exercise: Basic science perspective. *J Neuro Rehabil* 1991;5:49-61.

106. Ragnarsson KT, Pollack S, O'Daniel W Jr, et al: Clinical evaluation of computerized functional electrical stimulation after spinal cord injury: A multicenter pilot study. *Arch Phys Med Rehabil* 1988;69:672-677.

107. Ezenwa BN, Glaser RM, Couch W, et al: Adaptive control of functional neuromuscular stimulation-induced knee extension exercise. *J Rehabil Res Dev* 1991;28:1-8.

108. Collins SR, Glaser RM: Comparison of aerobic metabolism and cardiopulmonary responses for electrically-induced and voluntary exercise. *Proc 8th Ann RESNA Conf Rehabil Technol* 1985;391-393.

109. Figoni SF, Glaser RM, Rodgers MM, et al: Acute hemodynamic responses of spinal cord injured individuals to functional neuromuscular stimulation-induced knee extension exercise. *J Rehabil Res Dev* 1991;28:9-18.

110. Rodgers MM, Glaser RM, Figoni SF, et al: Musculoskeletal responses of spinal cord injured individuals to functional neuromuscular stimulation-induced knee extension exercise training. *J Rehabil Res Dev* 1991;28:19-26.

111. Petrofsky JS, Phillips CA, Heaton HH III, et al: Bicycle ergometer for paralyzed muscle. *J Clin Eng* 1984;9:13-19.

112. Glaser RM, Figoni SF, Collins SR, et al: Physiologic responses of SCI subjects to electrically induced leg cycle ergometry. *1988 IEEE Engineering in Medicine and Biology Tenth Annual Conference*. 1988;4:1638-1640.

113. Figoni SF, Glaser RM, Hendershot DM, et al: Hemodynamic responses of quadriplegics to maximal arm-cranking and FNS leg cycling exercise. *1988 IEEE Engineering in Medicine and Biology Tenth Annual Conference*. 1988;4:1636-1637.

114. Figoni SF, Glaser RM, Hooker SP, et al: Peak hemodynamic responses of SCI subjects during FNS leg cycle ergometry. *Proc 12th An RESNA Conf Rehab Tech* 1989;97-98.

115. Pollack SF, Axen K, Spielholz N, et al: Aerobic training effects of electrically induced lower extremity exercises in spinal cord injured people. *Arch Phys Med Rehabil* 1989;70:214-219.

116. Glaser RM, Figoni SF, Hooker SP, et al: Efficiency of FNS leg cycle ergometry. *1989 IEEE Engineereing in Medicine and Biology Eleventh Annual Conference.* 1989;3:961-963.

117. Figoni SF, Hooker SP, Glaser RM, et al: Physiologic responses to arm cranking and electrical stimulation leg cycling, part II: Quadriplegics (Abstract). *Med Sci Sports Exerc* 1990;22(suppl):S43.

118. Goss FL, McDermott A, Robertson RJ: Changes in peak oxygen uptake following computerized functional electrical stimulation in the spinal cord injured. *Res Quart Exerc Sport* 1992;63:76-79.

119. Faghri PD, Glaser RM, Figoni SF: Functional electrical stimulation leg cycle ergometer exercise: Training effects on cardiorespiratory responses of spinal cord injured subjects at rest and during submaximal exercise. *Arch Phys Med Rehabil* 1992;73:1085-1093.

120. Glaser RM, Strayer JR, May KP: Combined FES leg and voluntary arm exercise of SCI patients, in Lin JC, Feinberg BN (eds): *Frontiers of Engineering and Computing in Health Care.* 1985, vol 1, pp 308-313.

121. Glaser RM: Functional neuromuscular stimulation for physical fitness training of the disabled, in Kaneko M (ed): *Fitness for the Aged, Disabled and Industrial Worker.* Champaign, IL, Human Kinetics Books, 1990, pp 127-134.

122. Glaser RM: Spinal cord injuries and neuromuscular stimulation, in: Torg JS, Welsh RP, Shephard RJ (eds): *Current Therapy in Sports Medicine - 2.* Toronto, BC Decker, 1990, pp 166-170.

123. Hooker SP, Figoni SF, Rodgers MM, et al: Metabolic and hemodynamic responses to concurrent voluntary arm crank and electrical stimulation leg cycle exercise in quadriplegics. *J Rehabil Res Dev* 1992;29:1-11.

124. Figoni SF, Glaser RM, Rodgers MM, et al: Hemodynamic responses of quadriplegics to arm, ES-leg, and combined arm + ES-leg ergometry. *Med Sci Sports Exerc* 1989;21(suppl):S96.

Section Three

Training Programs in Midlife

Chapter 15

Cardiovascular Response to Isometric Exercise

J. Ricardo Serra Grima, MD

People over 40 years of age now spend more of their leisure time doing some type of physical exercise. One reason for this change in the life-style of subjects who had never previously taken part in any type of sport may be the relationship between physical exercise and good health.

Epidemiologic studies done during the last 25 years have shown that there is a direct correlation between heart disease and sedentary life-styles.[1-4] Smoking, high blood pressure, and hypercholesterolemia are the most important nongenetic coronary risk factors for the onset of heart disease. The earliest lesions of arteriosclerosis can usually be found in young children in the form of a lesion called fatty streak; whereas the advanced lesions (ie, fibrous plaque) generally appear during early adulthood and progress with age.[5] This time is the silent period of the disease. The clinical phase of the disease, angina pectoris and myocardial infarction, can be seen in predisposed individuals after the age of 40.

Prevention programs carried out in developed countries have reduced significantly the number of cases or delayed the onset of coronary heart disease. Blood pressure control, smoking cessation, and treatment of hypercholesterolemia are some of the measures that have helped.

Recently, several studies have been published that show the favorable effects of physical activity on high blood pressure[5-8] and hypercholesterolemia.[9] Suggestions that physical activity would act as an independent factor have increased the interest in exercise programs for the midlife population. However, the volume, intensity, and type of exercise required to attain the best effects without increasing other risk factors are not yet well defined.[10]

The success of an exercise program in the midlife population depends on previous regular physical activity, presence of coronary risk factors, and nature of work. For example, a subject whose work involves very intense physical activity will not need to increase his or her leisure-time activity if the only goal is improved health.

Before starting a physical exercise program in apparently healthy subjects older than 40 years, with or without coronary risk factors, the subject's physical capacity must be evaluated in order to determine the most adequate exercise. Stress testing results are necessary to adjust volume and intensity according to the particular conditions of each candidate. Bicycle or treadmill tests generally are used to evaluate physical capacity; these are valid systems for quantifying the work done during the stress test. The treadmill can easily be adapted to most subjects, and generally a higher effort level can be obtained with this test. The work performed with the ergometric bicycle also contains some isometric exercise because of the friction in the wheel and the difficulty in muscle coordination, especially during the last minutes of the test, when maximum effort is reached. The most important limitation is the easy onset of fatigue before reaching the physiologic limit of cardiovascular adaptation to exercise, especially in sedentary subjects.

The cardiovascular effects of bicycle exercise have been demonstrated in an echocardiogram study of competitive cyclists.[11] The left ventricular wall thickness is greater in the cyclists than in a similar group of runners. There is no sport activity in which the work is mainly dynamic or isometric. This should be kept in mind when designing a training program for patients with heart disease or high blood pressure.

The perfect ergometer is the one that reproduces regular exercise. The treadmill would be most adequate for evaluating the physical capacity of a subject who walks at a brisk pace several hours a day. When experienced runners are evaluated, a speed of over 20 kilometers per hour can be applied.

The end point of the test is when exhaustion appears, coincidental with the limit of the cardiovascular adaptation. Subjects with a sedentary life-style generally do not reach the maximum capacity of the cardiovascular system or maximum cardiac output because of muscle fatigue. In these subjects, and in those with heart disease, the maximum heart rate is the value reached at the end of the exercise. It is not advisable to use the maximum theoretical heart rate as a reference.[12]

The VO_2 max is commonly used to determine the capacity for physical activity; it serves as an indicator of the pulmonary function when the oxygen concentration is normal. The VO_2 max changes according to age, sex, physical activity, training, and genetic factors. It is expressed in cc/kg/minute or in relation to energy requirements. In the resting period, a subject uses up about 3.5 cc/kg/min O_2, which is also defined as 1 MET (metabolic equivalent).[12]

Analysis of the exchange of respiratory gases as determined in an exercise physiology laboratory helps to assess cardiovascular function, and thus provides more objective information on the functional capacity of the subject and the effect of the training.[13]

Blood pressure should be carefully recorded by a physician during each stage of exercise. Blood pressure increase during dynamic exercise is different than that produced during isometric exercise. During dynamic exercise, systolic blood pressure increases between 7 to 10 mm Hg and diastolic pressure remains the same or increases slightly.

With age, arteries lose their natural elasticity and become more rigid. These changes produce a greater increase in systolic and diastolic blood pressure during exercise. The hypertensive response during exercise, in apparently healthy subjects over 40 years old, and in patients with a previous myocardial infarction is of great clinical interest. The first case is of interest because the subject might develop hypertension in the future. The second case is of interest because the disproportionate increase in systolic blood pressure must be considered in order to program physical exercise. In cardiac rehabilitation programs, modifications of systolic and diastolic blood pressure must be evaluated in order to avoid a disproportionate rise of the heart rate blood pressure product, because such a rise could create severe complications in some patients.

Isometric Exercise and Cardiovascular Response

Isometric exercise produces changes in muscle tension with small changes in fiber length. A typical example is weightlifting.

Isometric contractions produce an abrupt pressure response, ie, an increase in systolic and diastolic blood pressure that seems disproportionate for the work done. This increase is influenced directly by the size of the contracting muscle mass; there is a direct relationship between the size of the active muscle mass and the magnitude of the increases in blood pressure.[14] In response to heavy resistance exercise, the arterial blood pressure shows extremely high values during the concentric contraction phase for each lift and declines with the eccentric contraction. MacDougall and associates[15] in a study of healthy young subjects performing weightlifting exercises found blood pressures over 320/250 mm Hg during double leg press. The mechanical compression of blood vessels combines with a strong pressure response and Valsalva response to produce extreme elevations in blood pressure.

Cardiovascular response of small muscle groups was measured using sustained contraction of a handgrip calibrated with a mercury manometer. These modifications occur in acute cardiovascular response. The sustained contraction decreases arterial flow by compressing the small arteries and impeding the venous return. The increase in systolic and diastolic blood pressure is disproportionate. The heart rate and stroke volume increase slightly. At the same percentage of maximal voluntary contraction there is a positive relationship between the increase in blood pressure and the size of the active muscle mass. There is a greater vascular response to leg extension (large muscle) than to handgrip (small muscle).

Outline 1 Cardiovascular response to isometric exercise

Increased systolic pressure
Increased diastolic pressure
Small change in stroke volume
Normal electrocardiogram

Isometric exercise produces changes at less than maximum loads. These changes may be evaluated with electrocardiography (ECG) and echocardiography studies. The ECG has low sensitivity to changes produced by isometric exercise and almost always appears normal (Outline 1).

The echocardiogram measures the wall thickness and dimensions of the left ventricle. In isometric exercise, the wall thickness increases in comparison with sedentary people, but the changes are not always significant.

In a comparative study done with 15 gymnasts and 15 long-distance runners, a significant difference in wall thickness was observed in both groups. There were no differences between sedentary people and runners. The most significant increase in wall thickness was seen in athletes who did mixed exercise (rowing, bicycle).

The normal thickness in sedentary subjects is not greater than 11 mm. In trained subjects, values of up to 13 mm are frequently found; values greater than 13 mm can be seen in only 2% of athletes (Fig. 1).

The limits of physiologic ventricle wall hypertrophy in the athlete are not well defined. In a study done with over 1,000 athletes, Pelliccia[16] found values of over 15 mm in very rare cases. These extreme values can be considered within the physiologic limits in rowing or cycling. A group of athletes who had a ventricle wall thickness of > 12 mm was studied to find the physiologic limit of cardiovascular adaptation to exercise.

Antimyosin uptake is another means of identifying ventrical wall hypertrophy. The antimyosin uptake in the myocardium is specific for myocyte cell membrane disruption. In the intact myocyte, cardiac myosin is protected from the extracellular fluid by the plasma cell's membrane. When the sarcolemma is disrupted via ischemia, the intracellular antigen becomes available to combine with the administered antibody, and positive antimyosin uptake in the myocardium is seen.

The athletes with a ventricle wall thickness of ≥12 mm had normal antimyosin scans. The results of this study suggest that a thickness over 13 mm corresponds to pathologic hypertrophy.[17] A study done after six weeks without training indicated that the athletes had a reduction in antimyosin uptake. These data show that it is necessary to follow up athletes with mixed, vigorous training, that is, isometric and dynamic or isometric alone.

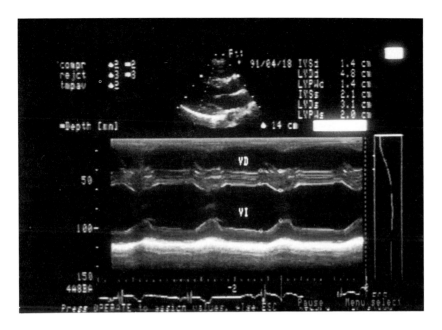

Fig. 1 *Abnormal interventricular septum thickness and abnormal posterior wall thickness measured by echocardiography (Mode M). VD: right ventricular; VI: left ventricular.*

Ventricular Function During the Isometric Exercise

Radionuclide ventriculography and echocardiography are used in the study of ventricular function. Left ventricular ejection fraction (EF) is determined using established methods. The isometric test for this study consists of the handgrip (contraction sustained) at 25% to 30% maximal voluntary contraction.

In normal subjects, a fall in the EF is related to an important increase in the systolic arterial pressure. During intense isometric exercise, the EF decreases initially, but it is recovered by the Frank-Starling mechanism.[18-21] The decrease in the EF probably is not actually a sign of abnormal ventricular function, but is instead a transitory mechanism of adaptation to isometric exercise.[19]

In summary, the work of strength training provokes an acute cardiovascular response that is characterized especially by a large increase in the systolic blood pressure over resting levels. Isometric work is part of most training programs for various sport activities. The predominance of isometric work in training requires continuous follow-up of the athletes because they have a greater tendency to myocardial hypertrophy.

In cardiac patients, circuit weight training appears to be safe and to result in significant increases in musculoskeletal strength and cardiac performance.[22]

References

1. León AS, Connett J, Jacobs DR Jr, et al: Leisure-time physical activity levels and risk of coronary heart disease and death: The multiple risk factor intervention trial. *JAMA* 1987;258:2388-2395.

2. Paffenbarger RS Jr, Hyde RT, Wing AL, et al: Physical activity, all-cause mortality, and longevity of college alumni. *N Engl J Med* 1986;314:605-613.

3. Salonen JT, Slater JS, Tuomilehto J, et al: Leisure time and occupational physical activity: Risk of death from ischemic heart disease. *Am J Epidemiol* 1988;127:87-94.

4. Kannel WB, Sorlie P: Some health benefits of physical activity: The Framingham study. *Arch Intern Med* 1979;139:857-861.

5. Russell R: The pathogenesis of atherosclerosis, in Braunwald E (ed): *Heart Disease: A Textbook of Cardiovascular Medicine*, ed 3. Philadelphia, PA, WB Saunders, 1988, p 1140.

6. Blair SN, Goodyear NN, Gibbons LW, et al: Physical fitness and incidence of hypertension in healthy normotensive men and women. *JAMA* 1984;252:487-490.

7. Boyer JL, Kasch FW: Exercise therapy in hypertensive men. *JAMA* 1970;211:1668-1671.

8. Kiyonaga A, Arakawa K, Tanaka H, et al: Blood pressure and hormonal responses to aerobic exercise. *Hypertension* 1985;7:125-131.

9. Krauss RM: Exercise, lipoproteins, and coronary artery disease. *Circulation* 1989;79:1143-1145.

10. Franklin BA, Gordon S, Timmis GC: Amount of exercise necessary for the patient with coronary artery disease. *Am J Cardiol* 1992;69:1426-1431.

11. Fagard R, Aubert A, Staessen J, et al: Cardiac structure and function in cyclists and runners: Comparative echocardiographic study. *Br Heart J* 1984;52:124-129.

12. Special Report: Guidelines for exercise testing: A report of the American College of Cardiology/American Heart Association Task Force on Assessment of Cardiovascular Procedures. *J Am Coll Cardiol* 1986;8:725-738.

13. Wasserman K: The Dickinson W. Richards lecture: New concepts in assessing cardiovascular function. *Circulation* 1988;78:1060-1071.

14. Seals DR, Washburn RA, Hanson PG, et al: Increased cardiovascular response to static contraction of larger muscle groups. *J Appl Physiol* 1983;54:434-437.

15. MacDougall JD, Tuxen D, Sale DG, et al: Arterial blood pressure response to heavy resistance exercise. *J Appl Physiol* 1985;58:785-790.

16. Pelliccia A, Maron BJ, Spataro A, et al: The upper limit of physiologic cardiac hypertrophy in highly trained elite athletes. *N Engl J Med* 1991;324:295-301.

17. Carrió I, Serra Grima JR, Martinez Dunker D, et al: Myocite damage in cardiac hypertrophy of athletes assessed by 111 In-antimyosin antibody studies, in press.

18. Sullivan J, Hanson P, Rahko PS, et al: Continuous measurement of left ventricular performance during and after maximal isometric deadlift exercise. *Circulation* 1992;85:1406-1413.

19. Ehsani AA, Heath GW, Hagberg JM, et al: Non-invasive assessment of changes in left ventricular function induced by graded isometric exercise in healthy subjects. *Chest* 1981;80:51-55.

20. Jones RI, Lahiri A, Cashman PM, et al: Left ventricular function during isometric hand grip and cold stress in normal subjects. *Br Heart J* 1986;55:246-252.

21. Vitcenda M, Hanson P, Folts J, et al: Impairment of left ventricular function during maximal isometric dead lifting. *J Appl Physiol* 1990;69:2062-2066.

22. Keleman MH, Stewart KJ, Gillilan RE, et al: Circuit weight training in cardiac patients. *J Am Coll Cardiol* 1986;7:38-42.

Chapter 16

Aerobic Training and Its Influence on Cardiovascular Fitness and Health

James C. Puffer, MD

It is well known that the geriatric population in the United States is increasing at an exponential rate. U.S. Census Bureau data indicate that by the year 2020, 20% of Americans will be over age 65. It follows that increasing numbers of Americans will also enter midlife in the next two decades, and this will have important implications for health care providers, who will be in a unique position to positively influence the health of baby boomers who are rapidly approaching or already in midlife.

A number of changes occur in the cardiac, respiratory, musculoskeletal, and nervous systems as we age.[1] Many of these changes may be related to the sedentary nature of older individuals rather than due to the inevitable process of aging, given that many of these changes appear to be retarded by regular aerobic activity.[2] This chapter will discuss the influence of aerobic training on the cardiovascular system by reviewing these age-related changes, investigating the manner in which aerobic activity can alter these changes, exploring current understanding about the threshold at which these changes occur, and finally, examining the implications these phenomena have on both fitness and health.

Aging and Its Influence on the Cardiovascular System

A number of changes have been demonstrated to occur in the cardiovascular system as a person ages. The myocardium experiences a progressive loss of myocytes, as well as an increase in lipid deposition, tubular dilatation, and lipofuscin deposition.[2] These changes may reflect alterations in protein synthesis, which subsequently influence the replacement of contractile fibers and other proteins. The left ventricle thickens with age and, in fact, is 25% thicker at age 80 than at age 30.[3] These ventricular changes negatively influence both myocardial contractility and cardiac output.

In the vasculature, thickening of the smooth muscle layers of the media, as well as greater fragmentation of elastin and increased calcification significantly decrease compliance.[2] This decrease in compliance results in increasing mean arterial blood pressure as age advances. Increasing afterload coupled with decreased maximum heart rate, contractility, and ventricular filling produce prominent decreases in cardiac output. In fact, it has been shown that cardiac output decreases 40% between the third and eighth decades.[3]

A number of concomitant changes in pulmonary function also influence cardiovascular performance. These changes include a decrease in vital capacity in the range of 17 to 22 milliliters per year; a reduction in forced expiratory volume of 32 milliliters per year in males and 25 milliliters per year in females; and an increase in residual volume.[3] Additionally, alveolar-capillary basement membrane thickening results in a well-demonstrated decline in mean arterial oxygen pressure of approximately 25% between the second and seventh decades.

These cumulative changes in the cardiovascular and respiratory systems contribute to the well-demonstrated age-related decline in maximal oxygen consumption ($\dot{V}O_2max$), an accepted marker of cardiorespiratory fitness. It has been shown that between the ages of 30 and 70, this marker declines approximately 1% per year (Fig. 1).[4] This decline is a consequence of the progressive loss of mean muscle mass, decreasing maximal heart rate, increased peripheral vascular resistance, and diminished myocardial contractility.

Exercise and Its Effect on Age-Related Changes in Cardiovascular Function

A number of investigators have demonstrated that regular exercise can retard the age-related decline in maximal oxygen consumption. Saltin and Grimby[5] studied former athletes in midlife who had been sedentary for at least 10 years and demonstrated that their average maximal oxygen consumption, which was 40 ml/kg/min, was 20% higher than that of sedentary nonathletes. However, the maximal oxygen consumption of active midlife athletes was found to be even 25% higher than that of these sedentary former athletes. This difference persisted with advancing age, as can be seen in Table 1.

Bottiger[6] compared physical work capacity in trained older Nordic skiers with that in younger athletes. Older men (55 years old) averaged 168 m/min during a 30-k cross-country race, while younger men (28 years old) averaged 193 m/min. This difference of 12% was much lower than the 25% to 27% difference that was expected as a result of age.[6] Pollock and associates[7] found similar results in study-

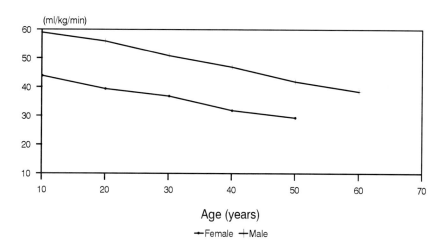

Fig. 1 *Maximal oxygen uptake.*

Table 1 Maximal oxygen consumption in sedentary and active former athletes.

Age Group	Maximal Oxygen Consumption (ml/kg LBW/min)	
	Sedentary Athletes	Active Athletes
44-49	44	57
50-59	38	53
60-67	37	43

n = 29 males; LBW = lean body weight

ing 24 regional or national master track champions over 10 years. Their ages ranged from 50 to 82 years; and 11 were still training at high intensity and competing regularly. All of these athletes were found to be aerobically fit, but all showed decreases in lean body weight and increases in body fat. When the 11 competitive athletes (considered the high-intensity group) were compared with the remaining 13 athletes (the low-intensity group), minimal declines were seen in maximal oxygen consumption. The high-intensity group demonstrated a maximal oxygen consumption of 54.2 ml/kg/min in 1971 and 53.3 ml/kg/min in 1981. The low-intensity group had maximal oxygen consumption values of 52.5 ml/kg/min and 45.9 ml/kg/min at the beginning and end of the same 10-year time period. Table 2 demonstrates maximal oxygen consumption and treadmill performance time as a function of age in these master athletes.

These data convincingly demonstrate that regular physical activity can retard the natural decline in cardiovascular fitness that might be expected to occur with age. Central (cardiovascular) or peripheral

Table 2 Comparison of treadmill performance time and maximal oxygen consumption as a function of age in master athletes.

	Age (years)		
	50-59	60-69	70-79
Treadmill Performance Time	NC	−15%	−27%
Max V̇O₂ (TBW)*	−4.3%	−9.0%	−10.5%
Max V̇O₂ (LBW)*	−4.3%	−3.2%	6.0%

*TBW = total body weight; LBW = lean body weight.

(skeletal muscle) adaptations may occur to preserve cardiorespiratory fitness. Forman and associates[8] demonstrated enhanced left ventricular diastolic filling in older individuals who participated in long-term endurance training. Child and associates[9] demonstrated important adaptive changes in left ventricular size of master athletes that may also favorably influence cardiac output. Most importantly, however, the efficiency of peripheral extraction of oxygen by skeletal muscle is preserved with regular physical activity.[10] This preserved efficiency results from the increased numbers and size of mitochondria in skeletal muscle, increased levels of myoglobin, increased activity of oxidative enzymes, and enhanced skeletal muscle to capillary density ratio in those who train aerobically.

Training Intensity

Given that exercise training has been shown to retard the decline in cardiovascular fitness with age, the critical question remaining is the intensity or threshold at which this decline can be retarded. The American College of Sports Medicine conducted a thorough review of the literature in preparation of its 1990 position paper, which recommended that exercise should occur at 60% to 90% of maximum heart rate, three to five times weekly, for a duration of 20 to 60 minutes, in order to be beneficial.[11] There is considerable work that demonstrates that beneficial changes may occur just as readily at the lower training intensities as at the higher training intensities.

Pollock and associates[12] evaluated the cardiovascular fitness of midlife men who walked for 40 minutes, four times weekly, over a 20-week period, and found that maximal oxygen consumption increased 28% when average heart rates from 63% to 76% of maximal heart rate were sustained during training. King and associates[13] recently evaluated cardiovascular fitness in 160 women and 197 men, aged 50 to 65 years, who were randomized into both high- and low-intensity training groups. The low-intensity group, which trained at 60% to 73% of maximal heart rate, achieved improvements in maximal oxygen consumption comparable with those of the high-intensity group, which trained at 73% to 88% of maximal heart rate. However, the most important factor to consider with respect to the issue of training intensity may not be cardiovascular fitness, but rather cardiovascular health and health in general.

Exercise Intensity and Health

A number of investigators have recently demonstrated the beneficial effect that regular exercise training has on both cardiovascular health and health in general. Paffenbarger and associates[14] studied the relationship between exercise and risk of heart disease in 17,000 Harvard alumni from 35 to older than 80 years of age. They found that sedentary men were at 64% higher risk for first myocardial infarction than those expending at least 2,000 kilocalories per week. Additionally, mortality from all causes declined as energy expenditure increased from 500 to 3,500 kilocalories per week, and this relationship persisted despite age. Blair and associates[15] similarly demonstrated a reduction in mortality from all causes in a longitudinal study of men and women from 20 to older than 60 years of age. They found a threshold level of approximately 8 to 9 mets (metabolic equivalents) in women and 9 to 10 mets in men at which the beneficial health effects of exercise were optimized. This threshold level is the equivalent of walking briskly for 30 minutes, three to four times weekly. Duncan and associates[16] studied the effect of walking on lipid profiles in 102 premenopausal women (20 to 40 years of age). The women were randomized into aerobic walking (8 km/h), brisk walking (6.4 km/h), strolling, and control (sedentary) groups. Although maximal oxygen consumption increased significantly in a dose-response manner when compared with that of controls, high density lipoprotein levels increased significantly, but to the same degree, in both the high- and low-intensity walking groups.

Similar findings have been demonstrated with respect to the risk of developing diabetes mellitus. It is well known that glucose tolerance declines at a rate of approximately 6.7 ml/dl per decade starting at midlife, and this decline is highly correlated with body mass index and hip to waist ratios.[17] Seals and associates[18] evaluated glucose tolerance in 11 healthy men and women after 12 months of endurance training, 6 months of which was low intensity and 6 months of which was high intensity. Maximal oxygen consumption increased 12% after 6 months of low-intensity training and an additional 18% after the 6 months of high-intensity training. Likewise, insulin activity decreased by 8% and 23%, respectively, and high-intensity exercise raised high-density lipoprotein levels and lowered triglyceride levels.

Helmrich and associates[19] studied the relationship between leisure time activity and the development of noninsulin dependent diabetes mellitus (NIDDM) in 5,990 male alumni (aged 39 to 68 years) at the University of Pennsylvania. Incidence rates for the development of NIDDM declined as energy expenditure increased from 500 to

3,500 kilocalories per week, and the age-adjusted risk of acquiring NIDDM decreased 6% for each 500-kcal increment of energy expenditure weekly. They found that the protective effect of physical activity was greatest for those who were at highest risk. Similarly, Manson and associates[20] prospectively evaluated the association between exercise and development of NIDDM in 21,271 male physicians from 40 to 84 years of age. Those physicians exercising at least once weekly had an age-adjusted relative risk of developing NIDDM of 0.64 when compared to those exercising less. The age-adjusted relative risk decreased with increasing exercise, and the inverse relationship of exercise to the risk of developing NIDDM was most pronounced in the obese physicians.

Prevalence of Regular Physical Activity

Given that regular physical exercise has been demonstrated to retard the decline in cardiovascular fitness and reduce the risks of cardiovascular disease, NIDDM, and mortality from all causes, it seems only reasonable that large numbers of midlife individuals would be exercising regularly to promote health. In fact, nothing could be further from the truth. The 1985 National Health Interview Survey demonstrated quite convincingly that midlife men between the ages of 45 and 64 are by and large sedentary.[21] Less than 5% of this population exercised regularly at levels sufficient to promote cardiovascular fitness, and over 30% were entirely sedentary (Fig. 2). Approximately 30% exercised regularly in a nonintensive manner and another 30% were irregularly active. Similar findings were reported for women in the same age group. Hence, a large population is at high risk for significant morbidity and mortality. The U.S. Department of Health and Human Services has recommended a reduction in the proportion of individuals aged 6 years and older who engage in no leisure time physical activity to no more than 15% by the year 2000.[22]

Because physical activity has been demonstrated to promote fitness and health, it is important to consider those factors that influence the decision to exercise regularly. Sallis and associates[23] examined physical activity patterns in 1,003 men and 716 women, aged 18 to 90 years. Prior exercise habits or sports participation strongly predicted the adoption or continuation of regular physical activity. Interestingly, women were found to be more strongly motivated by social factors than men, who were influenced primarily by convenience. Additionally, older women were found to be more likely to drop out from a regular physical activity program.

Summary

Regular aerobic training has been found to retard the natural age-related decline in cardiorespiratory fitness. Aerobic training at modest intensity has been shown to be effective in limiting this decline,

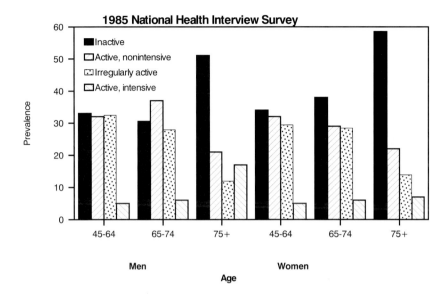

Fig. 2 *Prevalence of four patterns of physical activity. (Reproduced with permission from Casperson CJ, DiPietro L: National health interview survey: Health promotion/disease prevention supplement. Med Sci Sports Exerc 1985;23:5105.)*

although the absolute threshold at which this occurs has not been clearly established. However, health benefits have been demonstrated at training intensities well below those necessary to promote cardiovascular fitness.

A significant portion of the population is sedentary, and therefore, at increased risk for chronic disease. Health-care professionals are strongly encouraged to emphasize the benefits of regular physical activity as part of a well-designed health promotion program. Further information is required to identify those factors that motivate individuals to exercise regularly, so that physicians and health-care providers may optimize their ability to influence patients to exercise regularly. Regular exercise would not only significantly reduce morbidity and mortality from chronic disease, but also foster a greater sense of well-being and vitality in the midlife adult.

References

1. Menard D, Stanish WD: The aging athlete. *Am J Sports Med* 1989;17:187-196.

2. Wei JY: Age and the cardiovascular system: Review article. *N Engl J Med* 1992;327:1735-1739.

3. Siegel AJ, Warhol MJ, Lang G: Muscle injury and repair in ultra long distance runners, in Sutton JR, Brock RM (eds): *Sports Medicine for the Mature Athlete*. Indianapolis, IN, Benchmark Press, 1986, pp 35-43.

4. Åstrand I: Aerobic work capacity in men and women and with special reference to age. *Acta Physiol Scand Suppl* 1960;169:1-92.

5. Saltin B, Grimby G: Physiological analysis of middle-aged and old former athletes: Comparison with still active athletes of the same ages. *Circulation* 1968;38:1104-1115.

6. Bottiger LE: Regular decline in physical working capacity with age. *Br Med J* 1973;3:270-271.

7. Pollock ML, Foster C, Knapp D, et al: Effect of age and training on aerobic capacity and body composition of master athletes. *J Appl Physiol* 1987;62:725-731.

8. Forman DE, Manning WJ, Hauser R, et al: Enhanced left ventricular diastolic filling associated with long-term endurance training. *J Gerontol* 1992;47:M56-M58.

9. Child JS, Barnard RJ, Taw RL: Cardiac hypertrophy and function in master endurance runners and sprinters. *J Appl Physiol* 1984;57:176-181.

10. Kasch FW, Boyer JL, Van Camp SP, et al: The effect of physical activity and inactivity on aerobic power in older men (A longitudinal study). *Phys Sports Med* 1990;18:73-83.

11. American College of Sports Medicine. Position stand: The recommended quantity and quality of exercise for developing and maintaining cardiorespiratory and muscular fitness in healthy adults. *Med Sci Sports Exerc* 1990;22:265-274.

12. Pollock ML, Miller HS Jr, Janeway R, et al: Effects of walking on body composition and cardiovascular function of middle-aged man. *J Appl Physiol* 1971;30:126-130.

13. King AC, Haskell WL, Taylor CB, et al: Group- vs. home-based exercise training in healthy older men and women: A community-based clinical trial. *JAMA* 1991;266:1535-1542.

14. Paffenbarger RS Jr, Hyde RT, Wing AL, et al: Physical activity, all-cause mortality, and longevity of college alumni. *N Engl J Med* 1986;314:605-613.

15. Blair SN, Kohl HW III, Paffenbarger RS Jr, et al: Physical fitness and all-cause mortality: A prospective study of healthy men and women. *JAMA* 1989;262:2395-2401.

16. Duncan JJ, Gordon NF, Scott CB: Women walking for health and fitness: How much is enough? *JAMA* 1991;266:3295-3299.

17. Busby MJ, Bellantoni MF, Tobin JD, et al: Glucose tolerance in women: The effects of age, body composition, and sex hormones. *J Am Geriatr Soc* 1992;40:497-502.

18. Seals DR, Hagberg JM, Hurley BF, et al: Effects of endurance training on glucose tolerance and plasma lipid levels in older men and women. *JAMA* 1984;252:645-649.

19. Helmrich SP, Ragland DR, Leung RW, et al: Physical activity and reduced occurrence of non-insulin-dependent diabetes mellitus. *N Engl J Med* 1991;325:147-152.

20. Manson JE, Nathan DM, Krolewski AS, et al: A prospective study of exercise and incidence of diabetes among US male physicians. *JAMA* 1992;268:63-67.

21. Caspersen CJ, DiPietro L: National estimates of physical activity among older adults. *Med Sci Sports Exerc* 1991;23:S106.

22. *Promoting Health/Preventing Disease: Year 2000 Objectives for the Nation: Draft for Public Review and Comment*. Washington, DC, Public Health Service, US Department of Health and Human Services, 1989.

23. Sallis JF, Hovell MF, Hofstetter CR: Predictors of adoption and maintenance of vigorous physical activity in men and women. *Prev Med* 1992;21:237-251.

Chapter 17

Effects of Aerobic Training in Midlife Populations

Nicolás Terrados, MD, PhD

Introduction

Ever-increasing industrialization and more sedentary lifestyles, along with many of the customs of our consumer society, have brought about an increase in recent decades of so-called "diseases of civilization" (ie, diabetes, hypertension, arteriosclerosis, obesity, high cholesterol, etc). In spite of many information programs about the benefits of exercise during midlife, statistics reveal that few people in this age group take part in exercise programs during their leisure time.

The positive effects of regular aerobic exercise on health have been demonstrated in many studies. Nevertheless, the effects of physical activity on the different body systems differ depending on duration, intensity, number of sessions, type of exercise, and age. Most of these studies were performed with young subjects and, in some cases, a geriatric population, but very few were performed with a midlife population. It is important to emphasize that the scientific studies are carried out with well-controlled groups (with good coaches, training programs, gyms, etc), many times in an artificial situation. However, in real life situations, physicians see "normal" midlife people who exercise a few times per week, without professional supervision. It is of interest to know if the effects of aerobic exercise are as positive in these cases as in the scientific studies.

Aerobic Training

Aerobic Exercise

Dynamic aerobic exercise is defined as rhythmic contractions of skeletal muscle, with an intensity that would not produce an accumulation of lactate in blood, and could be maintained at least 20 minutes. Aerobic metabolism increases in proportion to the mass of muscle involved and the intensity of exercise. Blood flow increases more than tenfold, due to a decreased arterial resistance and opening or dilatation of the capillary beds of working muscle. Cardiac output and heart rate increase three to four times with increasing oxygen uptake, whereas stroke volume increases only to a minor extent.[1]

Repeated performance of dynamic aerobic exercise produces a training effect. The benefits are then maintained after the exercise is completed to yield benefits in the resting state, such as lower blood pressure, improved blood lipid profiles, and better heart efficiency.

Aerobic Training Effect

Generally, aerobic training promotes a combination of rather well-known adaptations in the skeletal muscles, the cardiovascular system, the autonomic nervous system, and the hormonal responses. In the skeletal muscle, there are two important adaptations with aerobic training. First, there is an increase in concentration of enzymes for the citric acid cycle, for fatty acid oxidation, and for the electron transport system. The net result is an augmentation of the metabolic capacities that are associated with the mitochondria (and the respiratory capacity) and an increase in the use of fat as a source of energy. Second, there is an increase in capillarization of the trained muscles, with both a greater number of capillaries per muscle fiber and a decrease of the area supplied by a single capillary.[2]

The cardiovascular adaptations include a greater stroke volume and maximum cardiac output, and an enhanced ability to lower peripheral resistance during strenuous exercise. The autonomic nervous system and hormonal adaptations to aerobic exercise training include increased vagal tone at rest and a blunted catecholamine response to submaximal exercise.[3]

One of the most important consequences of these adaptations is the shift to greater reliance on fat as a fuel for muscular exercise. This occurs with a glycogen-sparing effect that contributes to a greater endurance capacity and with a reduction in plasma triglyceride concentration and an increase in high-density lipoprotein (HDL) mass, due especially to increases in HDL_2 cholesterol and apolipoprotein A-I.[4]

Other consequences are that the heart rate and blood pressure are proportionately less for any given submaximal work load, sympathetic discharge is less, and peripheral vascular resistance is lower. In summary, aerobic training induces an increase in the aerobic capacity of the person.

Another important aspect is the psychological benefit of aerobic activity; it reduces anxiety and depression. Exercise improves functioning in a host of other life areas, including sleeping patterns and occupational satisfaction and efficiency.[5]

Aerobic Capacity and Age

Aerobic capacity is defined as the capacity to take in, transport, and use oxygen. The maximal oxygen uptake indicates the capacities of the systems, organs, and tissues involved. It is inversely related to a number of heart disease risk factors and directly related to long-term work performance.

Fries[6] has suggested the use of maximal oxygen uptake as an important marker for the determination of aging. It seems an excellent choice because it tells so much about health and performance, and because there is a substantial body of research describing its decline with age. However, the literature concerning the decline in maximal oxygen uptake with age is confusing. Although the majority of cross-sectional and longitudinal studies report an annual decline of 0.5 ml/kg/min,[7] others show a slower rate of decline, and in some cases an increase, depending on the level of physical activity.[8] When considering the changes in maximal oxygen uptake, it is important to take into account the increase in body fat with age. In some cases, the decrease in maximal oxygen intake per body weight with age could have been much less if the body fat had not increased.[9] It is generally accepted that in sedentary people there is a 5% to 10% loss of aerobic capacity per decade after 25 years; by 50 years the cumulative loss of function will be approximately 25%. However, training can give rise to a 20% increase in aerobic power, while eliminating surplus body fat. Thus, there is a potential to retain or restore aerobic capacity to levels of someone 20 years younger.[10,11]

Aerobic Training Effects in Midlife Population

There are very few studies about the effects of aerobic training in midlife people. Cross-sectional studies do not indicate the actual effect of time on those tested. Longitudinal studies show what actually happens with aerobic training but are scarce. In most of them, the effects are similar to those produced in younger populations. Many of the studies carried out with middle-aged populations focus on the effects of aerobic training on the plasma lipids profile and its relationship with coronary heart diseases. For example, in a study of 14 sedentary middle-aged men who increased their activity over two years by running approximately 12 miles per week, there was a decrease in their body fat content from 21.6% to 18% and, at the same time, an increase in their caloric intake by an average of 400 calories per day. During this time, their mean total cholesterol (T-C) concentration decreased while their HDL-cholesterol (HDL-C) concentration increased, both significantly.[12] The mechanism underlying these changes in lipoproteins after aerobic training is the enhanced capacity of skeletal muscle to use free fatty acids as fuel during exercise, due to the changes in mitochondrial size and number, enzyme activity, and capillary density. All of these improve the ability of the muscle to oxidize fat.

In our local community (Avilés, Asturias Spain), we studied the effects of aerobic training in a midlife population and focused on the type of aerobic exercise that ordinary people usually perform (aerobic classes, 3 to 4 times weekly). Below, we present in brief a description of one of these studies.

Aim of the Study

The aim of the study was to investigate two things. First, do midlife people exercising in standard activities three times per week obtain the same positive effects as the groups studied in highly controlled studies? Second, does the theoretical improvement continue year after year? For these purposes, we studied a group of midlife women who had taken part in an aerobic exercise program, with classes three times per week for at least two years. After four months, we studied the group again to determine the effects of this exercise program (three to four months is the time period normally used in longitudinal training studies).

Subjects and Methods

Twenty-four female subjects ranging in age from 26 to 56 years (mean $\pm$ SD $=$ 39. 1 $\pm$ 8.26) volunteered for this study. All of them had been regularly attending informal aerobic classes three times per week or less for 2 years at the start of the study (mean $=$ 4.4 years, SD $=$ 1.4, range $=$ 6.2 years). Four of them dropped out before the end of the study.

Aerobic Training Procedures　The aerobic exercise program consisted of a variety of repetitive rhythmic activities (eg, running, dancing, etc) for 60 minutes three times weekly. Each 60-minute class opens with warm-up activities, moves through more vigorous exercises for 20 to 35 minutes, and ends with a cool-down phase. During some classes, the heart rates of the subjects were recorded by telemetric pulsometers (Sport-Tester, Finland), to determine whether, in the middle portion of the class, the exercise raised the heart rate to at least 60% of the predicted maximal heart rate.

The subjects were tested before and after a four-month period of aerobic class training. The tests consisted of evaluation of their weight, height, body composition, and maximal oxygen uptake. All subjects had a complete medical examination before the study began.

Evaluation of Body Composition　Skinfold thickness measurements were made with a Harpender caliper at six sites (subscapular, triceps, chest, abdomen, suprailiac, and anterior thigh) using the

Table 1 Summary of the main physical and physiological characteristics of the participants in the aerobic training program, before and after four months of training

Parameter	Before	After
Weight (kg)		
mean	59.02	58.40
SD	6.57	6.04
% Fat		
mean	17.7	17.08
SD	3.93	3.30
Max HR (b/min)		
mean	182.7	183.5
SD	8.4	7.1
ExercTIME (sq)		
mean	586.5	617.3*
SD	82.4	84.6
$\dot{V}O_2$max (ml/min)		
mean	2171	2209
SD	371	367
$\dot{V}O_2$/kg(ml/kg/min)		
mean	37.4	37.9
SD	7.7	4.7
VEmax (l/min)		
mean	81.4	84.2
SD	12.1	12.6

n = 20
* significant differences between before and after ($p<0.01$).

landmarks described by Yuhasz.[13] Percentage of body fat was estimated from the skinfold measurements using the equations of Yuhasz.[13]

Maximal Oxygen Uptake Maximal oxygen uptake was evaluated through a progressive treadmill exercise test. Metabolic measurements were taken with an open circuit metabolic cart (MMC 4400tc, Sensormedics, USA).

Results After the four-month aerobic training period only the time of exercise performed appears to change significantly, whereas the other parameters do not show variations. The mean value and standard deviation are given in Table 1 for weight, percentage of body fat, maximal heart rate, time of exercise, maximal oxygen uptake in absolute and relative to body weight values, and maximal ventilation.

Discussion At the beginning of the study the group of active women selected had a higher aerobic capacity (mean value $\pm$SD = 37.4 $\pm$7.7 ml/kg/min) than sedentary women of the same age (29.8 $\pm$7.1),[14] as was expected after two years of physical activity. However, after the four months of aerobic training they did not show any clear additional improvements in aerobic capacity, weight, or body fat. The subjects demonstrated a small improvement in their exercise capacity.

Our results showed that midlife women who exercise regularly in a self-selected and nonvigorous program have already achieved a high level of fitness that is not improved further with a vigorous training program. If the informal program was not successful, then large aerobic gains would have been expected. It is encouraging that these active women had achieved gains in health status without requiring a highly organized program that would be difficult to implement.

References

1. Åstrand P-O, Rodahl K: *Textbook of Work Physiology: Physiological Bases of Exercise,* ed 3. New York, NY, McGraw-Hill, 1986.
2. Holloszy JO, Coyle EF: Adaptations of skeletal muscle to endurance exercise and their metabolic consequences. *J Appl Physiol* 1984;56:831-838.
3. Grimby G, Saltin B: Physiological analysis of physically well-trained middle-aged and old athletes. *Acta Med Scand* 1966;179:513-526.
4. Haskell WL, Stefanick ML, Superko R: Influence of exercise on plasma lipids and lipoproteins, in Horton ES, Terjung RL (eds): *Exercise, Nutrition, and Energy Metabolism*. New York, NY, Macmillan Publishing, 1988, pp 213-227.
5. Hayden RM, Allen GJ, Camaione DN: Some psychological benefits resulting from involvement in an aerobic fitness from the perspectives of participants and knowledgeable informants. *J Sports Med-Phys Fitness* 1986;26:67-76.
6. Fries JF: Aging, natural death, and the compression of morbidity. *N Engl J Med* 1980;303:130-135.
7. Shephard RJ: *Physical Activity and Aging*. London, Croom Helm, 1978, pp 52-145.
8. Kasch FW, Wallace JP: Physiological variables during 10 years of endurance exercise. *Med Sci Sports Exerc* 1976;8:5-8.
9. Sharkey BJ: Functional vs chronologic age. *Med Sci Sports Exerc* 1987;19:174-178.
10. Heath GW, Hagberg JM, Ehsani AA, et al: A physiological comparison of young and older endurance athletes. *J Appl Physiol* 1981;51:634-640.
11. Quirion A, DeCareful D, Laurencelle L, et al: The physiological response to exercise with special reference to age. *J Sports Med-Phys Fitness* 1987;27:143-150.
12. Wood PD, Terry RB, Haskell WL: Metabolism of substrates: Diet, lipoprotein metabolism, and exercise. *Fed Proc* 1985;44:358-363.
13. Yuhasz MS: *The Effects of Sports Training on Body Fat in Man With Prediction of Optimal Body Weight*. Urbana, IL, University of Illinois, 1962. Thesis.
14. Perez-Landaluce J, Fernandez B, Terrados N: Modificaciones de la Gimnasia de Mantenimiento en Mujeres. *V European Congress of Sports Medicine*. Barcelona, 1988.

Chapter 18

Endocrine Response to Training Programs in Midlife

Charles Y. Guezennec, MD, PhD

Introduction

The continuation of physical training through midlife is of major epidemiologic interest. The question is the extent to which physical training is able to prevent or forestall aging processes that typically start at midlife. To provide some answers to this question, I will successively review the aging theories and the consequences of aging on energy metabolism and supporting tissues, as well as the influence of hormones on this process. Using these data, I will compare the hormonal response to training of young, midlife, and old subjects, and I will try to define relationships between the hormonal response to physical training and protection against the aging process.

The Aging Process

The current state of knowledge on the aging mechanism has been comprehensively reviewed by Treton and Courton.[1] Without our conscious awareness, the continuous biologic process of senescence begins as soon as we are born and constantly changes the structure and operating processes of our bodies. Senescence occurs at different rates and in different patterns for various categories of cells, tissues, and organs. It affects all strata of living matter, from the simplest molecules to the most sophisticated organisms.

Two theories, not necessarily contradictory, have attracted the attention of gerontologists over these past 20 years, one implying that aging is an unpredictable (stochastic) phenomenon, the other defending the idea that aging is programmed. These theories rely on the general concept that each organism has its own quota of life to live and will age and die as a function of the use made of this quota. Numerous experiments have been run to try to modify this quota by various factors: body temperature, caloric restriction, and physical training. In cold-blooded animals, it is possible to shorten or prolong life span by modifying body temperature, which has a direct effect on their metabolism. In mammals, small species such as rats and mice, which have a high metabolism, live a short time, whereas larger species such as cows and horses, with a lower metabolism, live longer.

Dietary restriction in mice and rats resulted in a longer life span and reduced the normal decline in the immune system associated with aging. In various cases, dietary restriction also reduced the incidence of certain diseases, including cancer. While weight control has the strongest positive effects on life expectancy, too few long-term investigations have been performed to provide evidence of such results in humans.

Physical training has recently been recommended as a way to improve health and prolong life.[2] The life expectancy of laboratory rats is increased if regular moderate physical training (equivalent to jogging in man) is started in early life (Fig. 1). Regular exercise improves the performance of the heart and lungs, reinforces bone strength, and prevents cardiovascular diseases, yet the effects of physical training on life span are still unknown.

Several factors influenced by physical exercise may act upon aging. Free radicals, generated by muscular effort, can react with many biologic molecules, such as fatty acids, DNA, and proteins. Modified lipids, including peroxide, alter the structure of biologic membranes, causing lysosomes to rupture, releasing the peroxidized or undegradable polymerized elements, which can ultimately promote aging.

Hormonal and immune phenomena resulting from physical exercise may act on an internal clock or pacemaker that controls aging. There are two major categories of pacemaker: in one, the pacemaker is connected to the brain and is under the neuroendocrine control of the anterior hypophysis; in the other, the pacemaker is connected to the thymus or immune system.

Pacemaker Hypotheses

Pacemaker Connected to the Hypophysis   The hypophysis is a gland that plays a key role in the life cycle of vertebrates, providing neurohormonal control of such processes as growth and sexual maturity. Underfeeding depresses the function of the anterior hypophysis, delays maturation, and prolongs life span. A substantial increase in life span is observed in rats hypophysectomized in early life and administered a treatment of corticosteroids. The aging rates of collagen, the kidneys, and the immune system of these animals are lower than in control rats, and the incidence of vascular diseases is also reduced.

Pacemaker Connected to the Thymus and Immune System   The immune system changes with maturation and aging, and it could play the role of the aging pacemaker, resulting in a decline in immune control by T cells and growing autoimmunity. Changes in the T-cell immune system take place during aging and play a role in cer-

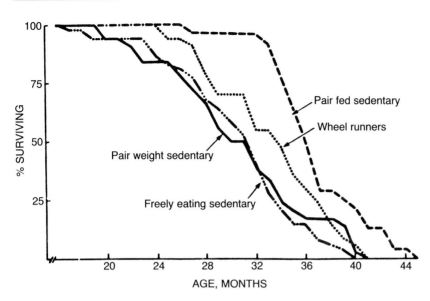

Fig. 1 *Survival curves for rats submitted to physical training (wheel runners) or food restricted (pair weight sedentary) compared to sedentary rates. (Reproduced with permission from Hagberg JM, Seals DR, Yerg JE, et al: Metabolic responses to exercise in young and older athletes and sedentary men. J Appl Physiol 1988;65:900-908.)*

tain age-related diseases, including rheumatisms. However, the question is the role of the immune phenomenon as a causal agent of aging. We will see later how it is possible to relate the hormonal response to physical exercise with its influences on the thymic and immune systems.

Metabolic and Degenerative Diseases Associated With Aging

Aside from unavoidable cell death, any of a number of diseases that occur at midlife may accelerate the aging process. The high epidemiologic prevalence of cardiovascular and metabolic diseases places them at the forefront of investigations. It has been unequivocally shown that the normal aging process is associated with enhanced resistance to insulin, which is one cause of increased concentrations of circulating lipids and, particularly, very-low-density lipids (VLDL). This increase is associated with a gradual elevation of insulin concentrations in rats fed *ad libitum*.[3] In rats, restricted feeding, which is associated with lower levels of serum insulin and circulating lipids, increases life span.[4] These data support the idea that initial variations in sensitivity to insulin are the cause of changes in circulating lipid concentrations. The effect of physical training on the prevention of metabolic diseases results largely from the effects of physical exercise on the regulation of insulin.

A decrease in the level of insulin and an increase in the utilization of glucose are observed during physical exercise. Considering the role of insulin in the entry of glucose into the muscle, this phenomenon may appear to be a paradox. However, this apparent contradiction disappears when the fact that exercise enhances glucose transportation into muscles is considered. This phenomenon occurs at low levels of insulin, but not in the absence of insulin, and is associated in part with a significant increase in sensitivity to insulin during physical exercise. Physical training makes this effect long-lasting and permanently increases sensitivity to insulin, thus playing a key role in the metabolic changes induced by physical exercise.

A study of animal models shows enhanced glucose transfer with the same concentration of insulin on rat muscles after 3 weeks of training (Fig. 2).[5] The mechanism of this enhanced sensitivity to insulin is associated with reinforced insulin-receptor binding, and also with an increase in tyrosine kinase activity at the postreceptor stage. These studies on animals explain the effects of physical training on healthy humans. Recent research by Sato and associates[6] using the glucose/insulin clamp method, which biochemically holds glucose at a constant level and challenges the system with insulin, showed a substantial increase in sensitivity to insulin in trained subjects compared to sedentary subjects.

However, another hormonal factor might explain the effects of physical training on metabolism. Recent results by Rivière and associates[7] show that lypolysis induced by increasing concentrations of epinephrine is greater in preparations of adipocytes sampled from trained women, which shows that sensitivity to catecholamines increases under the effect of physical training. Other studies indicate enhanced metabolization of lipids, depending on the activation of enzymatic systems such as muscle lipoprotein lipase activity. This system is activated by plasma catecholamines. Such actions, combined with the various levels of lipid metabolism, explain the difference in lipid concentrations in sedentary and trained subjects. The comparative study by Martin and associates[8] on changes in lipid concentrations as a function of three levels of physical activity demonstrated decreases in cholesterol and triglyceride levels and an increased high-density lipid (HDL) fraction. Such results can be associated with the enhanced sensitivity to insulin and catecholamines resulting from physical training.

The Effect of Aging on Support Tissues

The degeneration of support tissues, bones, and muscles, which gradually takes place with aging, is a significant problem because it influences the motor activity of older individuals. In this review, data obtained from immobilization protocols will be used, because the reduction in activity is one of the main factors causing a shrinkage of muscle mass in older subjects. Aging processes reduce muscle mass

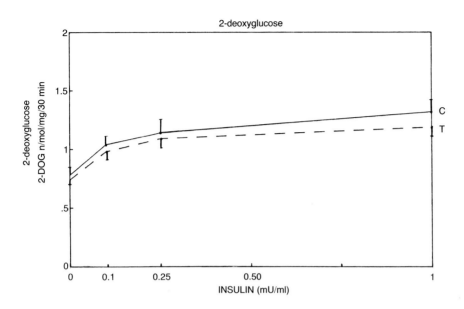

Fig. 2 *Effects of 3 weeks of treadmill running training on 2-deoxyglucose transport in soleus muscle of rat (C, trained rates; T, control sedentary rates). (Reproduced with permission from Guezennec CY, Pesquies PC, Satabin P: Etude comparative de la tolérance au glucose dans les populations de sportifs âgés et de sédentaires. Médecine du Sport 1983;6:324-327.)*

and contractility.[9] This muscular atrophy is associated with a preferential decrement in the number of fast-twitch fibers. Physical training is capable of reducing the muscular atrophy caused by aging (Fig. 3).[10] I will use my knowledge of the influence of hormones on muscle tissue to suggest hypotheses on the protective role of physical training through hormonal responses. The main hormones that can act on muscles are androgens, glucocorticoids, thyroid hormones, and growth hormone (GH).

Role of Androgens   Numerous studies have shown that androgenic steroids have an anabolic effect. Histologic analysis of this anabolic effect shows that the increase in muscle mass results from an increase in the number of noncontractile proteins. The administration of testosterone to immobilized rats prevents weight loss in postural muscles, but does not prevent changes affecting contractile proteins.[11,12] Immobilization also reduces the affinity of muscle testosterone receptors.[13,14]

Role of Glucocorticoids   Numerous investigations[13] have shown that hyperadrenocorticism is associated with a reduction in muscle mass. This muscular atrophy results from a negative nitrogen bal-

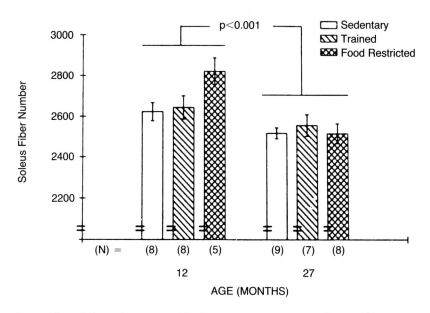

Fig. 3 *Effect of physical training and food restriction on soleus muscle mass of young and 27-month-old rats. (Reproduced with permission from Daw CK, Starnes JW, White TP: Muscle atrophy and hypoplasia with aging: Impact of training and food restriction. J Appl Physiol 1988;64:2428-2432.)*

ance impairing protein synthesis and enhancing protein degradation. This response is selective for the type of muscle fiber: protein catabolism is clearly greater for fast-twitch fibers, slow-twitch fibers being more resistant to the atrophying effect of glucocorticoids. Physical training interferes with the catabolic action of glucocorticoids on the skeletal muscle. This protective effect is much more efficient for slow-twitch fibers.

Role of Thyroid Hormones Skeletal muscle is a priority target for thyroid hormones, whose main role is to regulate the synthesis of the various types of contractile proteins. Elevated concentrations of thyroid hormones increase the synthesis of fast contractile proteins and the formation of fast-twitch fibers. Conversely, hypothyroidism reduces the number of fast-twitch fibers.[13]

Role of Growth Hormone The role of growth hormone on growth and protein synthesis of the skeletal muscle is well documented. Studies of animals with GH-secreting pituitary tumors show increases in the weight of muscles and in the surface area of slow-twitch fibers, the surface area of fast-twitch fibers being barely influenced by GH. This enlargement in muscle volume is the result of an increase in protein synthesis. There is an increase in the number of satellite cells in young animals, but not in adult animals. Such structural modifications in the skeletal muscle do not induce changes in fiber types. GH can act either in direct interaction with a muscle receptor or by increasing somatomedin concentrations in the muscle.

The Effect of Training on the Aging Process

The Effect of Aging and Physical Training on Bone Tissue

The decrease in bone density associated with age is a well-known phenomenon. Like other tissues, bone is a dynamic system that maintains its condition by constant renewal. Bone remodeling may diminish with age.[15] In most individuals in midlife and beyond, there is a trend toward a negative balance in bone remodeling, resulting in a loss of bone mineral. It has been shown that physical exercise is capable of counteracting this osteoporosis typically associated with aging, and that this is a long-term effect. The increase in bone mass (or minimized bone loss) by midlife resulting from intense physical activity could be the main protective factor against aging. This increase in bone mass is due mainly to mechanical factors acting on the bone.[16] However, the role of hormonal factors should also be mentioned. The metabolism of bone cells is influenced by the parathormone-calcitonin complex, but also by androgens, GH, and thyroid hormones. Bone demineralization is observed during overtraining, and is thought to be caused by the hypogonadism that may develop under such circumstances. We can, therefore, hypothesize that the hormonal response to physical training can affect bone.

Concerning support tissues, bones, and muscles, it can be hypothesized that the increased concentrations of anabolic hormones under the effect of well-structured physical training can explain muscle and bone anabolism.

The Effect of Physical Training on the Immune System

The effects of physical exercise on the immune system have recently been reviewed.[17] Isolated physical exercise increases almost all classes of leukocytes and lymphocytes. The appearance of leukocytes in blood probably results from the various shifts of immunocompetent cells among the various pools of the body. This mobilization of leukocyte classes is selective and does not exceed 24 hours. Chronic physical exercise seems to diminish the number of certain immunocompetent cells, although this has not been demonstrated uniformly. The meaning of changes in the numbers of cells induced by isolated physical exercise can be discussed. In the case of chronic exercise, the changes could be interpreted as a sign of immune deficiency in the athlete. They could also explain changes in the activities of immunocompetent cells.

The mechanisms of this immune deficiency observed in athletes remain to be unequivocally confirmed by clinical observation, and the many immune changes associated with physical exercise are, so far, mostly unknown. However, two mechanisms could be involved: changes in the number and in the activity of immunocompetent cells. Thus, changes in the activity of "natural killer" cells induced by exercise could be explained in part by changes in the numbers of these cells, whereas other activities could be affected by hormonal changes. The increased concentrations of glucocorticoids and catecholamines and the depressed concentrations of circulating androgens could induce a hormonal syndrome causing immune deficiency in the endurance athlete.

Hormonal Responses to Training in Young and Midlife Individuals

Hormonal Responses to Physical Exercise in Young Individuals

The hormonal responses to physical exercise in young people have been discussed in several reviews on this topic.[18,19] Short-term intense physical exercise induces a very rapid increase in catecholamine concentrations, resulting in a decrease in insulin and an increase in glucagon. This type of exercise also induces increases in the levels of GH, testosterone, and glucocorticoids. During prolonged exercise, these hormonal changes tend to amplify, except for plasma testosterone, which decreases. A high testosterone to cortisol ratio is observed in well-trained subjects. Conversely, overtraining depresses testosterone concentrations and hypophyseal reactivity to such stimuli as hypoglycemia.

Several hypotheses can be derived from these observations: (1) The effects of physical exercise on pancreatic hormones (insulin and glucagon) and catecholamines could cause the enhanced tolerance to glucose and lipid metabolism. (2) The effects of physical exercise on anabolic hormones (GH and androgens) could enhance bone and muscle protein metabolism. (3) The effects of very long and exhausting exercise, such as depressed levels of anabolic hormones and prolonged increases in glucocorticoids, could result in bone demineralization and depressed immune defenses.

The Effect of Physical Training on Metabolic Hormone Responses in Midlife Individuals

The tolerance to glucose of endurance-trained midlife subjects (mean age, 46 years) has been compared with that of young athletes and young sedentary individuals (mean age, 19 years).[5] The midlife male athletes ran 60 km/week and had a $\dot{V}O_2max$ of 63 ml/min per kg. Glucose and insulin responses were identical in the young and midlife endurance-trained groups and substantially lower than in the sedentary group. Two investigations have compared the resting insulin levels of older trained subjects (60 to 70 years old) with those of sedentary subjects of the same age or younger.[20,21] Improved sensitivity to insulin during training seems constant at all ages. A short period of inactivity reverses this effect, so that one could conclude that regular exercise protects against the development of insulin resistance and normalizes glucose tolerance in midlife subjects by means of a short-term effect of exercise.[21]

The response to prolonged submaximal exercise shows differences in the regulation of glycogen levels in trained and sedentary subjects. During 60 minutes of exercise at 70% $\dot{V}O_2$max, glycogen levels increased in young and midlife physically trained subjects, whereas they decreased in sedentary subjects of both age groups. This phenomenon can be due to a better ability of trained subjects to tap glycogen stores. The response to glucagon was much lower in both trained groups. A more substantial increase in catecholamine concentrations was observed in both trained groups, indicating that training enhances sympathetic stimulation.

A direct study using labeled norepinephrine perfusion confirmed that physical training significantly increased the production of catecholamines in midlife trained subjects, but did not affect clearance.[22] The authors correlated this increase in sympathetic stimulation with the increase in resting metabolism (Fig. 4).

In 40- to 70-year-old subjects, physical training thus significantly increases sensitivity to insulin and sympathetic tone. These two hormonal factors play a direct role in the improvement of lipid metabolism and reduction in fatty mass of midlife trained subjects when compared to their sedentary counterparts.[23] The first hypothesis regarding the role of hormones on energetic metabolism is confirmed: in midlife subjects, physical training increases the efficiency of insulin and circulating catecholamines on target tissues, controlling the regulation of the energy metabolism.

The Effect of Physical Training on Hormones That Influence Bone and Muscle Condition in Midlife Subjects

The gradual decrease in androgen concentrations with the progression of age has been extensively described. During an investigation of responses to stress, assays were made on midlife athletes competing in a modern pentathlon.[14] The mean age of the group was 44 years. At the time of this investigation, subjects were training 1 hour each day on average; three subjects had trained for 3 hours each day during the 3 weeks prior to the investigation. Resting plasma testosterone concentration in this population was 2.96 ± 0.28 mg/ml, lower than that of younger athletes (mean age, 23 years) participating in the same contest (4.88 mg/ml) and that of 45-year-old sedentary subjects (4.25 ± 0.18 mg/ml).

Under the effect of the stress associated with a rifle-shooting contest, testosterone concentration in populations of midlife and younger athletes increased by 63% and 56%, respectively. These re-

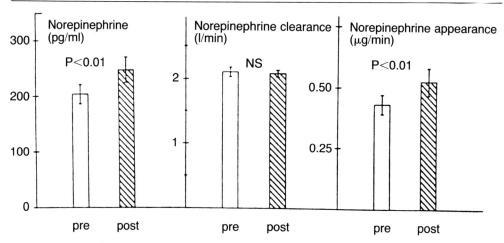

Fig. 4 *Norepinephrine metabolism before (pre) and after (post) endurance training at rest in aged subjects. (Reproduced with permission from Poehlman ET, Danforth E Jr: Endurance training increases metabolic rate and norepinephrine appearance rate in older individuals. Am J Physiol 1991;261:E233-E239.)*

sults show that intense physical training at a sport with several events, such as the modern pentathlon, decreases the plasma testosterone concentration in both younger and older athletes. Concentrations measured in the younger athletes were lower than those measured in a population of athletes practicing strength sports (4.88 ± 1.30 mg/ml versus 6.22 ± 0.12 mg/ml). These data confirmed those of Hackney and associates,[24] which showed a drop in plasma testosterone under the effect of intense endurance training. Midlife athletes reacted the same way as younger ones. The decrease takes place from a mean resting level lowered by age-related changes. In older, intensely trained athletes, the concurrence of these two factors reduce testosterone levels to very low absolute values. The case-by-case examination shows the lowest values in the three midlife athletes who prepared intensely for this contest. Their performance was good: one ranked second for all tests, the other two ranked among the first five places. These findings underline the fact that depressed testosterone levels resulting from intense physical training do not preclude good performance.

The resting levels and the response of glucocorticoids to stress were identical in both populations of athletes. If we consider as valid the fact that the ratio of testosterone to cortisol reflects the anabolic condition, we could believe that midlife athletes are in a catabolic phase. In the absence of clinical signs reflecting muscular or bone intolerance, other factors controlling muscular anabolism must be identified. GH has been considered as playing a possible role. The data of Hagberg and associates[20] show that resting GH concentrations were the same in young and midlife athletes and in their sedentary counterparts. However, the increase in GH under the effect of physical exercise was lower in midlife athletic and sedentary populations. The response of somatomedins to physical exercise was much higher in the younger athletes. These results seem to indicate that the anabolic stimulus resulting from the effect of physical exercise on GH secretion is lower in older subjects.

The tone of the two main hormonal pathways involved in muscle and bone anabolism seems, therefore, to be reduced in midlife high-level athletes. The beneficial muscle and bone adaptation of these subjects indicates that these pathways probably play a secondary role. Trophic factors resulting from mechanical constraints applying to bones and muscles and the role of innervation on muscles probably compensate for depressed hormonal secretions. A hypothesis could be suggested, correlating the depressed thyroid secretions with the increasing number of slow-twitch fibers under the effect of age, but results are controversial.

Poehlman and Danforth[22] reported that neither physical training nor aging modified the resting concentrations of thyroid hormones. Conversely, Hagberg and associates[20] showed that physical training reduced concentrations of thyroid hormones in young and older athletes. This effect could explain the increase in the number of slow-twitch fibers under the effect of endurance training.

Data published on the response of anabolic hormones in midlife subjects only concern endurance training. The results are not conclusive of an anabolic effect of hormonal adaptations and partly discredit our second hypothesis. However, it would be indispensable to study the hormonal response of midlife subjects to strength training protocols.

The third hypothesis concerns the effect of a prolonged increase in the concentrations of glucocorticoids, associated with a decrease in androgens on immune defenses and bone density. Results obtained on midlife subjects confirm the decrease in androgens under the effect of intense physical training. Resting glucocorticoid levels do not seem to be modified. The reactivity of glucocorticoids to physical exercise or stress is normal. It may, therefore, be suggested that overtraining can induce a catabolic condition in midlife subjects as it does in younger ones. However, no result has so far evidenced a reduction in bone density or immune defenses in intensively training midlife subjects. The only point that we can discuss is indirect: the number of cancers in physically trained populations. Although cancer genesis involves a variety of factors, results suggest that the incidence of this disease tends to diminish in physically active populations. If physical exercise really depresses immune defenses, it is possible that the total number of neoplasms tends to increase. However, the relationships among the ratio of testosterone to cortisol, the type of training, and the immune system should be investigated.

Summary

In conclusion, the study of the hormonal response of midlife subjects to physical exercise indicates a very strong relationship among the increased sensitivity to insulin, the increase in sympathetic tone, and the improvement of the lipid balance and body composition. Changes in the secretion of hormones acting on bone and muscle tissues, such as androgens, GH, and thyroid hormones, are not sufficient to completely explain the beneficial effects of physical training on the musculoskeletal system. The negative effect of intense physical training on the immune system or bone density should be further studied, with reference to the hormonal response of midlife subjects to physical exercise.

References

1. Treton C, Courton Y: Processus du vieillissement. *J Geriat* 1983;42:22-28.
2. Holloszy JO, Smith EK: Effects of exercise on longevity of rats. *Fed Proc* 1987;46:1850-1853.
3. Bracho-Romero E, Reaven GM: Effect of age and weight on plasma glucose and insulin responses in the rat. *J Am Geriatr Soc* 1977;25:299-302.
4. Masoro EJ, Compton C, Yu BP, et al: Temporal and compositional dietary restrictions modulate age-related changes in serum lipids. *J Nutr* 1983;113:880-892.
5. Guezennec CY, Pesquies PC, Satabin P: Etude comparative de la tolérance au glucose dans les populations de sportifs âgés et de sédentaires. *Médecine du Sport* 1983;6:324-327.
6. Sato Y, Iguchi A, Sakamoto N: Biochemical determination of training effects using insulin clamp technique. *Horm Metabol Res* 1984;16:483-486.
7. Rivière D, Crampes F, Beauville M, et al: Lipolytic response of fat cells to catecholamines in sedentary and exercise-trained women. *J Appl Physiol* 1989;66:330-335.
8. Martin RP, Haskell WL, Wood PD: Blood chemistry and lipid profiles of elite distance runners. *Ann NY Acad Sci* 1977;301:346-360.
9. Larsson L, Grimby G, Karlsson J: Muscle strength and speed of movement in relation to age and muscle morphology. *J Appl Physiol* 1979;46:451-456.
10. Daw CK, Starnes JW, White TP: Muscle atrophy and hypoplasia with aging: Impact of training and food restriction. *J Appl Physiol* 1988;64:2428-2432.
11. Tsika RW, Herrick RE, Baldwin KM: Effect of anabolic steroids on overloaded and overloaded suspended skeletal muscle. *J Appl Physiol* 1987;63:2128-2133.
12. Guezennec CY, Ferre P, Serrurier B, et al: Effects of prolonged physical exercise and fasting upon plasma testosterone level in rats. *Eur J Appl Physiol* 1982;49:159-168.
13. Guezennec CY, Serrurier B, Merino D, et al: Atrophie musculaire induite par l'immobilisation et l'hypokinésie. Influence hormonales et applications thérapeutiques. *Rev Franç d'Endocrinologie* 1991;32:149-164.
14. Guezennec CY, Serrurier B, Merino D: Stress et testostérone. *Rapport Ministére Jeunesse et Sport* 1992; n° 91228.
15. Mosekilde L, Viidik A: Age-related changes in bone mass, structure and strength—pathogenesis and prevention. *Int J Sports Med* 1989;10:S90-S92.
16. Pirnay F, Bodeux M, Crielaard JM, et al: Bone mineral content and physical activity. *Int J Sports Med* 1987;8:331-335.
17. Ferry A: Immunomodulations liées a l'exercice musculaire. *Science et Motricité* 1991;13:48-57.

18. Galbo H (ed): *Hormonal and Metabolic Adaptation to Exercise.* Stuttgard, Georg Thieme Verlag, 1983.
19. Terblanche SE: Recent advances in hormonal response to exercise. *Comp Biochem Physiol B* 1989;93:727-739.
20. Hagberg JM, Seals DR, Yerg JE, et al: Metabolic responses to exercise in young and older athletes and sedentary men. *J Appl Physiol* 1988;65:900-908.
21. Rogers MA, King DS, Hagberg JM, et al: Effect of 10 days of physical inactivity on glucose tolerance in master athletes. *J Appl Physiol* 1990;68:1833-1837.
22. Poehlman ET, Danforth E Jr: Endurance training increases metabolic rate and norepinephrine appearance rate in older individuals. *Am J Physiol* 1991;261:E233-E239.
23. Seals DR, Hagberg JM, Allen WK, et al: Glucose tolerance in young and older athletes and sedentary men. *J Appl Physiol* 1984;56:1521-1525.
24. Hackney AC, Sinning WE, Bruot BC: Reproductive hormonal profiles of endurance-trained and untrained males. *Med Sci Sports Exerc* 1988;20:60-65.

Chapter 19

The Reproductive Axis in Endurance Training Women

Alan D. Rogol, MD, PhD

Introduction

Alterations in menstrual cyclicity associated with endurance-type exercise have been widely reported. This association has been based mainly on cross-sectional (questionnaire) studies rather than on direct investigation of the effects of strenuous training on physiologic and endocrinologic parameters.[1-4] Interpretation of the available epidemiologic and cross-sectional data does not provide a clear explanation of the pathogenic mechanisms responsible for the reported alterations, even when multiple regression analysis is performed using some of the various factors associated with altered menstrual function (including amenorrhea) in athletes and nonathletes.[5,6]

The prevalence of "athletic amenorrhea" has been reported to vary widely, from 1% to 43%, compared to 2% to 5% in the general population.[7-9] This range reflects, to a large degree, methodological limitations; for example, the definitions of amenorrhea used include the absence of menstrual periods for anywhere from 4 to 12 months. Moreover, there are wide variations in chronologic age, age at menarche, gynecologic age, prior menstrual status, co-existing health problems, and extent of training (duration and intensity, particularly the latter) before and after menarche. Collectively, available cross-sectional studies indicate that the prevalence of amenorrhea is considerably higher in young, intensively training, competitive athletes than in the general population; however, it must be recognized that alterations in cycle length can occur without cessation of menses, eg, short luteal phase.[10] There are wide variations in cycle length at the extremes of gynecologic age.[11] Young women have great variability in their menstrual cycles and appear particularly susceptible to stressors (eg, psychological and athletic) that inhibit the hypothalamic-pituitary-gonadal axis. Thus, the maturity of this axis may play a dominant role in the prevalence of athletic menstrual cycle alterations.

Also, the age of menarche may be delayed.[12] However, it may be difficult to separate genetic from acquired factors, because Stager and Hatler[13] found that swimmers had a later age of menarche than their nonexercising sisters, whereas nonathletic controls and their sisters did not differ significantly. The nonexercising sisters of athletes were also significantly older at menarche than the controls and their sisters. Thus, although the age of menarche was later in athletes than in all other groups (suggesting a training effect), a genetic component may account for the older age at menarche.

There are no available data on alterations in hypothalamic-pituitary-ovarian function as older exercising women approach the climacteric. It would indeed be difficult to extract those effects due to exercise from those due to the natural waning of ovarian function, especially because the natural waning has such great variance.

Virtually all of the available studies that have sought mechanistic explanations for altered menstrual cycle function involve relatively young women.[14-16] Recently published data from my laboratory,[17] in which long-term training (12 to 24 months) produced very few alterations in the menstrual cycle or in the gonadal axis hormonal concentrations (see below) involved moderately older women, average age 31 years, average 17.2 years postmenarche.

The Menstrual Cycle

The human menstrual cycle is divided into the follicular phase, the luteal phase, and the ovulatory phase. The ovulatory phase is immediately preceded by a surge of gonadotropin release. The normal menstrual cycle requires the highly coordinated action of the hypothalamus, pituitary, ovaries, and uterus. Disorders anywhere along the pathway may cause primary (never having menstruated) or secondary (having previously menstruated) amenorrhea. These disorders may range from minor, including an imperforate hymen, to major, including congenital absence of the uterus, ovarian dysgenesis, or hormonal dysfunction affecting the hypothalamus, pituitary, or ovaries. Lack of menarche is considered pathologic above the age of 16 years, but medical attention should be sought if secondary sexual characteristics are not evident by 14 years. The more common pathologic conditions presenting with primary amenorrhea include gonadal dysgenesis (Turner syndrome), eating disorders (especially anorexia nervosa), and long-term endurance training with low body weight (eg, gymnasts, long-distance runners). Secondary amenorrhea is commonly associated with hypothalamic dysfunction, that is, with diminished gonadotropin-releasing hormone levels (see below). The phases of the menstrual cycle can be diagrammed as shown in Figure 1.

In one of the most comprehensive studies of menstrual cycle length, regularity, and variability, Vollman[11] recorded 31,645 menstrual cycles in 656 women. The follicular and luteal phases were determined in 656 women (31,645 cycles) by using the basal body tem-

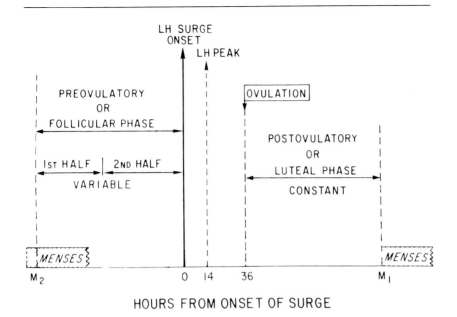

Fig. 1 *Phases of the human menstrual cycle. M₁ represents day 1 of the menstrual flow; M₂ denotes day 2 of the menstrual flow. The follicular phase terminates with the onset of luteinizing hormone (LH) surge, and the luteal phase begins following ovulation. (Reproduced with permission from Yen SSC: The human menstrual cycle, in Yen SSC, Jaffe RB (eds):* Reproductive Endocrinology: Physiology, Pathophysiology and Clinical Management, *ed 2. Philadelphia, PA, WB Saunders, 1986, pp 200-236.)*

perature method. The group of volunteers spanned the entirety of a woman's reproductive life. The mean cycle length decreased from 35.1 days at age 12 years to a minimum of 27.1 days at age 43; thereafter, it rose to 51.9 days by 55 years (Fig. 2). The greatest inter- and intra-individual variability in menstrual cycle length was observed in the early post-menarcheal and pre-menopausal years. At 20 and 30 years (the age of most subjects participating in exercise studies), the median length was 27.9 days, with fifth and ninety-fifth percentiles of 19.7 and 39.2 days (age 20) and 23.1 and 39.4 days (age 30), respectively. At 40 years, the median length was 26.7 days, with fifth and ninety-fifth percentiles of 22.0 and 33.6 days. Vollman[11] also pointed to the more pronounced heterogeneity when chronologic and not gynecologic ages were compared (see below). Based on basal body temperature determinations, he found that in normal menstrual cycles, the variability of the length is mainly determined by the highly variable length of the follicular phase, which ranges from 11 to 25 days, in cycles of 20 and 37 days, respectively. The luteal phase is, however, far more constant (10 to 16 days).

The pituitary gonadotropins, luteinizing hormone (LH) and follicle-stimulating hormone (FSH), stimulate the ovary to make gonad-

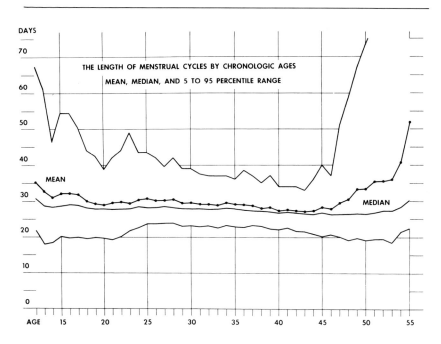

Fig. 2 *The length of the menstrual cycle from menarche to menopause. Menstrual cycles are charted by chronological ages of women, with mean, median, and 5th to 95th percentile range (31,645 menstrual cycles in 656 women). (Reproduced with permission from Vollman RF: The Menstrual Cycle. Philadelphia, PA, WB Saunders, 1977.)*

al steroid hormones and to mature an ovum for release at the midcycle. In females, LH stimulates the synthesis of estrogen and progesterone, and thus promotes oocyte maturation, ovulation, and maintenance of the corpus luteum. FSH is essential for oogenesis and promotes estrogen synthesis by stimulating the aromatase enzyme to convert androgens into estrogens. Receptors for both LH and FSH are linked to the stimulation of the enzyme adenylate cyclase and to the production of cyclic adenosine 3′, 5′-monophosphate (cAMP). Under the influence of FSH, the granulosa cells produce small amounts of estradiol, which permits the surrounding theca cells to develop. Acting together, FSH and estradiol induce LH receptors on the internal layer of the theca cells. Estrogen is thus considered a paracrine effector because it acts locally at adjacent cells. The interplay of the gonadotropins and the gonadal steroids on these two cell types matures the follicle and prepares it for ovulation at midcycle. Following ovulation, the luteal phase is initiated. Luteinization of cells begins immediately, and progesterone synthesis (also regulated by LH) greatly increases over baseline levels. The luteal phase of a nonfertile cycle ends spontaneously in luteolysis approximately 13 days after the ovulatory surge of LH.

The control of the waxing and waning of the ovarian cycle (ie, control of gonadotropin secretion) resides in the hypothalamus and higher centers and is mediated by gonadotropin-releasing hormone (GnRH). GnRH is released in an intermittent, pulsatile manner apparently controlled by unidentified "pacemaker" neurons located in the anterior hypothalamus. This pacemaker (oscillator) triggers one to two hourly pulses ("mini-surges") of LH and FSH (the former are larger) throughout life. The pulses are quite small in the prepubertal child, but they are present as defined recently by very sensitive immunofluorometric assay techniques.

As puberty begins, the pulsatile secretion of GnRH and LH (and thus, FSH) increases significantly in both frequency and amplitude, but only at night, following the onset of sleep. Based on data from infant rhesus monkeys, the LH pulse profiles suggest a GnRH pulse frequency of one per hour in the male[18] and one every three to four hours in the female.[19] The lower frequency favors FSH release and is probably responsible for the relatively high FSH-to-LH ratio in children, especially in girls. LH responses to exogenously administered GnRH are small, and the circulating gonadotropin levels are low during the first decade of life. During early- to midpuberty, the circulating concentrations of LH are kept low during most of the day by the GnRH pulse generator, which is exquisitely sensitive to the negative feedback actions of the gonadal steroid hormones. Later in puberty, there is decreased feedback inhibition by these steroid hormones (hypothalamic "maturation") and the pulsatile release of LH and FSH continues during the daytime as well. Thus, pubertal maturation involves an alteration in the responsivity to GnRH and the predominance of LH secretion (mature) over FSH secretion (prepubertal) (Fig. 3).

In the adult woman, the responsivity of the gonadotropins to GnRH is under complex regulation. High-level estrogen exposure over 36 to 48 hours "sensitizes" the gonadotropins to GnRH; LH responds more than FSH. The timing mechanism for this ovulatory surge resides in the ovary, which regulates the size of the midcycle surge of estradiol, itself requiring FSH, and the appearance of sufficient (low level) production of progesterone. Many extraneous factors can disrupt this orderly pattern. Stress, such as vigorous, endurance-type athletic training, may have profound effects on menstrual cyclicity. Psychological stress may be subjectively greater in amenorrheic compared to eumenorrheic runners.[20]

During the early follicular phase of the menstrual cycle, these ovarian steroid hormones feed back negatively at the GnRH pulse generator; however, critical to the function of this entire neuroendocrine system is its ability to alter the baseline GnRH pulse frequency. In the normal menstrual cycle, when circulating levels of estradiol and progesterone (Fig. 4) are low (early- to midfollicular phase), low-amplitude LH pulses occur once every 90 to 120 minutes. As the levels of estradiol and progesterone increase LH pulse frequency,

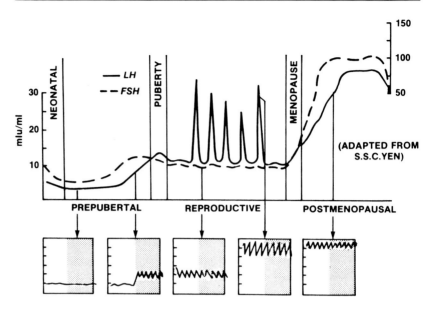

Fig. 3 *The changing pattern and FSH/LH ratio before, during, and following the reproductive phase of the human female's life cycle. The lower boxes illustrate the amplitude of pulsatile LH release through which circulating concentrations are maintained. The shaded areas represent periods of nocturnal sleep. Note that sleep-induced LH rise is uniquely found during pubertal sexual maturation. (Modified with permission from Yen SSC, in Ferin M (ed): Biorhythms and Human Reproduction. New York, NY, John Wiley & Sons, 1974, pp 219-238.)*

which presumably reflects GnRH release, increases to once every 60 to 90 minutes. LH pulse amplitude does not change significantly. The maturing follicle produces estradiol and inhibin, both of which decrease FSH concentrations. The preovulatory rise in LH concentration follows increases in both frequency and amplitude of the LH pulses (estradiol positive feedback), culminating in the ovulatory surge of LH and ovulation itself (Fig. 4). Thus, the ovulatory surge is a consequence of the positive effects of estradiol and progesterone in augmenting the responsivity of the gonadotropin (LH) as it receives the more rapid-frequency GnRH signal.

During the luteal phase (Fig. 4), with high circulating levels of estradiol and progesterone, the circulating pattern of LH shows slow frequency, one pulse every three to five hours, but often of high amplitude. As the corpus luteum ceases to function, and the levels of estradiol, progesterone, and inhibin decrease, the GnRH pulses begin to increase in frequency, and the next ovarian cycle is begun by recruitment of several follicles (Fig. 4). At this time (late luteal phase), FSH secretion is favored over LH, and together with the longer circulating half-life of FSH, there is dominance of FSH, which leads to the development of the next wave of ovarian follicles.

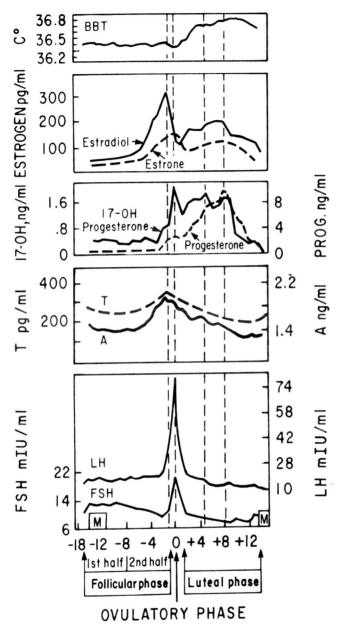

Fig. 4 *The cyclic hormone pattern of the human reproductive cycle centered on the day of peak (day 0). Basal body temperature (BBT) are shown on top, and gonadotropic levels are shown on the bottom. Ovarian steroids (estrogen, progestin, and androgens) are displayed in the center. Days of menstrual bleeding are indicated by M. (Reproduced with permission from Yen SSC: The human menstrual cycle, in Yen SSC, Jaffe RB (eds): Reproductive Endocrinology: Physiology, Pathophysiology and Clinical Management, ed 2. Philadelphia, PA, WB Saunders, 1986, pp 200-236.)*

Exercise and the Menstrual Cycle

Physiologic and psychological stress can have a major impact on the menstrual cycle, mediated in part by the hypothalamic-pituitary axis for the gonadotropins. Responses to exercise must be separated into those occurring acutely and those secondary to prolonged training (adaptive). Many studies have relied upon single hormonal measurements after an exercise session. Because these hormones are secreted in an intermittent, pulsatile manner, widely varying results are not unanticipated. Several studies, however, suggest that during and "immediately" after strenuous exercise, there is a decrease in LH pulse frequency.[21,22] Neither study determined the length of time following significant acute exercise that the gonadotropin release remained altered. Also, neither study was designed to detect a level of exercise intensity above which there were decrements in LH pulse frequency, nor was an effect of training on the acute response to endurance exercise sought.

Few prospective studies have evaluated the effects of endurance training on the menstrual cycle and the pulsatile release of gonadotropins. Boyden and associates[15,23] investigated 19 eumenorrheic (mean age 29.3 years), moderately trained women preparing for a 42-km run during 14 to 15 months of endurance training (running 66 to 110 km per week). Despite unaltered menstrual cyclicity, subtle reproductive system changes occurred. Bullen and associates[24] reported that modest training (at approximately 70% of $\dot{V}O_2max$) was followed by slightly decreased urinary sex-steroid hormone excretion; however, the menstrual cycle was virtually unaltered and all cycles were ovulatory. More recently, recreational runners were shown to have decreased gonadal steroid hormone excretion and disturbed follicular development as evaluated by ultrasound examination.[25] In an important follow-up study, Bullen and associates[14] were able to detect significant alterations in reproductive system function in a group of college-age women who undertook a very rigorous training program over 8 weeks. Many menstrual cycles did not have a midcycle LH surge, and thus, ovulation did not occur although there were few other indications of menstrual cycle disorders. It is possible to conclude that a sudden and marked increase in training volume or intensity is likely to alter the hormonal regulation of the reproductive cycle. These disrupted (anovulatory) cycles may have significant clinical implications for the longer term, ie, the hypoestrogenism of athletic amenorrhea can be accompanied by diminished mineralization of bone and the attendant increased risk for fractures.[26,27]

In hypothalamic amenorrhea, the reproductive axis is inhibited at all levels by products of the hypothalamic-pituitary-adrenal axis (see below). This restraint of the reproductive system conserves energy that might be put to more effective purposes than to prepare for a conception. In anorexia nervosa, hypogonadotropic hypogonadism and amenorrhea occur in virtually 100% of the women. The pulsatile pattern of LH appears to be of low frequency (however, this finding may change as the newer, more sensitive assays are employed) and low amplitude, as in the prepubertal child. Menstrual cycle alterations (short luteal phase, oligomenorrhea, or amenorrhea) occur in endurance training athletes to a greater degree than in nontraining women. Many mechanisms have been proposed (see below), but it is likely that altered release of GnRH and LH plays an important role. In some normally menstruating and other oligomenorrheic runners, Cumming and associates[21] found diminished LH pulse frequency. In established runners with amenorrhea, there was markedly diminished LH pulse frequency in the majority of the women.[16] However, three of nine had LH pulse frequency within the normal range. The data of Cumming and associates[21] are concordant with studies of women with hypothalamic amenorrhea of diverse etiology.[28]

What is the mechanism that transduces the effects of endurance training to diminished GnRH and LH pulse frequency? A critical weight and percentage body fat hypothesis states that a woman must attain a certain weight and body fat percentage to attain menarche or to regain menstrual cyclicity after becoming secondarily oligo- or amenorrheic.[29,30] Too many data are available that do not confirm this hypothesis to accept it as valid.[3] In addition, the original work has been criticized on theoretical and statistical grounds.[31-34] Using a computer algorithm to simulate retrospective sampling from a large population of young women for whom the ages of menarche and initiation of training were known and independently distributed, Stager and associates[33] did not detect a significant relationship between the two variables. More importantly, in a subpopulation that began endurance training before menarche, this milestone was reached later, precisely the result presented by Frisch and McArthur.[29] The concept of delayed menarche in pre-menarchal endurance training girls may thus be based upon flawed statistical reasoning. However, in groups of women, attainment of a "critical" body weight and menarche are well correlated.

The stress or "energy drain" of endurance training[35] is apparently transduced into diminished frequency of GnRH release through the hypothalamic-pituitary-adrenal axis.[36] Studies in animals show that activation of the hypothalamic-pituitary axis for corticotropin-releasing factor (CRH), pro-opiomelanocortin, and ACTH slows the GnRH pulse generator, leading to inadequate ovarian stimulation and suppression of ovarian cycles. Biller and associates[37] have proposed a similar mechanism in nontraining women with hypothalamic amenorrhea who have elevated cortisol levels and diminished cortisol responses to CRH. Another, perhaps larger, group of amenorrheic women with slowed LH pulse frequency may have enhanced suppression of GnRH and LH frequency by hypothalamic opioids, because they respond to opioid blocking agents with an increased LH pulse frequency.[38,39]

Possible mechanisms for the hypogonadism in endurance-trained athletes include disorders (adaptations) in the brain, pituitary, gonads, and other organs (Table 1).

Veldhuis and associates[16] and others[21,36] have presented data that implicate an alteration in the firing rate of the pulse generator for GnRH, demonstrated by slowing of the frequency of LH pulsations. Alteration in the feedback effects of estrogen remains a distinct possibility, because there is evidence[40] that such mechanisms are operative in some women with hypothalamic amenorrhea. There are to date no properly controlled studies in eu-, oligo- or amenorrheic endurance-training women to evaluate this proposed mechanism.

No data in an animal model or in the human are yet available to detect alteration in the synthesis of gonadotropins under running stress. Because the gonadotropin response to GnRH stimulus in amenorrheic runners was capable of augmenting ovarian estrogen production,[16] there must be biologic activity of the secreted LH. For the same reason, it is possible to conclude that the ovary is capable of responding after stimulation with biologically active LH.

It is difficult to completely rule out some of the other suggested mechanisms. Hyperprolactinemia clearly was not a cause in several studies.[16,21,23,36] Although endogenous opioids are capable of inhibiting rhythmic GnRH and LH release, and exercise does stimulate the release of these agents, there are no data to specifically link the slowed GnRH pulse generator to increased opioid peptides. In fact, much of the data presented may not even be relevant, because peripheral concentrations of the opioid peptides were measured, and it is CNS opioid activity that alters the function of the GnRH oscillator. Several investigators,[41-43] using the opioid peptide receptor antagonist naloxone or the orally active naltrexone, have found inconsistent results: either only a few subjects respond[42] or the responses found do not differ between athletes and controls.[43]

Diminished aromatization of androgens and variable metabolic clearance rates remain theoretical mechanisms for menstrual cycle alteration in athletes. However, no in vivo or in vitro data exist for either proposed mechanism in the exercising human.

Loucks and associates[36] assessed the functional integrity of the hypothalamic-pituitary-ovarian and hypothalamic-pituitary-adrenal axes during the early follicular phase of the menstrual cycle in eumenorrheic athletes and in regularly cycling sedentary women. Although the 24 hour pulsatile pattern of ACTH and cortisol did not differ between the groups, early morning serum cortisol levels were higher than normal in both groups of athletes, but in amenorrheic athletes, serum cortisol levels remained greater than in the relatively sedentary women throughout the day and evening. The athletic women had diminished 24-hour LH pulse frequency, but augmented pulse amplitude, which was reminiscent of an earlier stage in hypothalamic-pituitary-gonadal development. Although one could not determine with certainty the mechanism of diminished gonadotro-

Table 1 Possible mechanisms for hypogonadism in endurance-trained athletes

Site	Mechanism
Brain	Altered frequency or amplitude of basal pulsatile gonadotropin secretion
	Enhanced sensitivity to negative feedback from estrogen
	Diminished positive feedback to estrogen
Pituitary	Impaired synthesis or release of gonadotropins
	Gonadotropins with reduced biologic activity
Gonads	Diminished target organ sensitivity (steroid hormone synthesis)
Other	Hyperprolactinemia
	Hypersecretion of opioids and/or enkephalins
	Diminished aromatization of androgens
	Variable metabolic clearance rates for sex-steroid hormones

pin release, Loucks and associates[36] proposed that the degree to which the hypothalamic-pituitary-adrenal axis is activated in cyclic and amenorrheic endurance-training athletes is associated, perhaps causally, with the (perhaps adaptive) alterations in their hypothalamic-pituitary-gonadal axis. This remains a serious subject of study, but it is complicated by the multiple interactions of phase of the menstrual cycle (ie, gonadal steroid hormone concentrations) and degree of endurance stress (duration and intensity of training).

Exercise-induced alterations in long-distance running men have received less intense scrutiny than that described above for women. Several investigators have noted decreased total testosterone and free testosterone levels in male long-distance runners and in those who have undertaken a gradually increasing distance run-training program,[44,45] although others have not been able to show differences from controls.[46,47] In men who have had analysis of timed series of serum LH levels, either hypogonadotropism[46] or no alteration in gonadotropin release were found.[44,47,48] There do not appear to be any studies in which the age of the runners was taken into account, although many of the distance runners in these studies were in their fourth and fifth decades. It appears, therefore, that unless male endurance runners are overtrained,[49] there are few significant alterations in the reproductive endocrine system, including sperm function.[48]

Because the pathophysiologic mechanisms involved in the altered (adaptive) reproductive system function in women who exercise remained undefined, my associates and I[17] sought to define the nature of the interactions between volume (distance) and intensity (rate of oxygen consumption) and alterations within the hypothalamic-pituitary-gonadal axis. Because the intensity of exercise seemed to be a critical determinant of other physiologic and adaptive changes, we postulated that the intensity of exercise, independent of the distance run, would produce measurable changes in the function of the reproductive system. To test this hypothesis, we undertook a prospective (12 to 14 months), graded exercise program at different exercise intensities in two groups of relatively sedentary, eumenor-rheic women. A nonexercising (control) group was followed concur-rently. Twenty-three eumenorrheic, gynecologically mature (approx-imately 18 years beyond menarche), untrained women participated. Seventeen were assigned randomly to one of two training groups: one group trained within ±10 m/min of each individual's deter-mined lactate threshold and the other at a pace (±10 m/min) half-way between the velocity at the lactate threshold and the velocity at peak oxygen consumption for part of the training and at the velocity of the lactate threshold for the remainder. Each group began at 6.25 miles/week and progressed to 40 miles/week after week 39. Total mileage after 12 to 14 menstrual cycles (approximately 800 miles) did not differ between the groups. Physiologic tests were repeated every fourth menstrual cycle to adjust training pace. At the onset and at each of these "testing" menstrual cycles, body composition, pulsatile LH analysis, and the lengths of the follicular and luteal phases of the menstrual cycle were determined.[17]

Both groups of exercising women increased their oxygen con-sumption at the lactate threshold by the fourth menstrual cycle by approximately 20% for each group. However, for a continued in-crease in oxygen consumption at the lactate threshold, training above the lactate threshold (hence, a critical intensity) was required. By 12 to 14 menstrual cycles, both groups had further increased oxy-gen consumption at the lactate threshold and had a greater ratio of oxygen consumption at the lactate threshold to peak oxygen uptake (group training at the lactate threshold, a 28% increase; group train-ing above the lactate threshold, a 36% increase). These statistically significantly different responses indicate a differential training effect based on submaximal oxygen uptake values. Only minor changes in body weight or composition and none in dietary intake were found after one year of training.[17] Despite the differential training effect, there were no changes in the menstrual cycles of the exercising women, with the luteal phase length decrement of less than two days in the more intensively exercising group, as assessed by hormo-nal dating of LH and progesterone.

Quantitative alterations in the pattern of LH release were sought by analysis of LH concentrations obtained every 10 minutes over 24 hours during the early follicular phase. Despite sophisticated analy-sis,[50] we could not identify any significant alteration in the pulsatile pattern of circulating LH concentrations. Ten of our subjects exer-cised an additional four menstrual cycles and seven an additional eight cycles. Despite this great distance (approximately 1700 miles after 20 menstrual cycles), no abnormalities in the menstrual cycle or quantitative features of LH release could be identified.

In summary, we were unable to define significant, specific alter-ations in clinical reproductive status in eumenorrheic, previously nontraining women who undertook this progressive graded exercise program. Only minimal, and probably biologically irrelevant, alterations in sex-steroid hormone concentrations or pulsatile LH release were found. We concluded that a progressive, graded exercise program as performed by these two exercise groups does not substantially alter the robust reproductive system of initially eumenorrheic, gynecologically mature women. These women can attain the numerous benefits of a rigorous exercise program without interrupting their normal ovulatory cycles. Thus, the disrupted cycles reported by many other investigators from cross-sectional studies may result from associated or prior, nonexercise-dependent variables (eg, younger gynecologic age) that alone or in the aggregate disrupt the reproductive axis.[17]

These data cannot easily be extrapolated to either gynecologically younger or peri-menopausal women. Exercise training at these stages of a woman's reproductive life may have significantly different effects. Additionally, subtle deficits in other portions of the menstrual cycle (eg, late follicular or mid-luteal phases) may arise from such training at any age. These deficits would not have been detected during our study.[17]

References

1. Baker ER, Mathur RS, Kirk RF, et al: Female runners and secondary amenorrhea: correlation with age, parity, mileage, and plasma hormonal and sex-hormone-binding globulin concentrations. *Fertil Steril* 1981;36:183-187.

2. Feicht CB, Johnson TS, Martin BJ, et al: Secondary amenorrhea in athletes. *Lancet* 1978;2:1145-1146.

3. Loucks AB: Effects of exercise training on the menstrual cycle: Existence and mechanisms. *Med Sci Sports Exerc* 1990;22:275-280.

4. Speroff L, Redwine DB: Exercise and menstrual function. *Phys Sports Med* 1980;8:42-52.

5. Galle PC, Freeman EW, Galle MG, et al: Physiologic and psychologic profiles in a survey of women runners. *Fertil Steril* 1983;39:633-639.

6. Gray DP, Dale E: Variables associated with secondary amenorrhea in women runners. *J Sport Sci* 1983;1:55-67.

7. Bonen A, Keizer HA: Athletic menstrual cycle irregularity: Endocrine response to exercise and training (with self-test). *Phys Sports Med* 1984;12:78-94.

8. Fries H, Nillius SJ, Pettersson F: Epidemiology of secondary amenorrhea: II. A retrospective evaluation of etiology with special regard to psychogenic factors and weight loss. *Am J Obstet Gynecol* 1974;118:473-479.

9. Loucks AB, Horvath SM: Athletic amenorrhea: A review. *Med Sci Sport Exerc* 1985;17:56-72.

10. Prior JC, Yuen BH, Clement P, et al: Reversible luteal phase changes and infertility associated with marathon training. *Lancet* 1982;2:269-270.

11. Vollman RF: *The Menstrual Cycle*. Philadelphia, PA, WB Saunders, 1977.

12. Malina RM: Menarche in athletes: A synthesis and hypothesis. *Ann Hum Biol* 1983;10:1-24.

13. Stager JM, Hatler LK: Menarche in athletes: The influence of genetics and prepubertal training. *Med Sci Sports Exerc* 1988;20:369-373.

14. Bullen BA, Skrinar GS, Beitins IZ, et al: Induction of menstrual disorders by strenuous exercise in untrained women. *N Engl J Med* 1985;312:1349-1353.

15. Boyden TW, Pamenter RW, Stanforth P, et al: Sex steroids and endurance running in women. *Fertil Steril* 1983;39:629-632.

16. Veldhuis JD, Evans WS, Demers LM, et al: Altered neuroendocrine regulation of gonadotropin secretion in women distance runners. *J Clin Endocrinol Metab* 1985;61:557-563.

17. Rogol AD, Weltman A, Weltman JY, et al: Durability of the reproductive axis in eumenorrheic women during one year of endurance training. *J Appl Physiol* 1992;72:1571-1580.

18. Plant TM: Pulsatile luteinizing hormone secretion in the neonatal male rhesus monkey (Macaca mulatta). *J Endocrinol* 1982;93:71-74.

19. Plant TM: A striking sex difference in the gonadotropin response to gonadectomy during infantile development in the rhesus monkey (Macaca mulatta). *Endocrinology* 1986;119:539-545.

20. Schwartz B, Cumming DC, Riordan E, et al: Exercise-associated amenorrhea: A distinct entity? *Am J Obstet Gynecol* 1981;141:662-670.

21. Cumming DC, Vickovic MM, Wall SR, et al: Defects in pulsatile LH release in normally menstruating runners. *J Clin Endocrinol Metab* 1985;60:810-812.

22. Keizer HA, Platen P, Menheere PPCA, et al: The hypothalamic/pituitary axis under exercise stress: The effects of aerobic and anaerobic training, in Laron Z, Rogol AD (eds): *Hormones and Sport*. New York, NY, Raven Press, 1989, pp 101-115.

23. Boyden TW, Pamenter RW, Grosso D, et al: Prolactin responses, menstrual cycles, and body composition of women runners. *J Clin Endocrinol Metab* 1982;54:711-714.

24. Bullen BA, Skrinar GS, Beitins IZ, et al: Endurance training effects on plasma hormonal responsiveness and sex hormone excretion. *J Appl Physiol* 1984;56:1453-1463.

25. Broocks A, Pirke KM, Schweiger U, et al: Cyclic ovarian function in recreational athletes. *J Appl Physiol* 1990;68:2083-2086.

26. Drinkwater BL, Nilson K, Chesnut CH III, et al: Bone mineral content of amenorrheic and eumenorrheic athletes. *N Engl J Med* 1984;311:277-281.

27. Marcus R, Cann C, Madvig P, et al: Menstrual function and bone mass in elite women distance runners: Endocrine and metabolic features. *Ann Intern Med* 1985;102:158-163.

28. Reame NE, Sauder SE, Case GD, et al: Pulsatile gonadotropin secretion in women with hypothalamic amenorrhea: Evidence that reduced frequency of gonadotropin-releasing hormone secretion is the mechanism of persistent anovulation. *J Clin Endocrinol Metab* 1985;61:851-858.

29. Frisch RE, McArthur JW: Menstrual cycles: Fatness as a determinant of minimum weight for height necessary for their maintenance or onset. *Science* 1974;185:949-951.

30. Frisch RE: Fatness and fertility. *Sci Am* 1988;258:88-95.

31. Billewicz WZ, Fellowes HM, Hytten CA: Comments on the critical metabolic mass and the age of menarche. *Ann Hum Biol* 1976;3:51-59.

32. Reeves J: Estimating fatness. *Science* 1979;204:881.

33. Stager JM, Wigglesworth JK, Hatler LK: Interpreting the relationship between age of menarche and prepubertal training. *Med Sci Sports Exerc* 1990;22:54-58.

34. Trussell J: Statistical flaws in evidence for the Frisch hypothesis that fatness triggers menarche. *Hum Biol* 1980;52:711-720.

35. Warren MP: The effects of exercise on pubertal progression and reproductive function in girls. *J Clin Endocrinol Metab* 1980;51:1150-1157.

36. Loucks AB, Mortola JF, Girton L, et al: Alterations in the hypothalamic-pituitary-ovarian and the hypothalamic-pituitary-adrenal axes in athletic women. *J Clin Endocrinol Metab* 1989;68:402-411.

37. Biller BM, Federoff HJ, Koenig JI, et al: Abnormal cortisol secretion and responses to corticotropin-releasing hormone in women with hypothalamic amenorrhea. *J Clin Endocrinol Metab* 1990;70:311-317.

38. Khoury SA, Reame NE, Kelch RP, et al: Diurnal patterns of pulsatile luteinizing hormone secretion in hypothalamic amenorrhea: Reproducibility and responses to opiate blockade and an α2-adrenergic agonist. *J Clin Endocrinol Metab* 1987;64:755-762.

39. Wildt L, Leyendecker G: Induction of ovulation by the chronic administration of naltrexone in hypothalamic amenorrhea. *J Clin Endocrinol Metab* 1987;64:1334-1335.

40. Santen RJ, Friend JN, Trojanowski D, et al: Prolonged negative feedback suppression after estradiol administration: Proposed mechanism of eugonadal secondary amenorrhea. *J Clin Endocrinol Metab* 1978;47:1220-1229.

41. Dixon G, Eurman P, Stern BE, et al: Hypothalamic function in amenorrheic runners. *Fertil Steril* 1984;42:377-383.

42. McArthur JW, Bullen BA, Beitins IZ, et al: Hypothalamic amenorrhea in runners of normal body composition. *Endocr Res Commun* 1980;7:13-25.

43. Evans WS, Weltman JY, Johnson ML, et al: Effects of opioid receptor blockade on luteinizing hormone (LH) pulses and interpulse LH concentrations in normal women during the early phase of the menstrual cycle. *J Endocrinol Invest* 1992;15:525-531.

44. Wheeler GD, Singh M, Pierce WD, et al: Endurance training decreases serum testosterone levels in men without change in luteinizing hormone pulsatile release. *J Clin Endocrinol Metab* 1991;72:422-425.

45. Hackney AC, Sinning WE, Bruot BC: Reproductive hormonal profiles of endurance-trained and untrained males. *Med Sci Sports Exerc* 1988;20:60-65.

46. MacConnie SE, Barkan A, Lampman RM, et al: Decreased hypothalamic gonadotropin-releasing hormone secretion in male marathon runners. *N Engl J Med* 1986;315:411-417.

47. Rogol AD, Veldhuis JD, Williams FA, et al: Pulsatile secretion of gonadotropins and prolactin in male marathon runners: Relation to the endogenous opiate system. *J Androl* 1984;5:21-27.

48. Bagatell CJ, Bremner WJ: Sperm counts and reproductive hormones in male marathoners and lean controls. *Fertil Steril* 1990;53:688-692.

49. Barron JL, Noakes TD, Levy W, et al: Hypothalamic dysfunction in overtrained athletes. *J Clin Endocrinol Metab* 1985;60:803-806.

50. Veldhuis JD, Johnson ML: Cluster analysis: A simple, versatile, and robust algorithm for endocrine pulse detection. *Am J Physiol* 1986;250:E486-E493.

Chapter 20

Physical Exercise, Fatty Acids, and Midlife Obesity

Ramon Segura, MD, PhD

Introduction

Changes in some metabolic processes take place with advancing age. For example, men and women experience changes in body composition such that there is a greater amount of absolute and relative fat stored in the adipose tissue and there is a tendency to lose lean body mass, especially muscle tissue. A reduction in physical activity and variations in dietary habits could contribute to this phenomenon. In women, overweight peaks in the late 50s and early 60s; in men, overweight peaks in the early 40s.[1]

Weight gain after the young adult years increases the risk of cardiovascular disease in both sexes[2,3] and adiposity stands out as a major controllable contributor to hypertension.[4] Apart from the total degree of obesity, the distribution of the excess adipose tissue has a special relevance, visceral or intra-abdominal fat accumulation being associated with a higher frequency of metabolic disorders, hypertension, and ischemic heart disease.[5] Special emphasis should be placed on the prevention of obesity, because some of the deleterious effects of an increased adipose tissue mass (eg, steroid metabolism and lipoprotein lipase activity) do not disappear with weight reduction.[6]

During moderate or prolonged physical exercise, the muscle uses fatty acids and glucose as the main sources of energy. Both compounds furnish hydrogen atoms (reducing equivalents) that combine with oxygen to liberate the energy needed to regenerate adenosine triphosphate (ATP).

For the same mass, fatty acids liberate more energy than carbohydrates. For each mole of palmitic acid, 2,436 kcal can be liberated and 129 moles of ATP can be synthesized; for each mole of glucose, only 685 kcal can be liberated and 38 moles of ATP synthesized. This means that for each gram of palmitic acid and each gram of glucose, 9.5 kcal and 3.8 kcal, respectively, can be liberated.

In both cases, an adequate amount of oxygen must be present to oxidize the corresponding substrates. The amount of ATP generated by each volume of oxygen consumed is different depending on whether glucose or fatty acids are the substrate. For each liter of oxygen consumed, 0.283 moles of ATP can be generated, or 5.08 kcal can be liberated. When glucose is being utilized, only 0.250 moles of ATP can be synthesized. If fatty acids are the source of energy, 4.75 kcal can be liberated. This means that about 10% more energy can be obtained per liter of oxygen consumed when glucose is being oxidized than when fatty acids are being utilized.

Neither glucose nor fatty acids can be stored as such. Glucose is "condensed" in the form of glycogen, a polymer of glucose, and fatty acids are esterified with glycerol and stored as triglycerides. Because of their lack of attraction for water, the triglyceride molecules can be stored in a "dry" state. Glycogen molecules show a considerable number of hydrophilic groups, however, and must be stored as "wet" structures, surrounded by a watery environment.

Storage of energy in the form of glycogen is rather inefficient because for each gram of useful compound a dead load (one with no energetic value) of about 4 g of associated water has to be retained as well. For each gram of fat stored in the adipose tissue, about 9 kcal can be liberated, while for each gram of glucose, stored as glycogen, only 1 kcal can be obtained. This makes fat the preferred form of energy storage, the capacity of this system being exceedingly higher than that of the carbohydrates.

Thus, while an adult may store an average of around 0.3 to 0.4 kg of pure, "dry" glycogen, between 10 and 20 kg of fat can easily be stored in the adipose tissue. About 1,200 to 1,600 kcal can be obtained from the glycogen stores and 70 to 95 moles of ATP can be synthesized, while the total amount of kilocalories liberated from the adipose tissue will be on the order of 90,000 to 180,000, with a potential capacity to synthesize between 5,000 and 10,000 moles of ATP. This means that, in general, the energetic capacity of the adipose tissue is about 100 times higher than that of carbohydrates (Table 1).

The ability to store energy in the form of fat represents a major evolutionary step forward. However, in our modern industrialized society a considerable number of people carry an excessive amount of fat for their needs and show variable degrees of obesity. Obesity is the most prevalent chronic medical condition in our society. It is directly or indirectly associated with a considerable number of diseases (eg, increased blood pressure, diabetes, and heart disease) that, on the whole, account for a notable proportion of the mortality and morbidity rates in the developed countries. Physical exercise could contribute to the mobilization and oxidization of fat and, thus, to the reduction of adipose reserves of the body.

Physical Exercise and Fatty Acid Utilization

Because of the much larger amount of energy available from fat than from glycogen, the oxidation of fatty acids might be thought to be

Table 1 Energy reserves in the human body

	Reserves	
	Grams	Kilocalories
Glucose	16-20	64-80
(in blood and interstitial fluid)		
Glycogen	300-450	1,200-1,800
(in muscles and liver)		
Triacylglycerides		
(in adipose tissue)	10,000-20,000	90,000-180,000
(in plasma)	5-7	45-63
Protein		
(available only in part)	12,000-15,000	48,000-60,000

the preferred procedure for regenerating ATP during physical exercise. Conversely, in order to reduce the reserves of fat and, thus, treat or prevent obesity, physical exercise might appear to be quite useful; that is, theoretically, the higher the energy expenditure, the larger the reduction in the fat stores. However, it is necessary to remember that for the same amount of energy spent, the type of substrate being oxidized will be determined by the intensity and duration of the exercise, the physical condition and degree of training of the individual, and the nutritional status of the subject.

Thus, to complete a marathon race, a well-trained athlete will use about 3,000 kcal. Theoretically, that would reduce the weight of the adipose tissue by 350 g. However, the fat reserves will actually be reduced by only approximately 140 g. The reason for this is that for an intensity corresponding to a velocity of about 16 km/h, fatty acids alone cannot meet the energy demands and the individual must also resort to glycogen as a source of energy. Under these circumstances, about 1,200 of the 3,000 kcal will be furnished by fatty acids and the other 1,800 kcal will be obtained from glucose and, thus, from the glycogen stores.

Because reduction in the reserves of hepatic and muscle glycogen also implies a reduction in the amount of water associated with this compound, during a marathon race about 2 kg of weight will be lost from the body through the mobilization of the glucose stored in such a polymer.

Despite the very large amount of energy available in the form of fat, the quantity of fatty acids being used by the muscles and by the body as a whole is relatively small and limited by their rate of mobilization and transportation and by their rate of degradation in the mitochondria. Because a high concentration of fatty acids can be toxic for the cells, their concentration in the plasma and in the interstitial fluid, as well as in the cells, is usually kept at rather low levels. As a result, the amount of energy per unit time available from fatty acids may be relatively small and limited by a series of "safety" mechanisms.

A higher rate of fatty acid oxidation would reduce the amount of glucose that is being utilized by the muscle and would slow the release of stored glycogen,[7,8] thus delaying the onset of fatigue. If an exercise of moderate to high intensity, such as a marathon race, could be sustained by the oxidation of fatty acids alone, it would allow almost all the glycogen reserves to be preserved for the "extra" effort toward the end of the race and it would fuel a substantially higher speed during the last kilometers.

The steps by which fatty acids are made available to the muscle cells from the adipose reserves are outlined in Figure 1. Any one of these steps may limit the overall rate of metabolism and oxidation of fatty acids. As the uptake of fatty acids being utilized by an organ or a group of cells is not specific or selective, the availability of such compounds will depend on their concentration in the blood and on the blood flow through that particular organ or region. The rate at which the whole process takes place, through the steps described in Figure 1, can be modified up to a certain point by diet or pharmacologic manipulations (caffeine or heparin) as well as by training.

Liberation and Mobilization of Fatty Acids in the Adipose Tissue

The amount of fatty acids mobilized by the adipose tissue in a certain period of time is determined by the activity of adipose tissue lipase (triacylglycerol hydrolase). This enzyme is mainly controlled by the sympathetic nervous system[9] and, to a minor degree, the catabolic hormones. The hormonal factors or neurotransmitters that influence the activity of the adipose tissue lipase operate through a second messenger, cAMP. The intracellular concentration of cAMP is the net result of its rate of synthesis, through the action of the adenylate cyclase, and its rate of inactivation, through the effect of a phosphodiesterase. As shown in Figure 2, cAMP initiates a chain reaction during which large amounts of the phosphorylated form of triacylglycerol hydrolase (lipase) are activated.

The first step in the lipolytic process is the interaction of the catecholamines, mainly norepinephrine, with the β-adrenergic receptors located in the cell membrane. The rate of lipolysis thus may be increased by the actions of the corresponding agonists or may be reduced by the presence of adrenergic antagonists; ie, β blockers.

Human adipocytes contain both α- and β-adrenergic receptors in their cellular membranes. The stimulation of the α receptors inhibits intracellular lipolysis and the stimulation of β receptors activates lipolysis. Both types of receptors are linked to adenylate cyclase by means of a series of signal-transducing proteins, termed guanine nucleotide regulatory proteins GS and GI, which hydrolyze the nucleotide guanosine triphosphate (GTP).[10] The β1 and β2 agonist receptors, glucagon and the pituitary lipolytic peptides, activate adenylate cyclase by the stimulatory protein, GDS. Adenosine, certain types of prostaglandins, the neuropeptides Y (NPY) and YY (PYY) and, espe-

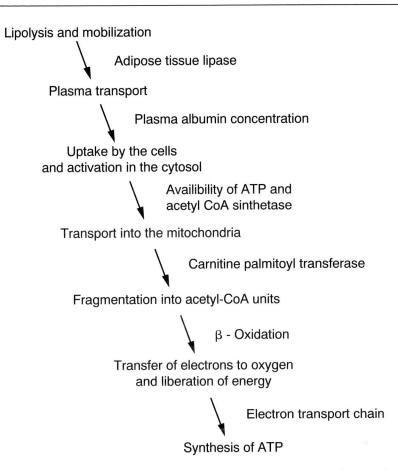

Lipolysis and mobilization

Adipose tissue lipase

Plasma transport

Plasma albumin concentration

Uptake by the cells
and activation in the cytosol

Availibility of ATP and
acetyl CoA sinthetase

Transport into the mitochondria

Carnitine palmitoyl transferase

Fragmentation into acetyl-CoA units

β - Oxidation

Transfer of electrons to oxygen
and liberation of energy

Electron transport chain

Synthesis of ATP

Fig. 1 *Steps involved in the liberation, mobilization, transportation, and utilization of fatty acids from adipose tissue.*

cially, the α-adrenergic agonists negatively influence the adenylate cyclase system by means of the inhibitory protein, GI.[11]

The most important physiological agonist of the adrenergic receptors found in the adipose tissue are epinephrine, which is released into the systemic circulation by the adrenal medulla, and norepinephrine, which is released by nerve endings in the blood vessels serving the adipose tissue and, to a lesser extent, by nerve terminals interacting directly with the adipocytes. Epinephrine and norepinephrine can stimulate both α and β receptors, which are the predominant receptor subclasses in the adipocyte. The combined effect on both types of receptors will determine the extent of lipolysis in a given adipocyte. Both males and females show a much less vigorous lipolytic activity at the buttocks and thighs than in the abdominal subcutaneous region. These notable differences are related to an in-

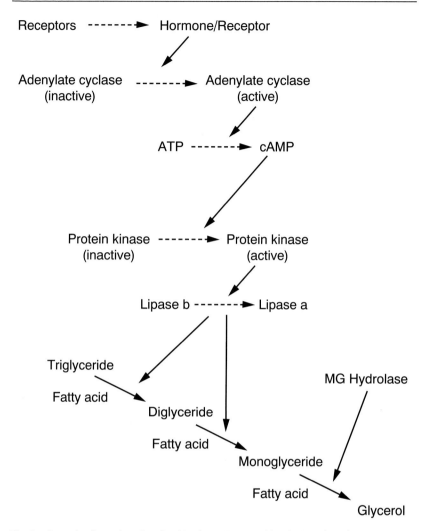

Fig. 2 *Cascade of reactions involved in the activation of lipolysis in the adipose tissue.*

creased density of abdominal β-adrenoreceptors, with a relative decrease in the affinity of the α-adrenoreceptors that results in an increased sensitivity of the abdominal adipocytes to adrenergic stimuli and an easy mobilization of fatty acids from that region.[12]

Abdominal subcutaneous adipocytes show greater α-adrenoreceptor activity in obese males than in obese females; on the other hand, an increased α-adrenergic receptor affinity in the gluteofemoral adipocytes of lean females compared to lean males also has been described.[13,14]

In relation to the factors mentioned above, the rate of lipolysis and fatty acid mobilization induced by physical exercise would be particularly rapid and elevated in the intra-abdominal fat reserves while it will be blunted and much more difficult to elicit in the adipocytes of the gluteofemoral region. This may explain the difficulty people at midlife have in trying to decrease buttock size and yet exercise regularly.

The subjects who are well trained or who regularly perform a moderate amount of physical exercise, have adipocyte β-adrenergic receptors that are more sensitive to the effects of catecholamines than sedentary individuals or those who have stopped training. Thus, in response to the stimulatory effect of physical activity, the former can mobilize and utilize a larger amount of fatty acids per unit time than the latter.

Modification of the cAMP Levels and of the Tissue Lipase Activity

Those factors that tend to increase the levels and/or the half-life of cAMP will stimulate lipolysis, while those that tend to reduce the concentration of this second messenger (ie, insulin[9]) will determine a lower rate of fatty acid mobilization.

The compounds that inhibit phosphodiesterase, the enzyme responsible for the termination of the effects of cAMP, induce an increase in the activity of the intracellular protein kinase system and, thus, favor lipolysis. Caffeine, a trimethylxanthine, inhibits phosphodiesterase and should, therefore, enhance lipolysis. Several studies[15-17] have shown that the ingestion of large amounts of caffeine (on the order of 5 to 10 mg/kg body weight), between half an hour and 1 hour before an exercise, induces a substantial increase in the plasma levels of nonesterified fatty acids. Costill and associates[15] have shown that after the ingestion of 330 g of caffeine 1 hour before the realization of an exercise of long duration, the concentration of nonesterified fatty acids in plasma increased between 50% and 100%, with a concomitant extension of the time of exercise, before exhaustion, of around 20% in relation to that observed after the ingestion of a placebo.

The amount of caffeine ingested with common beverages (ie, cola, coffee, tea) is much smaller than that utilized in the majority of the experimental work done thus far. Besides caffeine's metabolic effects, other actions (namely in the central nervous system) could contribute to increase the endurance capacity of the subjects. Lizarraga and Segura (personal communication, 1992) have observed that a dose of about 1 to 1.5 mg/kg body weight produces a substantial increase in the levels of plasma fatty acids if one waits long enough for the effects of caffeine to be completed. We have noted that the highest concentrations of nonesterified fatty acids in plasma appear between 2.5 and 3 hours after the ingestion of a cup of coffee containing about 100 mg of caffeine (Fig. 3). Apparently caffeine has to be

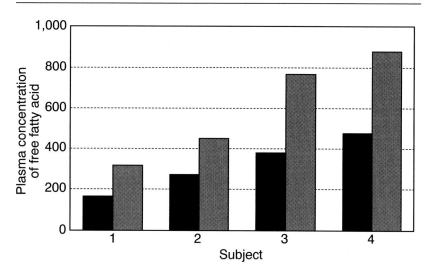

Fig. 3 *Effect of coffee on free fatty acid levels. Solid columns, before coffee is consumed; shaded columns, after coffee is consumed.*

transformed in the body into a derivative (paraxanthine) before it can act on the intracellular phosphodiesterase system.[18] This would explain, in part, the long lag phase between ingestion and action of this methylxanthine.

Following the mobilization of large amounts of fatty acids, it is necessary that these compounds be utilized and metabolized by oxidation, especially by the skeletal muscle cells and during exercise. If the uptake of fatty acids by the different tissues and organs does not match the amount liberated to the plasma, the levels of these compounds would tend to increase, with potential negative or toxic consequences for the organism. To avoid the build-up of fatty acids in plasma, the liver takes up a considerable proportion of these compounds and neutralizes them by esterification with glycerol, forming triglycerides. These products are later exported to the plasma packed in very-low-density lipoproteins (VLDL) and returned, mainly to the adipose tissue. As a result, even when a physical effort of moderate duration is performed, a discrete increase in the levels of triglycerides and VLDL may be observed, despite the fact that the muscles can obtain fatty acids from the triacylglycerides transported by this type of lipoproteins (Fig. 4).

Other factors induce a reduction in the rate of lipolysis and, thus, make exercise more dependent on glucose utilization. Insulin, and the factors or dietetic manipulations that promote an increase in the plasma levels of this hormone, determine a lower degree of fatty acid mobilization and utilization. Insulin, the only antilipolytichorone of physiologic importance, acts by conversion of the hor-

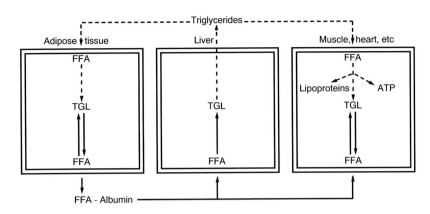

Fig. 4 *Fatty acid mobilization from the adipose tissue, cellular uptake, and recycling by the liver. FFA, free fatty acids; TGL, triglycerides. (Reproduced with permission from Brodie BR, Maickel RP, Stern DN: Automic nervous system and adipose tissue, in Handbook of Physiology. Washington, DC, American Physiological Society, 1965, section 5.)*

mone-sensitive lipase in adipose tissue from its phosphorylated (or active) form to its dephosphorylated (or inactive) form. This inhibitory effect appears to be secondary to a decrease in cAMP concentration, as insulin activates phosphodiesterase. On the other hand, this hormone reduces the activity of the adenylate cyclase system, leading to a decrease in the cAMP-dependent activity of phosphokinase.[19]

During exercise, sympathoadrenal activity is enhanced and circulating insulin concentration is depressed. Any factor or procedure that induces a higher insulin secretion or "activity" will counteract the lipolytic stimulation induced by exercise. It is worth noting that the plasma nonesterified fatty acid concentration is higher in fasted or fat-fed experimental subjects than in normal control subjects in which the plasma insulin concentration achieves higher levels. Thus, the ingestion of sugars shortly before exercise may influence negatively the mobilization and utilization of fatty acids if it is followed by an increase in the secretion of insulin. In this case, the subject will be more dependent on his or her own glucose reserves and will oxidize less fat. On the other hand, the amount of energy that is being ingested with this form of pre-exercise "feedings" or "drinks" does not supply too much of the energetic needs of the individual. For a marathon runner, who is using energy at a rate of about 20 kcal/min, the ingestion of 10 g of glucose (contained in about 200 ml of some commercial beverages) will not suffice to sustain the energetic needs of the subject for more than 4 minutes.

It is necessary to take into account that the antilipolytic activity of insulin does not disappear immediately after its plasma levels fall;

its metabolic effects fade away relatively slowly in such a way that the impact of a high insulin level can blunt the fatty acid mobilization induced by an exercise performed a few hours later.

The amount of fatty acid mobilized from the adipose tissue depends on the carrying capacity of the blood perfusing the tissue. During prolonged exercise blood flow through adipose tissue increases, a phenomenon that facilitates the removal of fatty acids from that tissue. On the other hand, as nonessential fatty acids circulate, not physically "free," but bound to plasma albumin, the capacity to mobilize fatty acids is dependent on the concentration of albumin in plasma. When the ratio between fatty acids and albumin reaches a certain value, an increase in the concentration of the unassociated or "free" form of the fatty acids will take place. In these circumstances, the rate of lipolysis will be counteracted by a considerable re-esterification in the same adipose tissue; as a consequence, net fatty acid mobilization will be reduced.[20,21]

The whole picture for fatty acid mobilization during exercise could be as follows: lipolysis increases rather quickly and, after a while, reaches a constant level because the adipose tissue is stimulated by the sympathoadrenal system; there is a concomitant reduction in the insulin levels. Increased lipolysis is perpetuated by increased adipose tissue blood flow, which promotes or facilitates the removal of fatty acids from that tissue. The amount of fatty acids mobilized from the adipose tissue is in excess of that being simultaneously utilized by the different organs, especially the working muscle, a fact that is reflected by an increase in the arterial fatty acid concentration. Finally, after a certain period of time, the plasma nonesterified fatty acid levels reach a plateau due mainly to two factors: uptake by the working muscle, which, under these circumstances, can obtain most of its energy from fatty acids, and uptake by the liver cells which re-esterify fatty acids with glycerol and transfer them, as triacylglycerides carried by the VLDL into the plasma. Therefore, utilization of free fatty acids is directly proportional to the circulating plasma concentrations of free fatty acids.

Utilization of Fatty Acids

The uptake of fatty acids from the blood by the different cells is a rapid process that depends on the gradient concentration of fatty acids. Thus, the higher the concentration of fatty acids in plasma the greater its uptake by the cell, a fact that leaves fatty acid mobilization as the major determination of fatty acid utilization by the muscle. Once inside the cell, the fatty acid is activated to the corresponding fatty acyl-CoA with the expenditure of energy. During exercise, most of the activated fatty acids are transferred to the mitochondria, where they will undergo β oxidation.

Transfer of Fatty Acids Into the Mitochondria

The transport of the fatty acyl-CoA complex across the mitochondrial membrane and into the mitochondrial matrix requires the presence of carnitine and the participation of two enzyme systems. The primary function of carnitine is to allow the transfer of long-chain fatty acids across the inner mitochondrial membrane.[22] These compounds, activated to their CoA esters, are first transesterified to carnitine by carnitine-palmitoyltransferase I, an enzyme located in the external surface of the inner mitochondrial membrane. Once the fatty acyl-carnitine ester has been formed, it diffuses across the inner mitochondrial membrane, a process mediated by an acyl carnitine translocase. This intramembrane transport takes place in exchange for carnitine from the intramitochondrial matrix. Once the carnitine-fatty acyl complex reaches the intramitochondial space, a second transfer system, carnitine-palmitoyltransferase II, regenerates the fatty acyl-CoA, leaving carnitine free to diffuse back to the outer surface (Fig. 5).

When carnitine is not available in sufficient amounts, disorders of fatty acids utilization and muscle energetics take place. This fact, and the essential role played by carnitine in fatty acid oxidation, tend to suggest that supplementation of the diet with carnitine would enhance fatty acid utilization and oxidation during prolonged exercise. However, the ingestion of carnitine does not appear to improve the rate of fatty acid oxidation during exercise. Actually, the changes in muscle carnitine with exercise are small (except when exercise is very intense). Enough carnitine should be available to the working cells through the endogenous biosynthetic process that starts with lysine, to assure the adequate activity of the carnitine-palmitoyltransferase systems and the carnitine-acylcarnitine translocase.

Other dietary manipulations also may influence the process of transferring fatty acids into the mitochondria. The acyl-CoA transferase systems are influenced by the phospholipid and fatty acid composition of the membranes in which they implant. Berge and associates[23,24] have shown that the activity of the carnitine palmitoyl CoA transferase systems is higher in rats fed a supplement of fish oil than in those that consume only a conventional diet. The change in the lipid environment, therefore, would modify the activity of the enzymatic systems and could, eventually, allow a higher rate of fatty acid uptake and oxidation during physical exercise.

Domingo and Segura (personal communication, 1993) have investigated the physical performance of the rat in relation to changes in the fatty acid composition of the cell membranes induced by a dietary supplementation with W-3 fish oil, especially rich in eicosapentaenoic acid (EPA) and docosahexaenoic acid (DHA). Notable changes in the fatty acid composition of the skeletal muscle membranes (and of the membranes of other cell systems) were observed

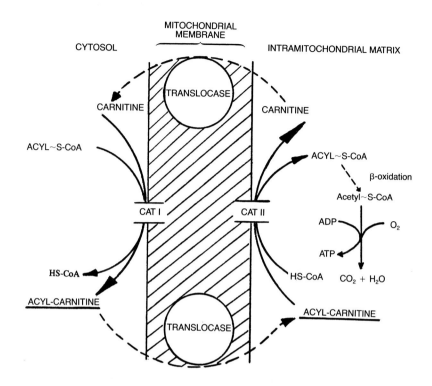

Fig. 5 *Intracellular transport of activated fatty acids.*

in rats fed the fish oil supplement for 2 months. The most important changes were a decrease in the proportion of 18:2 (n-6) and 20:4 (n-6) and an increase in the proportion of 20:5 (n-3) and 22:6 (n-3) in the phosphatidylcholine and phosphatidylethanolamine fractions of the sarcoplasmatic reticulum in the animals fed the fish oil in comparison with the animals that did not receive such a supplement. Similar changes were also observed in the mitochondrial membranes.

These changes in the lipid environment of the cellular membranes were associated with an increased endurance during physical exercise of a relatively long duration. Thus, the animals that were fed the fish oil supplement and subjected to a forced swim test were able to swim and stay afloat longer than the ones fed the regular diet (Table 2).

At this point, we do not know the mechanism by which these changes in lipid composition of the membrane structure can influence the physical performance of the animal. It can be assumed, however, that the mechanism should take place through modifications in the activities of the enzymatic systems (such as those observed in the carnitine-acyl CoA transferase by Berge and associ-

Table 2 Performance on a forced swim test by rats fed a conventional diet (control) and rats fed a conventional diet supplemented with fish oil (eicosapentaenoic acid)

Group	Number of Subjects	First trial Time (sec)	Second trial Time (sec)	Change (%)*
Eicosapentaenoic acid	16	736 ± 243	809 ± 265	115.5 ± 30.1
Control	17	691 ± 262	670 ± 272	96.9 ± 16.3
			$p < 0.05$	

*In relation to the first trial.

ates[23]), the calcium-dependent ATPase, or the intramitochondrial systems, or modifications in the physicochemical characteristics of the membranes and their impact on their permeability to certain compounds.

Plasma Lipoproteins and Physical Exercise

Besides the plasma free fatty acids, the muscle may use the fatty acids transported, in the form of triacylglycerides, by VLDL and, eventually, by the chylomicrons (large, low-density lipoproteins). While the uptake of nonesterified fatty acids is dependent on its concentration in plasma and the blood flow through the corresponding organ or tissue, the uptake of fatty acids from the lipoproteins is selective and subject to the presence of lipoprotein lipase, an enzyme responsible for the hydrolysis of lipoprotein triacylglycerides and the liberation of the corresponding fatty acids (Fig. 6).

Lipoprotein lipase is widely distributed in the body. The highest concentrations are found in the adipose tissue, the heart, the mammary glands, and the skeletal muscle, with the levels depending on the hormonal and nutritional status as well as on the degree, duration, and intensity of the exercise that is being performed.

After feeding, and under the influence of insulin, lipoprotein lipase is synthesized in large amounts by the adipose tissue and transferred to the intraluminal cell surface of the respective capillary endothelial cells; in these circumstances, most of the "fatty acids" transported by the chylomicrons and VLDLs will be taken up by the adipocytes. In contrast, when during fasting or physical exertion insulin levels are decreased, the activity of the lipoprotein lipase system of the adipose reserves will be very low, while the intracellular hormone-sensitive lipase will be stimulated.

The skeletal muscles can obtain a considerable amount of fatty acids, and therefore of energy, from the triglyceride-carrying lipoproteins because of their capacity to synthesize lipoprotein lipase in response to physical activity.[25,26] The amount of enzyme produced is not the same in all muscle as those integrated or composed mainly by slow-twitch, red fibers, which show a much larger lipoprotein lip-

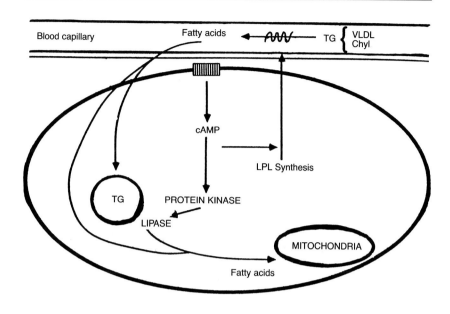

MUSCLE CELL

Fig. 6 *Hydrolysis of circulating and intracellular triglycerides and fatty acid utilization by the working muscle. LPL, lipoprotein lipase; VLDL, very-low-density lipoproteins; chyl, chylomicrons; TG, triglycerides.*

Table 3 Comparison of the levels of plasma lipids and lipoproteins in cross-sectional samples of male long-distance runners and sedentary males

	Runners	Nonrunners
Age	46.9 ±7.5 years	45.7 ± 6.1 years
Body mass index	22.6 ± 2.0 kg/m²	25.1 ± 3.3 kg/m²
Total cholesterol	190.0 ± 36.6 mg/dl	217.0 ± 31.1 mg/dl
LDL cholesterol	116.1 ± 30.7 mg/dl	147.0 ± 27.5 mg/dl
VLDL cholesterol	9.1 ± 8.3 mg/dl	20.4 ± 11.7 mg/dl
HDL cholesterol	64.9 ± 12.5 mg/dl	49.6 ± 8.7 mg/dl
HDL2 mass	88.8 ± 34.8 mg/dl	42.7 ± 31 mg/dl
HDL3 mass	245.4 ± 41.2 mg/dl	236.6 ± 35.7 mg/dl
Triglycerides	70.8 ± 35.0 mg/dl	123.0 ± 59.3 mg/dl

(Reproduced with permission from Williams PT, Krauss RM, Wood PD, et al: Lipoprotein subfractions of runners and sedentary men. *Metabolism* 1986;35:45-52.)

ase activity and fatty acid uptake from chylomicrons and VLDL than those composed by fast-twitch, pale fibers.

Runners and people engaged in prolonged aerobic activities in general have a lower concentration of plasma triglycerides, VLDL cholesterol, and LDL cholesterol, and higher levels of HDL cholesterol than sedentary people or individuals who perform short-term

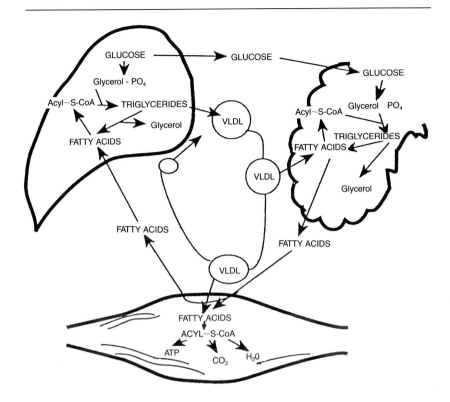

Fig. 7 *General overview of the dynamics of nonesterified or esterified fatty acids in the body. Synthesis of nonessential fatty acids and assembly of triglycerides (TG) in the liver; storage of fatty acids, as TG, in the adipose tissue. Utilization by the working muscles.*

physical activities. Due especially to the capacity of the red fibers to take up the fatty acids transported by VLDL and chylomicrons, the lipoprotein profile of the individuals who exercise regularly and for considerable periods of time approaches that typical of women in their fertile period, and diverges from that of sedentary men (Table 3).[27] The better lipoprotein profile of exercising people indicates that physical activity, practiced regularly and in sufficient amount, may reduce the risk of coronary heart disease and bring a series of beneficial effects through metabolic changes similar to those that operate in women and that, apparently, protect them from the risk of extensive atherosclerotic lesions.

Summary

Physical activity determines an increased mobilization of fatty acids from the adipose tissue reserves as well as the uptake of fatty acids from the triglycerides carrying lipoproteins (Fig. 7). Both actions or effects improve the metabolic and health status of the individuals and lower the number and degree of risk factors that tend to reduce life quality and expectancy.

References

1. Simopoulos AP: Characteristics of obesity: An overview. *Ann NY Acad Sci* 1987;499:4-13.

2. Hubert HB, Feinleib M, McNamara PM, et al: Obesity as an independent risk factor for cardiovascular disease: A 26 year follow-up of participants in the Framingham heart study. *Circulation* 1983;67:968-977.

3. Simopoulos AP: The health implications of overweight and obesity. *Nutr Rev* 1985;43:33-40.

4. Garrison RJ, Kannel WB, Stokes J III, et al: Incidence and precursors of hypertension in young adults: The Framingham offspring study. Cardiovascular Disease Epidemiology Newsletter, March 1985.

5. Kissebah AH, Freedman DS, Peiris AN: Health risks of obesity. *Med Clin North Am* 1989;73:111-138.

6. Siiteri PK, Williams JE, Takaki NK: Steroid abnormalities in endometrial and breast carcinoma: A unifying hypothesis. *J Steroid Biochem Mol Biol* 1976;7:897-903

7. Rennie MJ, Winder WW, Holloszy JO: A sparing effect of increased plasma fatty acids on muscle and liver glycogen content in the exercising rat. *Biochem J* 1976;156:647-655.

8. Ravussin E, Borgardus C, Scheidegger K, et al: Effect of elevated FFA on carbohydrate and lipid oxidation during prolonged exercise in humans. *J Appl Physiol* 1986;60:893-900

9. Havel RJ, Goldfien A: The role of the sympathetic nervous system in the metabolism of free fatty acids. *J Lipid Res* 1960;1:102-108.

10. Stryer L, Bourne HR: G-proteins: A family of signal transducers. *Ann Rev Cell Biol* 1986;2:391-419.

11. Lafontan M, Langin D, Portillo M, et al: Regulation of lipolysis by catecholamines and neuropeptides: Recent developments, in Oomura Y, Tarui S, Inoue S, et al (eds): *Progress in Obesity Research 1990*. Montrouge, France, J Libbey, 1991, pp 245-256.

12. Leibel RL, Hirsch J: Site and sex-related differences in adrenoreceptor status of human adipose tissue. *J Clin Endocrinol Metab* 1987;64:1205-1210.

13. Wahrenberg H, Loonqvist F, Arner P: Mechanisms underlying regional differences in lipolysis in human adipose tissue. *J Clin Invest* 1989;84:458-467.

14. Leibel RL, Rosenbaum M, Edens NK, et al: In vitro vs in vivo measures of lipolysis and re-esterification in human adipose tissue, in Oomura Y, Tarui S, Inoue S, et al (eds): *Progress in Obesity Research 1990*. Montrouge, France, J Libbey, 1991, pp 237-243.

15. Costill DL, Dalsky GP, Fink WJ: Effect of caffeine ingestion on metabolism and exercise performance. *Med Sci Sports Exerc* 1978;10:155-158.

16. Fisher SM, McMurray RG, Berry M, et al: Influence of caffeine on exercise performance in habitual caffeine users. *Int J Sports Med* 1986;7:276-280.

17. Flinn S, Gregory J, McNaughton LR, et al: Caffeine ingestion prior to incremental cycling to exhaustion in recreational cyclists. *Int J Sports Med* 1990;11:188-193.

18. Hetzler RK, Knowlton RG, Somani SM, et al: Effect of paraxanthine on FFA mobilization after intravenous caffeine administration in humans. *J Appl Physiol* 1990;68:44-47.

19. Leibel PC, Edens NK, Fried SK: Physiological basis for the control of body fat distribution in humans. *Am Rev Nutr* 1989;9:417-443.

20. Bulow J, Masden J: Influence of blood flow on fatty acid mobilization from lipolytically active adipose tissue. *Pflugers Arch* 1981;390:169-174.
21. Arner P, Kriecholm E, Engfeldt P, et al: Adrenergic regulation of lipolysis "in situ" at rest and during exercise. *J Clin Invest* 1990;85:893-898.
22. Cerretelli P, Marconi C: L-carnitine supplementation in humans: The effects on physical performance. *Int J Sports Med* 1990;11:1-14.
23. Berge RK, Nilsson A, Husoy AM: Rapid stimulation of liver palmitoyl-CoA synthetase carnitine palmitoyltransferase and glycerophosphate acyltransferase compared to peroxisomal beta-oxidation and palmitoyl-CoA hydrolase in rats fed high-fat diets. *Biochim Biophys Acta* 1988;960:417-426.
24. Aarsland A, Lundquist M, Borretsen B, et al: On the effect of peroxisomal beta-oxidation and carnitine palmitoyltransferase activity by eicosapentaenoic acid in liver and heart from rats. *Lipids* 1990;25:546-548.
25. Terjung RL, Budohoski LL, Nazar K, et al: Chylomicron triglyceride metabolism in resting and exercising fed dogs. *J Appl Physiol* 19821;52:815-820
26. Terjung RL, Mackie BG, Dudley GA, et al: Influence of exercise on chylomicron triacylglycerol metabolism: Plasma turnover and muscle uptake. *Med Sci Sports Exerc* 1983;15:340-347
27. Williams PT, Krauss RM, Wood PD, et al: Lipoprotein subfractions of runners and sedentary men. *Metabolism* 1986;35:45-52.

Chapter 21

Nutritional Habits of Spanish Athletes, Recreational Runners, and a Sedentary Population

Pedro Pujol, MD
R. Curco, PhD
E. Sanchez, PhD
M. Bellver, MD
S. Ribas, MD

Introduction

Adequate nutrition is an important factor in physical performance. Inadequate nutrition can lead to premature fatigue and can contribute to a greater risk of injuries. It also may precipitate other medical problems.

In recent years there has been increasing participation in athletic events (especially running) by the general public. In particular, many men and women older than 40 years have undertaken marathon running and other long-distance events. Our 16-year experience with the medical aspects of the Marathon of Barcelona has shown us that there is a growing interest in the nutritional aspects of long-distance running among participants in this sport. This has prompted us to study several aspects of nutrition in relation to distance running and athletic participation in general.

In this paper we will consider three nutrition studies recently conducted in Spain: (1) the nutritional habits of Spanish athletes of various sports as compared to the sedentary population; (2) the nutritional habits of runners in midlife as compared to younger runners (both competitive and recreational) and sedentary individuals; and (3) plasma cholesterol levels in Spanish marathon runners.

Nutritional Habits of Spanish Athletes of Various Sports as Compared to the Sedentary Population

Methods

The first study explored the nutritional habits of 130 athletes of various sports—69 men and 61 women—and a group of 58 sedentary controls—40 men and 18 women. The main characteristics of the subjects are depicted in Table 1.

To analyze the diet history we used the Professional Diet Balancer (Nutridata Software Corporation, Wappingers Falls, NY) software package, which has a data base of 1,600 foods with 23 nutrient values provided for each food. Fast foods are also included. This computer program compares the total of each nutrient with the US recommended dietary allowance (RDA) for each subject based on weight, age, sex, and physical activity or energy expenditure. Each individual in the first two studies was asked to keep a daily intake record for a minimum of 3 days and a maximum of 7 days. All vitamin and mineral supplements taken by the subjects were added after the food intake results were calculated. Once the 3-day diet history and the nutrient analysis were completed, a dietitian counseled the subjects about dietary weaknesses.

We realized that the data would not be as accurate as desired because of various potential sources of error. The 3-day diet record seems quite limited; however, the data reported in the literature justify using the 3-day rather than the 7-day intake record. The use of the RDA as a standard of intake adequacy is open to criticism; however, it is the most used standard in similar studies. Another possible source of error is the use of a program based on American foods rather than one prepared for the Spanish diet. Unfortunately, no such program exists in Spain.

Results and Discussion

The nutritional analysis shows that about 53% of the athletes consumed diets that provided less than 50% of energy intake as carbohydrates (Table 2). The vast majority of athletes consumed more than 30% of energy intake as total fat and the unsaturated:saturated ratio was less than 2 to 1 in almost all subjects. The cholesterol intake exceeded 250 mg/day in most athletes and controls. The number of athletes who ingested less than 15% of total daily calories from proteins was much higher than in the control group. Both controls and athletes ingested less than 25 g fiber/day.

Table 3 shows the percentages of athletes and controls who ingested less than two thirds of the RDA of vitamins. A significant number of athletes ingested less than two thirds of the RDA of vitamins A, E, and D, whereas the control group was most often deficient in vitamins A, E, and B6.

Table 1 Mean characteristics and calorie intake in 130 athletes and 58 controls

	Athletes	Controls
Number	69 men, 61 women	40 men, 18 women
Age (years)	11 to 41	18 to 43
Height (cm)	142 to 195	158 to 185
Weight (kg)	27.2 to 110	51 to 85
Total calorie intake/day	2,214	1,850

Table 2 Intake of nutrients*

	Athletes (n = 130)	Controls (n = 58)
Carbohydrates	53%	56%
Proteins	38%	1%
Total fat	96%	12%
Cholesterol	76%	77%
Unsaturated:saturated ratio (3:1)	97.6%	97%
Fiber	83%	100%

*Percentage of athletes and controls (men and women) in whom the total daily calorie intake is less than 50% carbohydrates, greater than 45% proteins, greater than 30% total fat, less than 2:1 unsaturated:saturated fat ratio, greater than 250 mg cholesterol, and less than 25 g fiber.

Table 4 shows that the great majority of athletes consumed normal amounts of calcium, whereas 43% of the control group consumed less than two thirds of the RDA of calcium. Thirty-six percent of the athletes and 27% of the control group consumed less than two thirds of the RDA of iron. A high proportion of the controls (77%) consumed less zinc as compared to the athletes (29%).

Nutritional Habits of Runners in Midlife as Compared to Younger Runners and Sedentary Individuals

In the second study, the nutritional habits of a group of 312 individuals were investigated. This group was composed of competitive runners (190 men), recreational runners (59 men), and relatively sedentary individuals (63 men). The individuals under study were further classified according to age, with each group divided into those younger than 40 and those 40 years and older.

The competitive group was composed of those who spent more than 1,500 kcal/week in physical exercise. Individuals with an expenditure of between 1,000 and 1,500 kcal/week were considered recreational runners and those with less than 1,000 kcal/week were categorized as sedentary.

Table 5 shows the main characteristics of the subjects of this study. The nutritional analysis was performed as described above.

Table 3 Vitamin intake

	Athletes* (n = 130)	Controls* (n = 58)
Vitamin A (IU)	40%	39%
Vitamin C (mg)	1.4%	17%
Vitamin D (IU)	60%	8%
Vitamin E (mg)	100%	58%
Vitamin B1 (mg)	4.9%	8%
Riboflavin (mg)	0%	6%
Niacin (mg)	9.8%	15%
Vitamin B6 (mg)	0%	43%
Vitamin B12 (μcg)	0%	10%
Folic acid (μcg)	0%	22%

*Subjects consuming less than two thirds of the RDA (%)

Table 4 Mineral intake

	Athletes* (n = 130)	Controls* (n = 58)
Sodium (mg)	48%	34%
Calcium (mg)	11%	43%
Magnesium (mg)	40%	0%
Iron (mg)	36%	27%
Potassium (mg)	0%	34%
Zinc (mg)	29%	77%

*Subjects consuming less than two thirds RDA (%)

Results and Discussion

Figure 1 shows that there was no difference between the competitive runners of either age group as regards the ingestion of carbohydrates, total fat, mono- and polyunsaturated fat, cholesterol, and proteins. When the intake of the same nutrients between individuals younger than 40 years of age at various levels of activity are compared, only the carbohydrate intake was higher in the group of competitive runners; no other differences were detected (Fig. 2).

In individuals older than 40 years of age, there was a small, but statistically higher intake of all nutrients except cholesterol in the competitive group (Fig. 3). Recreational and sedentary subjects had no difference in the amount of any other nutrient consumed.

Among individuals younger than 40 years of age, the competitive runners consumed significantly more saturated and unsaturated fat (Fig. 4). Among individuals older than 40 years, competitive runners consumed increased levels of saturated fats. In comparing older and younger individuals, there appears to be an increase in fat intake in the recreational and sedentary subgroups. No group consumed the recommended mono- and polyunsaturated:saturated ratio of 2 to 1 or more (Fig. 5). The competitive athletes consumed the highest levels of each type of fat.

Table 5 Participant characteristics for nutritional habits of runners study

	Age (years)	n	Weight (kg)	Height (m)	Age (years)	Expenditure* (kcal/week)
			Competitive Runners (n = 190)			
Range	<40	105	52-99	1.61-1.94	20-39	2,037-9,800
Mean			69.8	1.73	33.5	3,711
Range	≥40	85	59-90	1.61-1.95	40-61	2,030-9,660
Mean			70.4	1.72	46.8	3,530
			Recreational Runners (n = 59)			
Range	<40	18	59-92.5	1.60-1.90	26-38	1,078-1,946
Mean			75.9	1.75	34.7	1,531
Range	≥40	41	55.5-99.9	1.35-1.87	40-60	1,043-1,995
Mean			77.8	1.70	48.2	1,514
			Sedentary Controls (n = 63)			
Range	<40	21	60-95	1.63-1.80	35-39	266-959
Mean			77.0	1.70	37.5	683
Range	≥40	42	57-99.9	1.57-1.84	40-61	119-980
Mean			76.9	1.69	48.2	584.9

*Energy expenditure in physical exercise

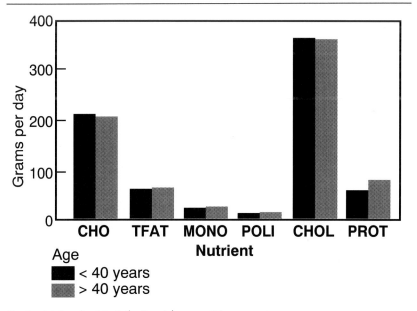

Fig. 1 *Intake of nutrients for Spanish competitive runners.*

Plasma Cholesterol Levels in Spanish Marathon Runners

Exercise literature for adults generally indicates that regular physical activity is associated with a healthy metabolic profile.[1] Several studies[2,3] have measured plasma cholesterol levels in Spanish sedentary

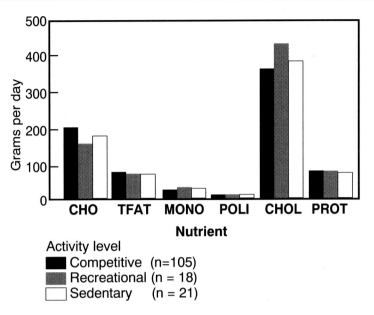

Fig. 2 *Intake of nutrients for individuals younger than 40 years of various activity levels* ($p < 0.05$).

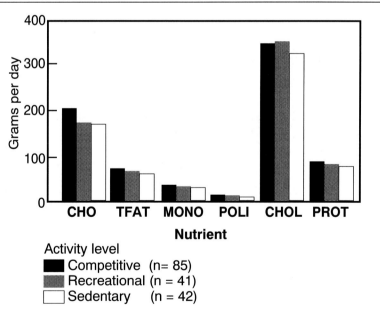

Fig. 3 *Intake of nutrients for individuals older than 40 years of various activity levels* ($p < 0.05$).

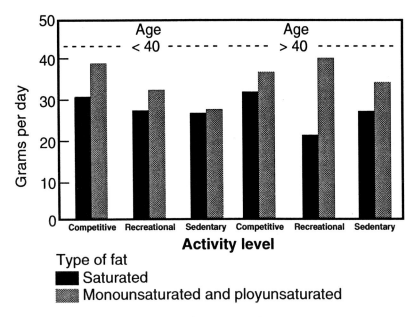

Fig. 4   *Fat intake for individuals at various activity levels.*

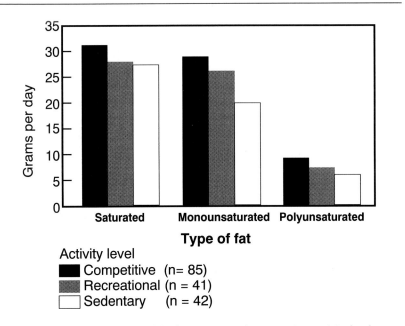

Fig. 5   *Fat intake for individuals older than 40 years of age at various activity levels (p < 0.05).*

individuals but there is no known such measurement in Spanish marathon runners. Marathon runners go through a very intensive training some months before a marathon and the vast majority of them are, according to our experience, very much concerned about diet. We thought it of interest to study plasma cholesterol levels in the participants of the pre-Olympic Barcelona marathon 4 months before the Olympic Games of 1992.

Methods

The study included 526 runners (496 men and 30 women) aged 19 to 74 years. Analyses were performed 1 to 2 days before the marathon by means of a quick (finger-stick sample) technique with a portable analyzer and with a coefficient of variation (CV) of greater than 3%. It is worth mentioning that portable analyzer values have been found significantly lower than those from an enzymatic assay (bias -2.5 and -3.7).[4]

Results and Discussion

The characteristics of the marathon runners who volunteered for the study and the mean of blood cholesterol levels are shown in Table 6.

The mean of the overall results (Table 6) showed that plasma cholesterol values for men were close to the "desirable levels" ($<$ 200 mg/100 ml), determined by the American National Cholesterol Education Program (NCEP), whereas levels for women were somewhat higher. When plasma cholesterol levels were adjusted for age, the highest values were obtained in 50- to 59-year-olds of both sexes (Table 7).

Table 8 shows the plasma cholesterol levels of the marathon runners and Table 9 shows the results reported by others[2] in a sedentary population from Catalunya, Spain. There are no differences among the total mean plasma cholesterol levels in the two studies. Also the mean percentages of the three cholesterol levels in both studies ($>$ 240, 200 to 240, and $<$ 200 mg/dl) are similar.

Discussion

One of the striking findings is that the amount of carbohydrate ingested by the great majority of the athletes is below the RDA. This is a limiting factor for optimal endurance capacity. The amount of carbohydrates needed to produce an optimal glycogen supply in the muscles is generally thought to be between 55% and 70% of the total daily calorie intake. Another noteworthy finding is the high level of saturated fat and cholesterol ingested by a large number of athletes. Almost all athletes and control subjects consumed less than 25 g fiber/day. Most of the athletes take vitamin and mineral supplements, which helps to compensate for their nutritional inadequacies.

Table 6 Individual characteristics and blood cholesterol levels of the marathon runners by sex

	Men*	Women*
Number	496	30
Age (years)	40 ± 10	42 ± 11
Running (km/week)	73 ± 29	48 ± 23
Years running	8 ± 6	7 ± 8
Completed marathons	6 ± 7	4 ± 8
Best marathon time (h)	3 ± 0	4 ± 0
Blood cholesterol (mg/dl)	202 ± 61	215 ± 45

* Value ± SD

Table 7 Marathon runners' total plasma cholesterol (mg/dl) by sex and age

Age (years)	Men (sample size)	Women (sample size)
<20	151.0 ± 24.5 (3)	—
20-29	170.6 ± 40.8 (69)	182.2 ± 29.5 (5)
30-39	193.5 ± 52.8 (162)*	211.2 ± 41.6 (5)
40-49	211.2 ± 61 (177)*	221.7 ± 47.7 (13)
50-59	233.8 ± 76.3 (64)	229.3 ± 48.3 (7)
60-69	198.5 ± 58.9 (13)	—
>70	168.1 ± 34.7 (8)	—

*p <0.003 between 30- to 39-year-old and 40- to 49-year-old men
± SD (n)

Table 8 Marathon runners' (466 men and 30 women) total plasma cholesterol (mg/dl)

Plasma Cholesterol* (mg/dl)	No. of Subjects			% of Subjects		
	Men	Women	Total	Men	Women	Average
>240	106	10	116	23	33	28
200-240	141	8	149	30	27	28
<200	219	12	231	47	40	43

* Average total plasma cholesterol: 208 mg/dl

Table 9 Total plasma cholesterol (mg/dl)* of sedentary Catalonian population (156 men and 158 women)

Plasma Cholesterol Cholesterol* (mg/dl)	No. of Subjects			% of Subjects		
	Men	Women	Total	Men	Women	Average
>240	39	38	77	25	24	24
200-240	52	51	103	33	32	33
<200	65	69	134	42	44	43

*Average total plasma cholesterol: 211 mg/dl
(Reproduced with permission from Planas P, et al: Cuantas personas son candidatas a reducir la concentración sérica de colesterol en la población adulta de Cataluña? *Clin Invest Atheros* 1991;3:149-156.)

The relationship between diet and dyslipoproteinemia is well described. The nature of the habitual diet—in particular the content of fat and cholesterol and the type of fat—clearly has a powerful influence on LDL-cholesterol and hence total cholesterol.

Grundy[5] has recently suggested that the Mediterranean diet is the healthiest diet for the prevention of cardiovascular diseases. This is mainly based on the generous use of olive oil, legumes (garbanzo beans, lentils, etc), cereals, fresh fruit, and fish, which provide monounsaturated fatty acids (olive oil), fiber, and antioxidants. Furthermore, Grundy reviewed the amount of fat consumed by Americans and established certain desirable levels. The American diet contains about 400 mg cholesterol/day, whereas only 200 mg/day is desirable. The content of saturated fatty acids of the American diet makes up 13% of the total calories, whereas no more than 7% is desirable. We believe that the advantages of the monounsaturated fatty acids are that they are safe, do not reduce HDL-cholesterol as opposed to polyunsaturated fatty acids, do not promote carcinogenesis in animals, and do not suppress the immune system.

These dietary patterns of the idealized Mediterranean diet are not reflected in the results of the studies outlined above. In my opinion, the main reasons for this are the proliferation of fast food restaurants, especially in Spanish cities, and changes in traditional eating habits as a result of more Spanish women entering the work force. The Mediterranean diet may still be preserved in some rural areas of the country.

The mean cholesterol levels obtained by Planas[2] do not differ markedly from those obtained in other studies of the general Spanish population; the same holds true even when the results are compared by age.

In chapter 3, Marrugat and associates found a mean total plasma cholesterol of 202 ± 36 mg/dl where the daily energy expenditure in training exceeded 285 kcal. These data are in close agreement with my findings. In their results, the most significant change was a marked decrease of plasma triglycerides. Our current results seem to support the view that cholesterol is not a parameter greatly affected by regular intensive physical training. The analysis of HDL-cholesterol in marathon runners probably would have given more marked differences with the general population.

The question of whether a single cholesterol measurement is enough to predict further levels is unresolved; however, the results of a recent study[6] have shown that one measurement is enough to predict future levels in healthy postmenopausal women.

Finally, the nutritional control and counseling of both the elite and the recreational athlete is important not only for an optimal performance but also for the maintenance of good health. The benefits of the modern Mediterranean diet should be reconsidered in light of modern nutritional changes in most Mediterranean urban areas where the influences of the American diet are being progressively introduced.

Acknowledgments

We are indebted to Boehringer-Mannheim for providing the portable analyzers (Reflotron) for conducting plasma cholesterol assays. Part of this work was supported by Laboratorios Menarini, Barcelona. We are also indebted to the nurses, M. Banquells, G. Coscolluela, M. A. Zamora, and C. Royo, for their technical assistance.

References

1. Wood PD, Stefanick ML: Exercise, fitness, and atherosclerosis, in Bouchard C, Shephard RJ, Stephens T, et al (eds): *Exercise, Fitness and Health: A Concensus of Current Knowledge.* Champaign, IL, Human Kinetics Books, 1990, pp 409-423.

2. Planas P: Cuantas personas son candidatas a reducir la concentración sérica de colesterol en la población adulta de Cataluña? *Clin Invest Atheros* 1991;3:149-156.

3. Muñiz J: Concentraciones séricas de colesterol en la población gallega de 40 - 49 años de edad. *Clin Invest Atheros* 1991;3:143-148.

4. Kaminsky LA, Whaley MH: Evaluation of within-day precision of serum cholesterol measured by a portable analyzer. *Med Sci Sports Exerc* 1992;24:134-138.

5. Grundy S: 39th Annual Meeting of the American College of Sports Medicine, Dallas, TX, May 1992.

6. Hetland ML, Haarbo J, Christiansen C: One measurement of serum total cholesterol is enough to predict future levels in healthy postmenopausal women. *Am J Med* 1992;92:25-28.

Chapter 22

Exercise and Nutrition at Midlife

Donna L. Wheeler, MS
James E. Graves, PhD
David T. Lowenthal, MD, PhD

Introduction

Midlife is typically identified chronologically as the years between 40 and 65.[1] However, there are differences in the aging process among individuals and even among organ systems of the same individual. This variability in functional loss may reflect disease processes, as well as a high-risk lifestyle throughout the years between childhood and adulthood. Inadequate physical activity and poor eating habits may lead to nutritional deficiencies or overnutrition and obesity, compromise the individual's athletic achievement, and increase the risk for chronic diseases such as heart disease and diabetes. Continuing proper nutritional habits and adequate physical activity into midlife and beyond may help minimize the physiologic changes associated with aging. Beginning a program of proper nutrition and exercise at midlife can even help to maintain an individual's physiologic status, prevent further declines in function, and perhaps even improve overall well-being. Nevertheless, an individual's genetic predisposition ultimately governs the nature of the interactions among exercise, nutrition, disease modification, and quality of life.

The purpose of this chapter is to discuss the effects of exercise and nutrition on overall body function at midlife. The first section reviews age-associated physiologic changes that typically manifest near midlife and then advance with age. The last two sections discuss the beneficial effects of exercise and proper nutrition in limiting or preventing age-associated physiologic changes and diseases.

Age-Associated Physiologic Changes

Outline 1 identifies some of the ways each body system is affected by the aging process. However, some changes are more apparent and typically present earlier in life. To understand the midlife transition,

Outline 1 Physiologic changes that occur with aging

Basal Metabolism, Energy Metabolism, and Body Composition
  ↓ Basal metabolic rate
  ↓ Lean body mass
  ↑ Body fat
  ↓ Intracellular and extracellular water

Cardiovascular System
  ↑ Atherosclerotic plaque
  ↓ Cardiac output
  ↓ Maximum heart rate
  ↓ Maximum oxygen consumption (functional capacity)
  ↑ Blood pressure

Respiratory System
  ↓ Vital capacity
  ↑ Residual volume
  ↓ Flow rate

Musculoskeletal Systems
  ↓ Bone mass
  ↓ Muscle mass
  ↓ Muscular strength
  ↓ Slow oxidative muscle fibers

Renal System
  ↓ Glomerular filtration rate
  ↓ Renal plasma flow

Hepatic System
  ↓ Hepatic blood flow
  ↓ Drug metabolizing capacity

Endocrine/Autonomic Nervous System
  ↓ Insulin sensitivity
  ↓ Pituitary function (growth hormone)
  ↑ Plasma catecholamines
  ↓ Renin-angiotensin-aldosterone responsiveness
  ↓ Baroreceptor responsiveness

Nervous System
  ↓ Reaction time
  ↓ Brain tissue mass
  ↓ Beta-receptor reactivity

it is important to recognize these changes and to be familiar with the influence of nutrition and exercise training.

Basal Metabolism, Energy Metabolism, and Body Composition

Both basal metabolic rate and daily energy expenditure decline with age. These decreases in metabolic function may be either the cause or the effect of associated changes in body composition. Metabolic activity may decline because of decreases in lean body mass (metabolically active tissue) and increases in total body fat (metabolically inactive tissue). Conversely, reduced activity may precipitate decreases in lean body mass and increases in total body fat. Whether the cause or the effect, energy expenditure and basal metabolic rate have been found to be highly correlated to body composition.[2] Proper nutrition and exercise become increasingly important with age because they stimulate metabolic function and prevent obesity and nutrient deficiencies.

The accumulation of excess fat with age is the most prevalent of the age-associated physiologic changes. With advancing age, most individuals lose an average of 6.3% of their lean body mass per decade, but they maintain or increase total body mass by gaining fat.[3,4] The typical American gains approximately 30 lb of fat from the age of 20 to 50. By midlife, approximately 20% of men and 40% of women are obese.[5]

The roles of physical exercise and nutrition cannot be separated when assessing age-associated changes in metabolism and body composition. Reducing dietary fat is recommended to control obesity and associated diseases, such as diabetes, hypertension, atherosclerosis, cardiovascular disease, renal disease, and hepatic disease.[6,7] Increasing activity level and energy expenditure not only promotes the exchange of fat for lean body tissue (muscle), but also enhances an individual's chance of meeting the recommended dietary allowance (RDA) of nutrients by increasing the amount of food consumed to maintain energy balance. At caloric intakes below 1,200 to 1,400 kcal/day, it is difficult to meet the RDAs for vitamins and minerals without supplementation. Åstrand[8] recommends a minimum of 1 hour of physical activity per day to boost energy expenditure and allow higher daily caloric intake. Exercise also tends to have psychological effects relating to better satiety control, adapted preference for nutritionally dense food, and enhanced self-image, which indirectly affect nutrition and body composiiton.

Conversely, deliberate overeating of a high-fat, high-carbohydrate diet can cause weight gain, a large percentage of which is lean body mass.[9] A gain of nearly 40%[9] in lean body mass is thought to be related to the anabolic actions of three hormones—testosterone, insulin, and somatomedin-C/insulin-like growth factor—the levels of which are increased by overfeeding.[10] These data included women aged 18 to 41 years, with 40 years being the lower end of the range for "midlife." No data are available for women aged 50 to 65 years. Postmenopausal weight gain is a significant problem in women and may, in part, be related to overfeeding and inactivity.

For previously sedentary individuals who are beginning an exercise program, the reported changes in body composition have been variable, depending on the intensity and duration of the program. While some researchers have found significant decreases in total body fat with accompanying increases in lean body mass,[11] others have failed to note changes in body mass composition with training.[12,13] When men in late midlife supplemented their diet by an additional 560 ± 16 kcal/day and participated in 12 weeks of strength training, they experienced increases in body weight, skinfold thickness (subcutaneous fat), and creatinine excretion. There was no discernable gain in strength over that seen in a control group whose diet was not supplemented.[14]

Long-term regular exercise alters age-associated changes in body composition. Oscai and associates[15] found that body composition can be maintained throughout midlife with regular exercise. This finding was substantiated by Heath and associates,[16] who evaluated the body composition of elite male master runners and cyclists, aged 50 to 75, and found no discernible change in percentage of body fat and lean body mass when compared to younger elite male athletes. The master athletes were also significantly leaner than both an age-matched untrained control group and a younger untrained group.

Other researchers have found body composition changes with age, even in lifelong athletes. Lundholm and associates[17] compared older lifelong athletes to their sedentary peers and noted that although the athletes trained intensely most of their lives, they did not have increased lean body mass when compared to their sedentary peers. However, the athletes had a significantly lower percentage of body fat. Meredith and associates[18] also found significant body composition changes with age when comparing young and midlife male endurance athletes. These results indicated that older male athletes had a greater percentage of body fat in spite of having similar body mass index (weight/height^2). Regular long-term exercise, therefore, may prevent age-associated increases in body fat, yet not affect lean body mass. These researchers hypothesized that body composition may be more closely related to time spent exercising per week (metabolic activity) rather than age.

In general, the daily energy expenditure with activity and the basal metabolic rate progressively decline throughout adult life. Maintaining the daily energy expenditure with exercise into midlife will help to obviate this decline in energy output and intake. Blair and associates[19] found that midlife runners' energy intake was 40% to 60% greater than that of sedentary men and women of the same age. These enhanced energy needs are similar to those demonstrated by young adults. Exercise requires more energy, which in turn requires a higher caloric demand to maintain energy balance. The more food consumed, the higher the total nutrient intake, thus assuring consumption of the daily RDAs.

Cardiovascular System

The most predominant debilitating age-related changes are associated with the cardiovascular system. Cardiovascular disease includes coronary artery disease, hypertension, stroke, congestive heart failure, and peripheral vascular disease; many of these diseases are precipitated by arteriosclerosis or atherosclerosis.

Arteriosclerosis is defined as any form of vascular degeneration (thickening or loss of resilience) of the arterial wall. Atherosclerosis specifically refers to the accumulation of fat in the intimal lining of the vessels, with an associated thickening of the connective tissue in the underlying subintima. Atherosclerosis is often referred to as a childhood disease because the mass of plaque (fatty deposits) originates in childhood and accumulates throughout life. Often the consequences or symptoms of atherosclerosis do not appear until midlife or late adulthood.[1]

The physiologic consequences of atherosclerosis depend on the site of accumulation. Coronary artery disease or ischemic heart disease involve the blockage of the coronary arteries and may lead to myocardial infarction. Blockage of the cerebral vessels often results in stroke. Blockage of the peripheral vessels, such as the femoral arteries, induces symptoms of intermittent claudication. Therefore, atherosclerosis is associated with many dangerous and often fatal diseases. The symptoms resulting from atherosclerotic plaque may be reduced or even eliminated by the adoption of a diet low in animal fats in conjunction with adequate amounts of aerobic exercise. Restricting dietary cholesterol to 300 mg/day and saturated fats to 10% of the total 30% fat intake is usually recommended to treat hypercholesterolemia and to treat and prevent atherosclerosis and cardiovascular disease.[20]

Vigorous exercise in the form of a stress test is used to induce symptoms and diagnose ischemic heart disease. Electrocardiograms taken during exercise usually reveal ST-wave depressions in those atherosclerotic individuals with angina. Anginal pain can severely limit physical activity and activity should be discontinued when symptoms develop.[21] Drugs such as beta-blockers and calcium channel blockers eliminate symptoms by reducing myocardial contractility, but they can cause other cardiac problems. The occurrence of anginal pain may, however, subside with regular, progressive, aerobic exercise of moderate intensity. This reduction in pain may be due to increased coronary blood flow or to neovascularization, which creates alternate routes for blood flow.[21] Exercise is used both to prevent myocardial infarction in midlife in individuals with angina[22] and as part of a cardiac rehabilitation program following myocardial infarction, where it has been proven to help patients return to a normal lifestyle and to decrease the mortality rate compared with sedentary patients.[21,23]

It is less clear that stroke and intermittent claudication are improved by exercise. Diabetes and cigarette smoking are the major risk factors associated with intermittent claudication, a condition that does not typically manifest at midlife. Stroke, however, is more common in midlife and is highly associated with hypertension, obesity, and cigarette smoking.[1]

There is a steady rise in systemic blood pressure from early adulthood to age 65 with little increase in pressure beyond midlife.[1] This increase in blood pressure with age promotes tissue perfusion through narrowed atherosclerotic vessels. Hypertension, however, is defined as the chronic elevation of blood pressure above levels considered desirable or healthy for the individual's age. For adults through midlife, a systolic blood pressure between 140 and 159 mm

Hg and/or diastolic pressures between 90 and 95 mm Hg are considered borderline hypertensive, with values above this range considered absolute hypertension.[21] Absolute hypertension is the most common cardiovascular disease and usually manifests early in adulthood, often before midlife.

Although antihypertensive drugs continue to be widely used for the treatment of hypertension, altering nutritional factors may also help to mitigate or control symptomatic hypertension. These factors include controlling obesity, maintaining appropriate dietary intakes of sodium, potassium, calcium, and fat, and limiting alcohol consumption. The use of regular aerobic exercise to control or reduce hypertension, once controversial, is now known to be beneficial.[1,12,24,25]

In young and midlife adults, the development of atherosclerosis and cardiovascular disease is very highly correlated with elevated levels of circulating triglycerides (TG), total cholesterol (TC), and low-density lipoproteins (LDL), and low levels of high-density lipoproteins (HDL).[2,26] Moderate aerobic exercise and consumption of a low-fat diet have been shown by many researchers to lower serum total cholesterol and low-density lipoproteins, while increasing high-density lipoproteins and the high-density lipoproteins/total cholesterol ratio, especially in those with hyperlipidemia.[20,27-29] Running (a minimum of 15 km/week) tends to be more effective than walking in raising high-density lipoprotein levels.[20,29] Lifetime exercisers maintain a more normal lipid profile with the advancement of chronologic age, and thus, may obviate or postpone atherosclerosis and associated problems.[30]

In addition to age-related changes associated with the onset and progression of cardiovascular diseases, the aerobic or functional capacity ($\dot{V}O_2max$) of the cardiovascular system to deliver oxygen to working muscles tends to decline with age.[31,32] Decreases in lean body mass, reductions in maximum heart rate, and compromised cardiac output are often attributed to this decrease in $\dot{V}O_2max$. The drop in $\dot{V}O_2max$ results from inadequate myocardial contractility, impaired coronary blood flow, reduced preload, increased afterload, and decreased sensitivity to catecholamine stimulation.[33] The arteriovenous oxygen difference may also contribute to reductions in $\dot{V}O_2max$ by deficient oxygenation of arterial blood, anemia, increased blood flow to the skin, and decreased oxygen extraction from working muscles. Rodeheffer and associates[34] suggest the decreases in functional capacity are primarily a result of general inactivity-related changes, rather than age-associated changes in the cardiovascular system.

Initiation of a regular exercise program has been shown to maintain or improve aerobic capacity throughout midlife, although the magnitude of cardiovascular training benefits in individuals older than 50 years of age is diminished compared to their younger counterparts.[35,36] Despite limitations for cardiovascular improvement,

Kasch and Wallace[37] demonstrated maintenance or improvement in $\dot{V}O_2$max of mature, previously sedentary adults, aged 45 to 55, with three 1-hour sessions running or swimming per week. Similarly, Pollock and associates[38] showed 18% improvement in $\dot{V}O_2$max in sedentary men, aged 49 to 65, in response to a regular aerobic training regimen (walking or jogging) for 20 weeks. In a more recent study in an older age group, a 22% change in $\dot{V}O_2$max was produced using a similar protocol to that used by Pollock.[39]

However, other researchers have shown declines in aerobic capacity with age, even with the use of similar exercise programs.[40-42] This discrepancy may have resulted from differences in the duration of the exercise program. Short-term exercise programs have very little effect on improving physiologic function, whereas prolonged training can improve $\dot{V}O_2$max, stroke volume, and cardiac output.[43] Other training studies have shown widening of the arteriovenous oxygen difference,[36] ie, an increase in oxygen uptake by muscle and enhanced peripheral circulation,[44] with the initiation of regular aerobic exercise. Although the initiation of exercise programs tends to improve cardiovascular parameters during physical activity, very few changes are seen in resting heart rate, cardiac output, and blood pressure.[45]

Continuing regular aerobic exercise throughout life does not prevent age-associated declines in functional capacity ($\dot{V}O_2$max), even when competitive athletes train regularly at a high intensity. Dill and associates[46] and Pollock and associates[47] report declines in oxygen transport of 0.67 ml/kg/min and 0.42 ml/kg/min, respectively, in longitudinal studies of active competitive athletes. This loss in aerobic power tends to be less than the loss experienced by the general population.[1] Vaccaro and associates[48] found similar decreases in $\dot{V}O_2$max in both competitive swimmers and sedentary individuals of 7% to 8% per decade; however, the aerobic capacity of the swimmers was significantly higher than that of the untrained individuals. Shephard[1] commented that although the master athlete may be losing aerobic power despite intense conditioning, an athlete's maximum oxygen uptake at age 65 is comparable with that of a sedentary 25-year-old individual. Many lifelong athletes experience cardiac hypertrophy. Typically, hypertrophy is not detrimental to cardiac function: echocardiographic findings in endurance-trained persons showed right and left ventricular chamber enlargement and left ventricular hypertrophy significantly greater than anticipated for the general population.[49]

Respiratory System

Respiratory function deteriorates with advancing age and inactivity.[50] Vital capacity decreases as residual volume increases, yet total lung capacity is typically unchanged. The decrease in vital capacity is caused by a reduction in thoracic compliance, which results in greater ventilatory energy expenditure. Aerobic exercise tends to increase the tidal volume.[12] However, because vital capacity is reduced in older athletes, increases in tidal volume exceeding 55% to 60% of vital capacity may cause shortness of breath, which may limit exercise potential.[50]

Neuromuscular System

The function of the neuromuscular system is extremely important for all athletes. Obviously exercise affects the size, strength, fiber composition, and function of the skeletal muscles. Often exercise can counteract or delay the detrimental effects of aging on the musculature.

Structural and functional changes in the muscle fibers of aging animals and humans adversely affect the neuromuscular junction, resulting in gradual reductions in synaptic contact and hormonal control.[51] Exercise tends to maintain nerve conduction velocity, which otherwise tends to decline with age.[52] These investigators[51,52] determined that the average difference in reaction time between young, active individuals (mean age, 23.6 years) and older active individuals (mean age, 57.2 years) was only 8%, whereas the difference between young, sedentary individuals (mean age, 25.4 years) and older, sedentary individuals (mean age, 56.3 years) was 22%. Regular aerobic exercise may preserve oxidative capacity in the brain, thereby preserving psychomotor processing as aging progresses.

Muscle strength and mass tend to decrease 30% to 50% between the ages of 30 and 70 years.[51,53] Larsson[54] noted age-related atrophy of the vastus lateralis muscle fiber in biopsy samples taken from 18 sedentary men, aged 18 to 65, prior to a 15-week strength training program. These previously untrained individuals showed significant increases in fiber size, proving that aged muscle retains its plasticity and potential for hypertrophy.

Muscular adaptation depends on the intensity, duration, frequency, and pattern of the stimulus. Endurance training and/or strength training are associated with muscle fiber hypertrophy and/or fiber interconversion. Fiber interconversion depends on changes in neural input.[55] When fast-twitch muscle fibers receive electric stimulation over several weeks in patterns and frequencies similar to those found in slow-twitch fibers, the fast-twitch fibers show increased oxidative capacities, decreased glycolytic enzyme activities, and decreased myosin ATPase activities.[56] Thus, the fast-twitch fibers were transformed to resemble slow-twitch fibers. Similarly, intense endurance training increases the oxidative capacity of all active muscle fibers.[57-59]

The interconversion of fast-twitch to slow-twitch fibers may play only a small role in an athlete's muscle fiber composition, a larger contributor is more likely to involve genetic endowment.[55] Endurance training (low-intensity contractions with a large number of repetitions) tends to increase the oxidative capacity of both type I (slow oxidative) and type II (fast glycolytic) fibers, whereas strength training (high-intensity contractions with a small number of repetitions) tends to be more effective in producing hypertrophy and type II fibers.[60] Frontera and associates[60] found that strength training increased the number of both type I and type II fibers in this area, with no changes in the proportion of fiber types when compared to age-matched control subjects. However, Lowenthal[61] has suggested, based on histologic evaluation of the plantaris muscle (type I, type IIa and type IIb fibers) and soleus muscle (predominately type I fibers) of aging rats, that aging tends to decrease the number of type I muscle fibers in sedentary age-matched controls. However, aerobic exercise tends to increase the number of type I muscle fibers in exercise, age-matched controls when the number of type I muscle fibers are compared over a 20 month period. Other work using human subjects[54,62] has shown that absence of stimulus and aging tend to decrease the proportional area of type II muscle fibers (fast glycolytic) to type I fiber area (slow oxidative).

The oxidative capacity (oxidative enzymes), ie, enzyme concentration, of muscle tends to decline with advancing age. Exercise can partially reverse this natural decrease in the muscle's oxidative capacity. Endurance training has been shown to increase mitochondrial cytochrome oxidase, as well as the activity of citric acid cycle (oxidative) enzymes in both young and old subjects.[40,63,64] Orlander and Aniansson[63] reported no changes in the volume fraction of mitochondria in older men following training, which suggests that the increase in oxidative capacity must have occurred within the existing mitochondrial volume (contrary to the increased volume fraction of mitochondria seen in younger men). Phosphofructokinase activity was also increased in these subjects, following training, indicating increased glycolytic capacity.

Moderate work or physical activity typically does not increase protein requirements; however, athletes in heavy training to build muscle mass may need to temporarily increase intake of dietary protein.[65] Gontzea and associates[66] conducted a controlled, long-term study to determine the protein requirements of endurance athletes. Intense endurance training tends to have a catabolic effect on protein balance in the first week of training; however, within 2 weeks, the body adapts to the added exercise stress and reestablishes the nitrogen balance without requiring additional dietary intake of protein. This initial increase in daily protein requirements in endurance athletes was confirmed by Tarnopolski and associates.[67] Protein supplements are rarely needed in nonvegetarian healthy athletes who eat balanced diets. In fact, protein utilization by skeletal muscle is enhanced by endurance training. Protein supplements, either predigested protein hydrolysates or free amino acid mixtures, are very popular among bodybuilders, yet there is no proof that these supplements have muscle-building capabilities.[68] The effects of strength training on protein metabolism are less clear than the effects of endurance training.[68]

Renal System

Renal function is typically maintained through the first 3 decades of life, after which there is a progressive functional decline of about 10% per decade.[69] Sluggish renal sodium conservation mechanisms in older athletes tend to make them more susceptible to dehydration.[70] Neuroendocrine influences also affect kidney function. Plasma renin and aldosterone concentrations decrease with advancing age as a result of reduced sympathetic input to the juxtaglomerular apparatus of the kidney.[69,70]

Endocrine System

Changes in whole-body carbohydrate metabolism and insulin sensitivity occur with advancing age. Levels of circulating glucose following an oral glucose tolerance test increase an average of 1 mg/dl per decade.[2] Impaired glucose tolerance has been associated with an increased risk of atherosclerosis, cataracts, non-insulin-dependent diabetes mellitus, and fat accumulation.[71] Obese individuals have reduced insulin sensitivity that is proportional to their degree of obesity.[1] Insulin sensitivity and glucose tolerance can be enhanced and maturity-onset diabetes can be controlled by increasing the percentage of complex carbohydrates in the diet, participating in regular physical exercise, and preventing or eliminating obesity.[1,2,71,72]

Hypopituitarism is more common with advancing age.[22] The reduction of circulating growth hormone with advancing age diminishes fat metabolism and protein synthesis.[11] Submaximal endurance training has been shown to increase levels of serum growth hormone,[73] which act to conserve body protein and augment fat mobilization. These effects are especially important in the older athlete, who may be experiencing such age-related changes as reductions in glycogen stores, diminished peripheral circulation, and decreased sensitivity of growth hormone target cells.[1,11,74]

The loss of androgens with advancing age can result in the loss of protein in muscle tissue. Intake of high-quality protein coupled with progressive exercise has been shown to offset the muscle wasting associated with decreased circulation of androgens.[75] Ingestion of protein encourages anabolism much more readily in young adults than older adults, however.

Liver

Hepatic blood flow and drug-metabolizing capacity, including plasma protein binding of drugs, decrease with age. Exercise does not result in further compromise of hepatic function.[76]

Skeletal System

More than 80% of individuals 60 years of age and older have radiographic evidence of osteoarthritis,[1] and almost 60% of Americans older than 55 years of age have symptoms of arthritis.[77] Joints afflicted with osteoarthritis are typically painful and stiff. Common treatment involves the administration of analgesics for pain, a reduction in weightbearing exercise, and an emphasis on increasing flexibility and muscular strength throughout appropriate exercises.

Primary osteoporosis is an age-related disorder characterized by decreased bone mass and increased susceptibility to fractures. Peak bone mass occurs about 35 years of age for cortical bone and earlier for trabecular bone; peak mass is influenced by sex, race, nutrition, exercise, and overall health. After reaching its peak, bone mass slowly and steadily declines with age because of an imbalance in bone remodeling: the rate of bone resorption exceeds the rate of bone formation.

Osteoporosis affects between 15 and 20 million Americans and is almost 10 times more common in women than in men. The higher incidence of osteoporosis among women is due to the fact that women have approximately 30% less bone mass than men. Bone mass declines rapidly after the onset of menopause due to the withdrawal of estrogen effect. Other risk factors include cigarette smoking, calcium deficiency, immobilization or prolonged bed rest, and a physically inactive lifestyle. Some dietary factors such as consumption of alcohol, vitamins A and C, magnesium, phosphorus, and protein may indirectly promote or prevent osteoporosis through their effects on calcium metabolism. A high-protein diet or protein supplements may produce a dose-related loss of calcium in the urine, and therefore, may have negative long-term effects on bone mass.[1,78]

The use of calcium supplements for the prevention and treatment of postmenopausal osteoporosis is controversial. Some investigators believe that supplementary calcium improves calcium balance and reduces bone loss,[79] but others believe that calcium supplementation is only effective when administered in conjunction with estrogen replacement.[80] Additionally, two thirds of American women between the ages of 18 and 30 (when peak bone mass is attained) consume less than the RDA for calcium, which may increase the incidence of osteoporosis later in life.[81]

Both exercise and calcium supplementation have been shown to prevent the loss of bone minerals in nonosteoporotic, midlife (age 30 to 60 years) and older women (older than 60 years). However, an additive effect was not seen in elderly women when the treatments were combined.[82] Mechanical loading of the skeleton through physical exercise has been associated with greater bone mass.[83] Yet, some young women who provide mechanical stimuli, ie, vigorous exercise, to their skeleton, consume adequate amounts of calcium, or have low caloric intake but diminished circulating estrogen have reduced bone mass.[84]

Nervous System

Both central and peripheral components of the nervous system slow in reactivity with age. This occurs independently of any cortical atrophy. Exercise may improve psychomotor responses.[76]

The Roles of Exercise and Nutrition in Preventing Age-Related Diseases

Most of the physiologic changes described in the preceding sections are found with advancing age. However, the magnitude of these changes can be influenced by active participation in a healthy lifestyle, including adequate exercise and proper nutrition, as shown in Outlines 2 and 3. Much of the available research on the effects exercise and nutrition have on physiologic function and age-related diseases is conducted on either younger or older adults; research involving adults in midlife is typically neglected. Therefore, more research is needed to identify the special needs of adults in midlife.[85] Where available, research specifically addressing exercise and nutrition in midlife is presented in the following sections. However, research findings on younger and older adults were often used to make recommendations about the needs of the midlife group.

Exercise in Midlife

More than 45% of American adults do not participate in physical activity outside the workplace.[86] In addition, the amount of physical activity seems to decrease with age for a variety of reasons, ranging from disability and disease to lack of knowledge about exercise, conditioning principles, and the availability of facilities. Individuals who are sedentary in early adulthood may have difficulty changing their unhealthy habits, whereas individuals with an active lifestyle in early adulthood tend to remain active throughout midlife and maintain a high level of fitness.[87]

In a classic study by Paffenbarger and associates,[88] the physical activity habits and incidence of disease in 36,500 Harvard University alumni were studied using questionnaires. The authors concluded that men with an activity index (caloric expenditure during physical activity or exercise) below 2,000 kcal/week were at 64% higher risk of cardiovascular disease. Paffenbarger and associates[89] also reported that less than 20% of the Harvard graduates spent more than 2 hours a week participating in physical exercise. The infrequency of exercise among adults also was revealed in the Sallis and associates[90] study of Californians, which showed that only 8% of men and 2% of women aged 50 to 64 years had exercised regularly during the previous year. Midlife obesity, cardiovascular disease, hypertension, and diabetes were among the reasons cited for inactivity. Although these conditions may prevent some individuals from exercising, exercise itself

Outline 2 Physiologic changes with aging that are positively influenced by exercise

↑ Lean body mass (fat-free mass)
↓ Body fat
↑ Sympathetic nervous system reactivity
↓ Blood pressure
↑ Maximum oxygen uptake (functional capacity)
↑ HDL-cholesterol
↓ LDL-cholesterol
↓ Triglycerides
↑ Respiratory function
↑ Muscular mass and strength
↑ Bone mass
↓ Insulin resistance

Outline 3 Physiologic changes with aging that are positively influenced by exercise and dietary intervention

↓ Blood pressure
↓ Body fat
↓ Blood lipids
↑ Bone mass
↓ Insulin resistance

actually has proven to be a means of preventing many of these age-related diseases.[91,92]

The following sections provide information on the special exercise concerns for adults in midlife. The needs of both untrained, sedentary midlife athletes who are just beginning an exercise program, as well as lifelong or competitive athletes, will be considered.

Exercise for the Sedentary Individual at Midlife   An individual's compliance with a healthy lifestyle of regular exercise and proper nutrition is an important issue. Although improved health and well-being can be motivating factors for some individuals, the majority of the population does not comply with the prescribed changes. Some factors that may increase the success of an exercise and nutrition program include social support, positive feedback, convenience, and minimal time and expense.[21] Initially, the changes in lifestyle may require some effort, but once these changes become habit, they require the same effort as an unhealthy lifestyle. Adults older than 45 years of age who are thinking about starting an intense exercise program should consult with their physician, even those in apparent good health and those involved in exercise as young adults.[42]

Exercise prescription depends on the baseline fitness of the individual. DeVries[42] has documented that older individuals can withstand and benefit from physical exercise in the same ways as their younger counterparts, yet he recommended that the intensity of the conditioning proceed at a slower pace. However, a training effect (improvement in cardiovascular fitness) is not typically seen unless the intensity of the exercise exceeds 50% $\dot{V}O_2$max or the duration of the exercise is prolonged.[93]

Exercise intensity is usually monitored with heart rate rather than oxygen consumption. Initially, maximum heart rates during exercise should be between 120 and 130 bpm for most healthy, mature adults. Exercise intensity should then be slowly increased to yield heart rates between 140 and 150 bpm. DeVries[42] suggested individuals maintain their heart rate at 60% of their heart rate range and not fall below 40% or exceed 75% of that range for optimal benefits of exercise.

Standard recommendations for duration of exercise sessions are 20 to 60 minutes three to four times per week.[21] A well-rounded exercise program that produces total body fitness incorporates aerobic exercise with muscle strengthening, flexibility, and stretching exercises, relaxation, and stress management, as well as proper nutrition. Pollock and Wilmore[21] discuss exercise prescriptions in more depth.

Safety and the prevention of injury are also important issues when dealing with sedentary untrained individuals, especially older adults. Injuries can discourage even the most motivated athlete from continuing or resuming exercise after recovery. Physiologic and psychomotor changes that occur around midlife can increase the risk of acute and chronic/overuse injuries.[1] These changes include the loss of muscle mass and gain of body fat (which increase body mass, placing more strain on musculotendinous units), loss of balance and psychomotor skills, shortening of tendons due to years of inactivity, training progression that is too rapid for appropriate adaptation and recovery, inadequate warm-up, and improper shoes.

Exercise and the Aging Athlete   Athletes in midlife who have exercised regularly most of their lives require special considerations.

These athletes typically have an established exercise routine, which may or may not be conducive to total body fitness. Often the exercise routines will focus on only one aspect of fitness, neglecting equally important areas. For example, they may emphasize aerobic training, while neglecting flexibility and strengthening exercises. Competitive master athletes often increase their training intensity in midlife. The cardiovascular fitness of these athletes tends to improve as the intensity of training is increased, often to levels greater than those seen in these same individuals at younger ages.[1]

Musculoskeletal injuries are common among master athletes. Shephard and Kavanagh[94] reported that 57.2% of master track athletes sustained an injury of sufficient severity to interrupt training within the previous year. Nutritional deficiencies may also predispose these older athletes to injury. However, of those athletes studied by Shephard and Kavanagh[94] who had a serious injury, 63% were taking dietary supplements. Large doses of vitamin C (500 mg/day or more) did not prove to be beneficial. It may be that occasional injuries are not completely avoidable in master athletes because of the intensity of training; however, proper recovery time, balanced muscle strength, and adequate muscle flexibility may reduce the frequency of injury.

Guidelines for Exercise in Midlife   There are several physiologic concerns that demand more attention as individuals at all skill levels approach midlife. The following guidelines may help an individual enhance performance, reduce injuries, and improve overall fitness: (1) Maintain adequate strength and flexibility. Strong, flexible muscles are less vulnerable to musculotendinous soreness and injuries. (2) Balance strength between the agonist and antagonist muscle groups to help avoid muscle and joint injuries. (3) Incorporate both aerobic and strength training to ensure complete cardiovascular and musculoskeletal fitness. (4) Vary training regimens to include both upper and lower body conditioning for complete, balanced fitness. (5) Allow time for recovery following an intense or long workout. With advancing age, the ability of the muscles to replenish glycogen stores and eliminate muscle waste products is reduced. Therefore, it is important to intersperse easy workout days with hard days and to rest when needed. Rest allows the musculoskeletal system to recover and heal, enabling older individuals to perform up to his or her potential.

Exercise, either for fitness or competition, increases metabolic expenditure and increases the energy demands of the body. A balanced diet is essential to fuel the athlete's increased energy expenditure. Proper nutrition becomes more important as individuals age due to physiologic changes in basal metabolism, gastrointestinal absorption of nutrients, glucose metabolism and glycogen storage, and body composition. Specific research on individuals in midlife is often lacking, and information acquired from studies of younger and older adults must be applied. The following section presents nutritional guidelines adapted to convey the special needs of individuals in midlife.

Nutrition

Food is composed of fat, protein, carbohydrates, vitamins, minerals, and dietary fiber. From a functional point of view, food is the fuel that runs the human engine. The energy content of food is based on the intake of fat, protein, and carbohydrate and is measured in calories (cal) or kilocalories (kcal). In addition to energy requirements, humans also have vitamin and mineral requirements, which can be met by eating the same foods used for energy sources. At least three guidelines have been developed to help individuals select nutritious meals and prevent malnutrition or overnutrition.

(1) Calories In = Calories Out. To maintain energy equilibrium, an individual's age, sex, body mass, and activity level are used to determine their metabolic rate or energy output, which is balanced by their caloric intake. Charts describing energy expenditure during

Table 1 Calorie output for sports and activities

Work Category	Men kcal/min/65 kg	METs	Women kcal/min/55 kg	METs	Activities
Light	2.0–4.9	1.6–3.9	1.5–3.4	1.2–2.7	Walking, reading a book, driving a car, shopping, bowling, fishing, golf, pleasure sailing
Moderate	5.0–7.4	4.0–5.9	3.5–5.4	2.8–4.3	Pleasure cycling, dancing, volleyball, badminton, calisthentics
Heavy	7.5–9.9	6.0–7.9	5.5–7.4	4.4–5.9	Ice skating, water skiing, competitive tennis, novice mountain climbing, jogging
Very heavy	10.0–12.4	8.0–9.9	7.5–9.4	6.0–7.5	Fencing, touch football, scuba diving, basketball, swimming (most strokes)
Unduly heavy	>12.5	>10.0	>9.5	>7.6	Handball, squash, cross-country skiing, paddleball, running (fast pace)

(Reproduced with permission from Pollock ML, Wilmore J: *Exercise in Health and Disease: Evaluation and Prescription for Prevention and Rehabilitation*, ed 2. Philadelphia, PA, WB Saunders, 1990.)

various physical activities can be found in the several texts (Table 1).[21,95] Many weight-conscious adults keep track of daily caloric consumption to burn more calories than they expend in order to lose weight or to maintain energy equilibrium. However, caloric equilibrium does not necessarily ensure adequate nutrition.

(2) Meet the Recommended Dietary Allowances (RDAs).[96] The RDAs provide information on the vitamin, mineral, and energy content of food. The RDAs are based on both age and sex. Although the consumption of the recommended RDA typically ensures adequate nutrition for the average adult, most individuals do not keep track of their daily intake of specific vitamins and minerals. These issues are addressed below.

(3) Select from the Four Basic Food Groups. Nutrition is often categorized according to the following four basic food groups: bread and grains; fruits and vegetables; dairy products; and meat and fish. Daily consumption of the appropriate number of servings from each food group provides a balanced diet, theoretically contributing both the RDAs and the required caloric intake for optimal nutrition. It is easier for the average individual to understand and use the concept of food categories in selecting a balanced diet than to compute the vitamin and mineral content of each food; thus, food categories may provide a more effective method of achieving dietary goals. Many popular and effective diets (such as Weight Watchers) are based on a balanced intake of food from these basic food groups.

Regardless of the methods used to promote consumption of nutritional food, the ultimate goal is to fulfill the RDAs because the RDAs are based on the latest scientific research. A large safety factor is built into each nutritional recommendation to account for the variability of individual requirements.

The publication of the 10th edition of the *Recommended Dietary Allowances*[96] was delayed to permit further examination of the special nutritional needs of individuals older than 50 years of age.[97] However, the 1989 edition of *Recommended Dietary Allowances* continued to group older Americans into one category, 51 years or more. The most recent guidelines do not contain the anticipated daily increases in vitamins A and C, and calcium for older individuals.[96,97]

The physiologic changes that occur between the ages of 50 and 90 are at least as numerous as those occurring in adolescence and therefore warrant modifications in the nutritional recommendations. For example, an active man in midlife who consumes more than 2,500 kcal/day would have different nutritional requirements than a 90-year-old man in a nursing home consuming fewer than 1,250 kcal/day. All individuals age at different rates based on lifelong nutritional intake, body composition, physical activity, and disease states; therefore, nutritional recommendations for the older individuals are, by necessity, very broad and general.[97] Chernoff and Lipschitz[7] suggest nutritional recommendations for individuals over 50 be made with reference to their level of physical fitness/health or disease state (ie, cancer, osteoporosis, obesity, atherogenesis, hypertension, and diabetes).

Daily energy expenditure tends to decline with age; thus, the total caloric intake needed to maintain energy balance is reduced. This reduction in caloric intake highlights the importance of eating nutritionally dense foods and carefully planning daily meals to include all important nutrients. Individuals with slower metabolism, inadequate nutrient absorption capabilities (due to aging, alcohol consumption, disease, or drug and nutrient interactions), and reduced nutrient intake are at risk for deficiencies of vitamin C, vitamin D, pyridoxine, thiamin, folate, riboflavin, and zinc.[98] The effects of chronic inadequate nutrient intake are cumulative and often do not materialize until the individual is under physical or emotional stress.

The physical signs and symptoms of nutritional deficiencies listed in Outline 4 are often nonspecific and may be easily overlooked. Symptoms of malnutrition are manifested in 17% to 44% of hospitalized patients treated for unrelated illnesses or trauma due to pivotal physical and emotional stress.[98]

Nutritional deficiencies in athletes are typically more apparent than their sedentary peers because physical stress tends to accentuate deficiencies and because below par performance is not well tolerated by most athletes. However, malnutrition is rarely seen in athletes because the quantity of food eaten to maintain energy equilibrium ensures consumption of the minimal requirements of vitamins and minerals (assuming a balanced diet is consumed). Nevertheless, the validity and accuracy of recall for food consumed is questionable, leading to inaccurate estimations of food intake.[99] Most Americans, including athletes, eat too much fat, too much protein, and too little carbohydrate.[100] Correction of small nutritional imbalances, such as too much dietary fat, may not necessarily enhance athletic perform-

Outline 4 Physical signs and symptoms of nutritional deficiency

Wasting of fat and muscle tissue
Generalized weakness
Flaking dermatitis
Sparse, thin hair that is easy to pull out
Peripheral edema
Transverse lines on nails
Abdominal distention
Hepatomegaly
Parotid gland enlargement
Changes in skin pigmentation
Anorexia
Depression

ance, yet may prevent suboptimal performance. Proper nutrition enables athletes of all ages to train effectively and perform up to their potential, but neither proper nutrition nor nutritional supplements can provide magical ergogenic powers.

There are three principal nutritional energy sources: fats, proteins, and carbohydrates. Consumption of these energy sources supply the body with not only energy, but also with vitamins and minerals. The importance of each energy source will be discussed, with attention to the relevance of specific minerals and vitamins for the midlife athlete. Human nutrition and its effects on the physiologic system are reviewed by Shils and Young.[101] The RDAs for vitamins and minerals for adults in midlife are summarized in Table 2.

Fats

Fats or lipids are composed primarily of triglycerides, phospholipids, and cholesterol. A triglyceride molecule is composed of a glycerol moiety with attached fatty acids, which provide the fuel for muscular work. Fatty acids are either saturated (consisting of single bonds to carbon atoms that cannot accept additional hydrogen atoms) or unsaturated (consisting of double bonds between carbon atoms that can accept additional hydrogen atoms). Phospholipids contain glycerol, fatty acids, phosphorus, and nitrogen and are typically incorporated into cell membranes. Cholesterol provides the substrate for the synthesis of steroid hormone and is also incorporated into cell membranes. Fats are the most calorie-dense nutrient, contributing 9.0 kcal/g. Optimally, only 30% of the daily caloric intake should come from fat.

Proteins

Protein consists of long chains of amino acids with a central nitrogen atom. Nine of the 22 amino acids are considered essential because they are not produced by the human body and must be consumed. The amino acids of ingested proteins provide the building blocks for structural tissue (bones, skin, and connective tissue), muscles, hormones,

Table 2 Summary of daily RDAs for midlife adults (Adapted from RDA, 1989)

Nutrient	Midlife Adult RDA	Food Sources
Vitamin A	14 µg/kg retinol	Retinol: liver, butter, whole milk, cheese, egg yolk
	28 µg/kg beta-carotene	Carotenes: carrots, leafy green vegetables, sweet potatoes, winter squash, cantaloupes
Vitamin D	5 µg	fortified dairy products, fish oils, egg yolk, sunlight
Vitamin E	1.4 mg/kg	vegetable oil, margarine, green leafy vegetables, wheat germ, whole grain products, egg yolk, butter, liver
Vitamin K	1.1 µg/kg	leafy green vegetables, gut flora
Vitamin C	60 mg	broccoli, peppers, collards, brussel sprouts, strawberries, oranges, kale, grapefruit, papayas, mangos, spinach, tomatoes
Thiamine (B_1)	0.5 mg/1000 kcal	pork, liver, meat, whole grains, enriched grain products, legumes, nuts
Riboflavin (B_2)	0.6 mg/1000 kcal	liver, milk, yogurt, cottage cheese, meat, enriched grain products
Niacin	6.6 mg/1000 kcal	liver, meat, fish, peanuts, enriched grain products
Pyridoxine (B_6)	0.016 mg/g protein 0.03 mg/kg	meat, fish, shellfish, green leafy vegetables, whole grains, legumes
Folic Acid	3 µg/kg	liver, legumes, green leafy vegetables
Cyanocobalamin (B_{12})	2.0 µg	meat, fish, shellfish, milk, milk products
Biotin	30-100 µg	kidney, liver, milk, egg yolk, most fresh vegetables
Pantothenic Acid	4-7 mg	liver, kidney, meats, milk, egg yolk, whole grains, legumes
Calcium	800 mg (1200-1500 mg)*	milk, dairy products, dry beans, peas, leafy green vegetables
Magnesium	4.5 mg/kg	dairy products, meat, fish, eggs, nuts, whole grains, vegetables
Phosphorus	800 mg	meats, milk, milk products, carbonated beverages
Chromium	50-200 µg	yeast, beer, liver, cheese, whole grains, meat
Copper	1.5-3.0 mg	liver, kidney, mushrooms, squash, cucumber, molasses, yeast
Fluoride	1.5-4.0 mg	beef, butter, cheese, tea, chicken, seafood, water
Iodine	150 µg	seafood, iodized salt
Iron	10 mg	enriched or whole grains and cereals, red meats, liver, dried beans and peas
Manganese	2.0-5.0 mg	wheat germ, seeds, nuts, meat, leafy green vegetables
Molybdenum	75-250 µg	whole grains, meats, legumes
Selenium	0.87 µg/kg	meat, seafood
Zinc	0.2 mg/kg	whole grains, cheese, meats, fish, shellfish, peas
Sodium	115 mg 300 mg NaCl	all foods
Potassium	1,600-2,000 mg	cantaloupe, bananas, leafy green vegetables
Chloride	300 mg NaCl	all foods
Water	1 ml/kcal/day 30 ml/kg	

*Recommended for prevention/treatment of osteoporosis

and enzymes. Protein has a caloric density of 4.0 kcal/g and should constitute approximately 15% of the total caloric intake. The recommended intake of protein in grams depends on the individual's body mass and age, typically 0.75 g/kg for adults older than 20 years of age.[96]

Adequate protein intake is reflected when a nitrogen equilibrium is maintained. Gersovitz and associates[102] found negative nitrogen balances in elderly men and women who consumed 0.8 g/kg of protein per day. As a result of their findings, these investigators suggested that protein requirements may increase with age, and they recommended that 1.0 g/kg be consumed by individuals older than 75 years of age. The RDA, however, has not increased the protein recommendation for adults older than 50 years of age. In all individuals, protein requirements may increase because of renal disease, surgery, sepsis, trauma, and severe psychological stress.[78]

Carbohydrates

Carbohydrates come in two basic forms, simple sugars and complex carbohydrates, and have a nutritional density of 4.0 kcal/g. The RDA recommendation is that carbohydrates constitute between 50% and 70% of the total caloric intake. Simple sugars include glucose, fructose, and galactose; they add flavor to the diet. The more complex carbohydrates, starches, glycogen, and fiber, consist of glucose polymers. Complex carbohydrates are more nutritionally dense, and they should constitute the majority of the carbohydrate intake.

Individuals with glucose intolerance should refrain from excess intake of simple sugars, which cause a rapid rise in blood glucose and trigger the release of insulin. Other diseases are exacerbated by the excessive intake of simple sugars, including dental caries, obesity, diabetes mellitus, cardiovascular disease, and cataracts.[103]

Dietary fiber is also considered a complex carbohydrate, yet fiber is the fraction of the foodstuff not hydrolyzed by digestive enzymes. The American diet currently contains approximately 20 g of dietary fiber per day; it is recommended this be increased to 30 g/day for treatment and prevention of constipation, irritable bowel syndrome, cardiovascular disease, hyperlipidemia, and colon cancer.[104] However, the use of high fiber diets may interfere with nutrient absorption, which could lead to vitamin and mineral deficiencies.[104,105]

In general, the fate of glucose is the same regardless of its source in a simple or complex carbohydrate. It is either burned as a fuel, stored as glycogen in the liver or muscles, or converted and stored as fat. Carbohydrate metabolism decreases with age. An older individual who consumes large amounts of simple sugars may experience a dramatic increase in serum glucose level, which triggers a corresponding increase in serum insulin level. Any unused glucose is then available for synthesis into triglycerides and very low-density lipoproteins, promoting atherosclerosis. To prevent these events, the individual should emphasize complex carbohydrates over simple carbohydrates in the diet.

Carbohydrates are the primary fuel source for muscles during endurance (aerobic) activities performed at submaximal levels. The amount of glycogen (stored carbohydrate), as well as the predominant muscle fiber type, which is genetically determined, influence the endurance limit of the individual. The glycogen reserves stored in the muscle tissue of untrained older individuals are significantly less than those of younger untrained adults.[74]

"Carbohydrate loading" or "supercompensation" has been shown to increase muscle glycogen stores, thus optimizing subsequent athletic performance for both young and old competitors.[106,107] Carbohydrate loading can be accomplished by three different methods: (1) conversion from a mixed diet to a carbohydrate-rich diet for 3 to 4 days before competition; (2) depletion of muscle glycogen stores 3 to 4 days prior to competition, with an exhaustive exercise session followed by a carbohydrate-rich diet until competition; or (3) depletion of muscle glycogen stores with an exhaustive exercise session followed by a carbohydrate-poor diet for 3 days, then another exhaustive exercise bout and a carbohydrate-rich diet for 3 to 4 days before competition.[108]

Aerobic conditioning can "train" the body to increase glycogen stores and to use other fuel sources (eg, fatty acids) preferentially, sparing glycogen stores and boosting endurance. Meredith and associates[74] found that aerobic endurance training augmented glycogen stores in older subjects (approximately 65 years of age), yet the post-training muscle glycogen level still remained well below that of younger subjects (approximately 25 years of age).

Athletes should eat a light meal 2 to 4 hours before endurance exercise to ensure that the labile liver glycogen stores are replenished and to prevent hypoglycemia during the exercise session.[108] However, carbohydrate ingestion in the final hour preceding exercise is not recommended, because it may induce hypoglycemia early in the exercise, place greater demands on muscle glycogen stores, and reduce endurance performance.[109]

Diminished insulin sensitivity in older athletes may reduce glucose uptake and limit glycogen storage capabilities. Endurance training improves insulin sensitivity and promotes glucose disposal. It is very important for athletes of all ages to eat a light meal of high-carbohydrate foods (preferably complex carbohydrates) within the first 2 hours after a strenuous training session or competitive endurance event.[110] This nourishment helps the muscles to replenish glycogen stores. Refueling of muscle glycogen is even more important with advancing age, because recovery, in general, tends to be slower in the midlife athlete than the younger athlete.

Vitamins

The vitamins are classified into two groups, the water-soluble vitamins and the fat-soluble vitamins. The water-soluble vitamins include vitamins C and the eight B vitamins (thiamine, riboflavin, niacin, B6, folate, B12, biotin, pantothenic acid). The fat-soluble vitamins include vitamins A, D, E, and K. Although Vitamin B12 and folate deficiencies are the most commonly observed vitamin deficiencies, biochemical tests are available to measure serum thiamine, riboflavin, and pyrodoxine, low levels of which may correlate with the onset of clinical disease.[111]

Vitamin C   Vitamin C (L-ascorbic acid) and vitamin E have been shown to have antioxidant activity.[112] Vitamin C is also involved in the synthesis of collagen, carnitine, epinephrine, norepinephrine, and serotonin.[113] Dietary deficiencies of vitamin C lead to scurvy, a disease characterized by weakening of collagenous structures and manifested by bleeding gums, easy bruising, hemorrhages, and joint pain. In spite of this vitamin's antioxidant potential, the RDA (1989) recommends only 60 mg/day of vitamin C for healthy adults. However, cigarette smokers may benefit by consuming additional vitamin C (100 mg/day) because of nicotine's interference with absorption.

Vitamin C enhances the absorption of nonheme iron sources, which is particularly important for vegetarians. Vitamin C has been reported to ease the symptoms of the common cold; however, the benefits of large doses of ascorbic acid are too small to justify recommendation.[114] Vitamin C is thought to play a role in connective tissue repair after athletic injuries. Bates[115] found a negative correlation between blood levels of ascorbic acid and the excretion of proline (a major connective tissue constituent) in subjects aged 74 to 86 years: as vitamin C consumption increased, connective tissue breakdown decreased. Much of the current research on vitamin C supplementation has produced conflicting reports; while vitamin C may enhance athletic performance,[113] vitamin C is a well-known cause of runners' diarrhea.

B Vitamins   Some aging individuals' intake of thiamine, riboflavin, and folic acid are below the recommended levels.[116] In theory, a reduction of physical activity could cause a shortage of the B vitamins, although this deficiency is rarely seen clinically except in alcoholics and persons with pathologic conditions affecting nutrient absorption.[117]

Thiamine is a coenzyme important in carbohydrate metabolism. Thiamine deficiency, traditionally known as beriberi, produces mental confusion, anorexia, muscular weakness, peripheral neuropathy, edema, tachycardia, and enlarged heart. Alcohol consumption can interfere with absorption of thiamine.[117] Dietary thiamine intake and overall caloric intake both tend to diminish with age and decreased physical activity. The recommended thiamine intake for adults is based on caloric consumption and is approximately 0.5 mg/1,000 kcal.

Riboflavin is a component of two important enzymes, flavin mononucleotide (FMN) and flavin adenine dinucleotide (FAD), involved in oxidation-reduction reactions. Riboflavin is also necessary to the metabolism of niacin and vitamin B6.[118] The recommended dietary allowances for riboflavin are based on caloric consumption, 0.6 mg/1,000 kcal.

Niacin is a generic term used to refer to both nicotinic acid and nicotinamide. Niacin is involved in forming two coenzymes, nicotinamide adenine dinucleotide (NAD) and nicotinamide adenine dinucleotide phosphate (NADP), which are intimately involved in the metabolic processes of glycolysis and fatty acid metabolism. Dietary niacin requirements can also be met, in part, by the consumption of tryptophan, which is metabolically converted to niacin (60 mg tryptophan = 1 mg niacin). Niacin deficiency, pellagra, is characterized by dermatitis, diarrhea, inflammation of mucous membranes, and dementia. Deficiencies are not common in the United States but are prevalent in other countries. The dietary requirements of niacin are also based on caloric consumption, 6.6 mg niacin per 1,000 kcal. There is some evidence to suggest that nicotinic acid supplementation impairs fatty acid mobilization and would, therefore, impair endurance performance if overconsumed.[113,119]

Vitamin B6 consists of three compounds, pyrodoxine, pyridoxal, and pyridoxamine, which function as coenzymes in protein metabolism. Therefore, vitamin B6 requirements increase as protein intake increases.[96] Deficiencies of vitamin B6 are rarely seen alone and most commonly are associated with other vitamin B deficiencies.[118] The current recommended dietary allowance for vitamin B6 is 0.016 mg per gram of protein.[96] This converts to approximately 2.0 and 1.6 mg for adult men and women respectively based on the recommended protein intake. Some animal models[120] suggest that absorption of vitamin B6 declines with age, warranting compensatory increases in dietary ingestion; however, more research is needed on humans before changes in the RDAs are contemplated.

Folates function as coenzymes involved in protein metabolism and nucleic acid synthesis. Deficiencies lead to altered protein synthesis and impaired cell divisions. Folate deficiency is rarely a problem in healthy adults, yet it is associated with dementia and intermittent episodes of depression in the elderly.[121] Folate deficiencies and vitamin B12 deficiencies produce similar symptoms and may be difficult to distinguish. The RDA for folate in adults is based on body mass, 3 μg/kg, which suggests 200 μg for men and 180 μg for women.

Vitamin B12, or cobalamin, is a metabolic coenzyme. Deficiencies of this vitamin are associated with pernicious anemia and neurologic symptoms due to demyelination of axons. Older adults sometimes become deficient in vitamin B12 because of inadequate absorption of the vitamin, which may manifest as psychiatric problems,[122] ie, confusion, dementia, psychoses. Vitamin B12 deficiency may also occur as a consequence of megadoses of vitamin C, which interferes with absorption. The RDA for this vitamin is 2 mg for healthy adults. However, older individuals with inadequate absorption may require injections of vitamin B12 instead of increased oral consumption.[123] Vitamin B12 is the most abused vitamin among athletes. Although many athletes reportedly received high-dose injections of vitamin B12 prior to competition,[124] there was no substantial evidence that the performance was enhanced.[113]

Biotin requirements are fulfilled either through dietary ingestion or through synthesis in the lower gastrointestinal tract by microorganisms. Biotin is an integral part of two enzymes, pyruvate carboxylase and acetyl-coenzyme A (CoA) carboxylase, which are involved in gluconeogenesis and fatty acid metabolism, respectively. Biotin deficiency is characterized by anorexia, nausea, vomiting, pallor, mental depression, hair loss, dry skin, and increase in serum cholesterol. The biotin content of many foods has not yet been established; therefore, the RDA spans a wide range, between 30 and 100 μg, for normal healthy adults.[96]

Pantothenic acid is a B-complex vitamin associated with fatty acid synthesis. This vitamin is, therefore, involved in glycolysis, gluconeogenesis, and fatty acid metabolism.[118] Deficiencies of pantothenic acid are very rare, but one symptom is extreme fatigue. The RDA for pantothenic acid has not been determined due to lack of research, yet intake between 4 and 7 mg/day should be safe and adequate for adults.[96]

Vitamin A   Vitamin A is essential for vision, growth, cellular differentiation and proliferation, reproduction, and immune system function. Deficiencies of vitamin A are uncommon, and symptoms include night blindness and skin dryness. In fact, excessive intake is more common as a result of multivitamin supplementation. Vitamin A toxicity produces headaches, vomiting, loss of hair, dryness of mucous membranes, bone abnormalities, and liver damage.[96] Vitamin A requirements do not change with aging for healthy individuals. Vitamin A is measured either in international units (IU) or in milligrams of carotenoids (retinol or β-carotene). One IU of vitamin A is equivalent to 0.3 μg retinol or 0.6 μg β-carotene. The vitamin A activity in food also is expressed as retinol equivalents (RE): 1 RE = 1 μg of retinol.[96] The recommended allowances for men and women are 1,000 RE and 800 RE per day, respectively.

Vitamin D   Vitamin D deficiencies are rare among healthy active individuals. Inadequate exposure to sunlight and decreased intake of milk products due to gastrointestinal intolerance can lead to vitamin D-associated metabolic disturbances, which result in bone and muscle weakness.[7] Vitamin D requirement for men and women older than 25 years of age is 5 μg/day.[96]

Vitamin E   The functions of vitamin E, or alpha-tocopherol, are not completely understood. Vitamin E has been associated with antioxidant activity, which protects tissue, particularly the lipid bilayer, from the oxygen-free radicals produced during oxidative phosphorylation. Vitamin E is also necessary for proper muscular function, contributing to calcium homeostasis and fiber and tissue integrity.[125] Vitamin E deficiencies in a rat model can decrease muscular endurance by 40%.[112] Vitamin E supplementation has been advocated by those endorsing the oxygen-free radical induced aging theory;[112] however, the benefits of excessive doses of vitamin E have not been consistently demonstrated. RDA requirements of 8 mg of alpha-tocopherol for women and 10 mg for men appear to be appropriate for all adults, even for people who exercise regularly.[96] Intense physical exercise, however, may significantly increase the need for vitamin E due to the activation of free-radical reactions. The need for vitamin E supplementation may be even greater when emotional stress is combined with exhaustive physical activity. Kagan and associates[125] recommend the RDA for vitamin E be increased between 25% and 30% in times of emotional and physical stress. Additionally, vitamin E supplementation in competitive runners and swimmers has been shown to improve $\dot{V}O_2max$, extend time to exhaustion, improve endurance at high altitude, and reduce lactate concentration in the blood following intense exercise.[126,127] Vitamin E supplementation, however, has not produced such dramatic positive effects for all researchers.[128]

Vitamin K　　Vitamin K deficiency rarely occurs due to inadequate dietary intake, but may result from antibiotic or sulfa drug therapy.[7] Adult requirements of vitamin K are 80 μg and 65 μg for men and women, respectively.[96]

Minerals and Electrolytes

Iron, calcium, and sodium in the diet have prominent physiologic effects that are important in athletes and in individuals with age-related diseases. However, the other minerals and electrolytes, including phosphorous, magnesium, zinc, iodine, selenium, copper, manganese, fluoride, chromium, molybdenum, potassium, chloride, and water, also play influential roles in maintaining physiologic homeostasis. The physiologic functions of the most important minerals and electrolytes will be reviewed.

Calcium　　The majority of the body's calcium (99%) is present in the skeleton. The body's ability to absorb dietary calcium and maintain calcium balance is affected by the presence of other physiologic factors, such as vitamin D intake, protein intake, age, pregnancy, lactation, disease states, mechanical loading (exercise), and levels of several hormones (eg, parathyroid hormone, calcitonin, insulin, estrogen, testosterone).

Dietary intake of calcium becomes increasingly important with age in order to maintain bone mass and prevent osteoporosis. The recommended allowance for dietary calcium is controversial.[129] The most recent RDA[96] suggests 800 mg/day for both men and women over the age of 50, yet it does indicate that additional calcium may be necessary to treat osteoporosis. Several investigators suggest that the allowances for calcium be raised to 1,200 to 1,500 mg/day, especially for postmenopausal women.[129] Intakes of dietary calcium up to 2,500 mg/day have not produced deleterious side effects in older adults. However, in rare cases high intakes may induce constipation and increase the risk of urinary stone formation in males.[130] Variations in gastrointestinal absorption, renal function, skeletal metabolism, nutrient interaction, and hormone levels create problems in defining adequate calcium intake in older adults. Also, there is increasing evidence that high levels of calcium may interfere with the absorption of trace minerals, particularly iron and zinc.[131] Often calcium intake must be prescribed on an individual basis.

Both passive and active transport are involved in intestinal calcium absorption, which tend to diminish in midlife.[129] The active transport of calcium is mediated by 1,25-(OH)$_2$ vitamin D (calcitriol). Serum calcitriol concentrations are adversely affected by inadequate renal function and by insufficient levels of parathyroid hormone (PTH). The reduction in circulating estrogen in postmenopausal women also adversely affects the absorption of calcium through a variety of mechanisms involving both PTH and calcitriol suppression. Several dietary factors have been shown to have an adverse effect on calcium absorption or calcium balance, including transitory high levels of dietary protein[132,133] and increases in dietary fiber.[129] In addition, the chronic use of diuretics increases renal absorption of calcium, and excessive use of alcohol and antacids decreases gastrointestinal absorption of calcium.[7,129] Physical activity enhances the gastrointestinal absorption of calcium and preserves bone mass; the latter function becomes more important with increasing age.[134]

Phosphorous   Phosphorous, along with calcium, is an essential bone mineral. In addition to enhancing skeletal integrity, phosphorous in the form of soluble phosphate is present in many soft tissues of the body. Soluble phosphate modulates enzyme activity and provides the phosphate ion for energy reactions (eg, adenosine triphosphate (ATP), creatine phosphate, etc). RDA[96] suggests that adults consume 800 mg of phosphorous per day. Typically, adequate intake is not a problem because practically all foods contain phosphorous.

Magnesium   Magnesium ions are essential for energy release; ie, adenosine triphosphate-adenosine diphosphate (ATP-ADP) reactions. They are also involved in maintaining the calcium and phosphorous balance as well and many other biochemical and physiologic processes. Magnesium deficiency could potentially impair myocardial and skeletal muscle contractility, but such a deficiency due to dietary inadequacy is rarely found in humans and is usually seen only in disease states. A magnesium deficiency, however, may be induced by drinking soft water, excessive diuretic use, sustained losses from burns or bedsores, alcoholism, and extended exposure to hot weather.[22] The RDA for magnesium is based on body mass (4.5 mg/kg) and is approximately 350 mg and 280 mg for adult men and women, respectively.

Iron   Iron is a constituent of many enzymes, as well as hemoglobin (Hb) and myoglobin (Mb), and therefore, is an essential dietary nutrient. Dietary iron exists as either heme iron, found in meat and readily absorbable, or nonheme sources, found in vegetables and beans, and requiring vitamin C for absorption. Iron requirements seem to diminish with age.[7] Hemoglobin (Hb) concentration can remain in the normal range, even when dietary intake is low, until approximately age 70, after which declines in Hb concentrations are often observed.[135] The daily recommended requirement of iron for adult males older than 20 years of age is 10 mg/day.[96] For women, the requirement is higher (15 mg/day) during the reproductive years because of iron loss with menstrual flow, yet after the age of 50 this requirement decreases to 10 mg/day.[96]

Anemia, one cause of which is the depletion of serum iron reserves, produces symptoms of fatiguability and lethargy as well as loss of aerobic capacity and endurance. The nutritional inadequacies producing anemia in the aging population generally result from poverty, physical handicaps, and lack of interest in cooking. However, the majority of anemia cases result from poor absorption of iron, copper, folic acid, and vitamin B12, and are exacerbated by the administration of salicylate drugs.[22] Additionally, iron absorption can be hampered by excessive dietary fiber intake and by protein deficiency.[1] Restoration of hemoglobin stores through iron and vitamin B supplements may restore oxygen transport, and, thus increase $\dot{V}O_2$max and alleviate fatiguability. Depletion and restoration of iron stores within the muscle (Mb) and within the blood (Hb) have similar effects.

"Sports anemia" (runner's anemia) sometimes develops in athletes during endurance-type training. This anemia is characterized by a reduction in the individual's Hb concentration and hematocrit to the low-normal range. Sports anemia may be induced by increases in plasma volume without proportional increases in hemoglobin concentration; intravascular hemolysis resulting from excessive pounding on the feet, as in running; iron losses in sweat; and gastrointestinal bleeding.[136] It has been suggested by Hallberg and Magnusson[137] that strenuous exercise resets the hemoglobin concentration to provide a higher extraction of oxygen from hemoglobin (less firmly bound oxygen), thus delivering more oxygen to exercising muscle. The hemoglobin concentration is thus reduced through a negative feedback mechanism, because ample oxygen is being extracted by the muscle. "Sports anemia" is usually self-limiting, transitory, and, therefore, not typically treated.[136] Additionally, sports anemia does not respond to iron supplementation.

Zinc   Zinc is a cofactor for an erythrocyte enzyme, carbonic anhydrase, which is important in maintaining the acid-base balance in the blood at rest and during exercise.[138] Zinc deficiency has been associated with loss of taste acuity, impaired wound healing, and depressed immune function, particularly in the older adult.[139] Zinc deficiency is exacerbated by alcoholism, malabsorption, bacterial infection, renal failure, chelating drugs, and antimetabolites. In spite of potential deficiencies for aging individuals, 15 mg/day and 12 mg/day for men and women, respectively,[96] is sufficient to meet the physiologic needs for all ages. Adequate zinc intake is especially important to the athlete, because exercise and stress stimulate zinc losses. Zinc deficiencies may be evident in vegetarian athletes because the foods highest in zinc content include oysters, beef, liver, chicken, and turkey (dark meat), and the poorest sources are sugar, citrus fruits, nonleafy vegetables, and tubers.[140] However, excessive intake of zinc (greater than 15 mg/day) may prevent the beneficial increase in high-density lipoprotein cholesterol that is normally associated with increased exercise in midlife and older adults.[141,142]

Iodine   Iodine is an essential part of the thyroid hormones, thyroxine and triiodothyronine. Deficiencies of iodine induce goiter production. Iodine or iodine derivatives are used in many processed foods such as iodized table salt. Deficiencies are rarely found and are typically confined to isolated geographical regions where environmental iodine is low. The RDA for iodine is 150 μg/day for adults.

Selenium   Selenium is a modulator for the antioxidant glutathione peroxidase.[141] Deficiencies are rare, with minimal manifestations. Selenium allowances are based on body weight (0.87 μg/kg) and are 70 and 55 μg/day for men and women, respectively.[96]

Copper   Copper is involved in many important physiologic functions, including the production of norepinephrine, carbohydrate and lipid metabolism, collagen and elastin formation, amino acid metabolism, hematopoiesis, and protection against cellular damage from the accumulation of toxic oxygen-free radicals. Copper deficiencies rarely occur except in disease states.[141] The daily requirement of 1.5 to 3.0 mg/day is adequately met in a balanced diet; supplementation is not recommended because excess copper is quite toxic.[96]

Manganese   Manganese is important for reproductive performance, growth, and glucose tolerance. Manganese deficiencies are rare. Between 2.0 and 5.0 mg/day is sufficient for adults.[96]

Fluoride   Fluoride, along with calcium and phosphorous, is important for development and for maintenance of bones and teeth. Food processing and water fluoridation plays an important role in maintaining appropriate consumption of fluoride. Safe and adequate intake of fluoride ranges from 1.5 to 4.0 mg/day for adults.

Chromium   Chromium is important in maintaining normal glucose metabolism. Chromium deficiency has been linked to impaired glucose tolerance and ischemic heart disease in older adults.[1,141] More research is needed to adequately determine dietary requirements in midlife individuals, athletes, and diabetics. A wide range, between 50 and 200 μg/day, of chromium intake is currently recommended for adults.[96]

Molybdenum   Molybdenum is involved in several physiologic enzymatic reactions. Deficiencies rarely occur. The concentration of molybdenum in food varies depending on the environment in which it is grown. An intake between 75 and 250 μg/day is considered sufficient for both children and adults.

Water   Fluid intake is extremely important because 40% to 60% of the total body weight comprises water. As the body ages, water accounts for less of the total body weight, reflecting a decrease in lean body mass and an increase in fat mass. The recommended fluid consumption for all adults is 1 ml/kcal/day or 30 ml/kg/day.[96] Age tends to blunt thirst sensation, therefore, special attention must be paid to preventing dehydration in aging individuals.

Physiologic requirements for water change with environmental stress, physical activity, and possibly drug therapy. The greatest water loss occurs in hot humid environments, where losses may exceed 3 liters, especially when exercising or working vigorously.[143] As body fluid losses in sweat approach 2% of body weight, the body's ability to circulate blood and regulate body temperature is compromised. As fluid loss approaches 5% loss of body weight, functional capacity may decline by 20% to 30%.[144]

Sodium   Sodium is the principal cation of extracellular fluid and regulates extracellular fluid volume in addition to regulating the osmolarity, acid-base balance, and the membrane potential of cells. Sodium homeostasis is maintained through the action of the hormone aldosterone. The minimum requirement of sodium in adults is no more than 5 mEq/day, which corresponds to 125 mg of sodium or 300 mg of sodium chloride per day.[96] The average American ingests between 1.8 g/day and 5 g/day, which well exceeds the amount needed for proper physiologic function.[145] Dietary sodium is often restricted for aging individuals if there is a propensity for hypertension, congestive heart failure, chronic renal disease, or cirrhosis. Sodium deficiencies are rare, but may occur with heavy and persistent sweating, trauma, chronic diarrhea, or renal disease.[96] High sodium levels may result from dehydration, central nervous system dysfunction, diabetes, or vomiting or diarrhea, and can produce neuromuscular irritability and mental confusion.[96]

Potassium   Potassium is the principal intracellular cation and contributes to the conduction of nerve impulses. Potassium deficiency may occur with diuretic therapy, vomiting, and diarrhea and is characterized by polyuria, cardiac arrhythmias, anorexia, fatigue, neuromuscular irritability, muscular weakness, postural hypertension, abdominal distention, and glucose intolerance. The minimum requirement for potassium is approximately 1,600 to 2,000 mg/day, yet those individuals taking diuretics may increase intake up to 3,500 mg/day.[96] Most individuals ingest adequate amounts of potassium from fresh fruits, vegetables, and meat; those individuals with greater needs can take supplements. Potassium excess rarely occurs except with impaired renal function or hemorrhage, and may result in fatal cardiac arrhythmias.[7]

Chloride   Chloride is an extracellular anion involved in maintaining electrolyte balance. Dietary deficiencies of chloride rarely occur. Chloride requirements parallel those of sodium: dietary chloride comes predominantly from sodium chloride ingestion.

Summary

Proper nutrition for a midlife athlete is not only important for prevention, treatment, and postponement of chronic, age-related diseases such as heart disease, hypertension, and atherosclerosis, but also to meet short-term energy needs for effective athletic perform-

Table 3 Adverse effects of insufficient or excessive consumption of vitamins and minerals

Vitamin/Mineral	Insufficient Intake	Excessive Intake
Vitamin C	scurvy, bleeding gums, easy bruising, hemorrhages, joint pain	diarrhea, impaired Vitamin B_{12} absorption
Thiamine (B_1)	beriberi, mental confusion, anorexia, muscle weakness, peripheral paralysis, edema, tachycardia, enlarged heart	nausea, anorexia, lethargy, ataxia
Riboflavin (B_2)	sore throat, seborrheic dermatitis, cheilosis, glossitis (magenta tongue)	none reported
Niacin	weakness, anorexia, indigestion, pellagra, dermatitis, diarrhea, mucous membrane inflammation, dementia	vascular dilation, abnormal glucose tolerance, hepatomegaly, impaired fatty acid mobilization, impaired endurance performance
Vitamin B_6	irritability, depression, seborrheic dermatosis, peripheral neuropathy	sensory ataxia, peripheral sensory neuropathy
Folate	peripheral neuropathy, pernicious anemia, skin hyperpigmentation, dementia, depression	renal toxicity, convulsions
Vitamin B_{12}	pernicious anemia, dementia, depression, jaundice, congestive heart failure, neuropathy	renal toxicity, convulsions
Biotin	anorexia, nausea, vomiting, pallor, depression, alopecia, dry skin, hypercholesterolism, swollen tongue, ECG abnormalities	reproductive abnormalities
Pantothenic acid	burning feet, extreme fatigue, vomiting, insomnia, muscle cramps	diarrhea
Vitamin A	night blindness, corneal abnormalities, skin dryness	drowsiness, headache, vomiting, alopecia, membrane dryness, bone pain, hyperlipemia, birth defects, liver damage
Vitamin E	myopathy, hemorrhages, oxygen free radical accumulation, decreased muscular endurance	none reported
Vitamin D	osteomalacia, rickets, muscle weakness	hypercalcemia, anorexia, nausea, vomiting, constipation, weakness, hypertension
Calcium	mental confusion, depression, dementia, muscular tetany, weakness, convulsions, osteomalacia, osteoporosis	anorexia, constipation, polyuria, kidney stone formation, decreased absorption of iron and zinc, muscle weakness
Phosphorous	anorexia, nausea, vomiting, confusion, peripheral neuropathy, anemia, osteoporosis	decreased calcium absorption
Magnesium	anorexia, nausea, vomiting, lethargy, weakness, muscle tremor, mental confusion, ataxia	absence of deep tendon relfex, ECG abnormalities, hypertension, respiratory depression, narcosis, cardiac arrest
Iron	fatigue, lethargy, reduced aerobic capacity	acute vomiting, pallor, cyanosis, diarrhea, diabetes, slate-grey skin, enlarged liver, cardiomyopathy, pituitary failure
Zinc	lethargy, loss of taste acuity, impaired wound healing, depressed immune function	nausea, vomiting, diarrhea, fever, decreased serum HDL
Iodine	goiter, hypotension, fatigue, bradycardia	inhibition of thyroid hormone synthesis
Copper	impaired energy metabolism, impaired collagen formation, accumulation of free radicals	liver cirrhosis, dementia, cataracts, renal failure
Fluoride	dental caries, osteopenia	bone deformities, tooth enamel abnormalities
Chromium	impaired glucose tolerance, ischemic heart	depressed insulin activity
Sodium	reduced plasma volume, reduced renal blood flow	neuromuscular irritability, mental confusion
Potassium	polyuria, cardiac arrhythmias, anorexia, fatigue, abdominal distension, glucose intolerance, muscular weakness, postural hypertension	cardiac arrhythmias
Water	decreased stroke volume, increased heart rate, reduced endurance	drowsiness, weakness, convulsions, coma

ance. In general, the older athlete's diet is no different from the younger athlete's diet, except possibly in total caloric content. There is a gradual fall in the basal metabolic rate, but there is no proportional decrease in essential nutrient requirements.[146] Most midlife athletes easily consume the recommended dietary allowances of all nutrients in foods; however, many athletes without vitamin deficiencies consume dietary vitamin and mineral supplements. In a survey of older male runners (50 to 64 years), 60% to 70% reported taking supplemental vitamins.[5] Similarly, Parr and associates[147] found that a large percentage (42% to 56%) of younger athletes also consumed dietary supplements (mostly multivitamin supplements). In most cases, these supplements are not necessary and do not improve the athlete's performance. Not only is the practice of megadose vitamin ingestion ineffective in helping to attain a high level of physical performance, but with certain vitamins (eg, vitamins A, B6, and niacin), megadoses can be toxic. Table 3 summarizes the adverse physiologic manifestations resulting from insufficient and excessive consumption of certain vitamins and minerals.

Conclusions

By contesting the natural physiologic declines that manifest in midlife with a healthy lifestyle of regular exercise and proper nutrition, the athlete is able to maintain peak performance for an extended period of time.

References

1. Shephard RJ: *Physical Activity and Aging*, ed 2. Rockville, MD, Aspen Publishers, 1987.
2. Evans WJ, Meredith CN: Exercise and nutrition in the elderly, in Munro HN, Danford DE (eds): *Nutrition, Aging and the Elderly*. New York, NY, Plenum Press, 1989, pp 89-126.
3. Forbes GB, Halloran E: The adult decline in lean body mass. *Hum Biol* 1976;48:162-173.
4. Buskirk ER, Mendez J: Sports science and body composition analysis: Emphasis on cell and muscle mass. *Med Sci Sports Exerc* 1984;16:584-595.
5. Wood PD: Dietary intake of the older athlete, in Haskell W, Scala J, Whittam J (eds): *Nutrition and Athletic Performance*. Palo Alto, CA, Bull Publishing, pp 260-273.
6. Arntzenius AC, Kromhout D, Barth JD, et al: Diet, lipoproteins, and the progression of coronary atherosclerosis: The Leiden Intervention Trial. *N Engl J Med* 1985;312:805-811.
7. Chernoff R, Lipschitz DA: Nutrition and aging, in Shils ME, Young VR (eds): *Modern Nutrition in Health and Disease*, ed 7. Philadelphia, PA, Lea & Febiger, 1988, pp 982-1000.
8. Åstrand PO: Whole-body metabolism, in Horton ES, Terjung RL (eds): *Exercise, Nutrition, and Energy Metabolism*. New York, NY, Macmillan Publishing, 1988, pp 1-8.
9. Forbes GB, Brown MR, Welle SL, et al: Deliberate overfeeding in women and men: Energy cost and composition of the weight gain. *Br J Nutr* 1986;56:1-9.

10. Forbes GB, Brown MR, Welle SL, et al: Hormonal response to overfeeding. *Am J Clin Nutr* 1989;49:608-611.

11. Sidney KH, Shephard RJ, Harrison J: Endurance training and body composition of the elderly. *Am J Clin Nutr* 1977;30:326-333.

12. deVries HA: Physiological effect of an exercise training regimen upon men aged 52 to 88. *J Gerontol* 1970;25:325-336.

13. Adams GM, deVries HA: Physiological effects of an exercise training regimen upon women aged 52 to 79. *J Gerontol* 1973;28:50-55.

14. Meredith CN, Frontera WR, O'Reilly KP, et al: Body composition in elderly men: Effect of dietary modification during strength training. *J Am Geriatr Soc* 1992;40:155-162.

15. Oscai LB, Babirak SP, Dubach FB, et al: Exercise or food restriction: Effect on adipose tissue cellularity. *Am J Physiol* 1974;227:901-904.

16. Heath GW, Hagberg JM, Ehsani AA, et al: A physiological comparison of young and older endurance athletes. *J Appl Physiol* 1981;51:634-640.

17. Lundholm K, Holm G, Lindmark L, et al: Thermogenic effect of food in physically well-trained elderly men. *Eur J Appl Physiol* 1986;55:486-492.

18. Meredith CN, Zackin MJ, Frontera WR, et al: Body composition and aerobic capacity in young and middle-aged endurance-trained men. *Med Sci Sports Exerc* 1987;19:557-563.

19. Blair SN, Ellsworth NM, Haskell WL, et al: Comparison of nutrient intake in middle-aged men and women runners and controls. *Med Sci Sports Exerc* 1981;13:310-315.

20. Kavanagh T, Shephard RJ, Lindley LT, et al: Influences of exercise and lifestyle variables upon high density lipoprotein cholesterol after myocardial infarction. *Arteriosclerosis* 1983;3:249-259.

21. Pollock ML, Wilmore JH (eds): *Exercise in Health and Disease: Evaluation and Prescription for Prevention and Rehabilitation*, ed 2. Philadelphia, PA, WB Saunders, 1990.

22. Shephard RJ: Exercise in coronary heart disease. *Sports Med* 1986;3:26-49.

23. Kavanagh T, Shephard RJ, Chisholm AW, et al: Prognostic indexes for patients with ischemic heart disease enrolled in an exercise-centered rehabilitation program. *Am J Cardiol* 1979;44:1230-1240.

24. Tipton CM: Exercise, training, and hypertension. *Exerc Sport Sci Rev* 1984;12:245-306.

25. Tipton CM (1991): Exercise, training, and hypertension: An Update. *Exerc Sport Sci Rev* 1991;19:447-505.

26. Kannel WB, Gorden T: Evaluation of cardiovascular risk in the elderly: The Framingham Study. *Bull N Y Acad Med* 1978;54:573-591.

27. Dufaux B, Assmann G, Hollmann W: Plasma lipoproteins and physical activity: A review. *Int J Sports Med* 1982;3:123-136.

28. Haskell WL: The influence of exercise training on plasma lipids and lipoproteins in health and disease. *Acta Med Scand* 1986;711(suppl):25-37.

29. Williams PT, Wood PD, Haskell WL, et al: The effects of running mileage and duration on plasma lipoprotein levels. *JAMA* 1982;247:2674-2679.

30. Hartung GH, Farge EJ, Mitchell RE: Effects of marathon running, jogging, and diet on coronary risk factors in middle-aged men. *Prev Med* 1981;10:316-323.

31. Hodgson JL, Buskirk ER: Physical fitness and age, with emphasis on cardiovascular function in the elderly. *J Am Geriatr Soc* 1977;25:385-392.

32. Plowman SA, Drinkwater BL, Horvath SM: Age and aerobic power in women: A longitudinal study. *J Gerontol* 1979;34:512-520.

33. Anton-Kuchly B, Roger P, Varene P: Determinants of increased energy cost of submaximal exercise in obese subjects. *J Appl Physiol* 1984;56:18-23.

34. Rodeheffer RD, Gerstenblith G, Becker LC, et al: Exercise cardiac output is maintained with advancing age in healthy human subjects: Cardiac dilation and increased stroke volume compensate for a diminished heart rate. *Circulation* 1984;69:203-213.

35. Wilmore JH, Royce J, Girandola RN, et al: Physiological alterations resulting from a 10-week program of jogging. *Med Sci Sports Exerc* 1970:2:7-14.

36. Kilbom A: Physical training in women. *Scand J Clin Lab Invest* 1971;119:1-34.

37. Kasch FW, Wallace JP: Physiological variable during 10 years of endurance exercise. *Med Sci Sports* 1976;8:5-8.

38. Pollock ML, Dawson DA, Miller HS Jr, et al: Physiological responses of men 49 to 65 years of age to endurance training. *J Am Geriatr Soc* 1976;24:97-104.

39. Hagberg JM, Graves JE, Limacher M, et al: Cardiovascular responses of 70-79 year old men and women to exercise training. *J Appl Physiol* 1989;66:2589-2594.

40. Suominen H, Heikkinen E, Parkatti T, et al: Effects of "lifelong" physical training on functional aging in men. *Scand J Soc Med Suppl* 1977;14:225-240.

41. Suominen H, Heikkinen E, Liesen H, et al: Effects of 8 weeks' endurance training on skeletal muscle metabolism in 56-70-year-old sedentary men. *Eur J Appl Physiol* 1977;37:173-180.

42. deVries HA: Tips on prescribing exercise regimens for your older patient. *Geriatrics* 1979;34:75-81.

43. Tzankoff SP, Robinson S, Pyke FS, et al: Physiological adjustments to work in older men as affected by physical training. *J Appl Physiol* 1972;33:346-350.

44. Clausen JP, Klausen K, Rasmussen B, et al: Central and peripheral circulatory changes after training of the arms or legs. *Am J Physiol* 1973;225:675-682.

45. Sidney KH: Cardiovascular benefits of physical activity in the exercising aged, in Smith EL, Serfass RC (eds): *Exercise and Aging: The Scientific Basis.* Hillside, NJ, Enslow Publishers, 1981, pp 131-147.

46. Dill DB, Robinson S, Ross JC: A longitudinal study of 16 champion runners. *J Sports Med Phys Fitness* 1967;7:4-27.

47. Pollock ML, Foster C, Rod J, et al: Ten year follow-up on the aerobic capacity of champion masters track athletes. *Med Sci Sports Exerc* 1982;14:105.

48. Vaccaro P, Ostrove SM, Vandervelden L, et al: Body composition and physiological responses of masters female swimmers 20 to 70 years of age. *Res Q* 1984;55:278-284.

49. Gilbert CA, Nutter DO, Felner JM, et al: Echocardiographic study of cardiac dimensions and function in the endurance-trained athlete. *Am J Cardiol* 1977;40:528-533.

50. Reddan WG: Respiratory system and aging, in Smith EL, Serfass RC (eds): *Exercise and Aging: The Scientific Basis.* Hillside, NJ, Enslow Publishers, 1981, pp 89-107.

51. Campbell MJ, McComas AJ, Petito F: Physiological changes in ageing muscles. *J Neurol Neurosurg Psych* 1973;36:174-182.

52. Spirduso WW: Reaction and movement time as a function of age and physical activity level. *J Gerontol* 1975;30:435-440.

53. Moritani T: Training adaptations in the muscles of older men, in Smith EL, Serfass RC (eds): *Exercise and Aging: The Scientific Basis.* Hillside, NJ, Enslow Publishers, 1981, pp 149-166.

54. Larsson L: Physical training effects on muscle morphology in sedentary males at different ages. *Med Sci Sports Exerc* 1982;14:203-206.

55. Armstrong RB: Muscle fiber recruitment patterns and their metabolic correlates, in Horton ES, Terjung RL (eds): *Exercise, Nutrition, and Energy Metabolism.* New York, NY, Macmillan Publishing Co, 1988, chap 2, pp 9-26.

56. Pette D, Vrbova G: Neural control of phenotypic expression in mammalian muscle fibers. *Muscle Nerve* 1985;8:676-689.

57. Holloszy JO, Booth FW: Biochemical adaptations to endurance exercise in muscle. *Ann Rev Physiol* 1976;38:273-291.

58. Saltin B, Gollnick PD: Skeletal muscle adaptability: Significance for metabolism and performance, in Peachey LD, Adrian RH, Geiger SR (eds): *Handbook of Physiology, Sect 10: Skeletal Muscle*. Bethesda, MD, American Physiological Society, 1983, pp 555-631.

59. Schantz P, Billeter R, Henriksson J, et al: Training-induced increase in myofibrillar ATPase intermediate fibers in human skeletal muscle. *Muscle Nerve* 1982;5:628-636.

60. Frontera WR, Meredith CN, O'Reilly KP, et al: Strength conditioning in older men: Skeletal muscle hypertrophy and improved function. *J Appl Physiol* 1988;64:1038-1044.

61. Lowenthal DT: The effect of aging, exercise and calorie restriction on skeletal muscle histochemistry in Fischer 344 rats. Philadelphia, PA, Temple University, 1986. Dissertation.

62. Larsson L, Karlsson J: Isometric and dynamic endurance as a function of age and skeletal muscle characteristics. *Acta Physiol Scand* 1978;104:129-136.

63. Orlander J, Aniansson A: Effects of physical training on skeletal muscle metabolism and ultrastructure in 70 to 75-year-old men. *Acta Physiol Scand* 1980;109:149-154.

64. Sanchez J, Bastien C, Monod H: Enzymatic adaptations to treadmill training in skeletal muscle of young and old rats. *Eur J Appl Physiol* 1983;52:69-74.

65. Torun B, Scrimshaw NS, Young VR: Effect of isometric exercises on body potassium and dietary protein requirements of young men. *Am J Clin Nutr* 1977;30:1983-1993.

66. Gontzea I, Sutzescu P, Dumitrache S: The influence of muscular activity on nitrogen balance and on the need of man for proteins. *Nutr Rep Int* 1974;10:35-43.

67. Tarnopolski MA, MacDougall VD, Atkinson SA: Influence of protein intake and training status on nitrogen balance and lean body mass. *J Appl Physiol* 1988;64:187-193.

68. Hickson JF Jr, Wolinsky I: Human protein intake and metabolism in exercise and sport, in Hickson JF Jr, Wolinsky I (eds): *Nutrition in Exercise and Sport*. Boca Raton, FL, CRC Press, 1989, pp 5-35.

69. Papper S: The effects of age in reducing renal function. *Geriatrics* 1973;28:83-87.

70. Epstein M, Hollenberg NK: Age as a determinant of renal sodium conservation in normal man. *J Lab Clin Med* 1976;87:411-417.

71. Holloszy JO, Schultz J, Kusnierkiewicz J, et al: Effects of exercise on glucose tolerance and insulin resistance: A brief review and some preliminary results. *Acta Med Scand Suppl* 1986;711:55-65.

72. Richter EA, Ruderman NB, Schneider SH: Diabetes and exercise. *Am J Med* 1981;70:201-209.

73. Sidney KH, Shephard RJ: Growth hormone and cortisol-age differences, effects of exercise and training. *Can J Appl Sport Sci* 1977;2:189-193.

74. Meredith CN, Frontera WR, Fisher EC, et al: Peripheral effects of endurance training in young and old subjects. *J Appl Physiol* 1989;66:2844-2849.

75. Munro HN, Young VR: Protein metabolism and requirements, in Exton-Smith AN, Caird FI (eds): *Metabolic and Nutritional Disorders in the Elderly*. Bristol, John Wright & Sons, 1980, pp 13-25.

76. Lowenthal DT, Kirschner DA, Tumer N, et al: The integration of exercise and its effects with age and disease. *South Med J*, in press.

77. Barney JL, Neukom JE: Use of arthritis care by the elderly. *Gerontologist* 1979;19:548-554.

78. Munro HN, Crim MC: The proteins and amino acids, in Shils ME, Young VR (eds): *Modern Nutrition in Health and Disease*, ed 7. Philadelphia, PA, Lea & Febiger, 1988, pp 1-37.

79. Recker RR, Saville PD, Heaney RP: Effect of estrogens and calcium carbonate on bone loss in postmenopausal women. *Ann Intern Med* 1977;87:649-655.

80. Riis B, Thomsen K, Christiansen C: Does calcium supplementation prevent post-menopausal bone loss? A double-blind controlled clinical study. *N Engl J Med* 1987;316:173-177.

81. Avioli LV: Calcium and osteoporosis. *Ann Rev Nutr* 1984;4:471-491.

82. Smith EL, Reddan W, Smith PE: Physical activity and calcium modalities for bone mineral increase in aged women. *Med Sci Sports Exerc* 1981;13:60-64.

83. Lane NE, Bloch DA, Jones HH, et al: Long-distance running, bone density and osteoarthritis. *JAMA* 1986;255:1147-1151.

84. Nelson ME, Fisher EC, Catsos PD, et al: Diet and bone status in amenorrheic athletes. *Am J Clin Nutr* 1986;43:910-916.

85. Ballor DL, Kessey RE: A meta-analysis of the factors affecting exercise-induced changes in body mass, fat mass, and fat-free mass in males and females. *Intl J Obesity* 1991;15:717-726.

86. *Promoting Health/Preventing Disease: Objectives for the Nation*. Washington, DC, Department of Health and Human Services, 1980, pp 79-81.

87. Pollock ML, Miller HS, Wilmore J: Physiological characteristics of champion American track athletes 40 to 75 years of age. *J Gerontol* 1974;29:645-649.

88. Paffenbarger RS Jr, Wing AL, Hyde RT: Physical activity as an index of heart attack risk in college alumni. *Am J Epidemiol* 1978;108:161-175.

89. Paffenbarger RS Jr, Hyde RT, Wing AL, et al: Physical activity, all-cause mortality, and longevity of college alumni. *N Engl J Med* 1986;314:605-613.

90. Sallis JF, Hadkell WL, Wood PD, et al: Physical activity assessment methodology in the Five-City project. *Am J Epidemiol* 1986;121:91-106.

91. Biegel L: Fitness: Who, what, and why, in Biegel L (ed): *Physical Fitness and the Older Person: A Guide to Exercise for Health Care Professionals*. Rockville, MD, Aspen Systems, chap 1, pp 1-12.

92. Tomporowski PD, Ellis NR: Effects of exercise on cognitive processes: A review. *Psychol Bull* 1986;99:338-346.

93. Pollock ML: The quantification of endurance training programs. *Exerc Sport Sci Rev* 1973;1:155-188.

94. Shephard RJ, Kavanagh T: The effect of training on the aging process. *Phys Sports Med* 1978;6:33-40.

95. Åstrand PO, Rodahl K (eds): *Textbook of Work Physiology: Physiological Basis of Exercise*, ed 3. New York, NY, McGraw-Hill, 1986.

96. *Recommended Dietary Allowances*, ed 10. Washington, DC, National Academy of Sciences, National Academy Press, 1989.

97. Schneider EL, Vining EM, Hadley EC: Recommended dietary allowances and the health of the elderly. *N Engl J Med* 1986;314:157-160.

98. Nelson RC, Franzi LR: Nutrition and aging. *Med Clin North Am* 1989;73:1531-1550.

99. Krall E, Dwyer JT: Validity of a food frequency questionnaire and a food diary in a short-term recall situation. *J Am Diet Assoc* 1987;87:1374-1377.

100. Pate TD, Brunn JC: Fundamentals of carbohydrate metabolism, in Hickson JF Jr, Wolinsky I (eds): *Nutrition in Exercise and Sport*. Boca Raton, FL, CRC Press, 1989, pp 37-49.

101. Shils ME, Young VR (eds): *Modern Nutrition in Health and Disease*, ed 7. Philadelphia, PA, Lea & Febiger, 1988.

102. Gersovitz M, Motil K, Munro HN: Human protein requirements: Assessment of the adequacy of the current Recommended Dietary Allowance for dietary protein in elderly men and women. *Am J Clin Nutr* 1982;35:6-14.

103. MacDonald I: Carbohydrates: General. In Shils ME, Young VR (eds): *Modern Nutrition in Health and Disease*, ed 7. Philadelphia, PA, Lea & Febiger, 1988, pp 38-51.

104. Jenkins DJA: Carbohydrates: Dietary Fiber, in Shils ME, Young VR (eds): *Modern Nutrition in Health and Disease*, ed 7. Philadelphia, PA, Lea & Febiger, 1988, pp 52-71.

105. Kay RM: Dietary fiber. *J Lipid Res* 1982;23:221-242.

106. Bergstrom J, Hermansen L, Hultman E, et al: Diet, muscle glycogen and physical performance. *Acta Physiol Scand* 1967;71:140-150.

107. Holloszy JO, Coyle EF: Adaptations of skeletal muscle to endurance exercise and their metabolic consequences. *J Appl Physiol* 1984;56:831-838.

108. Hultman E, Spriet LL: Dietary intake prior to and during exercise, in Horton ES, Terjung RL (eds): *Exercise, Nutrition, and Energy Metabolism*. New York, NY, Macmillan Publishing, 1988, pp 132-149.

109. Foster C, Costill DL, Fink WJ: Effects of preexercise findings on endurance performance. *Med Sci Sports* 1979;11:1-5.

110. Costill DL, Sherman WM, Fink WJ, et al: The role of dietary carbohydrates in muscle glycogen resynthesis after strenuous running. *Am J Clin Nutr* 1981;34:1831-1836.

111. Morrow FD: Assessment of nutritional status in the elderly: Application and interpretation of nutritional biochemistries. *Clin Nutr* 1986;5:112-120.

112. Davies KJ, Quintanilha AT, Brooks GA, et al: Free radicals and tissue damage produced by exercise. *Biochem Biophys Res Commun* 1982;107:1198-1205.

113. Keith RE: Vitamins in sport and exercise, in Hickson JF Jr, Wolinsky I (eds): *Nutrition in Exercise and Sport*. Boca Raton, FL, CRC Press, 1989, pp 233-253.

114. Chalmers TC: Effects of ascorbic acid on the common cold: An evaluation of the evidence. *Am J Med* 1975;58:532-536.

115. Bates CJ: Proline and hydroxyproline excretion and vitamin C status in elderly human subjects. *Clin Sci Mol Med* 1977;52:535-543.

116. Munro HN, Suter PM, Russell RM: Nutritional requirements of the elderly. *Annu Rev Nutr* 1987;7:23-49.

117. Iber FL, Blass JP, Brin M, et al: Thiamin in the elderly—relation to alcoholism and to neurological degenerative disease. *Am J Clin Nutr* 1982;36(5 suppl):1067-1082.

118. McCormick DB: Riboflavin, in Shils ME, Young VR (eds): *Modern Nutrition in Health and Disease*, ed 7. Philadelphia, PA, Lea & Febiger, 1988, pp 362-369.

119. Pernow B, Saltin B: Availability of substrates and capacity for prolonged heavy exercise. *J Appl Physiol* 1971;31:416-425.

120. Cochary EF, Gershoff SN, Sadowski JA: Aging and vitamin B-6 depletion: Effects on plasma pyridoxal-5′-phosphate and erythrocyte aspartate-aminotransferase activity coefficients in rats. *Am J Clin Nutr* 1990;51:446-452.

121. Marcus DL, Freedman ML: Folic acid deficiency in the elderly. *J Am Geriatr Soc* 1985;33:552-558.

122. Lindenbaum J, Healton EB, Savage DG, et al: Neuropsychiatric disorders caused by cobalamin deficiency in the absence of anemia or macrodytosis. *N Engl J Med* 1988;318:1720-1728.

123. Herbert VD, Colman N: Folic acid and vitamin B_{12}, in Shils ME, Young VR (eds): *Modern Nutrition in Health and Disease*, ed 7. Philadelphia, PA, Lea & Febiger, 1988, pp 388-416.

124. Ryan A: Round table: Nutritional practices in athletics abroad. *Phys Sportsmed* 1977;5:33-44.

125. Kagan VE, Spirichev VB, Erin AN: Vitamin E, physical exercise, and sport, in Hickson JF Jr, Wolinsky I (eds): *Nutrition in Exercise and Sport*. Boca Raton, FL, CRC Press, 1989, pp 255-278.

126. Nagawa T, Hiroshi K, Yunichiro A, et al: The effect of vitamine E on endurance. *Asian Med J* 1968;11:619-625.

127. Cureton TK: Influence of wheat germ oil as a dietary supplement in a program of conditioning exercises with middle-aged subjects. *Res Q* 1955;26:391-407.

128. Lawrance JP, Bower RC, Riche WP, et al: Effects of alpha-tocopherol acetate on the swimming endurance of trained swimmers. *Am J Clin Nutr* 1975;28:205-208.

129. Heaney RP, Gallagher JC, Johnston CC, et al: Calcium nutrition and bone health in the elderly. *Am J Clin Nutr* 1982;36(5 suppl):986-1013.

130. Heaney RP, Recker RR: Estimation of true calcium absorption. *Ann Int Med* 1985;103:516-521.

131. Spencer H, Kramer L, Norris C, et al: Effect of calcium and phosphorus on zinc metabolism in man. *Am J Clin Nutr* 1984;40:1213-1220.

132. Seeman E, Riggs BL: Dietary prevention of bone loss. *Geriatrics* 1981;36:71-76.

133. Spencer H, Kramer L, DeBartolo M, et al: Further studies of the effect of a high protein diet as meat on calcium metabolism. *Am J Clin Nutr* 1983;37:924-929.

134. Aloia JF: Exercise and skeletal health. *J Am Geriatr Soc* 1981;29:104-107.

135. Lynch SR, Finch CA, Monsen ER, et al: Iron status of elderly Americans. *Am J Clin Nutr* 1982;36(5 suppl):1032-1045.

136. Sherman AR, Kramer B: Iron nutrition and exercise, in Hickson JF Jr, Wolinsky I (eds): *Nutrition in Exercise and Sport*. Boca Raton, FL, CRC Press, 1989, pp 291-300.

137. Hallberg L, Magnusson B: The etiology of "sports anemia": A physiological adaptation of the oxygen-disassociation curve of hemoglobin to an unphysiological exercise load. *Acta Med Scand* 1984;216:145-154.

138. Ohno H, Yamashita K, Doi K, et al: Exercise-induced changes in blood zinc and related proteins in humans. *J Appl Physiol* 1985;58:1453-1460.

139. Sandstead HH, Henriksen LK, Greger JL, et al: Zinc nutriture in the elderly in relation to taste acuity, immune response, and wound healing. *Am J Clin Nutr* 1982;36(5 suppl):1046-1059.

140. Anderson RA, Guttman HN: Trace minerals and exercise, in Horton ES, Terjung RL (eds): *Exercise, Nutrition, & Energy Metabolism*. New York, NY, MacMillan, 1988, pp 180-195.

141. Lane HW: Some trace elements related to physical activity: Zinc, copper, selenium, chromium, and iodine, in Hickson JF Jr, Wolinsky I (eds): *Nutrition in Exercise and Sport*. Boca Raton, FL, CRC Press, 1989, pp 301-307.

142. Goodwin JS, Hunt WC, Hooper P, et al: Relationship between zinc intake, physical activity, and blood levels of high-denstiy lipoprotein cholesterol in a healthy elderly population. *Metabolism* 1985;34:519-523.

143. Randall HT: Water, electrolytes, and acid-base balance, in Shils ME, Young VR (eds): *Modern Nutrition in Health and Disease*, ed 7. Philadelphia, PA, Lea & Febiger, 1988, pp 108-141.

144. Saltin B: Aerobic and anaerobic work capacity after dehydration. *J Appl Physiol* 1964;19:1114-1118.

145. Pennington JA, Wilson DB, Newell RF, et al: Selected minerals in food surveys, 1974 to 1981/82. *J Am Diet Assoc* 1984;84:771-780.

146. Åstrand PO: JB Wolffe Memorial Lecture: Why exercise? *Med Sci Sports Exerc* 1992;24:153-162.

147. Parr RB, Porter MA, Hodgson SC: Nutrition knowledge and practice of coaches, trainers, and athletes. *Phys Sportsmed* 1984;12:127-136.

Chapter 23

The Physiologic Basis for Strength Training In Midlife

William J. Kraemer, PhD

Resistance training is the only way in which an individual can increase muscle mass. This makes resistance training a unique "modality" in an overall program for promoting health and fitness throughout a lifetime. Only within the last 10 years has resistance training become widely accepted as an important exercise modality in stimulating vital physiologic adaptations that appear important in fighting the aging process. Thus, resistance training can contribute to a better quality of life by improving various functional capacities, such as strength, body composition, and cardiovascular fitness.

Most research in resistance training has focused upon men in their 20s. Only in the last several years have investigators started to examine the effects of resistance training in individuals older than 60 years of age. Few studies have directly examined the effects of resistance training during midlife, which will be operationally defined in this chapter as individuals ranging in age from 35 to 55 years. The primary purpose of this chapter is to develop an overall paradigm illustrating the physiologic adaptations and benefits of a resistance training program for individuals during midlife.

Understanding the Exercise Prescription Process

A multitude of resistance training programs can be designed based upon a number of program design variables. As a result, a resistance training program can be designed to fit the specific needs of an individual. Over the past 3 years, studies have shown that changing one program design variable (eg, rest between sets and exercises or resistance lifted) can result in dramatic differences in the physiologic responses to an exercise session.[1,2] Subsequent physiologic adaptations are affected by the characteristics of the training sessions.[3,4]

Resistance training programs are really very individualized processes. A very specific configuration of exercise stimuli, or an exercise prescription, is created for an individual by using a combination of variables (eg, sets, repetitions, resistances).[3] In an effective training program, the exercise stimulus interacts with the individual's physiology and genetic predisposition, resulting in a physiologic adaptation. Because programs are individually designed, a program that is effective for one individual may not be as effective for another individual. Variations in program effectiveness may occur for a variety of reasons, ranging from the amount of physiologic adaptation already present for a given variable (eg, fitness level) to an individual's genetic predisposition. As the potential for physiologic adaptation of a given variable (eg, strength) increases toward an individual's theoretical genetic maximum, the exercise prescription must be changed. This change is necessary so that the training program remains an effective physiologic stimulus for either improving a given variable or maintaining a particular variable at a desired level of physiologic adaptation (eg, bone mineral density). During midlife, fitness levels vary widely due to differences in prior activity levels and life-style behavior patterns. Because a resistance training program can be designed to suit an individual's starting level of fitness and will also provide health benefits, resistance training is an important "tool" in preventive medicine and health care.[5]

A well-defined process for creating an exercise prescription for a resistance training program has been previously documented and discussed in detail.[3,6-8] Basic to this process is conducting a preliminary needs analysis prior to the start of a training program. The needs analysis should focus on issues related to the specific goals of the individual's resistance training program. Obtaining a complete information profile specific to the individual's functional capacities, medical history, prior exercise training background, job demands, and recreational sport interests is an integral part of the needs analysis.

After evaluating an individual's needs and starting levels of fitness, specific goals for a training program can be formulated. The resulting training program includes a specific, "individualized" exercise prescription that addresses the unique needs of the individual. The training program can then be started at a level consistent with the individual's level of fitness and health status to attain specific training goals. These goals represent the desire to achieve new levels of physiologic adaptation in specific variables.

Periodic reevaluation and testing helps assess program goals and overall program effectiveness. Changes are then made in the training program as goals are achieved and functional capacities improve to desired levels. Programs can be designed to either improve or maintain specific physiologic variables. Developing an exercise prescription as part of a resistance training program is a dynamic process that attempts to match desired physiologic adaptation with the most effective resistance program. Figure 1 is a graphic representation of the process.

The manipulation of short-term program variables and long-term program changes ultimately defines a given exercise session and the eventual effectiveness of the program to cause a physiologic

NEEDS ANALYSIS

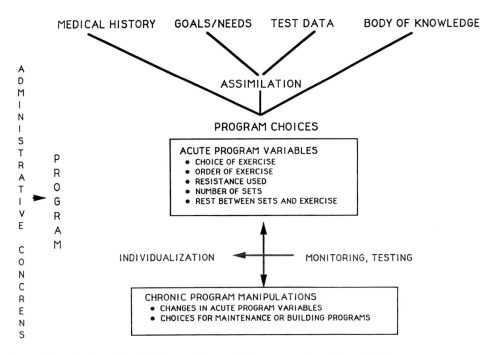

Fig. 1 *Theoretical paradigm for the exercise prescription process in resistance training.*

adaptation.[9,10] Research to date has only started to propose optimal exercise prescriptions for specific variables (eg, strength, muscle mass, bone density, etc). No real attempt has been made to devise an optimal exercise prescription that accounts for the effects of aging. To that end, however, empirical evidence has shown that recovery between exercise sessions changes as an individual grows older. In addition, individuals who maintain higher levels of strength fitness into their 40s and 50s do not appear to need the same frequency of training to maintain their level of fitness as do untrained individuals. Additional empirical research on specific programs needs for the individual in midlife is needed to better understand the effects of resistance training in this age group.

Physiologic Adaptations with Resistance Training

Adaptations In Muscular Strength

One of the most obvious physiologic adaptations resulting from a resistance training program is increased strength in the exercised musculature.[3,11,12] With training, strength increases from the individual's starting level of fitness to a point within the limits of the individual's genetic capacity to make the needed cellular changes for a physiologic adaptation. Increased muscular strength and other physiologic changes enhance both the individual's functional abilities and health status, due to associated training-induced adaptations, such as increased muscle mass.[5] These findings support the theoretical advantages associated with lifelong exercise training. Strength is defined as the ability of a muscle or muscle group to produce maximal force at a given or specified velocity.[13] It appears that even modest increases in muscle strength (ie, 20% to 35%) observed with training, when learning effects are removed, allow for associated physiologic adaptations. Such adaptations may have a dramatic impact upon the individual's health status and functional abilities in everyday life. Ultimately, these adaptations may reduce the amount of disability and subsequent medical and nursing home care that so many elderly people now require.

An individual with no previous resistance training can achieve increased muscle strength with training, even if the individual is well into midlife or old age before beginning such a program.[14] Studies can now track a larger number of individuals who have training histories of four or five decades; therefore, the absolute strength values that older people can achieve as a result of long-term training will continue to be redefined. Due to the enhanced functional abilities and health status of older individuals who have maintained a long-term program, it would appear that beginning a resistance training program during midlife would enhance the trainability and functional abilities realized.

One of the more intriguing questions concerns the possibility of whether individuals who participate in a long-term resistance training program can maintain a relatively high level of strength with age. Empirical data tend to suggest that they do. Therefore, a quite plausible hypothesis would be that while a decrease in strength might occur with aging, the magnitude of strength loss would be significantly less for trained individuals than for their untrained counterparts. Figure 2 shows the difference between the theoretical aging curves for strength of an upper body exercise (bench press) and a lower body exercise (squat exercise) for one repetition maximum (RM) strength.

The effects of a long-term resistance training program over the course of midlife are demonstrated in a number of case histories. Many factors contribute to decreased strength with aging, including amount of training time made available, differences in training goals, type of training program, health status, musculoskeletal injury status, and psychological factors.[15] However, a few master weightlifters have actually set age-group world records in their 40s; these records actually represented better personal performances than they achieved in their 20s. Again, there is a great deal of speculation about how this might occur. Possible factors explaining this enhanced performance may include improved training techniques, more training

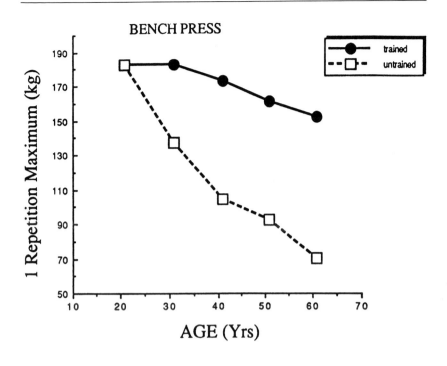

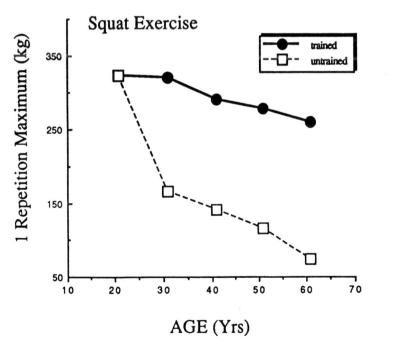

Fig. 2 *The theoretical responses for maximal 1 RM strength for the bench press and squat with age and case study response of a man who trained throughout midlife.*

time, and underachievement as a younger lifter. However, these examples demonstrate that very high levels of strength fitness are still possible during midlife. Detraining studies have shown that as a physiologic variable "strength performance" is maintained to a greater extent than aerobic fitness.[3,16,17]

Strength Changes with Age

Loss of muscle strength affects an individual's functional abilities both on the job and during recreational activities, and in later life may compromise health status and increase disability. The most prominent behavioral reason for the dramatic decline in muscle strength with age appears to be lack of use.[15,18-22] The lack of exertion beyond the demands of everyday activities results in a quantitative loss of muscle mass as well as a loss of force production capabilities.[15,23-25] Neural and metabolic processes may also contribute to limitations in strength development.[24,25]

When examining weightlifting and powerlifting records in both men and women, as shown in Figure 3, a dramatic decrease in strength can be observed with age. This decrease is most likely a function of the aging process, along with many other possible factors. The reason for this dramatic change is apparently quite different from other age-related reductions in strength previously observed in untrained individuals. Decreases in record performances probably reflect upper levels of genetic and training capacities for individuals as they grow older. As with other age-group records in athletic events, changes reflect a reduced capacity of the body to perform at its highest level. The decreases observed in athletes who are training and competing from midlife into old age may be influenced by several factors, including the following: neural changes associated with the motor performance of specific competitive lifts; decreases in the relative amount of training time dedicated to lifting; and the number of competitors (ie, genetic pool) involved with the various age-group competitions.

While it appears that strength decreases with age, overall health and functional ability status in individuals who train is quite a bit better than that of their untrained counterparts. Maintaining a resistance training program in midlife will help to offset the magnitude of physiologic decrements associated with the effects of aging. In studies based on job tasks, data comparing active to inactive individuals showed that job-related physical activity results in a higher functional ability in muscular performance through midlife for both men and women.[25-28] These results tend to support the need for "muscle overload" to obtain increases in muscular function and force production. However, while job tasks may strengthen the muscles used on the job, they do not provide for muscular balance around joints, sym-

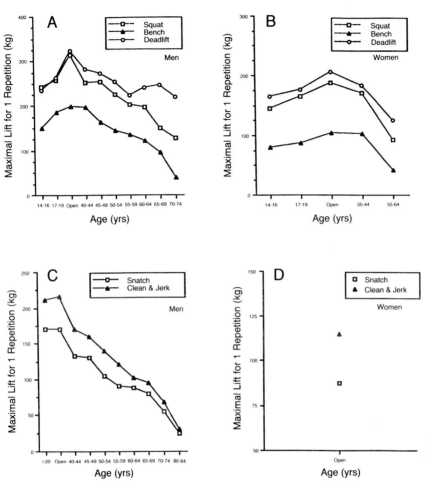

Fig. 3 *Profile of record performances for men and women. **A,** American Drug Free Powerlifting Association Men's 75 kg class records with age. (Bench Press, Squat and Dead Lift) **B,** American Drug Free Powerlifting Association Women's 63 kg class records with age. (Bench Press, Squat and Dead Lift) **C,** World Weightlifting Records Men's 75 kg class records with age.(Snatch Lift and the Clean and Jerk Lift) **D,** World Weightlifting Record for Women's 60 kg class record. (Snatch Lift and the Clean and Jerk Lift)*

metrical development of strength in the upper and lower body, changes in full range of joint motion, or prevention of overuse syndromes. Resistance training programs are more commonly used to compensate for limitations in muscular development from job-related adaptations. While some job-related adaptations may be positive, only a properly designed resistance training program can provide muscular development for the entire body. Many industrial fitness programs use weight training as an effective modality to prepare individuals for the rigors of the job, from sedentary jobs to heavy manual labor.

Previous research has suggested that there are differences in the relative trainability of men and women, but current studies indicate that the relative trainability of women appears to be similar to that of men.[3,29-31] When comparing the "normative male" with the "normative female," absolute gains in muscle size typically differ due to gender-related differences in muscle tissue mass mediated by differential hormonal mechanism(s), such as testosterone.[31,32] Care must be taken when interpreting gender differences from cross-sectional data. Such data are, in part, based on the limited exposure of women to intensive training. This is especially true for women over the age of 30 years, because intense resistance training was many times not socially acceptable. The strength performance of women participating in competitive lifting events indicates that women have considerably more absolute strength than previously thought possible (Fig. 3). Limited data are available concerning the effects of intense resistance training programs on women, especially during midlife. Still, the present data indicate that women are as capable as men at improving strength within their genetic capabilities. Examination of the competitive performances and training study data in women also indicates that many women are dramatically stronger than many men. Thus, beyond "normative" comparisons, individual evaluations must be made concerning the strength level and potential. Resistance training and its physiologic effects on women remain an important area of study as the health benefits become more obvious.[5,33] Further research will allow for more definitive conclusions concerning gender-related differences in resistance exercise prescription and resulting physiologic adaptations. Nevertheless, resistance training remains a potent exercise tool for both men and women in midlife to achieve increases in strength.[3,34-40]

Adaptations of Resistance Training on Muscle Fibers

Resistance training is the only way in which to increase the size of muscle cells. Chronic recruitment of motor units to perform heavy resistance exercise results in hypertrophy of the muscle cells exercised.[41] Therefore, if a proper resistance training program is used to recruit a large percentage of the musculature, changes in muscle tissue mass will occur as a result of training.[3,9] However, if muscle cells are not recruited, disuse muscle atrophy occurs, which depletes the muscle's contractile protein and results in a reduction in muscle tissue mass.[42,43] The loss of contractile protein leads to functional decreases in strength performance.[15] Resistance training increases the size of all muscle fibers, but greater increases can be seen in the type II muscle fibers recruited as a part of higher threshold motor units required for higher force production.[3,41,44,45]

The relative percentage of type I and type II muscle fibers in women is similar to that in men.[31,46] However, one of the few gender differences appears to be related to the cross-sectional size of type I and type II muscle fibers.[31,46] In women, type I cross-sectional muscle fibers are typically larger than type II muscle fibers—the opposite relationship in fiber size occurs in men. With heavy resistance training, the size of a woman's type II muscle fibers starts to equal and eventually surpasses the size of the type I fibers.[31,46] While this apparent gender difference is not completely understood, it may be due to the recruitment patterns involved with physical activities typically performed by untrained women.

Muscle cells are influenced by a variety of trophic factors, including neural stimulation, availability of nutrients, and hormonal influences. Such influences in the biologic environment of the muscle cell will directly impact the developmental timecourse of the muscle fiber. Behavioral changes in midlife probably also influence the biologic status of the muscle cell.[26,28,39] Behaviors related to nutrition practices, exercise habits, and other life-style activities, such as alcohol consumption and smoking, may alter the functional status of the muscle cell. In fact, nutrition may be one of the most important trophic factors affecting muscle cell growth and development in conjunction with exercise during the midlife, although an in-depth discussion is beyond the scope of this chapter.[47]

Long-term resistance training will affect a number of morphologic, biochemical, and histochemical adaptations in muscle.[45,48] Adaptations that occur with heavy resistance training are quite different from those associated with endurance training.[45] Endurance training results in a more oxidative muscle cell with less contractile protein and much lower force production capabilities.[49] Conversely, heavy resistance training results in the opposite end of the continuum in terms of cellular adaptation. Surprisingly, with resistance training muscle cells have only a slightly less oxidative potential, and greater amounts of protein accretion, and much higher force production capabilities. The exact way in which these two types of training opt for adaptational energy and morphologic change remains unclear. While decreases in both mitochondrial and capillary volume density measurements have been observed due to protein accretion in the muscle cell, no harmful effects on the whole body maximum oxygen consumption values have been observed.[4]

Table 1 presents an overview of some of the classic changes observed in the muscle cell as a result of resistance training. Limited data on older populations support the notion that similar muscle adaptations occur across the aging continuum as a result of heavy resistance training.[14,50] Trainability is probably the major determinant of the absolute magnitude of potential increase observed in a given muscle fiber variable and again argues for chronic exercise training and positive life-style interventions.

Dramatic program differences exist that are related to the effectiveness of the muscle to gain muscle mass and strength. If the resistance is not heavy enough, or if the volume of resistance exercise

Table 1 Adaptations in muscle cell with resistance training

Variable	Adaptation
Muscle fiber myofibrillar protein content	Increased
Capillary density	No change/decrease
Mitochondrial volume density	Decreased
Myoglobin	Decreased
Succinate dehydrogenase	No change/decrease
Malate dehydrogenase	No change/decrease
Citrate synthase	No change/decrease
C-Hydroxyacyl-CoA dehydrogenase	No change/decrease
Creatine phosphokinase	Increased
Myokinase	Increased
Phosphofructokinase	No change/decrease
Lactate dehydrogenase	No change/increase
Stored ATP	Increased
Stored PC	Increased
Stored glycogen	Increased
Stored triglycerides	?/increased
Myosin heavy chain composition	Slow to fast

stress (sets x repetitions) is not large enough for the given level of physiologic adaptation, little or no increase will be observed in strength or muscle mass. This illustrates the importance of the exercise prescription and its effectiveness as an exercise stimulus to change a given variable. These potential differences in program effectiveness directly affect other cellular adaptations linked to changes in the muscle cell itself. In a recent review, Tesch[45] indicates that there is some confusion about the metabolic and biochemical adaptations in muscle with resistance training. This confusion stems from the inconsistency in which results are reported. In some cases the training performed is referred to as "strength," while in others it is reported as "weight" or 'heavy resistance' training. Even though these terms are commonly used, the training does not result in any meaningful increases in strength and muscle mass. Therefore, changes must be evaluated within the context of a particular resistance training program's training effectiveness.

Increasing the muscle cell's metabolic and contractile function and its resistance to fatigue are important adaptations with resistance training. Cellular changes initiated during midlife may enhance the functional level of the muscle cell with older age. The structure and function of the muscle cell appear to provide the basis for adaptational changes in a variety of other physiologic systems, from the endocrine system to the cardiovascular system, as neuromuscular activation of movement is basic to changes in these other systems.

Adaptations With Connective Tissues

Connective tissues, specifically the major load-transmitting components (bone, tendon, ligament, and meniscus) are believed to increase in strength and undergo morphologic changes that enhance function as a result of resistance training.[51,52] Each of these connective tissue components has been found to be responsive to exercise stress. However, further research on the quantity and quality of physical activity is needed to evaluate exactly how these components respond to training.[50] A number of studies suggest that resistance training might be an effective tool in this process due to the multitude of stress configurations an exercise prescription can create. Previous research has examined in detail the theoretical framework that would make resistance training one of the most effective exercise tools to stimulate improved strength, growth, and quality of connective tissues.[33,51,52]

Increased strength in the connective tissues would help to increase the integrity of the joints and resistance to injury. Strong ligaments and stable cartilage would help offset or reduce the severity of a wide variety of joint disorders. In turn, movement, balance, and physical function are enhanced by the increases in the functional ability of the tendons and ligaments. Few studies have focused on ligament and tendon adaptation to exercise training, and these studies can only infer what might be happening with the more intense loading of the exercise stress that is characteristic of resistance training.[51,52]

Of particular concern and the principal focus of this chapter are the effects of exercise on bone, especially in women. Bone is one of the main connective and structural tissues that may benefit from resistance training initiated during midlife to protect and reduce the magnitude of bone loss with age, especially in women.

Bone Adaptations

Bone is a dynamic tissue that readily adapts to repetitive loading events, such as exercise, by creating additional bone. The type of exercise appropriate for stimulating formation of new bone is currently a topic of great interest. Changes in bone mineral density occur with age, and women are thought to experience greater decrements in bone mineral density with aging. In fact, during midlife dramatic changes in bone density begin in women with more subtle changes in men. Figure 4 presents a pattern of these changes.

Initiating a resistance training during youth is believed to increase peak bone mass, which allows an individual to start the aging process with more bone mass.[33] Conversely, resistance training programs begun during midlife require that the individual "stick to the program" in order to maintain improved bone mineral density. By starting a resistance training program during youth, or maintaining a resistance training program during midlife, an individual may experience benefits in bone health.[33,52] However, bone growth and modeling respond much more slowly than does the hypertrophic response of muscle. Therefore, longer periods of training are needed (6 months or greater) to observe increases in bone density.

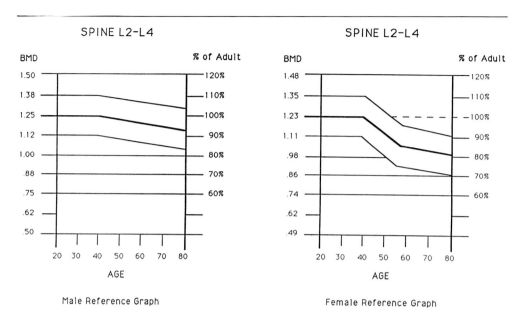

Fig. 4 *Reference graphs for spine L2-L4 with % age-matched for male and female changes in bone mineral density with age. (Reproduced with permission from Lunar Corporation, Madison, WI.)*

The demands of a resistance exercise program to develop bone appear to be more rigorous than that needed to develop muscle.[33] Midlife presents the individual with the last opportunity to obtain a higher level of trainability, which may provide more optimal conditions for training and maintaining bone health in old age. The functional capacity needed to perform the type of resistance exercises required for bone growth appears higher than that needed for the development of muscle tissue. This is because the type of resistance exercises needed for optimal bone modeling are more demanding. Several factors that affect the new bone growth have been identified, including the daily functional strain experienced by the bone, concentrations of various hormones, and availability of minerals.

Briefly, new bone growth is an adaptive response directed by strain-sensitive bone cells, such as osteocytes or osteoblasts.[53] Osteocytes are found throughout the extracellular matrix of the bone. They are ideally suited for monitoring deformations in the bone matrix consequent to mechanical loading. Osteoblast precursors are located on the outer surface of the bone and may be sensitive to strain at the periosteal surface. An important function of the osteoblast is to secrete the matrix proteins (eg, collagen) that make up the meshwork of mineralized connective tissues between neighboring bone cells. Once matrix proteins are established, they become "mineralized" as calcium phosphates (ie, hydroxyapatite) precipitate from the interstitial fluid binding to the matrix proteins.[54] This produces the rigid extracellular matrix that is characteristic of bone's resistance to deformation by external forces. Bone cells experience strain from mechanical loading and initiate a strain-specific response that results in new bone growth on the bone surfaces receiving the strain. The end result of these responses to strain is a series of signal transduction events that regulate the expression of the genes and their protein products that make up the matrix of bone. New matrix proteins, once in place and mineralized, increase the resistance of bone to deformation, thereby providing the bone with added protection against future loading events.

Bone strength is dictated by the mechanical strains routinely imposed upon the bone. In a recent study, some of the loading characteristics needed by exercise to alter bone were examined.[33] The results indicated that in response to repeated loading events, bone will alter its shape and increase its total mass in order to reduce the peak strain from the imposed load. Healthy bone fractures at approximately 25,000 μE (microstrain). Microstrain is a unit used to describe the force per unit area applied to bone. According to Frost,[55] a longitudinal compressive force equivalent to 1,000 μE will create a stress in the bone of approximately 1.4 kg/mm^2 and result in a change in bone length of approximately 0.1%. Forces generated by everyday activities, excluding intense exercise, rarely exceed 2,500 μE or one tenth of the fracture threshold. Forces that exceed 1,000 μE usually initiate new bone formation. Therefore, resistance training provides a controlled environment to present such forces through to the bone.

By understanding the strong relationship between bone and its attached musculature, and the effects of the configuration of the dynamic loading stimulus, a reasonable estimation can be made concerning the types of exercise required to bring about changes in bone mass.[33] It appears that the most effective type of exercise for increasing bone mass would involve intense muscular contractions during weightbearing activities. Effective exercise programs would need to produce increases in muscle mass and dynamic force production capabilities of the muscles. Such adaptations in muscular strength would allow an individual to use greater loads in training. The use of greater loads increases the osteogenic stimuli for bone formation due to the compressive forces on the supporting skeletal structures. The osteogenic stimuli created by the contracting musculature and compressive forces together stimulates bone formation only in those tissues that directly receive the mechanical strain.

The first longitudinal training study that showed significant bone formation in response to an exercise program involved postmenopausal women.[56] The women progressed from a moderate walking program to an exercise program that included a variety of more intense exercises, such as rowing, weight training, stair climbing, and running. The resulting adaptation to the higher intensity activities was a 5.2% increase in lumbar spine bone mineral density after only 9 months of training and a 6.4% increase in bone mineral density after 22 months of training. The bone mineral density of the control group did not significantly deviate from the baseline over the course of the study. To confirm that these increases were exercise induced, the women were observed for the next 13 months, a period in which their physical activity was reduced. The women retained only a 1.1% increase in bone mineral density above their baseline values. These changes in bone mineral density clearly indicated that a mechanical strain threshold for these women was reached when they participated in high-intensity exercises. Thus, exercise stimulated the bone cells to initiate a noticeable degree of new bone formation in the spine.

The most debilitating osteoporotic fractures occur in the axial skeleton at the hip and spine, due to low bone mass at these sites. In order for exercise to be an effective intervention for increasing bone mass in the axial skeleton, the hip and spine must receive direct mechanical loading to produce the functional adaptation of a localized increase in bone mass. However, the exercise must be appropriate for this area, and the individual must be capable of performing the exercise.

A group of world-class powerlifters were tested for bone mineral content at the lumbar spine while performing the dead lift exercise. Strain was placed on the third lumbar vertebra as the powerlifter grasped the barbell with both hands shoulder-width apart in a straight back squatting position. The lifter then lifted the barbell from the floor until he was in a standing position.[57] The forces acting on the lumbar spine during the dead lift exercise were observed to be 30 to 40 times the normal compression force created by the body weight of the individual. The magnitude of force exceeds the predicted fracture threshold of the vertebral bone. To withstand such forces, the vertebrae must act virtually as a solid block of bone. Analysis of the bone mineral content in these subjects revealed extremely high values in the lumbar spine. In addition, the bone mineral content values were found to correlate well (r = 0.85) with the annual "tonnage" each subject had lifted in the previous year. Other studies have subsequently shown that men who have a history of long-term training seem to have higher bone densities.[58,59] Also of note is the fact that athletes who have the highest bone mineral densities are powerlifters and weightlifters; both are types of resistance training that involve much greater loads than are used in other types of resistance training.

A significant point that is often overlooked by scientific study is that resistance training programs are not all the same. Even more dramatic are the differences among body building, powerlifting, and weightlifting. Again, the resistance exercise stimulus provides a dramatic tool for diverse configurations of exercise stress. Such evidence is provided by the wide continuum of adaptational responses observed after various resistance training programs. To establish a cause-and-effect relationship between specific exercise variables and their ability to stimulate new bone formation would require further longitudinal training studies.

In their attempt to evaluate the effects of resistance training and bone responses, several investigators have made mistakes in exercise prescription, making the results difficult to interpret or unable to demonstrate the effectiveness of resistance training during mid-life.[60,61] Typical errors have included the following: using too little resistance; using inadequate exercise volume; attempting to lift increasingly heavier resistance without adequate rest between sets; and selecting exercises that do not place the exercise stress vector in the proper orientation with the bone and the muscles acting on the bone (eg, leg extension rather than squatting to stress the long axis of the spine and femur).[33]

A recent review attempted to relate terms that describe the deformation of bone by external loading to terms that describe resistance exercise terminology.[33] The magnitude of the strain and the strain rate correspond to the load and intensity (power output) of the exercise, respectively. The magnitude of the load required to produce an effective stimulus for bone formation appears to be in the range of a 1 to 10 RM load, or about 85% to 100% of the 1 RM, as this is the magnitude of the loading used by powerlifters[57] and weightlifters,[58] groups who have the greatest values in bone mineral density. Studies involving training loads between 60% and 85% of 1 RM have also shown increases in bone mineral content.[59-61]

However, these values are not as dramatic as the adaptations seen in subjects using heavier loads in their training programs. It is important to note that the percentage of 1 RM that results in a given strength range of RM repetitions (ie, 1 to 10 RM) can vary with the size of the muscle being exercised.[3] Thus, exercises that use the larger muscle groups (eg, leg press, squat) usually require a higher percentage of 1 RM loads compared with exercises that use the smaller muscle groups (eg, biceps curl). This variation is important to ensure that the RM repetitions are maintained in the most effective range strength range (10 RM and below) for both trained and untrained men and women. Multiple sets (3 to 6) of structural exercises, such as squats, need to be performed to achieve the appropriate volume of exercise necessary to overload the musculoskeletal system, causing muscle hypertrophy and strength gains. This volume of loading corresponds to the findings of Rubin and Lanyon,[62] which demonstrated a minimum threshold of loading cycles (ie, volume of exercise) effective in stimulating new bone formation. Rubin and Lanyon found that 36 loading cycles were necessary to create an osteogenic stimulus in experimental animals, and increasing the number of loading cycles did not enhance the effectiveness of the stimulus. The effectiveness of a heavy resistance program may also be enhanced by including exercises that involve high strain rates (power output). Variations in weightlifting exercises, such as various cleans (eg, power cleans or hang cleans), snatch lifts, and jerks generate the highest values for power production. Higher power exercises may differ in their stimulus to bone when compared to high force, low power movement. Although both may be effective to increase bone density, the mechanisms by which power (strain rate) and high force (compression) achieve increases may differ.[57,62,63] The effectiveness of high strain rates was shown first by an artificial loading program in sheep,[62] and second by the incredibly high bone mineral content values of the junior weightlifters.[58]

Resistance exercise appears to have great potential for increasing peak bone mass and maintaining bone mineral content.[33,51,52] However, studies of specific loading programs that eliminate initial learning effects on strength are needed, including direct evaluations of the following: multiple sets and repetitions (loading cycles: three to six sets per exercise); load (magnitude of the strain—10 RM and under); intensity (strain rate: high power output exercises such as cleans, snatches, and jerks); and specific exercises directed at multiple target tissues (distribution of strain: squats rather than leg extensions to load the entire axial skeleton). Such direct evaluations are necessary to correctly determine how the prescription of heavy resistance exercise can be designed to most effectively stimulate new bone formation.

Cardiovascular Adaptations to Resistance Training

The cardiovascular system has been shown to adapt to resistance training, but only small increases in the oxidative capacity of muscle have been observed.[64-66] These adaptations are seen in the minimal increases (5% to 8%) in untrained men for maximal oxygen consumption values.[66] Resistance exercise has been used in a wide variety of situations and has proved to be a safe and effective means of increasing the strength and function of the peripheral musculature. In addition, it has positively contributed to enhanced cardiac morphology. Even cardiovascular rehabilitation programs commonly use resistance exercise as a part of a total exercise therapy program.[67] Individuals with cardiac problems during midlife have been observed to be able to tolerate relatively heavy resistance exercise (75% of 1 RM). In many instances, heavy resistance training is necessary for a patient to successfully resume a more active life-style and/or physically demanding occupation.[67] Resistance training has been found to be effective in reducing resting heart rate, most likely due to a combination of increased parasympathetic and diminished sympathetic tone.[64]

Positive effects on blood pressure have also been observed as a result of resistance training.[64,65] The ability to tolerate and develop a lower blood pressure response to the demands of heavy resistance exercise might be considered a positive training adaptation, and may very well be a necessity for many individuals in midlife as their jobs may require heavy physical exertion.[64,65]

Table 2 Cardiovascular adaptations to training with heavy resistance exercise

Variable*	Adaptation
AT REST	
Heart rate	Decrease or no change
Blood pressure	
Systolic	Decrease or no change
Diastolic	Decrease or no change
Double product	Decrease or no change
Stroke volume (absolute)	Increase or no change
Relative to BSA	No change
Relative to LBM	No change
Cardiac systolic function	Increase or no change
Cardiac distolic function	No change (increase?)
Lipid profile	
Total cholesterol	Decrease or no change
HDL-C	Increase or no change
LDL-C	Decrease or no change
Wall thickness	
Left ventricle	Increase
Septal	Increase
Right ventricle	No change
Chamber volume	
Left ventricle	Increase or no change
Right ventricle	No change
Left ventricular mass	Increase or no change
WITH EXERCISE CHALLENGE	
Maximal oxygen consumption	Slight increase (untrained) or no change

*BSA, body surface area; HDL-C, high-density lipoprotein cholesterol; LBM, lean body mass; LDL-C, low-density lipoprotein cholesterol.

Table 2 illustrates the many positive effects on the cardiovascular system associated with resistance training. It appears that resistance training is very specific in its adaptations in the heart's morphology, many of which cannot be achieved with endurance training alone.[68-70] These cardiovascular changes have been previously reviewed in detail.[64,66]

Summary

Resistance exercise training can be started during midlife and can result in many adaptations that benefit both health and fitness.[71] Individuals who eat properly and participate in a total conditioning program for both musculoskeletal strength and cardiovascular fitness may have a much higher functional capacity as they approach old age.[72-74] The ramifications of improved health and fitness may have a dramatic impact on the health care system and its corresponding costs for individuals in midlife and as they approach old age. It is important to realize that as an exercise tool, resistance exercise must be used properly in an attempt to achieve desired physical benefits and developmental goals. This modality is most beneficial when individualized exercise programs are developed to enhance an individual's physical function within his or her defined limits to ultimately stimulate physiologic adaptations.

Acknowledgments

The author would like to thank Carol Glunt, Brian Conroy, and L. Perry Koziris for their contributions to the preparation of this manuscript. This work was supported in part by a grant from the Robert F. and Sandra M. Leitzinger Research Fund in Sports Medicine at the Pennsylvania State University.

References

1. Kraemer WJ, Gordon SE, Fleck SJ, et al: Endogenous anabolic hormonal and growth factor responses to heavy resistance exercise in males and females. *Int J Sports Med* 1991;12:228-235.

2. Kraemer WJ, Marchitelli L, Gordon SE; et al: Hormonal and growth factor responses to heavy resistance exercise protocols. *J Appl Physiol* 1990;69:1442-1450.

3. Fleck SJ, Kraemer WJ: *Designing Resistance Training Programs*. Champaign, IL, Human Kinetics Publishers, 1987.

4. Kraemer WJ: Physiologic and cellular effects of exercise training, in Leadbetter WB, Buckwalter JA, Gordon SL (eds): *Sports-Induced Inflammation: Clinical and Basic Science Concepts*. Park Ridge, IL, American Academy of Orthopaedic Surgeons, 1990, pp 659-676.

5. Stone MH, Fleck SJ, Triplett NT, et al: Health- and performance-related potential of resistance training. *Sports Med* 1991;11:210-231.

6. Kraemer WJ: Exercise prescription in weight training: Manipulating program variables. *Natl Strength Cond Assoc J* 1983;5:58-59.

7. Kraemer WJ, Baechle TR: Development of a strength training program, in Ryan AJ, Allman FL Jr (eds): *Sports Medicine*, ed 2. San Diego, CA, Academic Press, 1989, pp 113-127.

8. Kraemer WJ, Fleck SJ: Resistance training: Exercise prescription (Part 4 of 4). *Phys Sportsmed* 1988;16:69-81.

9. Fleck SJ, Kraemer WJ: Resistance training: Physiological responses and adaptations (Part 2 of 4). *Phys Sportsmed* 1988;16:108-124.

10. Fleck SJ, Kraemer WJ: Resistance training: Physiological responses and adaptations (Part 3 of 4). *Phys Sportsmed* 1988;16:63-76.

11. Kraemer WJ, Deschenes MR, Fleck SJ: Physiological adaptations to resistance exercise: Implications for athletic conditioning. *Sports Med* 1988;6:246-256.

12. Atha J: Strengthening muscle. *Exerc Sport Sci Rev* 1981;9:1-73.

13. Knuttgen HG, Kraemer WJ: Terminology and measurement in exercise performance. *J Appl Sport Sci Res* 1987;1:1-10.

14. Frontera WR, Meredith CN, O'Reilly KP, et al: Strength training and determinants of VO2max in older men. *J Appl Physiol* 1990;68:329-333.

15. Frontera WR, Meredith CN, O,Reilly KP, et al: Strength conditioning in older men: Skeletal muscle hypertrophy and improved function. *J Appl Physiol* 1988;64:1038-1044.

16. Thorstensson A: Observations on strength training and detraining. *Acta Physiol Scand* 1977;100:491-493.

17. Berger RA: Effect of varied weight training programs on strength. *Res Quart* 1962;33:168-181.

18. Bassey EJ, Bendall MJ, Pearson M: Muscle strength in the triceps surae and objectively measured customary walking activity in men and women over 65 years of age. *Clin Sci* 1988;74:85-89.

19. Anderson WF, Cowan NR: Hand grip pressure in older people. *Brit J Prevent Soc Med* 1966;20:141-147.

20. Burke WE, Tuttle WW, Thompson CW, et al: The relation of grip strength and grip-strength endurance to age. *J Appl Physiol* 1953;5:628-630.

21. Montoye HJ, Lamphiear DE: Grip and arm strength in males and females, age 10 to 69. *Res Q* 1977;48:109-120.

22. Asmussen E, Heeboll-Neilsen K: Isometric muscle strength in relation to age in men and women. *Ergonomics* 1962;5:167-169.

23. Teraoka T: Studies on the peculiarity of grip strength in relation to body positions and aging. *Kobe J Med Sci* 1979;25:1-17.

24. Shephard RJ: Physiological aspects of sport and physical activity in the middle and later years of life, in McPherson BD (ed): *Sport and Aging*. Champaign, IL, Human Kinetics Publishers, 1986, pp 221-232.

25. Israel S: Age-related changes in strength and special groups, in Komi PV (ed): *The Encyclopaedia of Sports Medicine: Strength and Power in Sport*. Oxford, Blackwell Scientific Pub, 1991, pp 319-328.

26. Nygard CH, Luopajarvi T, Ilmarinen J: Musculoskeletal capacity of middle-aged women and men in physical, mental and mixed occupations: A 3-5-year follow-up. *Eur J Appl Physiol* 1988;57(2):181-188.

27. Nygard CH, Luopajarvi T, Cedercreutz G, et al: Musculoskeletal capacity of employees aged 44 to 58 years in physical, mental and mixed types of work. *Eur J Appl Physiol* 1987;56(5):555-561.

28. Yokomizo Y: Measurement of ability of older workers. *Ergonomics* 1985;28:843-854.

29. Hettinger TH: *Isometrisches Muskeltraining*. (Isometric Muscle Training). Stuttgart, George Thieme Verlag, 1968.

30. Kraemer WJ, Daniels WL: Physiological effects of training, in Bernhardt DB (ed): *Sports Physical Therapy*. New York, NY, Churchill Livingstone, 1986, pp 29-53.

31. Staron RS, Malicky ES, Leonardi MJ, et al: Muscle hypertrophy and fast fiber type conversions in heavy resistance-trained women. *Eur J Appl Physiol* 1990; 60:71-79.

32. Kraemer WJ: Hormonal mechanisms related to the expression of muscular strength and power, in Komi PV (ed): *The Encyclopaedia of Sports Medicine: Strength and Power*. Oxford, Blackwell Scientific Pub, 1991, pp 64-76.

33. Conroy BP, Kraemer WJ, Maresh CM, et al: Adaptive responses of bone to physical activity. *Med Exerc Nutri and Health*. 1992;1:64-74.

34. Howard JH, Cunningham DA, Rechnitzer PA: Personality and fitness decline in middle-aged men. *Intern J Sport Psychol* 1987;18:100-111.

35. Suominen H, Rahkila P, Era P, et al: Functional capacity in middle-aged male endurance and power athletes, in Harris R, Harris S (eds): *Physical Activity, Aging and Sports: Vol 1: Scientific and Medical Research*. Albany, NY, Center for the Study of Aging, 1989, pp 213-218.

36. Sinaki M, Grubbs NC: Back strengthening exercises: Quantitative evaluation of their efficacy for women aged 40 to 65 years. *Arch Phys Med Rehabil* 1989;70:16-20.

37. Brown RD, Harrison JM: The effects of a strength training program on the strength and self-concept of two female age groups. *Res Q Exer Sport* 1986;57:315-320.

38. Anderson T, Kearney JT: Effects of three resistance training programs on muscular strength and absolute and relative endurance. *Res Q Exer Sport* 1982;53:1-7.

39. Stone MH, Blessing D, Byrd R, et al: Physiological effects of a term resistive training program on middle-aged untrained men. *Natl Strength Cond Assoc J* 1982;4(5):16-20.

40. Gettman LR, Ayres JJ, Pollock ML, et al: Physiologic effects on adult men of circuit strength training and jogging. *Arch Phys Med Rehabil* 1979;60:115-120.

41. Sale DG: Neural adaptation to strength training, in Komi PV (ed): *The Encyclopaedia of Sports Medicine: Strength and Power in Sport*. Oxford, Blackwell Scientific Pub, 1991, pp 249-265.

42. MacDougall JD: Morphological changes in human skeletal muscle following strength training and immobilization, in Jones NL, McCartney N, McComas AJ (eds): *Human Muscle Power*. Champaign, IL, Human Kinetics Publishers, 1986, pp 269-288.

43. MacDougall JD, Elder GC, Sale DG, et al: Effects of strength training and immobilization on human muscle fibres. *Eur J Appl Physiol* 1980;43:25-34.

44. Billeter R, Hoppeler H: Muscular basis of strength, in Komi PV (ed): *The Encyclopaedia of Sports Medicine: Strength and Power in Sport*. Oxford, Blackwell Scientific Pub, 1991, pp 39-64.

45. Tesch PA: Short- and long-term histochemical and biochemical adaptations in muscle, in Komi PV (ed): *The Encyclopaedia of Sports Medicine: Strength and Power in Sport*. Oxford, Blackwell Scientific Pub, 1991, pp 239-248.

46. Staron RS, Leonardi MJ, Karapondo DL, et al: Strength and skeletal muscle adaptations in heavy resistance-trained women after detraining and retraining. *J Appl Physiol* 1991;70:631-640.

47. Chernoff R: Aging and Nutrition. *Nutr Today* 1987;22:4-11.

48. Larsson L: Physical training effects on muscle morphology in sedentary males at different ages. *Med Sci Sports Exerc* 1982;14:203-206.

49. Saltin B, Gollnick PD: Skeletal muscle adaptability: Significance for metabolism and performance, in Peachey LD, Adrian RH, Geiger SR (eds): *Handbook of Physiology: Section 10: Skeletal Muscle*. Baltimore, MD, Williams and Wilkins, 1983, pp 555-631.

50. Aniansson A, Gustafasson E: Physical training in old men with special reference to quadriceps muscle strength and morphology. *Clin Physiol* 1981;1:87-98.

51. Zernicke RF, Loitz BJ: Exercise-related adaptations in connective tissue, in Komi PV (ed): *The Encyclopaedia of Sports Medicine: Strength and Power in Sport*. Oxford, Blackwell Scientific Pub, 1991, pp 77-95.

52. Stone MH: Connective tissue and bone response to strength training, in Komi PV (ed): *The Encyclopaedia of Sports Medicine: Strength and Power in Sport*. Oxford, Blackwell Scientific Pub, 1991, pp 279-290.

53. Lanyon LE, Goodship AE, Pye CJ, et al: Mechanically adaptive bone remodelling. *J Biomech* 1982;15:141-154.

54. Vaughan JM (ed): *The Physiology of Bone*, ed 3. New York, NY, Oxford University Press, 1981.

55. Frost HM: Skeletal structural adaptations to mechanical usage (SATMU): 1. Redefining Wolff's law: The bone modeling problem. *Anat Rec* 1990;226:403-413.

56. Dalsky GP, Stocke KS, Ehsani AA, et al: Weight-bearing exercise training and lumbar bone mineral content in postmenopausal women. *Ann Intern Med* 1988;108:824-828.

57. Granhed H, Jonson R, Hansson T: The loads on the lumbar spine during extreme weight lifting. *Spine* 1987;12:146-149.

58. Virvidakis K, Georgiou E, Korkotsidis A, et al: Bone mineral content of junior competitive weightlifters. *Int J Sports Med* 1990;11:244-246.

59. Fiore CE, Cottini E, Fargetta C, et al: The effects of muscle-building exercise on forearm bone mineral content and osteoblast activity in drug-free and anabolic steroids self-administering young men. *Bone Miner* 1991;13:77-83.

60. Gleeson PB, Protas EJ, LeBlanc AD, et al: Effects of weight lifting on bone mineral density in premenopausal women. *J Bone Miner Res* 1990;5(2):153-158.

61. Notelovitz M, Martin D, Tesar R, et al: Estrogen therapy and variable-resistance weight training increase bone mineral in surgically menopausal women. *J Bone Miner Res* 1991;6:583-590.

62. Rubin CT, Lanyon LE: Regulation of bone formation by applied dynamic loads. *J Bone Joint Surg* 1984;66A:397-402.

63. O'Connor JA, Lanyon LE, MacFie H: The influence of strain rate on adaptive bone remodeling. *J Biomech* 1982;15:767-781.

64. Fleck SJ: Cardiovascular response to strength training, in Komi PV (ed): *The Encyclopaedia of Sports Medicine: Strength and Power in Sport*. Oxford, Blackwell Scientific Pub, 1991, pp 305-315.

65. Fleck SJ, Dean LS: Resistance-training experience and the pressor response during resistance exercise. *J Appl Physiol* 1987;63:116-120.

66. Fleck SJ: Cardiovascular adaptations to resistance training. *Med Sci Sports Exerc* 1988;20(suppl 5):S146-S151.

67. Faigenbaum AD, Skrinar GS, Cesare WF, et al: Physiologic and symptomatic responses of cardiac patients to resistance exercise. *Arch Phys Med Rehabil* 1990;71:395-398.

68. Fleck SJ, Bennett JB III, Kraemer WJ, et al: Left ventricular hypertrophy in highly strength trained males, in Lubich T, Venerando A, Zeppilli P (eds): *Proceedings of the 2nd International Conference on Sports Cardiology*. 1989, 2:302-311.

69. Hurley BF, Hagberg JM, Seals DR, et al: Glucose tolerance and lipid-lipoprotein levels in middle-aged powerlifters. *Clin Physiol* 1987;7(1):11-19.

70. Hurley BF, Seals DR, Ehsani AA, et al: Effects of high-intensity strength training on cardiovascular function. *Med Sci Sports Exerc* 1984;16:483-488.

71. Liemohn WP: Strength and aging: An exploratory study. *Int J Aging Hum Dev* 1975;6:347-357.

72. Tymn M, Oerter A, Ryan N: Training the older athlete: Part II. Practical considerations. *Natl Strength Cond Assoc J* 1989;10(6):10-14.

73. Dobrev PA: Complex experimental investigations of the influence of weight training on persons in middle, advanced and old age. *Sci Methodical Bull* 1980;3:27-28.

74. Carter DR, Fyhrie DP, Whalen RT: Trabecular bone density and loading history: Regulation of connective tissue biology by mechanical energy. *J Biomech* 1987;20:785-794.

Chapter 24

Aerobic Exercise and Musculoskeletal Injuries in Midlife Populations

Charles M. Tipton, PhD

Introduction

In this presentation, the primary emphasis will be on midlife individuals, those between 40 and 60 years of age. In addition, findings related to the "young-old" (60 to 75 years), "middle-old" (75 to 85 years), and the "old-old" (85 years or older) will also be included.[1]

By definition, the Greek word "aerobic" means to live or to be active only in the presence of oxygen.[2] Consequently, the focus of this presentation will be on exercise training programs that require oxygen in order for the activity to continue. The energy transformations necessary for the mechanical work to be performed at the organism level are in accordance with the first law of thermodynamics and are complicated physiologic and biochemical processes that involve mechanisms of oxygen delivery and utilization.[3] Although it is convenient to assign specific exercises to either aerobic or anaerobic categories on a time-dependent scale because of the profile of phosphagen changes,[3] it is important to remember that anaerobic or aerobic metabolic pathways can be simultaneously active in adjacent cells or tissues depending on the pattern of blood flow distribution to the region as well as the metabolic demands being placed on the tissues.

Classically, the energy requirements (also called energy costs) of different physical activities have been assessed by indirect calorimetry or by the measurement of oxygen consumption.[3] According to most exercise physiologists, the best single measure by which to evaluate aerobic capacity is the maximal oxygen consumption ($\dot{V}O_2max$). This measurement has also been used to assess physical performance, and the distinction between maximum oxygen consumption and physical performance are discussed in some detail by Rowell (chapter 5). However, to discuss and evaluate aerobic exercises, individuals must relate the intensity of exercise to the $\dot{V}O_2max$ requirement of the activity (Table 1).

Table 1 The classification of aerobic exercise

Classification	$\dot{V}O_2max$	Perceived exertion scale
A. The prescription		
Very light	<25%	<10
Light	26-49%	10-11
Moderate	50-74%	12-13
Heavy	75-89%	14-16
Strenuous	90-100%	>17

B. The energy sources during strenuous exercise

Source	Time (min)								
	0.17	0.50	1.00	2.00	4.00	10.00	30.00	60.00	120.00
Anaerobic									
%	90	80	70	50	35	15	5	2	1
Aerobic									
%	10	20	30	50	65	86	95	98	99

(Reproduced with permission from Pollock ML: Exercise prescriptions for the elderly, in Spirduso WW, Eckert HM (eds): *Physical Activity and Aging*. American Academy of Physical Education Paper No. 22. Champaign, IL, Human Kinetics, 1989, p 169, and Åstrand P-O, Rodahl K: *Textbook of Work Physiology*. New York, NY, McGraw Hill, 1977, p 303.)

Åstrand and Rodahl[3] tabulated oxygen consumption or caloric cost in more than 80 activities ranging from daily living essentials to occupational demands and athletic events. Few activities had an aerobic requirement exceeding 2 L of oxygen or essentially 10 kcal a minute. The significance of their results is that a large percentage of the total population in the industrialized work force has a daily energy expenditure that is sedentary in nature. It is unlikely that the percentage of active midlife individuals in either the United States or Spain would be higher than the figures cited in the text of Åstrand and Rodahl.[3] According to Nieman,[4] 20% of American adults participate in aerobic activities three times a week for 20 to 30 minutes per exercise session. Unfortunately, it is not clear what percentage of this specific population is in their midlife years, but it is probably less than 20%.

Fitness at the work site is a concern of community Wellness Councils and of Healthy People 2000.[5] The goal of these organizations is to have 50% to 80% of existing companies, depending on the number of employees, establish such programs in the immediate future. However, the percentage of companies with such programs currently ranges from only 14% to 54%.[5] Furthermore, we must recognize that in the United States, many midlife individuals do not exercise in their leisure time. Blair and associates[6] have carefully evaluated the patterns of physical activity in older populations and reported that the percentage of sedentary individuals between 30 and 44 years of age was 24%. This percentage increased to 33% for people between 45 and 64 years of age and became even larger, 43%, in young-old and middle-old groups. When efforts were made to determine the percentage of individuals who were participating regularly in "strenuous" exercise, presumably aerobic in nature, the number for the entire population was less than 10%.[4]

It is not known whether the information concerning participation in aerobic-type activities at the work site or during leisure time for individuals in other parts of the world is similar to what has been reported for the United States. Although a report from Tartu in Estonia[7] indicated that 2,000 or more midlife individuals participated regularly in 60-km ski races, it is not apparent that this form of aerobic activity is a way of life for older individuals in Estonia and nearby countries. The collective effect of this information[4-7] is that the midlife population in the United States has a sedentary occupation, a limited or a brief history of participating in regular physical activity, a sedentary fitness level, a limited knowledge of training principles, and a susceptibility for musculoskeletal injuries.

Historians will have to decide whether the publication in 1968 of *Aerobics* by K. H. Cooper[8] was a significant contributor to the modern fitness movement that began in the 1960s.[4] It is worth noting that Cooper considered the best exercises to be running, swimming, cycling, walking, stationary running, handball, basketball, and squash. Not included in his 1968 ratings were isometric exercises, weight lifting, and calisthenics.

Select Epidemiologic and Biomechanical Considerations

It is well accepted that injuries, like disease processes, follow specific biologic laws.[9] The relevant issues and questions that need to be addressed in current and future research projects are which biomechanical and physiologic factors cause musculoskeletal injuries; to what extent are these injuries related to aerobic activities; how can aerobic exercise programs minimize or prevent musculoskeletal injuries; and how should aerobic exercises be prescribed to aid the injury-recovery process, with emphasis on midlife and older individuals.

Biomechanical mechanisms responsible for musculoskeletal injuries are complex and beyond the scope of this chapter. However, it is evident that physical factors associated with impact, deformation, compression, acceleration, deceleration, rotation, extension, and combinations thereof can cause musculoskeletal injuries.[10,11]

In addition to the studies cited elsewhere in this book, several investigations deserve mention. DeHaven and Lintner[12] reported on the influences of age and gender on the nature of injuries observed in their clinic on a university campus. They noted that the incidence of inflammatory problems with injuries increased with age up to 70 years and that many older individuals had musculoskeletal re-injuries from their younger years. Hess and associates[13] stated that 50% of all sports-related injuries were caused by overuse, whereas Matheson and associates[14] reported that in a midlife population of 685 individuals (average age, 57 years), 85% of the musculoskeletal injuries were the result of overuse. Matheson and associates[14] noted that racket sports, walking, and low-intensity sports caused musculoskeletal problems in the midlife population, while running, fitness classes, and field sports required medical attention in their younger population of 722 individuals (average age, 30 years). For the midlife patients, the foot was the anatomic site that was injured most frequently, whereas the knee joint was the region requiring the most medical attention among the younger subjects.

It is generally accepted that when the forces generated with muscle contraction exceed the elastic properties of the tissues, muscle injuries will occur.[15] In recent years, research has clearly demonstrated that lengthening (eccentric) contractions induce more muscle soreness, damage, and injury than concentric-type contractions.[16] While others will discuss the mechanisms of injuries to ligaments and tendons in humans, it is apparent from experimental studies in animals that the junctions between muscles and tendons, as well as between ligaments and bones, are frequent sites for muscle tears and ligament separations.[17,18] In fact, Tipton and Vailas[18] concluded that the medial collateral ligament insertion site on the tibia in rats and dogs was extremely susceptible to experimental injury because it was the weakest of the junctions tested.

A recent investigation in Finland[19] measured the forces from the Achilles tendons of human subjects using a force transducer during walking, running, jumping, and hopping. In most running and jumping activities, forces ranging from 2,000 to 4,000 N were recorded. However, with hopping movements, values of 6,000 N were measured. The elevated values of hopping, when compared to running, may help to explain why aerobic dance instructors and students have a high incidence of musculoskeletal injuries and low back pain.[20,21] Cavanagh and associates[22] measured the forces experienced by the feet during running, cycling, and rowing and noted peak values ranging from 250 to 1,500 N, with running having the highest forces. Because of these differences, running has been advocated for astronauts in space as a countermeasure against the loss of bone. This information has two practical lessons for midlife populations concerned about musculoskeletal injuries: they should know the "impact ratings" via ground reaction forces of various aerobic exercises (Table 2) and they must understand that impact exercises can be either beneficial or detrimental to the structures and functions of bones, muscles, tendons, and ligaments, depending on their frequencies, intensities, and durations. These aspects will be discussed in more detail.

Paradoxically, the conditions of actual and simulated microgravity have been categorized with overuse as inciting factors for muscle injuries and damage.[23,24] This finding indicates that the responsible mechanisms are complex and that many factors must be considered to determine the etiology of a musculoskeletal injury.

Ongoing studies investigating the female athlete triad (anorexia, amenorrhea, osteoporosis) are trying to determine how and why this

Table 2 Classification of activities for their impact on biologic structures

High-impact activities	Low-impact activities
Aerobic dance	Swimming
Running/jogging	Walking
Volleyball	Bicycling
Basketball	Rowing
Skipping rope	Cross-country skiing
Hopping	Stair climbing
Jumping	

(Adapted with permission from Pollock ML: Exercise prescriptions for the elderly, in Spirduso WW, Eckert HM (eds): *Physical Activity and Aging*. American Academy of Physical Education Paper No. 22. Champaign, IL, Human Kinetics, 1989, p 168.)

condition occurs and how it might be prevented.[25,26] Data are sparse from midlife females who are experiencing menopause before, during, or after participating in an aerobic training program and more research is needed on this subject.

Exercise Specificity and Aerobic Exercise Training in Animals

One of the most important training principles to emerge in the past 40 years concerns exercise specificity. This concept, attributed to Franklin Henry,[27] indicates that the physiologic response and its cellular adaptations are specific to the exercise being performed. Three experiments help to illustrate the importance of exercise specificity when prescribing aerobic exercises for training or rehabilitation purposes. The first experiment involved individuals[28] whose $\dot{V}O_2max$ and maximal heart rates were measured before and after participating in either arm or leg training studies. The individuals who trained with their arms showed improvements in their $\dot{V}O_2max$ and maximal heart rate scores only when they were measured on an arm ergometer, whereas those who trained with their legs exhibited improvements in their scores only when they were measured using a leg ergometer. In the second study,[29] subjects were tested for $\dot{V}O_2max$ when swimming and while running on a treadmill before swim training for 10 weeks. When the subjects were tested for $\dot{V}O_2max$ when swimming, a significant improvement of 11% was noted. However, when tested for $\dot{V}O_2max$ while running, a nonsignificant improvement of 1.5% was recorded. The third experiment involved rats that were endurance trained either on a treadmill at 0 grade at high speeds or on a treadmill at moderate speeds but at grades that were progressively increased with the speed.[30] Both training programs significantly increased the activity of cytochrome oxidase, which is a mitochondrial enzyme in skeletal muscle; but, only the graded exercise program significantly improved the separation force measurements of the in situ tibia-medial collateral ligament-fibula preparation from the trained rats.

The measurement of $\dot{V}O_2$max in animals is a routine procedure in many laboratories and it is well documented that endurance training between 50% and 90% $\dot{V}O_2$max improves $\dot{V}O_2$max from 10% to 20%. When older rats were regularly exercised on a treadmill between 12 and 24 months of age, the trained rats consistently had significantly higher $\dot{V}O_2$max values than their sedentary controls, although the slope of the decline was similar in both groups.[31] The improved $\dot{V}O_2$max was attributed to enhanced cardiac contractility, elevated cardiac output, higher oxygen delivery, and better blood flow to the periphery.

Aging in rats is associated with a decrease in the number of mitochondria and in their ability to oxidize substrates, especially free fatty acids.[32] After training older (25-month-old) rats for 12 weeks on a treadmill at an intensity estimated to be between 50% and 75% of their $\dot{V}O_2$max, Beyer and associates[32] reported that the homogenates from the trained muscles catalyzed the oxidation of glucose, free fatty acid, and amino acid substrates at rates that were 55% faster than was found for the nontrained rats. Even though the mitochondrial yield per unit of muscle declined 32% with age, the trained rats had a yield that was 100% higher than their aged controls. The studies of Farrar and associates[33] also showed in rats that endurance training (approximately 60% to 90% $\dot{V}O_2$max) not only reduced the normal loss of mitochondrial protein that occurs with aging, but also limited the usual detrimental effects of aging on the respiratory characteristics of the mitochondria.

It was interesting to note in the previous rat studies that the expected decreases in the mass of select muscles were less in the trained than in the nontrained animals. Aging typically results in a reduction in muscle mass, which is associated with decreases in fiber number, muscle size, and central nervous system activity.[34,35] Daw and associates[36] investigated this matter in 3- to 27-month-old rats by examining the soleus (type I) and extensor digitorum longus (EDL, type II) muscles. They found that treadmill training at approximately 50% to 70% $\dot{V}O_2$max had no significant effect on the loss of muscle fibers or on EDL mass of the older rats, but chronic exercise did increase the mass of the soleus muscle by 13% when compared to their age-matched controls. One important point to be learned from these studies with rats is that regular aerobic exercise can minimize the loss in mass of select antigravity (type I) muscles that normally occurs with aging, even though traditionally we have believed that weight lifting exercises would be better for this purpose. No known studies have been conducted to resolve this point.

With the availability of labelled microspheres, it is possible to quantitate in animals the changes in cardiac output and muscle blood flow with acute and chronic exercise. Musch and associates[37] used this approach with foxhounds and reported that an aerobic exercise program for 8 to 12 weeks that was at approximately 80% of the maximal heart rate increased $\dot{V}O_2$max by 31%, elevated cardiac output by

28%, and diminished systemic vascular resistance by 25%. More importantly, maximal exercise before the training process began increased blood flow to an extensor muscle (gastrocnemius) by 395%; to a flexor muscle (flexor digitorum superficialis) by 273%; to an adductor muscle (adductor magnus) by 395%; and to the hindlimb muscles by 408%. When the effects of training were assessed, the absolute values were increased by 38% to 117%.

Related trends were found in rats trained by running. Laughlin and Ripperger[38] reported that blood flow to the hind limb muscles was increased by 85%, with the oxidative fiber types (type II) increasing by as much as 200%. In addition, the capillary exchange and the capillary diffusion capacities were elevated by 50% and 70%, respectively, in the trained rats. A recent study has demonstrated that treadmill running by rats is associated with a significant increase in the vasodilatory ability of muscle arterioles.[39] When the muscles of younger (7-month-old) and older (23-month-old) rats were electrically stimulated, the older rats fatigued sooner; this result was attributed, in part, to a decrease in muscle blood flow during the contraction phase and a reduction in the oxidative capacity of older muscle.[40] It is well documented in animals that endurance training increases muscle capillarity.[41] This fact, plus the results from the vast experimental literature on aerobic training in animals, provides a strong rationale for advocating aerobic exercises to improve the functional capacity of muscle, to enhance its ability to withstand the metabolic consequences of fatigue, and to possibly delay, minimize, or prevent musculoskeletal injuries. A similar viewpoint has been advanced by others.[15]

Studies with animals have shown that muscle damage and injury can occur with eccentric or lengthening type contractions.[42,43] Systematic aerobic exercise may facilitate the regeneration process for muscle tissue, provided the injury was not a recurrent insult (in which case the replacement cells are likely to be fibrous). White and associates[44,45] autografted the soleus muscle and reimplanted the nerve in rats. They found that light aerobic training (approximately 30% to 40% $\dot{V}O_2max$) did not increase the mass of the graft. However, when sprints (80% to 100% $\dot{V}O_2max$) or endurance exercise training were used (approximately 70% to 80% $\dot{V}O_2max$), the mass of the graft increased when compared to nontrained animals. Heavy to strenuous exercise also significantly increased the oxidative capability (muscle homogenates using pyruvate and malate as substrates) of the grafts, but to a lesser extent than the mass of the muscle. To date, similar experiments have not been conducted with older animals or with weight-resistive training programs, and these types of investigations are needed.

Animal studies with isolated ligaments and tendons or with intact bone-ligament-bone preparations have demonstrated that aerobic training programs exceeding 70% $\dot{V}O_2max$ or 85% of the maximal heart rate significantly increase tissue mass and cross-sectional area, as well as the forces necessary to separate the tissues from their osseous attachments.[18,46] These changes, which have been reported in rats, rabbits, dogs, pigs, and nonhuman primates, illustrate that connective tissue responds to the mechanical stimulation associated with a progressive aerobic training program. Because ligamentous separation forces can be increased in trained thyroidectomized and in hypophysectomized rats,[18,46] mechanical stimuli are believed to be as essential as endocrine influences for inducing cellular and tissue adaptations and for facilitating the repair process of these tissues. However, it must be conceded that it is not known whether heavy resistance exercises would be equal or superior to aerobic exercises in producing these tissue adaptations.

The creative and ingenious animal studies of Lanyon[47] and Rubin and Lanyon[48] have provided a quantitative basis for others[49,50] to use aerobic activities to examine the combined influences of mechanical loading, mechanical strain, and the frequency of application on bone structure and function. Although aerobic exercise programs in animals have clearly increased the biomechanical and remodeling properties of bone,[18] heavy and strenuous aerobic training can cause microfractures and retard bone growth and development.[51] Because of the experimental designs, it is not evident whether similar results could have been achieved if resistance training methods had been incorporated in these studies instead of aerobic programs.

The evidence in animals that aerobic training improves both the metabolic capacity and the blood flow to osseous and connective tissues and bones is limited.[18] As demonstrated by Tipton and Vailas,[18] ligaments and tendons have a low aerobic capacity and aerobic training has a marginal influence on the activity of cytochrome oxidase in these tissues when compared to tissues from nontrained rats. On the other hand, immobilization markedly decreased the activity of cytochrome oxidase. Based on surgical studies by Tipton and Vailas[18] and Tipton and associates,[46] it can be postulated that aerobic training hastens the repair process of lesioned ligaments because of the increased blood supply to the tissues and the beneficial influences of the increased plasma concentrations of hormones that promote glycosaminoglycan and collagen metabolism.

Aerobic Exercise in the Older Population

As discussed by Rowell in Chapter 5, and reported by others,[52-54] maximal oxygen consumption in sedentary men and women declines in a predictable manner with age (Fig. 1). Furthermore, short-term training programs (less than 1 year) are associated with significantly higher $\dot{V}O_2max$ values, whereas long-term programs (greater than several years) also appear to delay or shift the decline that occurs with time. The cardiovascular mechanisms discussed by Rowell will not be repeated except to state that restoring of plasma volume[55]

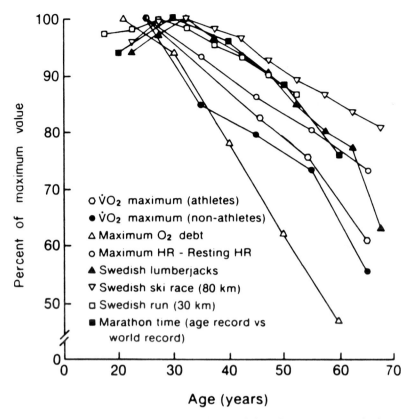

Fig. 1 *Influence of age on the percentage change of physiologic parameters of select aerobic activities. (Reproduced with permission from Skinner JS, Tipton CM, Vailas AC: Exercise, physical activity, and the ageing process, in Viidik A (ed): Lectures on Gerontology. London, England, Academic Press, 1982, vol 1, p 428.)*

or infusing red blood cells[56] increases $\dot{V}O_2$max in younger populations. A similar approach would likely be effective with midlife populations, but the crucial experiments have yet to be performed.

Of the multiple factors that should be considered as countermeasures to prevent or to minimize musculoskeletal injuries in humans, I believe that the best scientific rationale for prescribing aerobic exercises is to improve the metabolism and blood flow of muscles. It is well known that the propensity for musculoskeletal injuries increases when skeletal muscles are fatigued. Multiple and complex mechanisms are responsible for muscle fatigue,[57] and these mechanisms make it difficult to quantify fatigue-injury relationships. However, for muscles to sustain aerobic conditions, the cardiovascular system must transport and deliver oxygen and substrates to the tissues, and the mitochondria must utilize the oxygen at the cellular level. From the results of Andersen and Saltin[58] and Saltin[59] with their "isolated human muscle preparation," it is evident that during strenuous exercise the flow of blood through muscle is not maximal and the blood volume available for perfusion is influenced by the active muscle mass being perfused by the arteries and by the responsiveness of the receptors of the sympathetic nervous system. Muscle blood flow is also influenced by the ability of the myocardium to pump blood to the periphery; by the effectiveness of the cardiovascular regulatory centers to maintain blood pressure when the resistance of the vascular bed decreases; and by the vasodilatory potential or reserve of the vascular bed.[4,58-61] Cross-sectional studies by Snell and associates[62] on aerobically trained subjects and their untrained controls showed similar resting blood flow patterns, but when the subjects were challenged with ischemic exercise, the trained subjects had significantly higher values for lower leg muscle blood flow (approximately 35%) and maximal calf vascular conductance (approximately 37%) than the nontrained subjects.

As a consequence, the substrate available to the periphery can be altered, causing a shift from free fatty acid metabolism to one favoring glycogen utilization. There is some credence for this concept, as evidence from electric stimulation experiments shows higher lactate concentrations and lower phosphagens concentrations in older muscles,[40] presumably because they have poorer perfusion characteristics. As mentioned by Rowell in Chapter 5, trained midlife populations have been shown to have lower lactate concentrations than controls under standardized testing conditions. One intracellular effect of an increase in acidosis could be an inhibition of the contraction process,[3] leading to a cycling process of a decrease in the forces being generated, an increase in the recruitment of more fibers, a likely shift to glycogen metabolism, and a propensity for muscles to fatigue. Results summarized by Fry and associates[63] suggest that adenosine triphosphate (ATP) insufficiency was not associated with muscle injury, but that muscle pain was coupled with an increase in the inorganic phosphate concentration in the muscle. How these events change the production and availability of free radicals and their influences on muscle damage is not known, but this aspect deserves further investigation, especially in older populations.

There is sufficient evidence in human subjects to conclude that aerobic training increases the mitochondrial mass in skeletal muscles and the activity of its enzymes.[52,64] Kiessling and associates[64] studied younger (20 to 28 years) and older (56 to 59 years) healthy males and found the size of the mitochondria to be smaller in the older group. When they evaluated the influences of aerobic training, the younger subjects exhibited a 100% increase in the volume fraction of the mitochondria, whereas the older men had an increase of 20%. For the younger group, this change was associated with an increase in the number of mitochondria, while in the older group it was due to an increase in the size of the organelle. The mechanism responsible for this difference is not known.

Essen-Gustavsson and Borges[65] also used the muscle biopsy technique to examine the influences of age on select histochemical and biochemical characteristics of muscle obtained from "normal, healthy males." In men between the ages of 20 and 59 years, the activity of the enzyme citrate synthase in the Krebs cycle was similar regardless of age group, although it was 14% to 29% lower in the subjects between 60 and 70 years of age. The enzyme activity profile in the women they studied was so variable that it was difficult to generalize about its significance. From these findings, it appears that midlife and young-old populations have sufficient metabolic potential to adapt to aerobic exercise training programs.

Early investigations by Pollock and associates[66,67] studied young subjects (20 to 35 years) performing aerobic training (jogging) programs at 80% to 90% of their maximal heart rates for 20 weeks (including combinations of 15-, 30-, and 45-minute exercise sessions for 1, 3, and 5 times a week). They found that the improvement in $\dot{V}O_2max$ with training ranged from 8.3% to 17.4% and was related to the frequency and duration of the exercise program prescribed. The incidence of injuries that required subjects to lose week of training and the attrition rate of the subjects were also associated with the amount of exercise performed. Pollock's[68] findings are summarized in Table 3 and show that midlife and young-old populations experienced a higher percentage of musculoskeletal injuries in a standardized walk-jog aerobic program than their younger counterparts.

For some time, we have been advocating the use of circuit weight training programs as a countermeasure in space[69] (Table 4) to improve the strength, power, and endurance of skeletal muscles; to maintain the strength of ligament and tendons and their junctions with bones and muscles; to induce a cyclic stress on bones; and to modestly improve aerobic capacity. In the 10-station circuit training study conducted by Wilmore and associates[70] with college-aged men and women, subjects increased their $\dot{V}O_2max$ by 10%. Even though others have found either no changes or a slight improvement of 3%,[71] energy expenditure studies on circuit training indicate the caloric cost can range from 5.4 to 9.0 kcal/min depending on the gender and the equipment used.[72] Because of the potential value of impact on the mass and metabolism of osseous tissues, plus the need for improved muscular endurance to minimize the problems of fatigue, I agree with Wilmore's generic prescription[73] of adding running and stair-climbing stations to the others that promote the strength and mass of muscles, tendons, and ligaments. I advocate adding stations that emphasize the endurance capability of the arms and legs. The end result, I believe, is a model of an exercise prescription that provides adequate aerobic components that should help to reduce the incidence and severity of musculoskeletal injuries by midlife and older individuals.

Table 3 The influence of age on the percentage of injuries associated with aerobic training programs

Age range	Type of program	Percent of injuries
20 to 35 years	Walking and jogging	18
40 to 56 years	Walking	12
49 to 65 years	Walking and jogging	41
70 to 79 years	Walking and jogging	57

(Adapted with permission from Pollock ML: Exercise prescriptions for the elderly, in Spirduso WW, Eckert HM (eds): *Physical Activity and Aging*. American Academy of Physical Education Paper No. 22. Champaign, IL, Human Kinetics, 1989, p 167.)

Table 4 Possible circuit training stations for midlife populations

Bench press
Squat thrust
Chins
Stair climb
Extensions of lower legs
Two-arm curl
Half-squat
Sit-ups
Running laps

(Adapted with permission from Wilmore JH: *Training for Sport and Activity*, ed 2. Boston, MA, Allyn and Bacon, 1982, p 85.)

Conclusions

The advantages of regular aerobic training to reduce the risk factors associated with cardiovascular diseases have been extolled by numerous professional groups.[3,6,74] Moreover, the point has been made in this chapter that aerobic activity is highly desirable to minimize the musculoskeletal problems that are associated with the muscular fatigue caused by inadequate oxygen delivery, substrate availability, and substrate utilization. However, regular aerobic training is associated with a plethora of musculoskeletal injuries, warranting caution about its unrestricted use in midlife and older populations.

References

1. Morgan WP, O'Connor PJ, Koltyn KF: Psychological benefits of physical activity through the life span: Methodological issues, in Telema R (ed): *The Proceedings of the Jyvaskyla Sport Congress: Movement and Sport, Report 73*. Jyvaskyla, Finland, 1990, p 66.
2. Barnhart CL: *Thorndike-Barnhart Comprehensive Desk Dictionary*. Garden City, NJ, Doubleday, 1967, p 46.
3. Åstrand P-O, Rodahl K: *Textbook of Work Physiology: Physiological Basis of Exercise*, ed 3. New York, NY, McGraw Hill, 1986, pp 295-353, 487-522.
4. Nieman DC (ed): *The Sports Medicine Fitness Course*. Palo Alto, CA, Bull Publishing, 1986.
5. *Healthy People 2000*. DHHS Publication No. (PHS) 91-50212, Washington, DC, U.S. Public Health Service, 1991, pp 97-105.

6. Blair SN, Brill PA, Kohl HW III: Physical activity patterns in older individuals, in Spirduso WW, Eckert HM (eds): *Physical Activity and Aging.* American Academy of Physical Education Paper No. 22. Champaign, IL, Human Kinetics, 1989, pp 120-139.

7. Maaroos J, Landor A: Cardiac function and physical fitness in middle-aged participants in the Tartu ski marathon race, in Tekena R (ed): *The Proceedings of the Jyvaskyla Sport Congress: Movement and Sport, Report 73.* Jyvaskyla, Finland, 1990, pp 537-544.

8. Cooper KH: *Aerobics.* New York, NY, Bantam Books, 1968.

9. Kraus JH: Epidemiology of sports injuries, in *Football Injuries: Papers Presented at a Workshop.* Washington, DC, National Academy of Sciences, 1970, pp 1-16.

10. Henning CH: Injury prevention of the anterior cruciate ligament, in Maehlum S, Nilsson S, Renstrom P (eds): *An Update on Sports Medicine.* Oslo, Norway, Norwegian Sports Medicine Association, Swedish Society of Sports Medicine, 1987, pp 222-230.

11. Stapp JP: Human tolerance of impact, in *Football Injuries: Papers Presented at a Workshop.* Washington, DC, National Academy of Sciences, 1970, pp 23-46.

12. DeHaven KE, Lintner DM: Athletic injuries: comparison by age, sport, and gender. *Am J Sports Med* 1986;14:218-224.

13. Hess GP, Cappiello WL, Poole RM, et al: Prevention and treatment of overuse tendon injuries. *Sports Med* 1989;8:371-384.

14. Matheson GO, Macintyre JG, Taunton JE, et al: Musculoskeletal injuries associated with physical activity in older adults. *Med Sci Sports Exerc* 1989;21:379-385.

15. Safran MR, Seaber AV, Garrett WE Jr.: Warm up and muscle injury prevention: An update. *Sports Med* 1989;8:239-249.

16. Ebbeling CB, Clarkson PM: Exercise-induced muscle damage and adaptation. *Sports Med* 1989;7:207-234.

17. Tidball JG: Myotendinous junction injury in relation to junction structure and molecular composition. *Exerc Sport Sci Rev* 1991;19:419-445.

18. Tipton CM, Vailas AC: Bone and connective tissue adaptations to physical activity, in Bouchard C, Shephard RJ, Stephens T, et al (eds): *Exercise, Fitness and Health: A Consensus of Current Knowledge.* Champaign, IL, Human Kinetics, 1990, pp 331-344.

19. Komi PV, Salonen M, Jarvinen M, et al: In vivo registration of Achilles tendon forces in man: I. Methodological development. *Int J Sports Med* 1987;8(Suppl 1):3-8.

20. Richie DH Jr, Kelso SF, Bellucci PA: Aerobic dance injuries: A retrospective study of instructors and participants. *Phys Sportsmed* 1985;13:130-140.

21. Mutoh Y, Sawai S, Takanashi Y, et al: Aerobic dance injuries among instructors and students. *Phys Sportsmed* 1988;16:80-88.

22. Cavanagh PR, Davis BL, Miller TA: A biomechanical perspective on exercise countermeasures for long term spaceflight. *Aviat Space Environ Med* 1992;63:482-485.

23. Riley DA, Slocum GR, Bain JL, et al: Rat hindlimb unloading: Soleus histochemistry, ultrastructure, and electromyography. *J Appl Physiol* 1990;69:58-66.

24. Riley DA, Ilyina-Kakueva EI, Ellis S, et al: Skeletal muscle fiber, nerve and blood vessel breakdown in space flown rats. *FASEB J* 1990;4:84-91.

25. Munnings F: Osteoporosis: What is the role of exercise? *Phys Sports Med* 1992;20:127-138.

26. Myburgh KH, Watkin VA, Noakes TD: Are risk factors for menstrual dysfunction in runners cumulative? *Phys Sports Med* 1992;20:114-125.

27. Henry FH: Coordination and motor learning. *Proc Col Phys Ed Assoc* 1956;59:68-75.

28. Katch FI, McArdle WD (eds): *Nutrition, Weight Control, and Exercise.* Philadelphia, PA, Lea & Febiger, 1988, pp 229-230.

29. Magel JR, Foglia GF, McArdle WD, et al: Specificity of swim training on maximum oxygen uptake. *J Appl Physiol* 1975;38:151-155.

30. Tipton CM, Matthes RD, Vailas AC: Influences de l'exercise sur les structures ligamentaires, in Lacour J (ed): *Facteurs Limitant L' Endurance Humaine. Saint-Etienne Conference* 1977, pp 103-114.

31. Mazzeo RS, Brooks GA, Horvath SM: Effects of age on metabolic responses to endurance training in rats. *J Appl Physiol* 1984;57:1369-1374.

32. Beyer RE, Starnes JW, Eddington DW, et al: Exercise-induced reversal of age-related declines of oxidative reactions, mitochondrial yield, and flavins in skeletal muscle of the rat. *Mech Ageing Dev* 1984;24:309-323.

33. Farrar RP, Martin TP, Ardies CM: The interaction of aging and endurance exercise upon the mitochondrial function of skeletal muscle. *J Gerontol* 1981;36:642-647.

34. Everitt AV, Shorey CD, Ficarra MA: Skeletal muscle aging in the hind limb of the old male Wistar rat: Inhibitory effect of hypophysectomy and food restriction. *Arch Gerontol Geriatr* 1985;4:101-115.

35. Grimby G, Saltin B: The ageing muscle. *Clin Physiol* 1983; 3:209-218.

36. Daw CK, Starnes JW, White TP: Muscle atrophy and hypoplasia with aging: Impact of training and food restriction. *J Appl Physiol* 1988;64:2428-2432.

37. Musch TI, Haidet GC, Ordway GA, et al: Training effects on regional blood flow response to maximal exercise in foxhounds. *J Appl Physiol* 1987;62:1724-1732.

38. Laughlin MH, Ripperger J: Vascular transport capacity of hindlimb muscles of exercise-trained rats. *J Appl Physiol* 1987;62:438-443.

39. Lash JM, Bohlen HG: Functional adaptations of rat skeletal muscle arterioles to aerobic exercise training. *J Appl Physiol* 1992;72:2052-2062.

40. Dudley GA, Fleck SJ: Metabolite changes in aged muscle during stimulation. *J Gerontol* 1984;39:183-186.

41. Saltin B, Gollnick PD: Skeletal muscle adaptability: Significance for metabolism and performance, in Peachey LD, Adrian RH, Geiger SR (eds): *Handbook of Physiology: Skeletal Muscle.* Bethesda, MD, Waverly Press, 1983, sect 10, pp 555-631.

42. McCully KK, Faulkner JA: Characteristics of lengthening contractions associated with injury to skeletal muscle fibers. *J Appl Physiol* 1986;61:293-299.

43. Armstrong RB, Ogilvie RW, Schwane JA: Eccentric exercise-induced injury to rat skeletal muscle. *J Appl Physiol* 1983;54:80-93.

44. White TP, Villanacci JF, Morales PG, et al: Exercise-induced adaptations of rat soleus muscle grafts. *J Appl Physiol* 1984;56:1325-1334.

45. White TP: Adaptations of skeletal muscle grafts to chronic changes of physical activity. *Fed Proc* 1986;45:1470-1473.

46. Tipton CM, Vailas AC, Matthes RD: Experimental studies on the influences of physical activity on ligaments, tendons and joints: A brief review. *Acta Med Scand Suppl* 1986;711:157-168.

47. Lanyon LE: Functional strain in bone tissue as an objective, and controlling stimulus for adaptive bone remodelling. *J Biomech* 1987;20:1083-1093.

48. Rubin CT, Lanyon LE: Kappa Delta Award paper. Osteoregulatory nature of mechanical stimuli: Function as a determinant for adaptive remodelling in bone. *J Orthop Res* 1987;5:300-310.

49. Carter DR, Caler WE, Spengler DM, et al: Fatigue behavior of adult cortical bone: The influence of mean strain and strain range. *Acta Orthop Scand* 1981;52:481-490.

50. Whalen RT, Carter DR, Steele CR: Influence of physical activity on the regulation of bone density. *J Biomech* 1988;21:825-837.

51. Oakes BW, Parker AW: Discussion: Bone and connective tissue adaptations to physical activity, in Bouchard C, Shephard RJ, Stephens T, et al (eds): *Exercise, Fitness, and Health: A Consensus of Current Knowledge.* Champaign, IL, Human Kinetics, 1990, chap 29, pp 345-361.

52. Skinner JS, Tipton CM, Vailas AC: Exercise, physical training, and the ageing process, in Viidik A (ed): *Lectures on Gerontology: On the Biology of Ageing*. London, England, Academic Press, 1982, vol 1, part A, pp 407-439.

53. Heath GW, Hagberg JM, Ehsani AA, et al: A physiological comparison of young and older endurance athlethes. *J Appl Physiol* 1981;51:634-640.

54. Drinkwater BL: Women and exercise: Physiological aspects. *Exerc Sport Sci Rev* 1984;12:21-51.

55. Convertino VA: Exercise responses after inactivity, in Sandler H, Vernikos J (eds): *Inactivity: Physiological Effects*. Orlando, FL, Academic Press, 1986, chap 7, pp 149-191.

56. Thomson JM, Stone JA, Ginsburg AD, et al: O_2 transport during exercise following blood reinfusion. *J Appl Physiol* 1982;53:1213-1219.

57. Enoka RM, Stuart DG: Neurobiology of muscular fatigue. *J Appl Physiol* 1992;72:1631-1648.

58. Andersen P, Saltin B: Maximal perfusion of skeletal muscle in man. *J Physiol (Lond)* 1985;366:233-249.

59. Saltin B: Capacity of blood flow delivery to exercising skeletal muscle in humans. *Am J Cardiol* 1988;62:30E-35E.

60. Terjung RL, McAllister RM, Mackie-Engbretson B: The influence of exercise training on muscle blood flow, in Nazar K, Terjung RL, Kaciuba-Uscilko H, et al (eds): *International Perspectives in Exercise Physiology*. Champaign, IL, Human Kinetics, 1990, pp 19-25.

61. Saltin B: Maximal oxygen uptake: Limitation and malleability, in Nazar K, Terjung RL, Kaciuba-Uscilko H, et al (eds): *International Perspectives in Exercise Physiology*. Champaign, IL, Human Kinetics, 1990, pp 26-40.

62. Snell PG, Martin WH, Buckey JC, et al: Maximal vascular leg conductance in trained and untrained men. *J Appl Physiol* 1987;62:606-610.

63. Fry RW, Morton AR, Keast D: Overtraining in athletes: An update. *Sports Med* 1991;12:32-65.

64. Kiessling K-H, Pilstrom L, Karlsson J, et al: Mitochondrial volume in skeletal muscle from young and old physically untrained and trained healthy men and from alcoholics. *Clin Sci* 1973;44:547-554.

65. Essen-Gustavsson B, Borges O: Histochemical and metabolic characteristics of human skeletal muscle in relation to age. *Acta Physiol Scand* 1986;126:107-114.

66. Pollock ML, Cureton TK, Breninger L: Effects of frequency of training on working capacity, cardiovascular function and body composition of adult males. *Med Sci Sports* 1969;1:70-74.

67. Pollock ML, Gettman LR, Milesis CA, et al: Effects of frequency and duration of training on attrition and incidence of injury. *Med Sci Sports* 1977;9:31-36.

68. Pollock ML: Exercise prescriptions for the elderly, in Spirduso WW, Eckert HM (eds): *Physical Activity and Aging*. American Academy of Physical Education Paper No. 22. Champaign, IL, Human Kinetics, 1989, pp 163-174.

69. Tipton CM: Considerations for exercise prescriptions in future space flights. *Med Sci Sports Exerc* 1983;15:441-444.

70. Wilmore JH, Parr RB, Girandola RN, et al: Physiological alterations consequent to circuit weight training. *Med Sci Sports* 1978;10:79-84.

71. Gettman LR, Ayres JJ, Pollock ML, et al: The effect of circuit weight training on strength, cardiorespiratory function, and body composition of adult men. *Med Sci Sports* 1978;10:171-176.

72. Katch FI, Freedson PS, Jones CA: Evaluation of acute cardiorespiratory responses to hydraulic resistance exercise. *Med Sci Sports Exerc* 1985;17:168-173.

73. Wilmore JH: *Training for Sport and Activity: The Physiological Basis of the Conditioning Process*, ed 2. Boston, MA, Allyn and Bacon, 1982, chap 4, pp 73-92.

74. Tipton CM: Exercise, training and hypertension: An update. *Exerc Sport Sci Rev* 1991;19:447-505.

Section Four

Treatment of Musculoskeletal Disorders and Injuries

Chapter 25

Impingement of the Subacromial Space

Ramon Cugat, MD
Angel Ruiz-Cotorro, MD
Montse Garcia, MD
Xavier Cusco, MD
Juan Carlos Monllau, MD
Jaime Vilaro, MD
Xavier Juan, MD

Introduction

Shoulder injuries occur commonly in sports as well as daily activities; they can be caused by direct trauma or repetitive stress. Impingement of the subacromial space causes pain that must be diagnosed and treated promptly to avoid a chronic frozen shoulder condition. The anatomy of the subacromial space and the pathogenesis, diagnosis, and treatment of the impingement syndrome are reviewed in this chapter. A classification system is described that enables appropriate treatments to be instituted quickly.

Definition

Impingement of the subacromial space is a clinical syndrome. In 1972, Charles Neer[1] described the principal symptom as pain in the shoulder when the upper arm is raised from 60° to 120° with internal rotation and anteversion of 30°, while the scapula remains stable. Two possible zones of disorder can be defined: subcoracoid impingement and subacromial impingement.

Subcoracoid or Anteromedial Impingement

When the upper arm is adducted, flexed, and internally rotated, the biceps groove and the supraspinatus tendon come into contact with the coracoid process and the anteromedial edge of the coracoacromial ligament, producing acute pain in the shoulder (Fig. 1). This is experienced by many young people and by athletes, for example, a

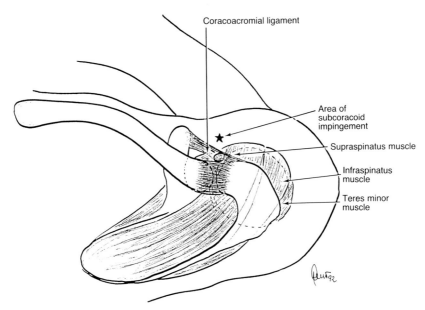

Fig. 1 *Right shoulder, superior view, internal rotation.*

tennis player at the final moment of serving.[2-6] The higher incidence among young people results from the greater intensity with which they take part in sport.

Subacromial or Anterosuperior Impingement

When the upper arm is abducted, flexed, and internally rotated, the anteroinferior edge of the acromion, the anterolateral edge of the coracoacromial ligament, and the acromioclavicular joint rub against the rotator cuff where the supraspinatus and the infraspinatus join. Anterosuperior impingement is not as acute as anteromedial impingement. It is caused by repeated and prolonged movements, and the principal symptom is impaired function. It is most common in midlife workers older than 40 years of age. If correct treatment is not instituted, subacromial impingement may become a chronic process, and the anatomic structures involved will degenerate.[4,7]

Functional Anatomy of the Subacromial Space

The borders of the subacromial space are superior, inferior, medial, lateral, anterior, and posterior. The superior border comprises the acromion, the coracoacromial ligament, the acromioclavicular joint, and the distal limb of the clavicle. At rest, the acromion covers one

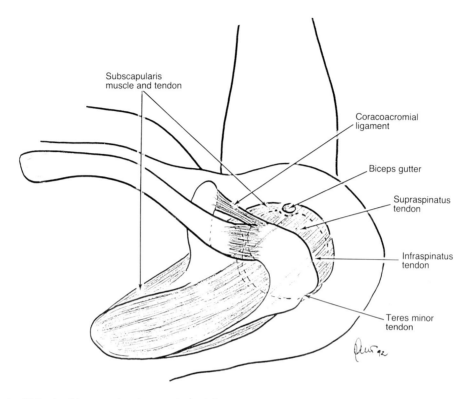

Fig. 2   *Right shoulder, superior view, neutral rotation.*

third of the rotator cuff and the coracoacromial ligament, two thirds. The inferior border comprises the rotator cuff, the long head of the biceps, and the greater tuberosity of the humerus. The rotator cuff is composed of the superior part of the supraspinatus tendon (60%), the superior part of the infraspinatus tendon (20%), and the superior part of the subscapularis tendon (20%). (The teres minor also has a small role; Fig. 2). The long head of the biceps is intra-articular. It crosses the space between the supraspinatus and the subscapularis tendons, then passes through the articular capsule between the coracohumeral, superior glenohumeral, and Gordon-Brodie ligaments. The medial border is the base of the coracoid process. Both the lateral border and the posterior border are formed by the deltoid muscle. The anterior border is the tip of the coracoid process and the coracoacromial ligament.

Subacromial impingement may affect the subacromial bursa, the rotator cuff, the long head of the biceps, the acromioclavicular complex, and the acromioclavicular joint. The anatomic characteristics of these elements are discussed below.

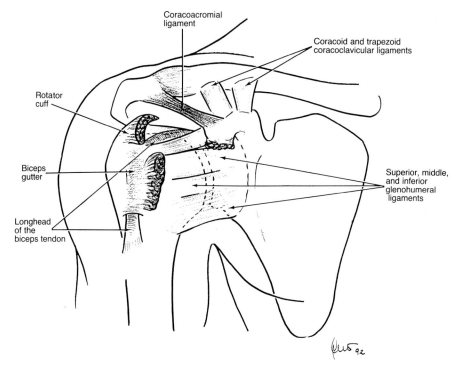

Fig. 3 *Right shoulder capsule and ligaments, rotator cuff, and subscapularis anchorages.*

The subacromial bursa is a fine and smooth membrane that lubricates the sliding area of the rotator cuff. It is often connected with the subcoracoid bursa. In patients with chronic pain and inflammation, the subacromial bursa may contain calcium deposits. There is a deep subscapularis bursa that can connect with the glenohumeral joint.

The rotator cuff comprises four elements (the supraspinatus tendon, the infraspinatus tendon, the teres minor muscle, and the subscapularis muscle) that function primarily to stabilize the humeral head. In addition, each of the muscles performs other functions: The supraspinatus tendon abducts the upper arm from 0° to 90°. The remainder of the range of motion is carried out by the deltoid muscle. The infraspinatus tendon, along with the teres minor muscle, rotates the arm externally and restricts elevation of the humeral head. An intact infraspinatus muscle can help to abduct the upper arm, even if the supraspinatus muscle is ruptured.[8] The teres minor muscle stabilizes and externally rotates the arm. The subscapularis muscle is a stabilizer and powerful internal rotator of the upper arm, aided by the latissimus dorsi, the pectoralis major, and the teres major muscles. It is also an adductor of the upper arm.

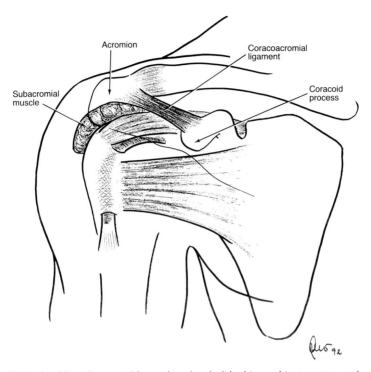

Acromion

Coracoacromial
ligament

Subacromial
muscle

Coracoid
process

Fig. 4 *Right shoulder subacromial bursa, long head of the biceps, biceps gutter, and rotator cuff.*

The long head of the biceps muscle (Fig. 3) acts to restrict elevation of the humeral head in abduction and in external rotation, at the same time contributing to the latter. It rotates the arm externally at the end of abduction, which allows the greater tuberosity to move behind the acromion and, thus, achieve maximum abduction. If the long head of the biceps is injured, the humeral head can elevate too far and subacromial impingement can develop on abduction.

The coracoacromial complex (Fig. 4) is a passive anterosuperior stabilizer of the glenohumeral joint, composed of the acromion and the coracoid process. The acromion, with the coracoid process, constitutes the bony structure of the complex. Anatomic variations in the size and shape of the acromion may predispose an individual to subacromial impingement. The acromion may be described as flat (type I), curved (type II), or hooked (type III).[9]

The coracoid process is the site of origin for the coracobiceps ligament and the site of insertion of the pectoralis minor muscle. Anatomic variations in the length and position of the coracoid process can cause differences in orientation and height of the coracoacromial ligament.

The coracoacromial ligament is actually a pseudoligament because it is a bridge between the acromion and the coracoid, two processes of the same bone (the scapula). It is a very solid and fibrous band that intermingles with the coracobiceps tendon, forming a fibrous pointed arch near the tip of the coracoid.

The acromioclavicular joint has certain anomalies that can contribute to a subacromial syndrome, such as osteoarthrtis.

Pathophysiology

Anatomic and vascular factors may be involved in the pathophysiology of the subacromial space.

Anatomic Factors

The coracoacromial arch may vary in form, size, and orientation; both the coracoid and the acromion may vary anatomically. These variations affect the relationship between the coracoacromial ligament and the rotator cuff. These anatomic variations may be due to primary causes (congenital) or secondary causes (fractures, pseudoarthrosis, osteoarthritis). The different spatial relationships of the elements during movement can cause impingement. This happens, for example, when there is internal rotation with flexion or elevation of the arm. The more vigorous these movements, the closer the rotator cuff comes to the coracoacromial ligament, the coracoid process, and the acromioclavicular joint, respectively.

Vascular Factors

Codman's 1934 studies[10] on the vascularization of the rotator cuff enabled him to label a zone of hypovascularization at the insertion of the rotator cuff, approximately 1 cm medial to the insertion of the supraspinatus in the greater tuberosity, which he called the "critical zone."

Rothman,[11] in 1965, proved that the vascular contribution to the rotator cuff is provided principally by three arteries: the suprascapular artery and the superior and inferior humeral arteries. Thus, he observed the existence of "critical zones" in other locations, such as the insertion of the infraspinatus tendon. Functional ischemia in these areas may predispose an individual to degenerative changes or ruptures, which frequently involve the insertion of the supraspinatus.

Rathbun and McNab[12] noted variations in the vascularization of the rotator cuff based on the functional position of the arm. That is, in abduction, the vascularization of the supraspinatus is maximal; in adduction, it is minimal. They also described a hypovascular zone in the long head of the biceps where it passes over the humeral head.

Pathomechanics of Impingement

In 1972, Neer[1] suggested that the pathology of the rotator cuff originates in mechanical defects and not in vascular defects. He described the types of impingement with specific pathophysiology and three stages of lesions.

Neer's Pathophysiology of Impingement

Neer described two types of impingement, outlet and nonoutlet. Outlet impingement, the most frequent type, occurs as a result of an anterior acromial spur, the shape and slope of the acromion, or a prominent acromioclavicular joint.

Nonoutlet impingement occurs less frequently and has multiple causes. It is caused by a prominent greater tuberosity (malunion or nonunion or a low-set humeral head), the loss of head depressors (rotator cuff tears or a biceps rupture), and the loss of glenohumeral fulcrum (the loss of all or part of the humeral head or glenoid caused by fracture, necrosis, arthropathy, osteoarthritis; ligamentous laxity; anomalies in the angle of the glenoid; or absence of inferior glenohumeral joint). Nonoutlet impingement also is caused by the loss of the suspensory mechanism (chronic acromioclavicular separation or trapezius palsy), defects of the acromion (unfused acromial apophysis or malunion or nonunion), nervous system deficiency (Erb's palsy, damaged suprascapular nerve—mechanisms of compression and stretching—and paraplegia), scapular dysfunction (disorders of the cervicodorsal column, for example scoliosis or kyphosis, and lesions of the Charles Bell's nerve), thickened bursa or cuff (large, chronic calcium deposit and chronic bursitis), and amputations.

Neer's Three Stages of Lesion

Stage I consists of edema and hemorrhage in the bursas and rotator cuff tendons. People under age 25 with overuse of the shoulder are most often affected. The principal symptom is moderate pain, which is relieved by rest.

Stage II involves fibrosis of the bursae, rotator cuff, and sometimes the long head of the biceps. It usually affects individuals under 40 years of age. The principal symptom is pain between 60° and 120° when the arm is in abduction, internally rotated, and flexed to 30°.

In stage III, there are spurs, and there may be partial or total ruptures of the rotator cuff or the long head of the biceps. Individuals over age 40 are most susceptible. The principal symptoms are constant pain (unrelieved by rest) and impaired mobility.

Other Classifications

J. C. Esch,[13] in 1990, described the impingement sequence as beginning with compression of the rotator cuff against the anteroinferior

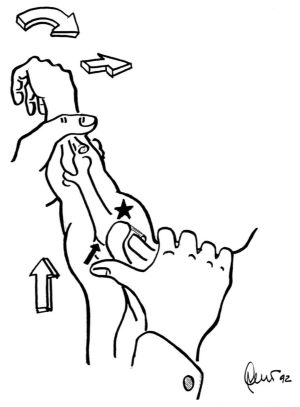

Fig. 5 *Neer's sign. Anteversion (flexion) abduction, internal rotation of the left shoulder: Pain is reproduced creating passive contact between the greater tuberosity of the humerus and the inferoanterolateral border of the acromion. The star indicates this point of contact.*

edge of the acromion. Trauma to the rotator cuff may create tension due to overuse, progressing to traumatic rupture of the rotator cuff, multidirectional instability, and calcific tendinitis.

Clinical Evaluation

History

Pain (generally chronic, but sometimes acute) is experienced in the anterolateral region of the shoulder, radiating out toward the biceps gutter and the distal insertion of the deltoid. Sometimes the pain reaches the elbow and the lower arm. The pain is aggravated by active movement, and the patient may find it uncomfortable to lie in the lateral decubitus position on the affected side. In extreme cases, a pseudopalsy may appear. When diagnosing subacromial impinge-

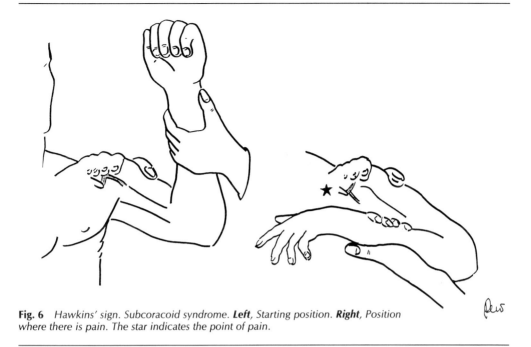

Fig. 6 *Hawkins' sign. Subcoracoid syndrome. **Left**, Starting position. **Right**, Position where there is pain. The star indicates the point of pain.*

ment, the most important factors are pain and loss of mobility, with resultant impaired function.

Physical Examination

On inspection, atrophy of the deltoid muscle and rupture of the long head of the biceps may be apparent. Palpation of most of the shoulder region produces pain.

Passive Tests   Passive tests for subacromial impingement are Neer's sign, Hawkins' sign, and Yocum's sign.

The examiner can provoke pain using passive motion to repeat the movements that originally caused it. When a study of mobility is undertaken, it is possible to establish a differential diagnosis from capsulitis.

To establish Neer's sign, the examiner begins by standing behind the patient. Blocking any movement of the scapula, the examiner passively flexes and abducts the inwardly rotated arm while looking for the contact between the greater tuberosity and the anteroinferior edge of the acromion (subacromioclavicular syndrome) (Fig. 5).

To elicit Hawkins' sign, the patient's arm is internally rotated. Pain occurs above the horizontal when the greater tuberosity comes into contact with the coracoid process and the coracoacromial ligament (Fig. 6). This reproduces the pain of the subcoracoid syndrome.

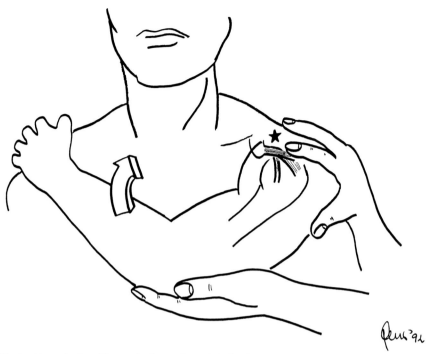

Fig. 7 *Yocum's sign. The star indicates the point of pain.*

Yocum's sign is seen when the hand of the injured shoulder is supported on the healthy shoulder. Anteversion of the shoulder creates pain because of friction between the greater tuberosity and the coracoacromial ligament or inferior spurs of the acromioclavicular joint (Fig. 7).

Active Tests Active tests for subacromial impingement result in pain with active motion of the affected joint, ie, anteversion and abduction with internal rotation. The tests that produce this pain are Jobe's test and the palm up test.

Jobe's test or supraspinatus test begins as the patient elevates his or her arm, rotates it internally, and also flexes it 30°. The examiner applies resistance to the movement. Diffuse pain and impaired function indicate a tendinitis of the supraspinatus. If the patient cannot overcome minimal force, a rotator cuff tear is likely (Fig. 8).

Palm up test, or large head of the biceps test, is conducted with the upper arm flexed and the elbow extended and in supination. The examiner tries to lower the arm (Fig. 9).

Other tests that can be helpful in diagnosing difficult cases include the impingement injection test and the suprascapular test. The impingement injection test begins after injection of local anesthesia (10 ml of 1% Xylocaine) into the subacromial space. With forceful for-

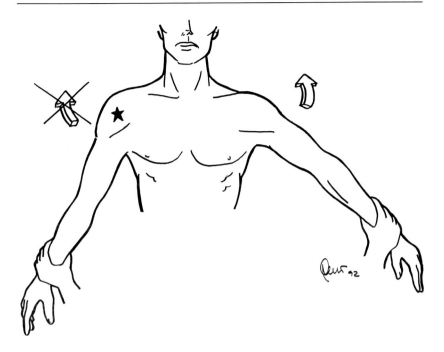

Fig. 8 *Jobe's test. Tendinitis of the supraspinatus. The star indicates the point of pain. Subject is unable to lift arm without pain.*

ward elevation of the humerus against the acromion as the examiner's opposite hand depresses the scapula, the pain completely disappears. The suprascapular test begins after injection of local anesthesia (5 ml of 1% Xylocaine) of the suprascapular nerve. The symptoms disappear if there is a supraspinatus lesion.

Radiologic Evaluation

Routine Radiographs

The impingement syndrome is not visible on early radiographs. If the problem persists and advances, alterations in the anteroinferior area of the acromion, deposits of calcium on the coracoacromial ligament, or alterations in the profile of the acromion may be seen on radiographs. Several views are recommended for the evaluation of impingement.[14]

Anteroposterior Views of the Glenohumeral Joint

Anteroposterior views of the glenohumeral joint should be taken with the arm in neutral position, in internal rotation, in external rotation, and centered in the coracoid.

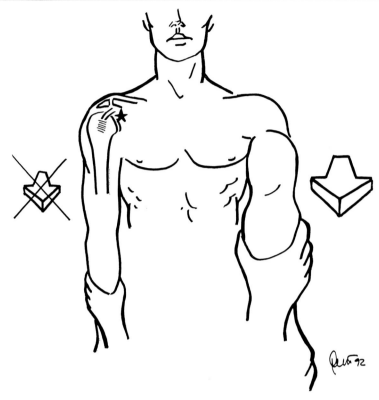

Fig. 9 *Palm test. Tendinitis of the right biceps. The star indicates the point of pain. The person is unable to lower the arm without pain.*

The pathologic findings may include calcium deposits on tendons, cysts or sclerosis in the greater or lesser tuberosity, degenerative changes in the acromioclavicular joint, sclerosis of the anterior part of the acromion, and a reduction in the humeral-acromial space. A reduction in the space of less than 7 mm on a properly taken radiologic view suggests a rotator cuff lesion.[15]

Thirty Degree Cephalic Angle View In cases where the routine anteroposterior views do not show pathologic findings, a 30° cephalic view of the glenohumeral joint can show spurs in the anteroinferior zone of the acromion or calcium deposits on the coracoacromial ligament. This view may even be clearer than the outlet view, and is easier to obtain.[14]

Outlet View To evaluate degenerative changes in the anteroinferior area of the acromion or in the coracoacromial arch above the tendon, an outlet view is helpful. The patient is placed in the same position as for a lateral view of the scapula, and the ray is angled

downward 5° to 10°. In this view, one can see where the supraspinatus tendon leaves the bone gutter and passes under the coracoacromial arch. Bigliani[9] described three types of acromial profile seen
from this view: type I (flat acromion), type II (curved acromion), type
III (hooked acromion).

This classification can be used to detect patients susceptible to
problems of impingement or problems of the rotator cuff. Patients
with a curved or hooked acromion are more susceptible to impingement.

Arthrography

Arthrography, whether it is simple, using radiologic contrast alone,
or double-contrast, using contrast and air, is very effective for diagnosing full-thickness tears of the rotator cuff and partial-thickness
tears on the articular surface of the rotator cuff. The presence of dye
in the bursa is conclusive evidence of a lesion in the rotator cuff. Arthrography (simple or double-contrast) is 95% to 100% sensitive in
diagnosing complete tears,[14,16] although double-contrast arthrography can provide more information about the size of the tear. Arthrography is not accurate with partial ruptures of the tendon where
the tear occurs on the subacromial surface or ruptures in the tendons
where there is no articular connection with the subacromial space.
Arthrograms combined with tomograms or axial computed
tomograms (CT) can also be used to quantify the size of the rotator
cuff tear.

Arthropneumotomography consists of taking tomograms of the
air-filled acromiohumeral joint. This test is used when routine radi-
ography or routine arthrography show signs of a tear. The anteroposterior views reveal the length of the tear, and the profile views
demonstrate whether the lesion involves only the supraspinatus, or
other tendons as well. This procedure, however, does not provide
any information on the state of the muscles of the rotator cuff. To
obtain this information it is necessary to use CT or CT scan arthrography.

When a surgical procedure is planned, CT can be helpful to establish the status of the muscle fibers; CT can be used to determine
whether there is greater infiltration of fatty tissue in the torn tendon
than in the healthy tendon. Tears of the subscapularis tendon, which
are very difficult to see with arthrography, also can be detected. In
studying instabilities, the CT arthrogram is useful, while for impingement and lesions of the rotator cuff, it is more cost-effective to
use arthrography.

Arthrography With Digital Substraction Arthrography with digital subtraction borrows techniques taken from the field of angiography. It requires costly special equipment. This test is done by injecting dye into the joint and taking images at 1-second intervals while

keeping the arm immobile. A master image (called the mask image), is taken prior to the injection of dye. The images are then processed by a computer. After the injection, a series of images shows the progression of the dye with the different structures that impede visualization "subtracted." Proponents of this technique argue that it is more sensitive in detecting smaller lesions and lesions on the inferior aspect of the rotator cuff and that it shows the location and size of the lesions with more precision than conventional techniques. Technically, it is much more complex than conventional arthrography, and its use has not gained wide acceptance.[15]

Bursagram   This easy-to-use technique has recently been described for the diagnosis of subacromial impingement. The subacromial bursa is a potentially large space that can hold between 5 and 10 ml of air or dye. If the bursa fills completely, the diagnosis of impingement can be excluded. If the bursa cannot be filled, it can be assumed that adhesions or impingement exist. Theoretically, lesions of the superior part of the rotator cuff can also be diagnosed in this way, although clinical correlation has not yet been demonstrated.[16]

Ultrasonography or Echography

Ultrasonography is a quick, noninvasive, and economical technique. It also facilitates comparative studies of both shoulders without inconvenience or additional costs for the patient. However, the reliability of the study depends a great deal on the expertise of the ultrasonographer and the quality of the equipment. Because the clarity of the images is not as good as that from conventional radiologic techniques, interpretation is difficult for the inexperienced evaluator. Ultrasonography is the only method that permits a dynamic study of the structures.[17,18]

In the presence of a rotator cuff lesion, ultrasonography demonstrates the absence of movement in the rotator cuff tissues; indirect signs of the lesions may also be present, although these are more difficult to interpret.

Lack of visualization of the rotator cuff, focal thinning, leveling, hyperechogenic focus, and central echogenic band on ultrasound[17] may be caused by a partial rotator cuff tear, edema, recent local injections of steroids, calcium deposits, or surgical scars. They may also be normal images in certain individuals; however, false positive results may occur from the echogenicity of the tendon varying with age or from differences in the angle of the projection and even the type of transductor.[18]

The technique is 91% to 100% sensitive, 75% to 100% specific, and its positive predictive value is 92% to 94%, according to various authors.[3,17,18] We prefer ultrasonography to other techniques because it is noninvasive, quick, and economical.

Magnetic Resonance Imaging (MRI)

MRI is a noninvasive technique that offers good visualization of the rotator cuff, the chondral structures, and the glenoid labrum. However, it is a costly technique and unavailable to many centers. In addition, it requires a prolonged time inside a confined space, which may be poorly tolerated by claustrophobic patients. MRI is similar to arthrography in terms of its predictive value, although some lesions shown by arthrography cannot be observed on MRI, and vice versa.[3]

As with ultrasonography, absolute agreement on the diagnostic criteria of a rotator cuff tear has not been reached.[3] In examining a rotator cuff with normal morphology and fatty tissue, an increase in the intensity of the signal or an intermittent signal probably indicates a degenerative area without a frank tear. The absence of fatty tissue or the presence of liquid in the bursa are also significant findings.[3]

In impingement syndrome, the MRI is very sensitive to degenerative processes of the rotator cuff. However, local injections of corticosteroids can provoke changes that simulate lesions. Thus, care must be taken when interpreting the MRI.

Discussion

The techniques based on conventional radiology continue to be basic in the exploration of the shoulder. The more modern techniques, such as ultrasonography, CT, and MRI have certain limitations, but they also have much to offer in the visualization of the soft tissues. Three-dimensional MRI and CT are being used in the United States today. They are capable of providing information not available with other techniques.

Differential Diagnosis

Several conditions may present with symptoms similar to shoulder impingement. These include cervical brachialgia (osteoarthritis of the cervical spine, disk lesions, cervical rib); long head of the biceps tear; tumors of the lungs, the thorax wall, or the scapula; capsulitis; articular disorders of the acromioclavicular joint; fractures and instability of the glenohumeral joint; and microtraumatic neurologic pathology of the shoulder.

Treatment

For a stage I lesion with edema and tendinitis, conservative treatment is recommended. This may consist of nonsteroidal and steroidal anti-inflammatory drugs (the latter may include local injections into the subacromial bursa or the biceps gutter), physiotherapy, and rehabilitation. Rehabilitation begins with passive motion, aided by gravity; as the pain decreases, active motion and muscle strengthening exercises are instituted.[19]

In stage II (fibrosis), conservative treatment is also recommended. If 6 months of treatment fails to relieve symptoms, surgical treatment consisting of arthroscopic subacromial decompression (bursectomy and anteroinferior acromioplasty) may be indicated.[19]

Treatment of state III lesion is the most controversial. Some authors advocate conservative treatment, with emphasis on strengthening shoulder muscles. Others recommend surgical treatment, either conventional surgery for decompression of the subacromial space and repair of the rotator cuff, or arthroscopic surgery for decompression alone without repairing the rotator cuff lesion.[19]

Based on our experience, we generally treat patients younger than 40 years of age with arthroscopic subacromial decompression (bursectomy and coracoacromial ligament resection). We treat patients older than 40 years with arthroscopic subacromial decompression (bursectomy, coracoacromial ligament resection, and acromioplasty). In cases with rotator cuff tears, if complete recovery is impossible after acromioplasty and rehabilitation, we repair the lesion with open surgery. In cases in which the impingement is secondary to cause, the primary cause must be treated.[20]

Technique of Subacromial Arthroscopy

The patient is placed in the lateral decubitus position, contralateral to the limb being explored, with the affected arm in 15° anteversion and abduction of 30°. Usually three portals are used: anterior, posterior (inferolateral to the acromion), and lateral or transdeltoid. After systematic inspection of the glenohumeral-scapular joint, the subacromial space is entered by changing the orientation, but not the portal. The objective of this technique is to create a space that allows evaluation of this anatomic area and to distend it so that its components can be identified and treatment initiated.

Small tears of the rotator cuff can be identified by injecting colored liquid (povidone) in the glenohumeral-scapular joint and looking at the superior or acromial surface of the rotator cuff from the subacromial space.

Results of Arthroscopic Subacromial Decompression

Several authors have evaluated the results of arthroscopic surgery as 82% to 97% satisfactory (Table 1).[21-26]

Conclusions

Impingement syndrome is a clinical disorder that may result from many different activities. To institute the appropriate treatment,

Table 1 Results of arthroscopic surgery

Study	Satisfactory results(%)
Esch and associates[21]	82
Ellman[22]	89
Paulos and associates[23]	86
Gartsman[24]	94*
Altcheck and associates[25]	97
Cugat and associates[26]	87

*Without rotator cuff rupture

early and careful diagnosis is essential. Conservative therapy followed, as appropriate, by arthroscopic surgery is the least aggressive approach and offers the possibility of evaluating the articular cavities and the surrounding spaces with a minimum of trauma while obtaining maximal information. In contrast to conventional open surgery, hospitalization is shorter and the postoperative period is more comfortable.

References

1. Neer CS II: Anterior acromioplasty for the chronic impingement syndrome in the shoulder: A preliminary report. *J Bone Joint Surg* 1972;54A:41-50.

2. Rodineau J, Saillant JG: *Pathologie du Membre Superieure du Joeur de Tennis*. Paris, Masson, 1986.

3. Borrell J, Henriquez A: Sindrome subacromial doloroso en el deportista. *Adv Traumatol Cir Rehab Prev Deport Med* 1989;19:159-166.

4. Blaimont P, Taheri A: Contribution to the biomechanics of impingement syndrome. *Orthop Trans* 1990;14:657.

5. Gine J: Biomecanica de la abduccion del hombro: Traumaticmos deportivos (no fracturas). *Fundacion Mapfre* 1990;167-207.

6. Patte D: Diagnostique des epaules douloureuses: Penser conflict antero-interne coraco-humerals. *J Traumatol Sport* 1987;4:92-95.

7. Eulert J, Gekeler J: Le ligament acromio-coracoidien et ses rapports avec le tendon du muscle sus-epineux. *Rev Chir Orthop Reparatrice Appar Mot* 1976:62 (Suppl):S60-S62.

8. Duchenne GB: *Physiologie des Mouvements*. Paris, Bailliere, 1867.

9. Bigliani LU, Morrison D, April EW: The morphology of the acromion and its relationship to rotator cuff tears. *Orthop Trans* 1986;10:228.

10. Codman EA (ed): *The Shoulder: Rupture of the Supraspinatus Tendon and Other Lesions in or About the Subacromial Bursa*. Boston, MA, Thomas Todd Co, 1934.

11. Rothman RH, Parke WW: The vascular anatomy of the rotator cuff. *Clin Orthop* 1965:41:176-186.

12. Rathbun JB, Macnab I: The microvascular pattern of the rotator cuff. *J Bone Joint Surg* 1970;52B:540-553.

13. Esch JC: Shoulder arthroscopy treatment of rotator cuff pathology. Abstracts Book of the Ninth Annual Meeting of the Arthroscopy Association of North America. Orlando, FL, 1990.

14. Rockwood CA Jr, Szalay EA, Curtis RJ Jr, et al: *The Shoulder*. Philadelphia, PA, WB Saunders, 1990, vol 2, pp 178-202.

15. Austin S: *Shoulder Arthroscopy*. London, Martin Dunitz Ltd, 1991, pp 41-50.

16. Rosenthal DI: Radiologic techniques, in Rowe CR (ed): *The Shoulder*. New York, NY, Churchill Livingstone, 1987, pp 67-78.

17. Gil P, Vila E, Lopez E, et al: Utilidad de la ecografia del hombro en el diagnostico de la roturas del manguito de los rotadores. *Radiologia* 1992;31:37-41.

18. Palacio A, Llauger J, Alexander C, et al: Estudio ecografico de la articulacion es-capulohumeral. *Rev Esp Reumatologia* 1988;31:37-41.

19. Bigliani LU, Flatow EL: History, physical examination, and diagnostic modalities, in McGinty JB (ed): *Operative Arthroscopy*. New York, NY, Raven Press, 1991, pp 453-464.

20. Zarins B: Arthroscopic treatment of calcific deposits in the supraspinatus tendon, in *Surgery of the Shoulder*. St. Louis, MO, Mosby Year Book, 1990, pp 50-52.

21. Esch JC, Ozerkis LR, Holgager JA, et al: Arthroscopic subacromial decompression: Results according to the degree of rotator cuff tear. *Arthroscopy* 1988;4:241-249.

22. Ellman H: Arthroscopic subacromial decompression: Analysis of one to three year results. *Arthroscopy* 1987;3:173-181.

23. Paulos LE, Harner CD, Parker RD: Arthroscopic subacromial decompression for impingment syndrome of the shoulder. *Techniques Orthop* 1988;3:33-39.

24. Gartsman GM: Arthroscopic acromioplasty for lesions of the rotator cuff. *J Bone Joint Surg* 1990;72A:169-180.

25. Altcheck DW, Warren RF, Wickiewicz TL, et al: Arthroscopic acromioplasty: Technique and results. *J Bone Joint Surg* 1990;72A:1198-1207.

26. Cugat R, Cusco X, Garcia M, et al: Follow-up de la artroscopia del espacio subacromio-deltoideo. Abstracts Book del VIII Congreso Nacional de la Asocia-cion Espanola de Artroscopia. Gijon, 1989.

Chapter 26

Tennis Elbow

Robert E. Leach, MD
Anthony Schepsis, MD
Arati Mallik, MD

Introduction

During the past quarter of a century, as the public has become more conscious of physical fitness and more actively involved in staying in shape, there has been a sharp increase in the number of chronic musculoskeletal injuries, including muscle strains, stress fractures, and chronic tendinitis. The diagnosis of some of these conditions may be difficult, but their treatment may be even more problematic. While the pain of a chronic tendinitis may interfere with athletic activity, it does not usually interfere with many of the activities of daily living. As a consequence, the individual may not seek help until the condition has become a long-term problem, by which time the condition may be less amenable to treatment. Even if medical attention is sought, the athlete may be disinclined to strictly follow the treatment regimen outlined by the physician.

Some chronic injuries, particularly muscle strains and chronic tendinitis, happen frequently in the athletic population of the midlife group. The muscle-tendon units of this population are less flexible than those of younger individuals, and yet, they are often exposed to the same stresses in sports as those of the younger age groups. Some people in their 40s, 50s, and even older who stay in very good shape sustain no more injuries than their younger counterparts do. Other midlife individuals are clearly out of shape and lack flexibility and strength; they are likely to be even more at risk for injury than active midlifers.

The topic of this paper is chronic tendinitis of the elbow, specifically, pain at the origin of the wrist extensor muscles on the lateral aspect of the humerus, which is common, or pain at the pronator teres and flexor origins on the medial aspect of the humerus, which is rarer. The usual "tennis elbow" causes pain that centers around the lateral epicondyle and is brought on by repetitive action of the wrist extensor muscles. The most common athletic activity that causes this condition is tennis, but other racquet sports, including squash, racquetball, and paddle ball may also cause tennis elbow. Sporting activities are the focus of this particular chapter, but tennis elbow may also be caused by other repetitive activities such as using a hammer or a screwdriver. "Do-it-yourself" homeowners may experience pain around the elbow brought on by sudden periods of more intense activity when using tools. The pathology of chronic tendinitis seems to be the same, whether it is caused by sporting or working activities, and the basic causative factors are similar (ie, overuse of the extensor or flexor muscles of the wrist).

Anatomy

Generally, when physicians or tennis players talk about tennis elbow, they are referring to pain occurring around the lateral epicondyle, in the area where the extensor carpi radialis brevis attaches to the humerus. This is the most common type of tennis elbow. However, the condition may also occur on the inside of the elbow, in the region of the attachments of the pronator teres and wrist flexors to the medial aspect of the humerus. Medial tennis elbow occurs less frequently than lateral tennis elbow, but medial tennis elbow is often more painful and less easy to treat.

Lateral tennis elbow has been referred to as lateral epicondylitis,[1] but this is an inaccurate term because the pathologic tissue is not the lateral epicondyle itself, but rather the tendinous attachment of the extensor tendons near the lateral epicondyle. The extensor carpi radialis longus and the anterior attachment of the extensor communis tendon are sometimes involved in chronic tennis elbow, but the extensor carpi radialis brevis[2,3] is the usual culprit.

The extensor brevis tendon originates from the extensor communis tendon, the lateral ligament of the elbow, the overlying fascia, and the intermuscular septum on each side. The anatomic relationship of the extensor brevis tendon with the lateral ligament of the elbow and the annular ligament of the radius demonstrates why release of the annular ligament of the radius,[4,5] a common operation in decades past for tennis elbow, may have caused symptomatic relief: because this also releases part of the extensor brevis tendon.[6] The extensor carpi radialis longus originates from the distal one-third of the lateral supracondylar ridge and from the lateral intramuscular septum; it overlies the extensor carpi radialis brevis. This anatomic proximity may cause difficulty when surgeons are looking for the area of pathology, because the extensor carpi radialis brevis is covered by the extensor carpi radialis longus. The extensor communis tendon arises from the anterior portion of the lateral border of the lateral epicondyle of the humerus and is only rarely involved in tennis elbow.

In medial tennis elbow, the pathologic process involves the flexor carpi radialis and the pronator teres, which arise from the medial epicondyle of the humerus and the adjacent fascia. The ulnar nerve passes behind the medial epicondyle and is frequently irritated as it goes through the heads of the flexor carpi ulnaris going distally to the forearm. The flexor carpi ulnaris also rises from the medial epicondyle, although more posteriorly than the flexor carpi radialis and is in some rare instances involved in medial tennis elbow.

History

Physicians hear two different patient histories from patients with tennis elbow. The most common history is that the athlete has been playing more tennis than usual over a period of months and gradually begins to feel pain around the elbow. At the onset of this process, the pain is typically present only when hitting with a backhand stroke. Pain is exacerbated by playing, but between periods of playing, the elbow may hurt very little or perhaps not at all. With time and continued playing, the pain gradually increases, and the elbow becomes painful not only while playing tennis, but also with daily activities such as lifting a milk carton, holding a briefcase, or shaking hands. The elbow may feel stiff after inactivity, and the patient may even keep it partially flexed as a means of avoiding pain. Gradually, the elbow becomes painful enough that the patient begins to avoid certain activities of daily living.

The other, less common history is that of a more acute onset of symptoms. This usually occurs when the individual has played a great deal of tennis over a 1- or 2-day period. The relatively severe pain usually prevents the athlete from playing any tennis and causes pain with daily activities. This player typically seeks medical attention much more quickly than the player with the more gradual onset of symptoms.

Diagnosis

Chronic lateral tennis elbow causes pain around the lateral epicondyle, where the extensor brevis tendon attaches, and pain frequently radiates down the extensor aspect of the forearm toward the fingers. While we do see tennis elbow in younger patients, the vast majority of patients are 35 to 55 years old and are playing tennis three or more times per week. Pain while playing tennis is caused by the impact of the ball on the racquet strings during the backhand stroke. Players with a less sophisticated backhand stroke who are hitting the ball improperly (catching the ball behind the plane of the body or hitting the ball without locking the wrist and extending the elbow) frequently have more pain with impact than those hitting the ball correctly.

The biomechanics of stroke production are often implicated in producing tennis elbow. To properly hit a backhand, the wrist extensor muscles should be contracted to firmly stabilize the wrist, and the elbow should be extended so that the stress of impact is passed proximally to the larger shoulder and back muscles. It appears that this repetitive stress in tennis players causes alterations in the extensor tendon tissue adjacent to the origin on the humerus, perhaps producing microtears of the tendon tissue, which instead of going through the normal reparative processes follows a chronic degenerative pattern that does not result in complete healing. However, these microtears have not been microscopically verified.

Acute rupture of the extensor muscle from the lateral epicondylar region is rare. It does occur, but when it happens it is usually in the athlete who has been experiencing symptoms and follows a major mishit or overpowering of the elbow muscles. The muscles on the extensor side are not as strong and powerful as those on the medial side, so rupture of the muscles from the medial side is more common than it is laterally, although it is still rare. We have not seen any extensor muscle ruptures in younger players, but have seen them in midlife players.

Medial tennis elbow in tennis players is a result of hitting the overhead, serve, or forehand strokes. Medial tennis elbow is likely to have had a more acute origin than that seen on the lateral side, but the inciting factors are the same: repetitive stress caused by the impact of the ball against the racquet strings that must be absorbed by the arm and forearm. Medial tennis elbow is also seen in athletes other than tennis players, such as javelin throwers,[7] and is common in baseball pitchers.[8-10] In these latter two groups, not only is stress placed on the medial muscle attachments, but also on the medial collateral ligament of the elbow; in some instances, the valgus stress generated by throwing causes underlying laxity of the medial collateral ligament, which may be a more serious problem for the baseball pitcher than the tennis elbow. Another problem in treating medial tennis elbow is that in tennis, the tension of the flexor muscle mass enables the athlete to flex the fingers and grip the racquet. Thus, the flexor muscle mass is always under some tension and subject to potential irritation.

Physical Examination

With chronic lateral tennis elbow, the patient usually has well-localized tenderness near the lateral epicondyle, in the region of the attachment of the extensor carpi radialis brevis. Elbow range of motion is generally complete, although in longer lasting cases there may be some loss of extension. Pronation and supination are normal. Epicondylar tenderness is exacerbated with the elbow fully extended. Examiner resistance to attempted wrist extension causes pain at the attachments of the wrist extensor muscles, which may be lessened if the elbow is flexed, or increased if the elbow is extended.

There is usually some weakness of the extensor muscle mass, although it may be difficult to discriminate between pain with extension and true weakness. If lateral tennis elbow is left untreated, weakness will likely increase. Radiation of pain down the forearm along the extensor muscle mass has been attributed to radial nerve involvement, but it is more likely due to referred pain along the extensor muscle mass. The physician should test for contractures of the wrist extensor muscles by fully extending the elbow and then flexing the wrist as far volarly as possible. Normal wrist flexion is 85° to 90°; restricted wrist flexion may indicate chronic contraction of the extensor muscle masses.

In medial tennis elbow, the athlete has tenderness where the flexor muscles and the pronator teres attach to the medial epicondylar region. Pain is increased with attempted wrist flexion against resistance and with pronation of the forearm against resistance. In some instances, full extension is lost. The ulnar nerve percussion test may be positive at the site where the nerve passes between the two heads of the flexor carpi ulnaris. Muscle weakness does occur, as in lateral tennis elbow, but must be differentiated from weakness caused by pain. In medial tennis elbow, the physician must test the elbow for medial instability. This test is done by placing the elbow in slight flexion as valgus stress is applied to the forearm. In the rare situation where there is tearing of the musculotendinous junction or avulsion of the tendon plus a small fragment of bone from the medial epicondyle, the athlete experiences severe local tenderness and the immediate loss of flexion strength.

Radiographic Examination

Most patients with lateral or medial tennis elbow have normal radiographs. If there is an acute rupture on the medial side, there may be a shadow where a bone fragment has been avulsed. An avulsed bone fragment is less common on the lateral side, and we have never personally seen a bone fragment pulled loose on the lateral side in the midlife group. If soft-tissue detailed radiographs are obtained, there are, in about 20% of the cases, soft-tissue changes seen around the lateral epicondyle, usually in the form of hazy calcification. The significance of this hazy calcification at present is questionable. It is probable, however, that as the use of magnetic resonance imaging (MRI) increases, we will learn more about the imaging of soft tissues in tennis elbow. Of course, the orthopaedist should always look for bony abnormalities around the elbow, such as loose bodies, traction or impingement spurs, or other findings that may indicate coexisting elbow problems.

Etiology

Much has been written over the years about etiology of tennis elbow, and some material previously published has been disproved and is no longer pertinent. At this time, we feel that the most logical theory is that lateral tennis elbow starts with chronic and repetitive stress at the origin of the extensor carpi radialis brevis, and as a consequence of this stress, changes occur in tendinous tissue. There is an early reparative response, with the formation of granulation tissue that should go on to form some collagen and eventual healing (Fig. 1). However, in some instances, this response ends, not with healing of the tissue, but with mucinoid degeneration of a portion of the tendinous tissue and the formation of reactive granulation tissue in this degenerated portion of the tendon (Fig. 2). This reactive granulation tissue is endowed with free nerve endings and may be the cause of pain. Why some individuals go on to heal over time is not known, but certainly most people do recover. Yet, there are some who do poorly with conservative treatment and may need surgery to recover from the chronic problem. Surgery is not a guaranteed cure, although the success rate is high for most of the procedures used to treat tennis elbow.

Pathology

The pathology involving the origin of the extensor carpi radialis brevis has been described by Nirschl.[3] He noticed immature scar tissue at the attachment to the humerus, which was described as being grayish and friable. Microscopically, there were areas of fibroblastic activity and ingrowth of vascular buds. Small clefts and mucinoid degeneration have also been described.[11]

Treatment

One obvious form of treatment for tennis elbow is rest. Unfortunately, it is not easy to persuade active athletes to forego playing the sport, even for a while. Yet, rest is an excellent treatment modality. Patients with an acute onset of pain are more easily treated than those who have had a long-term, chronic onset. First, those patients who have acute pain are more disabled by the pain, and thus, are more likely to follow directions. Second, the inflammatory response of the acute injury, if treated correctly, appears to progress to natural collagen formation and tendon healing in many instances. Patients who have lived with chronic pain are less disabled. Also, the chronic process appears to be less influenced by treatment methods, resulting in fewer outright cures.

We ask our patients to stop playing tennis for a period of time, perhaps only several weeks, in order to start the rehabilitation program considered to be critical to the ultimate healing of tennis elbow. In acute cases, the nonsteroidal anti-inflammatory drugs (NSAIDs) are useful to decrease pain and to allow the patient to start on a gradual rehabilitation program. In the chronic situations, these same

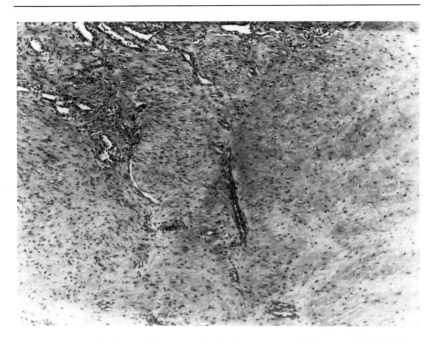

Fig. 1 *Section of tendon width neovascularization near area of microtear (H & E 79X). (Courtesy of Dr. Andrew Rosenberg)*

Fig. 2 *Longitudinal section of tendon. The upper half shows myxoid degeneration and splaying apart of the collagen fibers (H & E 31X). (Courtesy of Dr. Andrew Rosenberg)*

medications may relieve some pain, which has both a benefit and a drawback. The benefit is that the patient may be able to start on a rehabilitation program more quickly and more comfortably. The drawback is that if the patient feels better, he or she may be tempted to return to playing tennis when the underlying condition still remains unchanged.

We start patients on a program of stretching and strengthening the wrist extensor muscles.[1] The patient starts the forearm strengthening program by using very light weights with the elbow in a 90° flexed position. We ask patients to do sets of ten repetitions (two or three sets) two to three times per day, taking the wrist from flexion into extension (Fig. 3). We want them to do no exercise that increases the pain, but we do want them to exercise on a regular basis. The theory is to apply gradual stress to the wrist extensor tendons to stimulate nature to initiate or continue the reparative healing process without overpowering it. If the exercises can be done with the elbow in full extension without producing pain, we ask the athletes to perform them in that manner. In some instances, we instruct the patient to extend the wrist against no resistance. With others, we find it best to have the resistance provided by the patient's other hand or by use of various elastic devices; the resistance provided by the elastic can be carefully controlled so as not to produce pain. If the exercises increase pain, we ask the patient to decrease the resistance to a level that does not cause pain.

We have vacillated somewhat over a period of years as to the best use of heat and cold. At this point, we believe that mild heat for several minutes before doing the exercises is fine although we don't consider it to be a necessity. We do believe that the use of ice after playing tennis, even icing for five minutes, may be helpful in reducing the local inflammatory response, thus decreasing pain and allowing the patient to continue with the exercise program. However, we do not use ice beyond the first weeks of the rehabilitation program.

For medial tennis elbow, we ask athletes to move the wrist and hand into flexion and pronation, using light weights, with resistance applied manually or with rubber tubing. The pronation exercises are especially important (Fig. 4). We have also found it useful in both medial and lateral tennis elbow to have the patient hold a one- or two-pound weight in the affected hand and move from full elbow extension to full elbow flexion for ten repetitions repeated for two or three sets.

Stretching is an important component of the treatment. The patient with lateral tennis elbow stretches the wrist extensor muscles by extending the injured elbow fully (Fig. 5) and then trying to flex the wrist to 90° with the assistance of the opposite hand. Stretching is repeated six to ten times, holding for about 10 seconds each time. This stretching may initially produce discomfort. Some athletes may be unable to perform the stretching with the elbow fully extended at

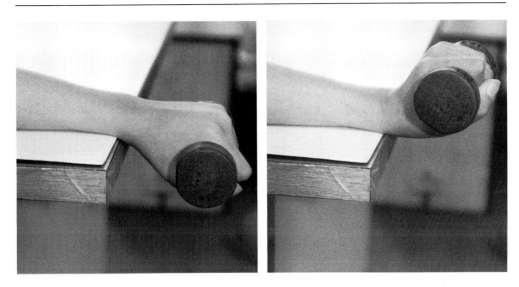

Fig. 3 *Left*, Wrist extension with weight. ***Right***, Wrist extension completed.

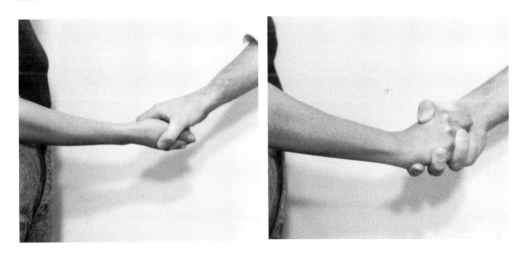

Fig. 4 *Left*, Pronation with weight. ***Right***, Pronation completed.

first, but this is a goal they should work to achieve. With medial tennis elbow, the stretching process is reversed. With the elbow fully extended, the patient tries to extend the wrist maximally.

Gradually the exercises are progressed. The strengthening and stretching exercises are increased by increasing first frequency and then resistance as the patient begins to improve. If these exercises

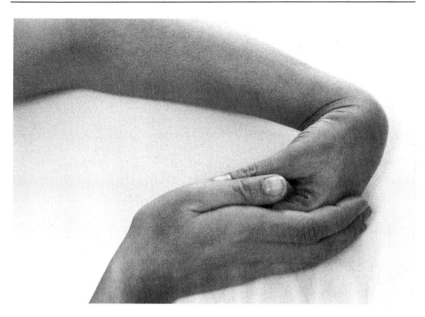

Fig. 5 *Stretching into full wrist flexion aided by the patient's other hand.*

begin to produce pain, then we must consider other treatment possibilities.

In our experience, there is a limited role for corticosteroid injections in the treatment of tennis elbow. If a patient fails to improve over a 6-week period, despite resting from playing tennis and following a good rehabilitation program, we consider the injection of a steroid preparation into the area of maximal tenderness, assuming this is near the attachment of the extensor radialis brevis to the humerus. Our intention is to insert the steroid into that subaponeurotic space. We ask the patient not to perform any major physical activities, including our exercises (other than range of motion exercise of the wrist and elbow, but not against resistance) for 2 weeks following an injection. After 2 weeks, we start with a program of light resistance exercises, perhaps starting with some Silly Putty in the hand. The patient squeezes the Silly Putty for several minutes 10 or 12 times a day, which helps finger flexion, but at the same time the wrist extensor muscles must act to stabilize the wrist. If this causes no pain, the patient progresses to the routine exercise program. If a patient has derived some benefit from an initial steroid injection, we consider a second steroid injection only after 3 to 6 weeks.

Physical therapy modalities, including ultrasound, iontophoresis, and high voltage galvanic stimulation, may be helpful to some athletes with tennis elbow. Ultrasound is a means of applying deep heat and may be of use when combined with a rehabilitation program, although we think moist heat is equally effective. Iontophoresis using a corticosteroid preparation or aspirin has been helpful in some patients; it should also be combined with a rehabilitation program. While galvanic stimulation has been popular with some clinicians, we have had little experience with this modality and cannot comment on its use. Each of these modalities may be helpful in decreasing the pain of tennis elbow and allowing the patient to begin a rehabilitation program. None of these physical therapy modalities is intended to cure by itself, and each one should be seen as an adjunct to the rehabilitation program.

As patients begin to recover and anticipate returning to tennis, factors such as technique, equipment, and the use of braces should be evaluated. The athlete's backhand technique should be observed. Under no circumstances should one assume that only players with poor backhands have tennis elbow. In fact, tennis elbow is not uncommon in world-class tennis players. Most elite players recover, but some have had long-term difficulties and shortened careers. However, the better the biomechanics are, the more likely the athlete is to avoid tennis elbow. Proper biomechanics consist of locking the wrist, extending the elbow, and hitting the ball with the racquet in front of the plane of the body.

A player hitting against a "big hitter" on a hard court may experience more impact stress against the racquet and may be more likely to have a late hit behind the plane of the body, which produces more stress and more pain. Clay surfaces slow the ball, but allow more hits. However, playing on clay would probably be easier and less stressful for a player who has a painful elbow or is coming back from a painful elbow.

Racquets with a large head have become increasingly popular; they seem to produce fewer off-center hits, and thus, should be less likely to cause pain.

Racquet frames and racquet grip size are other important factors. Racquet frames which are made of materials allowing fewer vibrations, such as graphite and epoxy, seem to be beneficial, but the stiffness of the racquet must be balanced with the playing ability of the athlete. If the strings are very tight, the force transmitted to the elbow is increased, suggesting that decreasing string tension might be a means of decreasing stress at the elbow. Nirschl[2] has stated that too many players use too small a racquet handle, and because of this, they must grip the handle very tightly.

There are a number of braces that are available to assist the athlete with tennis elbow. We believe that braces can be helpful, certainly for brief to moderate periods of time (3 to 12 weeks). After rehabilitation or after surgery, they are particularly efficacious. The concept of counterforce bracing as outlined by Nirschl[2] is to apply a firm brace around the bulkiest portion of the wrist extensor muscles near the elbow. As one contracts the extensor muscle mass while hitting the ball, the brace does not allow full contraction of the mass.

Therefore, less force is transmitted to the tendinous insertion at the humerus. We have not found the braces that include both the elbow and wrist to be any more effective, and they seem cumbersome.

If all of these conservative measures fail, then surgery seems the most reasonable choice if the patient continues to be symptomatic and wants to play tennis. It is beyond the scope of this chapter to discuss surgery for tennis elbow, which has been addressed in many published articles. We do, however, agree substantially with Nirschl's[3] surgical approach to the extensor carpi radialis brevis as the frequent source of pain. Following surgery, a strict rehabilitation program is necessary to return the player to tennis.

References

1. Leach RE, Miller JK: Lateral and medial epicondylitis of the elbow. *Clin Sports Med* 1987;6:259-272.
2. Nirschl RP: Tennis elbow. *Orthop Clin North Am* 1973;4:787-800.
3. Nirschl RP, Pettrone FA: Tennis elbow: The surgical treatment of lateral epicondylitis. *J Bone Joint Surg* 1979;61A:832-839.
4. Bosworth DM: Surgical treatment of tennis elbow: A follow-up study. *J Bone Joint Surg* 1965;47A:1533-1536.
5. Boyd HB, McLeod AC Jr: Tennis elbow. *J Bone Joint Surg* 1973;55A:1183-1187.
6. Goldberg EJ, Abraham E, Siegel I: The surgical treatment of chronic lateral humeral epicondylitis by common extensor release. *Clin Orthop* 1988;233:208-212.
7. Miller JE: Javelin thrower's elbow. *J Bone Joint Surg* 1960;42B:788-792.
8. King J, Brelsford HJ, Tullos HS: Analysis of the pitching arm of the professional baseball pitcher. *Clin Orthop* 1969;67:116-123.
9. Tullos HS, King JW: Throwing mechanism in sports. *Orthop Clin North Am* 1973;4:709-720.
10. DeHaven KE, Evarts CM: Throwing injuries of the elbow in athletes. *Orthop Clin North Am* 1973;4:801-808.
11. Goldie I: Epicondylitis lateralis humeri: (Epicondylalgia or tennis elbow) A pathogenetical study. *Acta Chir Scand (Suppl)* 1964;339:1-119.

Chapter 27

Pubic Pain in Athletes

Eugenio Diaz Ferreiro, MD

Introduction

Since Spinelli[1] first described pubic pain in fencers, many terms have been used to define this group of symptoms. Some authors have used as the basis the sport causing the discomfort: the rectus adductor syndrome in soccer players[2] or pubic symphysitis in long-distance runners,[3] for example. Others have taken the etiopathogenic character as a starting point: dynamic osteopathy of the pubis.[4] Still others,[5] given the etiologic and pathologic diversity, have given the syndrome a more general name: groin injury in athletes,[6] or simply pubalgia.

Like other authors,[7] I[8] prefer the term pubic disease in athletes, as it covers different phenomena in the pubis as a result of morbid action. Indeed, the disease consists of changes of the osteomyotendinous structures of the pubic area as a result of practicing different sports.

After a review of anatomy and biomechanical considerations, I will present a study that investigates the etiology, clinical manifestations, and treatment of this syndrome, as well as the results and some of the conclusions that can be made from this study.

Anatomic and Biomechanical Balance

A brief review of anatomy will remind us that the different fibers inserted in the pubis are from muscles with differing action (Fig. 1). In the superior region, there are the rectus abdomini and pyramidalis muscles, which exert their actions vertically and cranially, and the obliquus musculature (obliquus externus and internus), which do so cranially and obliquely. In the inferior region, the adductor muscles (longus, magnus, and brevis) and the gracilis act in a lengthwise (longitudinal and inferior) direction.

The abdominal musculature, together with the abductor muscles, stabilize the pelvis and trunk, while the adductor muscles, three times stronger, are protagonists. The dynamic balance is disrupted when demands for pelvic stability are multiplied, whether violently and occasionally (as happens when a soccer player shoots), sustained (as in fencing), or continuously (as in marathon or long-distance run-

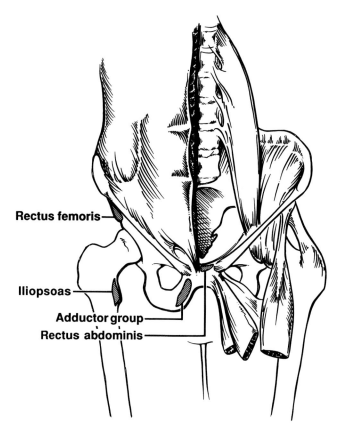

Fig. 1 *Muscles of the pubic region. (Reproduced with permission from Taylor DC, Meyers WC, Moylan JA, et al: Abdominal musculature abnormalities as a cause of groin pain in athletes. Am J Sports Med 1991;19:239-242.)*

ners). In a great many of the cases, and above all in young athletes, the first sign is usually pain and dysfunction of the adductor muscles at their pubic insertion brought about by the microtrauma.

Abdominal musculature can be involved in pubic disease in two ways: principally, by anomalies of the abdominal wall, which weaken it, or by the chronic inflexibility of adductor muscles responding to antialgie atitude. By this point, control of pubic articulation is lost, subject to axial scissoring forces that end up producing authentic arthrosis (arthropathic form).

Etiologic Factors

Based on anatomic and biomechanical factors, the role of certain sports in the genesis of pubic disease can be deduced. There is another series of factors, however, that may be present in isolation or in combination: (1) age, (2) improper conditioning, (3) morphologic and structural bone changes, and (4) abdominal muscle and tendon abnormalities.

Age

When we were drawing up a list of surgically treated cases 4 years ago,[8] we noted one peak of greater incidence around the age of 21 and another between 33 and 42 years of age (Fig. 2). In order to make our study more uniform, we selected a total of 46 long-distance, marathon, and ultramarathon runners from the latter group of athletes (ages 33 to 42 years) and carried out a follow-up for between 3 and 7 years. The results constitute the basis of the information presented here.

We know that with time, physiologic and structural changes take place in the musculoskeletal system. The most significant usually are:[9] (1) loss of osseous mass; (2) the maturation of cross-linkages of collagen fibers, which reduce the plasticity of tissue; (3) atrophy of the hyaline cartilage; and (4) decreased production of connective tissue.

There is no specific age for the start of these changes, as there are different factors that condition aging: genetic, structural, previous injuries, and, above all, physical inactivity. Indeed, all the changes mentioned can be prevented or reversed with proper physical activity.[10]

Muscle exertion and weightbearing activity have many positive benefits for building and maintaining bone and connective tissue. It is likely that a large portion of degenerative changes in the musculoskeletal system are due to inactivity rather than to the aging process.

Improper Conditioning

In order to evaluate this parameter more exactly, we have assigned the athletes to one of four levels, in accordance with their sporting standard and history (Table 1).

Overall, the following conclusions can be reached: Elite and competition athletes have periodic medical check-ups, assessment of their technique, and adequate preparation (warming up, stretching, etc). They usually suffer from pubic disease caused by overexercise and more frequent disease in adductors, whether or not associated with the parietal form (alterations of the abdominal wall, improper conditioning, etc.). Free-time runners and newcomer athletes start long-distance running without a prior medical check-up, and only go to the doctor several weeks after experiencing the first symptoms. Further, they have no technical assessment, longer periods of inactivity, and greater frequency of the abdominal form of pubic disease.

Alterations in Bone Morphology and Structure

For all our patients, we systematically carried out a radiologic study that included a simple radiograph of the pelvic ring, with the

OPERATED ATHLETES

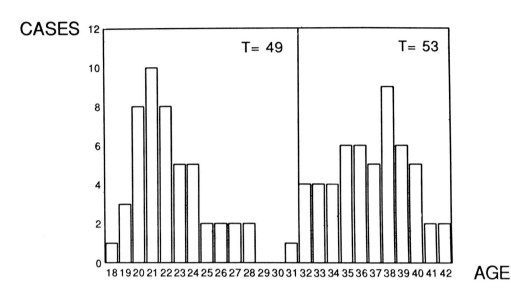

Fig. 2 *Athletes who were operated on for pubic disease.*

Table 1 Four levels of athletic conditioning

Level of Athlete	History
Elite	Long-distance runners for at least 10 years and participants in international competition.
Competition	Marathon or long-distance runners who have been preparing for national or regional competition for less than 10 years.
Free-time runners	Previously practiced other sports, and became long-distance runners to keep fit.
Newcomer	Practiced sports at school and then carried out some sporting activity sporadically and took part in long-distance runs for at least 1 year.

patient alternatively resting on each foot; a radiograph of the hip; a radiograph of the lumbar spine (in order to check axial deviation, spondylitis, etc); and weightbearing assessment in lower limbs.

Two conclusions can be reached from this examination: Most cases presented were normal based on radiographs and there was a clinicoradiologic discordance, that is, the cases presenting osseous injuries did not have an obvious clinical correspondence, either in the quality or extent of the symptoms.

Alterations in Abdominal Muscles and Tendons

In the clinical examination we carried out on the athletes who came to surgery, we tried to discover congenital or acquired alterations that could be connected to the illness. Therefore, we conducted muscular tests on the groups of muscles that are inserted in the pelvic ring. The abdominal wall was examined to discover possible hernias or constitutional anomalies. We looked for Malgaigne's sign: a fusiform protuberance in the abdominal wall, either with the patient standing on two feet and hyperlordosis, or carrying out Valsava's maneuver with the patient in dorsal decubitus. A positive sign would indicate a weakness of the abdominal wall as a result of muscular-aponeurotic insufficiency. Malgaigne's sign was positive in 15 cases and we were able to detect two hamstring retractions, five adductor muscle chronic inflexibilities, and two inguinal hernias.

All of the above clinical observations occurred in 20 patients, who presented them in isolation or in combination. In the other 26 patients, there was apparent normality. That is to say that in more than half of the patients, musculotendinous anomalies could not be verified.

Clinical Manifestations

The patients came to surgery with inguinal pain of several weeks' evolution, exacerbated by the intense physical activity, which forced them to interrupt their training. The pain has different manifestations, depending on the anatomopathologic form: in adductor disease, the pain is located in the insertion of the adductor tendons in the pubis (mainly the adductor longus and the gracilis muscles). This pain increases with the resisted maneuvers of adduction, and the abduction of the hip is limited by the pain. In the abdominal form, the pain is suprapubic, primarily in the upper area on the pubis tubercle, and spreads along the canalis inguinalis (occasionally to the testicles and root of the muscle) and increases with Valsava's maneuver. Finally, in the arthropathic form, the pain is seated in the symphyses of the pubis and has multiple radiations.

Treatment

The cases presented in this chapter, and which are the theme of this study, correspond to patients who were referred to our hospital at least 3 months after initial symptoms developed and after receiving conventional treatment with no positive results.

The following techniques were used: adductor disease (tenotomy of the adductor longus in the proximity of its insertion in the pelvis); parietoabdominal form (Nesovic-type herniorraphy—modification of Bassini's technique for treatment of inguinal hernias—

Table 2 Postoperative results

Result	Number	Explanation
Excellent	40	Activity same as preinjury level, with no discomfort and with a period of reincorporation into sport of 2.5 months
Good	3	Activity same as preinjury level, with sporadic discomfort that affected training for 4 months
Average	3	Limitation of activity that required additional therapies such as corticosteroid infiltrations and that slowed down the time taken to reincorporate into regular training
Bad	10	Impossible to practice sport continuously

which attempts to rebalance the muscular forces of the pubis, tightening the anterior wall of the canalis inguinalis);[11,12] and combined forms (association of both techniques).

Results

It is important to note that postoperative rehabilitation and the time taken to reincorporate the patient into sport did not vary in relation to the young athletes who were treated with similar procedures. The results were recorded as excellent, good, average, and bad (Table 2).

References

1. Spinelli A: Una nuova malattia sportiva: La pubalgia degli schermitori. *Ortop Traumatol Aparato Motore*. 1932;4:111-127.
2. Bandini T: Relievi su di una sindrome dei rett-addutori nei giocatori di calcio. *Inform Medico* 1948;2:10-12,285-287.
3. Koch RA, Jackson DW: Pubic symphysitis in runners: A report of two cases. *Am J Sports Med* 1981;9:62-63.
4. Cabot JR: Osteopatía dinámica del pubis, in Hanekopf G (ed): *World Congress of Sports Medicine*. Köln, Deutscher Aerzte Verlag, 1966, pp 359-364.
5. Villarrubias, et al: Conceptos actuales sobre la pubalgia en los deportistas. *Archiv Med Deporte* 1984;1:7-11.
6. Renström P, Peterson L: Groin injuries in athletes. *Br J Sports Med* 1980;14:30-36.
7. Arezki N, Zerguini Y, et al: La maladie pubienne chez le sportif: Priorité au traitement medicale. *J Traum Sport* 1991;8:91-97.
8. Diaz Ferreiro E, Marti D, Cabot A: La pubalgia del deportista. Fifth European Congress of Sports Medicine, Barcelona, Spain, Dec 7-10, 1988.
9. Green HJ: Characteristics of aging human skeletal muscles, in Sutton JR, Brock RM (eds): *Sports Medicine for the Mature Athlete*. Indianapolis, IN, Benchmark Press Inc, 1986, pp 17-26.
10. Bouvier J: Aspects cliniques et traitement medical del pubalgies. *Sports Med* 1984;34:4-5.
11. Jaeger JH: La pubalgie du sportif: Le traitement chirurgical. *J Traum Sport* 1984;1:56-59.
12. Nesovic Branislau: "El dolor en la ingle de los futbolistas." Simposium sobre la ingle dolorosa del futbolista: II. Curso de la Escuela Catalana de Traumatologia del deporte. Inst. Policlínico. Barcelona, Spain, April 1981.

Chapter 28

Osteoarthritis: Exercise and Other Factors

Robert C. Mulholland, MB, FRCS
Stephen L. Gordon, PhD

Introduction

Osteoarthritis (OA), the most common joint disorder throughout the world, is the cause of a great deal of pain and disability. Radiographic changes of osteoarthritis occur in the majority of individuals by age 65 and in more than 80% of those older than age 75. However, the problem originates at a younger age and is common in midlife. Osteoarthritis of the knee is more common in men before age 45, but more common in women after age 45.[1]

Exercise and Other Factors Leading to Osteoarthritis

For many individuals there is neither a clear pathogenesis nor are there definitive risk factors that would explain the origin of their OA. In addition, long symptom-free periods and episodes of steady, rapid deterioration are not yet well understood.

Many studies have attempted to link sports and physical exercise to the later onset of OA, but the majority of sports or activities studied so far have failed to demonstrate a cause and effect relationship.[1,2] Felson[1] has summarized five studies investigating a possible link between running and OA. Four of the five do not show an association (Table 1). Similarly, data from several studies of soccer players fail to document a clear relationship between that sport and OA.[1]

McKeag[2] identifies ten factors associated with exercise that affect the likelihood of developing OA: age, gender, ethnicity, geography, body habitus, bone density, hyperuricemia, hypertension, hypercholesteremia, and trauma. Table 2 documents some of the effects of these and other factors on the later occurrence of OA.

Two of these ten factors require specific explanation. Age may be a general risk factor for OA, but the normal changes in cartilage that occur with aging differ significantly from the changes observed

Table 1 Studies on running and osteoarthritis

Study	Joint	Number	Time elapsed since activity	Controls*	Results
Puranen and associates[3]	Hip	60	20 years	+	No increase in osteoarthritis
Lane and associates[4]	Knee	41	None	+	No increase in osteoarthritis
Panush and associates[5]	Knee	17	None	+	No increase in osteoarthritis
Sohn and Micheli[6]	Knee, hip	504	25 years	+	No increase in knee or hip pain over controls (swimmers)
McDermott and Freyne[7]	Knee	20	None	−	6/20 had definite radiographic osteoarthritis

* +, controls present; −, controls missing.
(Reproduced with permission from Felson DT: Epidemiology of hip and knee osteoarthritis. *Epidemiol Rev* 1988;10:1-28.)

in OA (Table 3). Evidence of normal aging of cartilage and joints does not mean that an individual also has OA.

Trauma is an important risk factor for developing OA; the more extensive the injury, the more likely is the development of OA. For example, in the knee, the more structures involved in the injury (anterior cruciate ligament, menisci, collateral ligaments, or bone), the higher the risk of developing OA. The role of direct injury to the hyaline cartilage in the development of OA is not clear.[1,2]

The risk factors for each joint (eg, knee, hip, and spine) are different. For example, obesity is strongly associated with knee OA, but not with hip OA. Even within the knee, patellofemoral OA may be distinct from tibiofemoral OA. Each type of OA should be considered separately.[8]

There are many aerobic and musculoskeletal benefits of exercise, and, conversely, there are many detrimental effects from a sedentary lifestyle. Because exercise does not appear to be a strong independent risk factor for developing OA, moderate levels of sports and physical activities can be recommended for most midlife individuals.

Diagnosis of Osteoarthritis

The late stages of OA are evidenced by moderate to severe pain, stiffness (especially after sleeping), functional impairment, joint enlargement, instability, changes in subchondral bone, and formation of new cartilage and bone at the joint margin. Few of these clinical symptoms are present in the early stages of disease. Radiographs may confirm the findings of OA in late stages, but may not provide clearly interpretable information in early stages. There are, as yet, no well-defined biochemical markers that distinguish normal subjects from OA patients.

Because mild to moderate pain, stiffness, and impairment may be symptomatic of many injuries and disorders of the joints, it is important not to label all joint pain as early OA. Telling patients that they may have a "wear and tear" disease and recommending a sed-

Table 2 Factors that may be associated with the development of sports-related osteoarthritis (SROA)

Possible Factors	Assertions
Physical Characteristics	
Age	Early participation may increase risk of OA
Gender	OA may be reduced in osteoporotic postmenopausal women with exercise
Ethnic background	Increased OA in the Native American; Decreased OA of hips in the Chinese population
Body habitus	Obesity may increase OA of the knee
Congenital abnormalities (ie, dislocations)	May increase risk of premature OA at the hip
Biomechanical Factors	
Gait	May alter normal cartilage stress sites of weightbearing joints
Joint alignment	Genu varum deformity may increase OA at the knee
Ligamentous instability (ie, injury)	Increased risk of OA
Impact stress loading	Increased risk of OA due to chondrocyte degeneration
Immobilization	Increased articular degeneration (fibrillation), which may increase OA
Overuse syndrome	May increase articular degeneration earlier in life
Prior injury	May increase risk of OA
Biochemical Factors	
Aging of articular cartilage	Loss of biophysical properties of articular cartilage (ie, chondrocytes) May increase risk of OA
Subchondral microfracture	May evolve with repetitive strenuous exercise and later increase risk of OA
Bone growth/remodeling	May be decreased at site of previous fractures Remodeling may be affected by chronic exercise
Joint lubrication	May be decreased with excessive impact: loading stress and later increase risk of OA
Local inflammation	May increase risk for development of early OA postinjury
Hormonal influences (ie, steroids)	An imbalance may affect bone metabolism in such a way as to increase the risk of OA
Synovial fluid characteristics	Alterations in hyaluronic acid, sulfates, structural glycosaminoglycans, and water content may increase risk of OA
Characteristics of the Playing Surface	
Asphalt	May increase OA
Clay	Unknown
Cement (concrete)	Increases stress loading, which may increase risk of OA
Grass	May decrease injury and thereby decrease risk of early OA
Ice	Unknown
Tarton surface (astroturf)	May increase risk of injuries (ie, turf toe), which may increase risk of premature OA
Water	May decrease the risk of OA by lessening stress and loading
Wood	May increase lower extremity injuries, which may increase risk of OA

(continued)

Table 2 Factors that may be associated with the development of sports-related osteoarthritis (SROA) *(continued)*

Possible Factors	Assertions
Characteristics of Sport	
Contact versus noncontact	May increase risk of OA with repetitive stress-loading
Duration of participation	May increase injuries and development of premature OA
Onset and Level of Participation	
Childhood/adolescence	May increase long-term risk of OA
Adult	May increase risk of OA with overuse syndrome
Professional/Competitive (Amateur)/ Recreational)	An increased risk of OA may be associated with antecedent injuries or length of participation
Miscellaneous	
Nutrition	
Protein diets	May cause electrolyte loss and accelerate osteoporosis
Phosphate loading	Unknown effect; may deplete magnesium sources
Calcium-deficient diets	May increase osteoporosis, which may increase risk of OA
Medical therapy	Accurate diagnosis and management of injury may decrease OA
Pharmacological therapy	Certain nonsteroidal anti-inflammatory drugs and steroids may have deleterious effects on cartilage. Ice, heat, and rest may decrease local inflammation and decrease risk of OA
Surgical therapy	Surgically or biomechanically altered joints may be more susceptible to OA (ie, meniscectomies) yet allow the individuals to continue participation
Preventative Measures	
Coaching methods	Proper techniques may decrease stress-load, prevent injury, and therefore prevent OA
Conditioning techniques	Well-conditioned athletes may have a decreased risk of OA
Training techniques	Overuse may increase risks of OA
Equipment design (ie, headgear, shoes)	May decrease OA by decreasing stress loading or preventing injuries
Rehabilitation of injury (ie, orthotics)	May decrease risk of OA and reinjury
Restricted participation postinjury	May decrease risk of premature OA in unstable, injured joints
Rule changes	May decrease incidence of injuries and risk of OA

OA = osteoarthritis
(Reproduced with permission from McKeag DB: The relationship of osteoarthritis and exercise. *Clin Sports Med* 1992;11:471-487.)

entary lifestyle may be detrimental to both the local joint health and general health of patients. In fact, a recent study by Michel and associates[9] demonstrated that in subjects with a mean age of 60 years, repetitive, painless, weightbearing exercise did not promote the formation of osteophytes (bone spurs) on knee radiographs. While complaints of joint problems are common in midlife, improper advice may lead to an unnecessarily sedentary lifestyle.

Table 3 Comparison of changes in articular cartilage in aging and osteoarthritis

Criterion	Aging	Osteoarthritis
Water content	Decreased	Increased
Glycosaminoglycans		
Chondroitin sulfate	Normal or slightly less	Decreased
Chondroitin sulfate 4:6 ratio	Decreased	Increased
Keratan sulfate	Increased	Decreased
Hyaluronate	Increased	Decreased
Proteoglycans		
Aggregation	Normal	Diminished
Monomer size	Decreased	Decreased
Link protein	Fragmented	Normal
Proteases	Normal	Increased

(Reproduced with permission from Hammerman D: Aging and the musculoskeletal system, in Hazzard WR, Andies R, Bierman EL, et al (eds): *Principles of Geriatric Medicine and Gerontology*, ed 2. New York, NY, McGraw-Hill, 1991.)

Many injuries and disorders can affect the joints and produce symptoms that must be distinguished from OA. For example, most instances of low back pain are not caused by OA, but rather by injuries or abnormalities of the disks, support structures, or muscles. Several shoulder conditions, such as capsulitis, rotator cuff tears, and coracoid impingement syndrome, may cause OA-like symptoms, but these conditions should be properly diagnosed and treated. Conditions of internal derangements of the knee often can be distinguished from OA by arthroscopic, radiographic, or clinical evaluation, and avascular necrosis of the knee can be identified by bone scan or magnetic resonance imaging (MRI). Most of these conditions, including chondromalacia patella, can be treated, so that midlife individuals are able to remain active. Whenever possible, joint problems should be distinguished from OA.[10-17]

Treatment of Osteoarthritis

There is no known therapy that reverses or completely arrests the progression of OA. Treatment is symptomatic and conservative, with the goals of controlling pain and allowing function to be maintained.

Nonimpact exercises have gained broad acceptance in the medical literature as a conservative treatment modality for OA. The goals of exercise include the following: maintaining or increasing joint motion; increasing strength and endurance of periarticular muscles; increasing aerobic capacity; assisting with weight loss; and improving functional capacity in activities of daily living.[18] However, exercise should not be initiated during an acute inflammatory phase of the disease, and in persons at risk for cardiac disease, aerobic exercises should be preceded by an exercise stress test. Summaries of exercise programs are provided by Semble and associates[18] and Bunning and Materson.[19]

Home- or hospital-based exercise programs are equally effective.[20] In either case, limited impact-loading exercise is usually recommended. Dexter[21] evaluated 110 individuals in a single community with OA, 96% of whom had seen a physician for the problem, and determined that fewer than half had received advice to exercise, and very few had received instruction or monitoring of their exercise. Exercise should be more widely used as a conservative therapy for OA, especially in midlife individuals.

Two recent clinical studies have considered the effects of a low-impact exercise, such as walking. Minor and associates[22] randomly assigned 120 patients with rheumatoid arthritis (mean age 54) and osteoarthritis (mean age 64) to groups performing aerobic walking, aerobic aquatics, or nonaerobic range of motion (controls). Both aerobic groups showed significant improvement over controls in aerobic capacity, 50-foot walking time, and Arthritis Impact Measurement Scales for physical activity after the 12-week exercise program. There were no significant differences in flexibility, duration of morning stiffness, or grip strength. There were no detrimental effects of walking and many benefits.

In another clinical study, Kovar and associates[23] randomized 120 OA patients to either an 8-week walking program (mean age 70) or routine medical care (mean age 68) with no exercise recommendaton. The walking group showed significant improvements in a 6-minute walking test, physical activity scale, arthritis pain scale, and reduced use of medication. Again, walking was a very successful intervention in the short term. Further information is required regarding the long-term impact of low-impact exercise on these pain and functional measures, as well as on the underlying pathophysiology. Based on these early results, low-impact exercise with physician monitoring of clinical progress seems to be a valuable adjunct to a complete, well-designed exercise program for patients with OA. Nonimpact and low-impact exercise may play vital roles in the overall health of the patient.

In addition to exercise, diet should be considered as a means to achieve weight loss in overweight OA patients. A recent study[24] demonstrated that weight loss may be effective in reducing symptoms of patients with mild to moderate OA.

The objectives of physiotherapy are to relieve pain, reduce stiffness, and improve strength of the affected joints. Also, the physical therapist teaches the patient about the benefits of movement and how to perform exercises at home. It is difficult to know whether the benefits of physiotherapy arise from the prescribed exercises alone or from the combined effects of exercise and therapeutic modalities. One clinical study by Jan and Lai[25] compared the effects of ultrasound therapy, shortwave diathermy, ultrasound plus exercise program, and shortwave diathermy plus exercise program in patients with knee OA. There was no placebo control. Ultrasound plus exercise and shortwave diathermy plus exercise showed similar improvement; however, exercise plus shortwave diathermy was significantly better in terms of improved functional measures and muscle torque.

There are several orthotic and support devices that may help OA patients. In selected patients, knee braces provide support and protection from further injury, while permitting a wide range of motion. Similarly, ankle orthotics and heel cups can support the ankle region. Walking canes and four-legged walkers are useful in patients with more advanced stages of OA. The patient should be reminded that these devices assist in walking and are not a signal to become inactive.

Analgesic medication and nonsteroidal anti-inflammatory drugs (NSAIDs) are commonly prescribed treatments for OA. One recent study[26] estimated that 94% of primary care physicians would prescribe a NSAID as initial treatment for a patient with uncomplicated hip OA. A number of issues makes this use of NSAIDs controversial. First, some NSAIDs inhibit the synthesis of proteoglycans by articular cartilage. Second, the role of synovial inflammation as a cause of joint pain and cartilage degeneration (especially in early stages of OA) is not clearly established. Third, while NSAIDs are superior to placebos in relieving joint pain, analgesics may be just as effective. Fourth, NSAIDs have potentially severe side effects that may be greatest in the elderly.

In a short-term, 4-week, randomized clinical trial[27] comparing a pure analgesic with a NSAID, the reported measures of pain and function were not significantly different. In a closely related study,[28] joint tenderness and swelling, which are often believed to be associated with inflammation, were not found to respond differently to analgesic or NSAID treatment. It appears that caution should be considered in prescribing NSAIDs as compared to analgesics, especially on a long-term, routine basis.

Osteoarthritis typically has a prolonged course, with many episodic flare-ups and other periods of no progression or even improvement. If the pain and disability become too great a burden for the patient, then surgical intervention is considered. Puhl[29] described arthroscopic surgery to abrade the cartilage surface with a shaver-like device and arthroscopic Excimer laser surgery to smooth the surface while sparing neighboring healthy tissue. These approaches are still experimental; further controlled clinical tests are necessary.

When conservative treatment and less invasive arthroscopy have failed to yield relief, osteotomy or arthroplasty (joint replacement) must be considered. Age is an important consideration in selecting the surgical procedure and type of device for each patient. For example, the decision to use cemented or noncemented devices is often based on the patient's age, weight, and exercise expectations.

Osteotomy has a role in the treatment of unicompartmental knee OA. This is particularly the case if the single compartment failure is clearly associated with a large varus or valgus anatomic defect. In the midlife patient, this option may substantially delay the need for total joint replacement.

Total hip and total knee joint replacements are now common procedures that provide great relief from pain and a return of mobility. After a 3- to 6-month period of rehabilitation, if they do not have other problems limiting mobility, most OA patients can walk unaided and participate in normal activities of daily living. While many sports activities may be resumed after total joint replacement, most patients are advised to avoid high-impact, shock-loading activities.[30-33]

Conclusion

An injury that significantly weakens the integrity of the joint may lead to OA, but age-related joint changes may be independent of changes induced by OA. In patients with OA, immobility is generally detrimental to musculoskeletal soft tissues and should be avoided whenever possible. Exercise is not an independent risk factor for developing osteoarthritis. In fact, exercise in the form of nonimpact or low-impact activities, including walking, appears to be beneficial for OA patients. As midlife is typically the time when OA first appears, the importance of exercise in this population is especially relevant.

References

1. Felson DT: Epidemiology of hip and knee osteoarthritis. *Epidemiol Rev* 1988;10:1-28.
2. McKeag DB: The relationship of osteoarthritis and exercise. *Clin Sports Med* 1992;11:471-487.
3. Puranen J, Ala-Ketola L, Peltokallio P, et al: Running and primary osteoarthritis of the hip. *Br Med J* 1975;1:424-425.
4. Lane NE, Bloch DA, Jones HH, et al: Long-distance running, bone density, and osteoarthritis. *JAMA* 1986;255:1147-1151.
5. Panush RS, Schmidt C, Caldwell JR, et al: Is running associated with degenerative joint disease? *JAMA* 1986;255:1152-1155.
6. Sohn RS, Micheli LJ: The effect of running on the pathogenesis of osteoarthritis of the hips and knees. *Clin Orthop* 1985;198:106-109.
7. McDermott M, Freyne P: Osteoarthritis in runners with knee pain. *Br J Sports Med* 1983;17:84-87.
8. Dieppe P, Cushnaghan J, McAlindon T: Epidemiology, clinical course, and outcome of knee osteoarthritis, in Kuettner KE, Schleyerbach R, Peyron JG, et al (eds): *Articular Cartilage and Osteoarthritis*. New York, NY, Raven Press, 1992, chap 44, pp 617-627.
9. Michel BA, Fries JF, Bloch DA, et al: Osteophytosis of the knee: Association with changes in weight-bearing exercise. *Clin Rheum* 1992;11:235-238.
10. Dandy DJ: Editorial: Arthroscopic debridement of the knee for osteoarthritis. *J Bone Joint Surg* 1991;73B:877-878.
11. Eriksson E, Häggmark T: Knee pain in the middle aged runner, in Mack RP (ed): *AAOS Symposium on The Foot and Leg in Running Sports*. St. Louis, MO, CV Mosby, 1982, chap 13, pp 106-108.
12. Brough B, Thakore J, Davies M, et al: Degeneration of the lumbar facet joints: Arthrography and pathology. *J Bone Joint Surg* 1990;72B:275-276.

13. Fairbank JC, Park WM, McCall IW, et al: Apophyseal injection of local anaesthetic as a diagnostic aid in primary low back pain syndromes. *Spine* 1981;6:598-605.

14. Dines DM, Warren RF, Inglis AE, et al: The coracoid impingement syndrome. *J Bone Joint Surg* 1990;72B:314-316.

15. Wasilewski SA, Frankl U: Rotator cuff pathology: Arthroscopic assessment and treatment. *Clin Orthop* 1991;267:65-70.

16. Watson M: Rotator cuff function in the impingement syndrome. *J Bone Joint Surg* 1989;71B:361-366.

17. Ellman H, Kay SP: Arthroscopic subacromial decompression for chronic impingement: Two- to five-year results. *J Bone Joint Surg* 1991;73B:395-398.

18. Semble EL, Loeser RF, Wise CM: Therapeutic exercise for rheumatoid arthritis and osteoarthritis. *Semin Arthritis Rheum* 1990;20:32-40.

19. Bunning RD, Materson RS: A rational program of exercise for patients with osteoarthritis. *Semin Arthritis Rheum* 1991;21(3 Suppl 2):33-43.

20. Chamberlain MA, Care G, Harfield B: Physiotherapy in osteoarthrosis of the knees: A controlled trial of hospital versus home exercises. *Int Rehab Med* 1982;4:101-106.

21. Dexter PA: Joint exercises in elderly persons with symptomatic osteoarthritis of the hip or knee: Performance patterns, medical support patterns, and the relationship between exercising and medical care. *Arthritis Care Res* 1992;5:36-41.

22. Minor MA, Hewett JE, Webel RR, et al: Efficacy of physical conditioning exercise in patients with rheumatoid arthritis and osteoarthritis. *Arthritis Rheum* 1989;32:1396-1405.

23. Kovar PA, Allegrante JP, MacKenzie CR, et al: Supervised fitness walking in patient with osteoarthritis of the knee: A randomized, controlled trial. *Ann Intern Med* 1992;116:529-534.

24. Felson DT, Zhang Y, Anthony JM, et al: Weight loss reduces the risk for symptomatic knee osteoarthritis in women: The Framingham study. *Ann Intern Med* 1992;116:535-539.

25. Jan M, Lai J: The effects of physiotherapy on osteoarthritic knees of females. *J Formosan Med Assoc* 1991;90:1008-1013.

26. Mazzuca SA, Brandt KD, Anderson SL, et al: The therapeutic approaches of community-based primary care practitioners to osteoarthritis of the hip in an elderly patient. *J Rheumatol* 1991;18:1593-1600.

27. Bradley JD, Brandt KD, Katz BP, et al: Comparison of an anti-inflammatory dose of ibuprofen, an analgesic dose of ibuprofen, and acetaminophen in the treatment of patients with osteoarthritis of the knee. *N Engl J Med* 1991;325:87-91.

28. Bradley JD, Brandt KD, Katz BP, et al: Treatment of knee osteoarthritis: Relationship of clinical features of joint inflammation to the response to a nonsteroidal anti-inflammatory drug or pure analgesic. *J Rheumatol* 1992;19:1950-1954.

29. Puhl W: Arthroscopy and Arthroplasty, in Kuettner KE, Schleyerbach R, Peyron JG, et al (eds): *Articular Cartilage and Osteoarthritis*. New York, NY, Raven Press, 1992, chap 46, pp 643-651.

30. Maquet P: The treatment of choice in osteoarthritis of the knee. *Clin Orthop* 1985;192:108-112.

31. Gill GS, Mills DM: Long term follow up evaluation of 1000 consecutive cemented total knee arthroplasties. *Clin Orthop* 1991;273:66-76.

32. Muller ME: Lessons of 30 years of total hip arthroplasty. *Clin Orthop* 1992;274:12-21.

33. Coventry MB: Lessons learned in 30 years of total hip arthroplasty. *Clin Orthop* 1992;274:22-29.

Chapter 29

Knee Injuries in the Mature Athlete

William J. Jason, MD
Erin L. Boynton, MD, FRCSC
Gerald M. Finerman, MD

Introduction

The mature athlete presents significant challenges in the management of injuries to the musculoskeletal system. Improved concepts of training and fitness enable mature athletes to participate at high levels of recreational, competitive, and even professional sports. The management of injuries to the knee joint in the mature athlete requires an assessment of the goals of the individual athlete and a knowledge of the stresses the athlete is likely to place on the knee. The physician's goal is to enable the patient to continue to participate in athletics while avoiding the development of osteoarthritis (OA).

Athletically active individuals obviously expose themselves to the risk of knee injury. In the absence of such injury, long-term athletic activity does not appear to be associated with degenerative joint changes; it can, in fact, be beneficial to the joint as well as to the body as a whole.[1]

Studies that compare athletically active adults to their sedentary counterparts exempt those injured or disabled from previous exercise. Nonetheless, such studies have shown that long distance running is not inevitably associated with osteoarthritic changes in knee joints; neither increased symptoms nor radiographic evidence of OA have been noted.[2,3] Although animal studies have shown that profound abuse to joints can cause early articular cartilage degeneration, more physiologic types of exercise did not appear to accelerate OA, even in knees with preexisting OA.[4,5] Similarly, magnetic resonance imaging (MRI) studies showed less subclinical meniscal damage in marathon runners with asymptomatic knees than was found in nonathletes and nonrunners; long-term loading of menisci may, in fact, have a beneficial effect.[6]

Some studies have attempted to eliminate the self-selection bias of long-term exercise by reviewing the progress of all athletes who were active at some point in time. One group of elite runners who had continued to run long distances over a 40-year period showed no increased incidence of OA by subjective, objective, or radiographic criteria when compared to controls matched for age, height, weight, and occupation.[1] Another study with long-term follow-up, in which former college runners were compared to nonrunning athletes, found no correlation between running or miles run with subjective complaints or treatments received for OA.[7]

While exercise by itself is not a risk factor for OA, injuries often associated with exercise, such as meniscal damage or other internal knee derangement, and their treatments, significantly increase a person's chance of developing OA.[8-10] Additional risk factors determined in an age-matched case control study included obesity and a history of heavy labor.[10]

Much has been learned about the formation and age-related decay of articular cartilage. During formation, chondrocytes proliferate rapidly and synthesize a large volume of intracellular matrix. With maturation, chondrocyte density in articular cartilage decreases because chondrocytes rarely, if ever, divide. There is a concomitant decrease in cell synthetic function. Because of this, the structure and composition of aggregating articular cartilage proteoglycans change with aging. Proteoglycan monomers have increased keratin sulfate and protein content, decreased chondroitin sulfate, decreased average monomer size, and increased monomer size variability with age. The proportion of these monomers that aggregate decreases, the aggregates become smaller, and average hyaluronidase filament length decreases because there is a decreasing concentration and increasing fragmentation of link proteins with aging.[11] This decline in the structure of aggregating proteoglycans may cause mature articular cartilage to lose some of its stiffness and resilience, and the age-related decline in chondrocyte density and synthetic function may limit the body's ability to restore a damaged cartilage matrix.[11] Softer, less resilient cartilage could thus be more susceptible to degenerative fibrillation and fissuring.[12,13]

Management of OA in the Mature Athlete

Management of OA in the mature athlete is a difficult challenge. Initial management should concentrate on decreasing inflammation and relieving pain with modification of activity programs, rest, ice, and nonsteroidal anti-inflammatory drugs. The ultimate goals of decreasing the mechanical loads on a specific joint compartment and improving dynamic stability may be achieved by weight loss, selective muscle strengthening and flexibility exercises, modification of the playing surfaces when possible, modification in footwear, orthotics, and knee bracing.

If this regime is unsuccessful and significant disability persists, the athlete must decide whether to permanently decrease his or her activities or undergo surgical intervention. In general, the surgical options are arthroscopic lavage and debridement, realignment, stabilization, or combined procedures. At this time, total or unicompartmental knee replacements are not considered an option for the mature patient who wishes to remain athletic. The surgical procedure selected will depend on the stage of the OA. One must assess which compartments in general are involved and the severity of OA within the specific compartment. Other important considerations are the overall alignment of the lower extremity and the presence or absence of instability.

For the patient with painful medial or lateral unicompartmental OA who has normal lower extremity alignment and a stable knee, arthroscopy may be performed for both diagnostic and therapeutic purposes. The extent of the OA may be assessed and graded, which will give both the surgeon and the patient some idea of the prognosis and recommendation for future participation in athletic endeavors. Any mechanical lesions, such as torn menisci or loose bodies, can be treated arthroscopically.

Arthroscopic saline lavage and debridement of fibrillated, degenerated articular cartilage in the knee can provide good symptomatic relief, albeit temporarily.[14] Lavage and debridement may, in effect, extract proteoglycans, allow or stimulate fibrin clot formation, and improve the repair process.[11]

Abrasion arthroplasty has not provided a predictable technique to stimulate the regrowth of articular cartilage. Mechanical perforation or abrasion of subchondral bone causes formation of a fibrin clot and local vascular invasion, eliciting a native repair response. Initially, fibrocartilage spreads over the repaired bone; in some patients, this tissue matures to a hyaline-like cartilage. With time, the tissue usually becomes more fibrous, then fibrillated, and broken down. This repair tissue occasionally functions well, but not predictably so.[11] Abrasion arthroplasty may be considered a palliative procedure in the well-aligned, stable knee, but it does not address the underlying cause of OA.

The patient with isolated medial or lateral compartment OA and a mechanically stable knee should be considered for a realignment procedure. Classically, a high tibial osteotomy (HTO) is performed to treat varus deformity and medial compartment OA, and a distal femoral varus osteotomy is performed to treat valgus malalignment and lateral compartment OA.

The objective of an osteotomy is to decrease the mechanical load on the diseased joint compartment, thereby allowing for cartilage repair and regeneration. Several authors have been able to demonstrate regeneration of fibrocartilage in overcorrected knees. However, the clinical results and arthroscopic staging at follow-up examination of these patients do not correlate with a regenerative process.[15,16] The results of HTO, as reported by Coventry and supported by others, show that 86% of patients were improved and pleased with their result at 2 to 5 years; however, this number decreased to 64% at 9 years after surgery.[17-19] Similar results are reported for distal femoral varus osteotomy.[20] The most important factor for achieving a good result with osteotomy is slight overcorrection of alignment. The major advantage of an osteotomy in the mature athlete is that it allows freedom of activity and unrestricted sports participation (Fig. 1).

Chronic anterior cruciate ligament (ACL) insufficiency in the athlete with deformity and OA is considered a relative contraindication to performing an osteotomy. In the most common situation, the athlete has medial compartment wear, varus deformity, and ACL deficiency. If an HTO is performed, the patient must understand that his or her instability may become more symptomatic postoperatively. Extra-articular reconstructions of the ACL combined with HTO have been described in this patient population. Of these patients, 50% had returned to some sporting activity at 2-year follow-up. However, objective assessment demonstrated that the repair stretches out over time.[21] In the future, surgeons may consider combining HTO with allograft ACL reconstruction as a staged procedure in the patient with symptomatic instability. Each athlete must be considered individually, taking into account the stage of the OA and the degree of instability and deformity of the knee.

Ligament Injuries

The approach to injuries of the knee ligaments is changing significantly for the mature athlete. Most previous research has looked at these injuries in young athletes, who generally place higher demands on their knees and incur more ligament injuries. With increasing numbers of midlife participants in vigorous athletics, orthopaedic surgeons must apply improvements in surgical techniques and their knowledge of ligament injuries to the mature athlete.

Posterior Cruciate Ligament Injury

Isolated posterior cruciate ligament (PCL) injury without other significant knee injury is relatively uncommon, but probably much more likely to occur with athletic trauma than other types of high energy trauma.[22] If the PCL is avulsed with a bony fragment, early reattachment is recommended.[23] An isolated midsubstance PCL rupture or a PCL-deficient knee requires neither activity modification nor operative repair or reconstruction. Athletes can return to their previous level of participation, regardless of objective posterior laxity and without protective bracing, provided they adequately rehabilitate their ipsilateral quadriceps muscles.[22,24]

Patients who have PCL injuries associated with other internal derangements of the knee, such as a meniscal injury or multidirec-

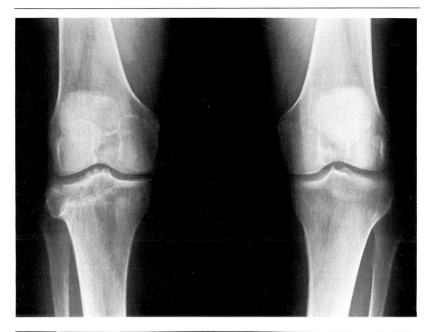

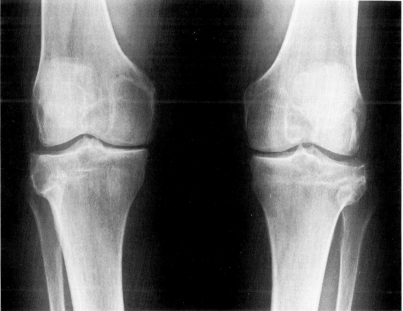

Fig. 1 *A 67-year-old competitive tennis player with varus knee deformity and increasing pain and swelling.* **Top,** *Initial radiograph demonstrates varus deformity on left knee and status following high tibial osteotomy on right knee.* **Bottom,** *Radiograph demonstrates status 2 years (**left**) and 5.3 years (**right**) after bilateral osteotomies, which have enabled return to age-group competitive tennis.*

tional laxity, or who have insufficiently rehabilitated quadriceps muscles, are unlikely to have a satisfactory return to their previous level of activity.[22,25] Injuries to the posterior-lateral complex (the arcuate ligament, fibular collateral ligament, and the popliteus tendon) often occur with the same mechanisms that disrupt the PCL, and can be very disabling for the active individual.[26-28] Hughston and associates have reported good results after operative repair and advancement of the arcuate ligament complex.[26,27]

Anterior Cruciate Ligament Injury

Few soft-tissue injuries to the knee have more bearing on an athlete's performance than ACL rupture; it renders the knee unstable to anterior tibial translation and vulnerable to episodes of "giving way."[29,30] This instability, along with symptoms of pain and swelling, makes such a knee unacceptable for strenuous or competitive sports that require running, cutting, or jumping movements. These drawbacks were once considered acceptable for older athletes because they placed lessening demands on their knees. The dim prospects for those wishing to continue competitive athletics after an ACL injury, and the improved reconstruction techniques, may be broadening the indications for operative ACL reconstruction in the mature athlete.

Mature ligaments have been shown to have greater tensile strength than immature ligaments in a rabbit model.[31] Ligament strength then declines as the individual gets older.[32] In animal models, the substance of exercised ligaments is stronger, stiffer, and weighs more than unexercised ones.[33,34] These changes are maximized by relatively low-duration, high-frequency endurance training.[33] Thus, lifelong exercise can probably retard the effects of aging on ligament properties, although one study found little difference between the medial collateral ligaments of exercised and caged dogs.[32] Studies of human ACLs by Noyes and Grood[35] and Woo and associates[36] have shown that as these ligaments age, they weaken. This weakening includes age-related decreases in stiffness, ultimate load, failure energy, ultimate deformation, elastic modulus, and maximum stress and strain energy.

Exercise also strengthens the bone-ligament junction, another site where ligaments may fail.[34,37] Conversely, limb immobilization decreases the strength of knee ligament-bone junctions,[34,35,38] in addition to stimulating the progression of generalized degenerative joint disease.[39] Both animal and human studies have demonstrated widespread, subperiosteal cortical resorption and bony replacement by loosely arranged fibrous tissue at the ligament-bone junction site.[34,35,38] Immobilized ligaments tend to fail at these weakened junction sites.[34,35] This fibrous tissue can remineralize with increased activity, although it may require months to return to normal.[38]

An ACL-deficient knee generally has increased anterior translation in Lachman testing, pivot-shift, or KT-1000 arthrometer testing, or ACL rupture verified by MRI study or arthroscopy. Partial ACL tears often will progress to complete ACL tears. This progression appears to be related to the extent of the partial tear, the amount of initial anterior translation, and subsequent knee injury; it appears to be independent of other intra-articular damage or future demands placed on the knee.[40,41]

Conservative treatment of ACL-deficient knees consists of muscular rehabilitation, bracing, and activity modification (Fig. 2). Rehabilitation concentrates on strengthening the ipsilateral quadriceps and hamstrings muscles; better results are achieved when these muscles are within 10% of the contralateral muscle strength on Cybex testing.[29,42-44] Rehabilitation procedures used for the treatment of the young injured athlete are appropriate for the older athlete as well; however, several age-related factors should be considered.[45] There is a natural decrease in muscle mass and an increase in the stiffness of connective tissue. Therefore, a slower rate of healing and a longer period of recovery can be expected with age. It has been shown that rehabilitation is twice as long in the athlete over 60 years old as in one of 20.[46] Each program should be individualized with emphasis on longer warm-up and cool-down periods and general conditioning exercises to minimize the effects of increased connective tissue stiffness and to prevent cardiopulmonary deconditioning.

Commonly used functional knee braces are designed to constrain joint motion and increase the patient's proprioception.[23] These braces can improve a patient's ability to run figures-of-eight and make quick cuts without decreasing running speed, while reducing pain, instability, and episodes of giving way.[29,47] Still, half of those patients who wear a stabilization brace feel it moderately to severely limits their athletic performance.[29]

Modification of athletic activity after an ACL rupture seems to be a necessity and reality, whether or not it is a voluntary decision of the patient's based on a physician's recommendations. Physicians often discourage high-risk activities, such as those that require the intense quadriceps contraction of cutting, jumping, and deceleration moves, and encourage sports in which some knee flexion is maintained. This flexion allows the hamstrings muscles to provide a mechanical advantage by working as an additional stabilizer.[14] Regardless of the quality of rehabilitation or bracing, a minority of ACL-deficient athletes (30%) will reach their desired postinjury activity level and even fewer (5% to 14%) their preinjury level.[14,29,30,41,43,44] Although some results suggest that disability from ACL deficiency decreases as the athlete ages and chooses to engage in less strenuous sports,[30] this finding may be less applicable to the competitive midlife athlete.

In active patients, ACL deficiency predisposes the knee to further injury. From 19% to 35% of patients with ACL-deficient knees will reinjure the knee within the first 2 years following the initial injury, regardless of the method of rehabilitation or sport activity;

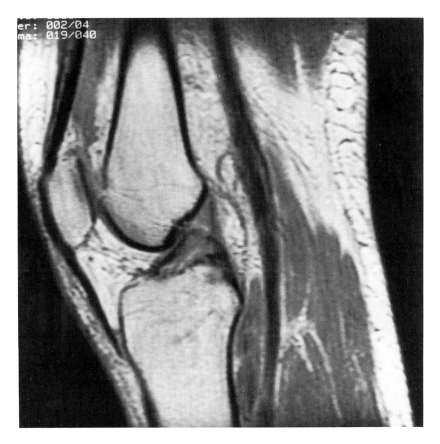

Fig. 2 *A 48-year-old with torn anterior cruciate ligament and torn posterior horn medial meniscus. The patient was treated with debridement of medial meniscal tear, physical therapy, and bracing.*

the risk of reinjury probably is related to the amount of initial instability and the frequency of giving way episodes.[30,40,41] Reinjuries include meniscal tears and articular cartilage damage, which may lead to accelerated joint destruction. Frequency of such injuries is inversely related to the patient's age.[29,43] Even without discrete, traumatic reinjury, the ACL deficient knee may develop mediolateral instability with time.[30,48] The overall laxity of the knee may predispose it to OA, although the incidence of OA seems to correlate more closely with related injuries such as meniscal tears.[48,49]

With longer follow-up, more patients (17% to 42%) become dissatisfied with their ACL-deficient knees and desire operative treatment.[29,30,42,43] The general indications for ACL reconstruction include high-grade instability, desire to continue participating in high-risk athletics, and relatively young age. However, advanced age should not be considered a contraindication to surgery if reconstruction is otherwise indicated.[50] Complete tear of another primary restraint, such as the medial collateral ligament, is also an indication for ACL reconstruction. ACL reconstruction alone is probably sufficient in combined ligamentous injuries, because complete collateral ligament tears can be treated nonsurgically.[51]

Earlier operative treatments, such as direct repair or augmented repair of the ruptured ACL, had unacceptably high failure rates.[42,52] Surgical techniques of extracapsular stabilization of ACL-deficient knees led to recurrent instability, even in short-term follow-up, and have been abandoned by most surgeons.[53,54]

Intra-articular ACL reconstruction has been performed using both dynamic transfers, such as semi-tendinous and biceps femoris tendon transfers, and static stabilizers, such as the middle third of the patella tendon, tendon allografts, and prosthetic ligaments. No published data directly compare dynamic transfers and static reconstruction; however, some authorities condemn the use of dynamic transfer for ACL reconstruction.[28] Reconstructions with prosthetic ligaments have been plagued by high failure rates and wear debris synovitis, and their use must still be considered experimental.[55] Autologous patella tendon ACL reconstruction, when combined with aggressive postoperative rehabilitation emphasizing early full extension and hamstring strengthening, has provided excellent patient satisfaction and ability to return to the preinjury level of athletic participation.[56] The morbidity of reconstruction is decreasing with arthroscopic-assisted techniques and the availability of allograft ligaments. The use of allograft bone-patella tendon-bone or Achilles tendon provides the surgeon with reliable tissue for reconstruction of the ACL and minimizes further insult to the knee[57] (Fig. 3). Although rehabilitation following ligament reconstruction is prolonged, the principles of early motion allow the mature athlete to resume daily activities after 3 to 4 months and full activities after 8 to 10 months.

Meniscus Injury

Although lower demand activities tend to place the mature athlete's knee at less risk for an injury such as an acute meniscal tear, aging itself renders the menisci more susceptible to injury. Increasing age is associated with meniscal changes. With maturation, the menisci develop an increased ratio of chondroitin-6-sulfate to chondroitin-4-sulfate, increased extractable proteoglycans, increased incidence of calcium pyrophosphate dihydrate deposition (CPPD) in the meniscal matrix and hydroxyapatite deposition in the meniscal vessels, and increasing foci of eosinophilic necrosis of collagen within the cartilage.[11,13] These microscopic changes probably contribute to the rising incidence of degenerative meniscal fraying, fissures, and horizontal splits found with increasing age.[13] These degenerative changes seem

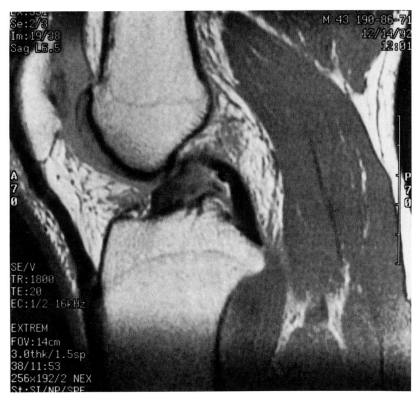

Fig. 3 *A 43-year-old recreational racquetball player sustained anterior cruciate tear left knee. The patient was treated with bone patellar tendon bone autograft for anterior cruciate reconstruction.*

to predispose the mature athlete to traumatic tears, particularly in the posterior horn of the medial meniscus.[13,49,58]

Total meniscectomy was once the accepted treatment for a symptomatic meniscal tear.[47,59] While this treatment provided short-term symptomatic relief of pain, follow-up studies have shown that the long-term effects of total meniscectomy include recurrent pain, knee joint laxity, instability and malalignment, and osteoarthritic changes such as joint space narrowing and flattening of the femoral condyles.[9,49,60]

Meniscal tears, particularly in the athlete over 30 years of age, are associated with degenerative chondromalacia of the articular surfaces.[58,61,62] This secondary chondromalacia may be inevitable once the meniscal damage has occurred, and its painful symptoms seem related to the amount of time passed since the meniscal tear.[58,62] Some authors feel the secondary chondromalacia may be avoided if the damaged meniscal tissue is removed promptly.[58] If significant intra-articular chondromalacia is present at the time of partial meniscectomy, results will be poorer than would be achieved with a more pristine knee.[58,61]

It is hoped that arthroscopic partial meniscectomy of meniscal tears in the mature athlete, like open total meniscectomy, can provide symptomatic relief without the common long-term effects of total meniscectomy.[58,61] Arthroscopic partial meniscectomy is now the treatment of choice for such lesions. The long-term results for mature athletes after an arthroscopic partial meniscectomy are not well documented; however, it is quite possible that many of these patients will experience the secondary degenerative changes of meniscal damage.

Vertical meniscal tears in the peripheral, vascularized region of the menisci have the potential to heal, thus avoiding the need for meniscectomy. Seventy percent of such "stable" tears will heal if the knee is adequately immobilized, and up to 90% heal if surgically repaired, even in the ligamentously unstable knee.[63-65] Unfortunately for the midlife athlete, the area of meniscal vascularization decreases with age, and these more benign tears tend to occur in younger athletes.[23] When one of these tears is later diagnosed as a chronic tear, it is unlikely to heal with repair and will probably require partial meniscectomy.[64] Avascular meniscal tears have been induced to heal in a canine model by placement of an exogenous fibrin clot at the site of the defect. The repair tissue was morphologically similar to reparative tissue found in the vascularized area of the meniscus.[66] The use of exogenous fibrin clots may extend the indications for meniscal repair in the mature athlete.

Chondromalacia

When malaligned, the patellofemoral joint experiences significant wear in athletes. Chondromalacia of the patella as a result of malalignment or dislocation is a frequent occurrence, and its sequelae often limit the intensity of athletic participation. The orthopaedic surgeon must carefully assess the patient clinically and radiographically to determine if the pain is secondary to articular cartilage lesions with or without malalignment, or evidence of tilt, subluxation, or a combination of these disorders.

If patients who have patellofemoral symptoms fail the nonoperative protocol described earlier for degenerative disorders of the knee joint, then they may be candidates for arthroscopic assessment. Patients who have isolated articular cartilage lesions and no malalignment or instability obviously will not benefit from realignment procedures. However, depending on the degree of articular cartilage wear, these patients may benefit from conservative arthroscopic debridement and lavage. Patients who have advanced patellofemoral arthritis are not candidates for realignment procedures, but age alone is not a contraindication.

Patients who have patellar tilt may respond to arthroscopic lateral release alone; however, adequate realignment may require more

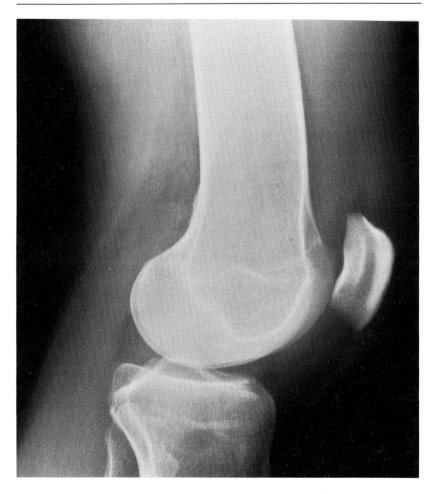

Fig. 4 *A 38-year-old with rupture of quadriceps tendon. Radiograph demonstrates knee effusion and defect in quadriceps tendon. The patient was treated with surgical repair of quadriceps mechanism.*

aggressive proximal and distal realignment procedures. Patients who have isolated patellar instability and those who have both instability and tilt usually will require both proximal and distal realignment procedures in addition to a lateral release.[67,68]

Extensor Mechanism Injury

Disruption of the extensor mechanism may occur in the older athlete. Both patellar ligament and quadriceps tendon ruptures have been described. Quadriceps tendon ruptures are reportedly more common in the older athlete.[69] Often there is a history of tendinitis prior to rupture, suggesting an underlying degenerative pathology. Quadriceps tendon ruptures should be repaired surgically. The prognosis for regaining full strength and resuming normal pain-free function is greater after patellar tendon than after quadriceps tendon disruptions[70] (Fig. 4).

Summary

The mature athlete faces not only the risk of acute athletic injuries, but also their effects combined with the aging process.[71] The physiologically aligned, ligamentously stable knee joint is capable of long-term athletic activity with minimal wear. The poorly aligned, unstable, or meniscus deficient knee will experience increased levels of articular cartilage wear and injury.

It is imperative that the dedicated midlife athlete maintain a program of cardiovascular fitness and appropriate resistive exercises in addition to specific sport participation. In that way, the mature athlete can extend participation in sport to later in life and maintain a high intensity level. It is the orthopaedist's challenge to assist these individuals in continuing to enjoy and compete in athletics while avoiding injuries or the development of disabling osteoarthritis.

References

1. Konradsen L, Hansen EMB, Sondergaard L: Long distance running and osteoarthrosis. *Am J Sports Med* 1990;18:379-381.

2. Lane NE, Bloch DA, Hubet HB, et al: Running, osteoarthritis, and bone density: Initial 2-year longitudinal study. *Am J Med* 1990;88:452-459.

3. Panush RS, Schmidt C, Caldwell JR, et al: Is running associated with degenerative joint disease? *JAMA* 1986;255:1152-1154.

4. Radin EL, Eyre D, Kelman JL, et al: Effect of prolonged walking on concrete on the joints of sheep. *Arthritis Rheum* 1979;22:649.

5. Videman T: The effect of running on the osteoarthritic joint: An experimental matched-pair study with rabbits. *Rheum Rehabil* 1982;21:1-8.

6. Shellock FG, Deutsch AL, Mink JH, et al: Do asymptomatic marathon runners have an increased prevalence of meniscal abnormalities? An MR study of the knee in 23 volunteers. *AJR* 1991;157:1239-1241.

7. Sohn RS, Micheli LJ: The effect of running on the pathogenesis of osteoarthritis of the hips and knees. *Clin Orthop* 1985;198:106-109.

8. Chantraine A: Knee joint in soccer players: Osteoarthritis and axis deviation. *Med Sci Sports Exerc* 1985;17:434-439.

9. Fairbank TJ: Knee joint changes after meniscectomy. *J Bone Joint Surg* 1948;30B:664-670.

10. Kohatsu ND, Schurman DJ: Risk factors for the development of osteoarthrosis of the knee. *Clin Orthop* 1990;261:242-246.

11. Woo SL-Y, Buckwalter JA (eds): *Injury and Repair of the Musculoskeletal Soft Tissues.* Park Ridge, IL, American Academy of Orthopaedic Surgeons, 1988.

12. Hastings D: Instability of the knee in mature athletes, in Sutton JR, Brock RM (eds): *Sports Medicine for the Mature Athlete.* Indianapolis, IN, Benchmark Press, 1986, chap 25, pp 265-269.

13. Meachim G: The state of knee meniscal fibrocartilage in Liverpool necropsies. *J Pathol* 1976;119:167-173.

14. Jackson RW: The masters knee: Past, present and future, in Sutton JR, Brock RM (eds): *Sports Medicine for the Mature Athlete*. Indianapolis, IN, Benchmark Press, 1986, chap 24 pp 257-263.

15. Fujisawa Y, Masuhara K, Shiomi S: The effect of high tibial osteotomy on osteoarthritis of the knee: An arthroscopic study of 54 knee joints. *Orthop Clin North Am* 1979;10:585-608.

16. Odenbring S, Egund N, Lindstrand A, et al: Cartilage regeneration after proximal tibial osteotomy for medial gonarthrosis. *Clin Orthop* 1992;277:210-216.

17. Coventry MB: Osteotomy about the knee for degenerative and rheumatoid arthritis: Indications, operative technique, and results. *J Bone Joint Surg* 1973;55A:23-48.

18. Ivarsson I, Myrnerts R, Gillquist J: High tibial osteotomy for medial osteoarthritis of the knee: A 5 to 7 and 11 year follow-up. *J Bone Joint Surg* 1990;72B:238-244.

19. Rudan JF, Simurda MA: Valgus high tibial osteotomy: A long-term follow-up study. *Clin Orthop* 1991;268:157-160.

20. McDermott AGP, Finklestein JA, Farine I, et al: Distal femoral varus osteotomy for valgus deformity of the knee. *J Bone Joint Surg* 1988;70A:110-116.

21. Johnson DP, Mansfield M: A new surgical procedure for treatment of cruciate deficient degenerative knee. Ninth Combined Meeting Orthopaedic Associations of the English Speaking World, Toronto, Canada, June 1992.

22. Parolie JM, Bergfeld JA: Long-term results of nonoperative treatment of isolated posterior cruciate ligament injuries in the athlete. *Am J Sports Med* 1986;14:35-38.

23. Daniel DM, Teitge RA, Grana WA, et al: Knee and leg: Soft tissue trauma, in *Orthopaedic Knowledge Update 3*. Park Ridge, IL, American Academy of Orthopaedic Surgeons, 1990, chap 43, pp 557-573.

24. Fowler PJ, Messieh SS: Isolated posterior cruciate ligament injuries in athletes. *Am J Sports Med* 1987;15:553-557.

25. Torg JS, Barton TM, Pavlov H, et al: Natural history of the posterior cruciate ligament-deficient knee. *Clin Orthop* 1989;246:208-216.

26. Baker CL, Norwood LA, Hughston JC: Acute combined posterior cruciate and posterolateral instability of the knee. *Am J Sports Med* 1984;12:204-208.

27. Hughston JC, Jacobson KE: Chronic posterolateral rotatory instability of the knee. *J Bone Joint Surg* 1985;67A:351-359.

28. Paulos L, Drawbert JP, Rosenberg TD: Knee and leg: Soft tissue trauma, in *Orthopaedic Knowledge Update 2*. Park Ridge, IL, American Academy of Orthopaedic Surgeons, 1987, chap 36, pp 411-425.

29. Bonamo JJ, Fay C, Firestone T: The conservative treatment of the anterior cruciate deficient knee. *Am J Sports Med* 1990;18:618-623.

30. Hawkins RJ, Misamore GW, Merritt TR: Followup of the acute nonoperated isolated anterior cruciate ligament tear. *Am J Sports Med* 1986;14:205-210.

31. Woo SL, Orlando CA, Gomez MA, et al: Tensile properties of the medial collateral ligament as a function of age. *J Orthop Res* 1986;4:133-141.

32. Wang CW, Weiss JA, Albright JP, et al: The effects of long term exercise of the structural and mechanical properties of the canine medial collateral ligament. *ASME Biomech Symp AMD* 1989;98:69.

33. Cabaud HE, Chatty A, Gildengorin V, et al: Exercise effects on the strength of the rat anterior cruciate ligament. *Am J Sports Med* 1980;8:79-86.

34. Tipton CM, Matthes RD, Maynard JA, et al: The influence of physical activity on ligaments and tendons. *Med Sci Sports* 1975;7:165-175.

35. Noyes FR, Grood ES: The strength of the anterior cruciate ligament in humans and rhesus monkeys: Age-related and species-related changes. *J Bone Joint Surg* 1976;58A:1074-1082.

36. Woo SL-Y, Young EP, Kwan MK: Fundamental studies in knee ligament mechanics, in Daniel DM, Akeson WH, O'Connor JJ (eds): *Knee Ligaments: Structure, Function, Injury, and Repair*. New York, NY, Raven Press, 1990, chap 7, pp 115-134.

37. Viidik A: Elasticity and tensile strength of the anterior cruciate ligament in rabbits as influenced by training. *Acta Physiol Scand* 1968;74:372-380.

38. Laros GS, Tipton CM, Cooper RR: Influence of physical activity on ligament insertions in the knees of dogs. *J Bone Joint Surg* 1971;53A:275-286.

39. Langenskild A, Michelsson JE, Videman T: Osteoarthritis of the knee in the rabbit produced by immobilization. *Acta Orthop Scand* 1979;50:1-14.

40. Finsterbush A, Frankl U, Matan Y, et al: Secondary damage to the knee after isolated injury of the anterior cruciate ligament. *Am J Sports Med* 1990;18:475-479.

41. Noyes FR, Mooar LA, Moorman CT III, et al: Partial tears of the anterior cruciate ligament: Progression to complete ligament deficiency. *J Bone Joint Surg* 1989;71B:825-833.

42. Andersson C, Odensten M, Gillquist J: Knee function after surgical or nonsurgical treatment of acute rupture of the anterior cruciate ligament: A randomized study with a long-term follow-up period. *Clin Orthop* 1991;264:255-263.

43. Noyes FR, Matthews DS, Mooar PA, et al: The symptomatic anterior cruciate-deficient knee: Part II. The results of rehabilitation, activity modification, and counseling on functional disability. *J Bone Joint Surg* 1983;65A:163-174.

44. Tegner Y, Lysholm J, Lysholm M, et al: Strengthening exercises for old cruciate ligament tears. *Acta Orthop Scand* 1986;57:130-134.

45. Perry J: Scientific basis of rehabilitation, in Stauffer ES (ed): *American Academy of Orthopaedic Surgeons Instructional Course Lectures XXIV*. St. Louis, MO, CV Mosby, 1985, chap 39, pp 385-388.

46. Brown M: Special considerations during rehabilitation of the aged athlete. *Clin Sports Med* 1989;8:893-901.

47. Marans HJ, Jackson RW, Piccinin J, et al: Functional testing of braces for anterior cruciate ligament-deficient knees. *Can J Surg* 1991;34:167-172.

48. McDaniel WJ Jr, Dameron TB Jr: Untreated ruptures of the anterior cruciate ligament: A follow-up study. *J Bone Joint Surg* 1980;62A:696-705.

49. Jones RE, Smith EC, Reisch JS: Effects of medial meniscectomy in patients older than forty years. *J Bone Joint Surg* 1978;60A:783-786.

50. Muller W: *The Knee: Form, Function, and Ligament Reconstruction*. Berlin, Germany, Springer-Verlag, 1983.

51. Indelicato PA: Non-operative treatment of complete tears of the medial collateral ligament of the knee. *J Bone Joint Surg* 1983;65A:323-329.

52. Kaplan N, Wickiewicz TL, Warren RF: Primary surgical treatment of anterior cruciate ligament ruptures: A long-term follow-up study. *Am J Sports Med* 1990;18:354-358.

53. Kochan A, Markolf KL, More RC: Anterior-posterior stiffness and laxity of the knee after major ligament reconstruction. *J Bone Joint Surg* 1984;66A:1460-1465.

54. Odensten M, Lysholm J, Gillquist J: Long-term follow-up study of a distal iliotibial band transfer (DIT) for anterolateral knee instability. *Clin Orthop* 1983;176:129-135.

55. Friedman MJ: Prosthetic anterior cruciate ligament. *Clin Sports Med* 1991;10:499-513.

56. Shelbourne KD, Whitaker HJ, McCarroll JR, et al: Anterior cruciate ligament injury: Evaluation of intraarticular reconstruction of acute tears without repair: Two to seven year follow-up of 155 athletes. *Am J Sports Med* 1990;18:484-489.

57. Indelicato PA, Linton RC, Huegel M: The results of fresh-frozen patellar tendon allografts for chronic anterior cruciate ligament deficiency of the knee. *Am J Sports Med* 1992;20:118-121.

58. Dandy DJ, Jackson RW: Meniscectomy and chondromalacia of the femoral condyle. *J Bone Joint Surg* 1975;57A:1116-1119.

59. Smillie IS: *Injuries of the Knee Joint*, ed 5. Edinburgh, Churchill Livingstone, 1978.

60. Jorgensen U, Sonne-Holm S, Lauridsen F, et al: Long-term follow-up of meniscectomy in athletes: A prospective longitudinal study. *J Bone Joint Surg* 1987;69B:80-83.

61. Jackson RW, Rouse DW: The results of partial arthroscopic meniscectomy in patients over 40 years of age. *J Bone Joint Surg* 1982;64B:481-485.

62. Litchman HM, Silver CM, Simon SD: Injuries to the medial meniscus in the aging patient. *JAMA* 1966;196:178-180.

63. Hanks GA, Gause TM, Handal JA, et al: Meniscus repair in the anterior cruciate deficient knee. *Am J Sports Med* 1990;18:606-613.

64. Sommerlath K, Hamberg P: Healed meniscal tears in unstable knees: A long-term follow-up of seven years. *Am J Sports Med* 1989;17:161-163.

65. Weiss CB, Lundberg M, Hamberg P, et al: Nonoperative treatment of meniscal tears. *J Bone Joint Surg* 1989;71A:811-822.

66. Arnoczky SP, Warren RF, Spivak JM: Meniscal repair using an exogenous fibrin clot: An experimental study in dogs. *J Bone Joint Surg* 1988;70A:1209-1217.

67. Fondren FB, Goldner JL, Bassett FH: Recurrent dislocation of the patella treated by the modified Roux-Goldthwait procedure: A prospecive study of fourty-seven knees. *J Bone Joint Surg* 1985;67A:993-1005.

68. Fulkerson JP, Shea KP: Disorders of patellofemoral alignment. *J Bone Joint Surg* 1990;72A:1424-1429.

69. Justis EJ Jr: Traumatic disorders, in Crenshaw AH (ed): *Campbell's Operative Orthoaedics*, ed 7. St. Louis, MO, CV Mosby, 1987, chap 53, vol 3, pp 2221-2246.

70. Kelly DW, Carter VS, Jobe FW, et al: Patellar and quadriceps tendon ruptures: Jumper's knee. *Am J Sports Med* 1984;12:375-380.

71. Menard D, Stanish WD: The aging athlete. *Am J Sports Med* 1989;17:187-196.

Chapter 30

The Effects of the Aging Process on Muscle and Tendon Injuries

Peter Jokl, MD

Introduction

"Each species has a characteristic average fixed life span that refers to the number of years of life expected from birth for an individual or a group. In contrast to the fixed human life span, life expectancy is increasing rapidly in most countries. Increasing life expectancy is thus converging with the fixed life span."[1] Fries and Crapo,[1] outline the current understanding of why life expectancy is increasing in all industrialized countries in the world. Although modern genetic engineering offers the future possibility of modifying life span, it is expected that present-day humans will not significantly surpass the maximal human life span, estimated to be 90 to 100 years.[1]

By controlling our environment, that is, providing adequate nutrition and preventing or curing most infectious diseases, the advances of modern science have significantly increased life expectancy. Presently, medical researchers are seeking cures for viral diseases, neoplasms, and degenerative diseases, such as cardiovascular and neurologic disorders, that limit maximal genetic potential.

Sports physicians are being introduced to a large pool of high-performance athletes of advanced age who are in virtually perfect health. These masters and senior athletes participate at a level of athletic achievement unforeseen at the beginning of the 20th century. Improvements in world records during this century for all athletic activities are reflected in similarly rapid improvements in masters and senior athletic performance records (Figs. 1 and 2).[2]

Despite these remarkable improvements, the average age for the world-record performer has remained relatively stable. In track and field, for example, power anaerobic activities such as sprinting events and field events are the domain of athletes with an average age of 22 to 23 years. In contrast, the longer, aerobic running events

Record Physiology

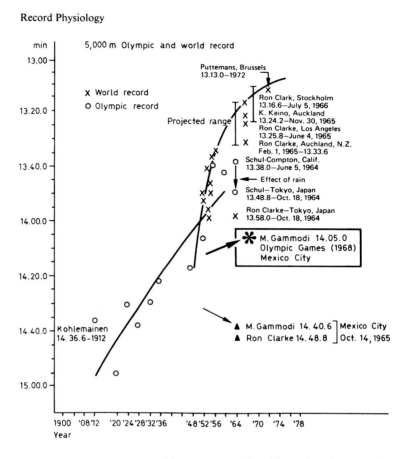

Fig. 1 *Graphic representation of the progression of world record performances in the 5,000 meter run for men. Of note is the steady improvement in world record performances since the beginning of this century. In more recent times, the curve is becoming asymptotic, predicting a decline in the rate of improvement of record performances. (Reproduced with permission from Jokl E: Record physiology, in Medicine and Sport. Basel, Switzerland, S Karger, 1976, vol 9, p 5.)*

favor slightly older athletes, averaging 27 years of age. This particular age difference for long- and short-duration athletic performances is not found in swimmers. Other sports, such as tennis and baseball, similarly favor slightly older individuals, averaging 30 years of age.[3]

Young age no longer appears to be the single requirement for an individual to maintain athletic competency. The main criteria for an athlete to achieve his or her potential are adequate nutrition, absence of disease, and the time and desire to continue to train and compete. Present observations indicate that the age-related decline in physiologic parameters can be modified or delayed, but not totally inhibited, by physical training.

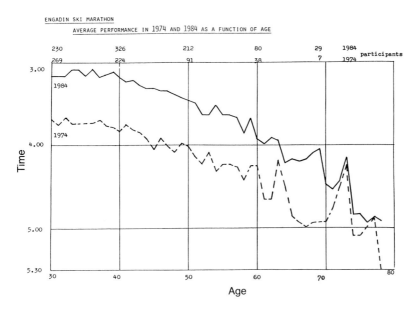

Fig. 2 *Graphic representation of Scandinavian long-distance ski performances in 1974 and 1984, showing improvement in performance times by all age groups during this period.*

Differentiation of disuse atrophy and age-related tissue changes are reviewed in this paper. Their impact from a physiologic and biochemical viewpoint are explored. Their potential effect on muscle and tendon function, overuse, and acute injury in the midlife athlete are discussed. Application of this information to appropriate training techniques and prophylaxis for the older athletes' muscle and tendon injuries are hypothesized.

Physiologic Changes in Normal Tendon and Muscle

Heretofore accepted age-related physiologic changes are modifiable by physical training. Many of the age-attributed degenerative changes in muscle function and, possibly, in tendon tissue appear, in part, to represent disuse atrophy. However, despite modifications in the aging process through training, genetically programmed degenerative changes in muscle and tendon are inevitable.

Physiologic Changes Related to Aging in Normal Muscle

Significant information is available to indicate that the general physiologic decline of various organ systems usually begins in the third to fourth decades (Fig. 3).[4] Some of the physiologic changes in muscle

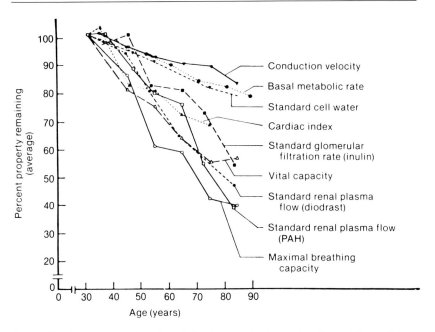

Fig. 3 *Graphic representation of declining human physiologic functions with age. It is generally accepted that between the ages of 30 and 40, all human physiologic functions begin a gradual decline. (Reproduced with permission from Shock NW: The science of gerontology, in Jeffers EC (ed): Proceedings of Seminars 1959-61, Durham, NC, Council on Gerontology. Durham, NC, Duke University Press, 1962.)*

that generally are attributed to aging are listed in Outline 1.[5] Age-related diminution of muscle strength, speed of contraction, reflex time, and muscle efficiency are all well documented.[6,7] Of historical significance is the study of Quetelet (1835),[8] indicating significant loss of muscle strength by age 65. In contrast, more modern studies have shown a modest decline of muscle function, averaging 18% to 20% between the ages of 45 and 65 years.[9] Macro-, micro-, and ultra-structural age-related changes in muscle are delineated in Outlines 2 and 3. Age-specific loss of type II fibers have been observed, explaining a greater loss of power and speed capability than of endurance in the older athlete.[5,10-13]

Studies of the aging process have raised the hypothesis that a significant number of the observed changes in muscle function attributed to aging may indeed represent disuse atrophy.[7] In a review article by Convertino,[14] which describes rapid atrophy of muscles in astronauts exposed to short periods of weightlessness, a selective atrophy of type II fibers is noted. Although the circumstances are different, many of the physiologic findings noted in Convertino's article on astronauts are similar to those "degenerative" musculoskeletal changes previously attributed to aging.[15] Table 1 indicates that in a

Outline 1 Physiologic changes of skeletal muscle with aging*

Decreased handgrip strength	Increased half relaxation time
Decreased functional motor units	Increased electromyographic recruitment
Decreased number muscle fibers	Increased endurance relative to type II anaerobic muscle function
Decreased quadriceps strength	Increased CA^{2+} transport by sarcoplasmic reticulum
Decreased isometric strength	
Decreased muscle contraction speed	

* Many of these parameters may, in fact, represent, to a significant degree, skeletal muscle accommodations to disuse atrophy.

Outline 2 Macro- and micro-anatomic changes in skeletal muscle with aging

Loss of lean tissue
Skeletal muscle wasting
Sarcoplasmal nuclei
Central nuclei
Interstitial fibrosis
Ragged red changes
Cell infiltration
Target information

Outline 3 Ultrastructural skeletal muscle changes with aging

Z-Band streaming
Nemaline rod formation
Lamellar figures
Myofilament whorls
Accumulation of lipopigment
Myelin figures
Curvilinear bodies
Deformity of muscle nuclei
Abnormal satellite cells
Increased mitochondria
Dilatation of sarcotubular system
Thickening of capillary basement membrane
Thickened subsynaptic fold
Decreased diameter of type II fibers
Hypertrophy of the sarcoplasmic reticulum

large group of midlife elite athletes, high levels of athletic performances can be maintained into the fifth and sixth decades of life. Other studies indicate "reversibility" of degenerative muscle changes attributed to aging. Specific training in the form of resistance and endurance exercise led to selective hypertrophy of muscle fibers of athletes into the sixth, seventh, and eighth decades of life.[12,13,15]

While certain age-related degenerative changes in muscle are reversible, other age-related changes of tissue structure and function seem to be irreversible.[16-18] Kavanagh and Shephard[19] noted an age-related diminution of best athletic performances, starting at age 40

Table 1 Performance of male contestants relative to current world record speed for their age and distance (mean percent ± standard deviation)

Age (years)	Sprint (meters)	Middle Distance (meters)	Long Distance (meters)
<40	88.8 ± 5.1	—	86.1 ± 10.3
40-50	86.4 ± 5.7	88.3 ± 7.2	82.8 + 8.1
50-60	88.2 ± 4.6	87.3 ± 6.6	82.9 ± 10.0
60-70	76.6 ± 3.9	73.1 ± 7.1	81.1 ± 6.7
70-90	63.8 ± 3.1	—	—

(Reproduced with permission from Kavanagh T, Shephard RJ: The effects of continued training on the aging process. *Ann N Y Acad Sci* 1977;301:658.)

and progressing to the ninth decade of life. It appears that despite high levels of training in elite masters and senior athletes, the aging process cannot be totally reversed.[20] Concentric muscle strength seems to be more vulnerable to maturation than eccentric muscle strength.[16] In contrast, aerobic capacity of aging muscle appears to be more resistant to changes with time than the anaerobic power function of type II muscle fibers.[21] Age-related changes of myosin heavy-chain isoforms have been noted in the contractile proteins of types I, IIA, and IIB fibers.[22] Although significant hypertrophy of muscle fibers can occur at all ages, the concomitant growth of surrounding capillaries that occurs with endurance training appears to become inhibited with increasing age.[23] Evidently, the aging process can be modified, but not reversed, with intense training throughout life.[12]

Physiologic Changes Relating to Aging in Normal Tendons and Ligaments

Physiologic changes in aging tendons and ligaments have been less intensively studied than those changes in muscle. Age-related tendon and ligament changes include an increase in collagen fibril size with age. A marked decrease in the ratio of cell to extracellular matrix is noted with increasing age in animal studies. An increase in the insoluble collagen content of tendon occurs with aging, although elastin and glycosaminoglycan levels appear to be unaffected. Water content in ligaments generally decreases with age, and this decrease is associated with age-related decreases in chondroitin sulfate and hyaluronic acid. The density of the capillary network in tendons also decreases with age.[20,24,25] Increased cross-linking of ligament collagen occurs with maturation, contributing to a stronger biomechanical structure.[26] Occasional areas of calcific metaplasia may be noted. A decrease in the ligament collagen turnover rate was noted in two-year-old rats.[24]

Biomechanical Changes With Aging in Normal Muscle and Tendon

Biomechanical Changes Related to Aging in Muscle

Little documentation is available on age-related biomechanical changes of muscle. There is no evidence that the general injury pattern in muscle strain injuries delineated by Garrett and Tidball[27,28] are changed with aging, the primary area of failure remaining at the musculotendinous junction. No data were found on the effect of direct trauma on muscle at different ages.

Biomechanical Changes Related to Aging in Normal Tendon

Studies of biomechanical changes in ligaments and tendons of young animals appear to show increasing strength and tension with maturation.[29,30] Ligament failure in young animals occurs at the ligament-bone junction. This site of failure changes after epiphyseal closure, with failure then occurring as a midsubstance tear.[30] In their studies of the changes of ligament properties in immature and mature rabbits, Woo and associates[29] showed that in immature rabbits ligaments gain strength at a faster rate than do their attachments to bone, thereby explaining the early avulsion of tendons under stress conditions from their bony insertions or origins. The bone-tendon junction strengthens with maturation and activity, causing failure to occur in the midsubstance of the ligaments.[31,32]

However, with increasing age, a diminution of ligament and tendon strength is noted. Tipton and associates[33] have shown that elastic stiffness, failure energy, and collagen concentration increase in rat ligaments with maturation; concomitantly, water content of the ligaments decreases. Although findings by Kennedy and associates[34] and Trent and associates[35] show variations of tendon and ligament strength with age, other studies on spinal ligaments by Nachemson and Evans[36] showed significant decreases in strength of human spinal ligaments and in ligamentum flavum with age. A more definitive study has been done on human cadaver knees by Noyes and Grood,[37] who compared anterior cruciate ligament failures in younger adults (16 to 26 years) and older adults (48 to 86 years). These studies showed a two- to threefold decrease in elastic modulus, ultimate tensile stress, and strain energy to failure in the older specimens compared to the younger specimens. Of interest is the fact that the method of failure in the older specimens was the immature mode of disruption at the bone-tendon junction due to osteoporotic changes in the bone.[37]

Many of the "degenerative changes" attributed to aging in tendons, may, as in muscles, be due to disuse. Butler and associates[38] have reviewed the effects of immobilization on the biomechanical properties of ligaments and found significant losses in stiffness, maximum load at failure, and energy absorbed to failure. Although reconditioning reverses these changes to a significant degree, the return to normal function requires a prolonged period of time, much longer than the period of enforced disuse.[38] It is possible that ligament failure associated with aging represents both the effects of disuse and the subsequent slow response of ligaments to reconditioning in midlife athletes.

Specific injury types noted in animal models may, in turn, explain clinically documented age-related ligamentous injuries. For example, soft-tissue injury of muscle or ligament, may largely represent atrophic tissue changes.[38] What is clear from this review[38] is that animal model studies do not evaluate the ligament changes with aging that are similar to those seen in midlife athletes. Furthermore, neither the animal nor human studies take into consideration the effects of continuous physical activities on age-related degenerative changes in tendon and muscle.

In summary, it appears that with increasing age, changes in the biomechanical properties of ligaments and tendons result in loss of strength and loss of energy-absorptive properties. Exercise increases the strength of tendons, reversing some, but probably not all, degenerative changes.[31,32]

Pathophysiology and Biomechanics of Sport-Related Injuries

Overuse Injuries

Soft-tissue injuries among athletes, and particularly in midlife participants, are a common occurrence.[39] The relatively high incidence of soft-tissue injuries in masters athletes, up to 50% per year, has been attributed to loss of muscle flexibility, slower relaxation time, and increased connective tissue stiffness, all of which are associated with aging.[40] Kavanagh and Shephard[19] have shown that almost 40% of masters athletes sustain injuries every year that prevent their participation in their individual sport activities. Almost 27% are incapacitated for 1 to 4 weeks. The fact that 53% of long-distance runners, compared to 26% of sprinters, sustained incapacitating injuries suggests that overuse activities may represent a major cause of disability to midlife athletes.[19] Table 2 displays the anatomic areas most commonly involved in overuse injuries in runners. Sporting activities other than running also show a relatively high incidence of injuries attributable to overuse.[41]

For purposes of this review, overuse injuries of soft tissue are divided into two categories: muscle tissue and tendon and connective tissue.

Muscle Overuse Injuries

Muscle overuse injuries can be categorized into two areas: injuries involving the muscle cell (the contractile proteins and the surround-

Table 2 Chronic prolonged problems reported by runners*

Anatomic Site	Injuries Reported (%)
Knee	23.2
Shin	14.6
Achilles	12.4
Forefoot	8.3
Hip	7.9
Thigh	7.5
Calf	7.0
Heel	7.0
Ankle	6.7
Arch	4.2
Groin	2.2

*Results of a poll of over 1,000 respondents of whom 60% reported prolonged injuries. (Reproduced with permission from Sheehan GA: An overview of overuse syndromes in distance runners. *Ann N Y Acad Sci* 1977;301:879.)

ing connective tissue envelope) and injuries involving the musculotendinous junction. A common example of overuse injury of muscle tissue is muscle pain, which occurs after athletic activities that are either new to the muscle groups involved or of an unaccustomed intensity.

Muscle appears to be particularly susceptible to injury following eccentric contraction overuse.[33,42] Eccentric muscle activity is defined as the lengthening of contracted muscle against resistance, more commonly known among body building aficionados as "negative lifting." Eccentric muscle contraction is in contrast to the more commonly discussed concentric contraction of muscle, in which the muscle actively shortens while lifting a given resistance ("positive lifting").

Although most athletic activities require coordination of both eccentric and concentric muscle activities, it appears that the eccentric portion of muscle contraction is particularly irritating and potentially damaging to contractile tissue.[42] Certain sporting activities, predominantly those involving eccentric muscle contraction, such as running downhill or lowering heavy weights, have been noted to induce muscle pain and inflammation. Various theories of how this type of eccentric muscle activity induces injury are described. The most probable cause is direct muscle fiber damage, which in turn induces an inflammatory response causing pain, edema, and transient muscle weakness.[43] Evidence of associated connective tissue damage within muscle as a result of eccentric contractions has also been hypothesized.[42] The release of the intracellular contents of damaged fibroblasts contributes to the inflammatory response as noted above.[28,42]

The second area of vulnerability in muscle associated with overuse activities is the musculotendinous junction.[44-46] Biomechanical studies on muscle under tension indicate consistent failure at the musculotendinous junction; weakness at this site may render the area susceptible to overuse activity, which causes inflammatory and reparative changes.[28] Tidball[28] wrote that the musculotendinous junction concentrates the forces that are generated by the contracting myofibrils; thus, on a molecular as well as on a biomechanical basis, the musculotendinous junction is susceptible to overuse injury.

Tendon and Ligament Overuse Injuries

Tendon and ligamentous injuries associated with overuse activities have been well documented. Nirschl[47] described the most susceptible areas of chronic discomfort associated with sporting activities as the tendon and ligament structures. His observations on overuse injuries do not appear to be specifically related to age. Overuse injuries are seen in athletes of all ages, although their effects are more difficult to overcome in midlife and senior athletes.[47]

A case in point is the well-studied Achilles tendon rupture, which occurs most commonly between 30 and 50 years of age.[48-50] There are few data explaining why this injury occurs in midlife, but two hypotheses have been proposed. One suggests that rupture is secondary to chronic, age-related degeneration of the tendon due to devitalization and fibrosis.[51] This observation, however, was contradicted in a study by Hooker,[52] who noted inconsistent findings of degenerative changes associated with Achilles tendon ruptures. The second theory suggests that a loss of protective inhibitory muscle contractile function allows uncoordinated muscle contractions causing rupture of the Achilles tendon.[53] Jozsa and associates,[48] in a study of Hungarian recreational athletes, noted a significantly higher incidence of Achilles tendon rupture in individuals who had relatively sedentary life-styles than in athletes. Christensen[53] seconded the findings of Jozsa, emphasizing lack of training and conditioning as a contributing cause of tendon ruptures. He observed that in 50% of the 26 Achilles tendon ruptures studied, the patients were not appropriately prepared for their athletic activities.[53] Josza speculated that an additional predisposing cause of this injury is a "disturbance" in the nutrition of the Achilles tendon due to a sedentary life-style. Of interest is another study by Jozsa and associates,[49] showing a correlation of blood group type O with Achilles tendon ruptures. Furthermore, tendon rerupture was also highly correlated with blood group type O. This particular finding, however, was not correlated with age.[49]

The example of Achilles tendon injuries again emphasizes the roles of disuse atrophy and inadequate training (allowing inadequate time for accommodation to increased stress) in contributing to the failure of the tendon. The fact that Achilles tendon ruptures are clustered around midlife indicates that a combination of disuse atrophy and age-related degenerative changes combine to produce failure of the tissue structures.

Age-Related Healing Responses in Muscle and Tendon

Normal Healing Response

The histologic and biomolecular processes involved in muscle and tendon healing are well documented.[45] In muscle injury, activation of satellite cells is required as part of the reparative process. Healing of a major muscle injury represents an imbalance between reconstitution of muscle fibers and proliferation of granulating scar tissue, the latter blocking the former.[54] Although some studies suggest that the healing process is retarded with age, little definitive evidence is available.[1,55] Similarly, the repair of tendon tissue appears to involve an organized process of healing induced by damaged connective tissue cells.[56]

Delayed Healing

Multiple factors may influence the healing process, including vascular insufficiency, diabetes, and age.[56] Nirschl[47] wrote that "physiologic age is probably a major cause of failed healing in connective tissue injuries." However, a controlled study of eccentric muscle contraction overuse injury in young (23.6 ± 3.3 years old) and older (60+ year old) women revealed no difference in time to recovery from this injury. In the acute phase, static contraction of overused muscle was greater in the older subjects; otherwise, recovery from the overuse injury was the same in both groups.[57]

Injury Prevention

The Effect of Training on Injury Prevention

The major determinant in preventing chronic athletic overuse injury is the appropriateness of training. Overuse injuries of muscle can be prevented by instituting a program that allows both the contractile elements and the surrounding connective tissue of muscle to accommodate to this repeated stress. A short period of training, as little as six weeks, can prevent muscle overuse injuries.[42] Furthermore, prophylactic training, including stretching and "warming up" of muscles prior to activity allows these structures to absorb a significantly greater amount of energy before failing.[58,59] Primary muscle injury represents almost half of all injuries noted in certain sporting activities.[60] Garrett and associates,[44] in an animal model, showed that a preconditioning maximal stimulation of muscle significantly increased the energy absorbed in the structures before failure. It did not, however, change the location of failure, which continued to be at the musculotendinous junction.[44]

Training Techniques

Proper training techniques can, in theory, help athletes to avoid chronic injuries. The possibility of muscle fatigue leading to greater susceptibility to injury has been suggested in an animal model.[61] Thus, appropriate training regimens that avoid excessive muscle fatigue are helpful in the prevention of muscle injury.[61] Overuse injuries represent a major proportion of incapacitating injuries in all athletes; therefore, training activities should be modified to prevent overuse of particular muscle or ligament complexes. Modern training programs advocating cross training to prevent overuse of particular anatomic structures may result in lower injury rates.

In addition, tissue adaptation to repeated stresses should be investigated to learn the appropriate increases in load that allow biologic accommodation.[62] It may be necessary in the older athletes to allow a longer period of time for physiologic tissue accommodation to occur. Klein and associates,[63] in a study on human subjects, demonstrated a longer recovery time in artificially stimulated muscles in trained, elderly individuals as compared to a younger group of athletes. Tissue turnover and repair may proceed at a slower rate with aging, thus requiring longer periods of adaptation.

The possibility that pharmacologic agents to enhance athletic performance may place the user at risk for increased soft-tissue injury has been proposed. The negative effects of anabolic steroids on the biomechanical and histologic properties of tendon have been documented in an animal model.[64] The potential for a small possible gain in muscle function with the use of anabolic steroids could well be nullified by the detrimental effects of these drugs on the biomechanical properties of the musculotendinous junction and on the tendon itself. The use of anabolic steroids in treating chronic tendon or muscle injuries appears to be contraindicated.[60]

In summary, there appears to be a genetically programmed aging of tissue that results in biologic, clinical, and performance changes. Loss of function associated with age can be slowed, but not reversed, through physical training. However, the risk of injury in midlife athletes can be modified or prevented through appropriate training.

References

1. Fries JF, Crapo LM: *Vitality and Aging: Implications of the Rectangular Curve*. San Francisco, CA, WH Freeman & Co, 1981.

2. Jokl E: *Physiology of Exercise*. Springfield, IL, Charles C. Thomas Publishers, 1964.

3. Schulz R, Curnow C: Peak performance and age among superathletes: Track and field, swimming, baseball, tennis, and golf. *J Gerontol* 1988;43:113-120.

4. Jeffers FC (ed): *Council on Gerontology*. Proceedings of Seminars, 1955-56. Durham, NC, Duke University Press, 1956.

5. Jokl P: The biology of aging muscle: Quantitative versus qualitative findings of performance capacity and age, in Nelson CL, Dwyer AP (eds): *The Aging Musculoskeletal System: Physiological and Pathological Problems*. Lexington, MA, Collamor Press, 1984, pp 49-58.

6. Reed RL, Pearlmutter L, Yochum K, et al: The relationship between muscle mass and muscle strength in the elderly. *J Am Geriatr Soc* 1991;39:555-561.

7. Bemben MG, Massey BH, Bemben DA, et al: Isometric muscle force production as a function of age in healthy 20- to 74-year-old men. *Med Sci Sports Exerc* 1991;23:1302-1310.

8. Quetelet A: *Sur L'Homme et le Developpement de ses Facultés.* Paris, Bachelier, Imprimeuer-Librarie, 1835.

9. Shephard RJ, Sidney KH: Exercise and aging. *Exerc Sport Sci Rev* 1978;6:1-57.

10. Caccia MR, Harris JB, Johnson MA: Morphology and physiology of skeletal muscle in aging rodents. *Muscle Nerve* 1979;2:202-212.

11. Clarkson PM, Kroll W, Melchionda AM: Age, isometric strength, rate of tension development and fiber type composition. *J Gerontol* 1981;36:648-653.

12. Brown AB, McCartney N, Sale DG: Positive adaptations to weight-lifting training in the elderly. *J Appl Physiol* 1990;69:1725-1733.

13. Melichna J, Zauner CW, Havlickova L, et al: Morphologic differences in skeletal muscle with age in normally active human males and their well-trained counterparts. *Hum Biol* 1990;62:205-220.

14. Convertino VA: Physiological adaptations to weightlessness: Effects on exercise and work performance. *Exerc Sport Sci Rev* 1990;18:119-166.

15. Charette SL, McEvoy L, Pykal G, et al: Muscle hypertrophy response of resistance training in older women. *J Appl Physiol* 1991;70:1912-1916.

16. Vandervoort AA, Kramer JF, Wharram ER: Eccentric knee strength of elderly females. *J Gerontol* 1990;43:125-128.

17. Grassi B, Cerretelli P, Norici MV, et al: Peak anaerobic power in master athletes. *Eur J Appl Physiol* 1991;62:394-399.

18. Kasch FW: The effects of exercise on the aging process. *Physician Sportsmed* 1976;4,64-69.

19. Kavanagh T, Shephard RJ: The effects of continued training on the aging process. *Ann N Y Acad Sci* 1977;301:656-670.

20. Butler DL, Siegel A: Alterations in tissue response: Conditioning effects at different ages, in Leadbetter WB, Buckwalter JA, Gordon SL (eds): *Sports-Induced Inflammation: Clinical and Basic Science Concepts.* Park Ridge, IL, American Academy of Orthopaedic Surgeons, 1990, pp 713-730.

21. Laforest S, St-Pierre DM, Cyr J, et al: Effects of age and regular exercise on muscle strength and endurance. *Eur J Appl Physiol* 1990;60:104-111.

22. Klitgaard H, Zhou M, Schiaffino S, et al: Ageing alters the myosin heavy chain composition of single fibres from human skeletal muscle. *Acta Physiol Scand* 1990;140:55-62.

23. Dennis C, Chatard JC, Dormois D, et al: Effects of endurance training on capillary supply of human skeletal muscle on two age groups (20 and 60 years). *J Physiol (Paris)* 1986;81:379-383.

24. Ippolito E, Natali PG, Postacchini F, et al: Morphological, immunochemical, and biochemical study of rabbit Achilles tendon at various ages. *J Bone Joint Surg* 1980;62A:583-598.

25. Ippolito E, Postacchini F, Ricciardi-Pollini PT: Biochemical variations in the matrix of human tendons in relation to age and pathological conditions. *Ital J Orthop Traumatol* 1975;1:133-139.

26. Viidik A: Connective tissues: Possible implications of the temporal changes for the aging process. *Mech Ageing Dev* 1979;9:267-285.

27. Garrett WE Jr, Tidball JG: Myotendinous junctions: Structure function, and failure, in Woo SL-Y, Buckwalter JA (eds): *Injury and Repair of the Musculoskeletal Soft Tissues.* Park Ridge, IL, American Academy of Orthopaedic Surgeons, 1988, pp 171-207.

28. Tidball JG: Myotendinous junction injury in relation to junction structure and molecular composition. *Exerc Sport Sci Rev* 1991;19:419-445.

29. Woo SL-Y, Orlando CA, Gomez MA, et al: Tensile properties of the medial collateral ligament as a function of age. *J Orthop Res* 1986;4:133-141.

30. Woo SL-Y, Weiss JA, Gomez MA, et al: Measurement of changes in ligament tension with knee motion and skeletal maturation. *J Biomech Eng* 1990;112:46-51.

31. Noyes FR, Torvik PJ, Hyde WB, et al: Biomechanics of ligament failure: II. An analysis of immobilization, exercise, and reconditioning effects in primates. *J Bone Joint Surg* 1974;56A:1406-1418.

32. Tipton CM, James SL, Mergner W, et al: Influence of exercise on strength of medial collateral knee ligaments of dogs. *Am J Physiol* 1970;218:894-902.

33. Tipton CM, Matthes RD, Martin RK: Influence of age and sex on the strength of bone-ligament junctions in knee joints of rats. *J Bone Joint Surg* 1978;60A:230-234.

34. Kennedy JC, Hawkins RJ, Willis RB, et al: Tension studies of human knee ligaments: Yield point, ultimate failure, and disruption of the cruciate and tibial collateral ligaments. *J Bone Joint Surg* 1976;58A:350-355.

35. Trent PS, Walker PS, Wolf B: Ligament length patterns, strength and rotational axes of the knee joint. *Clin Orthop* 1976;117:263-270.

36. Nachemson AL, Evans JH: Some mechanical properties of the third human lumbar interlaminar ligament (ligamentum flavum). *J Biomech* 1968;1:211-220.

37. Noyes FR, Grood ES: The strength of the anterior cruciate ligament in human and rhesus monkeys. *J Bone Joint Surg* 1976;58A:1074-1082.

38. Butler DL, Grood ES, Noyes FR, et al: Biomechanics of ligaments and tendons. *Exerc Sport Sci Rev* 1978;6:125-181.

39. Kilbom A, Hartley LH, Saltin B, et al: Physical training in sedentary middle-aged and older men: I. Medical evaluation. *Scand J Clin Lab Invest* 1969;24:315-322.

40. Hall DA: Metabolic and structural aspects of aging, in Brocklehurst JC (ed): *Textbook of Geriatric Medicine and Gerontology*. Edinburg, Churchill-Livingstone, 1973.

41. Sheehan GA: An overview of overuse syndromes in distance runners. *Ann N Y Acad Sci* 1977;301:877-880.

42. Stauber WT: Eccentric action of muscles: Physiology injury and adaptation. *Exerc Sport Sci Rev* 1989;17:157-185.

43. Evans WJ, Cannon JG: The metabolic effects of exercise-induced muscle damage. *Exerc Sport Sci Rev* 1991;19:99-125.

44. Garrett WE Jr, Safran MR, Seaber AV, et al: Biomechanical comparison of stimulated and nonstimulated skeletal muscle pulled to failure. *Am J Sports Med* 1987;15:448-454.

45. Russell B, Dix DJ, Haller DL, et al: Repair of injured skeletal muscle: A molecular approach. *Med Sci Sports Exerc* 1992;24:189-196.

46. Tidball JG, Chan M: Adhesive strength of single muscle cells to basement membrane at myotendinous junctions. *J Appl Physiol* 1989;67:1063-1069.

47. Nirschl RP: Patterns of failed healing in tendon injury, in Leadbetter WB, Buckwalter JA, Gordon SL (eds): *Sports-Induced Inflammation: Clinical and Basic Science Concepts*. Park Ridge, IL, American Academy of Orthopaedic Surgeons, 1990, pp 577-585.

48. Jozsa L, Kvist M, Balint BJ, et al: The role of recreational sport activity in Achilles tendon rupture: A clinical, pathoanatomical, and sociological study of 292 cases. *Am J Sports Med* 1989;17:338-343.

49. Jozsa L, Balint JB, Kannus P, et al: Distribution of blood groups in patients with tendon rupture: An analysis of 832 cases. *J Bone Joint Surg* 1989;71B:272-274.

50. Beskin JL, Sanders RA, Hunter SC, et al: Surgical repair of Achilles tendon ruptures. *Am J Sports Med* 1987;15:1-8.

51. Fox JM, Blazina ME, Jobe FW, et al: Degeneration and rupture of the Achilles tendon. *Clin Orthop* 1975;107:221-224.

52. Hooker CH: Rupture of the tendo calcaneus. *J Bone Joint Surg* 1963;45B:360-363.

53. Christensen IB: Rupture of the Achilles tendon: Analysis of 57 cases. *Acta Chir Scand* 1954;106:50-60.

54. Hurme T, Kalimo H: Activation of myogenic precursor cells after muscle injury. *Med Sci Sports Exerc* 1992;24:197-205.

55. Hayflick L: The cell biology of human aging. *Sci Am* 1980;242:58-65.

56. Postlethwaite AE: Failed healing responses in connective tissue and a comparison of medical conditions, in Leadbetter WB, Buckwalter JA, Gordon SL (eds): *Sports-Induced Inflammation: Clinical and Basic Science Concepts*. Park Ridge, IL, American Academy of Orthopaedic Surgeons, 1990, pp 597-607.

57. Clarkson PM, Dedrick ME: Exercise-induced muscle damage, repair, and adaptation in old and young subjects. *J Gerontol* 1988;43:M91-M96.

58. Safran MR, Garrett WE Jr, Seaber AV, et al: The role of warmup in muscular injury prevention. *Am J Sports Med* 1988;16:123-129.

59. Cole E, Malone T, Garrett WE Jr: Passive muscle stretch and the viscoelastic response. *Trans Orthop Res Soc* 1992;17:255.

60. Bass AL: Injuries of the leg in football and ballet. *Proc R Soc Med* 1967;60:527-532.

61. Chow GH, LeCroy CM, Seaber AV, et al: The effect of fatigue or muscle strain injury. *Trans Orthop Res Soc* 1990;15:148.

62. Lieber RL, Trestik CL, Schmitz MC, et al: Damage following cyclic eccentric contraction is not a function of muscle stress. *Trans Orthop Res Soc* 1992;17:259.

63. Klein C, Cunningham DA, Paterson DH, et al: Fatigue and recovery contractile properties of young and elderly men. *Eur J Appl Physiol* 1988;57:684-690.

64. Miles JW, Grana WA, Egle D, et al: The effect of anabolic steroids on the biomechanical and histological properties of rat tendon. *J Bone Joint Surg* 1992;74A:411-422.

Chapter 31

Diagnosis of Muscle Injuries

Josep Borrell, MD
Jose L. Bada, Jr, MD

Soft-tissue injuries, including muscle injuries, are the most common lesions in sports. They can occur in different forms depending on the trauma mechanism, and often they are underestimated because precise clinical diagnosis is difficult. It is very important to make an accurate diagnosis in order to treat the injury correctly.

Previously, immobilization had been the method used for treatment of this kind of pathology, but today, early mobilization techniques are used as part of the treatment.[1] Early mobilization avoids muscle atrophy, loss of muscle strength and extensibility, or muscle rupture; all of which are complications of prolonged immobilization.[2] The hamstring and calf muscles and the rectus femoris are the muscles most susceptible to this kind of lesion.[3]

Muscle injuries can be divided in two groups: injuries without muscle rupture and injuries with muscle rupture. In the first group, we can find either muscle contracture or strain and contusion without muscle rupture. The second group includes muscle strain and contusion with muscle fiber rupture and partial and total muscle rupture. In this kind of injury, a gap occurs in the muscle, and a hematoma fills the gap.

Several elements are instrumental in muscle injury. Some of these elements are sport related and others are based on individual characteristics. Muscle injury is more likely to occur in (1) persons having short and thick muscles; (2) muscles that cross two joints; (3) persons with bad training or warm-up technique;[4] (4) cold and damp weather; (5) older athletes; (6) athletes with bad diet, not enough sleeping hours, etc; (7) any condition that decreases the tensile properties of muscle; and (8) certain kinds of sport.

Muscle strain without macroscopic rupture of muscle fibers usually happens during an intensive muscular effort. The athlete stops because of sudden pain; there is a functional loss of power but the athlete can complete the game. It has been postulated that strength imbalance of antagonistic muscles may predispose the weaker muscle to injury.

Fig. 1 *If there is significant accumulation of fluid in the injured area, the hematoma could be punctured and aspirated.*

Muscle contusion is common, especially in contact sports. Contact may be with other players, but it can also be with the ground or a static element on the field. The contusion to the muscle usually results in a partial muscle fiber rupture and formation of a hematoma. The muscle still has some functional capacity but pain and disability are present.

In the case of muscle strain and contusion with muscle fiber rupture, active muscle contraction and passive muscle stretching are painful.[5] The pain is relieved with rest. There may be an elective point of pain. If there is a partial or total muscle rupture a depression as a "blow of an axe" can be felt on the surface of the muscle. When an injury is severe, the possibility of intramuscular hematoma and tissue damage should be considered. Ecchymosis can be found if the hematoma is superficial. If there is significant accumulation of fluid in the injured area, the hematoma could be punctured and aspirated (Fig. 1).

It is often helpful to corroborate clinical diagnosis of muscle injury with other techniques. The most important techniques are ultrasound, magnetic resonance imaging (MRI), and thermography.

Ultrasound is simple, sensible, reliable, and cheap; it is not invasive, and it can be used as many times as needed. It is very useful for diagnosis of muscle injuries, because it elucidates the anatomy of the injury, it can be localized, and its size can be determined. These pa-

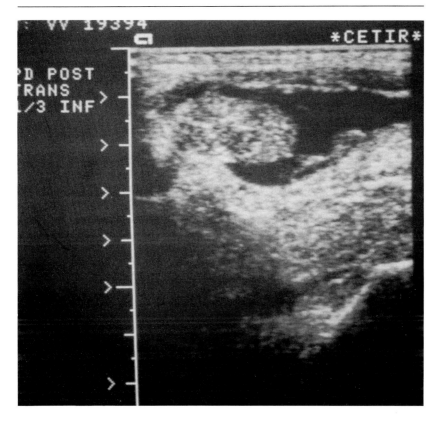

Fig. 2   *A muscle rupture is seen as a "bell clapper" image with hematoma surrounding it.*

rameters are very useful if surgery is required. The healing process can also be followed up by ultrasonography.

Ultrasound is used for diagnosis of acute injuries. Although ultrasound is useful after the third day of the lesion, it is more indicated after the tenth day. The injured area without hematoma appears as a hypoechogenic zone, similar to the neighboring area, without clear limits that depend on the edema of this area. A hematoma is seen as a nonechogenic area with posterior reinforcement. Puncture and aspiration of the hematoma can be done with ultrasound control. If more is aspirated than 50 ml, surgery can be considered. A muscle rupture is seen as a "bell clapper" image with hematoma surrounding it (Fig. 2).

Ultrasound also is useful for evaluation of chronic injuries. When there is absorption of the hematoma, the injured area is seen as a cavity with small echoes in it. The injured area and the hematoma can develop to a scar, seen as a hyperechogenic area; to an encysted hematoma, seen as a determined nonechogenic area; or to a myositis ossificans, seen as a hyperechogenic area with a nonechogenic "shadow."[6]

MRI is a very useful technique because it provides a detailed anatomic view of the extent of the injury in the muscle. It can be used to evaluate strains, muscle contracture, and sequelae of muscle injuries, such as myositis ossificans or compartment syndrome. MRI documents the distribution of affected muscles, the presence of focal hematoma or rupture and subsequent healing, fibrosis, fatty infiltration, or formation of an encysted hematoma.

Muscles are seen very well with T1-weighted images, but T2-weighted images, which have a higher signal intensity, are better for identifying intramuscular lesions. An increased signal intensity in T2-weighted images is caused by inflammatory processes, probably secondary to edematous changes. The high-contrast resolution of MRI, its great sensitivity to changes in water distribution and fat content of muscle, and its capability for multiplanar imaging facilitate depiction of these lesions.

MRI also is helpful because the contralateral extremity can be included for comparison with the injured one. Anomalous leg muscles can be discriminated from hematoma or other pathologic images, and it is possible to differentiate between individual and superficial muscles. However, because muscle exercises increase the signal intensity of T2-weighted MRI images, false diagnoses are possible.

Telethermography shows thermal alterations in the injured tissues. It is different from ultrasound because thermography shows the inflammatory reaction around the injured area, but not detailed anatomy. Some special conditions are needed for this exploration. Room temperature must be between 19° and 21°C, and no warming device can be present.

In acute muscle injuries, there can either be a normal image or, if the injury is small, a general hyperthermia of the injured muscle. In big contusions and sprains, the injured area is seen as a hyperthermic area with temperature 1° or 2°C higher than that of the healthy muscle. In neighboring areas of the limb, a hypothermia can be found. When the injury is healing, temperature becomes normal. In chronic injuries, such as encysted hematoma or myositis ossificans, there is an area of hyperthermia. If there is a fibrous scar, there is also a hypothermic area.

Treatment immediately after the injury must consist of rest, cold, compression, and elevation of the extremity. Rest should be for 1 to 3 days. Cold for more than 15 minutes is not useful because it is followed by increased circulation and increased bleeding, which will result in a larger hematoma. Massage should not be used within 48 to 72 hours following the muscular injury. Treatment with nonsteroidal drugs can be started early. Physiotherapy treatment with continuous ultrasound and stretching can begin 48 hours after the injury.[7]

If the lesion is a minor injury, treatment should be managed with support of the extremity with an elastic bandage, local cold,

NUMBER INJURIES/ SPORTS

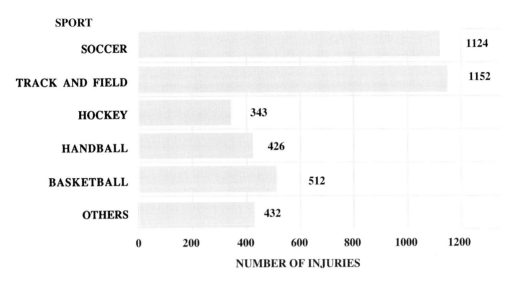

Fig. 3 *During a period of four playing seasons (1986/87, 1987/88, 1988/89, and 1989/90), 3,989 injuries were treated at the medical service of Football Club Barcelona.*

careful passive and active stretching of the affected muscle within the pain limit, and exercise of all the healthy muscles. Early mobilization techniques are used to avoid muscle atrophy, loss of muscle strength and flexibility, or muscle rupture. The process of recovery should follow coordination training and a gradual start of sport activity.[8] If the injury is severe enough, surgery could be considered. If there is a fibrous scar, heat can be used before stretching.

During a period of four playing seasons (1986/87, 1987/88, 1988/89, and 1989/90), 3,989 injuries were treated at the medical service of Football Club Barcelona (Fig. 3). The number of soccer injuries treated was 1,124. There were 312 muscle injuries (27.75%); of these, 127 (40.70%) were muscular strains or contractures; 132 patients (42.30%) had muscle fiber ruptures; 21 players had partial muscle rupture (6.73%); another 29 players had muscle contusion with hematoma (9.29%); and only three diagnoses were made of total muscle rupture (0.96%) (Fig. 4). Therefore, we can arguably state that even though muscle injuries are very common among athletes, most do not need surgery.

Muscle strains or contractures need 7 to 10 days for healing; muscle fiber ruptures healed in from 15 to 22 days. On the other hand, 20 to 35 days were enough for partial muscle ruptures, and 20 to 40 days for total muscle ruptures. When the lesion was a muscle

SOCCER TEAMS

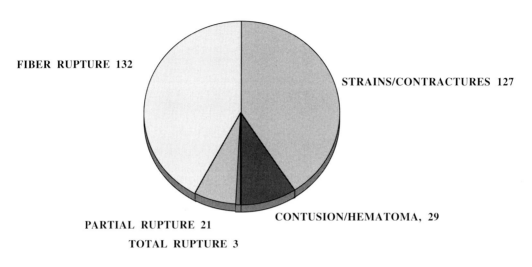

FIBER RUPTURE 132

STRAINS/CONTRACTURES 127

PARTIAL RUPTURE 21

TOTAL RUPTURE 3

CONTUSION/HEMATOMA, 29

TOTAL: 312

Fig. 4 *Types of muscle injuries in soccer players.*

SOCCER TEAMS

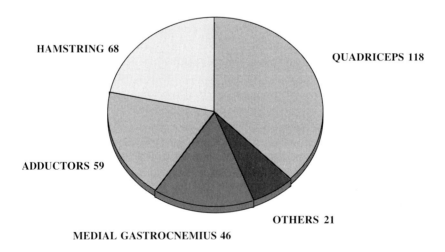

HAMSTRING 68

QUADRICEPS 118

ADDUCTORS 59

OTHERS 21

MEDIAL GASTROCNEMIUS 46

TOTAL: 312

Fig. 5 *Muscles injured among soccer players.*

contusion with hematoma the player needed from 5 to 20 days to play again.

Partial muscle ruptures affected more quadriceps and all three total muscle ruptures affected biceps femoris (Fig. 4). In general, the most affected muscle was the rectus femoris, the hamstring muscles (isquiotibial muscles) came second, the third place was for the hip adductors, and in fourth place we saw the medial gastrocnemius (Fig. 5).

Conclusions

Clinical diagnosis with an ultrasound examination is the most practical way to determine the kind of muscle injury the patient has. Short immobilization is needed following the injury to accelerate formation of the granulation tissue matrix and the scar. Mobilization is required to gain the original tensile strength of the muscle, for good results of the muscle repair, and to avoid muscle atrophy.

References

1. Kvist H, Järvinen M, Sorvari T: Effect of mobilization and immobilization on the healing of contusion injury in muscle. *Scand J Rehabil Med* 1974;6:134-140.

2. Lehto M, Duance VC, Restall D: Collagen and fibronectin in a healing skeletal muscle injury: An immunohistological study of the effects of physical activity on the repair of injured gastrocnemius muscle in the rat. *J Bone Joint Surg* 1985;67B:820-828.

3. Garrett WE Jr, Califf JC, Bassett FH III: Histochemical correlates of hamstring injuries. *Am J Sports Med* 1984;12:98-103.

4. Safran, MR, Seaber AV, Garrett WE Jr: Warm-up and muscular injury prevention: An update. *Sports Med* 1989;8:239-249.

5. Nikolaou PK, Macdonald BL, Glisson RR, et al: Biomechanical and histological evaluation of muscle after controlled strain injury. *Am J Sports Med* 1987;15:9-14.

6. Peetrons P, Moerman C, Djelassi L: Echographie et traumatismes musculaires du sportif. (English translation: Echography and muscular injuries in athletes.) *Acta Orthop Belg* 1991;57(Suppl 1):42-48.

7. Knight KL: Guidelines for rehabilitation of sports injuries. *Clin Sports Med* 1985;4:405-416.

8. Lehto MU, Järvinen MJ: Muscle injuries, their healing process and treatment. *Ann Chir Gynaecol* 1991;80:102-108.

Future Research Directions

The participants in the Workshop on Sports and Exercise in Midlife discussed directions for future research. The following recommendations are based on those discussions. There is no priority ranking assigned to the order in which they are presented. Other scientific ideas may be equally important.

The recommendations are listed in three categories: epidemiology, basic science, and clinical science. In some instances a recommendation may fit in more than one category.

Epidemiology of Sports Activity and Injury in Midlife

Define the relationship between extreme differences in temperature and humidity and the incidences of conditions like cardiac ischemia or musculoskeletal injuries in active midlife people. Environmental factors may play a role in an individual's ability to perform physical activity. Extreme variances in these conditions may affect the ability of the cardiovascular system to maintain good cardiac output and central blood flow, or to respond to increased metabolic demands. Metabolic homeostasis may be impaired. Physiologic responses change with age. There is inadequate information on the incidence of episodes attributable to environmental extremes to form a basis to recommend specific preventive measures.

Investigators could document the incidence rates of selected episodes in communities where environmental conditions may offer wide fluctuations. Seasonal changes in incidence rates should be related to seasonal changes in environmental conditions when other factors are chosen to be the same.

Determine among persons in midlife the frequency and economic impact (including absenteeism) of musculoskeletal injuries that are associated with commonly practiced exercises and sports, and the most common causes and mechanisms of these injuries. Current information on musculoskeletal injuries is provided by physicians or emergency centers, which serve selective and biased samples of the population. There is a need to conduct population-based studies of the incidence and economic impact of musculoskeletal injuries in midlife as a result of participation in exercise programs and sports. One way to achieve population-based studies is periodic surveillance of Health Maintenance Organizations (or health systems that serve large "captive" populations), identifying the individuals who have been treated for musculoskeletal injuries over a finite period of time, the cost of treating these injuries, and the overall economic impact. Identifying risk factors for these injuries would permit future development of prevention strategies.

Examine and evaluate musculoskeletal risks associated with the initiation of specific fitness/sports activities, specifying age and sex of the participants and type of exercise activity. Promotion of physical exercise and/or sports activities in midlife causes people to undertake activities without knowing the proper types and intensity of exercise and without taking proper precautions to avoid injuries or other risks (eg, exhaustion). Adequate information on the magnitude of these problems is currently unavailable; however, the problem may have importance and economic impact if people respond to community-wide programs promoting physical activity. Surveys of population samples should be conducted in community groups where promotion of exercise has been aggressively pursued and has been targeted to midlife persons.

Develop and validate simple methods to assess the levels of daily physical activity (at work and at leisure time) and of fitness, and express these levels in easily understood units. Current epidemiologic studies to assess the prevalence of sedentary and/or active lifestyles rely mainly on individuals' self-assessed participation in physical activities. There is limited ability to substantiate the validity and reliability of these assessments, and much less to express them in easily understood units (eg, energy expenditure expressed in kcal). It is clear that simple technologies could be developed to allow individuals to measure the level of their activity objectively to monitor it on a periodic basis. Incorporation of simple microchips to pedometers could help individuals in a controlled population assess their physical performance, and report it to their health-care providers or to epidemiologists.

Develop marketing strategies to promote participation in physical activities as means to enhance health, fitness, and well being. It is known that individuals in their early decades of life do not attach value to their health and do not follow simple prescriptions for health and disease prevention. There is ample experience in marketing strategies to promote the sale or consumption of a given product. It may be possible to develop strategies that would emphasize the value of health in specific terms that would be acceptable to young persons, such as self-esteem, well-being, and other incentives. Multidisciplinary groups of preventive medicine physicians, economists, and health-care administrators should convene to discuss this issue and develop specific proposals for future implementation.

Evaluate the impact of education programs targeted to primary health care providers. It is known that primary health care (PHC) providers can play a major role in emphasizing to their patients the value of health maintenance and disease prevention, but this is not routinely done.

It is necessary to organize continuing medical education (CME) programs targeted at PHC providers that convince them of the value of physical exercise in midlife and motivate them to change individuals' attitude and behavior regarding participation in physical exercise programs. The impact of such CME programs on physicians and eventually on their patients and the population at large could be assessed using evaluation techniques.

Determine factors that influence and motivate individuals to become physically active and that affect workplace fitness programs. A significant proportion of the population is sedentary, and the proportion increases with age. Physical inactivity has been associated with increased risk for cardiovascular disease and other chronic diseases. Determining those factors that individually influence the desire to exercise and using social and exercise behavior constructs might lead to programs that have a significant public health impact. These data would provide information that could increase the number of physically active people, thereby reducing risk for debilitating disease.

The number of programs that have been developed to promote fitness at the workplace has increased. The success of individual programs in promoting cardiovascular fitness, reducing absenteeism, and increasing productivity have been reported, but the ability to replicate successful programs on a wide scale has not been assessed. Specific elements of successful workplace fitness programs need to be identified and the generalizability of such elements studied. The replication of successful fitness programs for the workplace has significant ramifications for public health policy and the reduction of health care expense in the United States.

Basic Science Studies of Sports Activity and Injury in Midlife.

Study the role of physical training at midlife on relevant hormone receptor cell sensitivity. An increase in the secretory pattern of testosterone and growth hormone (GH) might be involved in the enhancement of muscle and fat-free mass after training, or there might be an enhanced hormone receptor sensitivity in target cells such as muscle, adipocyte, or liver. This topic could be investigated by means of animal studies.

Recent methods for assaying testosterone and GH receptors could be used in rats at various ages that have been exposed to endurance training or strength training. Several approaches could be used to evaluate protein synthesis as a function of higher GH or testosterone levels: muscle incubation with and without stimulation; whole body protein turnover with enhanced hormone levels; and the recent development of carbon 13 nuclear magnetic resonance, which allows study, in whole animals, of interorgan fluxes for nitrogen.

Develop synthetic or biologic prosthetic devices to improve surgical treatments for severe knee injuries in midlife. Some midlife sports enthusiasts experience severe knee trauma that requires surgical intervention to allow return to active participation. Most prosthetic devices used for ligament and meniscus repair do not have long-term success. Basic and clinical studies should be conducted to improve these allograft and synthetic biomaterials devices.

Studies are needed to elucidate the biomechanical and tissue compatibility requirements for prosthetic ligaments and the methods of using these devices. Studies are needed in which in vitro models are used to establish biomechanical parameters that will restore stability and provide appropriate stiffness to the prosthetic ligament. Studies of the synovial environment in animals are required to determine mechanical and host incorporation properties. Investigations can be performed to evaluate the capacity of animals and humans to duplicate ligament function and joint stability.

It is important to understand the biomechanical requirements for meniscus substitution with allografts, scaffolds, or combined scaffolds with cellular elements and to determine the efficacy of meniscus substitution for preserving joint function and preventing the development of osteoarthritis. Animal models must precede applications in humans of new technologies for meniscus replacement.

Develop agents to identify and prevent articular cartilage destruction and possibly enhance articular cartilage regeneration. Osteoarthritis may begin in midlife. It would be valuable to have early biochemical markers to identify the onset of osteoarthritis so that proper exercise could be prescribed. Studies of articular degradation may provide data regarding those biochemical processes that may be identified by assays or modified by pharmaceutical agents. Agents may be administered systemically or locally. Implantation of local lattices with cellular tissues and/or growth factors could provide a system for local cartilage regeneration.

Determine the biomechanical forces associated with common sports-related injuries and the age-related biochemical changes in the associated tissues. A study of the biomechanical forces associated with specific sporting activities (such as tennis or basketball) and their relationship to injury should be carried out to determine whether specific exercise and muscle strengthening programs can prevent injury. A study, at the histologic, ultrastructural, and biomechanical levels, of Achilles tendons from individuals of varying age and from individuals who have experienced rupture of this tendon would document its changes with age and with previous injury. Use of molecular biological techniques to assay differences in collagen and glycosaminoglycan synthesis in an animal model would assist in testing the hypothesis that exercise can prevent these changes.

Establish the effect of transition (significant change in activity level) on injuries in midlife. A salient feature of aging is a reduced ability to adapt to changes in environmental stress. The observed association of increased injury risk with rapid change in sports activity seems to represent a failure of adaptation of the dense connective tissue fibroblast and its surrounding matrix. In vitro analysis of senescent fibroblast response under conditions of changing levels of perturbation (eg, cyclic stimulation) is needed with attention to gene expression of extracellular protein synthesis and mediator release as well as intracellular organelle dysfunction.

Determine the role of tissue hypoxia in tendinopathy. In chronic overuse tendon injuries, recent studies have emphasized the pivotal role of mitochondrial damage secondary to hypoxia with resulting loss of Ca^{2+} ion balance, generation of oxygen free radical species, and subsequent cell membrane lipid peroxidation. The clinically observed pathology in tendinosis may represent such a failure of cell respiration. A limiting factor in current knowledge is the paucity of study beyond basic light microscopy analysis of clinical pathology in ligaments and tendons. In vitro studies of the senescent fibroblast under various oxygen tensions as well as in vivo study of the potential cell/matrix effect of induced ischemia and reperfusion may prove informative. Studies under such conditions should define the potential changes in collagen production, collagen cross-linking, and changes in biomechanical tissue properties. Limitations in such studies center on the logistics of methodology as well as on problems with unanticipated changes in cell behavior. Furthermore, because there is evidence that fibroblasts from different tissue sources vary in their phenotypic and genotypic expression, studies comparing responses from differing dense connective tissues (eg, ligament versus tendon, different tendons in same subject) are needed. In vivo studies of human tendon vascularity are needed to correlate characteristics of blood flow with observed patterns of tendinopathy. These studies need to be supported by histologic and biomechanical analysis of cell viability. In this respect, Doppler flowmetry combined with an intensive study of cell/matrix samples obtained by tissue biopsy may prove useful.

Determine the adequacy of injury response in midlife for specific connective tissues. Comparative study is needed of tissue-specific patterns of injury response as altered by aging because there are recognized differences among connective tissues. These differences exist in cell density, cell type, cell gene expression, load pattern, matrix composition, vascularity, and innervation. To date, studies have relied on laceration or explant-sponge ingrowth models to assess healing and the generation of granulation tissue. Using skin or subcutaneous sites, these models lack direct transferability to the most common injury mechanism in the aging athlete, namely overuse. Better models simulating the conditions of tissue stress in sports are needed. The fibroblast-like cell in vitro is known to be metabolically responsive and capable of initiating a reparative response. The endotenocyte (internal tendon fibroblast) in vivo seems to behave in a highly differentiated end-stage manner that may limit intratendinous healing as well as adaptive capability under stress. Studies that focus on such cells may unlock important clues to allow more effective therapeutic manipulation. A promising direction is the application of exogenous growth factors (eg, TGF-beta, PDGF, FGF) to stimulate repair. To understand the proper application of these growth factors will require in-depth understanding of the presence, time of appearance, concentration, and pattern of dissipation of these factors in injury response. Comparative studies of young versus old tissues are needed.

Study, in tissues of varying age, the role of rest in injury repair. The role of rest in cell/matrix recovery after injury remains controversial and paradoxical. Absolute rest seems detrimental, but too soon a return to activity results in reinjury. A physiologic "window" or mechanostat theory of connective tissue homeostasis has been proposed to explain these observations. Aging presumably delays cell recovery and creates a greater need for rest. Studies are needed to qualify and quantify cell/matrix response to rest, especially after the creation of a known level of injury. The methodology should take into account the differences in young versus aged animals as well as the influence of rate of change. The ideal model would provide a cyclic loading challenge and adequate opportunity for biomechanical testing. The medial collateral ligament rabbit model may be useful for study of ligament; a repetitive microtrauma model for the Achilles tendon has been described for study of tendon.

Establish an animal model that would be suitable for studying the problems of midlife individuals associated with musculoskeletal injuries and exercise training. Many of the sports injury problems of midlife individuals may be effectively studied in animal models. Epidemiologic surveys of humans may be used as a basis to indicate the musculoskeletal injury profile for this population, the anatomical regions involved, and the time for recovery from such injuries.

An animal model will allow the development of methods to produce specific musculoskeletal injuries and to study recovery processes. More importantly, scientists could use an animal model to study how exercise training could minimize the risk of injury and assist in rehabilitation. Animal models will permit biologic assays for mechanistic processes, such as free radical effects, substrate utilization, and blood flow distribution.

Determine the importance of musculoskeletal flexibility to health and injury prevention in midlife. It is commonly taught that musculoskeletal flexibility, full range of motion, is an important part of physical fitness because it improves performance and prevents injury in sports and occupational activities. However, very few basic or clinical studies have actually assessed the isolated effects of flexibility at any age. It is important to relate flexibility to general health maintenance and injury prevention as a function of age, because connective tissue elasticity appears to decrease with age, and the number of muscle-tendon injuries appear to increase with age. Changes in flexibility with age, the influence of training on flexibility, and the relationship of flexibility to injury all need more research. Basic science studies should be used to further evaluate the mechanisms underlying the decrease in connective tissue elasticity that occurs with aging. The muscle tendon junction, a common site of injury, is an important research area, which requires development of a model that considers degenerative and age-related changes.

Determine the biologic basis for the age-related mechanical/structural changes in ligaments and tendons. Although significant age-related deterioration of ligament and tendon mechanical/structural properties has been demonstrated in well-designed studies, the underlying biologic basis for these changes remains poorly understood. Detailed studies should be conducted on age-related changes in ligament and tendon matrix organization and composition, cell density, and cell function. Cell response to mechanical loading and strain will be essential to an understanding of the functional effects of these changes. Tissue culture stretching devices may allow the use of cell culture systems in preliminary research.

Determine the mechanisms by which ligaments and tendons respond to exercise. To develop better methods of preventing and treating ligament and joint capsule injuries and for maintaining optimal ligament and tendon function in midlife and beyond, more detailed information is needed concerning the training response of ligaments to exercise. This work should include in vivo studies using animal models and humans of the training effects of specific exercise programs on ligament and tendon structure and function.

Conduct studies on the exercise-training and age-related changes in cartilage properties. Very little is known regarding the effects of exercise training on the biochemical structures, metabolism, or properties of cartilage. While some exercise has been predicted to be of benefit to cartilage, it is not clear at what point the intensity exceeds a safety threshold and causes harm. Basic studies of normal adult animals and humans need to be performed before the age-related aspects can be determined. This information would be valuable guidance for those continuing or starting exercise programs in midlife.

Additionally, there have been few studies on the age-related changes in the material and structural properties of cartilage. Because many age-related changes have been noted in collagen and proteoglycan, of which cartilage is primarily composed, it is likely that research on this topic will provide a clear documentation of these age-related changes. The technology required to test small tissue samples is in place in many laboratories. Resulting age-related data can be incorporated into models for defining the activities and loads that may injure cartilage.

Establish the interaction of cartilage and joint stabilization tissues. Articular cartilage, as a major load-bearing material of joints within the body, depends on the support provided by joint stabilization tissues, such as tendon and muscle, ligament, meniscus (in the knee), and other connective tissues. The interaction of these supporting tissues during the growth, maturation, and aging of cartilage is not well defined. Establishing these relationships requires detailed, multidisciplinary studies of entire joint structures. The role of proprioceptive responses should be considered. This information may lead to a definition of specific exercises and activities that may be beneficial or harmful to cartilage (or other joint structures), especially in midlife and older individuals.

Clinical Science Studies of Sports Activity and Injury in Midlife.

Establish guidelines for the prevention or treatment of moderate hypertension by physical exercise. Arterial hypertension has a high prevalence in midlife people in our society and constitutes one of the most important risk factors for cardiovascular morbidity and mortality. Pharmacologic treatment of arterial hypertension has drawbacks (metabolic alterations, etc) and, in certain cases, important side effects. Physical exercise appears to be beneficial in prevention and treatment of moderate hypertension by itself or as a contributing factor with other interventions such as diet modification. More research related to type of exercise, intensity of the effort, duration and timing, total work load, and relation to work or labor activity is needed.

Develop an improved methodology for estimating nutritional status in midlife people. Current methods for nutritional assessment of people in primary care or even in most hospital settings are rather crude and rely mostly on anthropometric and, in a few cases, biochemical determinations. In any case, these are "static" measurements and do not give information about the "nutritional perform-ance" of the individual. In order to evaluate the working capacity and "the functional fitness" of midlife individuals, functional tests that are easily applicable in clinical practice are needed.

Establish the requirements for vitamins and micronutrients in mid-dle-aged individuals. Most of the emphasis on nutrition in the adult and midlife individual is placed on the major food components (carbohydrates, lipids, proteins), but not enough information is available about the effects of and needs for vitamins and certain mi-cronutrients. At the same time, the general population is subjected to a bombardment of confusing information and misinformation. Re-search should be performed on the effect of these factors on meta-bolic processes and functional performance.

Determine the specific cardiovascular adaptations that influence cardiac output and the threshold at which they occur in the midlife athlete. Regular physical activity has been shown to retard the age-related decline in maximum oxygen consumption in older ath-letes. The precise mechanisms that are responsible for this phenome-non and the specific thresholds at which they occur in the midlife athlete are not well understood. Noninvasive techniques, such as cardiac MRI and stress echocardiography, and graduated training regimens could be used to quantify the threshold at which cardiovas-cular adaptation occurs and to determine whether these changes are dose dependent. Such information would prove useful in designing exercise prescriptions for the sedentary. Study the effect of nonste-roidal anti-inflammatory drugs (NSAIDs) strength training, and/or high dietary protein on degenerative joint disease of the knee in mid-life men and women.

Nonsteroidal anti-inflammatory drugs have been widely used in the treatment of acute and chronic degenerative joint disease (osteo-arthritis). The toxicity of these drugs is directly related to the increas-ing age of the patient and the duration and dosage of the medication. Another problem is that some older patients are nutritionally de-prived, especially of protein, which is often less than 0.8 g/kg. The combination of protracted drug therapy and reduced protein intake, which is poor in the setting of a sedentary patient, provides no long-term benefit. It is possible to determine the ability of appropriate di-etary intake of protein and the incorporation of physical activity to increase muscle strength and decrease degenerative joint symptoms without the need for NSAID treatment.

Men and women, including minorities, in midlife who have os-teoarthritis of the knee could be evaluated. One group would remain on their customary diet and NSAID regimen; one group would re-ceive 1.5 g/kg protein in their diet plus NSAID; one group would receive 1.5 g/kg protein and strength training to the knee; and one group would receive NSAID and strength training plus high protein.

The strength training could be on isotonic or isokinetic equipment. Obstacles to designing such a clinical study include subject compliance, statistical power, and complications from NSAIDs. Clinical outcomes such as bioassay for urea, nitrogen, and creatinine as well as clinical and functional measures of osteoarthritis status would provide important clinical guidelines.

Determine the effects of calorie restrictions alone versus calorie restriction plus exercise in coronary heart disease prophylaxis when begun during midlife.   Calorie restriction in Fisher 344 rats results in an animal of lower weight that lives longer than rats that did not receive a calorie-restricted diet. Fisher 344 rats that exercise 5 out of 7 days per week and are fed ad lib live as long as the calorie-restricted sedentary rats. It is not clear that these results can be applied to midlife humans.

Under controlled conditions, the goals of this study would be to determine long-term results in midlife men and women of caloric restriction and exercise, alone and separately. The primary outcome measures would be fitness evaluation, coronary heart disease, and lipid and other predictors of coronary heart disease. Other factors could be assessed to uncover mechanisms by which these interventions may be acting. Subject compliance and statistical power are important obstacles in designing such a study. Results from this clinical study would have great public-health impact.

Determine if community exercise training programs are as effective as those under study conditions.   Scientific studies on the effects of physical training on midlife persons carried out under "artificial conditions" (well-controlled groups, good coaches, gyms, sophisticated equipment, etc) have shown the positive effects of exercise in the studied population. It would be valuable for public health recommendations to evaluate whether exercise training programs carried out by normal people are as beneficial as those in the scientific studies and to determine the means by which the programs could be improved.

Investigators might evaluate training gains in groups of midlife people exercising in different ways without changing their training programs. Because of the variety in exercise methods and varying starting point in levels of fitness, a large population will need to be sampled. The most successful "home" programs, in terms of adherence and fitness gains, could be recommended to the general public.

Determine the long-term adaptational effects of strength training in men and women of various age groups.   To date, limited data are available concerning long-term training adaptations to heavy resistance training. Several months of training may be needed to gain the fitness levels that allow for the initiation of more effective strength training programs. Adaptational changes in muscle and connective tissue appear to be more responsive to advanced programs. Such changes appear to affect the structural basis of cellular development. The problem is related to the fact that an individual's tolerance for advanced strength training, which demands higher levels of force production, higher rates of strain, and metabolic support, must be developed.

At present an unknown amount of initial training appears to be needed for the trainee to tolerate the exercise stress. The length of such preparatory training may be a function of prior training experience, age, injury, and disease status or a combination of these and other factors. The initial and longer-duration effects could be established by means of various longitudinal training studies ranging from 1 to 4 years. These studies would determine the effects of long-term strength training on a variety of physiologic and performance functions. Optimal training effects on specific muscles or bone could be determined in subsets of large clinical studies.

Determine the influence of strengthening peripheral musculature on cardiovascular function in healthy men and women of various ages and in those with cardiopulmonary disease. Most of the long-term epidemiologic studies of work and cardiovascular function have used forms of manual labor to provide the caloric expenditure each week. The question remains whether change in cardiovascular function is a peripheral or centrally-induced phenomenon. This information could be gathered by studying training in healthy and patient populations who are using appropriate strength training programs. Study topics could range from the microcirculation of peripheral muscles to intact cardiac function using MRI techniques. Such data would help address questions of how important the fitness of peripheral musculature is to cardiovascular function.

Determine the control mechanisms related to body composition during long-term health training in men and women of various ages. Maintaining lean body mass throughout a person's lifetime has been thought to lead to better health and function in old age. Understanding the physiologic mechanisms that control such phenomena may help promote health. This problem could be studied on a number of different levels, ranging from in vivo studies using human volunteers to animal models that allow determination of cellular changes with exercise. The first challenge would be demonstrating that the resistance training programs are effective in eliciting effective increases in fat-free body mass. This could be accomplished with a training program design using men and women of various age groups. Based on successful studies to show that exercise training can increase lean body mass, basic studies should define the underlying mechanisms.

Determine the role of training at midlife on the hormonal axis involved in bone density. Normal training enhances bone density while overtraining induces amenorrhea and decreases bone density in women. Aging decreases bone density. The practical problems are to define the optimum training to enhance bone density at midlife. This goal could be obtained by simultaneous studies of direct bone density, measured by absorptiometry, and bone hormone changes. Endurance exercise increases the levels of parathormone and calcitonin; strength training does not elevate these hormone concentrations. The basal status and the responses to strength and endurance exercise could be studied in control and trained subjects of different ages.

Study the effects of overtraining at midlife. It has been hypothesized that changes in steroid hormone and, more recently, in catecholamine metabolism are involved in the overtraining syndrome. The secretory capacity for these hormones seems decreased at midlife. It would be valuable to determine whether the threshold for overtraining is decreased at midlife. The problem is to observe clinically overtrained midlife subjects or to produce experimental animal models of overtraining at midlife. The peripheral hormone changes could be correlated with factors such as central nervous system change and precursors for neuromediators, compartmental changes, psychophysiologic variables, and serotonin metabolism.

Study the effects of physical training at midlife on anabolic hormones and on resulting muscle and protein metabolism. It has been shown that aging results in decreased testosterone and growth hormone (GH) levels associated with a diminished insulin sensitivity. It has been hypothesized that these hormonal changes are involved in the decrease of muscle mass and total body protein. In order to elucidate this hypothesis, the following points could be documented: (1) the role of training at midlife on the circadian rhythms of testosterone and GH secretions; (2) the mechanisms to explain the role of training on GH and testosterone secretory pattern; and (3) the role of these hormonal changes on muscle mass and protein metabolism.

Some methods to study this topic could be the following: (1) The 24-hour blood level pattern of GH and testosterone concentrations could be studied in several groups of human subjects differing by age and training. (2) The mechanisms of GH and testosterone secretions could be related with acute exercise-induced changes in catecholamine, endorphin, serotonin, and dopamine at peripheral and central levels (the probes for their role could be obtained by blockades or stimulation). (3) The stable isotope technique used to study protein metabolism (^{13}C-leucine) can be used to relate hormonal status and protein metabolism at rest, during exercise, and in recovery. In the future, the combined use of NMR spectroscopy with carbon 13 and imagery will enable the study of in vivo muscle mass and muscle protein metabolism.

Study the efficacy of therapeutic medical and physical modalities in injury repair in midlife.   The efficacy of current medical and physical modifiers of injury repair remains controversial and largely unsubstantiated, especially in midlife individuals. Emphasis should be placed on demonstrating a significant cell/matrix healing response. In this respect, conclusions to be drawn from current in vitro studies remain unproved as to clinical significance. It is important to control species variation in animal studies, for instance, the known variability in T lymphocyte response to glucocorticosteroid therapy. Clinical study designs need to include prospective protocols, blinding, use of age/gender matched populations, clear definitions of injury and populations at risk, control of therapeutic regimens, and documentation of tissue healing response (eg, synovial fluid analysis, temperature probes, scans, second-look arthroscopies, muscle biopsies, MRIs, biomechanical testing). The relief of pain is not in itself sufficient evidence of adequate healing because connective tissue pain is multifactorial and not always inflammatory.

Determine the effects of quantity and intensity of exercise on the cardiovascular and endocrinologic health of midlife men.   Cardiovascular disease is the greatest killer of midlife men and an even greater factor for morbidity. Exercise clearly can modify this risk factor, especially as it alters body composition and fat patterning. The latter is directly related to morbidity and mortality with the android type of visceral fat distribution being the most harmful.

A clinical study of men would be important to determine how modification of the circulating lipids and lipoproteins as well as fat topography by increased exercise will impact on their morbidity and mortality in midlife from cardiovascular disease.

In men, GH secretion declines with age. Growth hormone impacts bone positively, and it may be important to alter the negative aspects of GH deficiency on body composition and body fat distribution. Thus, study of the secretory dynamics of GH as well as longitudinal studies of the effects of GH administration, alone or in combination with exercise, on strength, blood lipids, and lipoproteins as well as body fat distribution are important to understanding the long-term health of midlife and older men.

Determine the separate and combined effects of estrogen and physical exercise on bone and cardiovascular health in women as they enter and pass through the climacteric.   The apparent partial immunity of menstruating women from cardiovascular disease wanes at menopause. Both estrogen replacement therapy and physical exercise have been suggested as important factors to ameliorate cardiovascular disease. It is imperative that clinical studies be conducted to determine whether these two factors are important to the continued cardiovascular health of women and whether there is a synergistic interaction between them. In a similar manner, further studies of midlife women are needed to determine the potential protective role of exercise in reducing postmenopausal bone loss at various anatomic sites.

It should be noted that there is a major deficiency of studies of exercise effects on women in midlife. In addition to the specific areas of investigation identified above, general studies on sport and exercise in midlife women are encouraged.

Study the mechanisms for declining maximum heart rate with increasing age. Maximum heart rate on average declines by one beat per miute per year after the age of 25. This is one of the dominant factors causing lowered VO_2 maximum with age. There is a large variation between individuals. Compensatory mechanisms, such as stroke volume, are not well defined as a function of aging.

Studies should not only document heart rate changes with aging, but also the mechanisms that induce these changes and factors, such as long-term endurance exercise, that may diminish the effects of aging. One such study might be a 5 to 10 year longitudinal study of midlife men and women who are sedentary, physically active, and very active. This study would follow resting, maximal, and intrinsic heart rate; maximum work performance (VO_2 maximum); cardiac dimensions (by echocardiography or cine MRI), and biochemical assays of blood and urine samples.

Investigate in midlife the activation of the central opioid system by endurance training. Activation of, for example, beta-endorphin production by long-term physical training causes lowered pain threshold, a sense of well-being, and posttraining lowered blood pressure. Studies should be conducted to determine if these effects are decreased in midlife; such a decrease may present a risk to the musculoskeletal or cardiovascular system. A possible study design would include comparing pain threshold, beta-endorphin in plasma, and blood pressure lowering after standardized long-term work (eg, in relation to VO_2) in three age groups (20, 40, and 60). An obstacle to completing this study is the discrepancy between plasma and brain endorphin levels. Research should include measuring factors that may explain the mechanisms underlying any changes in endorphin levels.

Study fluid and electrolyte balance in midlife women and men. Excessive fluid loss can lead to dehydration and even collapse following endurance exercise. Little is known regarding the effects of aging on changes in the physiology of fluid and electrolyte balance caused by extensive sweating, especially in warm environments. As more midlife athletes compete in marathons and other long-duration events, the risk of severe fluid loss has become more important. Some of the issues to be studied include: fluid absorption from the small bowel, optimal levels of fluid intake, optimal sodium and carbohydrate concentration in fluids, and treatment of exercise-associated collapse.

Development of specific rehabilitative and nonsurgical treatment programs for soft-tissue injury in midlife.   Painful conditions of muscles and tendons abound in the midlife athlete. The lack of understanding regarding these injuries is nowhere better seen than in the range of recommendations for treatment. A painful tennis elbow, rotator cuff, or heel cord may be treated by regimens ranging from complete immobilization to rest to stretching to strength training to steroid injections to early surgery. The costs in terms of patient satisfaction and the economic costs of therapy are significant. The emerging science of technology assessment and outcome studies should be applied to these soft-tissue injuries.

Develop recommendations for preventing joint injuries in midlife individuals during exercise and for treating these injuries to allow continued exercise.   With increasing age, individuals may become more vulnerable to joint injuries, especially if they have had previous joint injuries or participate in vigorous physical exercise. Clinical studies of the effects of training programs (for example, joint range of motion, muscle strengthening, and joint proprioception training programs, and different forms and intensities of exercise programs) are needed to determine their role in preventing joint injury during sports.

It has been hypothesized that in middle-aged and older people, ligament and joint capsule strains and ruptures often heal slowly and compromise or prevent exercise. Well-designed clinical studies of ligament and joint capsule injury treatments are needed to accelerate restoration of joint function following injury and thereby allow individuals to maintain their level of fitness.

Determine if exercise can retard the loss of muscle mass that occurs with aging.   The main reason for muscle mass becoming reduced in midlife and in the elderly is because of the loss of muscle fibers, which is secondary to the loss of motoneurons. Strengthening exercises can cause the remaining muscle fibers to increase in cross-sectional diameter and thereby, in part, compensate for the loss of fibers. The critical, but still unanswered question is whether exercise can reduce the rate at which skeletal muscle fibers are lost either by debth of fewer motoneurons dying or by accentuation of motor nerve sprouting and re-innervation of muscle fibers without nerve contact. These issues could be studied in appropriate animal models or in human volunteers.

A related topic concerns the optimal engagement of motor units. Young adults can maximally activate their muscles by voluntary tetanic tension. It is not clear if midlife individuals have lost the ability to engage all motor units. If not, can exercise conditioning restore this lost maximum power? And, is it safe to do so? These issues may be investigated along with the above studies on muscle mass.

A final objective of these muscle studies may be to determine specific types and intensities of exercise that optimize the restoration and maintenance of muscle strength in midlife. These optimal exercises are likely to be anatomic site specific because of the different muscle types present.

Conduct clinical and basic studies to determine optimum exercises that may have anatomic site specific benefit in protecting women and men from bone loss in midlife. In midlife, both men and women have attained peak bone mass and are slowly losing bone mass as they continue to age. During menopause, women may experience an accelerated loss of bone which is superimposed on the age-related effect. While some studies relating exercise to protection from reduced bone mass have been conducted, further studies are desired, especially regarding midlife and specific form of exercise (for example, protecting spinal bone mass).

Preliminary studies are required to determine strain induced by specific activities in order to provide safety measures in implementing an exercise program and to further understand the mechanisms (strain and strain history) that may be best for protecting bone mass. Dual energy X-ray absorptiometry is an accurate and noninvasive technique available for measuring bone mass. Hormonal status and markers of bone turnover will permit assessment of possible pathways to mediate the exercise effects.

Some preliminary studies of animal models may provide both valuable understanding of the mechanisms involved and design criteria for clinical tests. For example, several sites in rat bone remodel in a similar manner to human bone. Therefore, exercising rats with measured microstrain and bone density in the tibia and femur, may describe the results of a specific exercise program.

Develop exercise programs that might prevent and reverse changes in muscle due to paresis from a central nervous system injury. The neurologically disabled person has an impaired neuromuscular electrical activity pattern from central or peripheral causes. A growing body of experimental evidence suggests that daily mechanical loading at some minimum amount and frequency can ameliorate many of the deleterious changes in muscle mass and in the metabolic, enzymatic, protein, and physiologic properties that are associated with an altered firing pattern and disuse. Acute and chronic studies of muscle in patients with hemiplegic stroke and paraplegia would define the natural history of changes over time and serve as a model to try therapeutic interventions. Measures should include whole muscle MRI for fiber size; NMR spectroscopy for phosphorous, pH, etc; quantification of proteins and enzymes; changes in EMG activity, strength, fatigability, and functional performance in tasks that use the muscle groups.

Determine the long term-effects of exercise interventions for the spectrum of neurologically disabled people. Exercise provides a strengthening and conditioning benefit for neurologically disabled people. The mechanisms by which these gains can be enhanced and translated to activities of daily living require further study.

Specific adaptive interventions need to be defined to explore the complex and confounding factors that might limit exercise. Physiologic assessment and outcome tests may need to be modified to determine changes in this patient population. It also would be important to assess whether or not the rate of oxygen consumption required for locomotion and wheelchair activities can be reduced by exercise.

With or without measured physiologic gains in strength and fitness, it is critical to demonstrate that exercise efforts improve quality of life and reduce morbidity. Some of the important issues to be addressed include: increase in balance, mobility, and flexibility; decrease in hypertonicity, fatigability, and life-style restrictions; improvement in cognition and mood; enhancement of immune function in people who are at especially high risk for respiratory and urinary infections; and reduction in long-term health risk factors, such as coronary heart disease, hypertension, hyperlipidemia, noninsulin-dependent diabetes, osteoporosis, and obesity.

Develop enhanced mobility aids and exercise programs for spinal cord injury patients. Research should continue on devices that interact with the patient to provide mobility and strengthening. Two concepts are systems that use functional neuromuscular stimulation of paralyzed weakened lower-limb muscles to assist ambulation and leg-propelled vehicles to enable locomotion via functional neuromuscular stimulation of paralyzed, weakened lower-limb muscles.

It would be valuable to develop specific exercise programs and specialized instrumentation to increase muscle strength, power, and endurance, as well as cardiopulmonary function to enable improved mobility and general health. Functional neuromuscular stimulation should be further evaluated as an adjunct to voluntary arm exercise. For example, functional neuromuscular stimulation techniques may promote peripheral and central hemodynamics to prevent secondary problems such as blood pooling, edema, deep venous thrombosis, pulmonary embolism, and decubitus ulcers.

Clinical Questions

On July 20-24, 1992, the National Institute of Arthritis and Musculoskeletal and Skin Diseases, National Institutes of Health, and the Research Program, Institute for Studies of Health, Generalitat de Catalunya, Spain, sponsored a workshop on sports and exercise in midlife. While there are a variety of definitions of midlife, workshop participants considered the age range of midlife to be 35 to 65 years. A group of basic and clinical scientists from the United States and Europe gathered to discuss the state of knowledge and directions for future research in this field. These internationally recognized leaders in sports and exercise were asked to address six practical questions that a physician may be asked by a midlife person during a general examination. The answers are summarized below.

Question #1: Doctor, why should I exercise?

First, exercise can improve your quality of life. Enhanced fitness will give you greater strength and endurance. You will find that day-to-day activities, such as carrying packages, walking up steps, and running to catch a bus, are easier if you are fit. You will have more energy, feel better, and perhaps even live longer.

Second, it is important to either gain or maintain a strong heart and healthy skeletal muscles as you slowly begin to approach old age. Your improved endurance, strength, and coordination will allow you to continue an active and independent life-style.

Participation in an appropriate exercise program is invigorating and will give you a general sense of well being. After several weeks of regular exercise (both routine and vigorous), your body will perform better than before. For example, (1) your heart will pump blood more efficiently; (2) breathing will be easier, and you will have less shortness of breath after exertion; (3) your muscles will be stronger; (4) your joints will move more freely than before and may hurt less; and (5) your bones may become stronger and may lose less calcium, reducing the chance of broken bones in old age.

These changes may permit you to sleep better, to concentrate well in your work, to feel less depressed, to be more optimistic, and perhaps to fight infection better. In women who exercise regularly, the symptoms of premenstrual tension are usually less severe.

You can obtain these benefits with reasonable levels of conditioning. You do not need to take part in excessive or competitive training programs. A healthy diet is a good addition to your exercise activities and will help you in weight reduction, if necessary. Finally, I am pleased that you are seeking advice from a physician before starting an exercise program. This move is very valuable because different persons have different requirements. Your previous medical history and family medical history help to determine the type and level of exercise appropriate for you.

Question #2: Doctor, I am generally healthy, but out of shape. What can I do to become more physically fit?

The key to getting in shape is a successful exercise program. Pick an activity suited to your interests and abilities and then make it a part of your normal life-style. Recent studies have shown that even every-day activities, such as walking, house cleaning, and gardening, can result in measurable improvement.

The first step in getting into shape is a thorough medical evaluation. This is important because you exercise the heart, skeletal muscles, and other parts of the musculoskeletal system during activities to improve your fitness. Although the strength and endurance of these parts of the body decline slightly with age, most people in midlife can safely improve their fitness. However, your exercise program should advance more slowly than for a younger person.

Because you are out of shape, you should start your exercise program at a low level and build slowly from there. Walking is a great choice to begin with. It strengthens your legs, benefits your heart, and does not cause pounding on your joints. Start by walking for 15 minutes, at a comfortable pace, 3 to 4 times a week. Gradually increase your walks to 30 to 45 minutes each, and walk a little faster every day until you reach a brisk pace. If there are hills along your path, go slowly at first and build up to the point where you don't have to slow down to go up hill. Start each exercise session at a slower pace to warm up and stretch your muscles.

After about 1 to 2 months, your strength and stamina will increase. This is the point at which you should consider modifying your exercise program so that you do not get bored and quit.

If you want to continue walking, look for different (possibly more hilly) routes, find friends to walk with you, and find an enclosed shopping center for days with bad weather. At this point you may want to try other forms of exercise. Jogging, bicycling, and swimming are popular choices. One advantage to these more vigorous forms of exercise is that you can gain or maintain fitness in a shorter workout time. You may want to try an active recreational sport, such as tennis, racquetball, or basketball. Just remember, the key to success is regularity. Find one or more exercises and activities that will keep your interest. Missing an occasional exercise session will not leave you out of shape or reduce your exercise capacity. If you miss 2 or 3 weeks, restart slowly to avoid injury.

It is a good idea to seek further medical advice after about 2 to 3 months. At that time you may think about adding strengthening and flexibility exercises or increasing the intensity of your current exercises. If you need advice earlier, feel uncertain about the exercise program, or have problems, please call your doctor.

Question #3: Doctor, I have a disability and I am out of shape. Can I become more physically fit?

Most people with disabilities can become more physically fit. The first step is to carefully evaluate your medical condition. That will provide the information needed to develop a program that will improve your fitness and, if possible, your functional limitations without placing you at unnecessary risk for injury. You may require a more slowly advancing exercise program at your current age, but that should not prevent you from improving your strength and fitness and, perhaps, decreasing your risk of getting heart disease and diabetes in later years.

As I said, a thorough medical and neurologic examination is the first step. Because you have a neuromuscular disability, the range of motion of your joints; those movements that cause pain; your strength; the control you can exercise over individual muscles; how fast you fatigue; and your flexibility, balance, coordination, and general health must be taken into account. We will use that information to design a strategy for exercise and recreational sports that you find enjoyable, will strengthen weak muscles, and that will improve your overall condition. Perhaps we can develop a program that you can do with your spouse or a friend.

You should start each exercise or sport session by warming up with a series of stretches. If you need to strengthen muscles, a therapist may have to help you with light resistive exercises. Ideally, we'll test the strength of key muscles and then have you exercise at about 60% of your maximum strength for about ten repetitions and then repeat the exercise two to three times. If you enjoy working with weights, you can continue beyond the basic strengthening program. If you can walk safely, you can gradually build up your speed and distance traveled until you can manage your best pace for 20 to 30 minutes at a time at least 4 days each week. The equipment for stationary bicycling, pool exercises and swimming, or stair climbing can be adapted to make its use safer for persons with neuromuscular disabilities.

If you are confined to a wheelchair, you can still do strengthening and conditioning exercise. Many upper body exercises than can help you develop both strength and endurance, and there are many recreational sports that can help you maintain and enjoy your gains.

Question #4: Doctor, why do I have more aches and pains after exercising than I did when I was young?

The answer is based on two factors: (1) your generally inactive job and life-style and (2) some slow age-related changes that occur in your muscles, joints, ligaments, and tendons (the musculoskeletal system) independent of your activity level. Because you no longer run to classes or to catch the school bus, have daily gym exercise, or play sports and games on a regular basis, you may have decreased skills, endurance, or strength. In other words, you may have detrained your musculoskeletal system. The physiologic changes include a gradual decrease in flexibility, strength, and coordination of the musculoskeletal system. Also, you may have had a previous injury or other medical problem that may contribute to your aches and pains.

You also may have attempted too much activity for your current state of conditioning. To reestablish your strength, flexibility, and neuromuscular skill and coordination, you will need 1 to 2 months of training for strength, flexibility, and endurance specifically related to the sport or exercise in which you wish to participate. For example, you may learn to do exercises that will be very beneficial in preventing postexercise muscle pain. There are specific arm strengthening programs that will help prevent elbow pain from racquet ball sports. In general, the most common mistake that leads to pain or injury is to violate the "Rule of Too's"—too fast, too long, too little training, and too little rest between exercise activities.

The following eight-step program will help you avoid aches and pains. One, have a complete medical examination. Two, pick a sport or activity that is reasonable for your situation. Three, train for sport-specific strength, flexibility, and endurance before you participate. Four, warm up and stretch before and after each exercise period. Five, slowly develop the skills and purchase the proper clothing and equipment to participate safely. Six, continue the training program after you start to participate in the sport or activity. Seven, have adequate rest between exercise periods. Eight, don't be overly competitive; just have a good time.

Question #5: Doctor, I exercise regularly, but my knee hurts afterward. Should I continue to exercise and play sports?

Before I can specifically answer your question, I need more information about the nature and severity of the pain in your knee. Describe the intensity, location, and duration of the pain. Has the pattern changed in regard to the severity of the pain or the types of events that cause the pain? Have you significantly modified your exercise program? Have you injured your knee before? Is there swelling, stiffness, or instability in the knee joint? Does the pain wake you up while sleeping?

If the pain is not very severe and lasts for only a short period after exercising, it is probably safe to continue, but with a modified program. One modification is to adjust the duration and intensity of the workout. For example, jog for only half your usual time and choose a flat terrain. Also, check the condition of your running shoes. Another modification is to temporarily select another exercise, such as swimming or bicycling, that will not place the same types of load on your knees. You also may consider adding a flexibility and weight lifting program to benefit the knee joint.

There is no scientific evidence to indicate that properly trained individuals in your age group are more prone to injury than younger ones. People in midlife probably take a little longer to heal from an injury, but appropriate adjustment of your training and any necessary rehabilitation should allow you to return to full activity. The common sense you've gained with reaching midlife should compensate for the small declines in strength, endurance, and healing that come with age.

Do not use heavy doses of self-prescribed medication to suppress the pain. Further pain can be your guide to the effectiveness of reducing or modifying your level of activity. If you are pain free, very slowly increase toward your previous levels.

If the pain becomes more severe, lasts a long time after the exercise is finished, or is combined with joint swelling, instability, or locking, you will need a more thorough medical evaluation. The evaluation will include a detailed history of the pain and what causes it, as well as a history of any previous musculoskeletal problems. The physical examination of your knee will include joint alignment, range of motion, joint stability, and muscle strength testing. Based on these preliminary findings, other procedures, such as radiographs, imaging, or dynamic performance testing, may be required. The goal of this evaluation is to determine exactly what's wrong with your knee. A program (medical treatment, rehabilitation, and training) then can be developed to give you the quickest and safest return to sports and exercise activities.

Questions #6: Doctor, I participate in competitive tennis and cycling. Now that I am in midlife, what can I do to improve my performance?

Your reason for wanting to push the bounds of your performance is of prime importance. It is alright to have a healthy competitive spirit, but it is foolish to try to prove yourself as part of a "midlife crisis." If you exceed your physical limits, you may sustain an injury that will force you to discontinue all exercising for an extended period of time.

Increased performance will require further improvement in general strength and endurance as well as techniques and skill development. To advance to much higher levels of training at midlife, you should work closely with a sports medicine physician and/or a qualified sports trainer. You will need a higher level basic program for strength and endurance training and a special program that is sport specific. Your performance also depends on technique training; you should learn the proper form and methods, and then practice until you do them automatically. During competition you should drink plenty of water and eat a healthy diet that is rich in carbohydrates.

Because it may be difficult to advance in both cycling and tennis at the same time, it may be helpful to briefly discuss a few of the many training principles for each one separately.

For cycling, you need power in your legs for hills and cardiovascular and muscular endurance for competing in a long race. You should gradually lower your lean body mass by long, low-intensity training and a diet that is lower in calories. You should begin power interval training, which is an alternating mixture of high- and low-intensity exercise that is repeated between five to ten times. One example would be five repetitions for 10 minutes at 80% of maximum intensity with a 5-minute low-intensity recovery. When cycling, don't use the high gears until after the third or fourth week of training. Try to keep the frequency of pedaling around 80 to 90 revolutions per minute. If your body tells you that you are tired, decrease your intensity level.

In tennis, most of the power comes from the legs, so you will have to strengthen both your upper and lower extremities. Again, you will not only need strength for a powerful shot, but endurance to play out long points. You want to be able to hit the last ball as well as the first. Endurance training, such as jogging, swimming, or cycling, may be a good diversion from hours of hitting tennis balls. Weight training will be required to isolate and develop the many muscle groups involved in the various tennis shots. Because you may have to stretch or reach to make some shots, improved flexibility will be very valuable. Hitting your backhand shot with a firm elbow and racquet head in front of your body may help to avoid the common problem of tennis elbow.

Index

Page numbers in italics refer to figures or figure legends.